02/22/19
S0-AWZ-231

AUTO UPKEEP

Maintenance, Light Repair, Auto Ownership, and How Cars Work

EDITION
4TH

RESOURCES

39075057875715

Michael E. Gray and Linda E. Gray

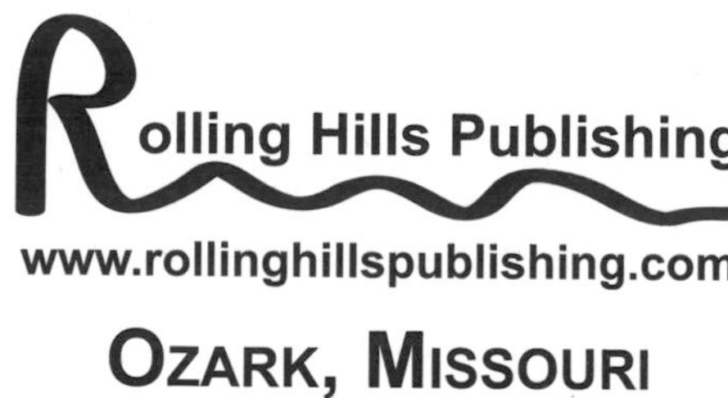

www.rollinghillspublishing.com
OZARK, MISSOURI

Auto Upkeep: Maintenance, Light Repair, Auto Ownership, and How Cars Work
4th Edition
Michael E. Gray and Linda E. Gray

Executive Editor, Illustrator, Production Director: Linda E. Gray
Assistant Editor: Nadia Riell

Copyright © 2018 by Rolling Hills Publishing. All rights reserved. No part of this book may be reproduced, stored in a retrieval system, or transmitted in any form or by any means (electronic, mechanical, photocopying, recording, or otherwise) without prior written permission from the publisher, except by a reviewer, who may quote brief passages in a review or as permitted by the United States Copyright Act.
Previous Editions Copyright: © 2013, 2007, 2003

Printed in the United States of America
24 23 22 21 20 19 18 10 9 8 7 6 5 4 3 2

Publisher's Cataloging-in-Publication
(Provided by Quality Books, Inc.)

Gray, Michael E., author.
Auto upkeep : maintenance, light repair, auto ownership, and how cars work / Michael E. Gray and Linda E. Gray. -- 4th edition.
pages cm
Includes index.
LCCN 2017941560
ISBN-13: 978-1-62702-011-4 (pbk.)
ISBN-10: 1-62702-011-X (pbk.)
ISBN-13: 978-1-62702-016-9 (hardcover)
ISBN-10: 1-62702-016-0 (hardcover)
ISBN-13: 978-1-62702-019-0 (e-book)
ISBN-10: 1-62702-019-5 (e-book)
1. Automobiles--Maintenance and repair--Popular works. I. Gray, Linda E., author. II. Title.

TL152.G6387 2017 629.28'72
QBI17-821

For more information contact: Rolling Hills Publishing
Phone: 1-800-918-READ (1-800-918-7323) Fax: 1-888-FAX-2RHP (1-888-329-2747)
Email: info@autoupkeep.com Website: www.autoupkeep.com

NOTICE TO THE READER
The publisher, authors, www.rollinghillspublishing.com, www.autoupkeep.com, reviewers, and those associated with the text do not warrant or guarantee any procedure, process, products, or websites presented in the text. Extensive effort has been made to ensure accuracy in the text and illustrations throughout the book. However, due to the vast number of automotive manufacturers and related products, the reader should follow all procedures provided with the vehicle or by the product manufacturer. The book is sold with the understanding that the publisher, authors, www.rollinghillspublishing.com, www.autoupkeep.com, reviewers, and those associated with the text are not engaged in rendering any specific mechanical, safety, diagnostic, legal, accounting, or any other professional advice. The reader assumes all risks while following activity procedures, is warned to follow all safety guidelines, and should avoid all potentially hazardous situations. The publisher, authors, www.rollinghillspublishing.com, www.autoupkeep.com, reviewers, and associates shall not be liable for damages to vehicles, their components, or injuries to individuals using or relying on this material.

PRODUCT DISCLAIMER
The publisher, authors, www.rollinghillspublishing.com, www.autoupkeep.com, reviewers, and associates do not endorse any company, product, service, or website mentioned or pictured in the book. The company names, products, services, and websites were noted and pictured because they are readily available, easily recognizable, and may help the reader understand the content. It is acknowledged that other company names, products, services, and websites could work as substitutes for those given throughout the text.

Preface

Introduction

Auto Upkeep: Maintenance, Light Repair, Auto Ownership, and How Cars Work is an introductory book that is intended to provide individuals with the knowledge to make economical decisions and take preventative measures to enhance the overall satisfaction of being an automotive consumer. The textbook content and workbook activities provide the fundamental knowledge and experience in owning and maintaining an automobile. The *Auto Upkeep* curriculum is used in over 500 high schools, technology centers, community colleges, and universities to teach the first course in an automotive sequence, commonly titled *Automotive Maintenance and Light Repair*.

Updates to the 4th Edition

Auto Upkeep has undergone a complete revision with over 300 new illustrations and 88 additional pages. This edition continues to focus on what every car owner should know and be able to do, while also introducing students to the rapidly advancing field of automotive technology. By learning how cars work, students develop a solid automotive foundation. They can continue to build upon this foundation, if they choose to become a technician, or use their knowledge throughout life as an educated consumer.

NATEF Correlations

The *Auto Upkeep* curriculum correlates to the entry level tasks within the 2017 National Automotive Technicians Education Foundation (NATEF) Maintenance and Light Repair task list. A correlation matrix can be accessed at **www.autoupkeep.com/standards**.

Reviewers

Thanks to all of the instructors, technicians, and readers who gave valuable input during the review process.

Technical Reviewers

Mitch Crowden
Automotive Technology Instructor
Casa Roble High School, Orangevale, CA

Mike Davidson AAM
ASE Certified Master Technician
President of American Skilled Labor Association

Ruben Delgado
Automotive Technology Instructor
W. H. Adamson High School, Dallas, TX

Ray Dove
Automotive Instructor
Weaver Academy for Advanced Tech., Greensboro, NC

John W. Duston Sr.
Automotive Faculty
Pueblo Community College/CCHS, Cañon City, CO

Carl Fedele
Automotive Program Instructor
Proviso West High School, Hillside, IL

Jonathan Gray
ASE Certified Master Technician
Gray's Garage LLC, Hibbing, MN

Matthew Griffin
Automotive Instructor
Verona Area High School, Verona, WI

Tim Kelly
Automotive Instructor
Decatur High School, Federal Way, WA

Randy Nussler
Automotive Instructor
New Market Skills Center, Tumwater, WA

Oudyalack Roddy Rampersad
Automotive Instructor
Mt. San Jacinto College, San Jacinto, CA

Bob Stockero
Automotive Instructor/Department Chair
Santa Barbara City College, Santa Barbara, CA

Wryann Van Riper
Automotive Instructor
Clackamas Community College, Oregon City, OR

Student Reviewers

McKade Brown
Frisco, TX

Cooper Gray
Frisco, TX

Features of the Text

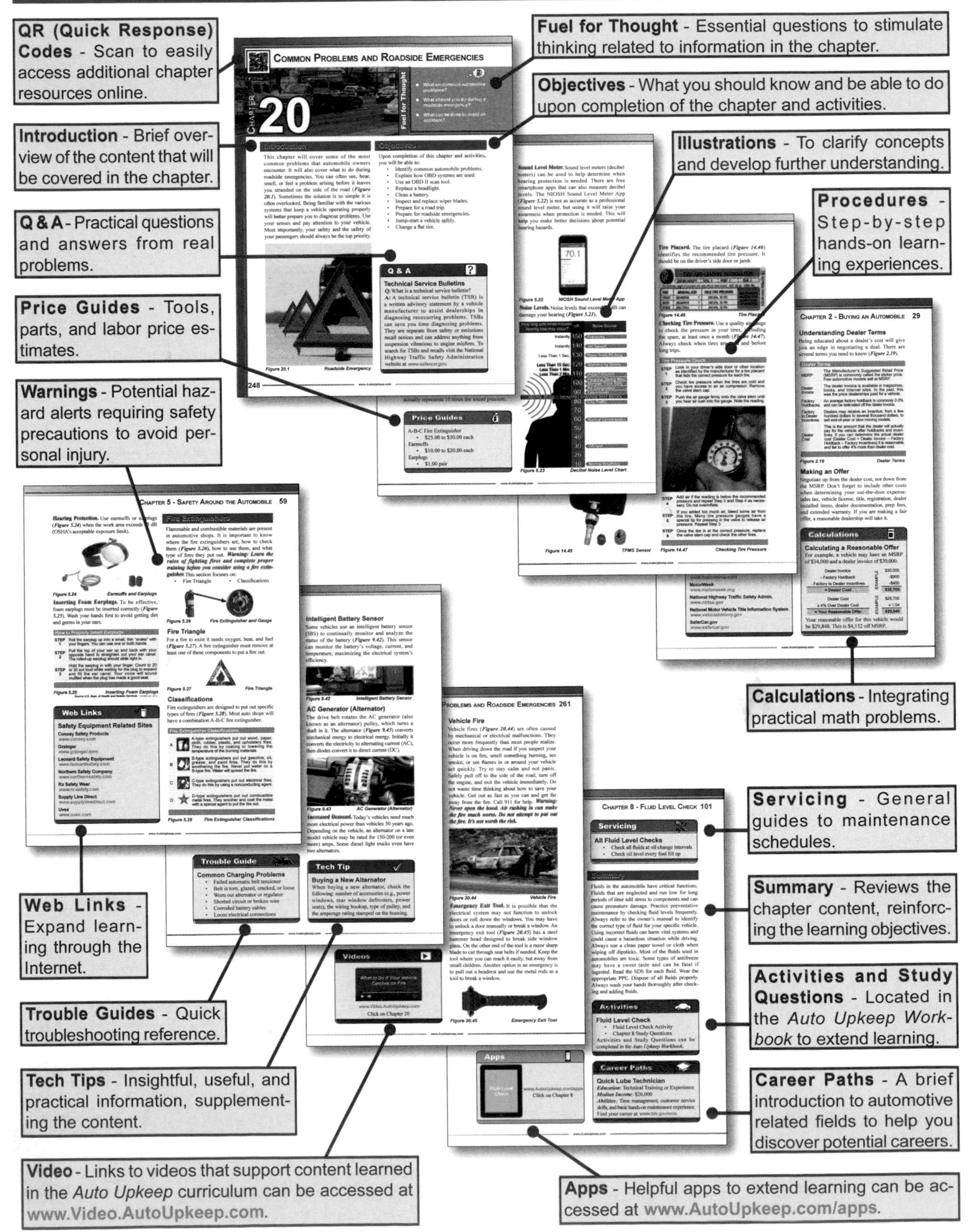

QR (Quick Response) Codes - Scan to easily access additional chapter resources online.
Introduction - Brief overview of the content that will be covered in the chapter.
Q & A - Practical questions and answers from real problems.
Price Guides - Tools, parts, and labor price estimates.
Warnings - Potential hazard alerts requiring safety precautions to avoid personal injury.
Fuel for Thought - Essential questions to stimulate thinking related to information in the chapter.
Objectives - What you should know and be able to do upon completion of the chapter and activities.
Illustrations - To clarify concepts and develop further understanding.
Procedures - Step-by-step hands-on learning experiences.
Calculations - Integrating practical math problems.
Servicing - General guides to maintenance schedules.
Summary - Reviews the chapter content, reinforcing the learning objectives.
Activities and Study Questions - Located in the *Auto Upkeep Workbook* to extend learning.
Career Paths - A brief introduction to automotive related fields to help you discover potential careers.
Web Links - Expand learning through the Internet.
Trouble Guides - Quick troubleshooting reference.
Tech Tips - Insightful, useful, and practical information, supplementing the content.
Video - Links to videos that support content learned in the *Auto Upkeep* curriculum can be accessed at www.Video.AutoUpkeep.com.
Apps - Helpful apps to extend learning can be accessed at www.AutoUpkeep.com/apps.

Curriculum Resources

Textbook

Auto Upkeep is available in both trade paperback and hardcover.

ISBN: 978-1-62702-011-4 (paperback)
ISBN: 978-1-62702-016-9 (hardcover)

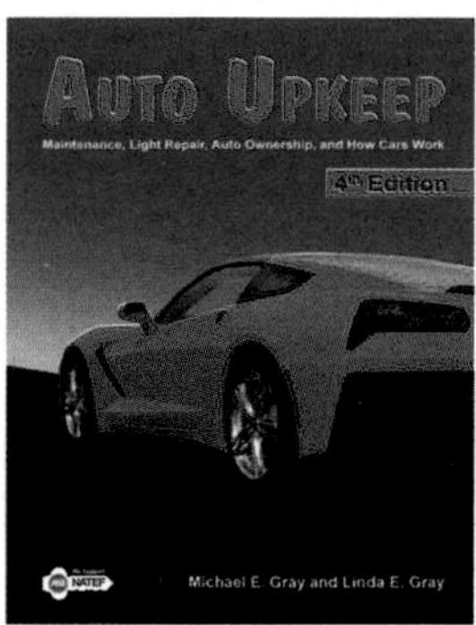

Workbook

Activities and study questions that correlate with the book's content can be accessed in the *Auto Upkeep Workbook.*

ISBN: 978-1-62702-012-1 (paperback)

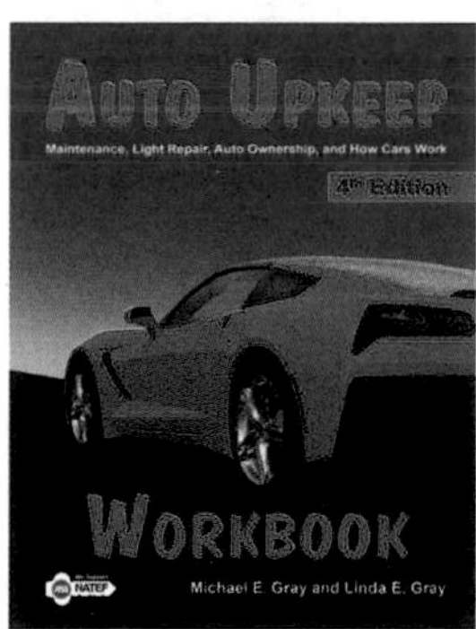

eBook

Auto Upkeep eTextbook and eWorkbook options are available at **www.autoupkeep.com/ebooks**.

Instructor Resources

The *Auto Upkeep Instructor Resource USB Flash Drive* assists instructors in delivering the curriculum. The resources include the following:

ISBN: 978-1-62702-013-8

- Course Syllabus Outline
- Competency Profile
- NATEF Correlation Matrix
- PowerPoint Slides
- Lab Activities
- Study Questions
- Chapter Tests
- Exams & Final
- Answer Keys

On the Internet

Additional *Auto Upkeep* resources can be experienced online at **www.autoupkeep.com**.

Videos

Links to videos that support content learned can be accessed at **www.video.autoupkeep.com**.

Authors

About Mike

Mike has roots in the automotive service industry. He began diagnosing and fixing cars at a young age in his family's service station. He has worked in automotive parts supply stores, towing companies, and service facilities. After graduating from St. Cloud State University (MN) with a Bachelor's degree, he implemented and taught a basic car care program at the high school level. During work on his Master's degree at Illinois State University (IL), he was a curriculum specialist on a National Science Foundation project where he co-authored ten integrated mathematics, science, and technology books designed for team teaching. Mike has also supervised teachers in Career and Technology Education as a school system administrator.

About Linda

Linda was motivated to learn about cars early on by her desire to be self-reliant and save money. As basic maintenance and repairs were needed on her car she figured out how to do them. She could often be found working on her Pontiac Fiero and reupholstering automotive interiors at her family's upholstery shop. She found guidance from automotive manuals, her family, friends, and husband Mike. During her studies at the University of Redlands (CA), she worked with classmates to design, build, and test a hybrid electric vehicle. After graduating with a Bachelor's degree in Engineering, Linda worked as a Project Engineer for a bicycle component company. Linda's other interests include alternative energies, home renovation, graphic design, and writing.

About Aiden

Aiden joined our team in 2010. He is learning the basics about cars and can already identify many of the parts. He really loves building Lego vehicles, riding his bike, reading, and playing baseball.

About Landen

Landen joined our team in 2013. He loves driving remote controlled cars, jumping monster trucks, having books read to him, and playing with his Thomas and Chuggington train sets.

Acknowledgments

Acknowledgments

The idea for this text came from Mike's student teaching experience. During that experience Mike worked under a talented and enthusiastic veteran teacher, Tim Goodner. Tim taught a class called *Car Upkeep*. Immediately Mike was impressed with the course. This wasn't another course just for future auto technicians, but a course for the average automotive consumer. This student teaching experience inspired Mike to implement a similar program. In the first year that the course was offered, it became one of the most popular elective courses at the school.

Thank You

We would like to thank all of our former teachers in giving us the classroom experiences and instilling positive work ethics that made us successful in our lives. A special thanks to all of our family, friends, and colleagues for inspiring us.

Table of Contents

CHAPTER 8
Fluid Level Check

CHAPTER 9
Electrical System

CHAPTER 10
Lubrication System

CHAPTER 11
Fuel System

CHAPTER 12
Cooling System and Climate Control

CHAPTER 13
Ignition System

CHAPTER 14
Suspension, Steering, and Tires

CHAPTER 15
Braking System
Fluid Reservoir

Brake Master Cylinder

Firewall

CHAPTER 16
Drivetrain

Chapter 17
Exhaust and Emission System

Chapter 18
Alternative Fuels and Designs

Photo: Tesla

Chapter 19
Automotive Accessories

Chapter 20
Common Problems and Roadside Emergencies

Appendix A

Appendix B

Appendix C

Introduction and How Cars Work

Chapter 1

Source: Library of Congress

Fuel for Thought

- How do cars work?
- How are vehicles classified?
- Why is it good to know the size of your vehicle's engine?

Introduction

For hundreds of years people have been compelled to find a better way to travel. It would be impossible to credit just one person for the development of the automobile. The word "automobile" literally means self-moving. People wanted a vehicle that could take them to new places. For many years people worked and lived within miles of where they were born and where they eventually died. Before the automobile, most people traveled on land from one place to another by foot, train, bicycle, or horse and carriage. Within a few years of the turn of the 20th century, the automobile would change society forever. Today, there are millions of vehicles on the roadways.

Objectives

Upon completion of this chapter and activities, you will be able to:

- Identify early automotive contributors.
- Differentiate between vehicle manufacturers, makes, models, and types.
- Describe how cars work.
- Locate and use an online owner's manual.

Automotive Timeline

Numerous milestones and significant automotive events (***Figure 1.1***) have made vehicles more efficient, comfortable, and reliable. This section focuses on:

- Early Years
- Henry Ford
- Growth Over 100 Years

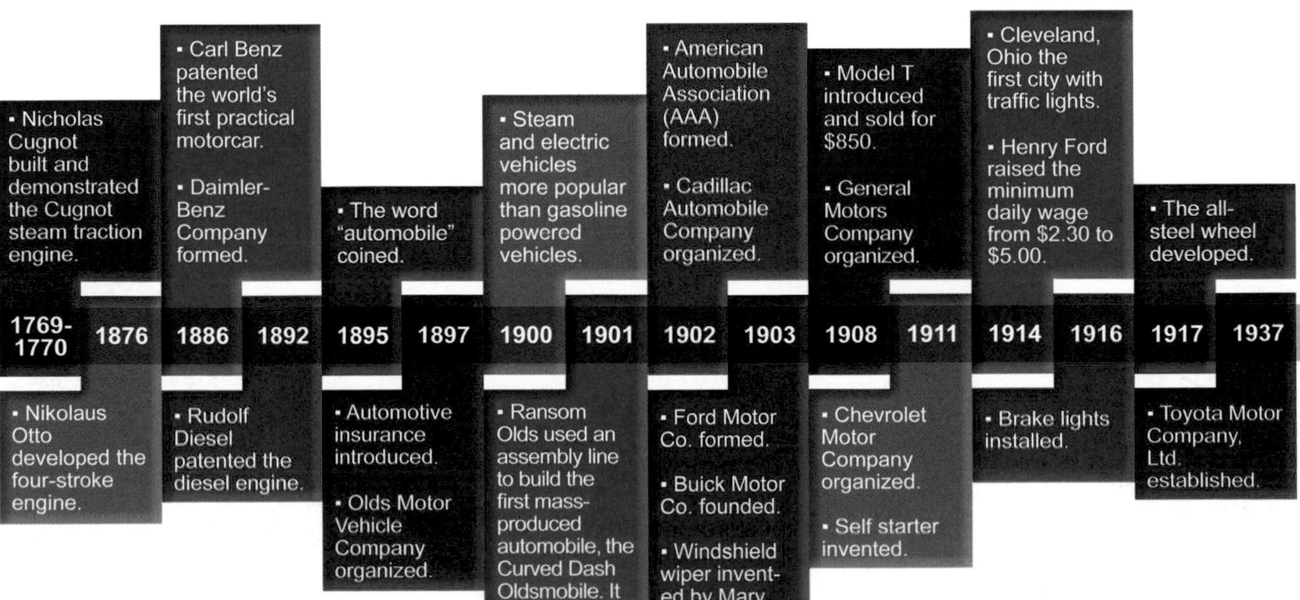

1769-1770 • Nicholas Cugnot built and demonstrated the Cugnot steam traction engine.
1876 • Nikolaus Otto developed the four-stroke engine.
1886 • Carl Benz patented the world's first practical motorcar. • Daimler-Benz Company formed.
1892 • Rudolf Diesel patented the diesel engine.
1895 • The word "automobile" coined.
1897 • Automotive insurance introduced. • Olds Motor Vehicle Company organized.
1900 • Steam and electric vehicles more popular than gasoline powered vehicles.
1901 • Ransom Olds used an assembly line to build the first mass-produced automobile, the Curved Dash Oldsmobile. It sold for $650.
1902 • American Automobile Association (AAA) formed. • Cadillac Automobile Company organized.
1903 • Ford Motor Co. formed. • Buick Motor Co. founded. • Windshield wiper invent-ed by Mary Anderson.
1908 • Model T introduced and sold for $850. • General Motors Company organized.
1911 • Chevrolet Motor Company organized. • Self starter invented.
1914 • Cleveland, Ohio the first city with traffic lights. • Henry Ford raised the minimum daily wage from $2.30 to $5.00.
1916 • Brake lights installed.
1917 • The all-steel wheel developed.
1937 • Toyota Motor Company, Ltd. established.

Figure 1.1

Early Years

One of the earliest recorded major milestones in the development of the automobile was the Cugnot steam traction engine in 1769-1770. Even though this self-powered road vehicle was rather impractical, it was a starting point for the automobile. The development of the internal combustion engine in 1860 made road vehicles more promising. Then in 1886 Carl Benz was credited with building the world's first practical motorcar. At the turn of the century, blacksmith shops around the country were hand-building cars.

Web Links

Automotive Museum Sites

Antique Automobile Club of America Museum
www.aacamuseum.org

Gilmore Car Museum
www.gilmorecarmuseum.org

Henry Ford Museum
www.thehenryford.org

Manitoba Antique Auto Museum
www.mbautomuseum.com

National Automobile Museum
www.automuseum.org

Petersen Automotive Museum
www.petersen.org

Henry Ford

Henry Ford, who introduced the Model T in 1908, put an end to many of the small hand-building automotive shops. By 1914, Ford was able to significantly decrease production time using a conveyor (moving) assembly line (***Figure 1.2***). Workers could put together a Model T in just 93 minutes. Originally introduced at $850 in 1908, the Model T eventually sold for as little as $260. By the 1920s, half the cars in the world were Model T Fords. In 1923 alone, Ford produced over 1.8 million Model Ts. The last Ford Model T rolled off of the assembly line in 1927. Ford produced over 15 million Model Ts.

Figure 1.2 ***Model T Ford Assembly Line***
Source: Library of Congress

Growth Over 100 Years

Over the last hundred years, automobile production has grown substantially. In 1900 about 9500 motor vehicles were produced in the world. That number grew to over 50 million per year just a century later.

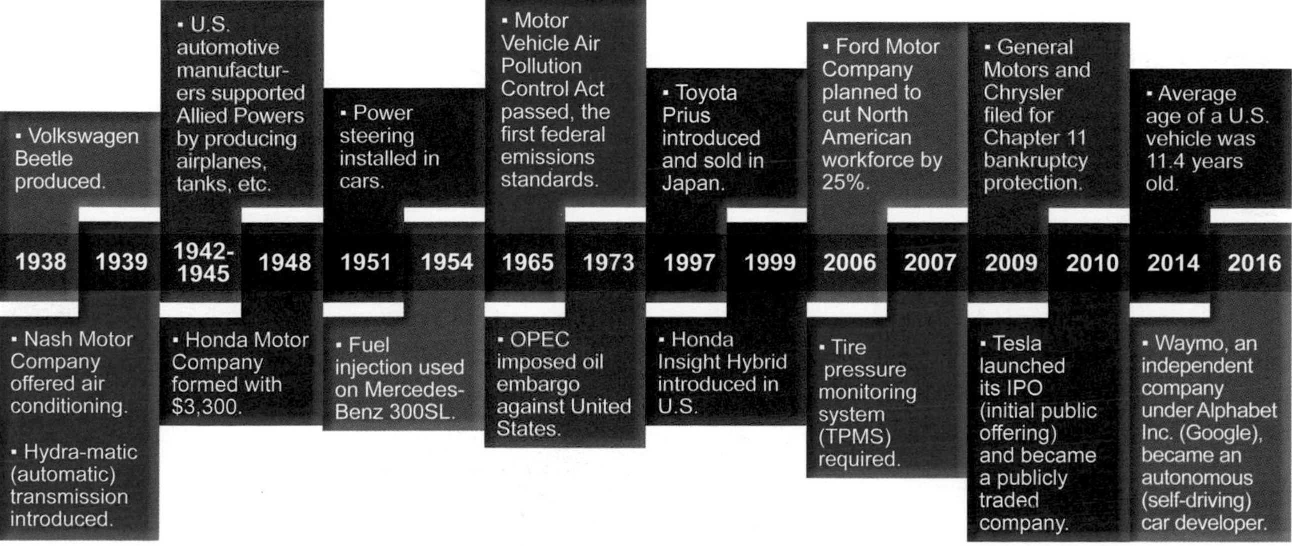

Significant Automotive Events

How Cars Work

Currently the most common propulsion system in an automobile is the internal combustion engine (ICE). ICEs burn fuel in a combustion chamber inside the engine. This section focuses on:

- Conservation of Energy
- Force, Work, Power, and Energy
- Measuring Engine Output
- Engine Components
- Four-Stoke Engines
- Power Transfer

Conservation of Energy

Vehicles need energy to move. The energy used is commonly gasoline, diesel, or electricity. A key concept to understand is that energy cannot be created or destroyed in the vehicle, it is just converted from one form to another. This is called the law of conservation of energy in physics (specifically in a closed system). Gasoline vehicles are not very efficient at moving down the road. They don't destroy energy, but they lose energy. These losses occur in the engine, drivetrain, braking, overcoming the wind (aerodynamic drag), rolling resistance (tires contacting the road), and running accessories (parasitic losses). The energy into the system is going to equal the energy out of the system, even if some of it is unwanted and not usable (*Figure 1.3*).

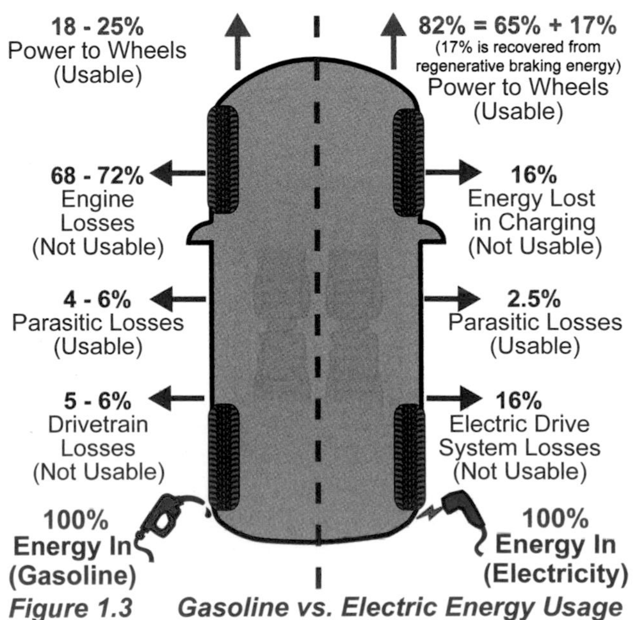

Figure 1.3 ***Gasoline vs. Electric Energy Usage***

Source: U.S. Department of Energy EERE - www.fueleconomy.gov

Force, Work, Power, and Energy

To learn how power is transferred in a vehicle, key terms (force, work, power, and energy) and the relationship between them need to be studied.

Force. Simply defined, force is a push or pull interaction between objects (***Figure 1.4***). This interaction can occur when objects are in physical contact with one another or when there is an action at a distance caused by magnetic forces, gravitational forces, and electric forces.

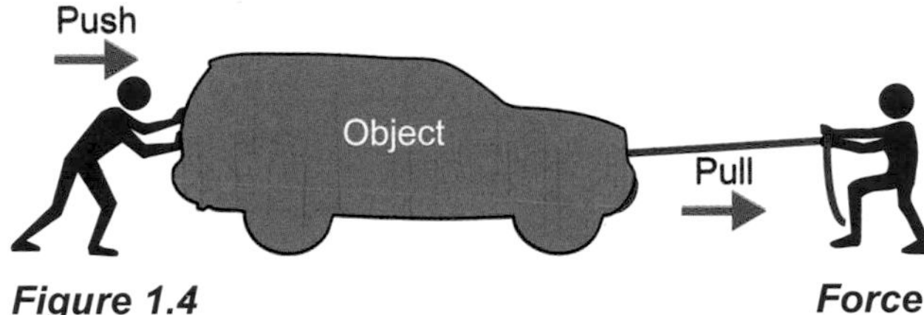

Figure 1.4 ***Force***

Work. When an object has moved from a force, the position of the object has changed and work has occurred. If no motion has occurred, no work has been done. Work is the transfer of energy from one object to another (***Figure 1.5***).

Work = Force x Distance

Figure 1.5 ***Work = Force x Distance***

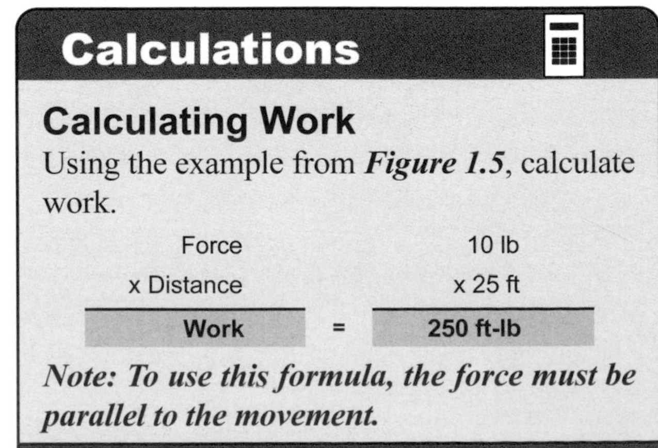

Calculations

Calculating Work

Using the example from ***Figure 1.5***, calculate work.

Force		10 lb
x Distance		x 25 ft
Work	=	**250 ft-lb**

Note: To use this formula, the force must be parallel to the movement.

Power. Power is the rate at which work is done (the amount of work done, energy delivered, in a given amount of time).

Power = Work/Time

Energy. Objects have the ability to do work when they have energy. Different forms of energy are classified into two categories: potential and kinetic. Potential energy is stored energy or energy of position. Kinetic energy is the energy of an object from its movement. Energy is required to do work. Gasoline, diesel, electricity, or some other source of energy is needed for a vehicle to do work. Energy and power are linked, but are not the same thing. This is helpful to know when looking at battery ratings on hybrid and electric vehicles. These batteries are usually rated in kilowatt hours (kWh).

Energy = Power x Time

1 kWh = 1 kilowatt x 1 hour

For example, an electric vehicle might have a battery capacity of 60 kWh. Think of energy as the amount of "fuel" stored or used to perform work.

Measuring Engine Output

Two numbers are commonly used in advertising a vehicle's output: torque and horsepower.

Torque. When force is in a twisting motion it is called torque. Tightening a bolt with a wrench is an example of torque (***Figure 1.6***). A special wrench, a torque wrench, is used to tighten bolts to an exact specification.

Torque = Force x Lever Length

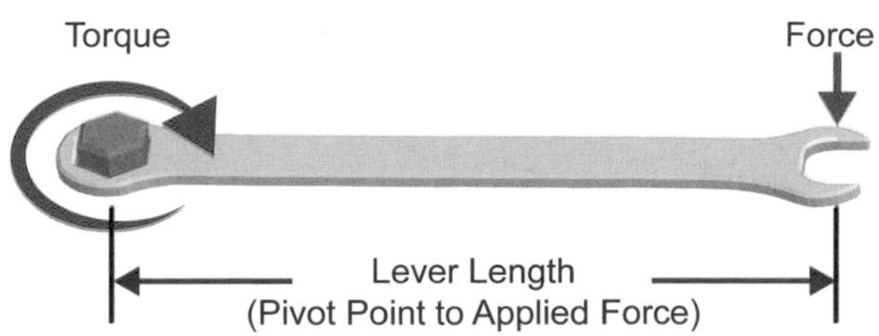

Figure 1.6 ***Torque = Force x Lever Length***

Crankshaft Torque. Torque is also used to describe the output rating of an engine, the crankshaft's turning force (***Figure 1.7***).

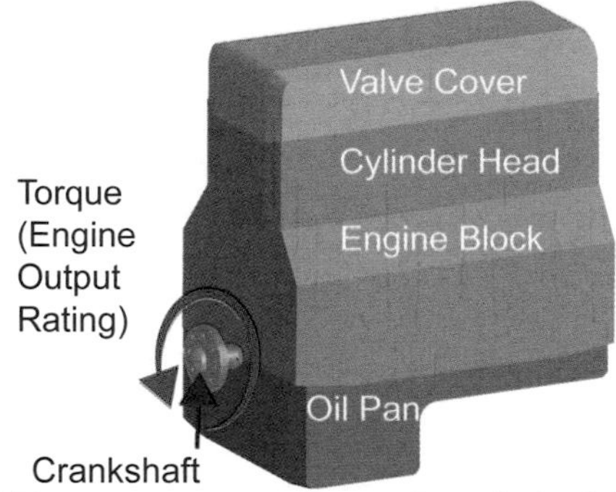

Figure 1.7 ***Crankshaft Torque***

Horsepower. A unit of power that is common in the automotive field is horsepower (hp). One horsepower is the work needed to lift 550 pounds a distance of 1 foot in 1 second (***Figure 1.8***).

Horsepower (English System)

1 Horsepower = 550 foot-pounds/second
1 Horsepower = 33,000 foot-pounds/minute

Watt (Metric System)

1 Horsepower = 746 watts = 0.746 kilowatts

Figure 1.8 ***One Horsepower***

Revolutions Per Minute (RPM). Torque and horsepower change as engine speed (revolutions per minute or rpm) changes, so these ratings are given at a specific rpm (***Figure 1.9***).

Vehicle	Engine	HP	Torque
1920 Ford Model T	2.9 L Gasoline	20 hp @ 1600 rpm	83 lb-ft @ 900 rpm
2017 Ford Super Duty	6.7 L Turbo Diesel	440 hp @ 2800 rpm	925 lb-ft @ 1800 rpm

Figure 1.9 ***Horsepower Comparison***

Engine Components

The basic parts in a four-stroke engine include intake valves, exhaust valves, pistons, connecting rods, engine block, cylinder head(s), crankshaft, camshaft(s), and oil pan (***Figure 1.10***).

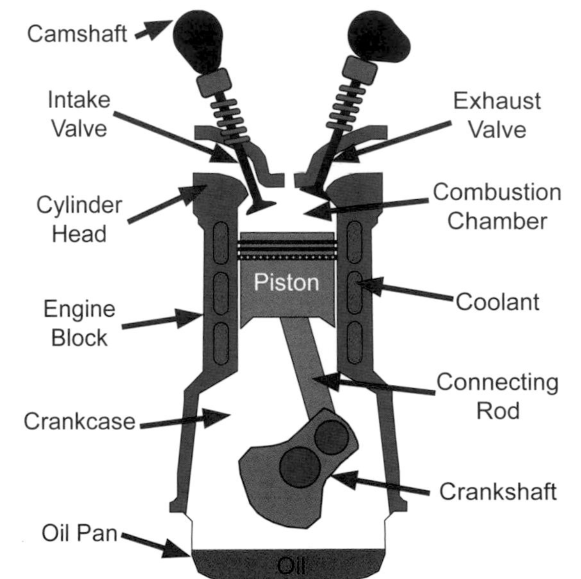

Figure 1.10 Dual Overhead Camshaft (DOHC) Engine

Four-Stroke Engines

The four-stroke internal combustion engine (also known as the Otto cycle, named after Nikolaus Otto) is the most common type used in automobiles. In a four-stroke engine the piston makes reciprocating (back and forth or up and down) movements to convert the chemical energy of fuel into mechanical energy of motion (kinetic energy).

Spark Ignition. Spark ignition (SI) engines are fueled by gasoline, propane, natural gas, or a gasoline/alcohol blend. A spark plug ignites the air-fuel mixture. The four-strokes of the spark ignition engine (***Figure 1.11***) are intake, compression, power (combustion), and exhaust. To complete the four strokes, the crankshaft makes two revolutions. Gasoline direct injection (GDI) engines, now becoming popular, will be explained in Chapter 11.

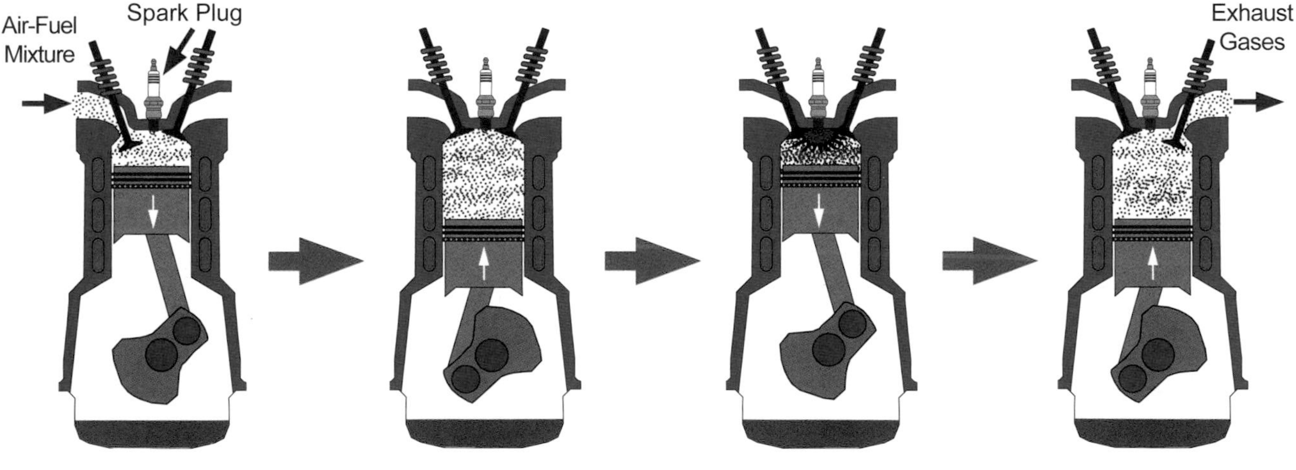

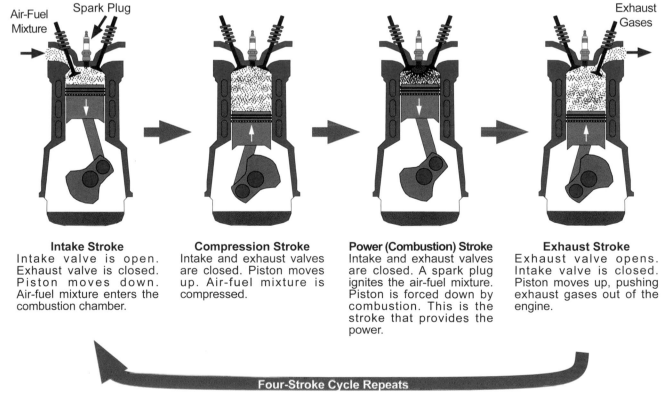

Intake Stroke
Intake valve is open. Exhaust valve is closed. Piston moves down. Air-fuel mixture enters the combustion chamber.

Compression Stroke
Intake and exhaust valves are closed. Piston moves up. Air-fuel mixture is compressed.

Power (Combustion) Stroke
Intake and exhaust valves are closed. A spark plug ignites the air-fuel mixture. Piston is forced down by combustion. This is the stroke that provides the power.

Exhaust Stroke
Exhaust valve opens. Intake valve is closed. Piston moves up, pushing exhaust gases out of the engine.

Figure 1.11 ***Four-Stroke Spark Ignition Engine***
Compression Ratio Commonly 8:1 to 12:1

Compression Ignition. Compression ignition (CI) engines are fueled by diesel. The four-strokes of the compression ignition engine (***Figure 1.12***) are similar to the spark ignition engine, except fuel is not mixed with air in the intake system. Instead diesel is injected directly into the combustion chamber or indirectly into a swirl (precombustion) chamber. Once in the combustion chamber, the diesel combusts spontaneously from the high pressure and heat. CI engines do not use spark plugs.

Videos

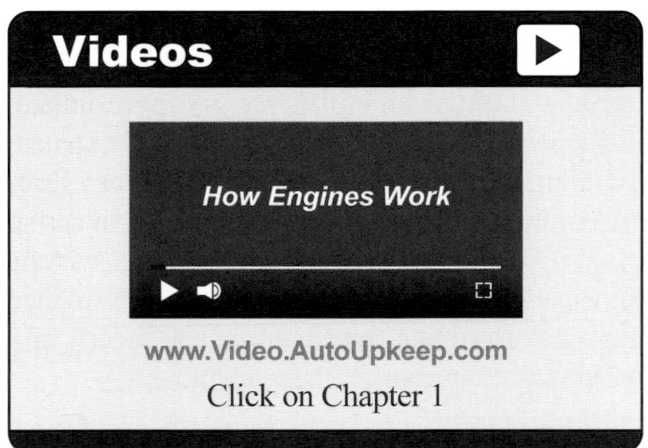

www.Video.AutoUpkeep.com

Click on Chapter 1

Tech Tip 

ICE Requirements

For efficient combustion to occur in an internal combustion engine (ICE), there needs to be the correct air-fuel mixture, sufficient compression, and an ignition source (heat or spark). These three things must function properly to achieve engine efficiency and minimize emissions.

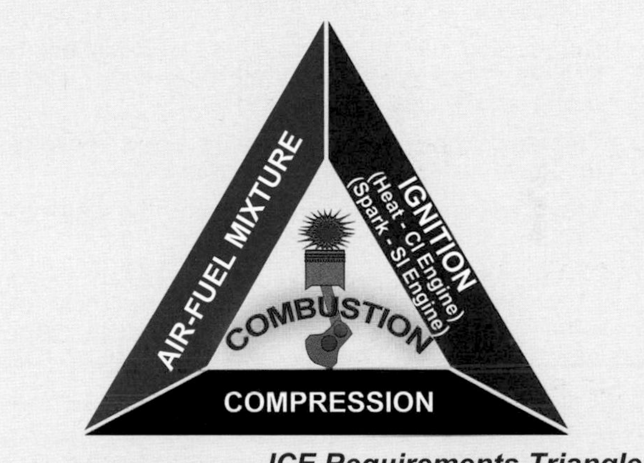

ICE Requirements Triangle

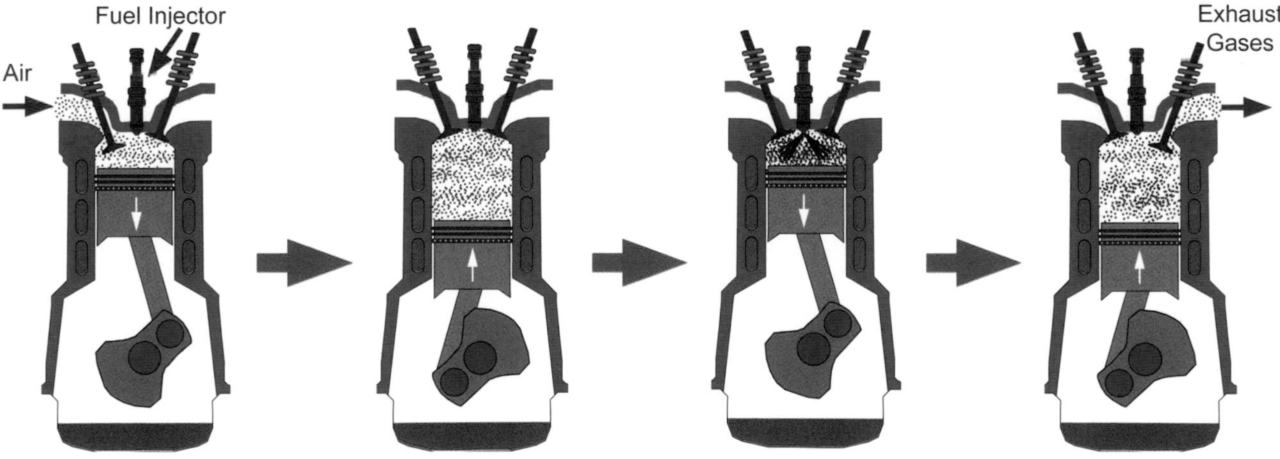

Intake Stroke
Intake valve is open. Exhaust valve is closed. Piston moves down. Air enters the combustion chamber.

Compression Stroke
Intake and exhaust valves are closed. Piston moves up. Air is compressed.

Power (Combustion) Stroke
Intake and exhaust valves are closed. Fuel is injected into the combustion chamber. The high pressure and heat ignite the fuel. Fuel combusts spontaneously. Piston is forced down by combustion. This is the stroke that provides the power.

Exhaust Stroke
Exhaust valve opens. Intake valve is closed. Piston moves up, pushing exhaust gases out of the engine.

Figure 1.12 ***Four-Stroke Compression Ignition Engine (Direct Injection Diesel)***
Compression Ratio Commonly 16:1 to 20:1

Power Transfer

Several processes have to happen in order for a vehicle to move. The following (***Figure 1.13***) explains how power is transferred in a common gasoline powered (non-hybrid) automobile.

Power Transfer Process	
1	Fuel is stored as chemical energy in the gas tank.
2	Fuel is transported to the engine by a fuel pump.
3	Air-fuel mixture enters the engine.
4	Electrical energy is used to create a spark at the spark plug.
5	Combustion occurs, converting the chemical energy to kinetic energy. The piston moves linearly, reciprocating up and down or back and forth.
6	The reciprocating motion of the pistons is converted to rotary (circular) motion of the crankshaft.
7	The crankshaft's rotary motion turns the transmission.
8	On front-wheel drive (FWD) vehicles, rotary motion is transferred through a transaxle (transmission and differential combined). From the transaxle, rotary power is moved through constant velocity (CV) shafts. On rear-wheel drive (RWD) vehicles, rotary motion is transferred from the transmission through the drive shaft then to a differential and final drive assembly. In this situation, the differential changes the power flow 90° and allows the drive wheels to turn at different speeds when cornering. Power is transferred from the differential to axle shafts.
9	The axle shafts or CV shafts turn the wheels.
10	The rotary motion of the wheels converts to linear motion on the roadway.

Figure 1.13 ***How Power is Transferred***

Fuels and Designs

Most of the 260 million vehicles registered in the United States today burn either gasoline or diesel in an internal combustion engine. This section focuses on:

- Gasoline Powered Vehicles
- Diesel Powered Vehicles
- Emerging Technologies

Gasoline Powered Vehicles

Passenger cars and light trucks powered solely by burning gasoline in an internal combustion engine are the most popular. Gasoline engines use spark plugs to ignite the air-fuel mixture in the engine. There are several reasons for the popularity of gasoline powered vehicles. They are currently affordable (this depends on the price of gas (***Figure 1.14***)), easy to refuel (gas stations in just about every town), they meet performance expectations (range, acceleration, and speed), and we are most familiar with the technology.

Gasoline Fuel. One of the major disadvantages of gasoline is that once the fuel is burned, it is gone forever. In addition, gasoline engines emit hydrocarbons (HC), nitrogen oxides (NO_X), carbon monoxide (CO), and carbon dioxide (CO_2). Gasoline emissions are discussed in Chapter 17.

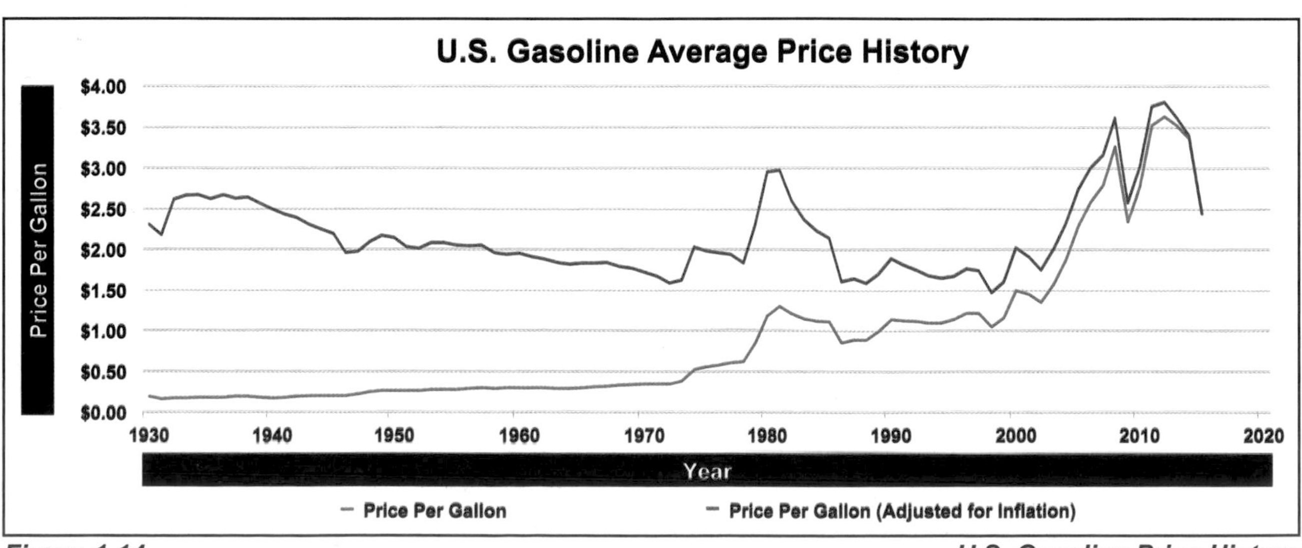

Figure 1.14 ***U.S. Gasoline Price History***

Diesel Powered Vehicles

Diesel engines are compression ignition engines; they do not have spark plugs. When thinking of diesel, a medium (***Figure 1.15***) or heavy-duty truck might come to mind. Diesel powered specialty vehicles (e.g., garbage trucks, school buses, and fire engines) and semi trucks pulling trailers are very common.

Figure 1.15 *Ford F 650 Medium Duty*
Courtesy of Ford Motor Company

Passenger Vehicles. Diesel engines have also become popular in light trucks. Recently in the United States there has been a resurgence of diesel powered cars. In Europe, diesel powered cars are fairly common, making up about one-half of new cars.

Diesel Fuel. Diesel fuel (***Figure 1.16***) has more energy per gallon as compared to gasoline, making it more efficient for every gallon of fuel burned. Diesels emit NO_X and particulate matter (PM), in addition to greenhouse gas pollutants. Ultra-low sulfur diesel and newer engine and emission systems have greatly decreased emissions. Diesel emissions are discussed in Chapter 17.

Figure 1.16 *Diesel Fuel Dispenser*

Emerging Technologies

In 2017, the following gas-free, 100% electric vehicles (EVs) were produced by auto manufacturers (***Figure 1.17***). ***Note: Miles per gallon of gasoline equivalent (MPGe) is a measure used to compare energy usage in advanced technology vehicles to the miles per gallon (MPG) rating in conventional vehicles.***

Electric Vehicles	MPGe
Hyundai Ioniq Electric	136 MPGe
BMW i3	124 MPGe
Nissan Leaf	112 MPGe
Mitsubishi i-MiEV	112 MPGe
Tesla Model X	93 MPGe
Mercedes-Benz B250e	84 MPGe

Figure 1.17 *Electric Vehicles*

EV Charging. EVs use only electricity for propulsion. The disadvantage is that their driving range is limited when the battery is discharged. In a sense, this is similar to your gasoline powered vehicle when your gas tank is empty. The difference is that there are many more gas stations than EV charging stations. Public and company owned charging stations (***Figure 1.18***) are strategically placed to extend the range of electric vehicles when you cannot recharge at home.

Figure 1.18 *Tesla Supercharger Station*
Photo: Tesla

Web Links

EV Charging Stations

PlugShare
www.plugshare.com

ChargePoint
www.chargepoint.com

Tesla Superchargers
www.tesla.com/supercharger

Engine Identification

A vehicle's engine is classified by its:

- Size/Displacement
- Configuration

Size/Displacement

The size of the engine is the combined volume of the cylinders. Engine size can be found on the vehicle emission control information sticker under the hood. Engine size is commonly listed in liters or cubic inches (***Figure 1.19***).
Note: 1 L = 61.02 cu. in.

International System of Units (Metric System)		U.S. Customary Units (English System)
1.8 L	=	110 cu. in.
2.4 L	=	147 cu. in.
4.6 L	=	281 cu. in.
5.0 L	=	305 cu. in.
5.3 L	=	323 cu. in.
6.8 L	=	415 cu. in.

Figure 1.19 ***Common Engine Sizes***

Configuration

Engine configuration is the design of the engine block. Common engine configurations include inline, opposed, or V (***Figure 1.20***). The configuration describes the way cylinders are arranged in the block. The number of cylinders within the engine block is also used to identify the type of engine design. Engines have 3, 4, 5, 6, 8, 10, or 12 cylinders. The most common engine configurations are inline 4s, V6s, and V8s.

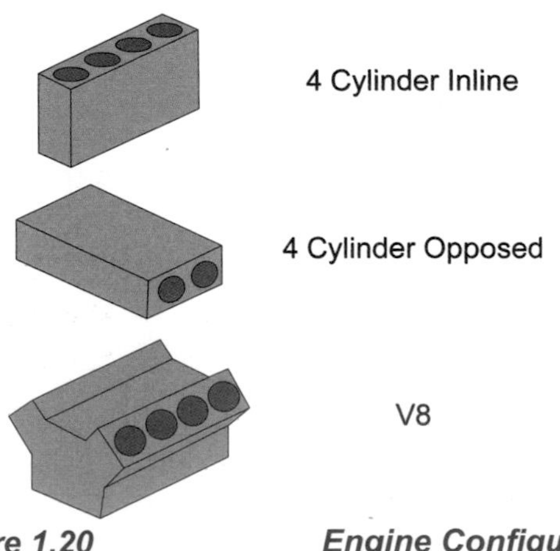

Figure 1.20 ***Engine Configurations***

Vehicle Identification

Vehicles can be identified by the:

- VIN
- Manufacturer
- Make
- Model
- Year
- Type

VIN

The Vehicle Identification Number (VIN) is an important number on a vehicle. This 17-character number can be seen on the left side of the dash from outside the vehicle through the windshield. Left and right sides are determined by sitting inside the vehicle facing forward. The VIN also appears on the vehicle certification label on the inside of the driver's doorjamb. Additionally, it is on the vehicle's title card.

VIN Information. The VIN contains information including codes that identify the engine type, body type, model year (MY), assembly plant, production sequence number, and other information specific to that vehicle. In the following figure, the tenth character "H" identifies the model year as 2017, even though the manufacture date was October 2016 (***Figure 1.21***). Keep the VIN handy, automotive parts stores may need it to find the correct replacement parts.

Figure 1.21 ***Doorjamb VIN***

Manufacturer

An automotive manufacturer (***Figure 1.22***) is a company that produces vehicles. Through the years some manufacturers have taken over others, joined forces, or completely gone out of business.

Figure 1.22 ***Automotive Manufacturer Logos***

Make

Automotive manufacturers (***Figure 1.23***) identify the various vehicles they produce by their "make" (also known as brands or divisions).

Manufacturer	Make/Brand/Division
GM	Buick, Cadillac, Chevrolet, and GMC
Fiat Chrysler Automobiles	Chrysler, Dodge, Jeep, Ram Truck, Alfa Romeo, Fiat, Lancia, Abarth, and Maserati
Daimler	Maybach, Mercedes-Benz, AMG, and smart
Ford	Ford and Lincoln
Toyota	Lexus and Toyota
Volkswagen Group	Volkswagen, Audi, Bentley, Bugatti, Lamborghini, Porsche, SEAT, and SKODA
Honda	Acura and Honda
Hyundai	Hyundai and Kia
Nissan	Infiniti, Nissan, and Datsun
Geely	Geely and Volvo
Tata	Jaguar, Land Rover, and Tata
BMW	BMW, MINI, and Rolls-Royce

Figure 1.23 ***Examples of Makes***

Model

The model (***Figure 1.24***) of a vehicle refers to the specific name of each vehicle within a make. Model names often change over time.

Make	Model
Chevrolet	Bolt EV, Camaro, Colorado, Corvette, Cruze, Equinox, Impala, Malibu, Silverado, Sonic, Spark, Suburban, Trax, Traverse, Tahoe, and Volt

Figure 1.24 ***Examples of Models***

Year

The model year of a vehicle is not necessarily the year in which it was built. A vehicle built in October 2017 most likely would be considered a 2018 model year vehicle. To find the actual model year of the vehicle look at the vehicle emission control information (VECI) sticker under the hood. This sticker indicates the year of pollution standards conformance, which is also the model year (MY). The date of manufacture is listed inside the driver's door on the vehicle certification label. This is the actual month and year that the vehicle rolled off the assembly line.

Type

Automotive manufacturers design many different types (***Figure 1.25***) of vehicles to meet consumer demands.

Type	Model
Microcar	GEM e2, Nano, and smart fortwo
Subcompact Car	Accent, Fiesta, Fit, Spark, Versa, and Yaris
Compact Car	Civic, Corolla, Focus, Golf, and Sentra
Mid-size Car	Accord, Camry, Fusion, and Malibu
Full-size Car	Avalon, Charger, Impala, and Maxima
Sports Car	Challenger, Corvette, Mustang, and Porsche 911
Compact SUV	Escape, RAV4, CR-V, and Wrangler
Mid-size SUV	Durango, Explorer, Grand Cherokee, Highlander, and Pathfinder
Crossover SUV	Edge, Flex, Murano, Outback, and Tiguan
Full-size SUV	Escalade, Expedition, Suburban, and Tahoe
Compact Pickup	Colorado, Frontier, Ridgeline, and Tacoma
Full-size Pickup	F-Series, Ram, Sierra, Silverado, Titan, and Tundra
Minivan	Caravan, Pacifica, Odyssey, Quest, Sedona, Sienna, and Transit Connect
Van	Express, Savana, and Transit

Figure 1.25 ***Examples of Types and Models***

Tech Tip 

Identifying Vehicle Parts

To purchase the correct maintenance items (e.g., filters) or replacement parts (e.g., an alternator or a starter), it is important to know a vehicle's VIN, make, model, engine size/configuration, production date, and model year. ***Note: The date of manufacture and the model year of a vehicle may differ. Manufacturers produce millions of vehicles each year by continuous manufacturing. Showroom floors often include vehicles from next year's model lineup six to nine months before that calendar year.***

Parts and Systems

The automobile is made up of:

- Parts
- Systems

Parts

The car's frame and body (sometimes integrated together into one unit called a unibody) are large parts of the automobile (***Figure 1.26***). Smaller parts (also called components) and assemblies (e.g., engine and transmission) work together to make the vehicle move.

Figure 1.26 ***Vehicle Body***
Photo: Tesla

Systems

Parts that work together to perform a specific task make up a system.

Electrical System. The job of the electrical system is to deliver electricity throughout the vehicle to various lights, motors, relays, and switches.

Lubrication System. The lubrication system moves oil throughout the engine to reduce wear.

Fuel System. Using fuel lines, injectors, and a fuel pump, the fuel system supplies the engine with the correct amount of fuel and air.

Cooling System and Climate Control. The cooling system carries away excess heat from the engine. Climate control is used to condition the air in the passenger's cabin.

Ignition System. The ignition system is designed to ignite the air-fuel mixture in a gasoline engine at the correct time.

Suspension, Steering, and Tires. The suspension system helps to control the vehicle's up and down movement. The steering system controls the vehicle's directional movements. The tires connect the vehicle to the road.

Braking System. The braking system slows and stops a vehicle.

Drivetrain. The drivetrain transfers the power from the engine to the wheels.

Exhaust and Emission System. The exhaust and emission system removes exhaust from the engine, quiets engine combustion, and lowers vehicle pollutants.

Web Links 

Automotive Manufacturer Sites

BMW of North America, LLC
www.bmwusa.com

Fiat Chrysler Automobiles
www.fiat.com

Fisker Inc.
www.fiskerinc.com

Ford Motor Company
www.ford.com

General Motors
www.gm.com

Honda Motor Company
www.honda.com

Hyundai Motor Company
www.hyundai.com

Mazda
www.mazda.com

Mitsubishi Motors North America, Inc.
www.mitsubishicars.com

Nissan Motor Company
www.nissanusa.com

Tata Motors
www.tatamotors.com

Tesla
www.tesla.com

Toyota Motor Corporation
www.toyota.com

Volkswagen of America
www.vw.com

Careers

Many careers exist in the automotive industry:

- Manufacturing Careers
- Service and Repair Careers
- Support Careers

Manufacturing Careers

Automotive manufacturers hire many different types of engineers that assist in pre-production, software and programming, automation, paint, and assembly. Designers, machinists, logistics personnel, production supervisors, and assembly line workers (***Figure 1.27***) are all needed to build highly complex vehicles.

Figure 1.27 ***Automotive Manufacturing***
Photo: Tesla

Service and Repair Careers

Automotive technicians can work in a variety of repair facilities (***Figure 1.28***) in different capacities to diagnose, service, and repair a vehicle. Service managers oversee the shop operations. Service writers communicate with the customers and convey the concern or scheduled service to the technician through a work order.

Figure 1.28 ***Repair Facility***
Courtesy of Ford Motor Company

Support Careers

Careers that support the automotive industry include automotive teachers, salespeople, parts specialists, auto body technicians, insurance adjusters, auto loan specialists, car rental managers, and installers at specialty shops.

Summary

In a little over one hundred years, automobiles have become extremely popular. The automobile has made personal land transportation easy, allowing people to work great distances from where they live. Cugnot, Benz, and Ford, among others, changed the development of the automobile forever. Today, manufacturers are mass-producing hybrid and 100% electric vehicles to increase efficiency, minimize pollution, and reduce our reliance on nonrenewable energy resources. See Chapter 18 to learn more about alternative fueled vehicles.

Activities

Introduction and How Cars Work

- Car Identification Activity
- Owner's Manual Activity
- Chapter 1 Study Questions

Activities and Study Questions can be completed in the *Auto Upkeep Workbook.*

Career Paths

Automotive Teacher

Education: Bachelor's Degree and/or ASE Cert.
Median Income: $52,800
Abilities: Good communication with students in a technical hands-on environment.
Find your career at www.bls.gov/ooh.

Buying an Automobile

Photo: Tesla

Fuel for Thought

- How do interest rates impact your buying power?
- What type of vehicle do you need or want?
- Where can you go to research buying a vehicle?

Introduction

Second to a home, the purchase of an automobile will probably be your next largest financial investment. The car buying process is amazing; you can walk into a car dealership and often within an hour drive away in an automobile. Take your time when buying an automobile. Remember, the new pretty red car that you just have to have will be there next week or dealers can often get another just like it (***Figure 2.1***). Since many people will buy a used car the first time, this chapter will present the process of buying a used as well as a new automobile.

Figure 2.1 ***New Vehicles at a Dealership***

Objectives

Upon completion of this chapter and activities, you will be able to:

- Determine your automobile budget.
- Differentiate between needs and wants in relation to good transportation.
- Identify the steps in buying an automobile.
- Identify the places to buy an automobile.

Purpose of Buying

Why do you need an automobile? This is an easy question to answer, right? You need to be able to get from place to place. Now think again. Do you need this vehicle to get to work? Do you need it for cruising on Saturday night? Automobiles are extremely expensive to own and operate. Do you need a car or do you want one? Either way, you will most likely own one someday.

Budgeting for a Vehicle

Buying a vehicle is a large financial decision. This section will briefly describe how to:

- Determine Your Budget
- Identify Your Wants and Needs
- Finance the Purchase

Determine Your Budget

The first thing you should do is develop a budget to determine what vehicle you can afford. Your choices may be limited if you only have $500 in the bank and work earning an entry level wage. For example, working 20 hours a week making $10 an hour will yield a gross income (before taxes and social security withholdings) of $200 a week or about $10,400 a year. Do you want to work one year of your life to own a car? There are also all of the expenses of owning: taxes, license plate tags, insurance, maintenance, unexpected repairs, and fuel. Don't get in over your head. If you can't put down at least 20% of the total cost, you probably can't afford the car. Chapter 3 will detail the total financial cost of owning and maintaining a car.

Identify Your Wants and Needs

Identifying wants and needs is important. You may want an off-road truck for fun on weekends, but need a car that is fuel efficient and reliable for commuting to work. Different types of vehicles provide for different needs and wants. With so many models available it might be a challenge to choose your best option.

Finance the Purchase

If you cannot afford to buy a vehicle outright, you may have to make monthly payments. If this is the case, you should go to several financial institutions to obtain financing information and loan qualifications. If you do not have any credit or are under 18, you may need to have someone co-sign the loan with you (that means they are responsible for the loan if you default).

Credit Report. If you have had a loan, you should request a credit report to see your credit history. The three consumer reporting companies (TransUnion, Equifax, and Experian) are each required under the Fair Credit Reporting Act to supply you with a free credit report once every 12 months. If you would like your report three times a year, alternate requests between these three companies every four months. A bank will use your credit report to quote an interest rate.

Credit Score. Your credit score (a complex calculated number based on your credit report) is an easy way for lenders to evaluate your credit status (***Figure 2.2***). The following factors contribute to your credit score: payment history, amount owed on credit, length of credit history, new credit, and types of credit used.

Credit Score Range

500	600	700	800	
Poor	Fair	Good	Very Good	Exceptional

Figure 2.2 ***Credit Score Range 300 to 850***

Q & A

Free Credit Report

Q: How do I get my credit report?

A: To request your free credit report, go to **www.annualcreditreport.com**. Be careful to only use this site. Imposter sites on the Internet also advertise free credit reports.

Interest Rates. Check current interest rates at several banks on automobile loans. Depending on the economy, financial institution, and your credit history, interest rates commonly range from 3.9 to 15.9%. However, automotive manufacturers may offer interest free (0.0%) or low (0.9 to 2.9%) interest loans to qualified buyers. The interest rate makes a big difference on the overall price you pay for a vehicle. The calculations in the table below are based on a loan of $6,000 for 36 months with interest rates from 3.9% up to 11.9% (***Figure 2.3***). Understanding interest rates is a necessity if you plan to borrow money. Once you have researched and mastered this, you will better understand what you will really be able to afford. Finding the lowest interest rate can save you hundreds or even thousands of dollars.

Interest Rate	Monthly Payment	Total Cost
3.9%	$177	$6,372
7.9%	$188	$6,768
11.9%	$199	$7,164
Note: Based on a $6,000 Loan for 36 Months		

Figure 2.3 ***Interest Rate Calculations***

Calculations

Auto Loan Calculator

Go to **www.autobytel.com/car-financing/car-calculators** for helpful calculators including: car payments, lease vs. buy, and rebate vs. 0% financing. You can determine monthly loan or lease payment options based on loan amount, term, and interest rate.

Buying or Leasing

Should you buy or lease a new car (***Figure 2.4***)? Leasing will generally get you into a new car for a lower monthly payment than buying with a loan. However, at the end of the lease term (commonly 36 months) you do not own anything. If you like driving a new car with the assurances of a factory warranty, then leasing may be for you. If you like driving a car without payments for a couple of years, then a loan may be for you. Purchasing makes more sense if you drive more than 15,000 miles (≈24,000 km) a year, drive the vehicle for 5+ years, or personalize the vehicle's appearance with accessories. If you use your car for business, check with a tax advisor for tax benefits that may apply when buying or leasing.

	Buying	Leasing
Ownership	You own it. It is yours for as long as you want to keep it.	You don't own it. You may have the option to buy it at the end of the lease or you can upgrade to a new car in another lease.
Monthly Payments	Higher cost than leasing, but once it is paid off, this monthly expense is eliminated.	Lower cost than buying, but if you continue to lease, you will have car payments throughout your driving life.
Up-front Costs	Down payment, taxes, and registration.	Security deposit, first month payment, taxes, and registration.
Mileage	As much as you want.	Designated allotment, such as 12,000 miles per year. If you go over, you pay extra charges.
Customizing	It's your car, do what you want.	You may be required to remove modifications at the end of the lease.
Equity	You are building equity because it is your car.	You have no equity in the car.
Depreciation	Your car starts to depreciate as soon as you drive off the lot.	Your leasing company accepts the depreciated value when the lease term ends.
Damage	If you get a dent or scratch, fix it if you want.	You may have to pay for damages beyond normal wear.
Selling	It's your car, sell or trade it in when you want.	You have to wait until the end of the lease to return it to the dealership. You cannot sell it. Early lease termination can be costly.

Figure 2.4 ***Buying vs. Leasing Comparison***

Buying a New Automobile

One of the main reasons to choose a new vehicle over a used one is the allure of a warranty. With a factory warranty, you won't have to worry about an expensive repair for years. A new vehicle will come with several different warranty packages: bumper-to-bumper, powertrain, corrosion perforation, emission, safety restraint, and hybrid related components (***Figure 2.5***). Some new vehicles even have complimentary maintenance (e.g., oil changes and tire rotations) for two or more years. Many even come with roadside assistance if you get a flat tire or need a jump start. This section will focus on:

- Locating Places to Purchase
- Reading Window Stickers
- Researching Vehicles
- Test Driving
- Understanding Dealer Terms
- Making an Offer

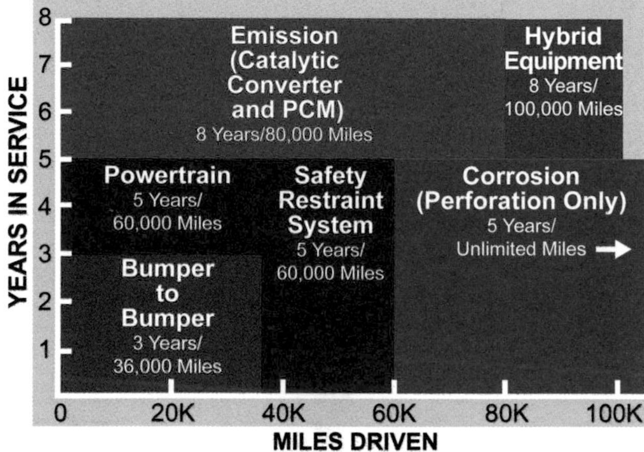

Figure 2.5 ***Example Warranty Packages***

Locating Places to Purchase

When purchasing a new vehicle you will normally buy it from a dealership. Some new car manufacturers, like Tesla, sell cars direct. Dealerships are independently owned or owned by a large corporation. You can enter the dealership through their front doors or through their website. The benefit of buying a new vehicle is that you can usually compare the same exact vehicle from one dealership to another. Use this to your advantage when negotiating a price.

Local Car Dealerships. Shopping local is beneficial because you are contributing to your community. A local car dealership (***Figure 2.6***) often gives back to the community, supporting causes and charities. A dealership close to home can reduce decision pressure by giving you more hands-on inspection time. In small communities you may already know the people working in the sales, service, and parts department.

Figure 2.6 ***Local Car Dealership***
Courtesy of Mayse Automotive Group - www.mayse.com

Dealership Internet Sales. Most dealerships have an Internet sales department. They know savvy buyers are comparing vehicles from one dealership to the next. If you have already settled on the vehicle that you want, taken a test drive for compatibility with your needs and wants, and decided on options - negotiating a deal through the Internet sales department might be the most hassle free way to buy a car. The salesperson you are chatting, texting, or emailing with knows you can choose another dealer with a click of your mouse. The Internet price will usually be lower than if you walked on the dealership lot.

Auto Buying Programs. Warehouse clubs like Sam's Club (***Figure 2.7***), Costco, and BJ's Wholesale Club have auto buying programs for their members. Auto club memberships like AAA also have discounted rates. Certified dealers work with these buying programs to give members specific pricing or additional discounts.

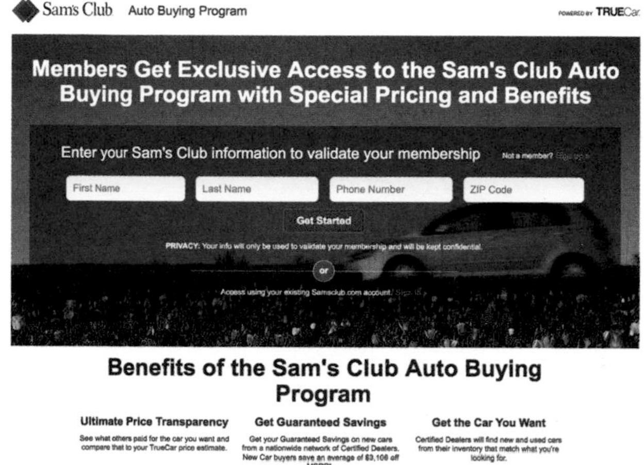

Figure 2.7 ***Auto Buying Program***
Screen Capture from samsclub.truecar.com

Fleet Sales Departments. Another way to enter a dealership is through their fleet sales department. This department works on high volume sales usually selling vehicles to businesses, but many will also sell to you directly. Keep in mind that their salespeople primarily work with businesses and may be on a normal 8 am to 5 pm weekday schedule. You can fax or email your vehicle specifications to the fleet departments at several dealerships to compare bids.

Lemon Law

Q: What is a lemon law?

A: Lemon laws vary depending on where you live. In general a new car is a lemon if it has been in a shop four times for the same problem or for an extended period of time (usually 30 days) in the first 12 to 24 months of ownership. Go to **www.autosafety.org** to read the lemon law for your area. Always keep detailed records to support a claim.

Reading Window Stickers

Every new vehicle is issued a window sticker full of information specific to that vehicle (***Figure 2.8***). It is also called the Monroney label or sticker, named after the United States Senator that sponsored the Automobile Information Disclosure Act of 1958. Keep a copy of the window sticker with the vehicle as a helpful reference when parts are needed or for resale details.

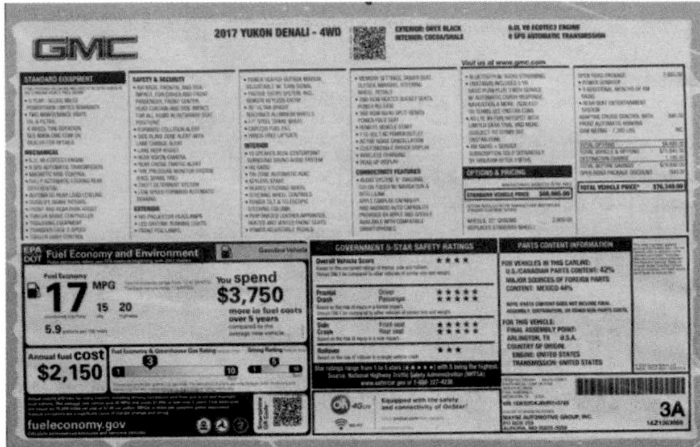

Figure 2.8 *Window Sticker with MSRP*

Window Sticker Requirements. The window sticker is required to include the MSRP (Manufacturer's Suggested Retail Price), engine and transmission specifications, standard equipment and warranty details, optional equipment and pricing, fuel economy ratings, and the National Highway Traffic Safety Administration's (NHTSA) crash test/safety ratings.

Window Sticker Additional Information. A sticker may also provide information on interior and exterior colors, part content information (foreign and domestic sources), final assembly plant (***Figure 2.9***), and wheelbase length.

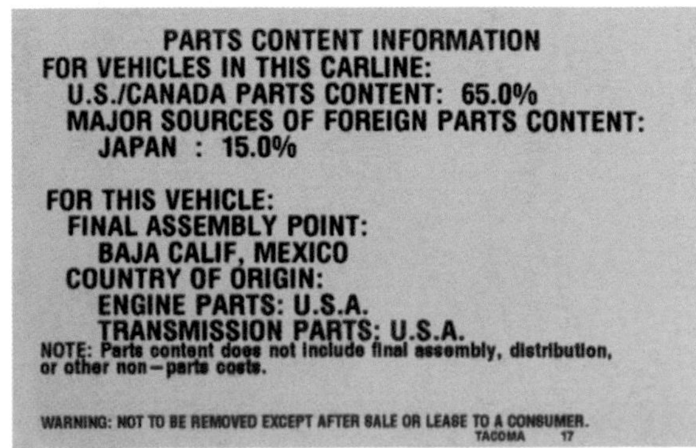

PARTS CONTENT INFORMATION
FOR VEHICLES IN THIS CARLINE:
U.S./CANADA PARTS CONTENT: 65.0%
MAJOR SOURCES OF FOREIGN PARTS CONTENT:
JAPAN : 15.0%

FOR THIS VEHICLE:
FINAL ASSEMBLY POINT:
BAJA CALIF, MEXICO
COUNTRY OF ORIGIN:
ENGINE PARTS: U.S.A.
TRANSMISSION PARTS: U.S.A.
NOTE: Parts content does not include final assembly, distribution, or other non–parts costs.

WARNING: NOT TO BE REMOVED EXCEPT AFTER SALE OR LEASE TO A CONSUMER.
TACOMA 17

Figure 2.9 *Additional Information*

Dealer Addendum Sticker. If the local car dealership added items to the vehicle, you may see an addendum sticker (***Figure 2.10***) next to the government required window sticker. This dealer installed sticker may list items like fabric protection, paint sealant, rustproofing, chrome exhaust tips, pin striping, nitrogen filled tires, floor mats, splash guards, cargo trays, window tinting, wheel locks, upgraded wheels, or even ADM (Additional Dealer Markup)/AMV (Adjusted Market Value) on high demand selling vehicles. ***Note: If you don't want the added items, consider asking the dealer to remove them or give them to you at a wholesale price.*** These are high profit items for the dealer. If all the additional items are difficult to remove or the dealer won't reduce their price on them, find a vehicle at another dealer that doesn't have the add-ons. If you do decide you want an additional item, like splash guards, get several price quotes from local reputable businesses. If you are handy, buy the accessories and install them yourself. Some items like paint sealant may be completely unnecessary. Review the standard warranty and determine if you really need any questionable add-on items.

DEALER NAME / ADDRESS MODEL:

STOCK NO. VEHICLE IDENTIFICATION NO: AVAIL. SERVICE AGREEMENT:

MANUFACTURER'S SUGGESTED RETAIL PRICE	$29,780.00
DEALER INSTALLED OPTIONS	
CUSTOM PINSTRIPE PLUS DOOR GUARDS	$195.00
PAINT SEALANT	$550.00
NITROGEN FILLED TIRES	$150.00
ADDED MARK-UP	
DEALER INSTALLED OPTIONS SUBTOTAL	$895.00
*Dealer's Asking Price (Not The Manufacturer's Suggested Retail Price)	$30,675.00

*Plus State and Local Taxes, License Fees, Documentary Fees or Finance Charges, if any.

FOR FUEL ECONOMY RATING CONSULT GAS MILEAGE GUIDE

THE ESTIMATED MILEAGE FOR THIS MODEL IS TO BE USED TO COMPARE VEHICLES OF THIS MODEL WITH OTHER VEHICLES. ACTUAL MILEAGE WILL VARY WITH OPTIONS, DRIVING CONDITIONS, DRIVING HABITS AND VEHICLE'S CONDITION.

Gas Mileage Information

THIS ADDENDUM HAS BEEN ADDED BY THE DEALER, NOT THE MANUFACTURER, TO REFLECT ANY ADDITIONAL CHARGES FOR ITEMS ADDED OR SERVICES PERFORMED.

THIS IS NOT AN AUTHORIZED FACTORY STICKER

Figure 2.10 *Dealer Addendum Sticker*

Fuel Economy and Environment Label. Part of the window sticker is a fuel economy and environment label (***Figure 2.11***). This label provides information to accurately compare fuel economy, greenhouse gas ratings, smog ratings, annual fuel cost estimates, driving range, and charging time (electric and plug-in hybrid vehicles). It shows how much you would spend on fuel for that vehicle as compared to the average new vehicle.

Figure 2.11 Fuel Economy and Environment Label
Source: U.S. Department of Energy - www.fueleconomy.gov

Driving Range. Driving range estimates (***Figure 2.12***) are helpful when considering an alternative fueled vehicle.

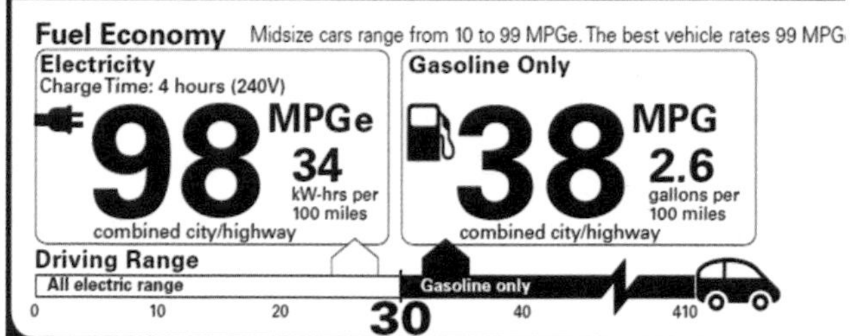

Figure 2.12 Driving Range Plug-In Hybrid
Source: U.S. Department of Energy - www.fueleconomy.gov

Types of Vehicles. The upper right hand corner of the fuel economy and environment label shows what type of vehicle it is (***Figure 2.13***).

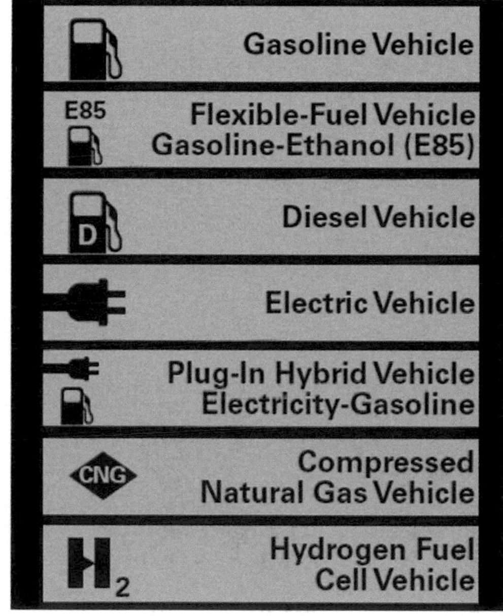

Figure 2.13 Types of Vehicles
Source: U.S. Department of Energy - www.fueleconomy.gov

Quick Reference (QR) Code. A smartphone QR code (***Figure 2.14***) is located in the lower right corner of the fuel economy and environment label. It can be scanned using a smartphone with a free scanning app to easily access more information specific to that vehicle online.

Figure 2.14 Smartphone QR Code
Source: U.S. Department of Energy - www.fueleconomy.gov

Q & A

Exchange a New Car

Q: Is there a three day cancellation policy mandated by law when buying a new car?

A: The three day cancellation (cooling off) policy generally applies to door-to-door sales or sales made away from normal business locations. When buying a new vehicle, unless it is written into the contract or mandated by local law, you cannot return it after you have signed the paperwork and taken possession. It is important to read the fine print before making your final decision. Check with your local consumer protection agency to find out if a "Car Buyer's Bill of Rights" is applicable in your area. For more information, go to www.consumer.ftc.gov.

Researching Vehicles

When purchasing a vehicle make sure you have done your homework. Safety features are constantly improving. Some of the features to look for include seat belt design, number of airbags, head restraint design and position, antilock braking system (ABS), electronic stability control (ESC), traction control system (TCS), visibility, tire pressure monitoring systems (TPMS), and tire quality. Factor vehicle history, safety, and reliability into your buying decision.

Model History. Check out a model's history. Does it have good reliability and consumer remarks? Sometimes a new vehicle with substantial model changes is not a good idea, the "bugs" may not be worked out. One source to use is J.D. Power (www.jdpower.com). They compile consumer data to issue ratings and awards in several categories: Dependability; Performance and Design; Quality; and Sales and Service.

IIHS Safety Ratings. The Insurance Institute for Highway Safety (www.iihs.org) is an independent non-profit organization (funded by auto insurance companies) that conducts tests to reduce injuries, deaths, and property damage from crashes. They provide vehicle safety ratings based on their tests (***Figure 2.15***).

G Good · A Acceptable · M Marginal · P Poor · SUPERIOR with optional equipment

CRASHWORTHINESS	
Small overlap front	G
Moderate overlap front	A
Side	G
Roof strength	G
Head restraints and seats	M
CRASH AVOIDANCE & MITIGATION	
Front crash prevention	SUPERIOR
Headlights	G
CHILD SEAT ANCHORS (LATCH) EASE OF USE	A

Figure 2.15 ***Sample Safety Ratings IIHS***

NHTSA Safety Ratings. The National Highway Traffic Safety Administration (www.nhtsa.gov) is a governmental agency in the United States. The NHTSA uses a 5-star rating system when evaluating vehicles (***Figure 2.16***). The more stars a vehicle has the safer it is. The safety ratings are based on frontal, side, and rollover tests.

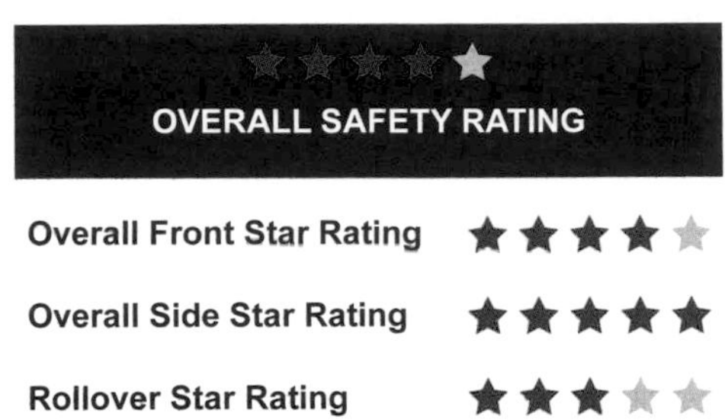

Figure 2.16 ***Sample Safety Ratings NHTSA***
Source: NHTSA - www.nhtsa.gov/ratings

Advanced Safety Technologies. Newer, more advanced technologies can help save lives. Safety features that are becoming popular on vehicles include: adaptive cruise control (ACC); automatic reverse braking (ARB); brake assist system (BAS); hill start assist (HSA); forward collision warning (FCW); lane departure warning; rearview video systems (NHTSA requirement after May 2018 on all new vehicles); and automatic (also called autonomous) emergency braking (AEB) (***Figure 2.17***). Control and safety systems are discussed further in Chapter 15.

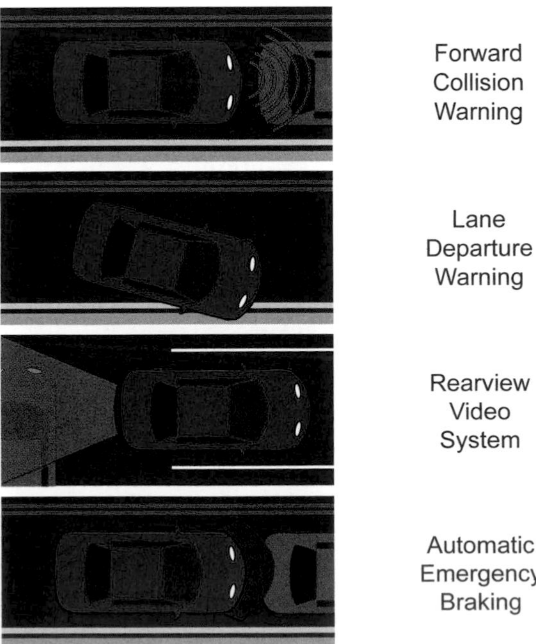

Figure 2.17 ***Advanced Safety Technologies***

Test Driving

After you have narrowed your vehicle search down to a couple of contenders, test drive them one after another if possible. This will let you compare their features (***Figure 2.18***).

Test Drive Checklist		
Drive home, if close. Does it fit in your garage?	■	■
Does it handle well on multiple road surfaces and at different speeds?	■	■
Does it have enough power to easily merge into highway traffic?	■	■
Is it easy to park in a parking space?	■	■
Does it have a suitable turning radius?	■	■
Do you have good visibility in all directions when behind the wheel?	■	■
Can you adjust and use the mirrors easily?	■	■
Does it have the brake stopping power you want?	■	■
Is the level of road, wind, and engine noise acceptable?	■	■
■ **YES** ■ **NO**		

Figure 2.18 ***Test Drive Checklist***

Web Links

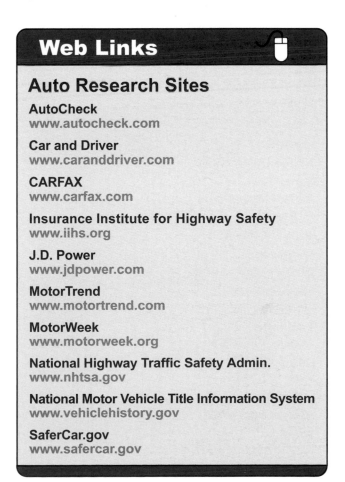

Auto Research Sites

AutoCheck
www.autocheck.com

Car and Driver
www.caranddriver.com

CARFAX
www.carfax.com

Insurance Institute for Highway Safety
www.iihs.org

J.D. Power
www.jdpower.com

MotorTrend
www.motortrend.com

MotorWeek
www.motorweek.org

National Highway Traffic Safety Admin.
www.nhtsa.gov

National Motor Vehicle Title Information System
www.vehiclehistory.gov

SaferCar.gov
www.safercar.gov

Understanding Dealer Terms

Being educated about a dealer's cost will give you an edge in negotiating a deal. There are several terms you need to know (***Figure 2.19***).

Dealer Terms	
MSRP	The Manufacturer's Suggested Retail Price (MSRP) is commonly called the sticker price. Few automotive models sell at MSRP.
Dealer Invoice	The dealer invoice is available in magazines, books, and Internet sites. In the past, this was the price dealerships paid for a vehicle.
Factory Holdbacks	An average factory holdback is commonly 2-3% and can be estimated off the dealer invoice.
Factory to Dealer Incentives	Dealers may receive an incentive, from a few hundred dollars to several thousand dollars, to sell end-of-year or slow moving models.
Dealer Cost	This is the amount that the dealer will actually pay for the vehicle after holdbacks and incentives. If you can determine the actual dealer cost (Dealer Cost = Dealer Invoice – Factory Holdback – Factory Incentives) it is reasonable and fair to offer 4% more than dealer cost.

Figure 2.19 ***Dealer Terms***

Making an Offer

Negotiate up from the dealer cost, not down from the MSRP. Don't forget to include other costs when determining your out-the-door expense: sales tax, vehicle license, title, registration, dealer installed items, dealer documentation, prep fees, and extended warranty. If you are making a fair offer, a reasonable dealership will take it.

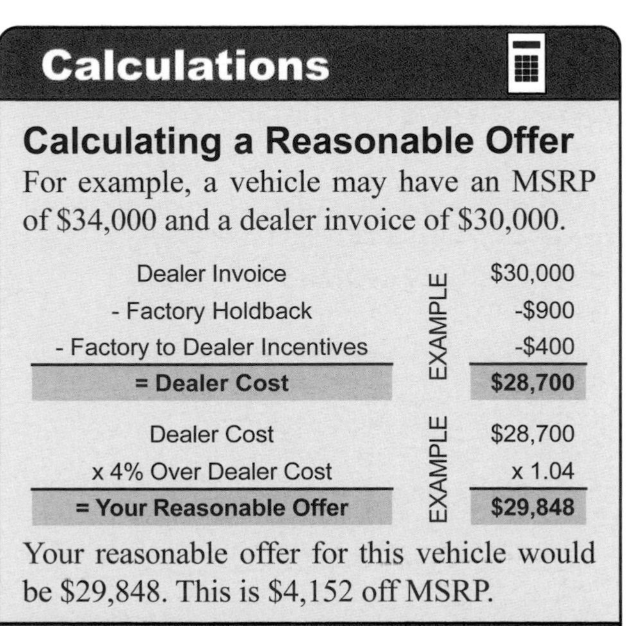

Calculations

Calculating a Reasonable Offer

For example, a vehicle may have an MSRP of $34,000 and a dealer invoice of $30,000.

EXAMPLE	
Dealer Invoice	$30,000
- Factory Holdback	-$900
- Factory to Dealer Incentives	-$400
= Dealer Cost	**$28,700**

EXAMPLE	
Dealer Cost	$28,700
x 4% Over Dealer Cost	x 1.04
= Your Reasonable Offer	**$29,848**

Your reasonable offer for this vehicle would be $29,848. This is $4,152 off MSRP.

Buying a Used Automobile

The main reason to choose a used (also known as pre-owned) vehicle over a new one is cost. If maintained properly, a used vehicle can be a great value. This section focuses on:

- Locating Places to Purchase
- Test Driving and Inspecting
- Vehicle History Reports
- Completing Comparables
- Making an Offer

Locating Places to Purchase

There are many places to buy a used vehicle.

Dealership. A dealership sells both new and used cars. They get their used car inventory through trade-ins, factory owned inventory, at auto auctions, from other dealers, and some cars are purchased directly from the public. Dealerships often keep more late model (commonly 5 years old or newer) cars and send off the older, less desirable cars to public auto auctions. Some dealers also sell certified pre-owned (CPO) cars. These cars, usually only a few years old with low miles, have met strict inspections and are backed by extended warranties by the manufacturer.

Internet. Use an online search to easily compare and locate vehicles. Hundreds of websites on the Internet offer used cars to consumers.

Web Links

Certified Pre-Owned Auto Sites

Dodge/Chrysler/Jeep/Ram Certified Pre-Owned
www.certifiedpreowned.chrysler.com

Ford Certified Pre-Owned
www.ford.com/certified-used

General Motors Certified Used Vehicles
www.gmcertified.com

Honda Certified Pre-Owned
www.hondacertified.com

Hyundai Certified Pre-Owned
www.hyundaicertified.com

Toyota Certified
www.toyotacertified.com

Auctions. Government and public auctions generally have higher mileage cars. Inspect an auto auction car thoroughly. These are cars that didn't make the grade at other car lots and may have significant underlying issues.

Independent Used Car Lot. A used car lot (***Figure 2.20***) is another place to find a car. If you do not know about a particular business, check the company's record with the Better Business Bureau (www.bbb.org).

Figure 2.20 ***Used Car Lot***

Web Links

Auto Buying Sites

Autobytel
www.autobytel.com

AutoTrader.com
www.autotrader.com

CarGurus
www.cargurus.com

Cars.com
www.cars.com

CarMax
www.carmax.com

craigslist
www.craigslist.org

eBay Motors
www.ebay.com/motors

Edmunds
www.edmunds.com

Kelley Blue Book
www.kbb.com

National Automotive Dealers Association (NADA)
www.nada.com

TrueCar
www.truecar.com

Private-Party Seller. Try to determine why someone is selling their "good" used car. Private-parties sell cars using newspapers, automotive publications, signs (***Figure 2.21***), or the Internet.

Figure 2.21 ***Private-Party Seller Sign***

Car Rental Sales. Car rental companies like to keep their fleets new. This means that they sell off late model vehicles with 20,000 to 40,000 miles (32,000 to 64,000 km) on them. These vehicles are usually meticulously maintained and cleaned. Several car rental companies offer an extended (up to a three day) test drive. Other rental companies will buy the car back within seven days if you are not happy with it. Read the contract carefully. If the factory warranty has expired, some offer an extended 12 month/12,000 mile (19,000 km) powertrain warranty and roadside assistance.

Independent Repair Facilities. Some independent auto repair facilities sell vehicles as a side business. A customer may have brought in their vehicle to have it repaired, but decided it wasn't worth it. The repair shop may have purchased the vehicle, fixed it, and are now reselling it. This is a way to keep their technicians busy if the repair business is slow.

Web Links

Car Rental Sales

Avis Car Sales
www.aviscarsales.com

Budget Car Sales
www.budgetcarsales.com

Enterprise Car Sales
www.enterprisecarsales.com

Hertz Car Sales
www.hertzcarsales.com

Thrifty Car Sales
www.thriftycarsales.com

Test Driving and Inspecting

Always inspect and drive a car before you buy, not after. Test driving a used car is different than test driving a new one. You want to make sure everything works. It is easier to test drive on familiar city streets and highways so you can focus on listening for suspicious noises and feeling how it handles. Take time to test accessories, windows, seats, door locks, and inspect all the vital systems (***Figure 2.22***). If you know a reputable technician or have friends that know about cars, ask them to look at it with you.

Exterior Inspection		
Body Condition – scratches, dents, rust, panel misalignments	■	■
Tires – matching tread design and brand, tire tread depth, even wear	■	■
Glass – windshield cracks and chips	■	■
Lights – headlights (low and high beam), turn signals, running lights, brake lights	■	■
Wiper Blades – cracks, streaking, missing pieces	■	■
Interior Inspection		
Upholstery – rips, worn seats, stains	■	■
Odors – unusually smells, mold, mildew, smoke	■	■
Power Functions – power seats, power windows, heater and A/C controls, audio system, sunroof	■	■
Instrument Cluster – gauges, malfunction indicator lights	■	■
Horn – function	■	■
Seat Belts – condition, latches	■	■
Under the Hood Inspection		
Fluids – oil, transmission, brake, power steering, coolant	■	■
Belts and Hoses – engine drive belts, upper and lower radiator hoses, heater hoses	■	■
Battery – terminals, load test	■	■
Charging System - voltage and amperage test	■	■
Under the Vehicle Inspection		
Brakes – brake pad/shoe thickness, brake hoses for cracks, parking brake function	■	■
Suspension and Steering – chassis lubrication, ride height, shocks, struts	■	■
Drivetrain – transmission, transaxle, or differential leaks; CV boots, U-Joints	■	■
Spare Tire – condition	■	■
Exhaust – leaks, holes, rust, noise	■	■
■ OK	■ NEEDS ATTENTION	

Figure 2.22 ***Used Car Inspection Checklist***

Vehicle History Reports

The National Motor Vehicle Title Information System (NMVTIS) (www.vehiclehistory.gov) helps you connect with approved data providers to view a used car's history. NMVTIS reports provide information in five areas that are commonly associated with automotive fraud and theft (***Figure 2.23***). These reports (e.g., title problems, ownership history, and accidents) are only as accurate as the databases that they search. State titling agencies, junk yards, salvage yards, auto recyclers, and insurance carriers are required to report data. Vehicle history reports should be used in conjunction with an inspection by an automotive professional and a review of the vehicle's service records.

NMVTIS Reporting Areas	
Title	This area lists the current state of title and last title date.
Brand History	Brand information is in relation to the status of the vehicle such as junk, salvage, or flood.
Odometer Information	An odometer reading history helps consumers identify any discrepancies with the vehicle's history.
Total Loss History	Knowing whether a vehicle was ever classified as a total loss by an insurance company helps buyers know if the vehicle has been significantly repaired.
Salvage History	This category also helps buyers determine a vehicle's history, knowing at one point in the vehicle's life if it had severe damage.

Figure 2.23 ***NMVTIS Reporting Areas***

Web Links

NMVTIS Data Providers

Auto Data Direct, Inc.
www.titlecheck.us

CARCO Group, Inc.
www.checkthatvin.com

instaVIN
www.instavin.com

VINAudit.com, Inc.
www.vinaudit.com

VINSmart
www.vinsmart.com

Completing Comparables

You should complete comparables to figure out if the vehicle you are looking at is a good deal. Many publications are available in book form or on the Internet. Some examples include *Kelley Blue Book*, *NADA*, and *Edmunds* (***Figure 2.24***). The actual value is dependent upon several factors such as paint quality, interior condition, or mileage on the vehicle.

Vehicles: 2015 4 Door Sedans	Private Party Value		Retail
	Edmunds	KBB	NADA
Honda Civic SE	$12,779	$12,815	$14,725
Toyota Corolla LE	$11,248	$11,628	$13,800
Ford Focus SE	$9,292	$10,321	$12,500

Note: Data Retrieved in 2017
Condition: Very Good/Clean
Mileage: 40,000 Miles

Figure 2.24 ***Sample Value Comparison***

Making an Offer

Making an offer on a used car is different than offering on a new one. With new cars, you can make a direct comparison. With used cars, the two vehicles may be the same year and model, but one vehicle might have more miles on it, have a small dent in the fender, or a tear in the upholstery. Before negotiating, know the approximate value of the vehicle by using the data you found during the completing comparables step. Make a reasonable offer, but on the low side. Work up in small increments from your offer, not down from the seller's asking price. You have more leverage in negotiations if you are willing to walk away from the deal that you believe is not fair. Lots of used cars are available, so don't get too attached to a specific one.

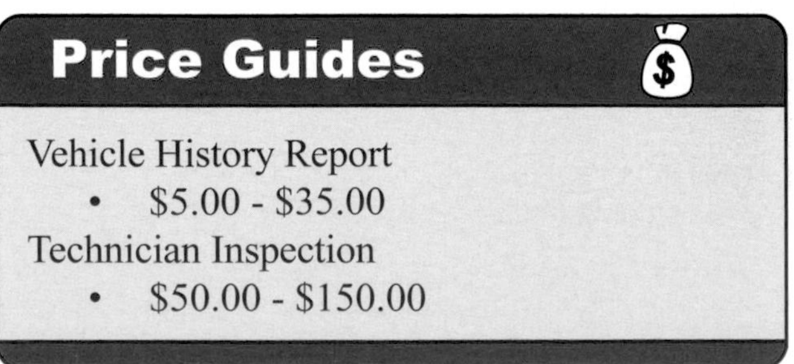

Price Guides

Vehicle History Report
- $5.00 - $35.00

Technician Inspection
- $50.00 - $150.00

Selling, Trading In, or Donating

When you are upgrading your current vehicle, you have choices on how to part with your old one. This section focuses on:

- Selling
- Trading In
- Donating

Selling

Selling your old car yourself will usually get you the most money, but it takes a considerable amount of work. You need to place advertisements online (***Figure 2.25***) or in newspapers, answer questions, and allow test drives to strangers.

Figure 2.25 ***Craigslist Ad***
Screen Capture from www.craigslist.org

Trading In

Trading in your old car has some advantages even if you only get a reduced wholesale price for it. It is easy and you can count the value as a down payment on the new car. Depending on where you live, you may have a tax advantage. If you purchased a new $30,000 vehicle and traded in a $10,000 vehicle you would only pay sales tax on $20,000. This law varies from state to state, so see what is applicable in your area. This tax savings may help you decide if selling your car yourself is worth the hassle.

Apps

www.AutoUpkeep.com/apps
Click on Chapter 2

Donating

Many charities accept old vehicles, even if they don't run. You may benefit from an income tax deduction (***Figure 2.26***) by donating an old vehicle to a qualified charity, but always check with your tax preparer. The other, non-financial benefit, is that you are helping the charity fulfill its mission.

1040 U.S. Individual Income Tax Return 2016

Filing Status

Figure 2.26 ***Income Tax Return***

Summary

Automobiles are expensive to own. Identifying your budget, wants, needs, ways to finance the deal, and the abundant places to purchase a vehicle will give you a step up. Remember that this is a large financial purchase – take your time, complete research, and be educated about the car buying process.

Activities

Buying an Automobile

- Buying a New Automobile Activity
- Buying a Used Automobile Activity
- Chapter 2 Study Questions

Activities and Study Questions can be completed in the *Auto Upkeep Workbook.*

Career Paths

Automobile Salesperson

Education: No Formal Education
Median Income: Commission System
Abilities: Strong communication skills, experience in sales, patience, and positive attitude.
Find your career at www.bls.gov/ooh.

CHAPTER 3 AUTOMOTIVE EXPENSES

Fuel for Thought

- What are some financial disadvantages of owning an automobile?
- Why is liability insurance commonly required?
- How can routine maintenance save you money?

Introduction

Before purchasing an automobile it is important to estimate all of the expenses that go along with ownership. Just because you can afford the monthly payment doesn't mean you can afford the vehicle. Sometimes the monthly payment is only half of your total monthly expenses. Many automotive expenses start after the vehicle purchase. When determining if you can afford a specific car, take into consideration car payments, insurance, fuel expenses, annual license and registration, routine maintenance, and unexpected repairs (***Figure 3.1***). This chapter will identify and describe the most common expense areas of owning and operating a vehicle.

Figure 3.1 ***Unexpected Repair***

Objectives

Upon completion of this chapter and activities, you will be able to:

- Identify automotive expenses.
- Identify ways to save money.
- Describe insurance coverage levels.
- Calculate specific automotive expenses.
- Determine the annual cost to own a car.

Auto Loan Payments

Often people take out a three-, four-, or five-year loan to pay for their vehicle. Remember that this is a long-term commitment between you and the bank. If you lose your job or other family income sources, a monthly car payment could negatively impact your remaining financial commitments. Your monthly payment is dependent on the amount you financed, duration of the loan, and interest rate (***Figure 3.2***). Use a free online loan calculator to simplify the calculation.

Monthly Loan Payment Calculation Factors	
$	Amount Financed (Vehicle Cost – Down Payment)
#	Duration of the Loan (Number of Months)
%	Interest Rate (Annual Percentage)

Figure 3.2 ***Auto Loan Calculation Factors***

Q & A

Auto Club Membership

Q: Are auto club memberships cost effective?

A: Auto clubs, such as AAA, can provide added assurance. Most clubs cover tows (up to a certain distance), jump starts, lockout services, limited fuel delivery, and recoveries (e.g., winched from a ditch). Memberships commonly cost between $50-150 a year depending on service level. ***Note: You may also be able to add emergency roadside service to an insurance policy for minimal cost. Contact your insurance agent for details.***

Insurance

Insurance premiums can be a major factor in your automotive decision. Most states/provinces require that automobiles be insured. If you have a loan on the vehicle, insurance is mandated by the bank to assure loan payment if the vehicle is wrecked. Auto insurance can protect against damage and theft, property damage, and personal bodily injury expenses. Many insurance coverage levels can be purchased. The contract that you decide on is called your insurance policy. Insurance costs depend on your age, driving record, gender, marital status, grades, vehicle model, where you live, and normal driving routes. For beginning drivers, auto insurance can be expensive. Speeding, moving violations, and accidents can substantially increase your insurance premiums. Insurance premiums are usually set up on a monthly, 3-month, 6-month, or yearly billing cycle. Be sure to have your insurance card (***Figure 3.3***) in your car at all times. Auto insurance coverage levels include:

- Deductible
- Liability Insurance
- Collision and Comprehensive Insurance
- Medical Payment, Personal Injury, and No-Fault Insurance
- Uninsured and Underinsured Motorist Insurance
- Umbrella Insurance
- Rental, Towing, and Total Replacement Insurance

INSURANCE COMPANY

Policy Identification Card

Policy Number	Effective Date	Expiration Date
2011-34-66-XX	06-31-17	06-31-18

Year/Make/Model/Vehicle Identification Number
2017 Honda Civic EX 1HGFA1687HL0269X

Insured: Your Name

INSURANCE COMPANY
Anytown, USA 12345

Figure 3.3 *Vehicle Insurance Card*

Deductible

An insurance deductible is the amount you must pay when you make a claim before your insurance kicks in. For example, if you have a claim for $1,000 and your deductible is $250, your insurance will pay $750. One way to decrease insurance premiums is to increase your deductible.

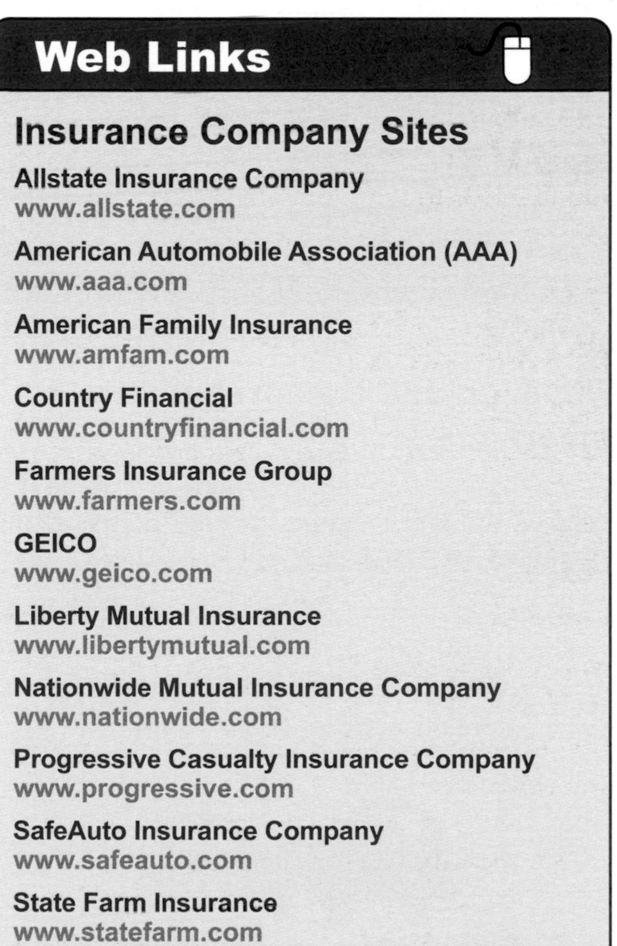

Web Links
Insurance Company Sites
Allstate Insurance Company
www.allstate.com
American Automobile Association (AAA)
www.aaa.com
American Family Insurance
www.amfam.com
Country Financial
www.countryfinancial.com
Farmers Insurance Group
www.farmers.com
GEICO
www.geico.com
Liberty Mutual Insurance
www.libertymutual.com
Nationwide Mutual Insurance Company
www.nationwide.com
Progressive Casualty Insurance Company
www.progressive.com
SafeAuto Insurance Company
www.safeauto.com
State Farm Insurance
www.statefarm.com

Liability Insurance

The minimum policy commonly required is liability insurance. It covers third party bodily injury or property damage claims that you cause. If you caused an accident, your liability insurance would pay the victim's claims (up to a certain dollar amount minus your deductible). Liability insurance policies are stated in numerical terms such as 20/40/10 (***Figure 3.4***). The first number indicates that this policy would have $20,000 bodily injury coverage per person. The second number indicates a limit of $40,000 bodily injury coverage per accident. The third number sets the property damage limit at $10,000. Minimum insurance requirements vary. A 20/40/10 policy, a minimum required by law in some areas, is usually inadequate considering the cost of medical and legal issues. For instance, if you did not have enough insurance and you caused a serious accident, a person could sue you and put a lien on your assets. Many insurance companies suggest drivers should have 100/300/50 coverage.

Liability Insurance Numbers	Bodily Injury per Person	Bodily Injury per Accident	Property Damage Limit
20/40/10	$20,000	$40,000	$10,000
100/300/50	$100,000	$300,000	$50,000

Figure 3.4 ***Liability Insurance Numbers***

Collision and Comprehensive Insurance

In addition to liability coverage, if you have a loan you will be required to add collision and comprehensive insurance on your policy.

Collision Insurance. If you were at fault in an accident, collision insurance covers the cost to repair your vehicle up to the vehicle's market value before the accident (***Figure 3.5***).

Figure 3.5 ***Collision Insurance***

Comprehensive Insurance. Comprehensive insurance covers the costs to repair your vehicle for damage that might occur from things such as natural disasters, vandalism, theft, fire, or hitting an animal on the road (***Figure 3.6***).

Figure 3.6 ***Comprehensive Damage Examples***

Medical Payment, Personal Injury, and No-Fault Insurance

Other protections that can be added to a policy are medical payment, personal injury protection, and no-fault insurance. Medical payment insurance covers you and your passengers if you were at fault in an accident. Personal injury protection covers such things as incurred lost wages if you could not work because of an accident. No-fault protection allows policyholders to submit a claim to their insurance company for reimbursement instead of waiting to see whom the insurance company tries to hold liable for the accident.

Q & A ?

Reducing Insurance Expense

Q: What types of cars are the most expensive to insure and what can be done to lower rates?

A: In general, sports cars and sport-utility vehicles are the most expensive to insure. Look for cars with advanced safety features. To find specific car safety ratings, visit the Insurance Institute for Highway Safety at www.iihs.org. Keep your driving record free of tickets and accidents. Discounts may be available for accredited driver education safety courses. Students on the honor roll can often get a 10 to 25% good student discount. Contacting several insurance companies for price quotes may save you hundreds of dollars per year.

Uninsured and Underinsured Motorist Insurance

Another insurance required in many areas is uninsured motorist coverage. This covers you if someone without insurance injures you or damages your car in an automobile accident. Underinsured motorist coverage will pay for damages or injuries that occur to you by someone else, if the damages exceed the other party's policy limits.

Umbrella Insurance

Umbrella insurance (***Figure 3.7***) is an additional form of liability protection. The term "umbrella" is used since it protects you from liability claims above and beyond your other policies – such as an auto or homeowners insurance. The insurance company would pay when damages exceed your other insurance limits if you are at fault in an accident and someone sues you for bodily injury, property damage, or lost wages. Without this coverage your personal assets are at risk in a lawsuit. Depending on your insurance company, umbrella insurance may add an additional 1 to 10 million dollars worth of coverage. It covers the cost of a legal defense, false arrest, slander, and provides you with personal liability coverage wherever you travel around the world. For so much additional protection you might be surprised to know that the cost is minimal to add umbrella insurance to an existing eligible policy. Keep in mind that it will not cover any business related claims, even if it is a home-based business.

Figure 3.7 ***Umbrella Insurance Protection***

Rental, Towing, and Total Replacement Insurance

Rental coverage will pay car rental fees while your vehicle is being repaired. Towing (***Figure 3.8***) coverage will pay for vehicle towing up to a certain limit. Total replacement coverage will pay the replacement cost of your vehicle if it is totaled (beyond fixing) instead of its depreciated value. Some insurance companies also offer an insurance coverage to get you into a newer vehicle with fewer miles if your vehicle was totaled.

Figure 3.8 ***Tow Truck***

Courtesy of Miller Industries – www.millerind.com

Q & A

Car Rental Insurance

Q: Should I pay for the insurance add-on when I rent a car?

A: If you have an auto insurance policy that includes third party liability, collision, and comprehensive it may cover the insurance on rental cars. Contact your insurance agent to clarify if you need to purchase additional coverage when renting. Some credit card companies offer rental insurance if you charge the car rental to your card. If your vehicle is being repaired and is covered by collision or comprehensive insurance, you may have an endorsement that covers a rental car while yours is in the shop. If you do not hold a car insurance policy, you should pay the rental company for rental insurance to protect you from lawsuits and property damage if you have an accident while renting.

Fuel Expenses

Fuel expenses depend on fuel prices at the pump and your vehicle's actual fuel economy. This section focuses on:

- Fuel Prices
- Fuel Economy

Fuel Prices

Fuel prices are set by crude oil prices (priced by the barrel), supply and demand, refinery production, octane rating, and specific regional formulation. Crude oil goes through a distillation process at a refinery to make gasoline and other products. The price per gallon of gasoline also includes federal and state taxes. ***Note: 1 gallon = 3.785 L***

Fuel Economy

Fuel economy varies depending on the vehicle. Pickups and sport utility vehicles commonly get 12-20 miles per gallon (MPG), compact cars can get 30-40 MPG, and hybrids can get 50-70 MPG (***Figure 3.9***). ***Note: In other countries fuel economy is calculated in L/100 km.***

MPG	Price per Gallon	1,000 Miles Monthly	12,000 Miles Yearly
20	$4.00	$200.00	$2,400.00
40	$4.00	$100.00	$1,200.00
60	$4.00	$66.67	$800.00

Figure 3.9 ***Effect of MPG on Fuel Cost***

License and Registration

You will be required by law to license and register your vehicle with your motor vehicle department. When buying a vehicle you also have to pay sales tax and title fees. If you have a loan on your vehicle the title (***Figure 3.10***) will identify the lien holder.

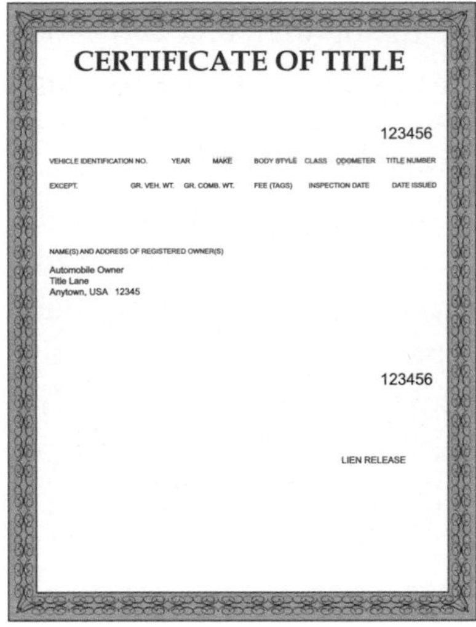

Figure 3.10 ***Vehicle Title***

License plate tags (***Figure 3.11***) need to be periodically renewed. Convenient online tag renewal services are becoming more popular.

Figure 3.11 ***License Plate with Tags***

Calculations

Monthly Fuel Expense

	EXAMPLE
Miles Driven Between Fill-ups	300
÷ Gallons of Fuel Used	÷ 12
= MPG	**25**

	EXAMPLE
(Miles Per Month ÷ MPG)	(1,000 ÷ 25)
x Fuel Cost Per Gallon	x $3.00
= Fuel Cost Per Month	**$120.00**

Driving a vehicle with high fuel mileage will lower your monthly expenses.

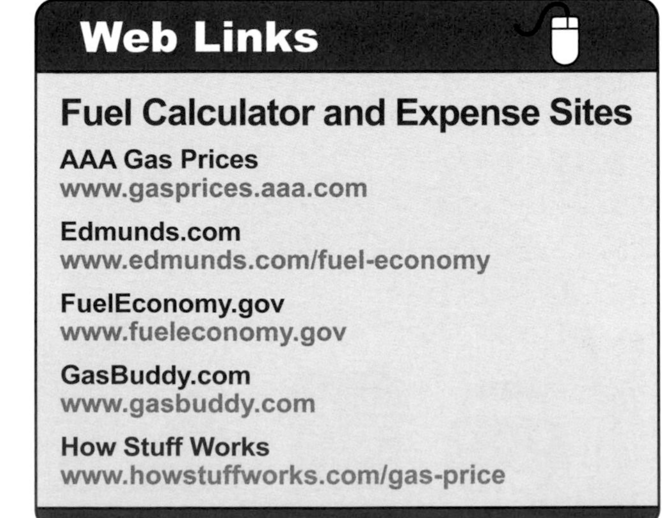

Web Links

Fuel Calculator and Expense Sites

AAA Gas Prices
www.gasprices.aaa.com

Edmunds.com
www.edmunds.com/fuel-economy

FuelEconomy.gov
www.fueleconomy.gov

GasBuddy.com
www.gasbuddy.com

How Stuff Works
www.howstuffworks.com/gas-price

Maintenance and Repairs

Vehicles are generally very reliable, but still need maintenance and may experience an unexpected repair. This section focuses on:

- Maintenance
- Repairs

Maintenance

Maintenance expenses include oil changes, tire rotations, lubricating the chassis, replacing filters, checking/changing fluids, performing tune-ups, and more. An owner's manual may identify two or three recommended service schedules: normal service, severe service, and extreme service.

Normal Service Schedule. A normal service schedule (***Figure 3.12***) includes carrying passengers and cargo within the recommended limits; driving on reasonably well-maintained road surfaces; not exceeding speed limits; and having a balance between city and highway driving.

Tech Tip

Do Maintenance When Required

It is easy to ignore maintenance if there is no apparent problem. Skipping oil changes can cause costly engine damage. Worn or damaged tires and brakes can lead to a safety hazard. Don't ignore a new sound or vibration, it probably means it's time for service.

Severe Service Schedule. A severe service schedule includes vehicles that are driven in extremely cold, hot, or humid climates; driven in mostly city traffic or for short trips; frequently used for towing; driven in mountainous or hilly terrain; are commonly idled for extended periods of time; experience travel on dusty, muddy, or rough roads; and have their brakes used extensively.

Extreme Service Schedule. Some manuals add a third service schedule. If you operate your vehicle continuously in hot/cold/humid climates or under maximum load and towing, the extreme service schedule should be followed.

Repairs

If scheduled maintenance is ignored, it usually costs more as an unexpected repair and possible tow. Unexpected repair expenses may include electrical problems, internal engine damage, or transmission issues. Other problems include replacing suspension and steering parts, the alternator, the starter, belts, or hoses. New vehicles commonly come with a standard 3-year/36,000 mile (57,000 km) bumper-to-bumper warranty. Some manufacturers have a much longer powertrain (e.g., engine, transmission, and drivetrain) warranty. Warranties apply as long as scheduled maintenance has been performed. After the manufacturer warranty expires, repairs will be your responsibility. It is good to have money in reserve for unexpected repairs.

Example Maintenance Schedule in Miles	7,500	15,000	22,500	30,000	37,500	45,000	52,500	60,000	67,500	75,000	82,500	90,000	97,500	105,000
Change oil and filter, if needed, and reset oil life system.	✓	✓	✓	✓	✓	✓	✓	✓	✓	✓	✓	✓	✓	✓
Lubricate suspension and steering components.	✓	✓	✓	✓	✓	✓	✓	✓	✓	✓	✓	✓	✓	✓
Rotate tires. Check tire inflation pressure. Inspect tire wear.	✓	✓	✓	✓	✓	✓	✓	✓	✓	✓	✓	✓	✓	✓
Check all fluid levels and conditions.	✓	✓	✓	✓	✓	✓	✓	✓	✓	✓	✓	✓	✓	✓
Replace cabin air filter.			✓			✓			✓			✓		
Replace engine air filter.						✓						✓		
Replace spark plugs. Inspect spark plug wires.													✓	
Replace brake fluid.						✓						✓		
Note: 1 Mile = 1.60934 Kilometers														

Figure 3.12 ***Example Maintenance Schedule***

Depreciation

Depreciation is a term used to describe how an asset, like a vehicle, has its value reduced over time. Depreciation is impacted by a vehicle's wear and how much demand there is for it when it is used. Some vehicles depreciate less than others and have a higher resale value when trading or selling it. A newer car depreciates faster than an older one. A significant change in gas prices may make less fuel efficient vehicles (e.g., SUVs) depreciate faster than those with better mileage. If fuel prices decline again, the demand for SUVs and trucks can also increase. If you plan to keep your vehicle for a long time, let's say 10 or more years, then the depreciation rate is less meaningful.

- Years 1-5
- Buying Used

Years 1-5

A new car can easily lose 10-20% of its value as you drive off the lot. At the end of five years, depreciation can reduce the value well over 50% of the original cost (***Figure 3.13***).

Buying Used

Knowing that a vehicle depreciates significantly in the first few years can be used to your advantage. Consider purchasing a vehicle that's two to three years old. If you drive it for three years and then sell it when it is about six years old, you have missed the biggest depreciation spots in a vehicle's life.

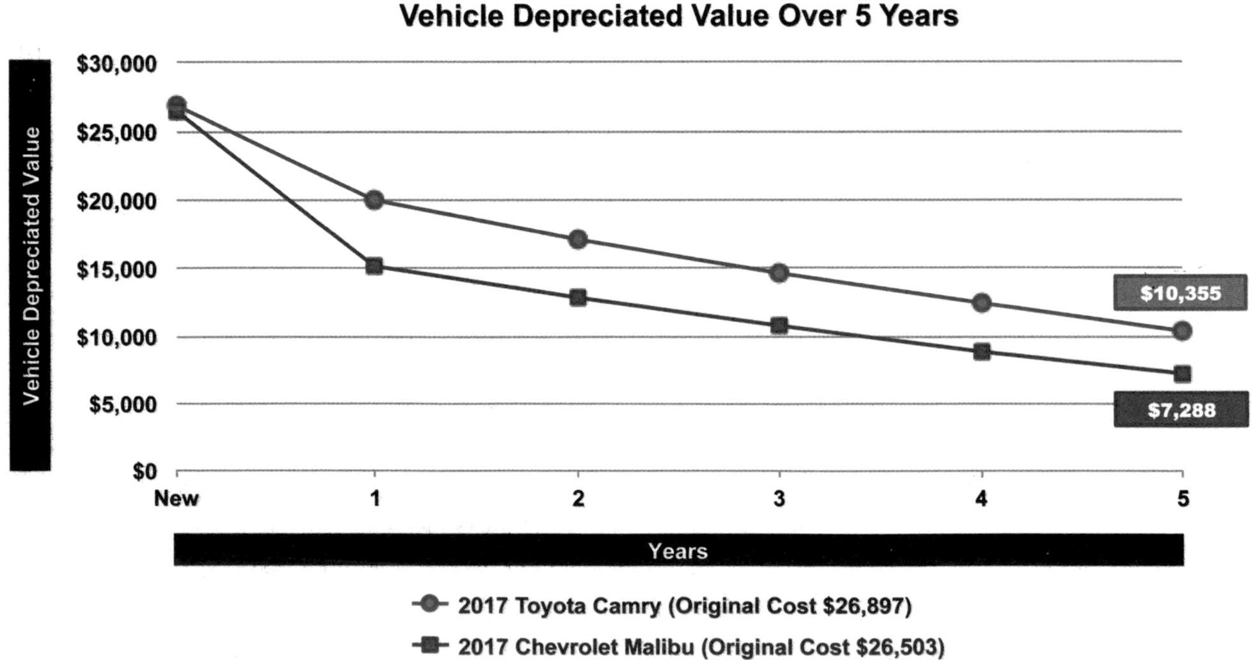

Figure 3.13 *Depreciation Comparison*

Annual Cost to Own a Car

Cars are more reliable than ever. The average vehicle on the road in the United States is over 11 years old. A new car buyer will generally keep their vehicle about six to seven years. Vehicles with the same purchase price can have very different costs to own over time. Your annual costs include depreciation, insurance, fuel, maintenance, repairs, finance charges, and license and registration fees (***Figure 3.14***). According to the U.S. Bureau of Transportation Statistics, over the past five years, the average annual cost to own and operate a vehicle for 15,000 miles was $8840.

2017 GMC Yukon
Annual Cost Averaged Over 5 Years

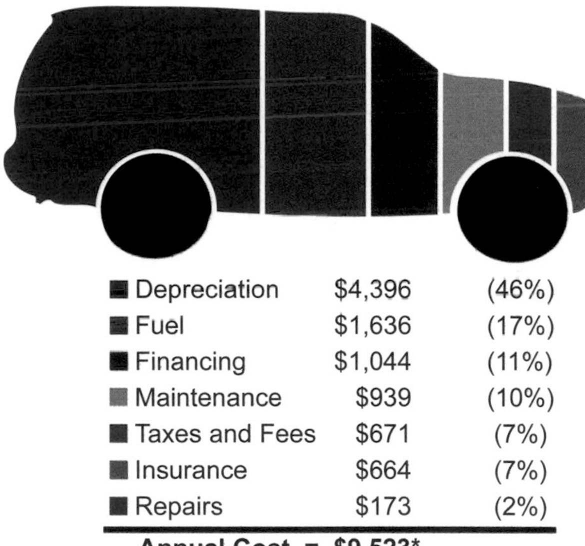

Depreciation $4,396 (46%)
Fuel $1,636 (17%)
Financing $1,044 (11%)
Maintenance $939 (10%)
Taxes and Fees $671 (7%)
Insurance $664 (7%)
Repairs $173 (2%)
Annual Cost = $9,523*

*Based on 15,000 Miles per Year

Cost per Mile = 64¢

Figure 3.14 ***2017 GMC Yukon***

Calculations

Costs to Own a Car

Edmunds created a cost calculator called True Cost to Own® that includes depreciation, interest on your loan, taxes and fees, insurance premiums, fuel costs, maintenance, and repairs. You can check it out and search different vehicles at www.edmunds.com.

Summary

Automobiles are expensive to own. The financial obligations to own and operate a vehicle range from monthly car payments to insurance premiums to unexpected repairs. Understanding depreciation, knowing your budget, and planning for routine maintenance and unexpected expenses will prepare you for the financial responsibility of vehicle ownership.

Activities

Automotive Expenses

- Automotive Expense Activity
- Chapter 3 Study Questions

Activities and Study Questions can be completed in the *Auto Upkeep Workbook*.

Career Paths

Insurance Claims Adjuster

Education: Collision Repair Training

Median Income: $63,060

Abilities: Estimating, investigating, negotiation, communication, and computer skills.

Find your career at www.bls.gov/ooh.

Repair Facilities

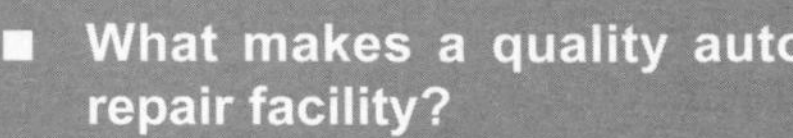

Fuel for Thought

- What makes a quality auto repair facility?
- What are the different types of auto repair facilities?
- What types of auto repair warranties are available?

Introduction

Even do-it-yourselfers may periodically need to visit a repair facility. Being an educated consumer can save you time, money, and headaches. Repair facilities come in a variety of sizes. Some facilities are one person operations, while others may have many employees. Remember to check the warranty (***Figure 4.1***) on your vehicle first to see if a repair is covered by the manufacturer. If unsure, call your local dealer for more information.

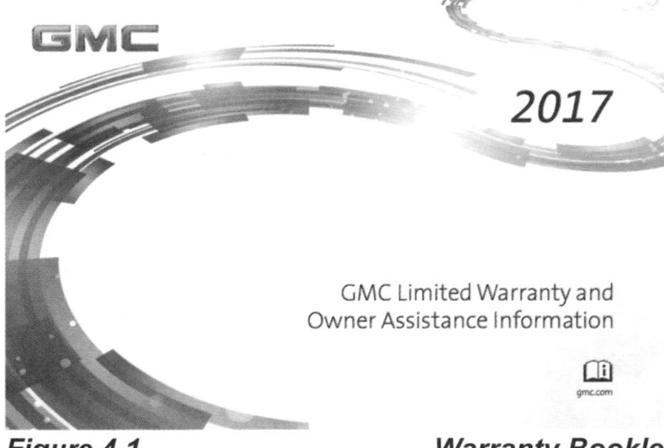

Figure 4.1 ***Warranty Booklet***

Objectives

Upon completion of this chapter and activities, you will be able to:

- Identify a quality repair facility.
- Communicate effectively with a technician or service writer.
- Interpret a repair invoice.
- Locate a car care education program.
- Understand different types of warranties.
- Search for safety recalls.

Key Characteristics of a Quality Repair Facility

Quality repair facilities take pride in their work and keep a clean and organized workspace. They provide written estimates, charge a reasonable rate, hire certified technicians, and are honest with their customers. Before choosing a repair facility, complete research and get recommendations to find a highly qualified company. This section focuses on:

- ASE Certified Technicians
- Business Ethics
- Better Business Bureau (BBB)
- AAA Approved Auto Repair
- Reasonable Costs

ASE Certified Technicians

Repair facility quality depends on the quality of the technicians, support staff, tools, and equipment.

Tech Tip 

Community Education Programs

Local dealerships, specialized repair centers, and independent repair facilities will often hold "Saturday Car Care Clinics" or something similar to educate consumers in the community. These education programs help businesses build a positive relationship with clients and better serve the public.

Technician Training. Troubleshooting automotive problems takes expert training and often high dollar diagnostic equipment. In the past automotive technicians were called mechanics. Today's technicians require extensive training that needs to be updated frequently because the technology on vehicles continuously changes. The National Institute for Automotive Service Excellence (ASE), an independent non-profit organization, certifies technicians through national certification tests. Exams are grouped by specific content area to test technician competence in diagnosing and repairing automobiles. In addition to passing an exam, a technician is also required to have two years of related experience to be certified.

ASE Certifications. Automotive and light truck technicians can become certified in nine areas (***Figure 4.2***). Technicians passing tests A1 through A8 achieve ASE Master Technician status, becoming the best of the best. ASE also tests service consultants, collision repair technicians, engine machinists, parts specialists, and many more in the transportation field. To stay current, ASE requires technicians to retest every five years. Look for a shop posting an ASE sign. Check if their certified technician has several years of experience in the area in which your vehicle needs servicing. ***Note: In Canada look for Journeyperson Automotive Service Technicians.***

Automotive and Light Truck ASE Test Areas	
A1	Engine Repair
A2	Automatic Transmission/Transaxle
A3	Manual Drive Train and Axles
A4	Suspension and Steering
A5	Brakes
A6	Electrical/Electronic Systems
A7	Heating and Air Conditioning
A8	Engine Performance
A9	Light Vehicle Diesel Engines*
*Test A9 not required for Master Status	

ASE
CERTIFIED
We employ technicians certified by the National Institute for
AUTOMOTIVE SERVICE EXCELLENCE
Let us show you their credentials

ASE Repair Facility Sign
Courtesy of National Institute for Automotive Service Excellence

Figure 4.2 ***ASE Certified - A Series Tests***

Business Ethics

It is critical to find a service facility that is honest and reliable. Just as these characteristics are important in everyday life, they are also important in business. Unfortunately a few service facilities take advantage of customers because the automobile is an extremely complex machine. Look for service writers and technicians that are courteous and willing to explain the diagnosis. Reliable facilities have few customer complaints and get the job done right the first time. ASE technicians pledge a Code of Ethics (***Figure 4.3***).

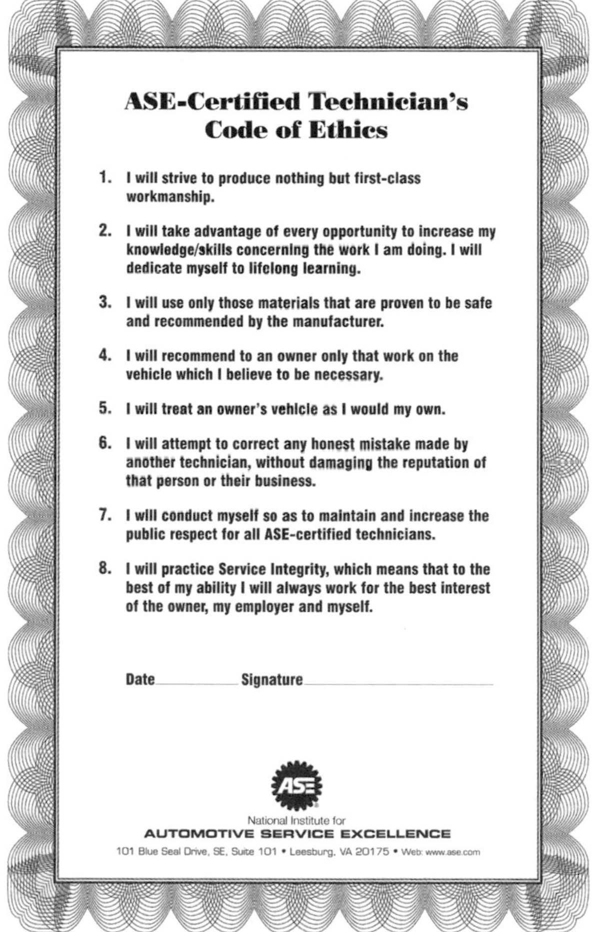

ASE-Certified Technician's Code of Ethics

1. I will strive to produce nothing but first-class workmanship.
2. I will take advantage of every opportunity to increase my knowledge/skills concerning the work I am doing. I will dedicate myself to lifelong learning.
3. I will use only those materials that are proven to be safe and recommended by the manufacturer.
4. I will recommend to an owner only that work on the vehicle which I believe to be necessary.
5. I will treat an owner's vehicle as I would my own.
6. I will attempt to correct any honest mistake made by another technician, without damaging the reputation of that person or their business.
7. I will conduct myself so as to maintain and increase the public respect for all ASE-certified technicians.
8. I will practice Service Integrity, which means that to the best of my ability I will always work for the best interest of the owner, my employer and myself.

Date________ Signature________

ASE
National Institute for
AUTOMOTIVE SERVICE EXCELLENCE
101 Blue Seal Drive, SE, Suite 101 • Leesburg, VA 20175 • Web: www.ase.com

Figure 4.3 ***ASE Technician's Code of Ethics***
Courtesy of National Institute for Automotive Service Excellence

Better Business Bureau (BBB)

The BBB (**www.bbb.org**) is a neutral non-profit organization. It is a go-between connecting consumers to businesses, helping to resolve issues, prevent fraud, and promote ethical practices. The BBB reports on public complaints, scams, and a company's reliability.

AAA Approved Auto Repair

The American Automobile Association (AAA) approves auto repair facilities that meet strict standards in repair, service, and facility cleanliness. AAA Approved Auto Repair facilities also have to provide a 1 year/12,000 mile (20,000 km) repair warranty. Look for a facility that proudly displays the AAA Approved Auto Repair sign (***Figure 4.4***).

Figure 4.4 ***AAA Approved Auto Repair***
Courtesy of AAA

Reasonable Costs

Repairing a vehicle can be costly. That is why it is extremely important to follow the manufacturer's service interval recommendations. If your car is in need of a repair be cautious when shopping around, the lowest price may not be your best choice. Most facilities charge labor rates in two ways: actual time or flat rate (also known as book time). Flat rate uses a manual to look up the time it should take to complete that repair. If it takes more or less time than the flat rate, you are still charged the same. Facilities that charge actual time bill out the real time that it takes to repair your vehicle. Some services may have an advertised set cost (e.g., oil change for $29.95).

Facility Types

Repair facilities can be small, medium, and large. Some are corporate owned, while others are independently owned. The key is to find a quality facility with competent technicians. Communicating your vehicle's problem clearly with the service writer or technician is critical and can save valuable time during diagnosis. This section focuses on:

- Dealership Repair Facilities
- Independent Repair Facilities
- Specialized Repair Facilities
- Auto Repair Chains

Dealership Repair Facilities

Automotive dealerships sell and service specific makes and models of vehicles (***Figure 4.5***). Dealerships are known for having up-to-date repair information on cars that they sell. Technicians are frequently factory trained for new vehicles being released. New car warranties are handled through dealerships. Some dealerships service all makes of vehicles, but it is best to use a dealership specific to your vehicle for major repairs.

Figure 4.5 ***Dealership Repair Facility***
Courtesy of Mayse Automotive Group - www.mayse.com

Q & A

Choosing an Auto Repair Facility

Q: How do I choose an auto repair facility?
A: Look for shops that display its employees' ASE certifications. Ask your co-workers and friends for recommendations. Find a shop that specializes in the service you need. For example, some facilities specialize in suspension repair, tires, and alignments. Others may specialize in transmission repair and service. If you don't know what your vehicle needs your best bet may be to go to the dealership. Dealerships will be able to fix any problem. Once you find a shop you trust, build a rapport with the service writers and technicians. This relationship will help you if you ever get in a bind and need emergency service.

Independent Repair Facilities

Independent repair facilities (***Figure 4.6***) are usually started by a technician that wants to run his or her own business. Some of these are quite large and have highly skilled technicians. An independent shop may have several family members contributing in various roles offering a personal touch. At these establishments you can build long-lasting relationships, especially if the owner is dedicated to providing high quality service at a reasonable price.

Figure 4.6 ***Independent Repair Facility***

Specialized Repair Facilities

Repair facilities that specialize in one area of service are gaining popularity. Common areas of specialty include brakes, mufflers, tires (***Figure 4.7***), oil changes, alignments, transmission repairs, audio/entertainment systems, off-road accessories, or electrical problems. Specialized repair facilities can sometimes save you money due to the volume of business that they complete in one specific area. For example, facilities that specialize in tire replacement may purchase such large quantities of tires that they can pass the savings on to the customer. Technicians employed by specialty shops can become extremely skilled in one area of the automobile. They also only have to buy and maintain the tools that relate directly to their specialty.

Figure 4.7 ***Specialized Tire Repair Facility***

Auto Repair Chains

Corporate or privately owned auto repair chains may be run as a franchise system. Franchised auto repair facilities provide the same products and services, even though the businesses may be owned by different people or companies. A franchisor grants a franchisee the right to conduct business under their trade name and trademark.

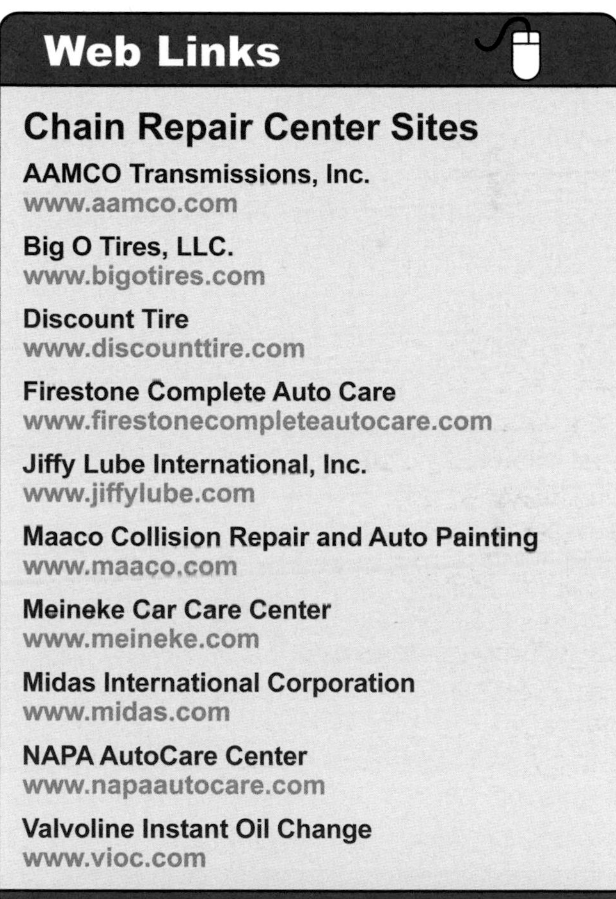

Web Links

Chain Repair Center Sites

AAMCO Transmissions, Inc.
www.aamco.com

Big O Tires, LLC.
www.bigotires.com

Discount Tire
www.discounttire.com

Firestone Complete Auto Care
www.firestonecompleteautocare.com

Jiffy Lube International, Inc.
www.jiffylube.com

Maaco Collision Repair and Auto Painting
www.maaco.com

Meineke Car Care Center
www.meineke.com

Midas International Corporation
www.midas.com

NAPA AutoCare Center
www.napaautocare.com

Valvoline Instant Oil Change
www.vioc.com

Videos
Choosing
a
Repair Facility
www.Video.AutoUpkeep.com
Click on Chapter 4

Estimates and Repair Orders

A repair order is a legal document between the repair facility and the customer. It is a form used to collect vehicle information to communicate the customer's concern to the technician. This section focuses on:

- Estimates
- Repair Orders

Estimates

Estimates should be prepared before a repair is performed. An estimate should include a repair description, the labor rate, estimated time to complete, and a list of parts. Ask the repair facility to review your customer rights and get them in writing for your records (***Figure 4.8***). Identifying your preferences will let the facility know what you want if they run into unforeseen problems that would put the repair over the original estimated cost.

Customer Rights (Repair Estimate/Order)	
Do you want your parts returned?	Yes ☐ No ☐
Do you want a written estimate?	Yes ☐ No ☐
If the job exceeds the estimate by 10% or more, do you authorize us in proceeding?	Yes ☐ No ☐
If additional repairs are found necessary, do you authorize us in proceeding?	Yes ☐ No ☐
Do you request a written estimate for repairs with cost in excess of $50.00?	Yes ☐ No ☐

Figure 4.8 ***Customer Rights Questions***

Price Guides

Oil Change
- $20.00 to $70.00 (parts and labor)

Brake Fluid Flush
- $75.00 to $150.00 (parts and labor)

Headlight Bulb Replacement
- $20.00 to $100.00 (parts and labor)

Serpentine Belt Replacement
- $50.00 to $100.00 (parts and labor)

Wheel Alignment
- $50.00 to $150.00 (parts and labor)

Repair Orders

A repair order (also known as a repair ticket, service order, shop ticket, invoice, or work order) summarizes work completed (***Figure 4.9***). The repair order should list the labor, parts, shop supplies used, environmental fees, and taxes. The VIN, odometer reading, and warranty information (if applicable) should also be listed. Many repair facilities use software management systems to electronically track vehicle records and send text/email service reminders.

Concern. The technician or service writer should clearly write down your concerns, identifying what you believe is wrong with your vehicle and any services you request.

Cause. Once the service writer knows the concern, a possible cause or what the technician should check is noted. Sometimes an estimate can be completed before a technician inspection. For example, if a customer wants the brake fluid flushed as part of their vehicle's scheduled maintenance, a service writer can complete that estimate right away. If the concern needs diagnosing, such as determining why a malfunction indicator light is on, an estimate on the diagnosing service can be completed first. After the technician inspects the vehicle and verifies the cause of the problem, an estimate can be completed for the specific repair.

Correction. Finally the repair order contains the correction to the problem by listing repairs performed, parts used, and labor charged.

Tech Tip

Part Replacement

Depending on the repair and faulty component, a part may be new, rebuilt, remanufactured, or from a salvage yard. Before having work completed, ask the service writer what type of parts will be used. Some replacement parts like starters, alternators, and water pumps are commonly remanufactured.

Repair and Service Facility
123 Anytown, USA
(555) 555-0100

Work Order Number: __________
Date & Time Received: ___/___/___ ___:___A.M. P.M.
Promised: ___/___/___ ___:___A.M. P.M.
Order Written By: ______________________________

Customer Contact Information		
Name:		
Address:		
City:	State:	Zip:
Phone Home: ( )		
Work: ( )	Cell: ( )	

Vehicle Information		
Make and Model		
Year/Color		
License Number		
Odometer Reading	IN	OUT
Engine Size		
VIN		

Description of Customer Concern

Customer Rights	
Do you want your parts returned?	Yes ❑ No ❑
If the job exceeds the estimate by 10% or more, do you authorize us in proceeding?	Yes ❑ No ❑
If additional repairs are found necessary, do you authorize us in proceeding?	Yes ❑ No ❑
Do you request a written estimate for repairs with cost in excess of $50.00?	Yes ❑ No ❑

Possible Cause

Estimate of Repair	
Parts	$
Labor Rate $ ____ Per Hr. x ___ Hrs.	$
Other/Supplies	$
Preliminary Estimate Total	$

I hereby authorize the above repair work to be done with the necessary material, and hereby grant you and/or your employees permission to operate the vehicle herein described on streets, highways, or elsewhere for the purpose of testing and/or inspection. An express mechanic's lien is hereby acknowledged on above vehicle to secure the amount of repairs thereof.

Authorized By______________________________

❑ **Lubricate Chassis** ❑ **Change Oil** ❑ **Check All Fluids** ❑ **Rotate Tires** ❑ **Wash**

Parts Required			
Qty.	Item No.	Description	Price
		Total Parts	

Labor Required		
Service Description	Hours	Charge
	Total Labor	

Other/Supplies Required			
Qty.	Item No.	Description	Price
Towing			
Environmental Fees			
Supplies			
		Total Other/Supplies	

Repair Total	
Total Parts	$
Total Labor	$
Total Other/Supplies	$
Subtotal	$
Tax	$
Total Amount Due ►	$

Repair Summary - Correction to Problem

Signed______________________________

Date______________________________

Figure 4.9 ***Repair Order***

Warranties and Recalls

This section focuses on:

- Warranties
- Safety Recalls

Warranties

It is important to know whether or not your vehicle is covered under warranty. It would be unfortunate if you spent your money at an independent repair facility to find out afterwards that the service would have been covered by the factory warranty at no charge by the dealership.

Factory Warranties. New cars often come with several different types of factory warranties: bumper-to-bumper, powertrain, corrosion perforation, emission, safety restraint, and hybrid related components. You should understand each of the warranties that your vehicle manufacturer provides. Each type of warranty may have different time periods.

Certified Used Car Warranties. Certified used car warranties have become popular in recent years. These are different than used cars sold with extended warranties. Certified used cars have met strict inspections by the dealership and are backed by extended warranties by the manufacturer (***Figure 4.10***). Sometimes the word "certified" gets thrown around to mean less than it was intended. Be sure if you are looking at a certified used car that it is backed by the manufacturer, not just the dealer. Then when you need warranty repair work while traveling, any dealership should be able to assist you.

Figure 4.10 *Certified Used Cars*

Extended Warranties. If you purchased an extended warranty on a new vehicle it is important to read the details on the reimbursement procedure so you are not denied a claim. Identify what is and what is not covered. A used vehicle may also come with an extended warranty. Look for a warranty sign in the window (***Figure 4.11***) to learn the details of what the seller will cover.

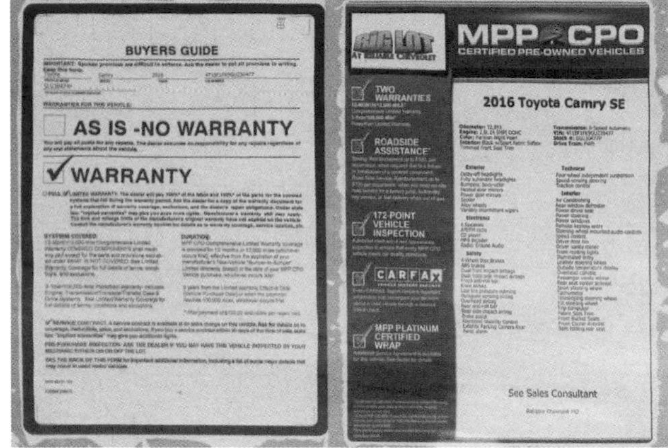

Figure 4.11 *Warranty and Certified Pre-Owned*

Chain Warranties. If you have your car repaired at a chain service center a warranty may be included. The benefit of a chain warranty is that it is guaranteed by any repair facility within the chain.

Independent Warranties. Independent repair facilities may have their own warranties to stand behind their work. Like any warranty, be sure it is in writing. The disadvantage here is that you will most likely have to bring it back to the shop where it was fixed. This may be an impractical task if you are traveling on a trip or if you move away from the area.

Battery and Tire Warranties. Automotive batteries and tires have their own warranties. If you have trouble with a tire or battery, any dealer that sells that brand should warranty it. Most tires and batteries have prorated warranties. Prorated means you will have to pay for part of the replacement cost, depending on how old or worn the component is that you want covered. Some tire and battery manufacturers have a full replacement period that lasts for a designated time. Batteries have a date stamp code on the label or engraved on the casing signifying the start of the warranty period. For a tire warranty to be honored, you are required to maintain the proper tire pressure, perform rotations as recommended, and may need to show the warranty booklet with your receipt and maintenance records. Tire warranties will not be honored if the tire is damaged from poor wheel alignment, a faulty tire repair, improper tire mounting, or overloading.

Tech Tip

Search for Safety Recalls

You can search to find out if there is a safety recall with your vehicle, tires, or child car seat at the National Highway Traffic Safety Administration's website - www.nhtsa.gov.

Web Links

Automotive Group Sites

AAA Foundation for Traffic Safety
www.aaafoundation.org

Automotive Service Association
www.asashop.org

Car Care Council
www.carcare.org

Consumer Reports
www.consumerreports.org

Motorists Assurance Program
www.motorist.org

National Inst. for Automotive Service Excellence
www.ase.com

Safety Recalls

Automotive safety recalls can be initiated by the manufacturer or ordered by the National Highway Traffic Safety Administration (NHTSA). If a recall is issued due to a safety related defect or non-compliance with a federal safety standard, the manufacturer is required to provide the vehicle owner a safe, free, and effective remedy. The manufacturer is obligated to attempt to notify you of the safety recall within a reasonable period of time.

Summary

Whether your vehicle needs an oil change or transmission overhaul, there is a wide choice of repair centers. When choosing a facility, check its quality, service, price, reputation, and warranties. Have a clear understanding of what service work is being completed and how you are being charged for that service with a written estimate. Maintain an open communication with the technician and service writer. Keep good records of all work completed on your vehicle.

Activities

Repair Facilities

- Repair Facilities Activity
- Chapter 4 Study Questions

Activities and Study Questions can be completed in the *Auto Upkeep Workbook*.

Career Paths

Automotive Technician

Education: Technical Experience or ASE Cert.
Median Income: $37,850
Abilities: Diagnostic, communication, problem solving, and hands-on technical skills. Look for schools that are NATEF certified. Find your career at www.bls.gov/ooh.

Chapter 5 Safety Around the Automobile

Fuel for Thought

- What safety equipment is required when working on vehicles?
- How can you safely lift and support a vehicle?
- How are fire extinguishers classified?

Introduction

If the correct precautions are not taken, working on automobiles can be dangerous. The Occupational Safety and Health Administration (OSHA) (***Figure 5.1***) and the Environmental Protection Agency (EPA) publish information and create regulations to help keep you safe and to protect the environment. In a school lab, in your garage, or at an automotive repair facility you need to be aware of people and your surroundings at all times. People are hurt each year through carelessness. This chapter provides information necessary to safely work on the automobile. When safety precautions are followed, working on the automobile can be a rewarding experience. Safety glasses, eyewash stations, first aid kits, fire extinguishers, and Safety Data Sheets (SDSs) are some of the items that should be available in an automotive work area.

Figure 5.1 **OSHA Website**
Screen Capture from www.osha.gov

Objectives

Upon completion of this chapter and activities, you will be able to:

- Describe auto shop hazards.
- Interpret safety data sheets.
- Choose appropriate personal protective equipment.
- Safely use auto shop tools and equipment.

Laboratory Safety

In a laboratory setting it is important to think safety. Moving engine parts, explosive fuels, and hot components can make working on vehicles dangerous. The following is a list of safety rules (***Figure 5.2***) for the general vehicle lab. This list is not all-inclusive. ***Warning: Follow safety guidelines provided by OSHA, EPA, safety data sheets, your instructor, and tool, equipment, and chemical manufacturers.***

Tech Tip

Learn Automotive Safety Online

S/P2 (**www.sp2.org**) offers online safety and pollution prevention training for automotive businesses and students. This program covers safety topics such as personal protection, safety data sheets, jump starting, hybrid vehicles, bloodborne pathogens, air quality, lifts and jacks, and more. Pollution topics include antifreeze, oil, solvents, refrigerants, and many others.

SAFETY RULES*

Personal Protection

- Safety glasses are not optional. Wear them at all times when working on a vehicle. ***Note: Ordinary prescription glasses are not safety glasses. You can purchase approved prescription safety glasses with side shields.***
- Do not have bare feet or wear open-toed sandals. Wear shoes that protect your feet.
- Loud noises can damage your hearing, so wear ear protection (e.g., earplugs or earmuffs).
- Keep your tools and hands free of grease and oil. Wearing mechanic gloves is smart, but do not wear gloves when moving parts are present. Keep your hands away from moving parts. Never use your hands to stop components that are moving.
- Remove your rings, watch, and other jewelry. If you have long hair, tie it back. It could get caught in moving parts. Do not wear loose or baggy clothing that could get caught in moving parts.
- Use the appropriate respirator when hazardous dust or airborne chemicals are present.
- Do not touch spark plug wires while the engine is running. Tens of thousands of volts are present.
- Never put your hands on or near the cooling fan. Many fans are electric and can start at anytime, even if the ignition is off.
- Do not work on a hot engine. Never open a hot radiator cap.
- Use proper lifting procedures to avoid injury. Use your legs, not your back.

Shop/Lab Procedures

- Know the location and operational procedures of fire extinguishers, first-aid kits, safety data sheets, eyewash stations, and a telephone. Dial 911 for emergencies. Have an evacuation route out of the shop identified.
- Someone must be sitting in the driver's seat whenever a car is started and/or running.
- The exhaust system of a running engine must be connected to a ventilation system if the vehicle is in an enclosed location such as a garage. ***Warning: Carbon monoxide is a colorless, odorless, and poisonous gas. Proper ventilation is required.***
- Always engage the parking brake to prevent the vehicle from moving.
- Put oily rags in an approved can for combustible materials.
- Always clean up spilled oil and grease off the floor. Sawdust, kitty litter, and oil dry work well for this.
- Never pour chemicals, solvents, antifreeze, or oil down the sanitary drain. Put them in their proper containers to be recycled.
- Use an approved safety cabinet for flammable materials. Do not use gasoline to clean parts.
- OSHA states that compressed air shall not be used for cleaning purposes (parts or objects) except where reduced to less than 30 pounds per square inch (psi) and then only with effective chip guarding and appropriate personal protective equipment. Never (at any pressure or under any circumstances) use compressed air to clean off clothes or your body. Never point an airline toward your skin, your body, or another person.

Hand Tools, Power Tools, and Shop Equipment Safety

- Use the proper tool for each job. Make sure tools and equipment have all the proper guards installed. Operate tools and equipment according to the manufacturers' instructions. Do not put sharp or pointed tools in your pocket.
- Avoid tripping hazards. Stand creepers up and place floor jack handles in the up position when not being used.
- Be cautious where sparks are falling when grinding, cutting, or welding.
- If a car is off the ground (except when on an automotive lift) it must be supported by jack stands.
- Do not use chisels or punches with mushroomed heads. When striking the ends with a hammer, the heads might shatter on impact, causing fragments to become airborne.
- Wrenches must not be used when jaws are sprung, malformed, or bent. Slippage can occur.
- Secure work with a vise or clamp. Operate a tool with both hands as recommended by the manufacturer.
- Maintain good footing and keep yourself balanced when operating power tools.
- Do not put tools on top of a vehicle's battery. Accidentally touching both terminals will cause a spark, which could lead to an explosion.
- Inspect electrical cords for fraying before use. Do not use electric tools in damp or wet locations. Electric tools must have a three-wire cord with a ground and be plugged into a properly grounded receptacle or be double-insulated.
- Prior to grinding stand off to the side and allow the grinder to get up to full operating speed. A grinding wheel can explode during start-up.

*** Note: This list is not all-inclusive. Follow safety guidelines provided by OSHA, EPA, safety data sheets, your instructor, and tool, equipment, and chemical manufacturers.**

Figure 5.2 ***Safety Rules***

EPA

The United States Environmental Protection Agency (EPA), established in 1970, is a federal agency with a mission to protect human health and the environment. The EPA develops and enforces environmental regulations, studies environmental issues, and teaches people about environmental topics. This section focuses on:

- Hazardous Wastes
- Product Life Cycle

Hazardous Wastes

When servicing and caring for vehicles, hazardous wastes can result that could harm the environment (land, air, and water) if not properly disposed (***Figure 5.3***).

Oil and Fluid Replacement	
Wastes Generated	• Used oil, oil filters, and fuel filters contaminated with cadmium, chromium, lead, benzopyrene; ethylene glycol (antifreeze) contaminated with lead; petroleum distillates; and chlorinated hydrocarbons.
Potential Recycling, Treatment, and Disposal Methods	• Store fluids separately to make it easier to recycle. Recycle used oil and antifreeze. • Recycle drained oil filters and fuel filters as scrap metal. • Ship hazardous waste using a registered transporter to a hazardous waste treatment, storage, and disposal facility for treatment and disposal.
Potential Pollution Prevention Methods	• Use drip pans to prevent contamination of the floor and subsequent floor-cleaning solutions. • Use a long-lasting, high-performance oil that needs less frequent changing. • Use fluids that do not contain chlorinated hydrocarbons.

Figure 5.3 ***Sample Automotive Wastes***
Source: U.S. EPA - www.epa.gov

EPA has identified the following hazardous waste characteristics: ignitability, reactivity, corrosivity and toxicity.

Ignitability. Ignitable (flammable) wastes are those that easily combust (catch on fire).

Reactivity. Reactive wastes are those that are unstable under normal conditions. They can go through violent reactions, can easily explode, might react to water, or give off toxic gases.

Corrosivity. Corrosive wastes are very acidic (low pH) or very alkaline (high pH). When these wastes come in contact with materials, they can readily corrode or dissolve them. The pH scale (***Figure 5.4***) is used to identify the acidity or alkalinity of a solution.

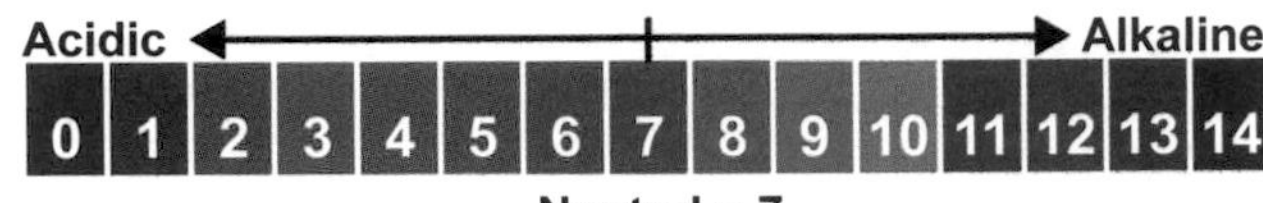

Figure 5.4 ***pH Scale***

Toxicity. Toxic (poisonous) wastes are capable of causing harm to living organisms or have negative environmental effects.

Product Life Cycle

Raw materials and energy are used to make automotive products. Understanding a product's life cycle helps in waste management and in assessing environmental impacts (***Figure 5.5***).

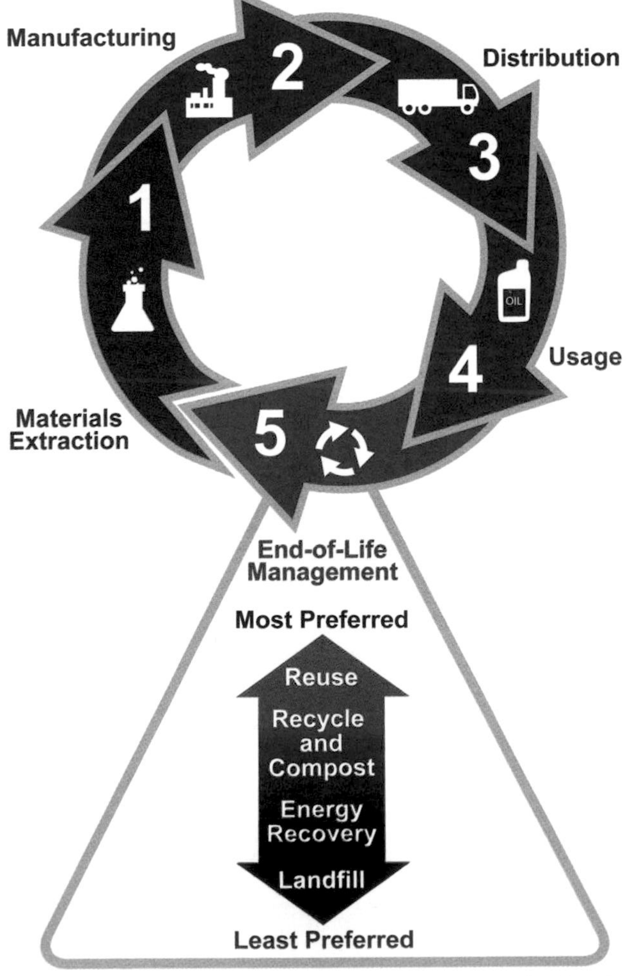

Figure 5.5 ***Product Life Cycle***

OSHA

The Occupational Safety and Health Administration (OSHA) was created in 1971 in the United States to prevent work related deaths, illnesses, and injuries. This section focuses on:

- OSHA Regulations
- Employer Responsibilities

OSHA Regulations

OSHA sets and enforces health and safety standards (***Figure 5.6***) for the workplace. Even though OSHA only regulates safety in the workplace, it is still a good idea when working at home to follow these safe work practices.

Title	Regulation
Eye and Face Protection 1910.133 (a)(1)	The employer shall ensure that each affected employee uses appropriate eye or face protection when exposed to eye or face hazards from flying particles, molten metal, liquid chemicals, acids or caustic liquids, chemical gases or vapors, or potentially injurious light radiation.
Jacks 1910.244 (a)(1)(i)	The operator shall make sure that the jack used has a rating sufficient to lift and sustain the load.
Hand and Body Protection 1915.157 (a)	The employer shall ensure that each affected employee uses appropriate hand protection and other protective clothing where there is exposure to hazards such as skin absorption of harmful substances, severe cuts or lacerations, severe abrasions, punctures, chemical burns, thermal burns, harmful temperature extremes, and sharp objects.

Figure 5.6 ***OSHA Regulation Examples***
Source: U.S. Department of Labor - www.osha.gov

Tech Tip

Right-to-Know Laws

You are entitled to a safe and healthy workplace under federal law. Employers are responsible for knowing when personal protection equipment is needed and providing most of it free of charge. If you feel your workplace is unsafe or unhealthy, you can file a complaint with OSHA. These reports are confidential and an employer cannot retaliate against you for speaking your concerns. For more information visit www.whistleblowers.gov.

Employer Responsibilities

Employers have many responsibilities under OSHA. Most importantly, they must provide a safe work environment free of known dangers. An official OSHA poster must be prominently displayed for employees (***Figure 5.7***). To learn more about OSHA go to www.osha.gov. ***Note: In Canada, the federal agency is the Canadian Center for Occupational Health and Safety. For more information, go to*** www.ccohs.ca.

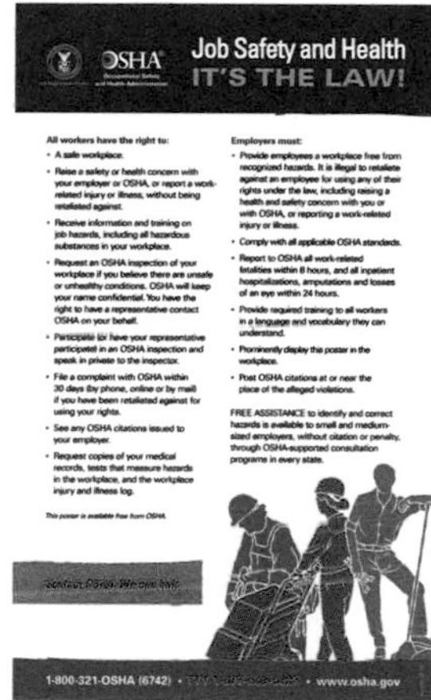

Figure 5.7 ***Sample OSHA Poster***
Source: U.S. Department of Labor - www.osha.gov

Web Links

Safety Training

AdvanceOnline Solutions, Inc.
www.advanceonline.com

American Red Cross
www.redcross.org

CareerSafe
www.careersafeonline.com

ClickSafety.com, Inc.
www.clicksafety.com

Health and Safety Institute
www.hsi.com

PureSafety On Demand
www.puresafetyondemand.com

S/P2
www.sp2.org

University of South Florida
www.usfoticenter.org

360training.com, Inc.
www.360training.com

Safety Data Sheets (SDSs)

Chemicals used in car care, repair, and maintenance can be hazardous to your health. You need to be aware of the potential hazards in order to properly protect yourself. SDSs (formerly known as Material Safety Data Sheets or MSDSs) provide detailed information on the possible hazards of working with a chemical product. It explains emergency procedures, physical properties, and how to handle, store, and dispose of the specific material. This section focuses on:

- Format
- Accessibility
- Availability

Format

Since 2015, each SDS has to follow a specific uniform format (***Figure 5.8***).

Section	Information
1	Identification
2	Hazard(s) identification
3	Composition/information on ingredients
4	First-aid measures
5	Fire-fighting measures
6	Accidental release measures
7	Handling and storage
8	Exposure controls/personal protection
9	Physical and chemical properties
10	Stability and reactivity
11	Toxicological information
12	Ecological information
13	Disposal considerations
14	Transport information
15	Regulatory information
16	Other information

Figure 5.8 ***OSHA SDS***
Source: U.S. Department of Labor - www.osha.gov

Accessibility

Employers are required to have SDSs for each hazardous product in a shop readily accessible to employees. Many shops use a binder system to store all their SDSs.

Availability

SDSs are readily available online by chemical producers. Just search the product's name and then SDS after it and you will usually get a direct hit from the search engine (***Figure 5.9***). From gasoline to antifreeze to brake cleaner to glass cleaner, all hazardous chemical products are required to have SDSs. Complete SDSs for each product can be several pages long.

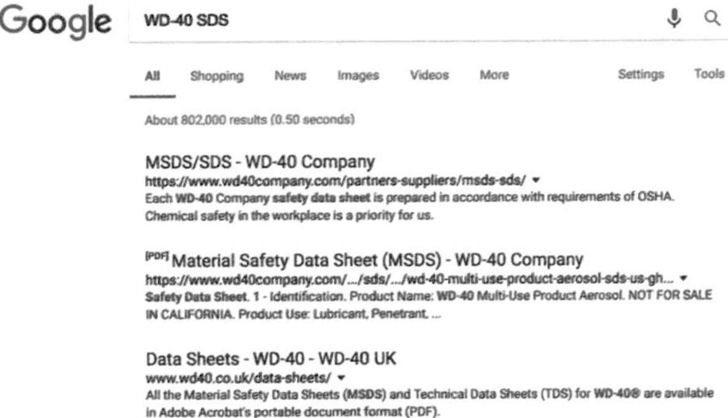

Figure 5.9 ***SDS Web Search***
Screen Capture from www.google.com

Web Links

Safety Related Sites

American National Standards Institute
www.ansi.org

Canadian Center for Occ. Health and Safety
www.ccohs.ca

Dangerous Decibels
www.dangerousdecibels.org

FireExtinguisherTraining.com
www.fireextinguishertraining.com

International Safety Equipment Association
www.safetyequipment.org

National Highway Traffic Safety Administration
www.nhtsa.gov

National Institute for Occ. Safety and Health
www.cdc.gov/niosh

National Safety Council
www.nsc.org

Occ. Safety and Health Administration
www.osha.gov

U.S. Fire Administration
www.usfa.fema.gov

First Aid

First aid is the initial intervention before medical personnel arrive. Sometimes this may involve a cut or scrape, while other times it may be much more serious like a bone fracture, heavy bleeding, or poisoning. This section focuses on:

- First Aid Kit
- Bloodborne Pathogens

First Aid Kit

When an accident or illness occurs, you should know basic first aid steps. You also need to know where your first aid kit (***Figure 5.10***) is and how to use it. A first aid kit should contain supplies and equipment appropriate for injuries that may occur while working on an automobile such as cuts, burns, and slivers. ***Note: If the situation warrants it, do not hesitate to call 911.***

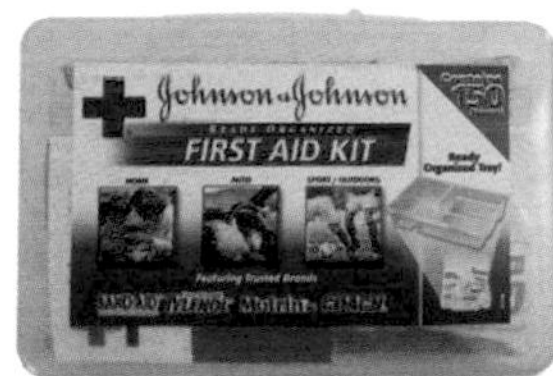

Figure 5.10 ***First Aid Kit***

Bloodborne Pathogens

Be aware and protect yourself from bloodborne pathogens (infectious microorganisms that can cause diseases). Use appropriate personal protection equipment (PPE), such as a pair of sterile gloves from the first aid kit.

Tech Tip 

Know What to Do

It is good to prepare for the unexpected. Take a class online or in person to know what to do. You may encounter many different types of emergency situations throughout your life. You could save a person's life by administering care before Emergency Medical Services (ambulance/paramedics) arrive at the scene. Visit www.redcross.org to sign up for a first aid class.

Lifting and Carrying Safety

Car parts (e.g, tires and batteries) are heavy and can be in awkward positions. Lifting, carrying, and moving heavy objects can injure you. Know what your limits are and apply smart lifting and material handling practices (***Figure 5.11***). Consider the position, weight, shape, and size of the object before lifting. Get someone to assist you when necessary.

Hazard	Possible Solution
Heavy Loads - Lifting loads heavier than about 50 pounds will increase the risk of injury.	• Lift items in the "Power Zone". The power zone for lifting is close to the body, between mid-thigh and mid-chest height. • Maintain neutral and straight spine alignment whenever possible. Usually, bending at the knees, not the waist, helps maintain proper spine alignment.
Awkward Positions - Bending while lifting moves the load away from the body and allows leverage to significantly increase the effective load on the back.	• Keep the load close to the body. • Avoid twisting. Turn by moving the feet rather than twisting the torso. • If possible, break down loads into smaller units and carry one in each hand to equalize loads.
Pushing vs. Pulling	• Pushing is generally preferable to pulling. Pushing allows you to use large muscle groups and apply more force to the load. Pulling carries a greater risk of strain and injury.
Inadequate handholds make lifting more difficult.	• Utilize proper handholds, including handles, slots, or holes. • Ensure that gloves fit properly and provide adequate grip to reduce the chance of dropping the load.

Figure 5.11 ***Material Handling Practices***
Source: U.S. Department of Labor - www.osha.gov

Personal Protection Equipment

When working on vehicles, think safety first. You should use the proper tools and clothing to protect yourself. Personal protection equipment, often referred to as PPE, is equipment that you wear to prevent injuries and illnesses. Some examples of PPE are safety glasses, safety goggles, respirators, gloves, safety shoes, and earplugs. This section focuses on:

- Eye and Face Protection
- Respiratory Protection
- Hand Protection
- Foot Protection
- Ear Protection

Eye and Face Protection

Eye protection is a must when working on cars. Eyes are very fragile.

Safety Glasses. Safety glasses (***Figure 5.12***) will help prevent foreign materials from entering your eyes. Sports, fashion/sun glasses (non-safety eyewear) are not built like safety glasses that protect against high impacts. Safety glasses are especially important when inspecting the underbody of a vehicle.

Figure 5.12 ***Safety Glasses***

Safety Goggles. Goggles (***Figure 5.13***) can be used over prescription glasses or when working around chemicals.

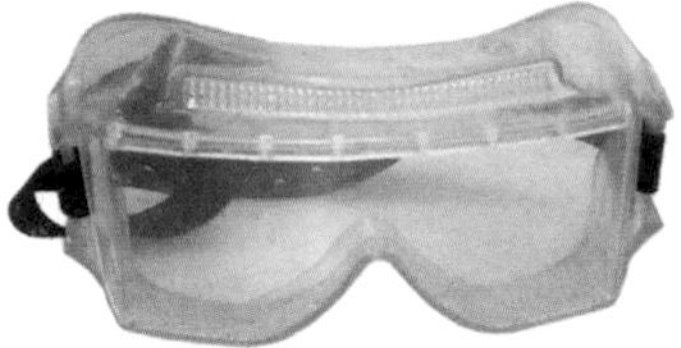

Figure 5.13 ***Safety Goggles***

Face Shield. A face shield (***Figure 5.14***), used in conjunction with safety goggles, provides maximum protection when working with chemicals or grinding.

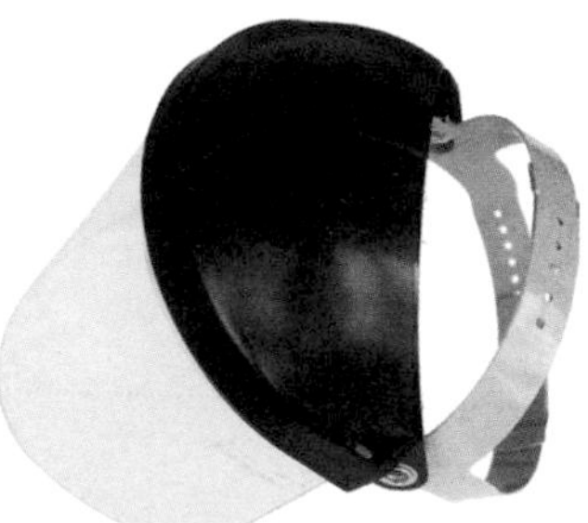

Figure 5.14 ***Face Shield***

Eyewash Station. An eyewash station (***Figure 5.15***) is used to flush foreign bodies from eyes.

Figure 5.15 ***Eyewash Station***
Courtesy of Guardian Equipment Company

Respiratory Protection

Use the appropriate respirator when hazardous dust or airborne chemicals are present (***Figure 5.16***). Protect your respiratory system. ***Warning: Friction materials used in brake and clutch systems may contain asbestos.***

Figure 5.16 ***Air Respirator***

Hand Protection

To protect your hands from cuts, scratches, burns, bruises, and chemicals use hand protection. ***Warning: Do not wear gloves around rotating machinery or parts. Gloves can get caught on rotating machines, pulling your hands into the rotating parts causing an entanglement hazard.***

Work Gloves. Work gloves (***Figure 5.17***) are great for performing work on tires and exhaust. Extremely worn tires can have sharp steel belts poking out from the tread. Exhaust systems can be hot and have rusty holes that can cut your hands.

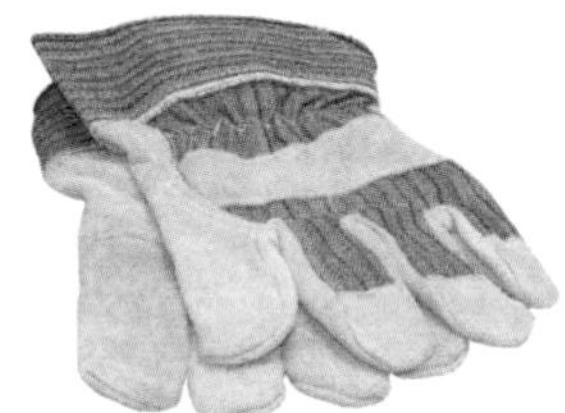

Figure 5.17 *Work Gloves*

Mechanic Gloves. Form fitting mechanic gloves can help you grip tools. Some gloves use conductive material on the finger tips making them touchscreen compatible (***Figure 5.18***).

Figure 5.18 *Mechanic Gloves*
Photo: Bosch Automotive Service Solutions, Inc.

Price Guides

Disposable Gloves
- $5.00 box of 100

Mechanic Gloves
- $15.00 to $30.00

Respirator
- $20.00 to $40.00

Safety Glasses
- $5.00 to $15.00 each

Disposable Gloves. Use disposable gloves that are resistant to chemicals (***Figure 5.19***) when you are working with oils, greases, and chemicals. If you need to administer first aid to another person wear the appropriate sterile disposable gloves. ***Note: Always read the glove manufacturer's recommendations to make sure the gloves are appropriate for your application.***

Figure 5.19 *Blue Nitrile Gloves*

Foot Protection

To protect your feet, do not have bare feet or open toed sandals when working on vehicles. Wear shoes or boots. Steel toe boots or shoes provide the best protection for heavy falling objects. Shoe soles that are nonslip and chemical/oil resistant are recommended (***Figure 5.20***).

Figure 5.20 *Oil Resistant Shoe Soles*

Q & A

Used Oil Precaution

Q: Why should I wear disposable gloves when changing the oil in my car?

A: Prolonged exposure to used oil on your skin can increase your chances of developing skin and health problems. Used oil has been shown to cause cancer in laboratory animals. Your body will absorb chemicals that come in contact with your skin. If you do get any chemicals on your skin, thoroughly wash them off with soap and water.

Ear Protection

Noise-induced hearing loss (NIHL) is permanent, but also preventable. NIHL can be caused by an intense impulse sound (e.g., fireworks or an explosion), intermittent sounds (those that come and go), or by continuous loud sounds over time (e.g., using an impact wrench).

Factors Affecting NIHL. Factors that affect hearing loss are sound level, distance to the sound, and the exposure time (***Figure 5.21***).

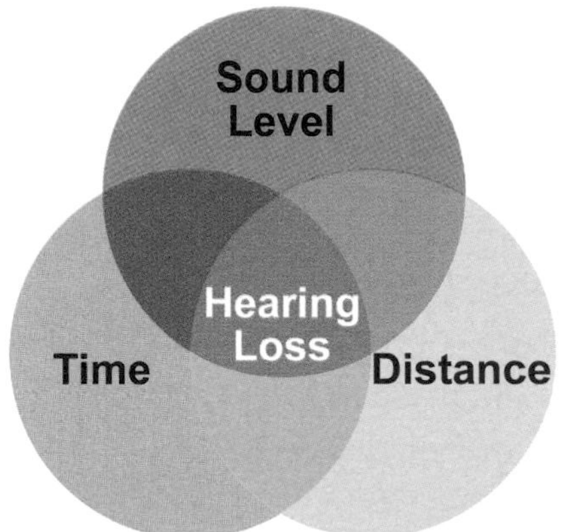

Figure 5.21 ***Factors Affecting NIHL***

Decibel. Sound travels in waves. How loud a sound is depends on the pressure of the sound wave. A unit used to measure sound level is called a decibel (dB). The dB scale is a logarithmic (based on multiplication) scale. A sound at 20 dB has ten times greater pressure than a sound at 10 dB. A sound at 30 dB has 100 times greater pressure than a sound at 10 dB. This means that an impact wrench at 110 dB has 100,000 times the sound pressure than a normal conversation at 60 dB. The problem is that a 10 dB increase may only sound twice as loud in your ears, but it actually represents 10 times the sound pressure.

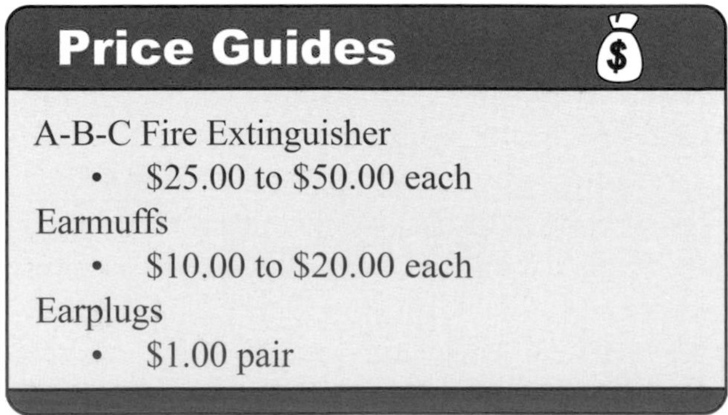

Price Guides

A-B-C Fire Extinguisher
- $25.00 to $50.00 each

Earmuffs
- $10.00 to $20.00 each

Earplugs
- $1.00 pair

Sound Level Meter. Sound level meters (decibel meters) can be used to help determine when hearing protection is needed. There are free smartphone apps that can also measure decibel levels. The NIOSH Sound Level Meter App (***Figure 5.22***) is not as accurate as a professional sound level meter, but using it will raise your awareness when protection is needed. This will help you make better decisions about potential hearing hazards.

Figure 5.22 ***NIOSH Sound Level Meter App***

Noise Levels. Noise levels that exceed 85 dB can damage your hearing (***Figure 5.23***).

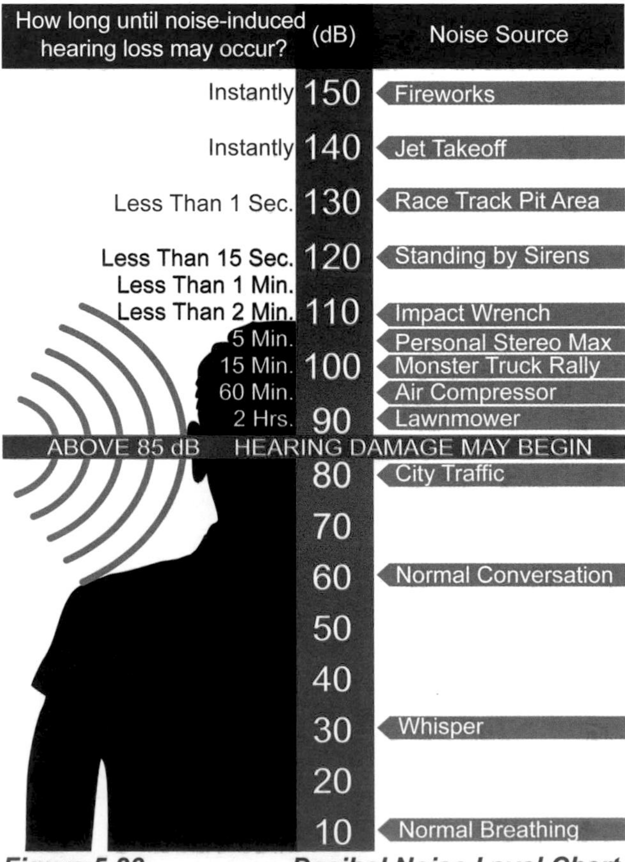

Figure 5.23 ***Decibel Noise Level Chart***

Hearing Protection. Use earmuffs or earplugs (***Figure 5.24***) when the work area exceeds 85 dB (OSHA's acceptable exposure limit).

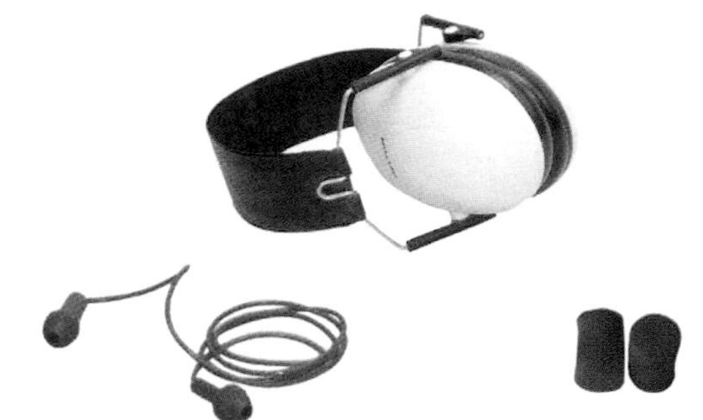

Figure 5.24 ***Earmuffs and Earplugs***

Inserting Foam Earplugs. To be effective, foam earplugs must be inserted correctly (***Figure 5.25***). Wash your hands first to avoid getting dirt and germs in your ears.

How to Properly Insert Foam Earplugs	
STEP 1	Roll the earplug up into a small, thin "snake" with your fingers. You can use one or both hands.
STEP 2	Pull the top of your ear up and back with your opposite hand to straighten out your ear canal. The rolled-up earplug should slide right in.
STEP 3	Hold the earplug in with your finger. Count to 20 or 30 out loud while waiting for the plug to expand and fill the ear canal. Your voice will sound muffled when the plug has made a good seal.

Figure 5.25 ***Inserting Foam Earplugs***
Source: U.S. Dept. of Health and Human Services - www.cdc.gov

Web Links

Safety Equipment Related Sites

Conney Safety Products
www.conney.com

Grainger
www.grainger.com

Industrial Safety
www.industrialsafety.com

Leonard Safety Equipment
www.leonardsafety.com

Northern Safety Company
www.northernsafety.com

Rx Safety Wear
www.rx-safety.com

Uvex
www.uvex.com

Fire Extinguishers

Flammable and combustible materials are present in automotive shops. It is important to know where the fire extinguishers are, how to check them (***Figure 5.26***), how to use them, and what type of fires they put out. ***Warning: Learn the rules of fighting fires and complete proper training before you consider using a fire extinguisher.*** This section focuses on:

- Fire Triangle
- Classifications

Figure 5.26 ***Fire Extinguisher and Gauge***

Fire Triangle

For a fire to exist it needs oxygen, heat, and fuel (***Figure 5.27***). A fire extinguisher must remove at least one of these components to put a fire out.

Figure 5.27 ***Fire Triangle***

Classifications

Fire extinguishers are designed to put out specific types of fires (***Figure 5.28***). Most auto shops will have a combination A-B-C fire extinguisher.

Fire Extinguisher Classifications		
A		A-type extinguishers put out wood, paper, cloth, rubber, plastic, and upholstery fires. They do this by coating or lowering the temperature of the burning materials.
B		B-type extinguishers put out gasoline, oil, grease, and paint fires. They do this by smothering the fire. Never put water on a B-type fire. Water will spread the fire.
C		C-type extinguishers put out electrical fires. They do this by using a nonconducting agent.
D		D-type extinguishers put out combustible metal fires. They smother and coat the metal with a special agent to put the fire out.

Figure 5.28 ***Fire Extinguisher Classifications***

Lifting a Vehicle Safely

It is imperative to read and review lift safety procedures. If an accident occurs, it could easily be fatal. A person is no match for a vehicle. Several different types of lifts are available. The two most common are the two-post lift and the four-post lift. The four-post lift is sometimes called a multi-post runway lift, since you drive onto runways that lift the vehicle by its tires. Safely lifting a vehicle requires reading and understanding the following:

- Safety, Caution, and Warning Labels
- Lift Constraints
- Lift Manuals
- Two-Post Lift Operating Procedure
- Four-Post Lift Operating Procedure

Safety, Caution, and Warning Labels

Automotive lifts should have safety, caution, and warning labels (***Figure 5.29***) attached to the column that houses the controls for the lift. Frequently review these labels for safety.

Lift Constraints

Vehicle lifts are designed to only lift vehicles. Never use a lift to remove an engine or other heavy component from a vehicle. Also, never overload the lift. The load capacity of the lift is located on the manufacturer's nameplate.

Lift Manuals

The Automotive Lift Institute (www.autolift.org) has up-to-date manuals and online courses to help you safely operate automotive lifts.

Figure 5.29 ***Safety, Caution, and Warning Labels for Automotive Lifts***
Courtesy of Automotive Lift Institute, Inc. - www.autolift.org

Two-Post Lift Operating Procedure

Always refer to the lift manufacturer instructions for specific lifting procedures. The following is a general procedure.

Driving into the Area. When using a lift have a partner direct you into the lifting area. ***Warning: Stand to one side, not in front of the vehicle.***

Center of Gravity. Line the center of gravity of the vehicle with the posts or as required by the lift manufacturer. On rear-wheel drive vehicles the center of gravity is usually directly below the driver's seat. However, on front-wheel drive vehicles, it is usually slightly in front of the driver's seat (***Figure 5.30***).

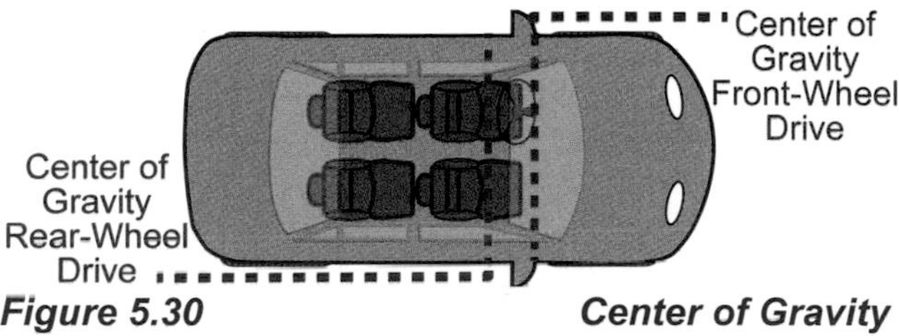

Figure 5.30 ***Center of Gravity***

Vehicle Lifting Points. Make sure the lift arms are contacting the vehicle's lift points. When vehicles still had full frames, the lifting points were easy – the frame. Today many automobiles do not have full frames, but unibodies. The frames on unibody vehicles are integrated with the body. When lifting a vehicle, use a manual to identify the correct lift points (***Figure 5.31***).

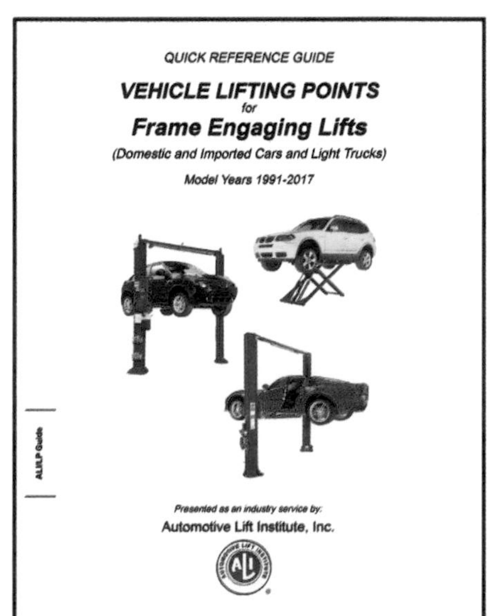

QUICK REFERENCE GUIDE

VEHICLE LIFTING POINTS

for

Frame Engaging Lifts

(Domestic and Imported Cars and Light Trucks)

Model Years 1991-2017

Presented as an industry service by:

Automotive Lift Institute, Inc.

Figure 5.31 ***Vehicle Lifting Points Guide***

Courtesy of Automotive Lift Institute, Inc. – www.autolift.org

Raising the Vehicle. Lift the vehicle about a foot off the ground. Then gently push on the front and rear bumper to make sure the vehicle is stable. Visually recheck the lift point connections. Raise the vehicle to the desired height and inspect the lift points again. ***Warning: Some two-post lifts have overhead devices.*** Do not lift the vehicle so that the roof of the vehicle comes in contact with overhead devices. Once at the desired height lower the lift onto the load holding devices (safety locks).

Lowering the Vehicle. After work is completed remove everything from under the vehicle. First raise the vehicle off the load holding devices to disengage the latches, then lower it to the ground.

Four-Post Lift Operating Procedure

Always refer to the lift manufacturer instructions for specific lifting procedures. The following is a general procedure.

Driving into the Area. Drive the vehicle on the runways, centering the weight of the vehicle on the lift. Apply the parking brake and chock both sides of at least one wheel.

Vehicle Lifting Points. Four-post lifts are easier to use since the vehicle's lift points are the tires (***Figure 5.32***).

Figure 5.32 ***Four-Post Lift***

Courtesy of of BendPak, Inc. – www.bendpak.com

Raising the Vehicle. Raise the vehicle to the desired height. Once at the desired height lower the lift onto the load holding devices (safety locks).

Lowering the Vehicle. After work is completed remove everything from under the vehicle. First raise the vehicle off the load holding devices to disengage the latches, then lower it to the ground.

Using Jacks and Jack Stands

You should never go under a jacked-up vehicle unless it is supported by jack stands. Safety jack stands are inexpensive and a must when completing repairs or service procedures under a vehicle. The following are the steps for jacking up a vehicle (***Figure 5.33***). ***Warning: Never use concrete blocks or other inadequate devices for supporting a vehicle.***

Jacking a Vehicle

STEP 1	Chock the wheels that will be on the ground. Wheel chocks are used to minimize the risk of the vehicle rolling and falling off the jack.

Figure 5.33a ***Chocked Wheel***

STEP 2	Position the floor jack so that it comes in contact with the frame or another solid chassis component. Do not use the oil pan, body, or other fragile component as lifting points when jacking up the vehicle. Serious damage could result. Check the owner's manual for specific lift points.
STEP 3	Slowly pump the jack and lift the vehicle.
STEP 4	Once at the desired height, position the jack stands under the frame or specified jacking points. Ratchet the jack stands to the desired height.
STEP 5	Slowly lower the vehicle onto the jack stands and remove the floor jack.

Figure 5.33b ***Jack Stands in Position***

STEP 6	Reposition the floor jack, lift the vehicle off the jack stands, remove the jack stands from under the vehicle, lower the jack, and remove chocks.

Figure 5.33 ***Jacking a Vehicle***

Safety Around Airbags

Since 1998, dual frontal airbags for the driver and front passenger have been standard equipment for all passenger cars sold in the United States. Since 1999, all light trucks, vans, and SUVs were also required to have dual airbags. This section focuses on:

- Airbag Deployment
- Working on Airbag Systems
- Working Near Airbag Components

Airbag Deployment

Over the years, airbag improvements have been made. They are made to deploy in moderate to severe crashes.

Types of Airbags. Frontal airbags are required, but most vehicles have many more. Side-impact (curtain, torso, and head) airbags, knee airbags, rollover airbags, rear airbags, inflatable seat belts, and even pedestrian airbags are available.

Advanced Systems. Advanced systems use various sensors to minimize the risk of being injured by an airbag deployment during an accident, especially for children and small adults. These sensors commonly detect the size of the person sitting in the seat, the severity of the crash, the position of the seat, and whether or not the occupant is wearing a seat belt. The advanced systems inflate according to the sensor input.

Supplemental Restraint System (SRS). Injuries can occur if an occupant is not properly seated (***Figure 5.34***). Airbags are supplemental restraint systems and designed to work with seat belts. Read about your vehicle's specific airbag system in your owner's manual. Go to www.safercar.gov for more information.

Airbag Safety - General Recommendations*

- Use your seat belt.
- Never use a rear facing infant seat in the front seat of an airbag equipped vehicle.
- Stay at least 10 inches from the airbag cover.
- Have children 12 and under sit in the back seat. The back seat is the safest location during a crash.

*** Follow instructions in your owner's manual.**

Figure 5.34 ***Airbag Safety***

Working on Airbag Systems

Do not attempt to work on airbags, part of the Supplemental Restraint System (SRS), without professional training. Do not disturb, hit, or tamper with airbag system components when working on a vehicle (***Figure 5.35***). ***Warning: Airbags may deploy rapidly without warning causing serious injury or death.***

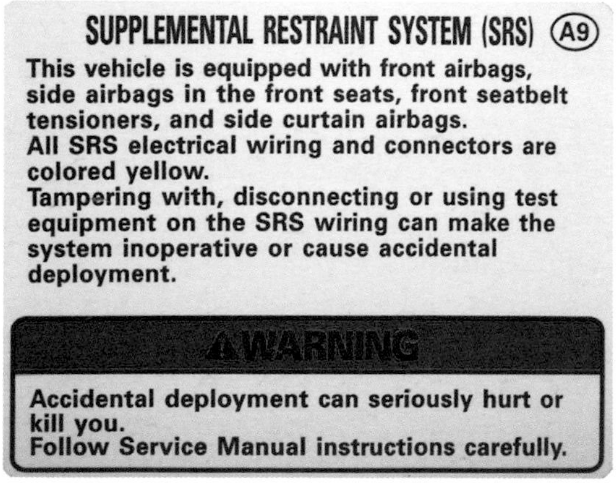

SUPPLEMENTAL RESTRAINT SYSTEM (SRS) (A9)

This vehicle is equipped with front airbags, side airbags in the front seats, front seatbelt tensioners, and side curtain airbags.
All SRS electrical wiring and connectors are colored yellow.
Tampering with, disconnecting or using test equipment on the SRS wiring can make the system inoperative or cause accidental deployment.

⚠ WARNING

Accidental deployment can seriously hurt or kill you.
Follow Service Manual instructions carefully.

Figure 5.35 ***SRS Warning Label***

Working Near Airbag Components

It is generally recommended to disconnect the battery about 30 minutes before working in areas of a vehicle that may be near airbag related components (e.g., inside the console, steering wheel/column, doors, seats) (***Figure 5.36***).When in doubt, don't take the risk, take your vehicle to a qualified technician.

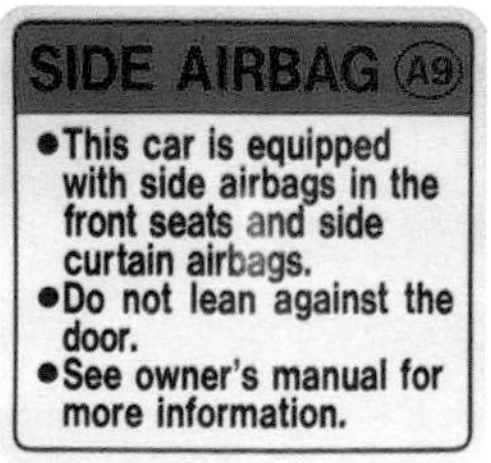

SIDE AIRBAG (A9)

- This car is equipped with side airbags in the front seats and side curtain airbags.
- Do not lean against the door.
- See owner's manual for more information.

Figure 5.36 ***Side Airbag Warning Label***

Airbag Error Code. If you do inadvertently disconnect or disturb part of the airbag system an error code will set off the dash airbag light (***Figure 5.37***). The light should come on for several seconds when starting the vehicle. If it stays on, have it checked right away.

Figure 5.37 ***Airbag Indicator Light Example***

Summary

Safety in an automotive lab or shop is essential. EPA's mission is to protect human health and the environment. OSHA works to prevent work related deaths, illnesses, and injuries. When lifting heavy or awkward objects, consider its position, weight, shape, and size. To protect against injuries and illnesses, the proper PPE must be worn. SDSs provide detailed information on the possible hazards of working with a chemical product. Know where they are located. NIHL is permanent, but also preventable. A decibel (dB) is the unit to measure sound level. Wear ear protection when noises are over 85 dB. Fires are classified by the type of material burning. The best type of fire extinguisher to have when working on an automobile is a combination A-B-C. Follow lift manufacturer instructions when operating a vehicle lift. Proper jack procedures enable you to lift a vehicle safely and without damage. Always use jack stands to support a vehicle that has been lifted by a jack. Be extremely careful when working around airbag system components. They can be dangerous if accidentally deployed.

Activities

Safety Around the Automobile

- Automotive Safety Activity
- Safety Data Sheet (SDS) Activity
- PPE and Fire Safety Activity
- Chapter 5 Study Questions

Activities and Study Questions can be completed in the *Auto Upkeep Workbook*.

Career Paths

Health and Safety Specialist

Education: Cert. and/or Bachelor's Degree
Median Income: $70,210
Abilities: Good at data collection, analysis, and at identifying hazardous conditions.
Find your career at **www.bls.gov/ooh**.

Chapter 6 Tools and Equipment

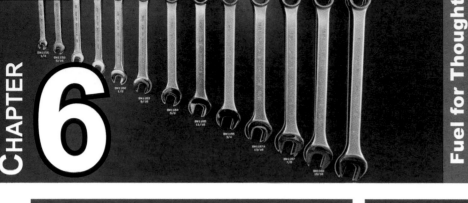

Fuel for Thought

- What hand tools are commonly used on an automobile?
- Why is it important to use the correct tool?
- Where can you find information to help with a vehicle repair?

Introduction

Using the right tools and equipment when working on cars makes the job easier, safer, and more enjoyable. An ASE certified technician typically has hundreds of common and specialty tools to work on a variety of vehicles (***Figure 6.1***). However, every auto owner should have some basic tools to perform periodic maintenance and minor repairs. ***Warning: Always read the user manual for each tool or piece of equipment you plan to use. Follow all safety warnings and precautions and receive the proper training.***

Figure 6.1 ***Automotive Technician Tool Set***
Courtesy of Matco Tools - www.matcotools.com

Objectives

Upon completion of this chapter and activities, you will be able to:

- Recognize basic tools and equipment.
- Identify the correct tool for the job.
- Use tools properly.
- Identify types of service manuals.
- Navigate an online service manual.

Common Hand Tools

Common hand tools are necessary when performing basic vehicle maintenance and repair work. You may find that you already own many of these tools. Use a toolbox to store, organize, and protect your tools. Put similar tools in the same drawer. Keep your tools clean. Tools that are greasy or oily can cause your hands to slip. This section focuses on:

- Wrenches
- Ratchets
- Sockets
- Pliers
- Screwdrivers
- Hammers
- Pry Bars

Wrenches

Wrenches, important tools for maintenance and repair, come in various sizes and designs. Both standard and metric wrenches should be in a basic tool kit. Metric sizes commonly increase by 1 millimeter (mm), so a metric wrench set may have these sizes: 7mm, 8mm, 9mm, 10mm, 11mm, 12mm, 13mm, 14mm, etc. Standard wrenches commonly increase by 1/16″, so a standard set may have these sizes: 1/4″, 5/16″, 3/8″, 7/16″, 1/2″, 9/16″, 5/8″, 11/16″, 3/4″, etc. ***Note: The double prime sign (″) is a symbol for inch units.*** The size corresponds to the distance between the two jaws in an open-end wrench.

Combination Wrench. A combination wrench (***Figure 6.2***) has the two most common ends, a box-end and an open-end. Use the box-end whenever possible.

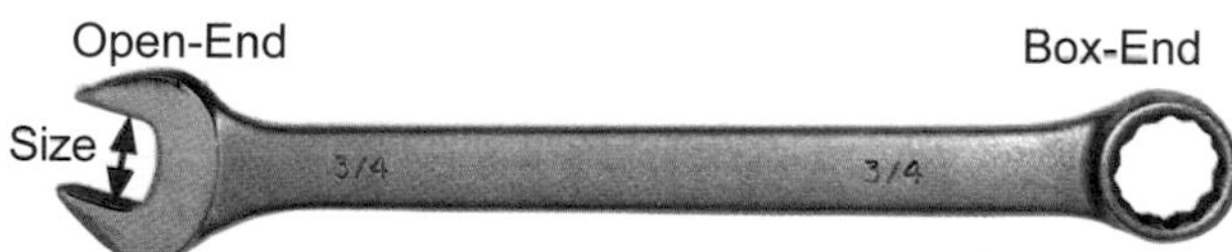

Figure 6.2 ***Combination Wrench***

Wrench Ends. The box-end usually has 6-points or 12-points (***Figure 6.3***). Use the 6-point box-end when a great amount of torque is required to reduce the chance of rounding off the fastener (i.e., a nut or bolt). ***Note: Torque is a rotational force used to turn an object around a pivot point.*** An open-end is handy when the fastener position will not allow access with the box-end. If you need more leverage, use a longer wrench.

Figure 6.3 ***6-Point and 12-Point Box-Ends***

Tech Tip

Flip the Wrench

The end of an open-end wrench is offset. In a tight area flip the wrench over to grip the fastener in a different location. You may need to flip the wrench after each turn.

Adjustable Wrench. An adjustable wrench (sometimes called a Crescent® wrench) is a versatile second choice if a fixed-sized jaw wrench is not available (***Figure 6.4***). The jaw can be adjusted to fit metric or standard fasteners, but it does not fit as snugly as a fixed-sized jaw wrench. If you are going to have only one wrench in your tool box, choose an adjustable wrench.

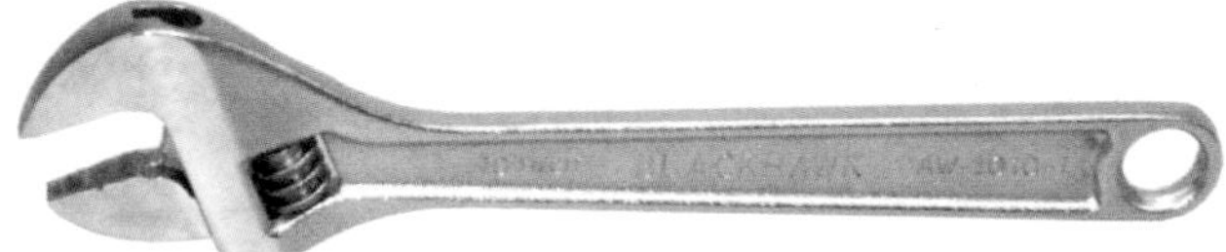

Figure 6.4 ***Adjustable Wrench***

Ratchets

Ratchets, in combination with sockets, are used to quickly turn nuts and bolts. A ratchet is basically a lever with a pivoting mechanism, which allows the user to tighten or loosen a fastener without removing the tool. Ratchets are sized according to the square driver head (***Figure 6.5***). For example, 1/4″ drive ratchets have driver heads that are 1/4″ x 1/4″. Common ratchet sizes are 1/4″, 3/8″, and 1/2″. A 3/8″ ratchet is the most common size found in a basic tool kit.

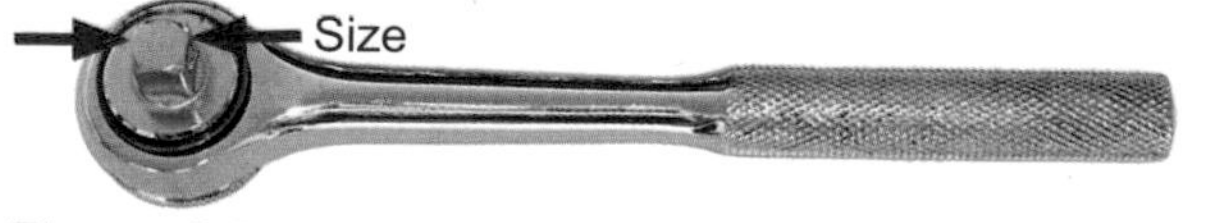

Figure 6.5 ***Ratchet***

Tech Tip

Wrench and Socket Selection

Use a wrench or socket that fits the fastener snugly. If it is a little loose it may round the fastener corners. If the head of a fastener is slightly rounded, use a 6-point socket or box-end wrench to lessen the likelihood of further rounding. If you have a limited amount of space for movement, the 12-points allow for twice the placements on the fastener. A bolt/nut extractor can be used if a wrench or socket continues to slip and will not lock on to a rounded fastener head.

Sockets

Sockets can be directly connected to the ratchet or first connected to a universal joint or driver extension.

Standard Sockets. Sockets are classified as regular or deep well (***Figure 6.6***). Deep well sockets can fit over the threads of a long bolt. Sockets, like wrenches, have points inside that fit over the fastener and come in both metric and standard sizes. Common sockets will have either 6-points or 12-points.

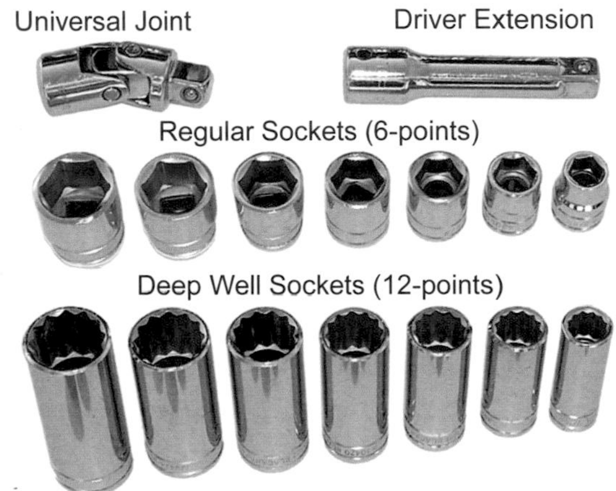

Figure 6.6 *Socket Set*

Specialty Sockets. Some sockets are specially designed. Do not use them on common nuts and bolts. For example, a spark plug socket (***Figure 6.7***) has a rubber boot insert to hold and protect the spark plug from cracking.

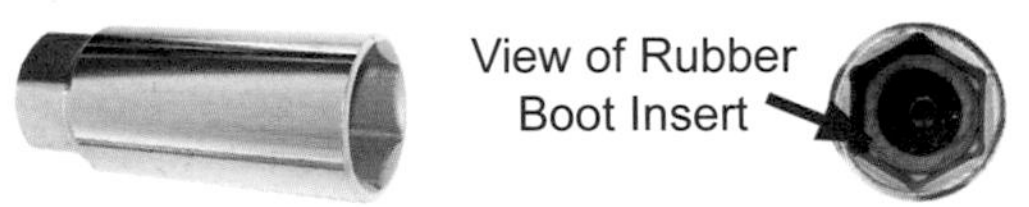

Figure 6.7 *Spark Plug Socket*

Impact Sockets. Impact sockets (***Figure 6.8***) are used where high torque and speed are needed, especially when using an electric or pneumatic (air-powered) impact wrench. ***Warning: Never use a non-impact socket on a power tool. Always wear safety glasses.*** Impact sockets have thicker sides than standard sockets and are often black.

Figure 6.8 *Impact Sockets*

Pliers

Pliers are handy adjustable tools that can be used in a variety of situations. Types include slip joint, locking, groove joint, needle nose, and diagonal cutters. Pliers are used to grab, turn, cut, or bend. Pliers consist of two levers that pivot at one point. This pivoting point is called a fulcrum.

Slip Joint Pliers. Slip joint pliers (***Figure 6.9***) are one of the most basic and versatile hand tools. However, do not use slip joint pliers in situations where a wrench would be better (e.g., turning a nut or bolt). Trying to loosen a stubborn nut with slip joint pliers can round off the head. Also if the pliers slip your knuckles could get bruised or cut.

Figure 6.9 *Slip Joint Pliers*

Groove Joint Pliers. Also called adjustable pliers or Channellocks® (an industry brand name), groove joint pliers (***Figure 6.10***) adjust to a wide range of sizes. These are especially useful for gripping cylindrical objects, like pipes.

Figure 6.10 *Groove Joint Pliers*

Needle Nose Pliers. Needle nose pliers (***Figure 6.11***) have long pointed jaws. These can be used to grip or pull objects that are in hard-to-reach areas. Sometimes there is also a cutting mechanism next to the fulcrum.

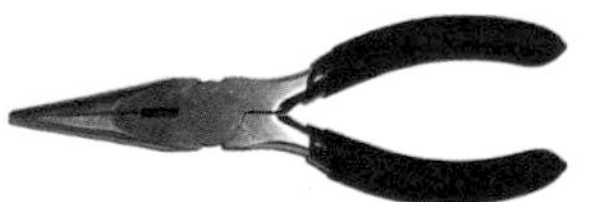

Figure 6.11 *Needle Nose Pliers*

Diagonal Pliers. Also called side cutters, diagonal pliers (***Figure 6.12***) have sharp edges instead of gripping jaws like most pliers. They are commonly used for cutting wires.

Figure 6.12 *Diagonal Pliers*

Locking Pliers. Locking pliers (***Figure 6.13***) are sometimes called Vise-Grips® (an industry brand name). Locking pliers are used to tightly grip and then lock on an object. These pliers come in handy when a bolt or nut is already rounded off beyond the point where a wrench will work. Grabbing onto flat or oddly shaped items are additional functions of locking pliers.

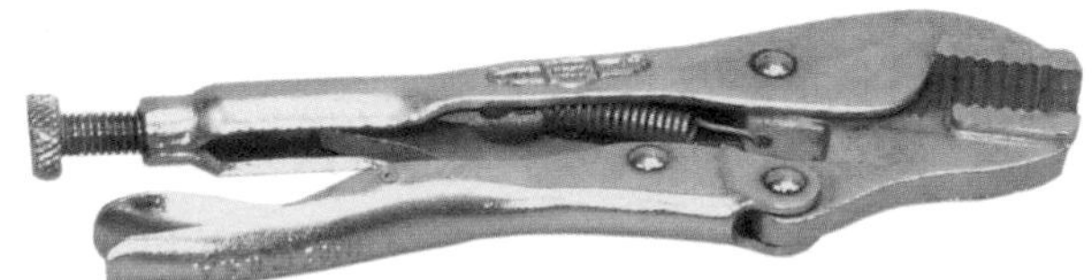

Figure 6.13 ***Locking Pliers***

Screwdrivers

Screwdrivers (***Figure 6.14***) turn screws or other fasteners. Some screwdrivers have magnetic tips to help with positioning fasteners in tight spaces. ***Warning: Do not use screwdrivers as pry bars.***

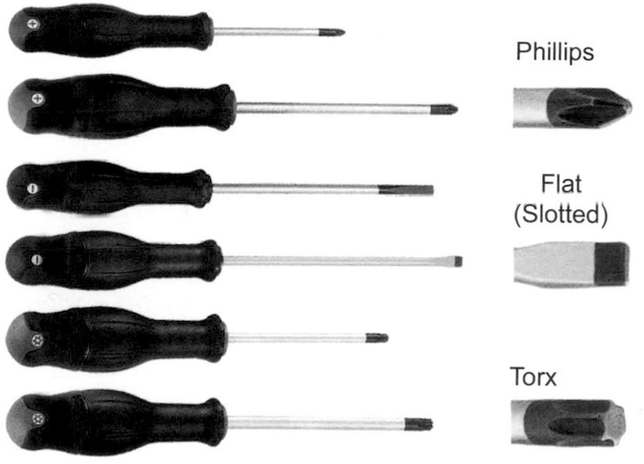

Figure 6.14 ***Screwdriver Set***

Fastener Head Types. The head of a fastener determines the type and size of screwdriver tip that is needed. The proper tip will fit in a fastener head snugly. Damage or tool slippage may occur if an incorrect sized tip is used. Common types of screwdriver tips include Phillips, slotted, square, Allen, Torx, and hex (***Figure 6.15***). Screwdriver tips are also made as bits that can be placed in a socket to ratchet in tight places.

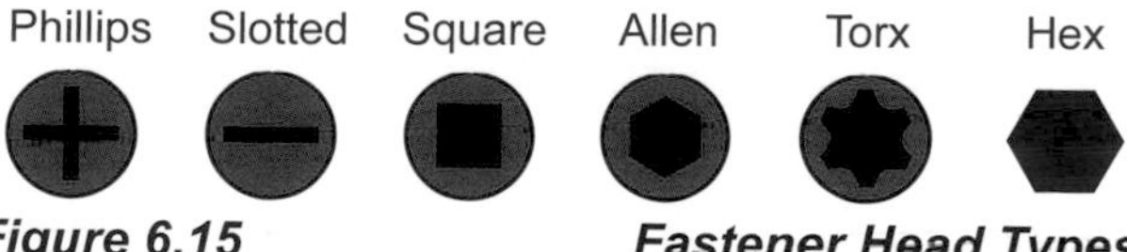

Figure 6.15 ***Fastener Head Types***

Hammers

Sometimes what you are working on needs a little more persuasion. Using the correct hammer will ensure that you don't damage components.

Ball Peen Hammer. A ball peen hammer (***Figure 6.16***) is commonly used to drive a chisel or a punch. ***Warning: Always wear eye protection.***

Figure 6.16 ***Ball Peen Hammer***

Courtesy of Matco Tools - www.matcotools.com

Rubber Mallet. A rubber mallet (***Figure 6.17***), a hammer with a rubber head, comes in handy to drive on stubborn wheel covers and other parts without damaging them.

Figure 6.17 ***Rubber Mallet***

Pry Bars

Pry bars (***Figure 6.18***) are long bars with handles that come in a variety of sizes and styles. They can be useful for gaining leverage on a component that is heavy or stuck.

Figure 6.18 ***Pry Bar***

Price Guides

Ball Peen Hammer
- $10.00 to $15.00

Combination Plier Set
- $15.00 to $50.00

Locking Pliers
- $10.00 to $15.00

Pry Bar
- $10.00 to $20.00

Ratchet and Socket Set
- $50.00 to $150.00

Screwdriver Set
- $15.00 to $50.00

Lifting Tools

When performing work under a vehicle it is often necessary and convenient to raise the vehicle off the ground with a floor jack and jack stands or drive-on ramps. Work safely by using lifting equipment on a surface that is solid and chock the wheels still on the ground. ***Warning: The weight of the vehicle being lifted should not exceed the lift ratings on the equipment.*** This section focuses on:

- Floor Jack
- Drive-on Ramps
- Wheel Chocks
- Jack Stands

Floor Jack

A floor jack (***Figure 6.19***) is used to lift a vehicle. Be sure to place the jack's lifting pad under the frame or other solid chassis component. Lifting by the sheet metal underbody may cause damage to a vehicle and make it more likely to fall off the jack. ***Warning: To prevent serious injury or death, jack stands must be used. Do not go under a vehicle that is only supported by a jack.***

Figure 6.19 *Hydraulic Floor Jack*
Photo: Bosch Automotive Service Solutions, Inc.

Drive-on Ramps

Drive-on ramps (***Figure 6.20***) can make raising one end of a vehicle very easy. Line the ramps up in front of the tires, carefully drive onto them, set the parking brake, and chock the wheels remaining on the ground. Since the vehicle is still resting on its tires, don't plan on doing any wheel work. Ramps are convenient for oil changes and undercarriage inspections. ***Warning: Drive-on ramps may move when driving up them.***

Figure 6.20 *Drive-on Ramps*

Wheel Chocks

To prevent a vehicle from moving forward or backward, wheel chocks (***Figure 6.21***) are used to block a wheel when jacking. Place the wheel chocks in front and in back of the wheels that are not being lifted.

Figure 6.21 *Wheel Chocks*

Jack Stands

Jack stands (***Figure 6.22***) are used to hold a vehicle up after a jack has raised it. ***Warning: Do not use concrete blocks or other non-approved stands to hold up a vehicle.***

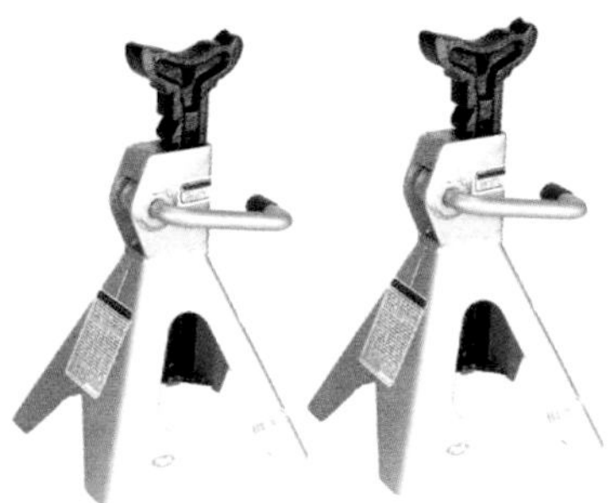

Figure 6.22 *Jack Stands*

Price Guides 

Air Pressure Gauge
- $1.00 to $15.00

Drive-on Ramps
- $40.00 to $60.00

Hydraulic Floor Jack
- $40.00 to $150.00

Safety Jack Stands
- $20.00 to $50.00 pair

Tread Depth Gauge
- $1.00 to $3.00

Tire Pressure Monitoring Tool
- $50.00 to $250.00

Wheel Chocks
- $10.00 to $20.00

4-Way Tire Tool
- $10.00 to $20.00

Tire Tools

Basic tire tools will allow you to change a tire, check the tread depth, and maintain the recommended air pressure. This section focuses on:

- Tire Pressure Gauges
- Bottle and Scissor Jacks
- 4-Way Tire Tool/Cross/Lug Wrench
- Tread Depth Gauge
- TPMS Tool

Tire Pressure Gauges

Tire pressure is measured with a tire pressure gauge (***Figure 6.23***) in pounds per square inch (psi) or kilopascals (kPa) and should be checked at least once a month. Recommended tire pressure is calculated according to the tire type, vehicle weight, and the desired ride. Maintaining the recommended tire pressure is critical to minimizing tire wear and optimizing handling stability. For every 10 degrees Fahrenheit (°F) the temperature drops, tire pressure drops by 1 psi (6.9 kPa). The inverse also occurs as temperature rises.

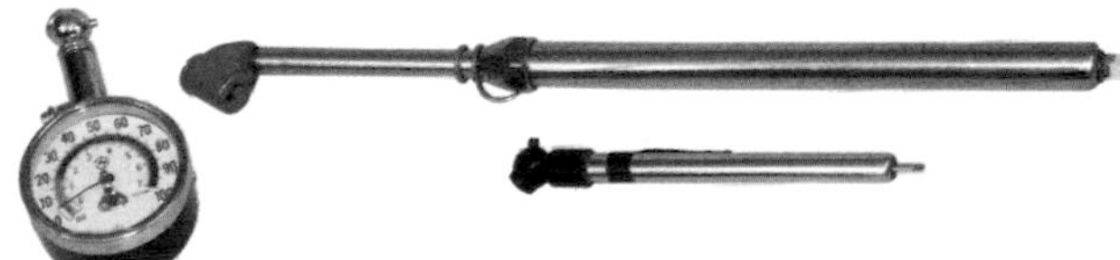

Figure 6.23 ***Dial and Stick Pressure Gauges***

Bottle and Scissor Jacks

Many vehicles have a bottle jack (***Figure 6.24***) or scissor jack stored in the trunk for emergency tire changes. These manufacturer supplied jacks are not as easy or as safe to use as a hydraulic floor jack. Save them for roadside emergencies and invest in a hydraulic floor jack for your garage.

Figure 6.24 ***Bottle Jack with Lug Wrench***

4-Way Tire Tool/Cross/Lug Wrench

A 4-way tire tool (***Figure 6.25***) is more versatile for removing lug nuts than the basic manufacturer lug wrench (i.e., tire iron) supplied with your vehicle. A 4-way has a different size on each end and allows for more leverage.

Figure 6.25 ***4-Way Tire Tool***

Tread Depth Gauge

A tread depth gauge (***Figure 6.26***) is a simple measuring device to help determine the actual amount of tread remaining on your tires. It provides a depth reading from the top of the tread surface to the bottom of the tread groove.

Figure 6.26 ***Tread Depth Gauge***

TPMS Tool

Tire pressure monitoring system (TPMS) sensors monitor tire pressure and transmit the pressure reading to a receiver in the vehicle. These systems have been standard on 2008 and later model year vehicles. A TPMS tool ***(Figure 6.27)*** is used when performing a tire rotation. Some systems relearn the new tire location automatically, while others need you to use a compatible tool. Often called a TPMS reset, relearn, activation, or scan tool, it identifies the new location of the tire. Read your owner's manual to identify the TPMS relearn procedure for your vehicle.

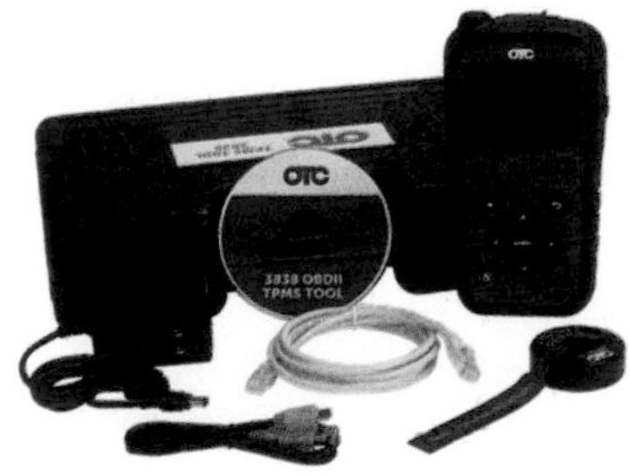

Figure 6.27 ***TPMS Tool***
Photo: Bosch Automotive Service Solutions, Inc.

Measuring Tools

Measuring accurately requires the use of measuring tools like rulers, gauges, and micrometers. This section focuses on:

- Systems of Measurement
- Rulers
- Torque Wrench
- Infrared Thermometer
- Coolant Testers
- Spark Plug Gauge
- Precision Measuring Tools

Systems of Measurement

Two systems of measurement (***Figure 6.28***) are used: International System of Units (metric system) and U.S. customary units (English system).

	Metric System	English System
Length	meter	inch, foot, mile
Mass	gram	ounce, pound, ton
Volume	liter	cubic inches, pint, quart, gallon
Power	watt	horsepower
Torque	Newton-meter	pound-foot
Temperature	degree Celsius	degree Fahrenheit

Figure 6.28 Common Metric and English Units

Web Links

Tool Manufacturer Related Sites

Bosch
www.boschtools.com

Mac Tools
www.mactools.com

Matco Tools
www.matcotools.com

Milwaukee Tool
www.milwaukeetool.com

OTC Tools
www.otctools.com

Robinair
www.robinair.com

Snap-on Tools
www.snapon.com

Rulers

Rulers are used to measure linear distances. Measuring tapes are used to measure large distances whereas small rigid rulers are used to measure short linear distances.

Torque Wrench

A torque wrench, either beam or clicker style (***Figure 6.29***), can be used to tighten a fastener to a specific amount of force. For example, wheel lug nuts should be tightened to the manufacturer's specifications. Lug nuts that are not tight enough could loosen over time. Lug nuts that are too tight are hard to remove, can cause runout on brake rotors, and can damage the stud's threads. A torque wrench is also critically important when completing internal engine repairs.

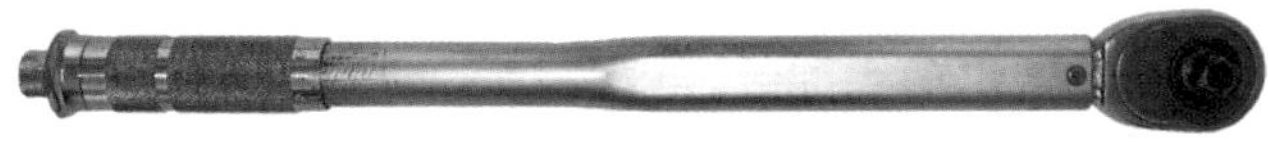

Figure 6.29 Clicker Style Torque Wrench

Infrared Thermometer

An infrared thermometer, also called a temperature gun, (***Figure 6.30***) is used to measure the surface temperature of an object.

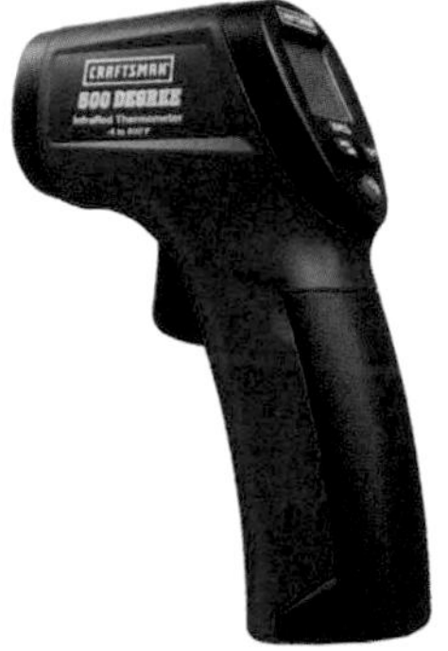

Figure 6.30 Infrared Thermometer

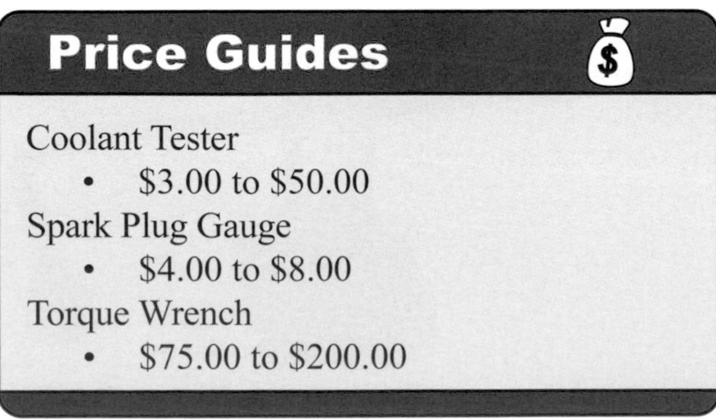

Price Guides

Coolant Tester
- $3.00 to $50.00

Spark Plug Gauge
- $4.00 to $8.00

Torque Wrench
- $75.00 to $200.00

Coolant Testers

Coolant testers are used to determine coolant freeze and boilover protection.

Hydrometer. A hydrometer tester (***Figure 6.31***) measures specific gravity of the coolant, which can give you approximate freeze and boil points. Hydrometers cannot be used with propylene glycol coolant.

Figure 6.31 ***Hydrometer***

Refractometer. A refractometer (***Figure 6.32***) is an optical device. It calculates freeze protection by measuring how light passes through a coolant sample.

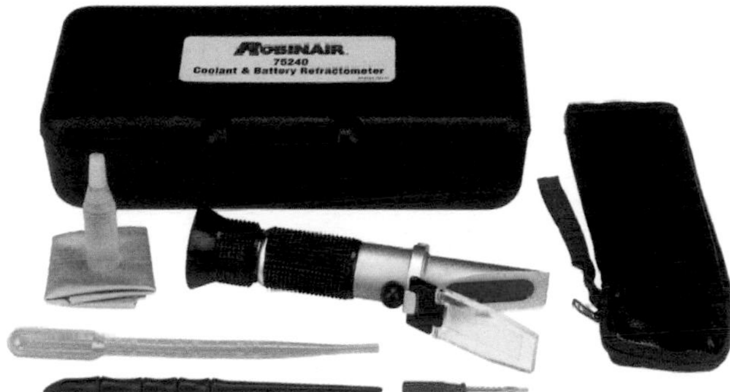

Figure 6.32 ***Refractometer***
Photo: Bosch Automotive Service Solutions, Inc.

Spark Plug Gauge

A spark plug gauge (***Figure 6.33***) has various diameter wires for checking the electrode gap and benders to adjust the gap. The gap is the distance between the center and side electrodes on the spark plug. A spark must arc across the gap in order to ignite the air-fuel mixture in a cylinder. The correct gap may be located on the vehicle emission control information (VECI) sticker in the engine compartment.

Figure 6.33 ***Spark Plug Gauge***

Precision Measuring Tools

Feeler gauges, calipers, micrometers, and dial indicators are used to obtain very precise measurements. These tools can provide measurements to the nearest thousandths (0.001) of an inch or to the nearest hundredths (0.01) of a millimeter.

Feeler Gauge. Feeler gauges (***Figure 6.34***) consist of flat metal blades that are a specific thickness. You can put several feeler blades together to obtain a desired thickness.

Figure 6.34 ***Feeler Gauge Set***

Caliper. A caliper (***Figure 6.35***) is an especially versatile measuring tool able to measure inside, outside, and depth dimensions. However, when extremely precise measurements are required consider using a micrometer.

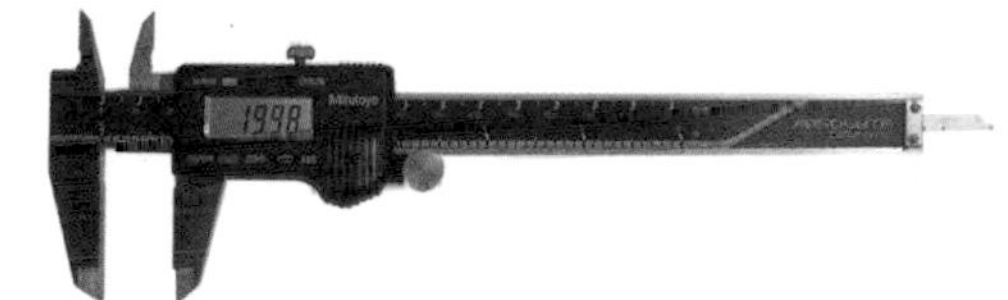

Figure 6.35 ***Digital Caliper***

Micrometer. Micrometers (***Figure 6.36***) are particularly good for measuring the diameter of objects.

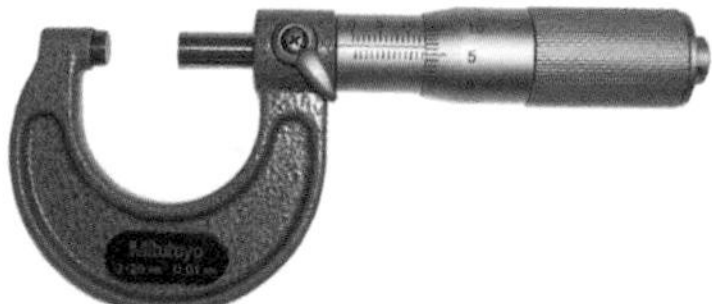

Figure 6.36 ***Outside Micrometer***

Web Links

Measurement Related Sites

Measurement Conversions
www.convert-me.com

Starrett (Precision Measuring Tools)
www.starrett.com

Electric Related Tools

If you plan to maintain a vehicle's electrical system some electrical tools will be necessary. At the very least every vehicle should carry a set of jumper cables. This section focuses on:

- Test Light
- Multimeter
- Fuse Puller
- Wire Stripper
- Battery Tester
- Battery Terminal Puller
- Battery Brush
- Battery Hydrometer
- Battery Terminal Spreader
- Jumper Cables

Test Light

A test light (***Figure 6.37***), also known as a circuit tester or voltage tester, is a basic tool to detect electricity. To use a test light attach the ground clip to a solid ground and touch the probe end where the test for electricity is needed. If the test light is self-powered it can be used as a continuity tester. For example, a bulb can be tested out of the vehicle with a self-powered test light.

Figure 6.37 ***Test Light***
Courtesy of Matco Tools - www.matcotools.com

Price Guides

Battery Brush
- $4.00 to $8.00

Battery Terminal Spreader
- $5.00 to $10.00

Fuse Puller
- $1.00 to $2.00

Jumper Cables
- $10.00 to $250.00

Multimeter
- $25.00 to $200.00

Test Light
- $10.00 to $20.00

Wire Stripper
- $10.00 to $15.00

Multimeter

A digital multimeter (DMM) makes a great addition to any toolbox. DMMs (***Figure 6.38***) measure voltage (volts), resistance (ohms), and current (amps). ***Warning: As a safety measure use a fusible test lead.*** See Chapter 9 to learn how to use a multimeter.

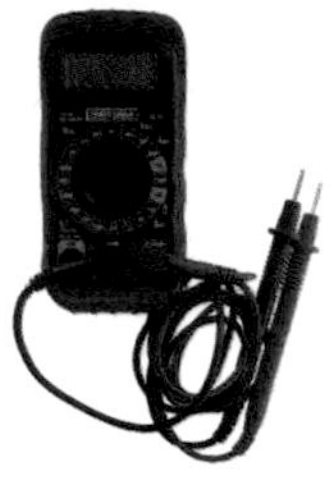

Figure 6.38 ***Multimeter***

Fuse Puller

Fuses are fairly small, very close to one another in a fuse junction block, and often tightly held, making it difficult to pull them out. A fuse puller (***Figure 6.39***) is a small plastic device designed to grasp a fuse so it can be pulled out easily.

Figure 6.39 ***Fuse Puller***

Wire Stripper

A wire stripper (***Figure 6.40***) can be used to remove wire insulation, cut wires, and to crimp solderless connectors and terminals.

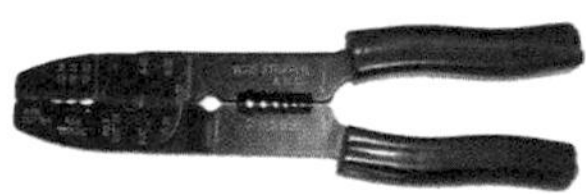

Figure 6.40 ***Wire Stripper***

Battery Tester

A battery tester (***Figure 6.41***) is a specialty tool used to evaluate a battery's condition. ***Note: Some automotive parts stores will test your battery for free.***

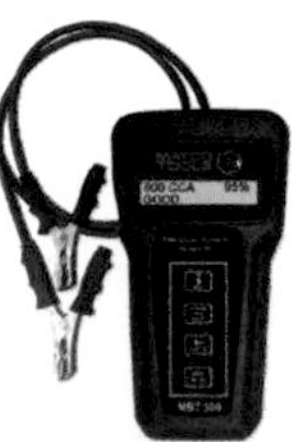

Figure 6.41 ***Battery Tester***
Courtesy of Matco Tools - www.matcotools.com

Battery Terminal Puller

The battery terminal puller (***Figure 6.42***) is designed to remove a stubborn or corroded battery terminal clamp after the battery terminal nut has been loosened. The lower jaws of the puller are placed under the battery terminal clamp and then the top lever is turned to lower the center screw onto the terminal post until it forces the clamp free. This type of puller is only used on top post batteries.

Figure 6.42 *Battery Terminal Puller*
Photo: Bosch Automotive Service Solutions, Inc.

Battery Brush

Once the battery terminal clamps have been disconnected from the battery posts, use battery brushes (***Figure 6.43***) to scrape off any visible corrosion. Rotate the external wire battery brush inside each clamp and the internal wire battery brush over each post. See Chapter 20 for steps on cleaning a battery. ***Warning: Always wear eye protection and gloves when cleaning a battery.***

Figure 6.43 *Battery Brushes*

Battery Hydrometer

A battery hydrometer (***Figure 6.44***) measures the specific gravity of the battery's electrolyte (water and sulfuric acid) solution. Knowing the specific gravity of the solution will indicate the cell's state of charge. The specific gravity can be measured in each cell. A 12V DC battery has six cells. See the Battery Activity in Chapter 9 of the workbook for specific steps. ***Warning: Be sure to wear safety goggles and gloves.***

Figure 6.44 *Battery Hydrometer*
Photo: Bosch Automotive Service Solutions, Inc.

Battery Terminal Spreader

A battery terminal spreader (***Figure 6.45***) is specially designed to spread battery terminal post clamps. It can also be used to scrape corrosion from the inside of terminal clamps.

Figure 6.45 *Battery Terminal Spreader*

Jumper Cables

A battery can become discharged simply by leaving your lights on, a door ajar, or it can be a sign of an electrical problem. You should know how to select good jumper cables (***Figure 6.46***) and how to properly hook them up. For steps on safely hooking up jumper cables refer to the owner's manual and the procedure in Chapter 20. ***Warning: Incorrectly jump-starting a battery can be dangerous. If cables are hooked up incorrectly the battery could explode or electrical components could be damaged.***

Figure 6.46 *Jumper Cables*

Choosing Jumper Cables. Make sure your jumper cables have a cable diameter of at least 6 gauge, insulation which stays flexible in cold weather, strong terminal clamps, and are 16 ft (4.88 m) long (***Figure 6.47***). If cables are short, it may be necessary to line up the booster vehicle next to the discharged vehicle, which can be dangerous on a road.

	BEST	GOOD	POOR
Gauge	1	6	12
Amps	800	400	150
Length	30 ft.	16 ft.	6 ft.
Price	$250.00	$30.00	$10.00

Figure 6.47 *Jumper Cable Quality*

Oil Change and Lube Tools

To perform an oil change and lube you will need lifting equipment, an oil drain pan, an oil filter wrench, a funnel, a grease gun, and a socket or wrench to remove the drain plug. See Chapter 10 for oil change steps. This section focuses on:

- Oil Drain Pan
- Oil Filter Wrench
- Funnel
- Grease Gun

Oil Drain Pan

An oil drain pan (***Figure 6.48***) helps to keep used oil from spilling. It should have a wide collection area, a place for the oil filter to sit while draining, enough capacity to hold at least one oil change, and a cap to prevent spilling during transportation to an oil recycling facility. Used oil is considered a carcinogen (causes cancer) and a hazardous waste. ***Warning: Always wear disposable gloves to prevent skin contact with used oil.***

Figure 6.48 ***Oil Drain Pan***

Oil Filter Wrench

Two oil filter wrench styles are the most common.

Band Filter Wrench. The band filter wrench (***Figure 6.49***) is made to adjust to several different sized filters within a range. For hard to reach filters get a filter wrench with a swivel handle.

Figure 6.49 ***Band Oil Filter Wrench***

Tech Tip

Oil Filter Wrench Size

Use a replacement filter as a guide when selecting a wrench if unsure of the size.

Cup Oil Filter Wrench. The cup oil filter wrench (***Figure 6.50***) is used with a ratchet for leverage. Select the cup size that fits snugly on your filter.

Figure 6.50 ***Cup Oil Filter Wrench***

Funnel

A funnel (***Figure 6.51***) helps prevent spills when adding oil to the engine. Always make sure the funnel is clean so you don't contaminate the engine with other fluids or dirt.

Figure 6.51 ***Funnel***

Grease Gun

A grease gun (***Figure 6.52***), containing a grease cartridge, is used to lubricate steering, suspension, and drivetrain components. A vehicle's service manual should identify the lubrication fittings (grease zerks) location (if applicable) and the type of grease recommended. See Chapter 14 to learn how to use a grease gun. Many automotive parts are being manufactured with a permanent seal, so grease can't be added.

Figure 6.52 ***Hand Operated Grease Gun***

Price Guides

Grease Gun
- $10.00 to $40.00

Oil Drain Pan
- $5.00 to $20.00

Oil Filter Wrench
- $5.00 to $15.00

Metalworking Tools

Sometimes it is necessary to remove a piece of metal, align parts, cut an exhaust pipe, drill a hole, or repair damaged nuts and bolts. ***Warning: Always wear eye protection when working with metal.*** This section focuses on:

- File
- Cold Chisel
- Punch
- Hacksaw
- Drill Bit
- Tap and Die Set

File

A file can be used to smooth, shape, and de-burr surfaces by removing metal. Common machinist files come in square, flat, half-round, and round types (***Figure 6.53***).

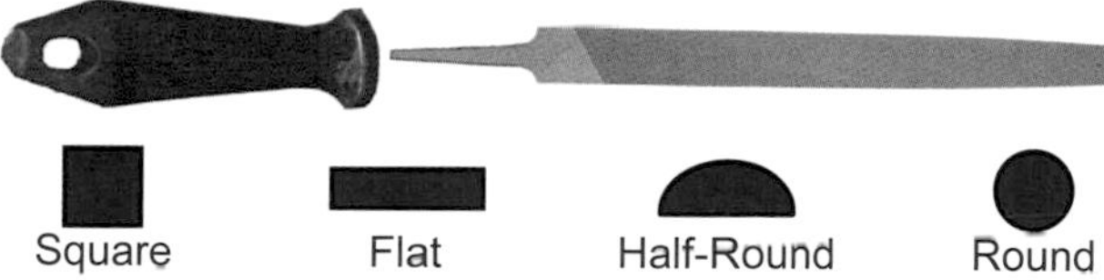

Figure 6.53 Machinist File and Common Shapes

Cold Chisel

To use a cold chisel (***Figure 6.54***), place the chiseled end on an object, such as a seized/rusted nut or rivet, and hit the blunt end with a hammer.

Figure 6.54 ***Cold Chisel***

Punch

Punches (***Figure 6.55***) can be used to drive parts during removal or installation, mark points, or align objects. To use a punch, place the driving end on the object you want to move, mark, or align and hit the blunt end with a hammer.

Figure 6.55 ***Punch***

Warning: Punches and chisels can get mushroomed heads from the hammer's impact. These parts can become projectiles when they are hit. OSHA requires that punches and chisels be kept free of mushroomed heads. Remove the mushroomed part with a file or grinder following the manufacturer's instructions.

Hacksaw

Hacksaws (***Figure 6.56***) cut metal using thin blades. Blades commonly have 18, 24, or 32 teeth per inch (25 mm). Blades with more teeth cut cleaner and slower. Point the teeth away from the handle to cut on the forward stroke.

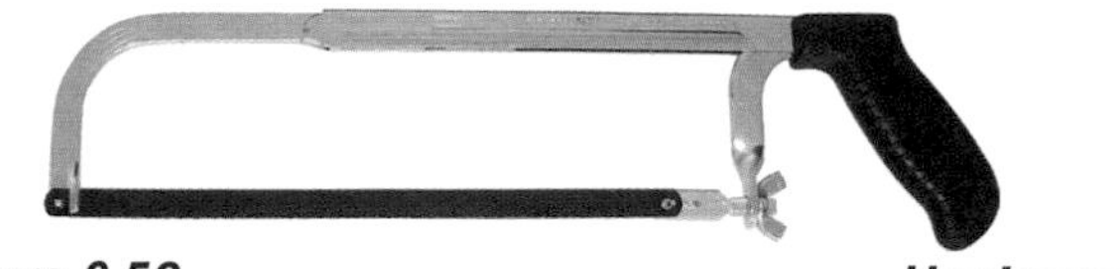

Figure 6.56 ***Hacksaw***

Drill Bit

A drill bit (***Figure 6.57***) used with a drill can create new holes.

Figure 6.57 ***Drill Bit***

Tap and Die Set

Internal threads are cut with a tap. A die cuts external threads (***Figure 6.58***). When a thread is cleaned or restored, it is called chasing a thread. Special thread chaser/restorer/rethreading kits are used to clean up threads.

Figure 6.58 ***Tap and Die Set***
Photo: Bosch Automotive Service Solutions, Inc.

Apps
Drill, Tap, Bolt, and Nut Charts
www.AutoUpkeep.com/apps
Click on Chapter 6

Power Tools

Power tools make work easier. If used improperly, they can be hazardous. ***Warning: Read the user (also known as operator or instruction) manual for each tool you plan to use. Follow all safety warnings and precautions.*** Power tools can be categorized by their power source:

- Electric-Powered Tools
- Air-Powered (Pneumatic) Tools
- Battery-Powered Tools

Electric-Powered Tools

Electric-powered drills, grinders, heat guns, impact wrenches, and vacuums can be found in an automotive shop (***Figure 6.59***).

Figure 6.59 ***Electric-Powered Tools***
Courtesy of Milwaukee Tool - www.milwaukeetool.com

Air-Powered (Pneumatic) Tools

Common air-powered (pneumatic) tools used in automotive shops are impact wrenches, ratchets, chisels, die grinders, and drills (***Figure 6.60***).

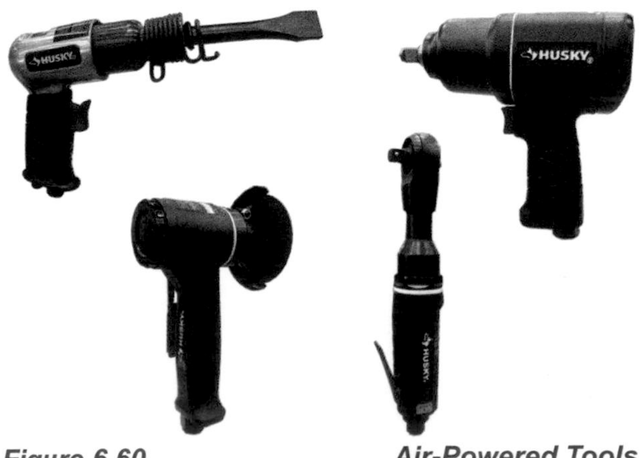

Figure 6.60 ***Air-Powered Tools***

Air Compressor. Air-powered tools need an air compressor (***Figure 6.61***) to work. An air compressor pressurizes the air, storing potential energy in a tank. An air hose connects the compressor to the air tool. When the air tool is activated, using a trigger mechanism, air is transferred from the tank to the tool. During this process the stored potential energy is converted to kinetic energy.

Figure 6.61 ***Air Compressor***
Courtesy of of BendPak, Inc. – www.bendpak.com

Battery-Powered Tools

Battery-powered, also called cordless, tools are becoming more and more popular. Cordless tools have many advantages over air and electric tools. If your are using an air or electric tool, you or someone near you could trip on the electric cord or air hose. This could even cause you to lose control of the tool and get injured. Without being tied to an air hose or electric cord, you have the freedom of mobility. Lithium-ion batteries are light, compact, and high-powered. Battery-powered impact wrenches, ratchets, drills, and inspection lights are very handy (***Figure 6.62***).

Figure 6.62 ***Battery-Powered Tools***
Courtesy of Milwaukee Tool - www.milwaukeetool.com

Inspection Tools

If you are going to diagnose, maintain, and repair a vehicle, consider owning the following:

- Creeper
- Fender Cover
- Work Light

Creeper

A creeper (***Figure 6.63***) allows easier access to the undercarriage of a vehicle. With your head and body supported, you can comfortably roll around on your back in a low clearance space.

Figure 6.63 ***Creeper***

Fender Cover

A fender cover helps to protect a vehicle's finish from scratches and dings while inspecting or working in the engine compartment.

Work Light

Seeing things in a quality light can really help when doing inspections and completing service work. Features to look for in a portable work light (***Figure 6.64***) include: impact and chemical resistant, ample light, low glare, and a hook or clip for positioning.

Figure 6.64 ***LED Work Light***
Photo: Bosch Automotive Service Solutions, Inc.

Price Guides

Creeper
- $25.00 to $50.00

Fender Cover
- $15.00 to $25.00

Work Light
- $10.00 to $50.00

General Shop Equipment

Most repair facilities will have general shop equipment for all their technicians to use. Many do-it-yourselfers (DIYers) also have the following equipment in their garage. This section focuses on:

- Battery Charger
- Bench Vise
- Bench Grinder

Battery Charger

When a battery has a low state of charge, a battery charger (***Figure 6.65***) can be used to put energy back into it. ***Note: Different battery chargers will vary slightly in their charging procedure. Be sure to read the manufacturer's instructions.***

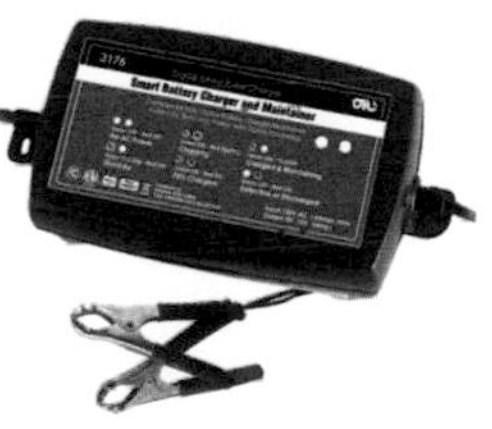

Figure 6.65 ***Battery Charger***
Photo: Bosch Automotive Service Solutions, Inc.

Bench Vise

A bench vise (***Figure 6.66***), attached to a workbench, is handy to hold the object you are working on in place.

Figure 6.66 ***Bench Vise***

Bench Grinder

A bench grinder (***Figure 6.67***) will have grinding wheels, wire wheels, or a combination of the two. The grinding wheel can be used to sharpen tools or grind metal. The wire wheel is used for cleaning parts.

Figure 6.67 ***Bench Grinder***

Automotive Lifts

Most repair shops and educational automotive labs have automotive lifts. Automotive lifts are more convenient than using a jack and jack stands. The greatest advantage is that they allow the technician to access the whole underside of the vehicle. This section focuses on:

- Inground Lifts
- Surface-Mounted Lifts

Inground Lifts

Inground lifts (***Figure 6.68***) generally take up less space. Their configuration varies depending on design and age of lift.

Figure 6.68 ***Inground Vehicle Lift***
Courtesy of Rotary Lift - www.rotarylift.com

Web Links 

Auto Lift and Equipment Sites

Automotive Lift Institute
www.autolift.org

BendPak, Inc.
www.bendpak.com

Bosch
www.bosch.com

Challenger Lifts
www.challengerlifts.com

Dannmar Equipment
www.dannmar.com

Hunter Engineering Company
www.hunter.com

Mohawk Lifts
www.mohawklifts.com

Rotary Lift
www.rotarylift.com

Surface-Mounted Lifts

A surface-mounted lift, powered by an electric motor, is bolted to the garage floor. A hydraulic pump pushes fluid in hydraulic cylinders to lift the vehicle. Types of surface-mounted lifts include two-column and four-column lifts.

Two-Column Lifts. The two-column drive through frame engaging lift is often called a two-post lift (***Figure 6.69***). Two-post lifts have synchronized lift arms that ride up each column evenly. This type of lift is commonly used for doing under-the-car service work. Since the lift contacts the frame, and not the wheels, it is an ideal setup for completing tire rotations, brake inspections, and suspension work. It is also used for doing undercarriage work on exhaust systems and performing oil changes. By far, the two-post lift is the most popular type of surface-mounted automotive lift.

Figure 6.69 ***Two-Post Vehicle Lift***
Courtesy of of BendPak, Inc. – www.bendpak.com

Tech Tip 

Buying a Lift

Surface-mounted lifts have become extremely popular. With the advent of the "extreme" garage, more and more automotive enthusiasts are installing lifts at home. If you buy a lift make sure it is certified through the Automotive Lift Institute. For a list of complying manufacturers and the latest lift safety information go to www.autolift.org.

Four-Column Lifts. The four-column drive on lift is often called a four-post lift. Four-post lifts have runways. Once the vehicle is driven onto the runways, it is raised by its tires exposing the underside. This type of lift is most common in muffler and oil change shops. It is relatively safe and easy to use. The main disadvantage is the inability to perform services that require the removal of wheels without adding special adapters to lift the vehicle off the runways. These special adapters, called rolling lift jacks (***Figure 6.70***), are available from many manufacturers.

Figure 6.70 Four-Post Lift with Rolling Lift Jacks
Courtesy of Rotary Lift - www.rotarylift.com

Specialty Tools and Equipment

Technicians and repair facilities have many specialty tools and equipment, which are often only used for one purpose. Specializing, becoming an expert in a certain automotive area, will require having more tools and equipment in that particular area. For example, a repair facility that specializes in tires and alignments would have a tire machine, wheel balancer, and an alignment system. If you plan to become a professional technician you will need to learn more about the tools and equipment that will make your work possible. A technician commonly purchases the handheld specialty tools, while a shop usually purchases the specialty equipment. This section focuses on:

- Handheld Specialty Tools
- Specialty Equipment

Handheld Specialty Tools

As technicians specialize in an automotive area, they may add tools to aid their expertise. Their specialty commonly focuses on ASE Certification areas: Engine Repair, Automatic Transmission/Transaxle, Manual Drivetrain and Axles, Suspension and Steering, Brakes, Electrical/Electronic Systems, Heating and Air Conditioning, Engine Performance, and Light Vehicle Diesel Engines. Some technicians specialize working on particular vehicles and add vehicle manufacturer specific tools to their toolbox.

Scan Tool. One tool that will work on all vehicles since 1996 is an OBD II scan tool (***Figure 6.71***). A scan tool connects to the vehicle's data link connector (DLC) to retrieve diagnostic trouble codes (DTC).

Figure 6.71 Scan Tool
Courtesy of Matco Tools - www.matcotools.com

Specialty Equipment

Repair facilities purchase specialized shop equipment to meet their needs.

Tire Equipment. Common at repair facilities that repair and sell tires are tire changing machines and wheel balancers (***Figure 6.72***).

Figure 6.72 Wheel Balancer and Tire Changer
Courtesy of of BendPak, Inc. – www.bendpak.com

Vehicle Service Manuals

As you perform repair or service procedures, it is essential you have the correct reference material. Vehicle service information is available in books, videos, online, and at some public libraries. This section focuses on:

- Owner's Manual
- Online Service Manuals
- Consumer Service Manuals
- Professional Service Manuals

Owner's Manual

Reading your owner's manual should be the first step to maintaining your vehicle correctly. It describes specific vehicle features, instructions, warnings, and maintenance requirements. If you don't have your print manual, you can usually download an electronic version free from the manufacturer's website (***Figure 6.73***).

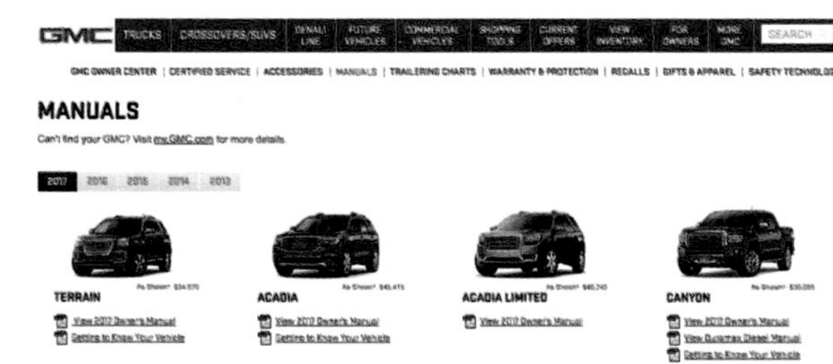

Figure 6.73 ***Online Owner's Manuals***
Screen Capture from www.gmc.com/owners/manuals

Online Service Manuals

Online service manuals (***Figure 6.74***) have the benefit of taking up less space than print manuals with everything accessible through your computer, tablet, or smartphone. Another benefit is that these manuals are constantly updated.

Figure 6.74 ***Mitchell 1 Online Service Manual***
Screen Capture from www.mitchell1diy.com

Consumer Service Manuals

Most individuals who do some of their own mechanic work may eventually purchase a general service and repair manual. These manuals cover a vehicle through a range of years, makes, and models in a condensed format. They are written for the average auto owner and often contain specific vehicle photos (***Figure 6.75***).

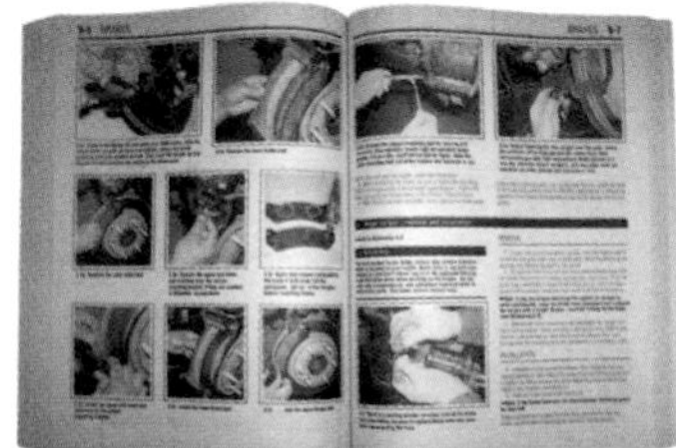

Figure 6.75 ***Consumer Service Manual***

Professional Service Manuals

Each professional service manual, often containing several volumes, is specific to one year of a vehicle make and model (***Figure 6.76***). They cover almost every component and system with detailed illustrations, diagnostic checks, wiring diagrams, and step-by-step repair procedures.

Figure 6.76 ***Professional Service Manuals***

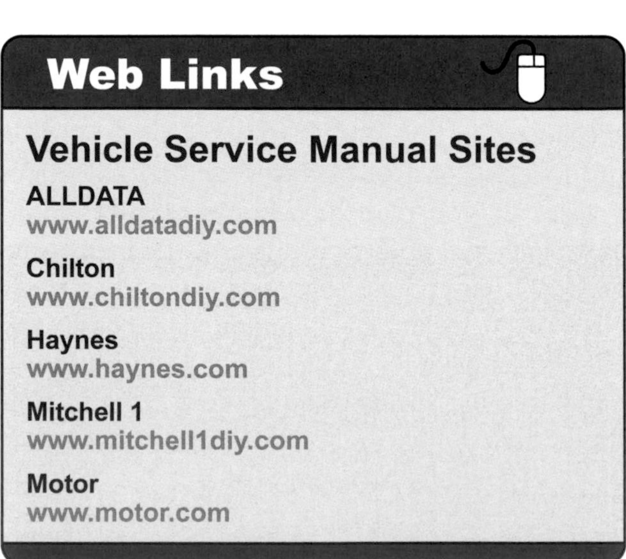

Web Links

Vehicle Service Manual Sites

ALLDATA
www.alldatadiy.com

Chilton
www.chiltondiy.com

Haynes
www.haynes.com

Mitchell 1
www.mitchell1diy.com

Motor
www.motor.com

Cleaning Supplies

It is important to keep your hands and work area clean. This section focuses on:

- Shop Towels
- Hand Cleaner
- Floor Dry

Shop Towels

Shop towels (***Figure 6.77***) and rags help you to keep your hands, tools, and vehicle components clean. If they have been used to wipe up combustible materials such as oil, fuel, or chemicals they should be stored in an approved container until they can be properly disposed or cleaned.

Figure 6.77 ***Shop Towels***

Floor Dry

To prevent accidents and to keep your work area safe, use floor dry (***Figure 6.78***) to absorb oil and other spills. If you don't have floor dry, kitty litter also works.

Figure 6.78 ***Floor Dry***

Hand Cleaner

If you do not wear gloves you will probably want an effective hand cleaner (***Figure 6.79***). Some automotive hand cleaners can be rubbed on and wiped off without water.

Figure 6.79 ***Hand Cleaner***

Summary

Quality tools can be expensive, but having the right tool can make a difficult job easier. Start off with a basic tool set and then periodically add more specialized tools as you see a need and as your budget permits. Remember that caring for and cleaning your tools will help them last longer. Having the proper tools makes working on a vehicle easier, faster, and ultimately more enjoyable. Automotive repair facilities purchase equipment to make work easier. One of the most common pieces of equipment found in an automotive repair facility is an automotive lift. Other shop equipment includes things such as bench grinders, bench vises, battery chargers, and specialty equipment. ***Note: Always read the user manual for each tool or piece of equipment you plan to use. Follow all safety warnings and precautions and receive the proper training. If you are unsure how to operate something, ask for help.*** Be sure to use the correct reference manual for the vehicle being serviced or repaired.

Activities 

Tools and Equipment

- Tools and Equipment Identification Activity
- Service Manual Activity
- Chapter 6 Study Questions

Activities and Study Questions can be completed in the *Auto Upkeep Workbook*.

Career Paths 

Industrial Designer

Education: Bachelor's Degree
Median Income: $67,130
Abilities: Apply math, science, technology, and ingenuity to solve technical problems.
Find your career at **www.bls.gov/ooh**.

AUTO CARE AND CLEANING

CHAPTER 7

Fuel for Thought

- What is the difference between a basecoat and a clearcoat finish?
- What type of soap should you use to wash a vehicle?
- Why is it so important to keep your windows clean?

Introduction

Some people say that when their vehicle is clean it actually runs better. With today's fast paced society, many people take their vehicle to a detail center or a car wash instead of doing the work themselves. Detailing a car personally, however, can be very rewarding and can save money. The appearance of a vehicle does not actually change its performance, but it does improve its longevity. A vehicle that is kept clean inside and out will surely render a better value at trade-in time. Conserve water by using a spray nozzle to control flow and consider using cleaning products that are environmentally safe.

Objectives

Upon completion of this chapter and activities, you will be able to:

- Identify different automotive finishes.
- Explain the importance of washing, drying, and waxing a vehicle.
- Explain the importance of cleaning the inside of a vehicle.
- Correctly clean, wax, and detail a vehicle inside and out.
- Repair paint chips and scratches.

Automotive Finishes

Automotive finishes have advanced significantly. The finish used on most vehicles today is a clearcoat finish. This section focuses on:

- Finish Types
- Finish Failure

Finish Types

The paint covers and protects the vehicle's body.

Basecoat. Up until the 1980s, most vehicles had a basecoat finish where the color was the topcoat. When waxing, the rag used would turn the color of the vehicle. The oxidized layer of paint would come off revealing fresh paint.

Clearcoat. On a clearcoat finish, the basecoat is covered with a topcoat that contains no color pigment. This extra layer adds protection and appearance to the basecoat. When waxing this type of finish, the rag does not turn the pigmented color because the oxidized layer is on the clearcoat.

Finish Failure

Peeling paint (or clearcoat) can be caused by improper paint preparation during the paint process, incompatible paint products, or when the finish (primer, basecoat, or clearcoat) is compromised with a chip or a scratch. Once compromised, dirt and moisture may enter. Moisture can lead to rust or peeling. The sun's ultraviolet (UV) rays, chemical exposure, and infrequent waxing can also lead to paint failure (***Figure 7.1***).

Figure 7.1 ***Peeling Finish***

Exterior Care and Cleaning

A vehicle's exterior has to withstand extreme conditions from the environment. Intense sun, road dirt, rain, dust, mud, snow, ice, and salt are all harsh elements. This section focuses on:

- Washing
- Drying
- Polishing
- Waxing
- Trim Detailing

Washing

Keeping the exterior finish clean is the first step in maintaining a vehicle's shine and endurance. If you brush up against a dirty vehicle you could scratch the finish. ***Note: Sunscreens/suntan lotions and insect repellents can severely damage paint. If these inadvertently get on your paint, wash them off immediately.***

Hand Washing. Many owner's manuals indicate that hand washing a vehicle is preferred over automatic car washes or even hand-held pressure washers. Pressure washers can damage paint and decals if not used properly (***Figure 7.2***).

Pressure Washer Recommendations

- Keep the water pressure below 1200 psi.
- Do not heat the water above 179°F.
- Avoid moving the pressure washer's nozzle (tip) closer than 12 inches to the vehicle's surface.
- Maintain a 90 degree angle to vehicle's surface.

Figure 7.2 Pressure Washer Recommendations

Car Wash Soap. Use only specifically formulated car wash soap (***Figure 7.3***). Car wash soap is designed to float away dirt and grime without harming the finish. Some car wash soaps are biodegradable, providing an environmentally-safer cleaner. Dish detergents are not chemically designed for vehicle finishes. They may strip the wax and dry out the finish, so don't use them.

Figure 7.3 Car Wash Soap, Bucket, and Mitt

Washing Tips. Do not wash a vehicle while it is hot. Park in the shade and hose off any loose dirt by rinsing the vehicle from the roof down. Hose off the underbody, wheel wells, and wheels. Keep all body and door water drain holes clear and open, free of dirt and debris. As you are washing keep your mitt clean to avoid scratching the finish. After washing an area rinse the soap off before it dries. To avoid water spots keep the vehicle's finish wet until you are ready to dry it.

Removing Bugs and Tar. Bug and road tar removers come in wipes, aerosol cans, gels, spray bottles (***Figure 7.4***), and pour bottles. Often you only have to apply the product, wait as directed, and wipe it off with a shop towel. Stubborn spots may require rubbing. Follow instructions on the product. Bug and tar remover may strip the wax off the paint. After using, wash the area with car wash soap, rinse, dry, and then apply a new coat of wax. ***Note: Remove any bird droppings, bug deposits, and tar as soon as possible. Over time, they can damage your vehicle's finish.***

Figure 7.4 Bug and Tar Removers

Tech Tip

Automatic Car Washes

The most popular automatic car washes are touchless, using high-pressure nozzles to clean a vehicle. High pressure can be hard on a vehicle's finish, especially if it is already peeling or flaking. If you use an automatic brush wash, remove the antenna and exterior accessories (e.g., roof racks) that the brushes could get caught on. To be safe, it is best to wash your vehicle by hand.

Lenses. Be extremely careful cleaning headlight lenses and other lamp covers. Use car wash soap mixed with cold or lukewarm water. Clean with a soft cloth or microfiber towel while wet. Do not try to clean them when they are dry. Read your owner's manual for the specific procedure. Over time, some headlight lenses get cloudy. This can cause a driving hazard. If your headlight lenses are cloudy or frosted, use a headlight restoration kit to polish them (***Figure** 7.5*). Follow the instructions with the product.

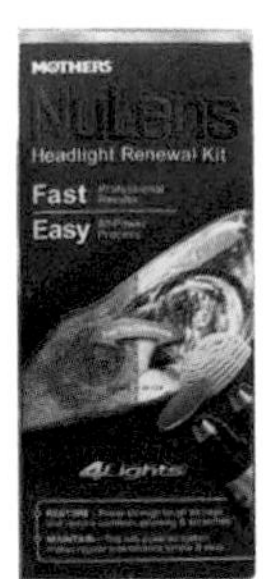

Figure 7.5 ***Headlight Restoration Kits***

Windshield. A dirty windshield reduces visibility. Clean the windshield with glass cleaner. Using a windshield treatment product like Rain-X® on the outside of the windshield will smooth the glass surface and repel water, providing protection similar to wax on a vehicle's finish (***Figure** 7.6*). Wipers moving across a smooth windshield are less likely to skip.

Figure 7.6 ***Rain-X® Windshield Treatment***

Wiper Blades. Dirty wipers result in poor wiper operation. Using a microfiber cloth, clean the rubber wiper blades with a soapy water solution (***Figure** 7.7*) or windshield washer fluid. Inspect for damage and replace if necessary.

Figure 7.7 ***Cleaning Wiper Blades***

Wheels. Use a soft brush, cloth, or sponge to scrub the tire walls and rims. It is best to clean your wheels last to avoid contaminating the wash bucket with dirt that can scratch your vehicle's finish. Special tire and whitewall cleaners and conditioners (***Figure** 7.8*) are available to protect your tires and can really make them shine.

Figure 7.8 ***Tire Care Products***

Q & A

Dirty Front Wheels

Q: Why do front wheels get dirty quicker than rear wheels?

A: When braking, a small amount of brake pad material wears off as dust and collects on your wheel or hubcap. The front brakes do more of the braking than the rear brakes, making them wear quicker. Also, if your car's rear brakes are drum style, the dust usually collects in the drum and then falls out on the backside of the wheel.

Drying

Water accelerates corrosion and hard water can leave damaging spots on a vehicle's finish. After washing, dry a vehicle with a clean microfiber detail towel or a super absorbent chamois (***Figure 7.9***). Make sure your chamois or detail towel remains clean to prevent scratches.

Figure 7.9 Microfiber Towel and Chamois

Microfiber Towel. A microfiber towel is made from ultra-fine synthetic fibers. They are highly adsorbent, soft, durable, and lint free. Microfiber towels that have a waffle weave design are best for drying.

Chamois. A chamois, usually made from sheepskin, will be hard and abrasive when dry, so wet it and wring it out first. Drag it across the finish to pull water off and then wring out the excess until the chamois is just damp.

Detailing. It is also important to open the doors, trunk, and hood to wipe around them with a shop towel. Do not use a chamois or detail towel in these areas because you will pick up contaminants that were missed when you washed.

Evaluate the Finish. Once the vehicle is dry you should evaluate the finish condition. Slide a clean, dry detail towel across your hood. If it does not glide effortlessly, then the finish should be waxed. Next move your finger along the paint, if it feels rough there are contaminants and oxidation on the surface. This roughness indicates that the finish also needs to be polished.

Price Guides

Chamois
- $10.00 to $25.00 each

Microfiber Waffle Weave Drying Towel
- $10.00 to $25.00 each

Polishing

Washing only removes surface dirt. To remove deeper oxidation, minor scratches, and old wax you may need to use a polish or more aggressive rubbing compound before waxing (***Figure 7.10***). Polishes use abrasives and/or chemicals to rub off the very top layer of finish, so don't overuse them. On clearcoat finishes only use a polish that is specially formulated "clearcoat safe" and nonabrasive. If a polish rubbed between your fingers feels granular or gritty then it definitely contains abrasives and should not be used on a clearcoat finish. Always read the product label for specific recommendations.

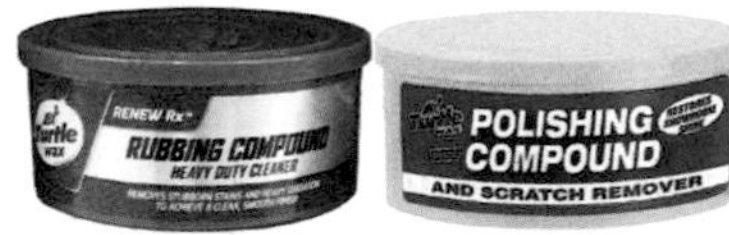

Figure 7.10 Rubbing and Polishing Compounds

Q & A

Wax or Polish

Q: Is polish different from wax?

A: A polish removes minor scratches and oxidation by using special chemicals and abrasives. A wax is generally used after the car is polished to add a thin layer of protection over the vehicle's finish. Some cleaners combine a polish and wax into one product. However, a two step process using a polish first and then a wax generally produces a better overall finish.

Waxing

Waxing adds shine and enhances the look of a vehicle's finish, while also providing a final layer of protection (***Figure 7.11***) from UV rays, pollution, and other damaging environmental conditions.

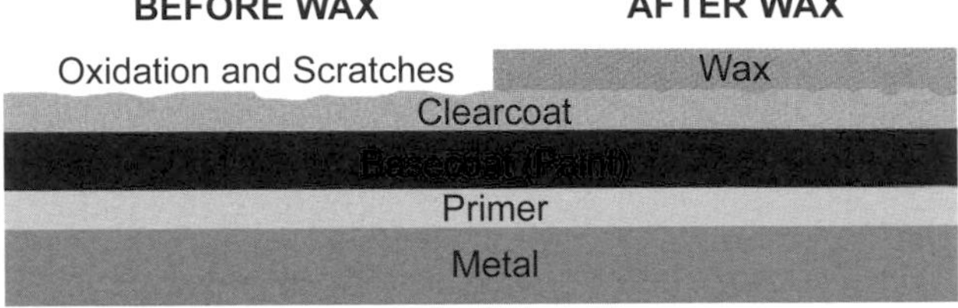

Figure 7.11 Clearcoat Finish Layers with Wax

Types of Wax. Carnauba, a natural wax, tends to shed water by making the water bead and run off. Some synthetic waxes add an extra agent like silicone polymers to increase the slickness, shedding water even better. Water contacting waxed finishes slides right off, allowing a vehicle to dry much faster. The less time water and impurities sit on a vehicle's finish, the less chance they have to contribute to corrosion and oxidation. Some "cleaner waxes" (***Figure 7.12***) are also formulated to remove oxidation and minor scratches more gently than polishes.

Figure 7.12 Cleaner Waxes

Applying Wax. Like washing, you should never apply wax on a hot vehicle or in direct sunlight. Remember to read the labels on the wax container for specific application information. Make sure the wax that you buy is suitable for your car's finish (***Figure 7.13***). ***Note: Some waxes are safe for both basecoat and clearcoat finishes, others are not.*** Pure wax for a clearcoat finish should be nonabrasive.

Figure 7.13 Automotive Waxes

Trim Detailing

Once you are done waxing your vehicle's finish it is time to focus on detailing the mirrors, plastic accessories, and metal trim pieces. There are many different kinds of polishes (***Figure 7.14***) available, so find the ones appropriate for your vehicle.

Figure 7.14 Metal Polish

Tech Tip

Wash Before You Wax

To avoid scratching the finish and trapping dust in fresh wax always wash your vehicle before you wax it, even if it looks clean.

Q & A ?

Gasoline on Paint

Q: Will gas spilled on a car's finish damage it?

A: Gas may strip the wax, which could eventually lead to fading in that area. You should wash the area right away and wax it. Waxing will help to maintain the shine and protect the finish.

Engine Compartment Cleaning

Make sure the engine is cool before cleaning in the engine compartment. Spray an engine cleaner or an all purpose cleaner like Simple Green® (***Figure 7.15***) on a rag and then wipe down the surfaces. Do not spray the cleaner directly on engine components. Today's cars have lots of wires, connectors, and fuse blocks in the engine compartment. Moisture will cause damage to the electrical components. Again, spray the cleaner on a rag and then wipe. Take your time. After everything is clean, spray a product like Armor All® on a rag and wipe the rubber and plastic components. Don't use a hose or pressure washer to spray the engine. If your vehicle's engine compartment is dirty beyond wiping, it is best to take it to a professional engine cleaner.

Figure 7.15 ***All Purpose Cleaner***

Q & A

Pressure Washing an Engine

Q: Why did my check engine light come on after I pressure washed my engine?

A: Pressure washing an engine without properly covering all electrical connectors, fuse blocks, and sensors can cause a variety of problems. The force from the pressure washer may have caused water to get into some of the wiring connectors or sensors. If water is in a connector it may be shorting out the electrical component or giving false voltage signals to the car's computer, which could trigger the check engine light.

Weatherstripping

In hot and dry climates, weatherstripping can dry out and crack. Dielectric silicone grease is commonly used to condition weatherstripping (***Figure 7.16***). Refer to your owner's manual to find out what your vehicle manufacturer recommends. Look under the title "Vehicle Care" or something similar. Condition weatherstripping once a year.

Figure 7.16 ***Dielectric Silicone Grease***

Price Guides

Wax

- $5.00 to $15.00 each bottle/can

Car Wash Soap

- $10.00 to $25.00 each

Web Links

Automotive Care Sites

Armor All Products
www.armorall.com

Dupli-Color Automotive Paints
www.duplicolor.com

Radiator Specialty Company - Gunk
www.gunk.com

Meguiar's
www.meguiars.com

Microfinish LLC
www.automotivetouchup.com

Mothers Polishes-Waxes-Cleaners
www.mothers.com

Nu Finish
www.nufinish.com

STP
www.stp.com

Turtle Wax Inc.
www.turtlewax.com

Interior Care and Cleaning

This section focuses on:

- Windows
- Vacuuming
- Floor Mats
- Upholstery Cleaning
- Stain Treatment
- Surface Protection
- Vehicle Information Displays

Windows

Dirty windows can lead to unsafe driving. At night, windows that have a film over them glare. Use an auto-approved glass cleaner with old newspapers, lint free cloths, or microfiber cloths. Clean the rearview mirror too. ***Note: If you have custom tinted windows, where the tint is not part of the glass, do not use a window cleaner that contains ammonia.***

Vacuuming

Vacuuming cleans the inside of the vehicle. Vacuum the carpet, floor mats, seats, headliner, door panels, and trunk. Dirty fabric will wear out quicker. Dirt accelerates wear by grinding away at the material's fibers.

Floor Mats

Remove your floor mats and shake them out. Rubber mats can be rinsed off and scrubbed as necessary. Carpet mats can be vacuumed thoroughly. Clean under the mats too. Secure the mat with the vehicle's floor mat retainers (***Figure 7.17***). ***Warning: Only use floor mats designed for your vehicle, especially for the driver's side. A loose floor mat can interfere with the brake and accelerator pedals.***

Figure 7.17 ***Custom Floor Mat with Retainers***
Courtesy of Husky Liners, Inc. – www.huskyliners.com

Upholstery Cleaning

Fabric, vinyl, leather, and carpet should be cleaned periodically with an interior or upholstery cleaner (***Figure 7.18***), even if there are no stains. Vacuuming will not remove all of the dirt that gets trapped in your upholstery and carpet fibers. Use a fabric cleaner made for your vehicle's material and follow the manufacturer's label. Remember to use fresh rags frequently to help lift the dirt away. You might consider using a power carpet or steam cleaner.

Figure 7.18 ***Carpet and Upholstery Cleaners***

Stain Treatment

Not all treatment products should be used on all stains and materials. Try to identify your vehicle's upholstery or carpet fabric and what caused the stain. Leather is especially unique. Find a product that best fits the stain and material. Follow the product instructions, which usually includes testing the product first in a hidden area to avoid potential discoloration problems. Without spreading the stain any further, remove any loose material with a vacuum, brush, or clean rag. Blot the stain (***Figure 7.19***) with a white paper towel or clean white rag to draw the stain out. Apply the stain remover as directed. Repetition may be needed to lift the stain. Finally clean the whole area. If you only spot treat the stain the surrounding area may appear dirty.

Figure 7.19 ***Blot the Stain***

Surface Protection

It is important to wipe down and condition interior vinyl, plastic, and rubber components, because they have a tendency to dry out. Specially formulated interior protectants (***Figure 7.20***) are safe for most types of vinyl, plastic, and rubber, but always read the manufacturer's label. Leather should also be conditioned with the appropriate product. Use cotton swabs to get into hard to reach areas like vents. ***Warning: To avoid hazardous driving conditions, do not use surface protectants on the driving controls (pedals, shifter, and steering wheel) or floor mats.***

Figure 7.20 ***Interior Protectants***

Vehicle Information Displays

Vehicle information displays (***Figure 7.21***), such as touch and navigation screens, are very delicate. Read your owner's manual for specific recommendations. Many new vehicles that have touch screens include a microfiber cleaning cloth in the glove box. A soft microfiber towel slightly dampened with lukewarm water is usually recommended to clean the screen. Apply minimal pressure. ***Note: Do not use window cleaners, solvents, or paper towels.***

Figure 7.21 ***Vehicle Information Display***

Forgotten Part Lubrication

Lubrication helps to reduce wear, rust, and corrosion, while keeping moving parts operating smoothly. This section focuses on:

- Forgotten Parts
- Lubrication

Forgotten Parts

If you hate the sound of annoying squeaks and creaks when you open your door, move your seat, or have difficulty releasing the hood latch, then it is time to lubricate your vehicle's forgotten, but important moving parts (***Figure 7.22***).

Area	Lubrication Part
Doors	Hinges, Latches, and Locks
Trunk	Hinges, Latch, and Lock
Seat	Rails
Hood	Hinges and Latch
Fuel Door	Hinges

Figure 7.22 ***Lubrication Locations***

Lubrication

Refer to your owner's manual for specific lubrication locations and lubricant recommendations. Read product labels for exact procedures and applications.

Types of Lubricants. Various types of lubricants are available, such as WD-40®, 3-In-One® oil, silicone spray, silicone paste, dry graphite spray, and lithium grease.

Lubrication Application. Before applying lubrication wipe off any dirt from the area. After application be sure to clean up any excess lubricant.

Finish Repair

While cleaning the finish of your vehicle you may have noticed a scratch, chip, or dent. With a little bit of effort and know-how you can keep these imperfections from being so noticeable, while also preserving your vehicle's finish. This section focuses on:

- Paintless Dent Repair
- Paint Color Code
- Chip and Scratch Repair

Paintless Dent Repair

Paintless dent repair (PDR) is a process that removes dents, dings, creases, and even hail damage up to the size of a football without effecting the paint. No sanding or body filler is used with this technique. Paintless dent repair methods can be used if the paint has not been scratched or cracked. However, not all dents can be repaired using this method. Since paintless dent repair requires special tools and training it is probably best to leave this to the professionals, especially if the damaged area is located near an airbag sensor. If you don't know what you are doing, you can make the dent worse. Another option is to obtain an old door or hood from a salvage yard and practice on that first. Two types of tools are commonly used - PDR glue pullers and PDR rods.

PDR Glue Pullers. PDR glue pulling (***Figure 7.23***) is a method where you use hot glue to attach a pulling tab onto the dented panel. Then you connect a dent lifter or slide hammer onto the tab to pull out the dent.

Figure 7.23 *PDR Glue Pulling Set*
Courtesy of Blehm Tool Company - www.pdrtoolstore.com

PDR Rods. Using PDR rods (***Figure 7.24***), you go behind the panel to work out the dent.

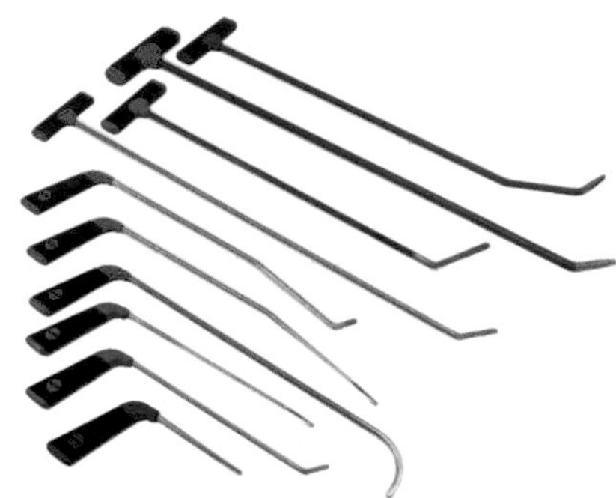

Figure 7.24 *PDR Rod Set*
Courtesy of Blehm Tool Company - www.pdrtoolstore.com

Paint Color Code

A vehicle's paint color code can be located in various places. Not all manufacturers keep paint code locations consistent. This information is often on the certification label in the driver's side doorjamb (***Figure 7.25***). At the bottom of the label below, BC/CC identifies the basecoat/clearcoat and then a color code is given. You can search a specific vehicle's make, model, and year on the Internet to find the color code location.

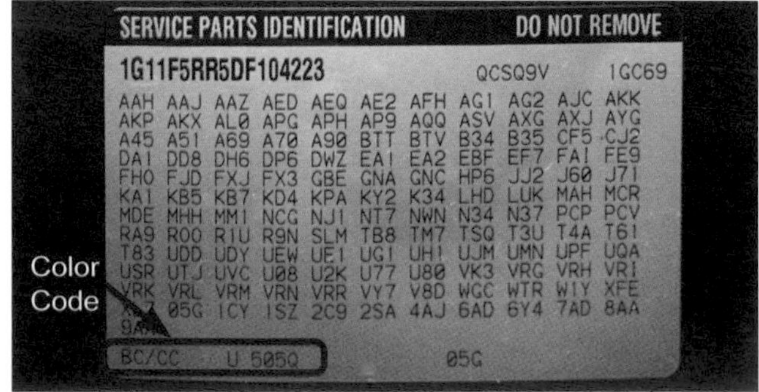

Figure 7.25 *Vehicle Paint Color Code*

Chip and Scratch Repair

The following is a general procedure for repairing a chip or scratch (***Figure** 7.26*). Start by finding touch up paint in a small bottle or pen to match the color code, along with rust remover, a sanding pen, touch up primer, and clearcoat at an auto parts store or dealer. Check the owner's manual for any specific suggestions.

Chip and Scratch Repair

STEP 1	Start by removing any rust or flakes. A rust remover can be used to dissolve larger rust areas.

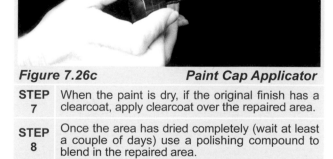

Figure 7.26a ***Rust Remover***

STEP 2	If you only have a small chip with surface rust, consider using a sanding pen. The tip of a sanding pen is small to minimize disturbing the surrounding painted areas.

Figure 7.26b ***Sanding Pen***

STEP 3	Clean the area with soap and water. Allow time for it to completely dry.
STEP 4	If rust was removed or metal is exposed you need to apply primer for the new paint to bond properly. Read the label for primer drying time.
STEP 5	You should be able to find a small bottle or pen of touch up paint. Stir the touch up paint and test in a hidden area for a color match.
STEP 6	Apply the paint with the cap applicator. Do not apply too much at once. Use several thin coats if necessary to fill the chip or scratch. Allow each coat to dry before applying another coat.

Figure 7.26c ***Paint Cap Applicator***

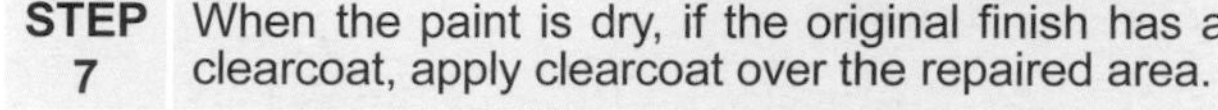

STEP 7	When the paint is dry, if the original finish has a clearcoat, apply clearcoat over the repaired area.
STEP 8	Once the area has dried completely (wait at least a couple of days) use a polishing compound to blend in the repaired area.
STEP 9	As a final step, protect the repaired area and the rest of your vehicle's finish by waxing.

Figure 7.26 ***Chip and Scratch Repair***

Servicing

Care and Cleaning

- Wash when dirty or every two weeks
- Wax at least twice a year
- Vacuum when dirty or every two weeks

Summary

Keeping a vehicle clean is not difficult; it just takes a little time. Washing, waxing, and vacuuming will make your vehicle worth more and make it more appealing to drive and own. Finishes on vehicles have changed over time from basecoats to basecoat/clearcoats. Clearcoats add a deeper shine and a more durable finish. By spending a little extra time on paint repair and forgotten part lubrication you can keep your vehicle looking good and functioning properly.

Activities

Auto Care and Cleaning

- Interior Cleaning Activity
- Exterior Cleaning Activity
- Waxing Activity
- Chapter 7 Study Questions

Activities and Study Questions can be completed in the *Auto Upkeep Workbook*.

Career Paths

Collision Repair Technician

Education: Technical Training or ASE Cert.
Median Income: $39,880
Abilities: Detail oriented and fast learner. Math, reading, and computer literate.
Find your career at **www.bls.gov/ooh**.

Fluid Level Check

CHAPTER 8

Fuel for Thought

- Why is it best to check engine oil when the engine is cold?
- What fluids should be checked on an automobile?
- Why is it important not to mix fluids?

Introduction

Fluids provide cooling, cleaning, lubricating, and sealing to vehicle components. The do-it-yourselfer can maintain the different systems by checking fluid levels and conditions. This chapter will guide you through checking and adding fluids to vehicle components.

Objectives

Upon completion of this chapter and activities, you will be able to:

- Identify different types of automotive fluids.
- Analyze fluid conditions.
- Perform basic fluid level checks.

Opening the Hood

In order to check fluids you will need to know how to open and close the hood (***Figure 8.1***).

Opening and Closing the Hood	
STEP 1	From the driver's seat locate the hood release latch. It will commonly have a hood symbol on it. Pull the handle. The hood will pop up slightly.
STEP 2	Go to the hood. There is a secondary (safety) catch with a handle underneath, near the center of the hood's front lip. Depending on the vehicle, pull up or push down the handle.
STEP 3	Lift the hood. Some hoods are held up automatically by lift supports, while others use a hood prop (support) rod that you manual set.
STEP 4	Before closing the hood, make sure all fluid caps are on correctly. If your vehicle had a manual prop rod, reset it. Slowly lower the hood about 6 to 12 inches from the fully closed position. Then remove your hands and let the hood close. Make sure it is completely closed.

Figure 8.1 ***Opening and Closing the Hood***

Fluid Specifications

Always check the owner's manual for the correct type of fluid that is recommended for a specific vehicle. Do not add fluid unless you are sure the fluid meets the specifications. Fluids are not interchangeable. Always use a clean paper towel or cloth when wiping off dipsticks. Damage caused by adding incorrect fluids will not be covered by your vehicle warranty and may lead to premature component failures. Do not let foreign contaminants enter into the systems through accidental contact of the dipstick, cap, or fluid. Wear the appropriate PPE when handling fluids. Read the product's SDS. Wash your hands thoroughly after handling.

Types of Fluids

Vehicles have specific fluid requirements based on their features. When checking any fluid, it is important to park on a level surface. The most common fluids (***Figure 8.2***) to check are:

- Windshield Washer Fluid
- Engine Oil
- Automatic Transmission Fluid
- Manual Transmission Fluid
- Continuously Variable Transmission Fluid
- Coolant
- EV and HEV Cooling Systems
- Differential Fluid
- Power Steering Fluid
- Brake Fluid
- Clutch Fluid (Manual Transmission)
- Diesel Exhaust Fluid (DEF)
- Battery Electrolyte (Maintenance Style)

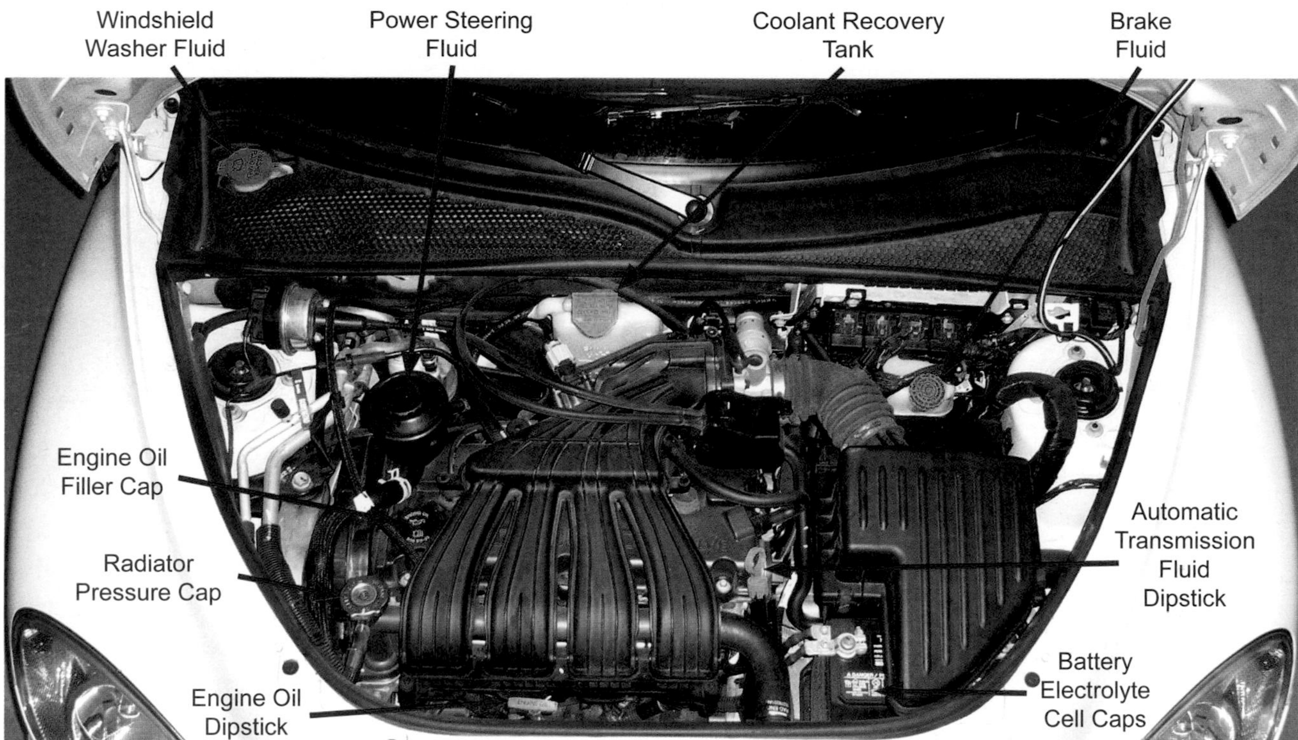

Figure 8.2 *Engine Compartment Common Fluid Locations*

Windshield Washer Fluid

Windshield washer fluid is easy to check.

Windshield Washer Fluid Types. Windshield washer fluid is specially formulated to clean road grime from the windshield. Various types of windshield washer fluid have different freezing points and colors (***Figure 8.3***). The color is not important other than helping you identify that it is not water. Colors can be mixed. Read the label and choose the correct type for the freeze protection needed. ***Note: Do not use only water. If the temperature drops below 32°F (0°C) and the water freezes, you will risk cracking the windshield washer fluid reservoir and pump. It could also freeze on your windshield.***

Figure 8.3 *Windshield Washer Fluids*

Checking Windshield Washer Fluid. The cap on a windshield washer fluid reservoir usually has a wiper symbol on it (***Figure 8.4***). Do not confuse this reservoir with the coolant recovery tank – they often look similar. ***Note: Never use cooling system antifreeze as it is not made for window cleaning and can damage a vehicle's finish.***

Figure 8.4 *Windshield Washer Fluid Reservoir*

Adding Windshield Washer Fluid. To add windshield washer fluid, locate the cap and fill almost to the top. ***Note: When adding windshield washer fluid, take a moment to inspect the windshield wipers. The wipers should be soft and without cracks. If the wipers are streaking or skipping across the windshield they need to be replaced.*** See Chapter 20 for more information on replacing wiper blades.

Engine Oil

An important fluid to check is engine oil because it cools, cleans, lubricates, and seals the internal engine components.

Engine Oil Types. Clean engine oil is gold in color, while dirty engine oil is black. Common multigrade engine oils are 0W-20, 5W-20 (***Figure 8.5***), and 5W-30 but always refer to the owner's manual because there are many different viscosities and brands available. Synthetic and semi-synthetic oils are also available. See Chapter 10 to learn more about engine oil types.

Figure 8.5 *5W-20 Engine Oil Bottle*

Checking Engine Oil. To check the engine oil, shut off the engine, apply the parking brake, open the hood, and look for the engine oil dipstick (***Figure 8.6***). To get an accurate reading it is best to check the engine oil when the engine is cold. The engine oil dipstick runs through a metal tube that is usually located on the side of the engine on rear-wheel drive vehicles or on the front of the engine on front-wheel drive vehicles. Refer to the owner's manual if you have questions on the location of the dipstick. ***Note: Some vehicles do not have an oil dipstick. They use an electronic oil level monitor. Check the owner's manual.***

Figure 8.6 *Engine Oil Dipstick*

Trouble Guide

Excessive Oil Consumption

- Broken or worn piston rings
- Worn valve guides or seals
- Improper oil viscosity
- PCV problems

Reading the Dipstick. Pull out the dipstick, wipe it off with a paper towel, reinsert it completely into the tube, remove again, and note the reading. The engine oil should be in the safe range (***Figure 8.7***). Most automotive engines have an oil capacity between four to five quarts (3.8 to 4.7 L). Vehicle manufacturers suggest adding oil when the engine is low one quart (≈1 L).

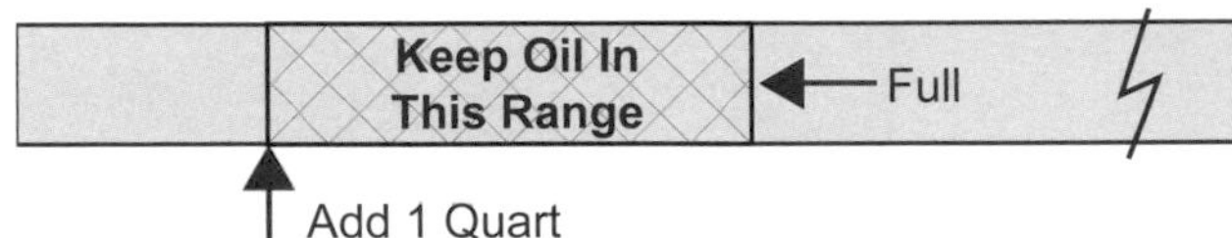

Figure 8.7 *Engine Oil Dipstick Reading*

Adding Engine Oil. To add engine oil, locate the oil filler cap (***Figure 8.8***) on the engine valve cover. Use a clean funnel to add the correct amount of engine oil. Give the engine oil time to flow to the oil pan. Recheck the level and correct if necessary. Do not overfill.

Figure 8.8 *Engine Oil Filler Cap*

Q & A

When to Add Oil

Q: Should I wait to add oil until it reaches the ADD mark?

A: Keep the oil at the full mark. If you allow the engine to get to the ADD mark and your engine only holds four quarts of oil, you are running the engine oil 25% low. Keeping the oil at the full mark helps in lubrication, disperses contaminants through a larger volume of oil, and dissipates heat more efficiently. Be sure not to overfill the crankcase. Engine oil contains detergents to help clean the engine. Too much oil causes foam (air bubbles) to form if the crankshaft whips the oil, lessening lubricating qualities.

Automatic Transmission Fluid

Automatic transmission fluid is used in self-shifting (automatic) transmissions.

Automatic Transmission Fluid (ATF) Types. Clean ATF (***Figure 8.9***) is usually pinkish-red. Always use the ATF recommended by the manufacturer. Manufacturers have strict requirements.

Figure 8.9 ***Automatic Transmission Fluid***

Checking ATF. For accurate results, most manufacturers recommend checking ATF while it is hot with the gear selector in park. Park on a level surface and apply the parking brake. Locate the automatic transmission oil dipstick (***Figure 8.10***).

Figure 8.10 ***Automatic Transmission Dipstick***

Reading the Dipstick. With the engine idling, pull out the dipstick, wipe it off with a paper towel, reinsert it completely into the tube, remove again, and note the reading. The ATF should be between the "full cold" and the "full hot" marks (***Figure 8.11***). ***Note: To minimize the risk of internal damage from overfilling or adding the incorrect type of fluid, some automatic transmissions do not have a dipstick and must be checked with a special tool and/or procedure.***

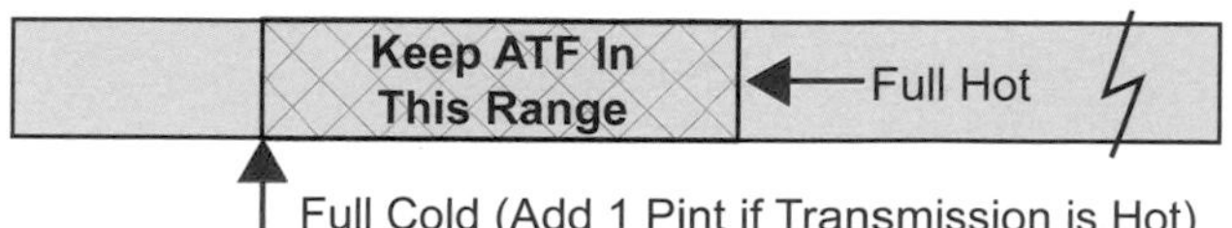

Figure 8.11 ***Automatic Transmission Reading***

Adding ATF. If low, use a clean funnel to pour the ATF directly into the tube. It usually takes only one pint (½ quart or 0.47 L) of fluid to bring the level from the "full cold" to the "full hot" mark. Recheck the level and add more if necessary. Do not overfill.

Manual Transmission Fluid

A manual transmission usually has a plug (***Figure 8.12***) on the side of the transmission housing.

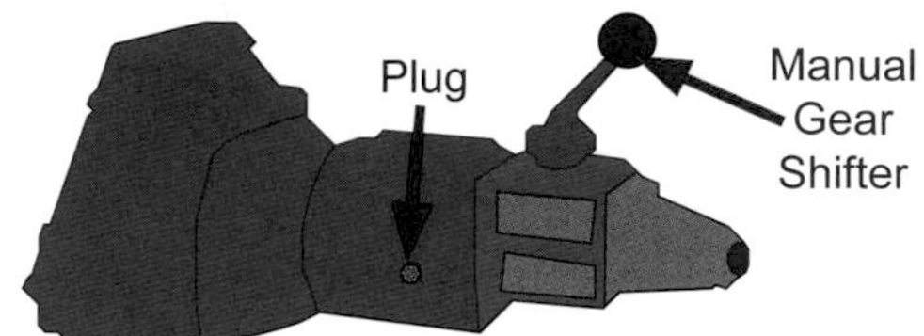

Figure 8.12 ***Manual Transmission Plug***

Manual Transmission Fluid Type. Manual transmissions take ATF, heavyweight/high-viscosity (e.g., SAE 75W-90, 75W-140, 80W-90, 80W-140, 85W-140) gear oil, synchromesh fluid, or motor oil. Always check the owner's manual.

Checking/Adding Manual Transmission Fluid. To check the fluid level you must turn the engine off, apply the parking brake, clean around the area, and then remove the plug with a wrench. The fluid should be level to the plug hole bottom (***Figure 8.13***). Fill as necessary. You may need an adapter that fits on the bottle to transfer the fluid.

Figure 8.13 ***Correct Fluid Level Check***

Continuously Variable Transmission (CVT) Fluid

Although a CVT is a type of automatic transmission, the method for checking this fluid varies.

CVT Fluid Types. If the recommended CVT fluid is a proprietary formula, specific to your vehicle's make and model, you may have to buy it from the dealer. ***Note: If you take your vehicle in for service, make sure the recommended CVT fluid is added. Do not assume that standard ATF is adequate for a CVT.***

Checking/Adding CVT Fluid. Some CVTs have a dipstick, some have two plugs, while others have three plugs. If your CVT has plugs instead of a dipstick, you need to find the fill/level plug. On plug types, the fluid should be level to the bottom of the plug hole threads. Review the owner's manual or contact the dealer for fluid checking and filling instructions.

Coolant

Engine coolant is used to remove excess heat from the engine. Coolant/antifreeze raises the boiling temperature, lowers the freezing point, and protects against corrosion in the cooling system. Coolant is made up of glycol, corrosion inhibitors, lubricants, and dye. ***Note: The terms antifreeze and coolant are used interchangeably.***

Types of Glycol. Ethylene glycol, which is the base of many coolants, is a toxic substance. ***Warning: Ethylene glycol can be fatal if ingested.*** Some coolant manufacturers are formulating more environmentally friendly coolants. Propylene glycol, another glycol used, is less toxic and safer if spilled or accidentally ingested. ***Note: Both types of coolant need to be properly stored and disposed.***

Types of Coolant. Three types of coolant are used (***Figure 8.14***). A quarter of a century ago, most automakers used conventional (usually green) coolant. This coolant is called inorganic acid technology (IAT). The corrosion inhibitors are based on inorganic salts. Today, two types of extended life coolants are used. Organic acid technology (OAT) is silicate and phosphate free. Hybrid organic acid technology (HOAT) is a combination of inorganic and organic acids.

	Types of Coolant	Service Interval	Typical Color*	Additives/ Corrosion Inhibitors
Conventional	Inorganic Acid Technology (IAT)	2 years 48,000 miles	Usually Green	Inorganic Salts
Extended Life	Organic Acid Technology (OAT)	5 years 150,000 miles	Typically Amber, Orange, or Red	Organic Acids Silicate and Phosphate Free
	Hybrid Organic Acid Technology (HOAT)	5 years 150,000 miles	Typically Yellow or Red	Combination of Inorganic Salts and Organic Acids

*** These are typical colors, but they cannot be relied upon for identification.**

Figure 8.14 *Types of Coolant*

Coolant Dye Color. Coolants are dyed many different colors (green, yellow, orange, pink, blue, gold, amber, and red). However, color is no longer an indicator of the correct type of coolant to use. The dye in the coolant helps identify if there is a leak when comparing to other fluid colors on a vehicle, but does not identify the type of coolant to add.

Universal Coolants. Some aftermarket coolants (***Figure 8.15***) are formulated to mix with many different types of OEM coolants regardless of color. ***Note: Always refer to the owner's manual to be sure you add the proper type of coolant.*** See Chapter 12 to learn more about coolant characteristics.

Figure 8.15 *Coolants*

Price Guides

Antifreeze/Coolant
- $6.00 to $30.00 a gallon

Automatic Transmission Fluid (ATF)
- $2.00 to $5.00 a quart

Brake Fluid/Clutch Fluid
- $2.00 to $4.00 a 12 oz. bottle

Distilled Water
- $1.00 to $2.00 a gallon

Manual Transmission Fluid/Differential Fluid
- $2.00 to $5.00 a quart

Oil
- $3.00 to $12.00 a quart

Power Steering Fluid
- $2.00 to $4.00 a pint

Windshield Washer Fluid
- $1.00 to $2.00 a gallon

Note:
1 gal = 3.785 L
1 qt = 0.946 L
1 pt = 0.473 L
12 oz = 0.355 L

Requirements. Automotive manufacturers design vehicles to use coolant with different types of additive and corrosion inhibitors. These substances bind to metal, forming a thin layer of protection in the cooling system, which is critical to the performance of the coolant.

Mixing Coolant. Concentrated (full strength) coolant is diluted (mixed) with water for the best boiling and freezing characteristics. Generally a 50% water (use distilled/demineralized water) to 50% coolant is the most common mixture for freeze and boilover protection. Coolant is also available in premixed, ready-to-use bottles.

Checking/Adding Coolant at Recovery Tank. ***Warning: Wear the appropriate PPE and be sure the engine is cool.*** First, check the level in the coolant recovery tank (expansion tank). It is usually translucent with a "full cold" (or MIN) and a "full hot" (or MAX) mark or a "cold fill range" (***Figure 8.16***). If low, remove the cap and add the manufacturer's recommended coolant type and mixture. ***Note: The coolant may be a different color.***

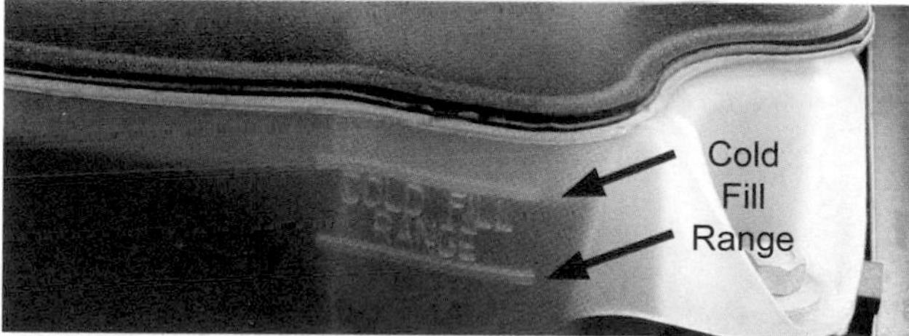

Figure 8.16 **Coolant Recovery Tank Fill Range**

Checking/Adding Coolant at Radiator. Second, check the level in the radiator. This requires removing a cool radiator cap (***Figure 8.17***) and looking into the radiator. ***Warning: Never remove a hot radiator cap – severe burns could result.*** The fluid should be at or near the top. If low add the manufacturer's recommended coolant type and mixture as needed. Reinstall the cap. ***Note: On some engines the pressure cap is on the coolant recovery tank.***

Figure 8.17 **Radiator Cap**

EV and HEV Cooling Systems

Some electric vehicles (EVs) and hybrid electric vehicles (HEVs) use separate cooling systems for their high voltage batteries and power electronics. Both systems can be checked visually while parked on a level surface, but don't open the systems (***Figure 8.18***). If the coolant is low, there may be a leak. ***Note: Not all hybrid and electric vehicles use the same type of system. Check your owner's manual to see how your system works and what checks you should perform.***

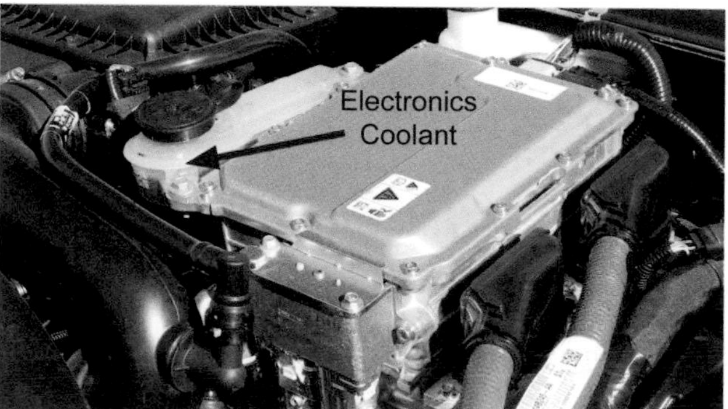

Figure 8.18 **Battery/Power Electronics Coolant**

High Voltage Battery Coolant. High voltage battery coolant is used to keep the batteries within a normal operating temperature, which is essential to the performance and life of the battery cells. Additional fans or cool air from the air conditioning system may also be used if the battery temperature increases above normal. In cold weather, a heating element is used to bring the battery coolant temperature up to normal.

Power Electronics Coolant. Another cooling system used on some electric and hybrid vehicles is a power electronics cooling system. This is used to cool the power electronics and charger modules. Electronic components are sensitive to high temperatures. As temperatures exceed the acceptable limits, cooling fans reduce the temperature of the coolant. ***Warning: Servicing (topping off or replacing) the high voltage battery coolant and power electronics coolant should be left to a professional certified technician. This coolant is critical to the advanced electronics which are integral to the operation of the vehicle. Some manufacturers void the warranty if damage was caused by opening the system.***

Differential Fluid

Rear and front axle housings, which contain the axles and differential gears, also require fluid.

Types of Differential Fluid. Gear oil (e.g., SAE 75W-90, 75W-140, 80W-90, 80W-140, 85W-140) is the most common differential fluid (***Figure 8.19***). Some differentials use limited slip additives. Always check the owner's manual for the specific fluid.

Figure 8.19 ***Gear Oil***

Checking/Adding Differential Fluid. This fluid check is performed on rear-wheel drive (RWD) and four-wheel drive (4WD) vehicles. The process is similar to checking manual transmission fluid. Remove the check plug (***Figure 8.20***), check the level, and fill as necessary. On most vehicles the oil should be at the bottom of the plug hole, but check the owner's manual for the required level.

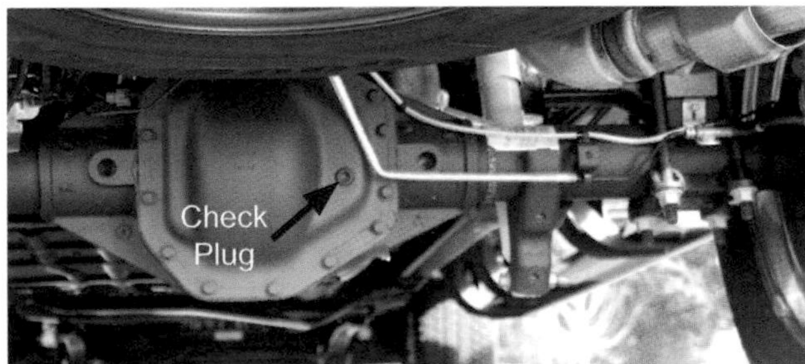

Figure 8.20 ***Differential Check Plug***

Tech Tip

Leaking Fluids

Most fluids have distinct colors. If you see a leak, note its color, texture, and position under the vehicle. This may lead you to the component that is failing.

Power Steering Fluid

Some vehicles have hydraulic power steering. The power steering pump is located off an engine drive belt. ***Note: All electric power steering (EPS) systems are becoming more popular. They eliminate the power steering fluid, pump, and hoses - so there is no fluid to check.***

Types of Power Steering Fluid. Power steering fluid (***Figure 8.21***) can be clear, gold, or red. Check the owner's manual for specifications.

Figure 8.21 ***Power Steering Fluid***

Checking Power Steering Fluid. To check the power steering fluid, shut off the engine and locate the power steering reservoir (***Figure 8.22***).

Figure 8.22 ***Power Steering Fluid Reservoir***

Reading the Dipstick/Adding Fluid. The cap and the dipstick are commonly one unit (***Figure 8.23***). The dipstick usually has a "full hot" and a "full cold" line. Remove the dipstick, wipe it off, reinstall, remove again, and note the reading. Using a clean funnel, add fluid as necessary.

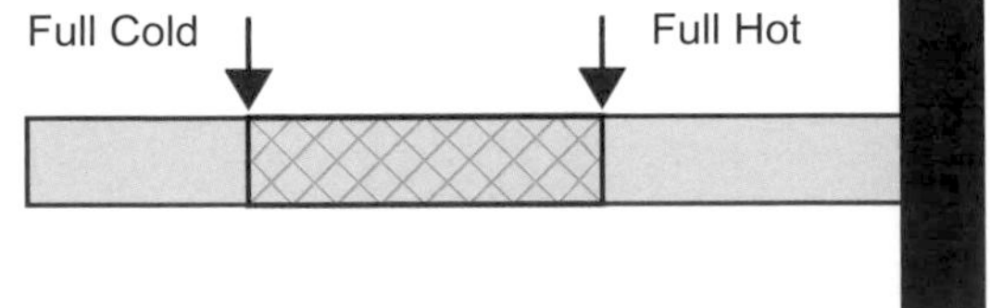

Figure 8.23 ***Power Steering Dipstick and Cap***

Brake Fluid

Brake fluid provides the transfer of hydraulic pressure to the wheels.

Types of Brake Fluid. The most common type of brake fluid (***Figure 8.24***) is DOT 3, but DOT 4, DOT 5, and DOT 5.1 are also available. Clean brake fluid is clear in color (except DOT 5, which is often dyed purple). Always refer to your manufacturer's recommendations because brake system damage can occur with the incorrect type. ***Warning: Use extreme caution when handling. Brake fluid is harmful to your eyes and if spilled on a vehicle's finish, it will strip paint. Wear safety goggles and chemical resistant gloves.***

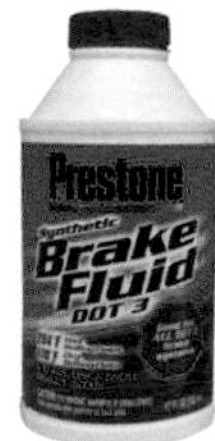

Figure 8.24 **Brake Fluids**

Checking Brake Fluid. The brake master cylinder that houses the fluid is usually mounted on the driver's side firewall in the engine compartment. Most vehicles today have a plastic translucent reservoir with "MIN" and "MAX" marks (***Figure 8.25***). Some fluid level drop may be normal. As the brake pads wear the level will fall as more fluid fills the brake caliper pistons or wheel cylinders.

Figure 8.25 **Brake Fluid Reservoir**

Adding Brake Fluid. To add brake fluid, park on a level surface, turn the engine off, clean around the cap and reservoir, remove the cap, and add as necessary. When reinstalling the cap, make sure that the rubber gasket seats properly.

Clutch Fluid (Manual Transmission)

Vehicles that have manual transmissions with hydraulic clutches have a clutch master cylinder fluid reservoir. It is usually mounted next to the brake master cylinder (***Figure 8.26***).

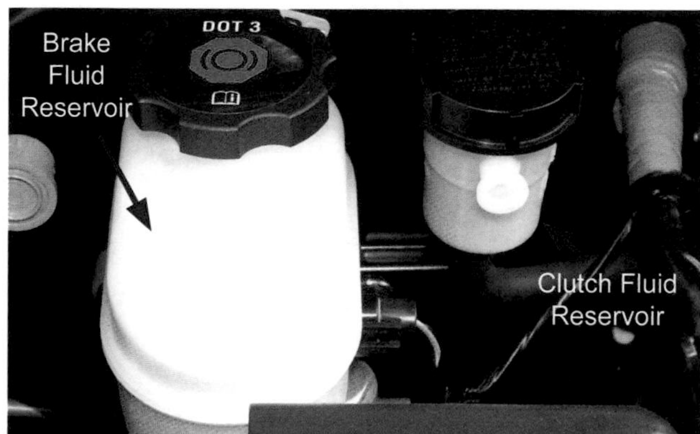

Figure 8.26 **Brake and Clutch Fluid Reservoirs**

Types of Clutch Fluid. Clutch fluid is commonly DOT 3 brake fluid, but always check the owner's manual. ***Warning: Wear the appropriate PPE.***

Checking Clutch Fluid. To check the clutch fluid, park on a level surface, turn the engine off, and look through the translucent reservoir. The fluid should be at or near the top.

Adding Clutch Fluid. To add clutch fluid, remove the cap, and add as necessary. When reinstalling the cap, make sure the rubber gasket seats properly.

Q & A ?

Brake Fluid Mix-Up

Q: I poured windshield wiper fluid in my brake fluid reservoir. What should I do?

A: Brake fluid is critically important to the safe operation of your vehicle. You will need to have the braking system flushed (all of the brake fluid completely removed) and refilled. If contaminated fluid is left in the braking system, it could end up ruining brake components – leading to brake failure. To be on the safe side, have the vehicle towed to your dealer or repair facility, tell them what you did, and get their recommendation.

Diesel Exhaust Fluid (DEF)

Some diesel engines use a technology called selective catalytic reduction (SCR) to meet emission standards.

DEF. SCR systems inject diesel exhaust fluid (DEF) into a special catalyst located in the exhaust system to reduce emissions. Chapter 17 will give details on how SCR systems work. Not all diesel vehicles use the same technology. Read your owner's manual to see how your diesel engine reduces emissions.

Checking DEF Level. DEF level is indicated on the instrument panel or through a warning system using the vehicle's information center. ***Note: If the DEF tank is allowed to go to empty, the speed of the vehicle may be limited.***

DEF Cap. The DEF cap is blue (***Figure 8.27***). Do not add DEF to the diesel fuel tank, it never mixes with the diesel fuel system. The diesel cap is green.

Figure 8.27 *DEF Cap is Blue*

Adding DEF. Only add DEF in a well ventilated area. A full DEF tank generally lasts thousands of miles, but it depends on the driving conditions. Fill using the instructions on the DEF container (***Figure 8.28***) or at the DEF pump. Do not overfill. ***Warning: DEF is corrosive. It may cause skin, eye, and respiratory irritation. Read the warnings on the product label and SDS. Wear disposable gloves and eye protection.***

Figure 8.28 *DEF Container*

Battery Electrolyte (Maintenance Style)

The electrolyte in a lead acid battery is a mixture of sulfuric acid and distilled water. Some batteries are sealed so the electrolyte cannot be checked. Refer to the owner's manual or read on the battery to determine if it is a maintenance or maintenance-free battery. On maintenance batteries some of the water may evaporate over time.

Checking Battery Electrolyte/Adding Water. To check the level, take off your rings and watch. ***Warning: Battery electrolyte can cause severe skin burns and eye damage. Read the warnings on the SDS. Wear safety goggles and chemical resistant gloves.*** After putting on the appropriate PPE, remove the cell caps (***Figure 8.29***). Shine a flashlight into the cells and inspect the level in each cell. Commonly a split ring indicator in each cell identifies the correct electrolyte level. Add only distilled water to any cell that is low, making all cell levels equal. Be sure the electrolyte covers the plates. Do not overfill. Replace the caps.

Figure 8.29 *Battery Cell Caps*

Warning: Wash hands thoroughly to remove any battery acid after removing gloves (Figure 8.30).

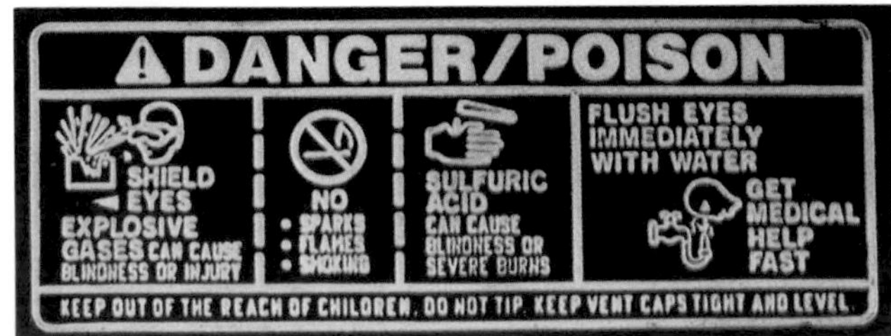

Figure 8.30 *Battery Warning Label on Cell Cap*

Storage and Disposal

Obtain the SDS for each chemical/fluid used. Section 7, Handling and Storage, on the SDS indicates how a chemical is safely handled and stored. It also includes chemical incompatibilities. Follow the recommendations on the SDS for safe storage and use an appropriate cabinet when necessary (***Figure 8.31***). Section 13, Disposal Considerations, on the SDS indicates how a chemical (or the container) can be disposed or recycled.

Figure 8.31 **Materials Safety Cabinet**
Courtesy of Justrite Manufacturing Company

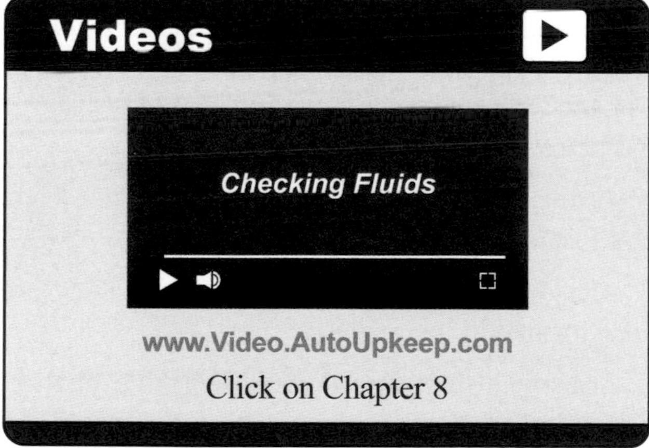

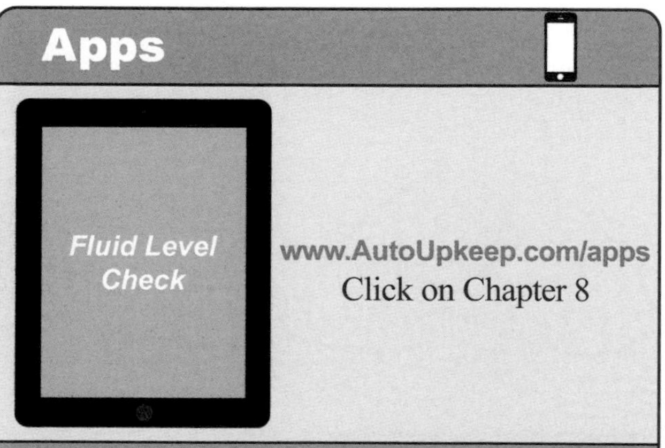

Servicing

All Fluid Level Checks

- Check all fluids at oil change intervals
- Check oil level every fuel fill up

Summary

Fluids in the automobile have critical functions. Fluids that are neglected and run low for long periods of time add stress to components and can cause premature damage. Practice preventative maintenance by checking fluid levels frequently. Always refer to the owner's manual to identify the correct type of fluid for your specific vehicle. Using incorrect fluids can harm vital systems and could cause a hazardous situation while driving. Always use a clean paper towel or cloth when wiping off dipsticks. Most of the fluids used in automobiles are toxic. Some types of antifreeze may have a sweet taste and can be fatal if ingested. Read the SDS for each fluid. Wear the appropriate PPE. Dispose of all fluids properly. Always wash your hands thoroughly after checking and adding fluids.

Activities

Fluid Level Check

- Fluid Level Check Activity
- Chapter 8 Study Questions

Activities and Study Questions can be completed in the *Auto Upkeep Workbook.*

Career Paths

Quick Lube Technician

Education: Technical Training or Experience
Median Income: $26,000
Abilities: Time management, customer service skills, and basic hands-on maintenance experience.
Find your career at www.bls.gov/ooh.

Electrical System

Chapter 9

Fuel for Thought

- What is electricity?
- What is the purpose of an automotive battery?
- What is the difference between voltage, current, and resistance?

Introduction

The automotive electrical system consists of wires, lights, motors, circuits, fuses, relays, and switches. Even though the electrical system is extremely complex, there are still many repairs that you can do without taking your vehicle to a service facility. A simple thing like a headlight burning out can stop you from driving safely down the road. This chapter provides the basics on how to maintain, test, and repair electrical system components.

Objectives

Upon completion of this chapter and activities, you will be able to:

- Define electricity in terms of voltage, current, and resistance.
- Explain different types of electrical circuits.
- Locate and interpret a wiring diagram.
- Analyze different types of circuit problems.
- Use a digital multimeter to test for voltage, resistance, and amperage.
- Inspect belt conditions.
- Identify and describe the components in the starting and charging system.
- Explain battery performance ratings.
- Identify the importance of fuses.
- Test the starter and alternator.
- Clean and test a battery safely.

Electrical Principles

Vehicles need electricity to work. Starting systems, charging systems, ignition systems, and vehicle electronics need electricity. Electricity is defined as the movement of electrons in a conductor. This section focuses on:

- Atoms
- Electricity
- Electrical Terms
- Electrical Symbols
- Ohm's Law
- Watt's Law

Atoms

Atoms make up all solids, liquids, and gases. They are extremely small. The center of the atom is called the nucleus. Each atom consists of three particles: protons, neutrons, and electrons.

Protons. Protons have a positive charge. They are located in the nucleus.

Neutrons. Neutrons have no charge. They are also located in the nucleus.

Electrons. Electrons have a negative charge. Electrons orbit the nucleus of an atom much like the Moon goes around the Earth (***Figure 9.1***).

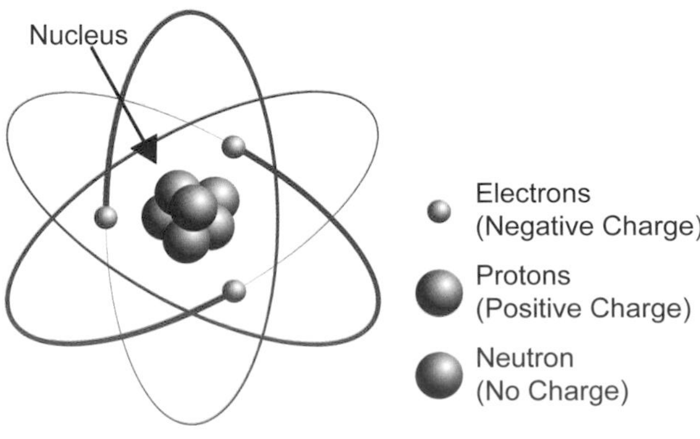

Figure 9.1 ***Parts of an Atom***

Electricity

Electrons can move from one atom to another, causing electricity.

Conductors and Insulators. Electricity flows through a conductor, which is usually in the form of a wire covered by an insulator (***Figure 9.2***). Copper is a well known conductor, which is full of copper atoms. An insulator, such as plastic, is something that restricts the flow of electrons.

Figure 9.2 ***Cross-section of Stranded Wire***

Potential Difference. In order for the electrons to flow through a conductor, they must jump from one atom to another. There has to be a force to push the electrons. When there is a potential difference, a pushing force from one end of a conductor to the other, electrons can move. For example, a common AA battery has 1.5 volts of potential difference between its terminals (***Figure 9.3***).

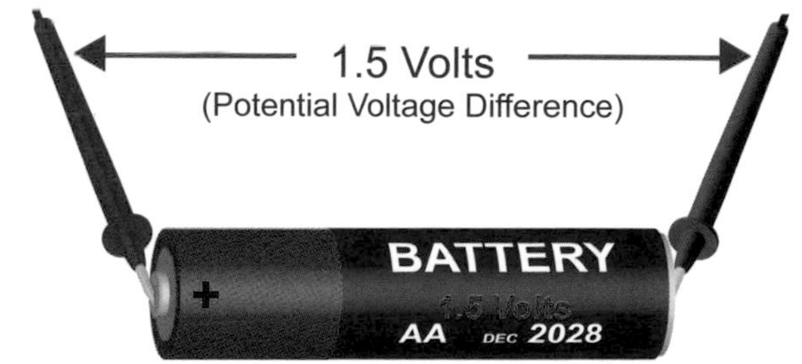

Figure 9.3 ***Potential Difference Example***

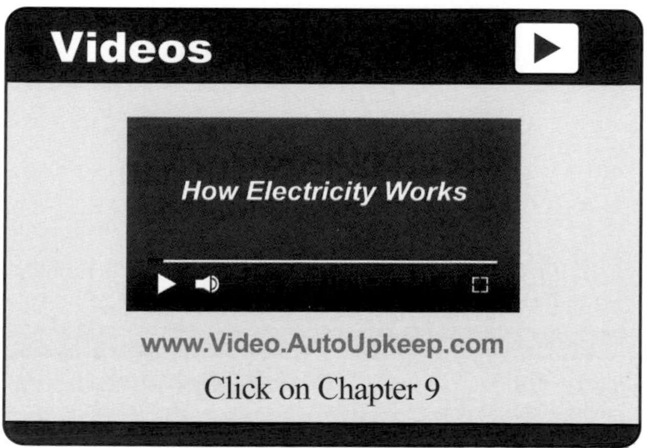

Videos
How Electricity Works
www.Video.AutoUpkeep.com
Click on Chapter 9

Electrical Terms

Before discussing the electrical system, you need to be able to identify and describe voltage, current, and resistance.

Voltage. A volt is the measure of voltage or pressure pushing electrons. Voltage is the electrical pressure that causes current to flow. In technical terms, one volt is the amount of pressure required to move one ampere (amp) of current through a resistance of one ohm. (Amps and ohms will be discussed later.) Most vehicles have 12-volt systems, while most homes have 120-volt systems. Another difference in most home and vehicle electrical systems is the current. Automotive batteries provide direct current (DC), while homes use alternating current (AC).

Current. An ampere (amp) is the unit of measure for electrical current. Amperage, the electrical current measured in amperes, is the quantity of electrons moving through a conductor. There are two types of electrical current: DC and AC. In DC systems the electrons are moving through the conductor in one direction. In AC systems the electrons change direction at a given rate (***Figure 9.4***). The alternator (AC generator) in a vehicle generates AC, but then converts the current to DC to recharge the battery.

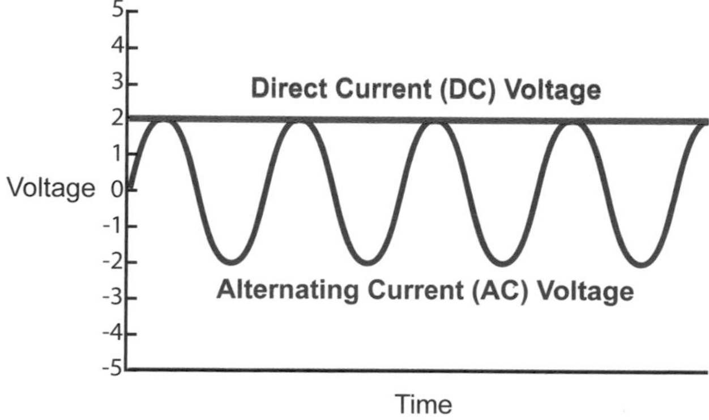

Figure 9.4 ***DC and AC Waveforms***

Resistance. An ohm (Ω) is a measure of electrical resistance. The resistance in a circuit is usually a load such as a light, radio, electrical motor, or sensor. For example, there needs to be resistance in the filament of an incandescent light bulb for it to produce light.

Electrical Symbols

Symbols, or abbreviations, are used in mathematical equations and to simplify communication (*Figure 9.5*).

Math Symbol	Unit of Measure	Unit Symbol	What is being Measured
E	Volts	V	Electromotive Force
I	Amps	A	Current (the Intensity)
R	Ohms	Ω	Resistance
P	Watts	W	Electrical Power

Figure 9.5 ***Electrical Symbols***

Ohm's Law

Ohm's Law shows the direct relationship between volts, amps, and ohms. The following simple mathematical equation can be used to find any unknown variable if the other two variables are known (*Figure 9.6*).

Voltage = Current x Resistance **E = I x R**

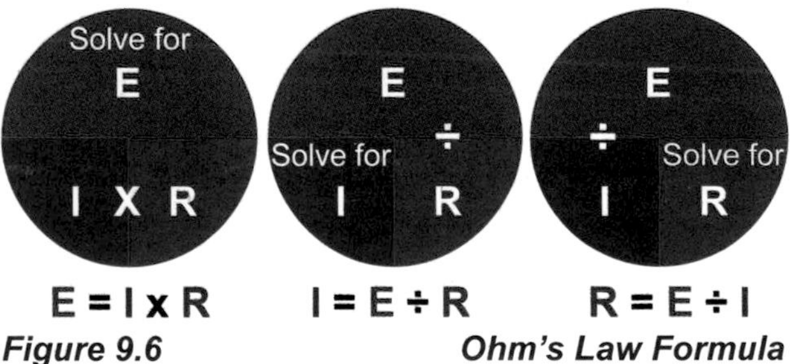

Figure 9.6 ***Ohm's Law Formula***

Watt's Law

Watts's Law shows the direct relationship between volts, amps, and watts. Watts (or wattage) is a measure of electrical power. ***Note: 1000 watts (W) = 1 kilowatt (kW).*** Any one unknown variable can be found if the other two variables are known (*Figure 9.7*).

Power = Current x Voltage **P = I x E**

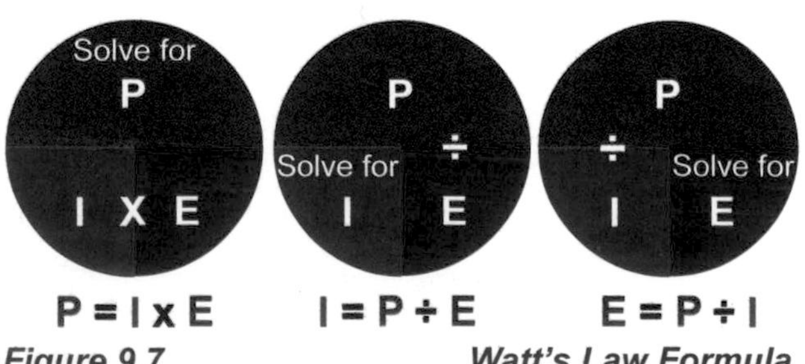

Figure 9.7 ***Watt's Law Formula***

Electrical Circuits

The path for electrons to flow is called an electrical circuit. An electrical circuit starts and ends at the same point. For electricity to flow, the circuit must be a closed, unbroken loop. This section focuses on:

- Wiring Diagram Symbols
- Parts
- Simple Circuit
- Types of Circuits

Wiring Diagram Symbols

Wiring diagrams use symbols to represent actual components and lines to depict wires in an electrical circuit. The following table contains only a few of the more common symbols (*Figure 9.8*). ***Note: There are many more symbols and symbols may vary, so always check for a symbol chart specific to the wiring diagram being reviewed.***

Wiring Diagram Symbols	
+	Positive
−	Negative
	Ground
	Fuse
	Circuit Breaker
	Resistor
	Closed Switch
	Open Switch
	Single Filament Lamp
	Single Cell Battery
	12 Volt Automotive Battery (Six Cells)

Figure 9.8 ***Wiring Diagram Symbols***

Parts

All electrical circuits need three things: a power source, a conductor, and a load.

Power Source. A power source provides the voltage for the electrical circuit.

Conductor. A conductor, such as a wire, provides a path for electricity to flow. The frame or body of the vehicle can also be a conductor.

Load. A load is the resistance in the circuit. This could be a light bulb, coil, wiper motor, power window, horn, or anything that requires electricity to operate.

Simple Circuit

A simple circuit has a power source, a pathway for electricity to flow, and a load. The load uses the electricity (***Figure 9.9***).

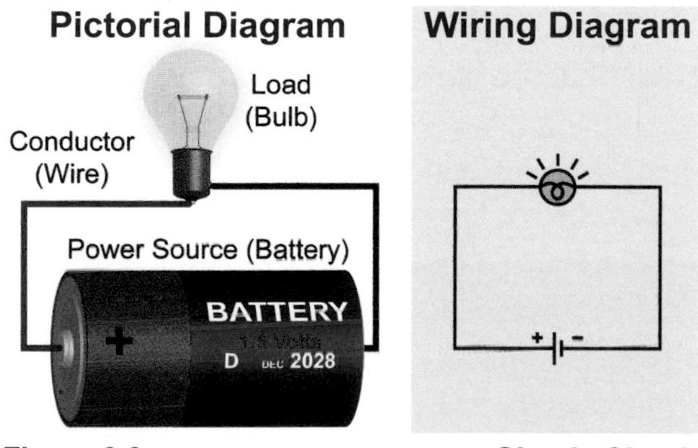

Figure 9.9 ***Simple Circuit***

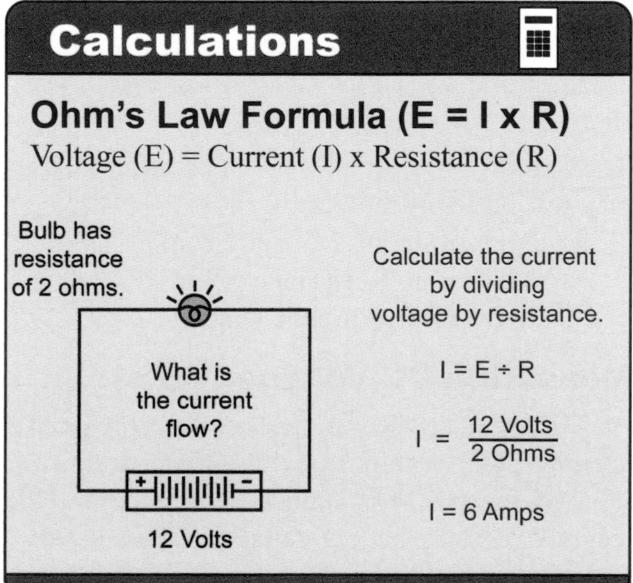

Calculations
Ohm's Law Formula (E = I x R)
Voltage (E) = Current (I) x Resistance (R)
Bulb has resistance of 2 ohms.
What is the current flow?
12 Volts
Calculate the current by dividing voltage by resistance.
I = E ÷ R
I = 12 Volts / 2 Ohms
I = 6 Amps

Types of Circuits

There are three types of electrical circuits: series, parallel, and series-parallel. Automotive circuits also have control devices (e.g., switches) and protection devices (e.g., fuses) in addition to a power source, conductor, and a load.

Series Circuit. In a series circuit, two or more electrical loads are wired in a single path (***Figure 9.10***). In this type of circuit, if any part of the circuit is broken, the whole circuit will not work.

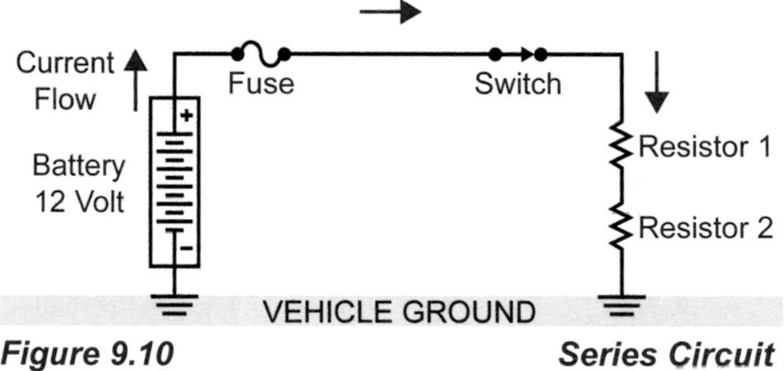

Figure 9.10 ***Series Circuit***

Parallel Circuit. In a parallel circuit, two or more electrical loads are wired in separate paths (***Figure 9.11***). These paths can operate independently from one another. If one resistor path is broken, the other will still work.

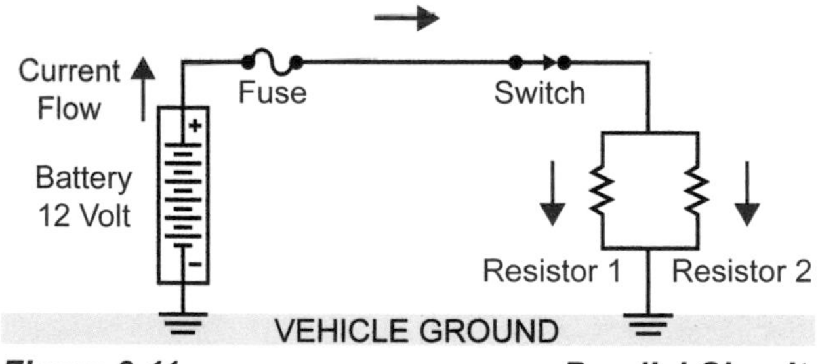

Figure 9.11 ***Parallel Circuit***

Series-Parallel Circuit. In a series-parallel circuit, a combination of series and parallel characteristics are built into a single circuit (***Figure 9.12***).

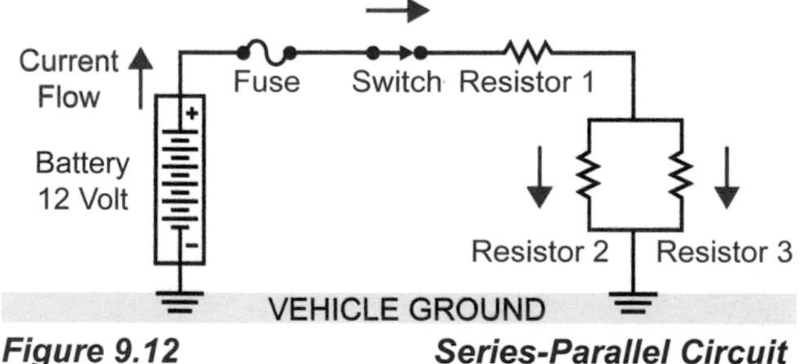

Figure 9.12 ***Series-Parallel Circuit***

Circuit Problems

Electrical circuits may develop problems where they no longer work as intended. This section focuses on:

- Open Circuit
- Short Circuit
- High Resistance Circuit

Open Circuit

When an electrical circuit does not make a complete loop due to a break, it is called an open circuit (***Figure 9.13***). The circuit has no continuity, no path for the electricity to flow. The open could be a faulty component (e.g., a burned out bulb), broken wire, or loose connection.

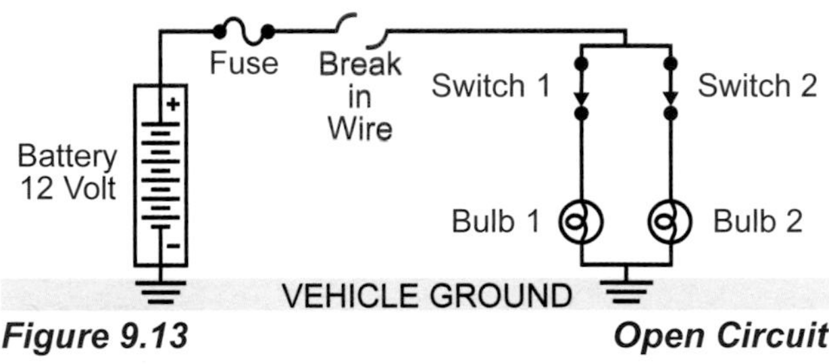

Figure 9.13 ***Open Circuit***

Short Circuit

The term short is used because the current is taking a shorter, less resistant, unintended and unwanted path to complete the circuit.

Short to Power. When an unwanted path is created between two conductors on the power side, it is called a short to power or short to voltage (***Figure 9.14***). This unwanted path is usually caused by damaged insulation on a wire. The short may be within a component (e.g., faulty coil), between two power sides of same circuit, or it may be between the power side of one circuit to the power side of another circuit. The current flow can fully or partially bypass the load. It can also cause a circuit to be live with a switch off.

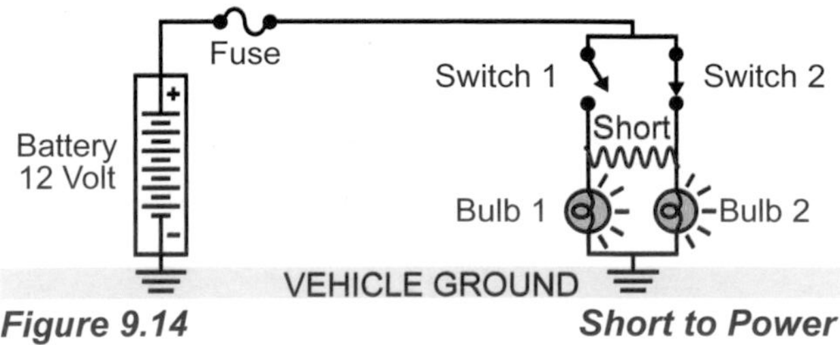

Figure 9.14 ***Short to Power***

Short to Ground (Grounded Circuit). When an unwanted path is created within a circuit between a conductor on the power side and ground, it is called a short to ground or a grounded circuit (***Figure 9.15***). This unwanted path is usually caused by damaged insulation on a power side wire touching a vehicle part that is grounded (e.g., the engine, frame, or body). Without going to an intended load in the circuit, there is very low resistance. The current increases and usually causes the fuse to blow, wires to melt, or causes excessive battery drain.

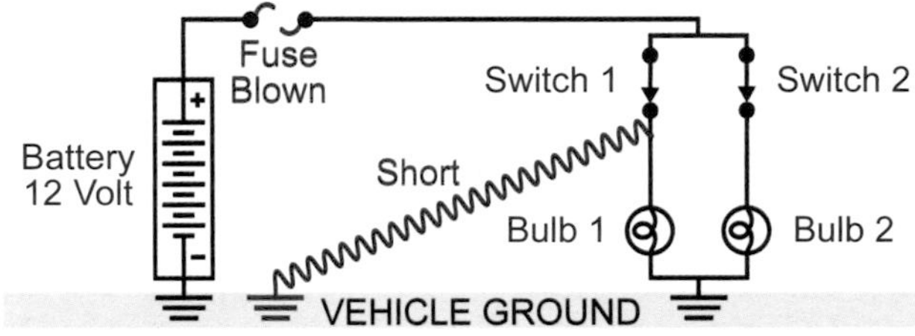

Figure 9.15 Short to Ground (Grounded Circuit)

High Resistance Circuit

Another problem a circuit might have is excessively high resistance. This is commonly caused by corroded or loose connections.

Digital Multimeter

A digital multimeter (DMM) can measure voltage (volts), resistance (ohms), and current (amps). Many different kinds of electrical tests can be completed with a DMM. ***Warning: Always follow the directions in your user's manual to correctly operate your DMM. Read all safety precautions, operating instructions, and device limitations. Incorrectly connecting to electrical wires could result in injury.*** This section focuses on a few basic procedures:

- Measuring DC Voltage (Volts)
- Measuring Resistance (Ohms)
- Measuring Current (Amps)

Measuring DC Voltage (Volts)

A DMM can be used to measure the voltage at a specific point within a circuit. When testing for voltage, the DMM is connected in parallel. One test is to measure battery voltage (***Figure 9.16***).

Measuring DC Voltage

STEP 1	Turn the DMM's range selector to $\overline{\text{V}}$ (also identified as VDC or DCV). If you are unsure of the voltage, start with the highest setting first. Some meters have one setting with a built in automatic range selector.
STEP 2	Insert the black test lead into the DMM's COM jack and the red test lead into the DMM's V jack.
STEP 3	Connect the test leads to the circuit. Red lead to positive (+) side, black lead to negative (-) side.

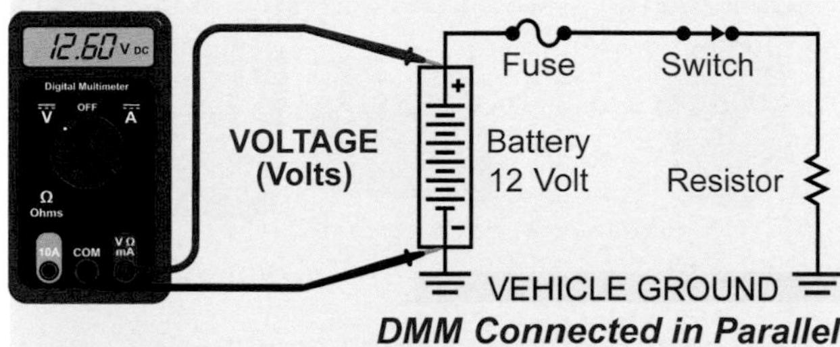

DMM Connected in Parallel

STEP 4	Read the DC voltage on the display. If you need to select a different $\overline{\text{V}}$ range to obtain a better resolution, adjust the range selector.

Figure 9.16 *Measuring DC Voltage*

Measuring Resistance (Ohms)

A DMM can be used to measure resistance in a circuit or component (*Figure 9.17*). Isolate the part being tested. ***Warning: Never use the resistance function on the DMM with voltage running through the circuit. Circuit power must be off and any capacitors discharged.***

Measuring Resistance

STEP 1	Turn the DMM's range selector to Ω. Start with the highest setting first. Some meters have one setting with a built in automatic range selector.
STEP 2	Insert the black test lead into the DMM's COM jack and the red test lead into the DMM's Ω jack.
STEP 3	Turn circuit power off. Isolate the part being tested. Connect the test leads across the part. Make sure you have good contact points.

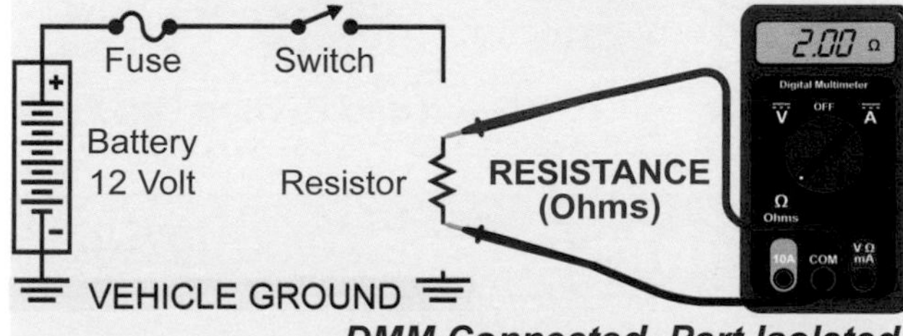

DMM Connected, Part Isolated

STEP 4	Read the ohms on the display. If you need to select a different Ω range to obtain a better resolution, adjust the range selector.

Figure 9.17 *Measuring Resistance*

Measuring Current (Amps)

A DMM can be used to measure current in a circuit (*Figure 9.18*). To measure current, the DMM is placed in series. ***Note: Some automotive manufacturers do not recommend breaking (opening) a circuit to measure current. A less intrusive way is to use a current clamp (also known as a current probe). Low amp and high amp clamps are available. Warning: Most DMMs can only test up to 10 amps. Use a current clamp when testing amperage over the DMM's rating.***

Measuring Current

STEP 1	Turn the DMM's range selector to $\overline{\text{A}}$ (also identified as ADC or DCA) or the 10A setting. Some meters have one setting with a built in automatic range selector.
STEP 2	Insert the black test lead into the DMM's COM jack and the red test lead into the DMM's 10A jack.
STEP 3	Turn circuit power off. Break (open) the circuit where you want to test. Put the DMM in series. Turn circuit power on.

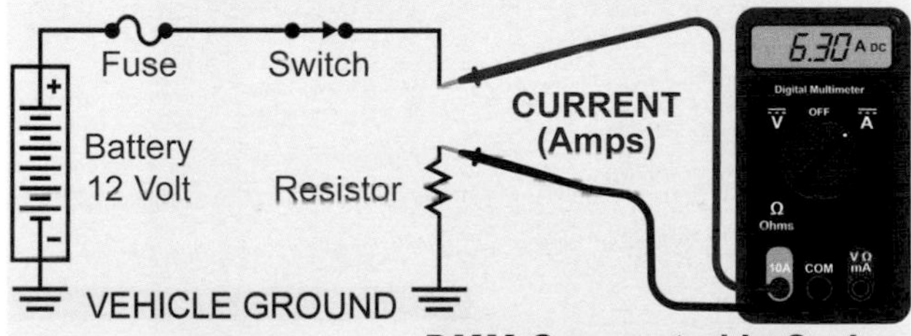

DMM Connected in Series

STEP 4	Read the amps on the display. Do not leave connected for over 30 seconds.

Figure 9.18 *Measuring Current*

Current Clamp/Clamp on Meter. To measure current without opening a circuit or if you have exceeded the DMM's capabilities, clamp on meters are available (*Figure 9.19*). You just clamp over the wires carrying the current to obtain an amp reading. The clamp measures the magnetic field around a wire as current is moving through it.

Figure 9.19 *1000 Amp Current Probe/DMM*
Courtesy of Electronics Specialties, Inc.

Fuse Box

A fuse box containing circuit protection and control devices can be found under the hood, under the dash, on the driver's side edge of the instrument panel, in the trunk, or in the glove box. It is also called a fuse block, fuse panel, power distribution box, or electrical center. There may be more than one panel and some fuses may be in-line, especially on aftermarket installed accessories. A cover on the fuse box often identifies the purpose of each device (***Figure 9.20***). If the cover is unclear, refer to the owner's manual for a fuse box diagram. ***Warning: Always have the ignition switch off before working on any electrical component. On push button keyless ignition vehicles follow the owner's manual for specific safety procedures. When servicing some electrical components, you may need to disconnect the negative battery cable.***

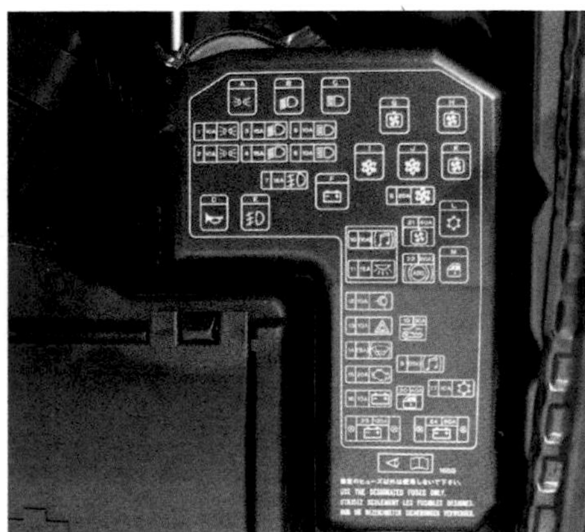

Figure 9.20 **Fuse Box**

Circuit Protection Devices

Circuit protection devices safeguard electrical circuits from excessive current. Excessive current, which leads to high heat, can damage the electrical system. This section focuses on:

- Fuses
- Fusible Links
- Circuit Breakers
- Capacitors

Fuses

Fuses are used in electrical circuits to safeguard the vital components. A fuse has a sacrificial metal strip that will melt if too much current is trying to get to the intended load.

Fuse Types. Fuses are designed in many shapes and sizes. Common types include glass cylinder, blade, and cartridge (***Figure 9.21***).

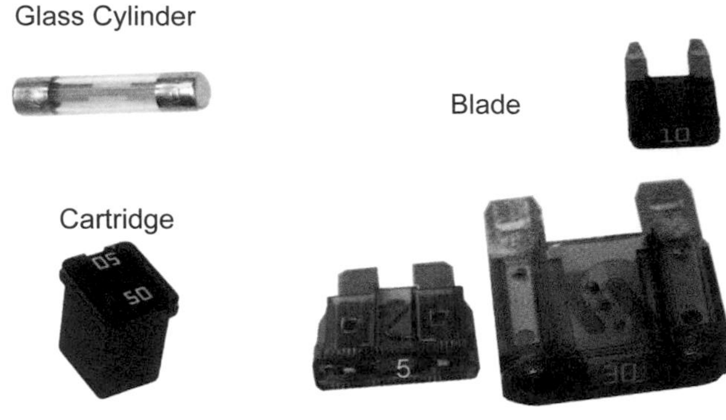

Figure 9.21 ***Automotive Fuses***

Fuse Ratings. Fuses are rated in amps such as: 3, 5, 10, 15, 20, 25, 30, and up. Always refer to the owner's manual for fuse specifications.

Blown Fuse. When experiencing an electrical problem the first and easiest check is to look for a blown fuse (***Figure 9.22***). Look through the plastic part of the fuse for a wire filament. If it is broken, you have found your problem. A fuse is rated so it is the weakest link in the electrical circuit to protect all of the components in that circuit. If you don't have a spare and are in a bind, remove a fuse with the same amperage rating from an accessory that you could temporarily be without (e.g., power seats). ***Warning: Never replace a blown fuse with a larger amperage rated fuse and never bypass the fuse completely by using a jumper wire or steel stock. Severe electrical damage could result.***

Figure 9.22 ***Good and Burned Out Fuse***

Trouble Guide

Fuse Continues to Blow

- Shorted circuit
- Accessory pulling too much current
- Wrong fuse rating

Fusible Links

Some circuits have fusible links (***Figure 9.23***). A fusible link is a type of circuit protector. It is a short piece of wire that has a smaller diameter than the rest of the circuit. If too much current runs through the circuit, the wire overheats and melts, opening the circuit. When a circuit is open, no electricity can flow. A fusible link has a nonflammable insulation that bubbles to indicate that it has blown.

Figure 9.23 ***Fusible Link***

Circuit Breakers

Circuit breakers (***Figure 9.24***) are used to protect overloaded circuits. Unlike fuses that blowout, circuit breakers reset automatically after they have cooled. Headlights and other high current components may be on circuit breakers.

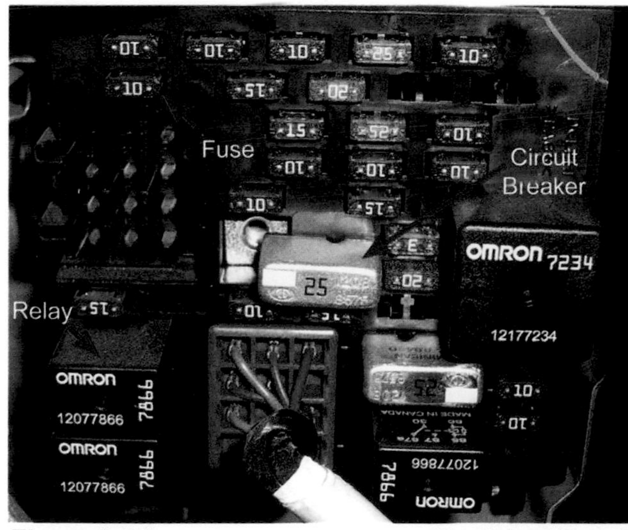

Figure 9.24 ***Electrical Panel***

Capacitors

Some circuits use capacitors (***Figure 9.25***) to store electricity like a mini battery. Capacitors provide protection to electronic components by absorbing potentially damaging voltage spikes.

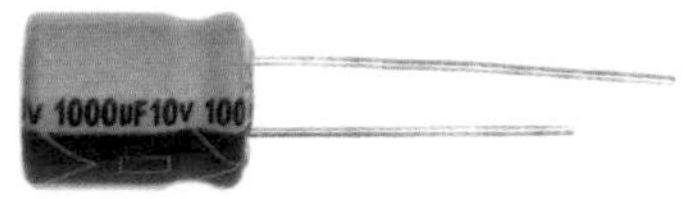

Figure 9.25 ***Capacitor***

Circuit Control Devices

Circuit control devices are used to regulate how the circuit works. For example, the circuit might simply need to be turned on or off with a switch. Another circuit, such as a dome light dimmer, may need the electrical current to vary to work properly. This section focuses on:

- Switches
- Solid State Devices

Switches

A switch allows a circuit to be turned off or on. It does this by opening (turning off) or closing (turning on) the circuit.

Manual Switches. Headlights, brake lights, windshield wipers, power windows, power seats, and many more devices have manual switches (***Figure 9.26***).

Figure 9.26 ***Power Seat Switches***

Flashers. Flashers (***Figure 9.27***) are what cause turn signals and hazard lights to blink or flash at a regular rate. Some systems use an electronic lighting control module to complete this operation.

Figure 9.27 ***Flashers***

Relays. Relays allow a small current to turn on or off a circuit requiring a high current (***Figure 9.28***).

Figure 9.28 ***Relay***

Solid State Devices

Solid state switches have no moving parts. They use semiconductors, which can act like a conductor or insulator, to switch the circuit on or off. They are extremely durable, compact, quiet, and fast-switching.

Battery

A vehicle battery stores chemical energy, supplies electrical energy to the starter when the engine is cranking, and supplements the AC generator (alternator) in running accessories (e.g., lights, blower motor fan, and radio). The battery is the heart of the electrical system with primary functions in the starting, charging, and ignition systems. This section focuses on:

- Types of 12-Volt Batteries
- Groups, Ratings, and Maintenance
- Higher Voltage Systems

Types of 12-Volt Batteries

Most automotive batteries are lead acid 12-volt DC. Each of the six cells in a 12-volt DC battery produces 2 to 2.1 volts. A fully charged 12-volt battery will actually have about 12.6 volts.

Flooded Battery. In a flooded battery the plates are covered with a liquid electrolyte.

Dry Battery (Absorbed Glass Mat). In an Absorbed Glass Mat (AGM) battery a thin ultra-fine fiberglass mat separator absorbs the electrolyte. An AGM battery is referred to as a dry battery and can be mounted in various positions without concern of it leaking electrolyte.

Groups, Ratings, and Maintenance

When purchasing a vehicle battery it is important to identify the correct BCI group, rating, and maintenance needed. Take note of how the battery cables connect. Make sure the positive and negative terminals are on the correct side and the replacement battery mounts safely, using the same factory holddown as the original battery.

Battery Terminals. Some new batteries have top and side dual mount systems (***Figure 9.29***). Others will have just top or side mounts.

Figure 9.29 *Dual Mount Battery*

BCI Groups. Battery Council International (BCI) (www.batterycouncil.org), a trade organization, works with battery manufacturers to maintain standardized battery sizes within the industry. When purchasing a battery, look at the BCI group number to compare replacement options between brands. Any battery within that group number will have the same physical dimensions. The BCI group number may be within the battery's model number (***Figure 9.30***).

Figure 9.30 *BCI Group Number 78*

CCA and CA Ratings. Besides being the correct physical size, a battery must meet the amperage requirements to start the engine and run accessories. When comparing batteries from different vendors make sure you are comparing the same type of rating. Battery manufacturers basically use two ratings: cold cranking amps (CCA) and cranking amps (CA) (***Figure 9.31***). A battery that is rated with cold cranking amps has been tested to deliver the specified number of amperes at 0ºF (-18ºC) for a duration of 30 seconds. A battery that is rated with cranking amps has been tested to deliver the specified number of amperes at 32ºF (0ºC) for a duration of 30 seconds.

Figure 9.31 *Battery Rating Label*

Battery Life and Warranty. Batteries commonly last about five years. Battery warranties can vary. Some manufacturers have a free replacement period and then prorate the remaining part of the warranty. This means that after the free replacement period you will have to pay part of the cost to get a new battery (***Figure 9.32***). Read the fine print on the warranty conditions.

Replacement Warranty	Year 1	Year 2	Year 3	Year 4	Year 5
Battery - 2 Year	FREE		45%*	25%*	10%*
* Percentage Off Suggested Retail Price					

Figure 9.32 *Battery Prorated Warranty*

Battery Safety. Batteries are poisonous and extremely dangerous (***Figure 9.33***).

Battery Warnings*

- Battery terminals, accessories, and posts contain lead. Wash hands thoroughly after handling.
- Do not tip flooded batteries, keep upright.
- Batteries emit gases that are explosive and flammable. Recharge batteries only in well ventilated areas. A spark or flame can cause a battery to explode.
- Remove rings and metal jewelry when working on a battery. Do not set metal objects on top of a battery.
- Avoid contact with skin and eyes. Wear safety goggles and gloves. Batteries contain sulfuric acid that can cause blindness and severe skin burns.
- Keep out of reach of children.

*** Read battery warning labels and the SDS.**

Figure 9.33 ***Sample Battery Warnings***

Visual Inspection and Cleaning. Make sure terminals are free from corrosion. Inspect the battery for loose connections. Make sure the holddown is secure. Also check the casing for cracks. See Chapter 20 for procedures on cleaning a battery and minimizing future corrosion.

Maintenance-Free Battery. Many maintenance-free flooded lead acid batteries are permanently sealed with a hydrometer built into the battery casing. An indicator on the top of the battery identifies a battery's charge condition (***Figure 9.34***). Instructions for understanding the indicator are usually next to the indicator. An AGM battery is completely carefree, just inspect the terminal connections for a clean and tight fit.

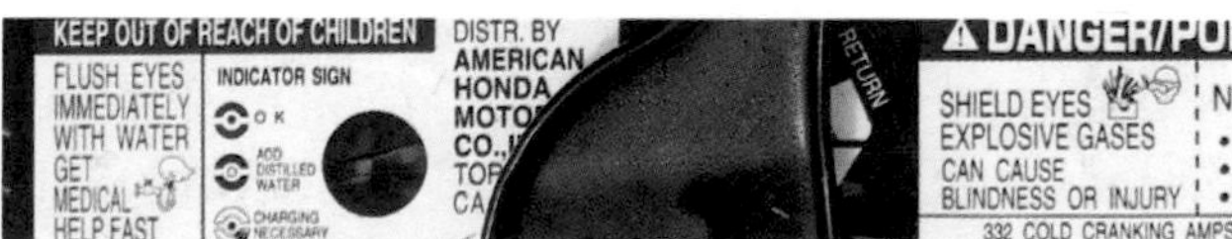

Figure 9.34 Built-in Battery Hydrometer Indicator

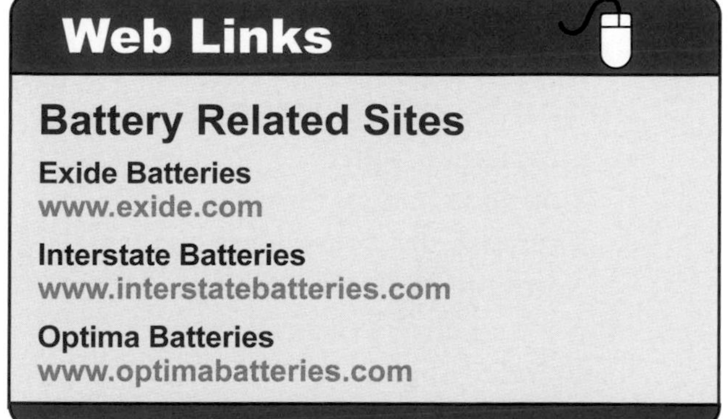

Web Links

Battery Related Sites

Exide Batteries
www.exide.com

Interstate Batteries
www.interstatebatteries.com

Optima Batteries
www.optimabatteries.com

Maintenance Battery. If a flooded lead acid battery is not maintenance-free, use a hydrometer to check the battery electrolyte's specific gravity (***Figure 9.35***). See the Battery Activity in Chapter 9 of the workbook for instructions. ***Warning: Never recharge a battery that has a low electrolyte level or is frozen.***

State of Charge Electrolyte Temperature 80°F (26.7°C)	Specific Gravity	Volts	Electrolyte Freezing Point	
			°F	(°C)
100%	1.265	12.6	-77	(-67)
75%	1.225	12.4	-35	(-37)
50%	1.190	12.2	-10	(-23)
25%	1.155	12.0	5	(-15)
Discharged	≤1.120	≤11.7	20	(-7)

Figure 9.35 ***Battery Electrolyte Readings***

Charging. When using a battery charger, be sure to read the manufacturer's instructions for the charging procedure specific to your battery type.

Recycle. Batteries contain lead. Return your old battery where you purchased your new one.

Higher Voltage Systems

As electrical energy demands increase on cars, other higher voltage systems are needed. Nickel Metal Hydride (NiMH), Lithium-ion (Li-ion), and Lithium-ion polymer (Li-poly) batteries are used in hybrid and electric vehicles. See Chapter 18 to learn more about hybrid and electric vehicles.

Orange Cables. Higher voltage systems can be identified by their orange cables (***Figure 9.36***). ***Warning: Be extra careful around high voltage systems. High voltage can kill.***

Figure 9.36 ***High Voltage Orange Cables***

Kilowatt Hour Rating. High voltage batteries are commonly rated in kilowatt hours (kWh). A kWh is a measure of energy equivalent to the power of 1 kW for 1 hour. In equation form:

Energy = Power x Time

Starting System

The starting system (***Figure 9.37***) converts chemical energy (molecular energy) to electrical energy (electrons moving through a conductor) to mechanical energy (energy of motion). The main components of the starting system are:

- Battery
- Ignition Switch
- Starter Relay
- Solenoid
- Starter
- Park/Neutral Safety Switch
- Computer Controlled Starting

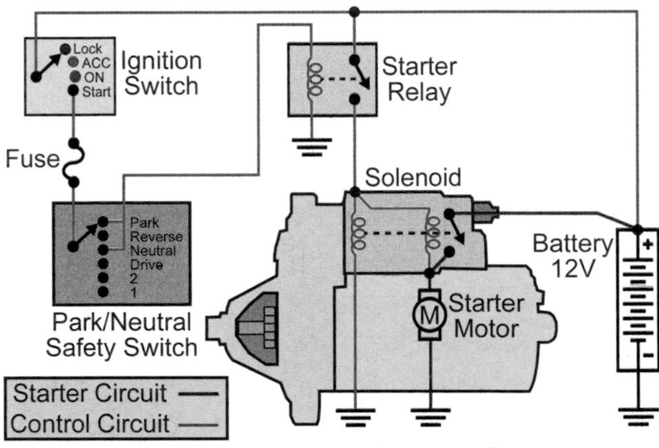

Figure 9.37 ***Starting System Components***

Price Guides

AC Generator (Alternator)
- $50.00 to $500.00

Battery 12-volt DC
- $40.00 to $100.00

Fuse
- $0.50 to $5.00 each

Headlight - Composite or Sealed Beam
- $5.00 to $40.00 each

Headlight Bulb - High-Intensity Discharge
- $20.00 to $100.00 each

Miniature Light Bulb
- $1.00 to $4.00 each

Serpentine Belt
- $20.00 to $50.00

Starter
- $30.00 to $300.00

V-Belt
- $5.00 to $20.00

Battery

In the starting system, the battery converts chemical energy to electrical energy when the operator closes the circuit by engaging the ignition switch.

Ignition Switch

The ignition switch is turned or pushed to start a vehicle (***Figure 9.38***). The ignition switch turns on the starter control circuit when it is in the start position. It sends low current to the starter relay. ***Warning: On push button keyless ignition vehicles follow the owner's manual for specific safety procedures before working on electrical components.***

Figure 9.38 ***Push to Start System***

Starter Relay

When electricity is sent to the starter relay, contacts in the relay close. When the contacts close, current is sent to the solenoid energizing it.

Solenoid

A solenoid is an electromechanical switch. The current from the starter relay energizes a coil in the solenoid creating a magnetic field. The magnetic field closes the circuit for a higher current to go from the battery to the starter. A solenoid that mounts directly on the starter mechanically engages the starter pinion gear with the engine's flywheel gear.

Trouble Guide

Common Starting Problems

- Discharged battery
- Corroded battery terminal
- Corroded electrical connections
- Worn out starter or solenoid
- Shorted circuit or broken wire
- Flooded engine

Starter

Current from the solenoid travels to the starter. The starter converts electrical energy to mechanical energy to crank over the engine. A small gear on the starter meshes with the engine's flywheel gear. As the starter turns the flywheel, the flywheel turns the crankshaft and the pistons move up and down. This movement (compression), along with the air-fuel mixture, and ignition, begins the combustion process. The starter is usually mounted on the underside of the engine.

Start-Stop Technology. Automakers are incorporating start-stop technology in conventional vehicles utilizing a specially adapted starter (***Figure 9.39***) and dedicated programming to shut down the engine when not under a load. This is a cost effective way (only a few hundred dollars to implement) to increase fuel efficiency by 3-10% and reduce emissions.

Figure 9.39 ***Start-Stop Starter and Solenoid***
Photo: Bosch

Web Links
Electrical Related Sites
AC Delco
www.acdelco.com
Bosch
www.boschautoparts.com
Cooper Bussmann
www.cooperindustries.com
Littel Fuse
www.littelfuse.com
Remy International, Inc.
www.remyautoparts.com
Wagner Lighting Products
www.federalmogul.com

Park/Neutral Safety Switch

The park/neutral safety switch only allows current to flow in the starting system if the clutch is depressed (manual transmission) or if the shifter is in park or neutral (automatic transmission) to prevent the vehicle from being started while in gear.

Computer Controlled Starting

Computer controlled starting circuits require certain conditions to be present before a starter will engage. The powertrain control module (PCM) requires that the brake pedal is pressed, the transmission is in park or neutral, and that the key fob (smart key) is in the vehicle (***Figure 9.40***). On many push switch systems, one firm push is required. You do not need to hold the button in continuously. The PCM will determine when the engine has started and disengage the starter. If the engine doesn't start after a preset maximum cranking time, for example 15 seconds, the PCM will disengage the starter to prevent it from overheating. The system may prevent you from rapidly re-engaging the starter by initiating a delay between cranking sessions. It will also prevent you from engaging the starter if the vehicle is already running. See Chapter 19 for information on remote starting systems.

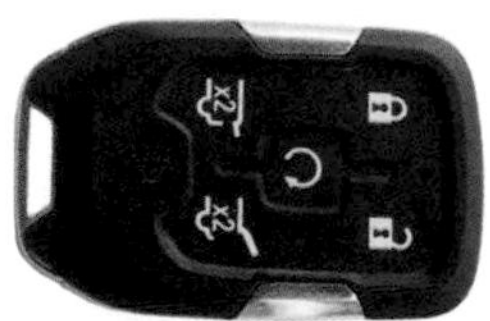

Figure 9.40 ***Key Fob***

Charging System

The charging system (***Figure 9.41***) is somewhat a reverse of the starting system. The charging system converts mechanical energy to electrical energy to chemical energy. The charging system keeps the battery charged and provides power for a vehicle's electrical accessories. The main components of the charging system are:

- Battery
- Intelligent Battery Sensor
- AC Generator (Alternator)
- Voltage Regulation

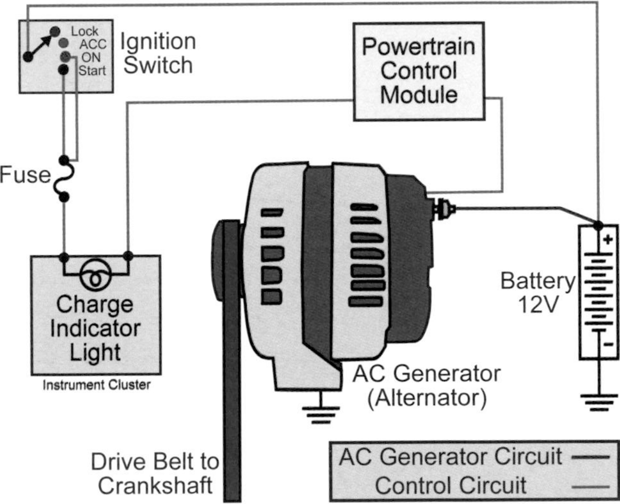

Figure 9.41 ***Charging System Components***

Battery

The battery converts electrical energy to chemical energy during charging and then converts chemical energy to electrical energy during starting. The battery stores energy for future use.

Trouble Guide

Common Charging Problems

- Failed automatic belt tensioner
- Belt is torn, glazed, cracked, or loose
- Worn out alternator or regulator
- Shorted circuit or broken wire
- Corroded battery cables
- Loose electrical connections

Intelligent Battery Sensor

Some vehicles use an intelligent battery sensor (IBS) to continually monitor and analyze the status of the battery (***Figure 9.42***). This sensor can monitor the battery's voltage, current, and temperature, maximizing the electrical system's efficiency.

Figure 9.42 ***Intelligent Battery Sensor***

AC Generator (Alternator)

The drive belt rotates the AC generator (also known as an alternator) pulley, which turns a shaft in it. The alternator (***Figure 9.43***) converts mechanical energy to electrical energy. Initially it converts the electricity to alternating current (AC), then diodes convert it to direct current (DC).

Figure 9.43 ***AC Generator (Alternator)***

Increased Demand. Today's vehicles need much more electrical power than vehicles 50 years ago. Depending on the vehicle, an alternator on a late model vehicle may be rated for 150-200 (or even more) amps. Some diesel light trucks even have two alternators.

Tech Tip

Buying a New Alternator

When buying a new alternator, check the following: number of accessories (e.g., power windows, rear window defrosters, power seats), the wiring hookup, type of pulley, and the amperage rating stamped on the housing.

Voltage Regulation

Voltage regulation is critical in protecting electrical system components. It reduces battery drain during high accessory load situations and prevents the battery from becoming overcharged during times of low load.

Voltage Regulator. The voltage regulator is commonly located in or near the alternator. It regulates the alternator's voltage output by measuring the system voltage and controlling the amount of current that is sent into the alternator's field windings. For example, if a heavy load is put on the battery such as a rear window defroster, the battery voltage decreases. The voltage regulator senses this decrease and thereby increases the current to the field windings to increase the alternator's output. Charging system voltage while the engine is running is commonly 13.8 to 14.8 volts. During very cold weather, the voltage may increase to 15.2 volts. If the alternator is putting out too much or too little voltage, the battery could be overcharged or undercharged. Electrical system components could also be damaged by excessive voltage.

Computer Controlled Voltage Regulation. Newer vehicles use computer regulation instead of a standard voltage regulator. Voltage regulated with a powertrain control module (PCM) (***Figure 9.44***) or other control module is more precise and efficient. Keeping a precise regulated voltage helps extend battery life. It can also increase fuel economy by charging only as necessary and during the most optimal times. The PCM, by monitoring multiple vehicle systems, can determine when more or less output is needed. The vehicle's computer will also be able to track problems by triggering a diagnostic trouble code (DTC) for easier troubleshooting.

Figure 9.44 ***Powertrain Control Module (PCM)***

Computer

Advances in vehicles today are often only possible with the integration of computer technology. At least one computer, microprocessor, or electronic control module provides accurate and instant commands to almost every major mechanical or electrical system (e.g., ignition, fuel, emission, transmission, brake, safety restraint, navigation, and traction control).

Powertrain Control Module. The main computer is commonly called the engine control unit (ECU), electronic engine control (EEC), electronic control module (ECM), or the powertrain control module (PCM). PCM is the standardized name used by the Society of Automotive Engineers and will be used throughout this book. Sensors are constantly inputting raw information, in the form of electrical signals, into the PCM where the data is analyzed, processed, and sometimes stored (***Figure 9.45***). The type and number of sensors and computers on vehicles vary. Computers monitor and adjust engine controls by performing self checks to make sure the engine is running efficiently.

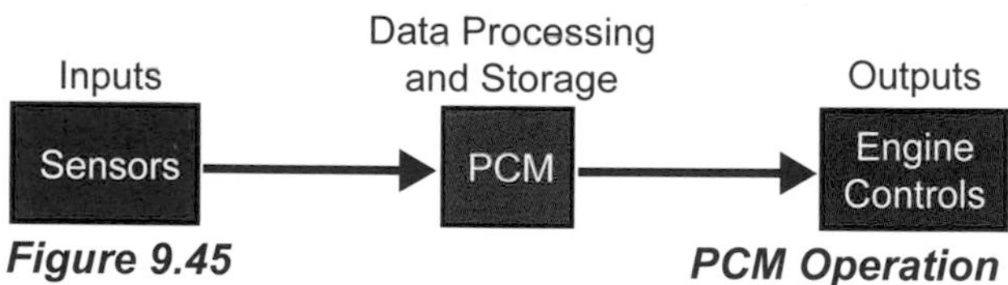

Figure 9.45 ***PCM Operation***

On-Board Diagnostics. When something is not working properly a trouble code will normally be stored in the computer. The check engine light (***Figure 9.46***) will go on if a code is stored. A scan tool is used to retrieve stored on-board diagnostics (OBD) codes. See Chapter 20 to learn more about OBD. Most computers never need maintenance, but if they fail they will need to be replaced. Often the problem is sensor input. If you are having trouble with diagnosis take your vehicle to the dealer. A computer is covered under an extended federal emission warranty.

Figure 9.46 ***Service Engine Soon Light***

Drive Belt

The drive belt turns the pulley on the AC generator (alternator) and may connect to other accessories such as the water pump and air conditioning (A/C) compressor. Belts come in three types: serpentine (V-ribbed), stretch, and V-belt. This section focuses on:

- Engine Drive Belt Routing
- Serpentine Belt
- Stretch Belt
- V-Belt
- Belt Wear
- Buying Belts

Engine Drive Belt Routing

An engine drive belt routing diagram (***Figure 9.47***) is commonly located on an engine compartment label or in the owner's manual.

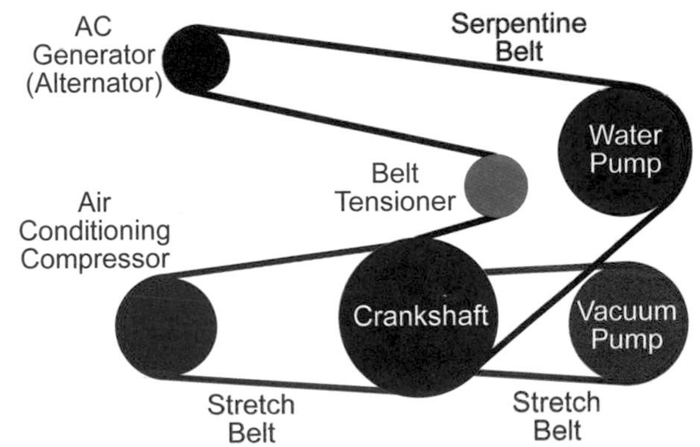

Figure 9.47 ***Engine Drive Belt Routing***

Serpentine Belt

A serpentine belt (***Figure 9.48***), also called a multi-ribbed or multi V-ribbed belt, is usually flat on one side and has grooves that run parallel with the belt on the other side. Commonly, serpentine belts will have 2 to 8 grooves on one side and are usually ½ to 1 inch (1.27 to 2.54 cm) wide depending on the number of grooves and application. Some have ribs on both sides.

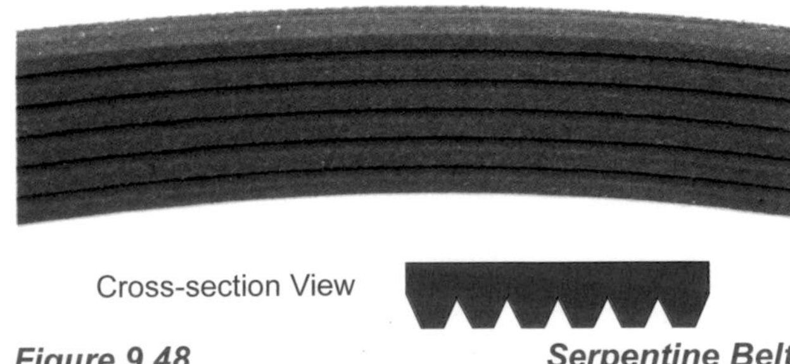

Figure 9.48 ***Serpentine Belt***

Belt Construction. Older belts were made from neoprene material. Neoprene belts crack and lose rib pieces when worn. Neoprene belts commonly had a life of about 50,000 miles. Serpentine belts today are made from EPDM (Ethylene Propylene Diene Monomer) rubber. EPDM wears similar to a tire, losing rubber, but not necessarily cracking. An EPDM belt that isn't cracked or visibly damaged, could still be worn out and need replacing. EPDM belts commonly last about 90,000 miles.

Automatic Belt Tensioner. The automatic belt tensioner (***Figure 9.49***), a critical component in the belt drive system, keeps a serpentine belt tight with the correct amount of tension and minimizes vibrations. Tensioners wear over time and must be replaced. If the tensioner spring is worn the belt can slip creating excessive heat - glazing the belt's surface. Glazing leads to belt squealing. A worn tensioner spring will exhibit excessive vibrations. If the bearing on the tensioner is worn, the belt may get out of alignment causing side wear and fraying. Worn bearings can also put stress on the AC generator (alternator), water pump, air conditioning compressor, or other accessories - resulting in premature component failure. It is generally recommended to replace the belt tensioner when an EPDM belt is replaced.

Figure 9.49 ***Belt Tensioner***

Stretch Belt

Some belt systems do not use belt tensioners, they use a special stretch belt (***Figure 9.50***). Stretch belts look similar to conventional serpentine V-ribbed belts, but they are not the same. Some vehicles have a conventional serpentine belt and stretch belts. ***Note: Serpentine V-ribbed belts and stretch belts are not interchangeable.***

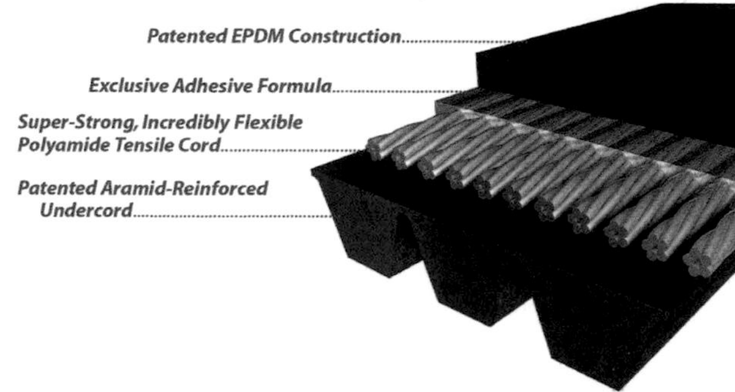

Figure 9.50 **Stretch Belt**
Courtesy of Gates Corporation - www.gates.com

Installation. A stretch belt cannot be removed and reused. To remove an old stretch belt, you simply cut it off. A new stretch belt is designed to be stretched over pulleys during installation. Once they are installed, they automatically tension. Do not use a screwdriver to slip the belt over the pulley. Some manufacturers recommend a special installation tool, while others allow you to use a zip tie to help during installation.

V-Belt

V-belts (***Figure 9.51***) are usually less than ½ inch (1.27 cm) in width and have a cross-section that looks like a "V".

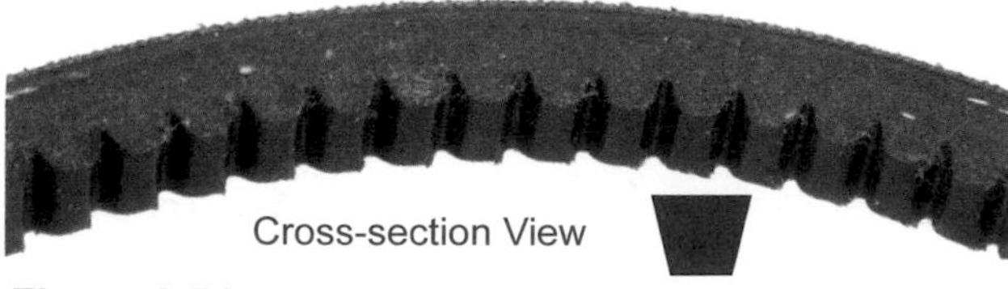

Figure 9.51 ***V-Belt***

Servicing

Replace Belts

- Inspect and replace as recommended by the manufacturer

Belt Wear

A worn belt can slip, hydroplane, elongate, or become misaligned. Worn belts can have side abrasion from misalignment (***Figure 9.52***), cracking, glazing, or pilling.

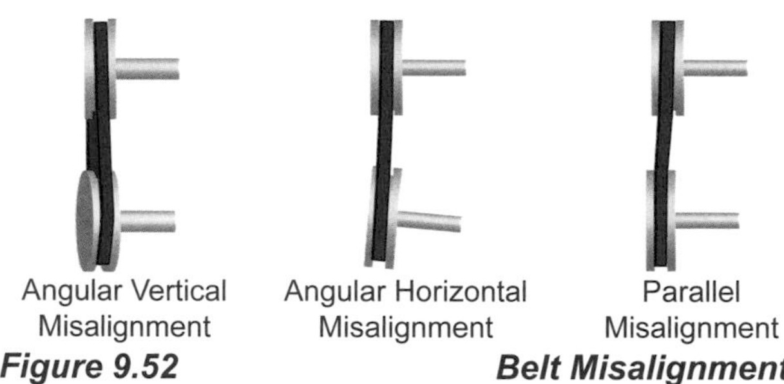

Figure 9.52 ***Belt Misalignment***

EPDM Belt Wear Gauges. Two major belt manufacturers, Gates (***Figure 9.53***) and Dayco, have designed simple tools to inspect EPDM belts for wear. You can get these for free at parts stores. Start inspecting belts at 60,000 miles.

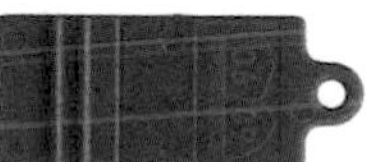

Figure 9.53 ***Gates Belt Wear Gauge***

Buying Belts

When buying a new belt check the number and type of accessories the belt goes around. Determine if it is a serpentine (V-ribbed), stretch, or V-belt. Then note the factory numbers (***Figure 9.54***) on the old belt to assist in cross-referencing if necessary.

Figure 9.54 ***Belt Number***

Apps

www.AutoUpkeep.com/apps
Click on Chapter 9

Lights

Lights are an important safety feature. Without them we could not see at night or notice when someone is braking, turning, or changing lanes. Some lights are controlled by sensors so they automatically illuminate in low-light conditions. Other lights are turned on by manual switches. As a safety feature, daytime running lights (DRL) make it easier for approaching drivers to see each other. Lights burn out with age. When replacing bulbs, use the number on the bulb as a guide. This is not true for most automotive replacement parts, but it is true for headlights and other bulbs. It is recommended to replace blown out headlights in pairs. This section focuses on:

- Light Sources
- Miniature Light Bulbs
- Sealed Beam Headlights
- Composite Headlights
- Non-serviceable Assemblies

Light Sources

Light is emitted using different technologies (***Figure 9.55***). A tungsten filament bulb uses a resistive wire that heats up to create light. Filament bulbs consume large amounts of energy compared to the light they emit. To increase light output, halogen gas can be used with the filament. Halogen lamps run at a higher temperature which leads to increased light over a standard filament bulb. High-intensity discharge (HID), also called xenon lights, use an electric arc to create light. ***Warning: HID lights operate at high voltage. Follow the warnings in your owner's manual to avoid injury while servicing.*** Light-emitting diode (LED) lights use a semiconductor chip to emit light, consuming significantly less energy than the other technologies.

Figure 9.55 ***Composite Replacement Bulbs***

Miniature Light Bulbs

Miniature light bulbs (e.g., taillights, brake lights, side markers) are designed as push-in or bayonet (***Figure 9.56***).

Figure 9.56 ***Automotive Miniature Bulbs***

Sealed Beam Headlights

Sealed beam headlights (***Figure 9.57***) come as a unit with the bulb sealed inside. When replacing a sealed beam headlight the all-in-one unit (bulb and glass lens) is replaced.

Figure 9.57 ***Sealed Beam Headlight***

Composite Headlights

Composite headlights (***Figure 9.58***) are integrated aerodynamically into a vehicle's body. Their housing consists of a reflective surface covered by a lens. When a composite style headlight burns out only the bulb needs to be replaced. See Chapter 20 for a general procedure on how to replace a composite headlight.

Figure 9.58 ***Composite Headlights***

Non-Serviceable Assemblies

Some light assemblies are non-serviceable (***Figure 9.59***). This means that the bulbs cannot be replaced. When this happens you need to replace the whole light assembly. This is common for LED light assemblies.

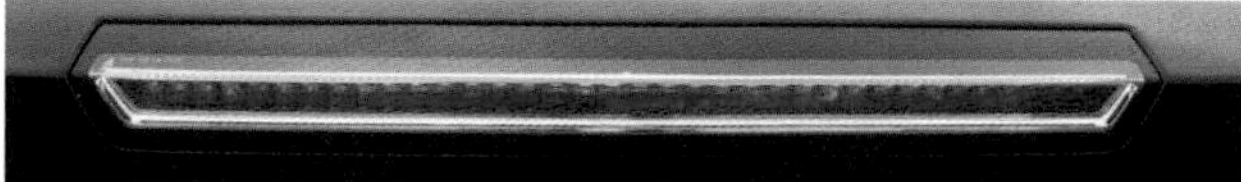

Figure 9.59 ***Non-Serviceable Assembly***

Accessory Power Points

Newer vehicles may have accessory USB ports (DC) and power outlets (120V AC) (***Figure 9.60***). These are designed to run and charge electronic equipment (e.g., cell phones, laptops) within limits (commonly a max of 15 amps or 150 watts). Read the specific recommendations in your owner's manual and find the wattage rating of the device before plugging in or you may blow a fuse. Some electrical equipment (e.g., vacuum cleaner, medical devices) use at least 1000 watts.

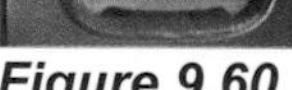

Figure 9.60 ***Power Outlets and USB Ports***

Q & A

Bulb Keeps Burning Out

Q: What would cause my headlight bulb to blow out frequently?

A: Moisture from a cracked lens will make it burn out quicker. If the electrical socket is corroded, use an electrical cleaner and then put a dab of dielectric grease in the socket. When replacing a composite style headlight bulb, do not touch the glass. Oil from your fingers can shorten the life of the bulb. Another possibility is that an overcharge condition is present.

Summary

The electrical system may seem quite complex to the do-it-yourselfer, but there are simple ways to maintain it and save money. Start by keeping your 12-volt DC battery maintained. The starting system converts chemical energy to electrical energy to mechanical energy in order to start the engine. The charging system converts mechanical energy to electrical energy to chemical energy to recharge the battery. Fuses are overcurrent protection devices. Lights are used in many places on the automobile and periodically need replacing. Electric and hybrid vehicles have an additional high voltage electrical system that runs electric motors for propulsion. The electrical system activities will assist you in testing and replacing automotive electrical system components. Keep in mind that integrated computer technology can help you keep your vehicle running smoothly and help diagnose problems with trouble codes.

Activities

Electrical System

- Ohm's Law Activity
- Wiring Diagram Activity
- Battery Activity
- Charging Activity
- Starting Activity
- Chapter 9 Study Questions

Activities and Study Questions can be completed in the *Auto Upkeep Workbook.*

Career Paths

Electrical Engineer

Education: Bachelor's Degree in Engineering

Median Income: $95,230

Abilities: Apply math, science, technology, and ingenuity to solve electrical problems.

Find your career at www.bls.gov/ooh.

Lubrication System

Chapter 10

Fuel for Thought

- What is the function of engine oil in the lubrication system?
- How are oils rated?
- What are synthetic oils?

Introduction

The engine is the heart of a vehicle with hundreds of moving parts that must be lubricated. While the engine burns fuel, it also takes in outside air. Road dust and dirt are brought in with this air. While most of the air is cleaned, some dust may get by the air filter. In addition, incomplete combustion adds carbon deposits to the oil. Water can also come in contact with the oil from humidity in the air and gaskets leaking. All of these factors can lead to engine oil failure. Engine oil, processed from crude oil, is the substance that keeps your engine going day after day. It is extremely important to keep the oil clean and at the correct level to prevent engine oil failure.

Q & A

Oil Recycling

Q: Why is it important to recycle used motor oil and where do I take it?

A: According to the EPA (Environmental Protection Agency), improperly dumping oil from one oil change can contaminate one million gallons of groundwater. To learn more about used engine oil recycling visit www.recycleoil.org. Many auto parts stores and service centers recycle used oil for free. Recycled oil can be reprocessed as fuel oil or re-refined as a base for new lubricants. The properties of lubrication in engine oil last indefinitely when recycled and re-refined.

Objectives

Upon completion of this chapter and activities, you will be able to:

- Define the purpose of engine oil.
- Explain oil service and viscosity ratings.
- Discuss the advantages and disadvantages of synthetic oils.
- Discuss the importance of oil filters.
- Change the oil and filter on a vehicle.

Web Links

Motor Oil Company Sites

AMSOIL Inc.
www.amsoil.com

Castrol
www.castrol.com

Havoline
www.havoline.com

Mobil Oil
www.mobil.com

Mystik Lubricants
www.mystiklubes.com

Pennzoil
www.pennzoil.com

Phillips 66 Lubricants
www.phillips66lubricants.com

Quaker State
www.quakerstate.com

Royal Purple
www.royalpurple.com

Valvoline
www.valvoline.com

Purpose of Engine Oil

Modern engine oils perform many tasks. Engine oil has to protect against corrosion, clean the engine, carry away excess heat, improve sealing, and lubricate moving parts to reduce engine wear. This section focuses on:

- Lubricates
- Cools
- Cleans
- Seals

Lubricates

The most important function of engine oil is to lubricate. Within the engine there are parts rubbing up against each other. This rubbing creates friction.

Friction. Friction is the force that resists motion between two bodies in contact. Friction creates heat (thermal energy). Engine oil molecules are like little ball bearings (***Figure 10.1***). The oil molecules have a tendency to stick to metal surfaces, but have less of a tendency to stick to each other. Oil decreases resistance and friction between two sliding bodies, resulting in a reduction of engine wear.

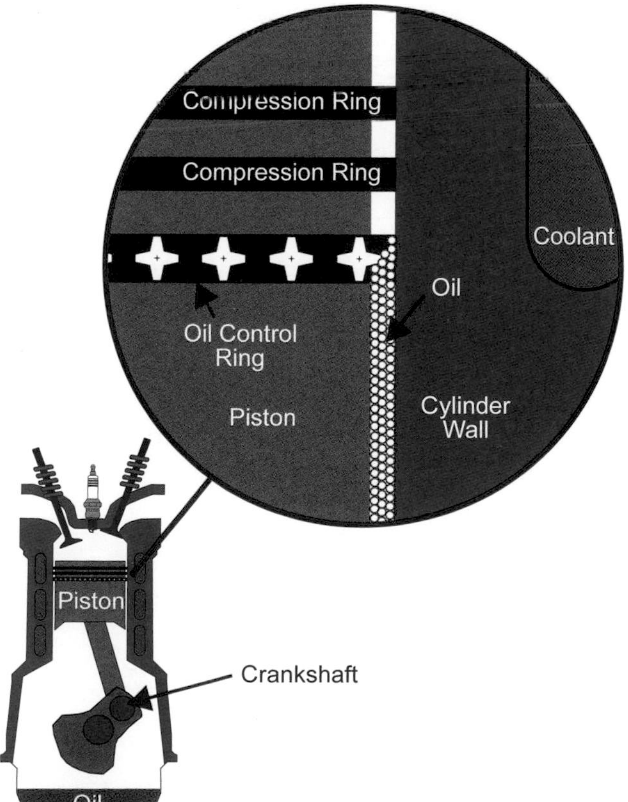

Figure 10.1 Oil Lubrication in an Engine Cylinder

Cools

While engine oil does reduce friction, it cannot eliminate it. Friction would build up undesirable heat without engine oil. Overheating can damage engine components.

Heat Dissipation. Engine oil is pumped throughout the engine, moving into various parts, and then back to the oil pan. In the oil pan and in some vehicles through an engine oil cooler, heat is dissipated to the outside air. Engine oil helps cool your engine in this process.

Cleans

Conventional gasoline-fueled vehicles are not very efficient. Approximately 25% of money spent on fuel is used for propulsion (movement) or running accessories, like the A/C. Inefficiency in the internal combustion engine causes unburned deposits to build up in the engine. Dirty air may also come in through the air filter during the intake process. While the engine oil is lubricating all the critical engine components, it also cleans by removing particles of carbon and other contaminants.

Oil Filter. As the oil is pumped throughout the engine, the dirty particles are screened out by the oil filter. Clean engine components help ensure proper lubrication.

Seals

During engine operation, the pistons are rapidly moving up and down. Engine oil is also moving up and down with the pistons. Not only does engine oil lubricate, cool, and clean; it also seals between vital components.

Blow-by. Engine oil seals between pistons and the cylinder walls to reduce blow-by. Blow-by is the gas that escapes past the piston rings and into the crankcase, causing power loss and piston wear.

Seals Gaskets. Engine oil acts as a seal between components that are separated by gaskets. For example, you should put a thin film of oil on the oil filter gasket before installation to seal the connection between the filter and engine.

Understanding Oil Ratings

Reading and understanding an oil bottle can be challenging. The oil ratings you need to become familiar with are (***Figure 10.2***):

- Society of Automotive Engineers (SAE)
- American Petroleum Institute (API)
- Energy or Resource Conserving
- International Lubricant Standardization and Approval Committee (ILSAC)
- European Automobile Manufacturers' Association (ACEA)
- Manufacturer Specifications

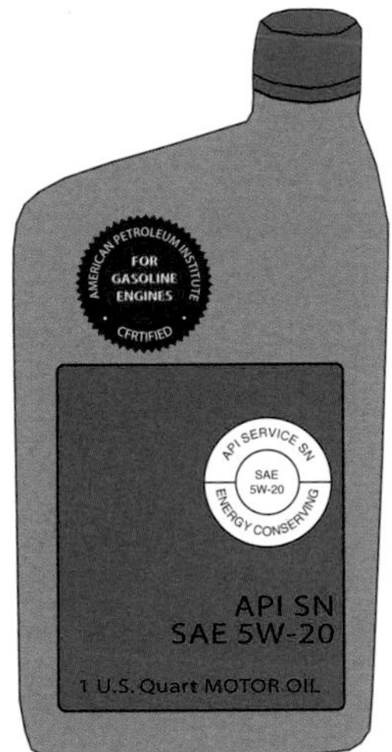

Figure 10.2 ***Bottle of Oil with Ratings***

Q & A

Wrong Oil in Engine

Q: What will happen if I use 10W-30 instead of the recommended 5W-30?

A: The difference between 5W-30 and 10W-30 is the viscosity (thickness). Many new cars recommend using 5W-30 or 0W-20 all year long, while others indicate that it is OK to use 10W-30 in warm climates. The lower viscosity oil (5W-30) circulates quicker throughout the engine when it is cold. Check the owner's manual to see if the manufacturer allows the use of 10W-30 during warmer climatic conditions. Using the incorrect viscosity of oil may void the warranty and decrease fuel economy by 1-2%.

Society of Automotive Engineers

SAE rates engine oil viscosity. Viscosity is defined as the resistance to flow. Engine oil is available in single (e.g., SAE 30) and multigrade (e.g., SAE 5W-30) viscosity ratings.

Multigrade Oils. An oil that has two numbers in the rating is called a multigrade oil. Multigrade oils have been tested at various temperatures and can be used in a wide range of climates (***Figure 10.3***). The W after a rating signifies that the oil has been tested for a winter weather temperature at 0°F (-18°C). If there is not a W after the number the oil was tested at 210°F (99°C). The higher the viscosity number the thicker the oil. 5W-30 oil acts like SAE 5 when cold and SAE 30 when warm. It is thin enough when the engine is cold to get to all of the components and thick enough when the engine warms up to protect against engine wear. This is why multigrade oils have become so popular – they meet the viscosity ratings in multiple temperature ranges.

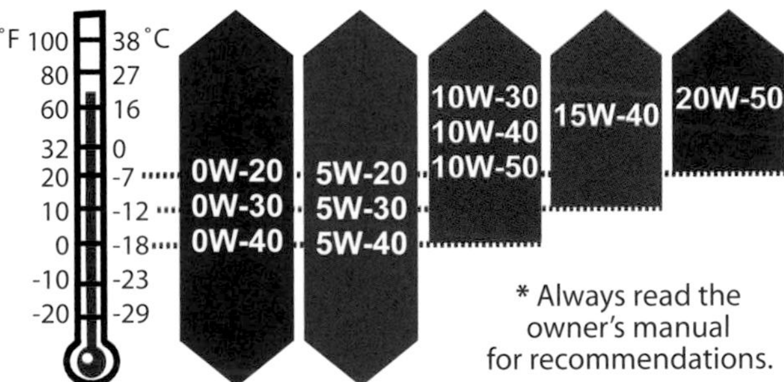

Figure 10.3 ***Engine Oil SAE Viscosity Ratings***

Common Viscosity Ratings. Common engine oil viscosity ratings for newer vehicles are 0W-20, 5W-20, and 5W-30, but always check the owner's manual for the manufacturer's recommendations.

Web Links

Oil Rating Related Sites

American Petroleum Institute
www.api.org

Society of Automotive Engineers
www.sae.org

American Petroleum Institute

API rates the engine oil service (***Figure 10.4***). SA, SB, SC, SD, SE, SF, SG, SH, SJ, SL, SM, and SN are API rated engine oils.

API Rating Defined. The first letter "**S**" stands for **S**park ignition (gasoline) engines (also referred to as **S**ervice categories). The later the second letter is in the alphabet, the newer and more advanced the oil. For example, SC oil was used in vehicles in the 1960s and is not suitable for current vehicles. Sometimes you'll see designations such as CK-4. The "**C**" stands for **C**ompression ignition (diesel) engines (also referred to as **C**ommercial categories). A new diesel oil, FA-4 was designed to meet 2017 greenhouse gas emissions. It is specifically formulated for vehicles that require diesel fuel sulfur content that doesn't exceed 15 ppm (parts per million). Some oils are not compatible with others, so always refer to your manufacturer's recommendations.

Gas Engine (Spark Ignition)	Diesel Engine (Compression Ignition)
SN	CK-4 and FA-4

Figure 10.4 Engine API Ratings in 2017

API Standards. Newer engines are requiring more strenuous standards. When the API determines that current oils cannot meet newer engine needs or when current technology can improve engine oil qualities, it establishes a new set of standards. The key is that SN oils replace all the previous oils and can be used in any spark ignition engine with any of the previous letter designations. Look for the API symbols (***Figure 10.5***) when identifying the correct engine oil for your vehicle. Over time, API will come out with more advanced oil standards to replace SN oils.

Figure 10.5 API Donut and Starburst Symbols

Energy or Resource Conserving

Labeled as either energy conserving or resource conserving, these oils have increased additives to lower friction between components. By lowering the friction, the engine becomes more efficient which in turn improves fuel economy.

ILSAC

The International Lubricant Standardization and Approval Committee (ILSAC) was formed in the 1990s by Japanese and American automotive manufacturers. ILSAC develops and identifies standards for gasoline-fueled (GF) engine oils. The back of the oil bottle will list the standards met (***Figure 10.6***).

Exceeds:
- **API Service SN/SM/SL/SJ**
- **ILSAC GF-5/GF-4/GF-3**
- **API Certified Gasoline Engine Oils**
- **Meets the Performance of GM6094M**
- **Ford WSS-M2C946-A and Ford WSS-M2C929-A**

Exceeds all passenger car and light truck manufacturer's warranty requirements for the protection of gasoline and turbo charged engines where API SN, SM, SL, or SJ is recommended.

Figure 10.6 Standards Listed on an Oil Bottle

ACEA

The European Automobile Manufacturers' Association (also known as Association des Constructeurs Européens d'Automobiles - ACEA) develops oil ratings. Read the owner's manual for the standard that is right for your engine.

Manufacturer Specifications

Vehicle manufacturers may have specific ratings (***Figure 10.7***) for the vehicles they produce. Always be sure to compare the oil bottle ratings to those listed in the owner's manual. Oil information is commonly under section titles "Capacities and Specifications" or "Service and Maintenance".

	Specification*	Engine Type
Ford	WSS-M2C946-A	Gas Engines
	WSS-M2C171-E	Diesel Engines
General Motors	dexos1	Gas Engines
	dexos2	Diesel Engines (except some Duramax)

* This list is not all-inclusive.

Figure 10.7 Sample Oil Manufacturer Standards

Engine Oil Additives

Engine oil is a mixture of a base oil (about 70 to 90% of total composition) and an additive package (the remaining 10 to 30%). Additive packages enhance an oil's ability to properly protect the engine, improving performance. Oil additives are chemical compounds that perform many functions (***Figure 10.8***). ***Note: Don't confuse engine oil additives with aftermarket oil additives. Aftermarket additives are put into your engine in addition to the engine oil. Most manufacturers do not recommend adding anything to the specified oil.***

Additive	Function
Detergents	Cleans, helps prevent deposits.
Dispersants	Keeps contaminants suspended, helps prevent sludge from forming.
Corrosion and Rust Inhibitors	Coats metal, slows down oxidation.
Antifoam Agents	Helps prevent air bubbles from forming.
Antioxidants	Slows oxidation in oil.
Viscosity Modifiers	Helps prevent high temperature oil from becoming too thin.
Pour Point Depressants	Improves low temperature fluidity.
Extreme Pressure Agents	Helps oil stick to metal even under high pressure.
Friction Modifiers	Helps reduce friction between moving parts.
Antiwear Additives	Helps coat and surround objects, maintaining a very thin film around them.

Figure 10.8 ***Engine Oil Additives***

Price Guides

Conventional Oil
- $3.00 to $8.00 a quart

100% Synthetic Oil
- $8.00 to $12.00 a quart

Semi-Synthetic Oil
- $5.00 to $8.00 a quart

Oil Filters
- $3.00 to $20.00 each

Note: 1 qt = 0.946 L

Types of Engine Oil

Advancements in oil technology have dramatically increased the life of automobile engines. A properly maintained engine can easily have a life lasting over 200,000 miles. This section focuses on the three common types of oil used in engines (***Figure 10.9***):

- Conventional Engine Oil
- Synthetic Engine Oil
- Semi-Synthetic Engine Oil

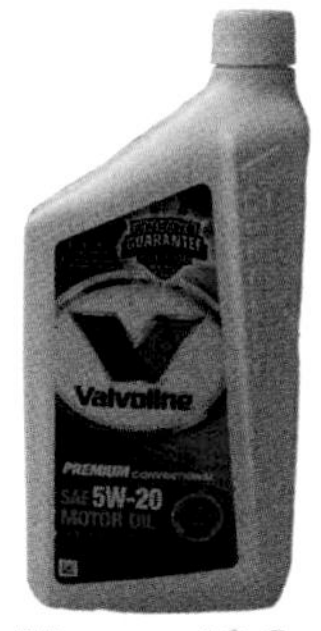

Figure 10.9 ***Types of Engine Oil***

Conventional Engine Oil

Conventional engine oil, also referred to as mineral oil, is crude oil that has been pumped from oil wells and refined into a base oil. The base oil then gets an additive package. The main problem with conventional oil is that even though it goes through a high level of production/distillation to remove impurities, it still is left with molecular compounds that vary in size and shape. This variation can impact the oil's film strength, allowing for the possibility of conventional oil to deteriorate under extreme temperatures. When oil film deteriorates, wear can occur.

Tech Tip

Oil Warning Light

The oil light comes on when your engine has little or no oil pressure. Without oil pressure, severe engine damage can result. If the light stays on for more than 5 seconds, turn the engine off and check your oil. If it is at the correct level and the light still stays on, do not run the engine.

Synthetic Engine Oil

Instead of going through a distillation process like conventional oil, synthetic oils are engineered from various chemicals and hydrocarbons. This engineered base oil then gets an additive package. The main advantage of synthetic oils is that their molecular structure is consistent (***Figure 10.10***). With structurally consistent molecules, a synthetic oil's film strength is superior over conventional oil. It is extremely durable under high temperatures.

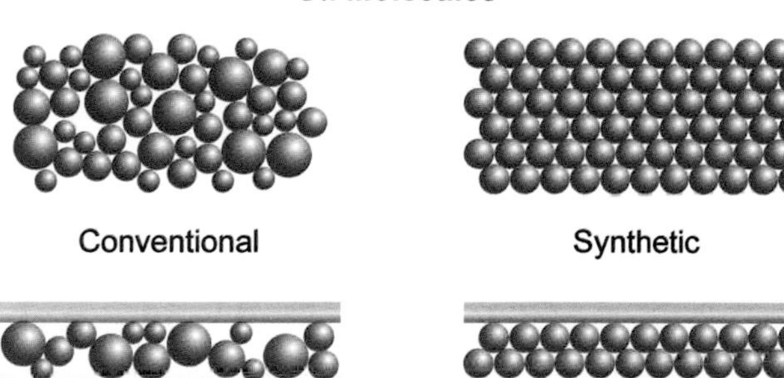

Figure 10.10 *Molecule Comparison*

Applications. Synthetic oils have been used by military organizations since World War II, but they have only become more common in the automotive sector since the 1990s. Today, synthetic oils are commonly used to factory fill new vehicle engines.

Advantages and Disadvantages. Synthetic oils have advantages and disadvantages (***Figure 10.11***).

Advantages of Synthetic Oil
• Contains low levels of impurities.
• Increases lubricating qualities improving fuel mileage.
• Resists sludge from forming.
• Maintains lubricating abilities for longer oil change intervals.
• Flows well in extreme cold and during initial start up.
• Protects at extremely high temperatures.
Disadvantages of Synthetic Oil
• Higher cost.
• Some manufacturer warranties require regular oil change intervals that reflect conventional oil use.

Figure 10.11 *Synthetic Oil Factors*

Semi-Synthetic Engine Oil

Semi-synthetic oils, also called synthetic blends, are a combination of fully synthetic and conventional base oils. They will provide some of the advantages of a fully synthetic oil, but at a lower cost.

Oil Filters

As oil circulates through the engine, it is cleaned by an oil filter (***Figure 10.12***). The oil filter should be replaced every time your engine oil is changed. Oil filters are composed of paper screening materials that collect contaminants from the engine oil. Once the contaminants are removed from the engine oil, the oil is recirculated through the engine.

Figure 10.12 *Oil Filter*

Web Links

Filter Related Sites

Fram Filters
www.fram.com

Hastings Premium Filters
www.hastingsfilters.com

Wix Filters
www.wixfilters.com

Trouble Guide

Engine Oil Leaks

- Engine oil plug loose or not sealing
- Oil filter loose or not sealing
- Other various seals or gaskets leaking

Oil Change

As oil is circulated throughout your engine, it picks up contaminants. This section focuses on:

- Oil Life Monitoring System
- Example Intervals
- Changing the Oil and Filter

Oil Life Monitoring System

Most newer vehicles have an oil life monitoring system. A computer on the vehicle monitors miles driven, engine revolutions, engine temperature, and driving conditions. The computer then calculates the effective life of the engine oil. When the life percentage approaches 0%, it is time for an oil change. To work properly, the oil life system must be reset (***Figure 10.13***) after changing the oil. ***Note: An oil life monitoring system does not sense oil level. Check oil level every fuel fill up or as recommended by the manufacturer.***

Figure 10.13 ***Oil Life Monitoring System***

Example Intervals

Vehicle usage will determine how often you are required to change the oil (***Figure 10.14***).

Service	Typical Miles	Vehicle Use
Normal	7,500 to 10,000	• City and Highway Driving • Typical Cargo Loads • Infrequent Towing • Mostly Flat Terrain • Well-Maintained Roads
Severe	5,000 to 7,499	• Mostly City Driving • Heavy Cargo Loads • Frequent Towing • Mountainous or Hilly Terrain • Dusty Roads
Extreme	3,000 to 4,999	• Maximum Load or Towing • Continuous Extreme Climates • Extreme Road Terrain and Conditions

Figure 10.14 Oil Life Monitoring System Intervals

Changing the Oil and Filter

To reduce engine wear, the oil and filter must be changed (***Figure 10.15***).

Steps to Remove Old Oil and Filter

STEP 1	After warming the engine to loosen contaminants and to thin the oil, shut it off and remove the ignition key. ***Warning: On push button keyless ignition vehicles follow the owner's manual for specific safety procedures to prevent an unintended engine startup.***
STEP 2	Wear eye protection and disposable gloves.
STEP 3	Chock the wheels, lift the vehicle, and support it with jack stands. Or, use drive-on ramps, wheel chocks, and then jack stands. Apply the parking brake. See Chapter 5 for safe lifting information.

Figure 10.15a ***Drive-on Ramps***

STEP 4	Remove oil filler cap. Position an oil drain pan under the oil drain plug and filter. If the oil is extremely hot, allow it to cool some.
STEP 5	Loosen the oil drain plug with the correct size wrench or socket and then carefully remove it by hand.

Figure 10.15b ***Loosen Oil Drain Plug***

STEP 6	While the oil is draining (at least 5 minutes) inspect the oil plug threads, gasket (washer), and oil pan threads for cracks, damage, or wear. Purchase a new oil plug or gasket if needed.
STEP 7	Use an oil filter wrench to remove the old oil filter and gasket. Be careful, the oil filter is full of warm oil. Set the old filter into the oil drain pan to drain.

Figure 10.15c ***Loosen Oil Filter***

STEP 8	Use a rag to wipe off the filter mounting base, the drain plug, and the drain plug area after the oil has drained.

Steps to Install New Oil and Filter	
STEP 1	Reinstall the oil plug finger tight by hand and then tighten to the recommended torque with a wrench. Do not cross-thread or over-tighten.
STEP 2	Apply a thin film of clean oil on the new oil filter gasket.
STEP 3	Install the oil filter by hand by rotating it clockwise. Once the gasket contacts the engine, tighten it further according to the instructions - usually ½ to 1 full turn.

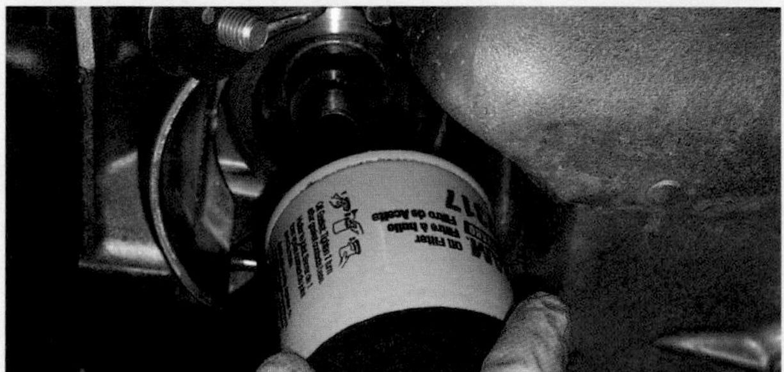

Figure 10.15d ***Install a New Oil Filter***

STEP 4	Remove the oil drain pan and tools from under the vehicle. Lower the vehicle if you used a jack and jack stands.
STEP 5	With the filler cap removed, use a funnel to add the correct amount and type of oil. Check the owner's manual for recommendations. Reinstall the oil filler cap. ***Note: Never overfill the crankcase with oil. Too much oil causes foam (air bubbles) to form if the crankshaft whips the oil, lessening lubricating qualities.***

Figure 10.15e ***Add Oil using a Funnel***

STEP 6	Start the engine and let it idle for a minute. Check that the oil gauge or light is normal. If you used drive-on ramps remove the jack stands and carefully back down the ramps. Shut off the engine for safety and inspect the filter and oil plug for leaks.
STEP 7	If there are no leaks, wait a couple of minutes and then check the oil dipstick level. Be sure the car is on level ground to get an accurate reading. Correct if needed.
STEP 8	Clean up and properly recycle your old oil and filter.
STEP 9	Write down in your vehicle records the odometer reading and date of service.

Resetting the Engine Oil Life System	
STEP 1	Read your owner's manual on how to reset the oil life monitoring system.
STEP 2	Reset the system. Make sure the display now shows 100%.

Figure 10.15 ***Oil and Filter Change Procedure***

Videos

www.Video.AutoUpkeep.com

Click on Chapter 10

Summary

Engine oil lubricates, cools, cleans, and seals engine components. While engine oil is a vital component to the longevity of an engine and may seem extremely complex, it is not very difficult to service. When purchasing oil look for the SAE, API, and other ratings that meet the manufacturer's recommended requirements. Oil filters are used to remove contaminants from the engine oil and should be changed at oil change intervals. Synthetic oils are becoming more popular and accepted due to stringent engine tolerances. Always refer to the owner's manual for oil recommendations and change intervals.

Activities

Lubrication System

- Oil and Filter Change Activity
- Chapter 10 Study Questions

Activities and Study Questions can be completed in the *Auto Upkeep Workbook*.

Career Paths

Service Writer

Education: Technical Experience or ASE Cert.
Median Income: $37,850
Abilities: Diagnostic, communication, problem solving, and time management skills.
Find your career at www.bls.gov/ooh.

FUEL SYSTEM

CHAPTER 11

Fuel for Thought

- How are gasoline and diesel produced?
- What is the purpose of the fuel system?
- How are gasoline prices determined?

Introduction

Most automobiles in production today depend on either gasoline or diesel. Many problems arise from using gasoline and diesel. Once these fuels are burned, they are gone forever. Driving habits, maintenance procedures, and technological advancements can improve the efficiency of vehicles. This chapter provides information on fuel properties, automotive fuel components, and ways to increase fuel efficiency.

Objectives

Upon completion of this chapter and activities, you will be able to:

- Explain the purpose of the fuel system.
- Describe the parts of the fuel system.
- Use an online parts catalog to identify fuel system components.
- Remove and replace an air filter.
- Remove and replace a fuel filter.
- State gasoline and diesel properties.
- Explain how fuel is priced.
- Identify ways to improve fuel economy.

Fuel System Purpose

The purpose of the fuel system is to store, transfer, clean, and then mix the fuel with air. Fuel (chemical energy) is stored in the fuel tank until it is pumped, filtered, pressurized, and delivered to the injection system. The fuel must be mixed with air either before the combustion chamber (indirect injection - low pressure system) or inside the combustion chamber (direct injection - high pressure system), where it is then burned.

Air-Fuel Mixtures

In gasoline engines the cleanest burning and most efficient mixture under moderate load conditions is when the mass ratio is close to 14.7 parts of air to 1 part of gasoline (i.e., stoichiometric ratio). This is called the air-fuel ratio or AFR. This section focuses on:

- Lean Air-Fuel Mixture
- Rich Air-Fuel Mixture

Lean Air-Fuel Mixture

When there is more air above the ideal 14.7:1 AFR, it is considered a lean air-fuel mixture. For example, an AFR of 16:1 is lean.

Rich Air-Fuel Mixture

When there is less air than the ideal 14.7:1 AFR, it is considered a rich air-fuel mixture. For example, an AFR of 12:1 is rich.

Q & A

Fuel Pump Replacement

Q: My technician gave me an estimate over $800 for a new fuel pump. Why is it so high?

A: The fuel pumps on most vehicles today are located in the fuel tank. Some pumps are a complete fuel assembly module that includes the pump and the fuel level sender. The technician has to drain and then remove the fuel tank from the vehicle to access the fuel pump. The part itself can cost over $300.

Fuel System Components

The fuel system parts that will be discussed are:

- Fuel Filler
- Fuel Tank
- Fuel Pump
- Fuel Lines
- Fuel Filter
- Fuel Injectors
- PCV Valve
- Air Filter
- Throttle Valve
- Powertrain Control Module
- Sensors and Controls

Fuel Filler

Most vehicles come with a standard fuel (gas) cap. However, Ford Motor Company introduced a capless fuel filler called Easy Fuel™ in 2008. Both systems keep the fuel from spilling out and foreign objects from entering the fuel tank. The Ford Easy Fuel™ capless system has a built-in spring loaded flapper door. When refueling, this system allows you to simply insert the fuel filler nozzle directly into the filler neck. A special funnel is provided and required when refilling with a gas can (***Figure 11.1***).

Figure 11.1 ***Capless Easy Fuel™***

Fuel Tank

The fuel (gas) tank, made of either steel or plastic, stores the fuel. The most common reason for having to remove the fuel tank is replacement of a faulty or worn-out in-tank electric fuel pump.

Price Guides

Fuel Filter
- $5.00 to $50.00 each

Fuel Pump
- $20.00 to $800.00 each

Fuel Pump

The fuel pump, either mechanical or electric (***Figure 11.2***), supplies the engine with fuel. Mechanical fuel pumps are usually located on the engine. Electric fuel pumps are usually located in the fuel tank. In addition to an in-tank electric fuel pump, gasoline direct injection (GDI) vehicles use a mechanical high pressure (up to 2900 psi) fuel pump.

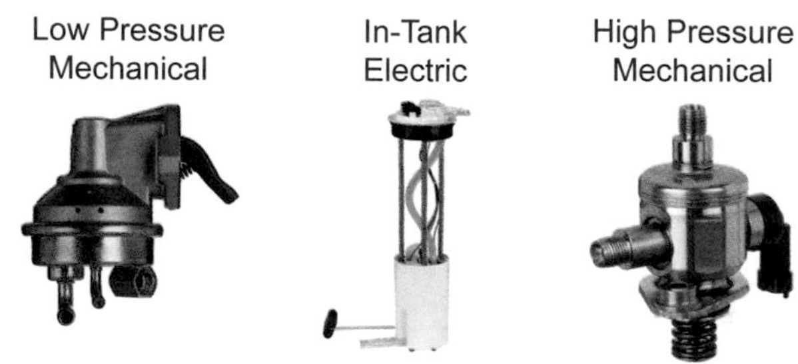

Figure 11.2 ***Fuel Pumps***

Courtesy of Spectra Premium, Inc. - www.spectrapremium.com

Fuel Lines

Fuel lines (***Figure 11.3***), made of steel or rubber, carry fuel to the carburetor or fuel injectors.

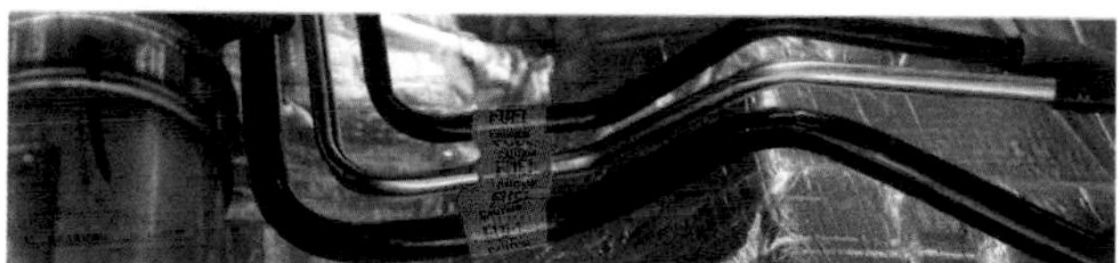

Figure 11.3 ***Fuel Lines***

Fuel Filter

The fuel filter (***Figure 11.4***), located between the fuel tank and the injection system, cleans the fuel entering the engine. Fuel filters contain a paper type element to collect contaminants. A clogged fuel filter slows fuel delivery, lowers engine performance, and causes excessive fuel pump wear. ***Note: Late model vehicles may have a non-serviceable fuel filter as part of the fuel pump module assembly. Warning: Complete fuel system services in a well-ventilated area. Allow engine to cool, wear goggles, disposable gloves, and follow the manufacturer's procedure to safely relieve fuel pressure.***

Figure 11.4 ***Fuel Filter***

Fuel Injectors

Vehicles today use fuel injectors to mix fuel with air. Fuel injection has evolved over time.

Throttle Body Injection (TBI). TBI systems replaced carburetors. In a TBI system (***Figure 11.5***), a fuel injector is placed above the throttle body, supplying fuel to all the cylinders.

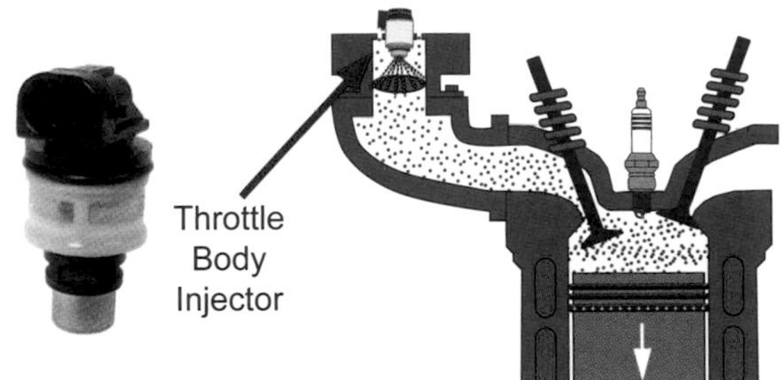

Figure 11.5 ***Throttle Body Injection System***

Port Fuel Injection (PFI). TBI systems were eventually replaced by PFI. In a PFI system (***Figure 11.6***), there is a fuel injector located near the intake port (before the intake valve) for each cylinder. PFI systems achieve greater precision over TBI systems by delivering equal amounts of fuel to each cylinder.

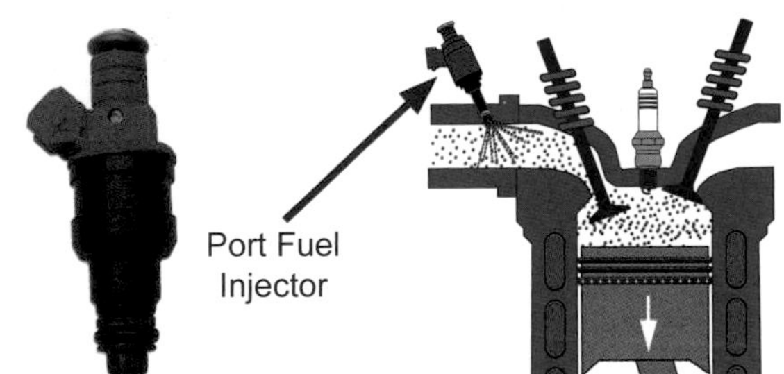

Figure 11.6 ***Port Fuel Injection System***

Gasoline Direct Injection (GDI). Today, GDI is gaining popularity. In a GDI system (***Figure 11.7***), each cylinder has a fuel injector that sprays a high-pressure fuel mist directly into the combustion chamber. GDI systems will be discussed in more detail later in this chapter.

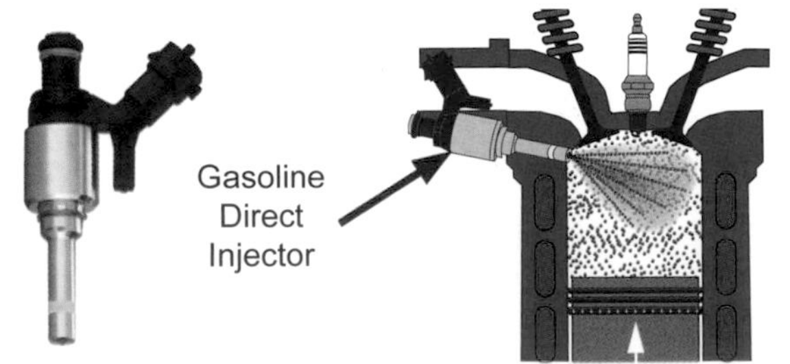

Figure 11.7 ***Gasoline Direct Injection System***

PCV Valve

The positive crankcase ventilation (PCV) valve (***Figure 11.8***) redirects blow-by, the unburned air-fuel mixture that is forced past the piston rings into the crankcase during combustion, back to the combustion chamber. Reducing this unwanted crankcase pressure lowers crankcase emissions, decreases oil contamination, and increases fuel economy.

Figure 11.8 ***PCV Valve***

Air Filter

An air filter (***Figure 11.9***) cleans dirt and dust from air that is drawn into the engine. A large volume of air is drawn into the engine when fuel is burned. A dirty air filter can reduce engine performance and can cause premature failure to vital engine components (e.g., bearings, valves, and piston rings).

Figure 11.9 ***Air Filter***

Trouble Guide

Engine Lacks Power (sluggish)

- Clogged fuel filter
- Impurities in fuel
- Fuel octane too low

Price Guides

Air Filter

- $5.00 to $35.00 each

Fuel Injector

- $25.00 to $100.00 each

PCV Valve

- $5.00 to $25.00 each

Air Filter Replacement. The following is a general procedure for replacing an air filter (***Figure 11.10***).

Air Filter Replacement

STEP 1	Locate the air filter housing by looking for the cold air intake system on your engine.

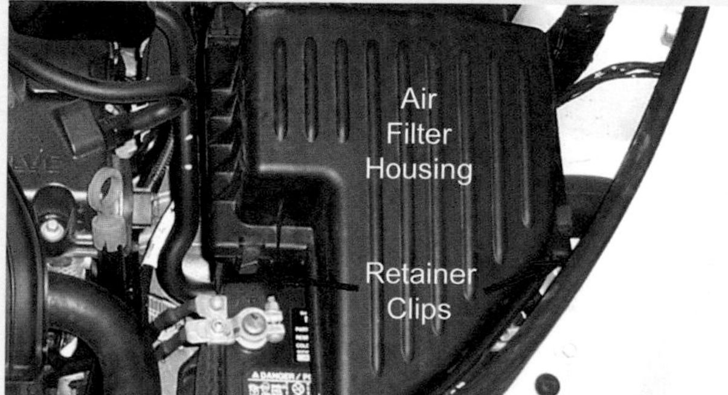

Figure 11.10a ***Locate Air Filter Housing***

STEP 2	Identify how the air filter housing cover secures the air filter. This is usually done by retainer clips or screws. Remove air intake hoses if necessary.

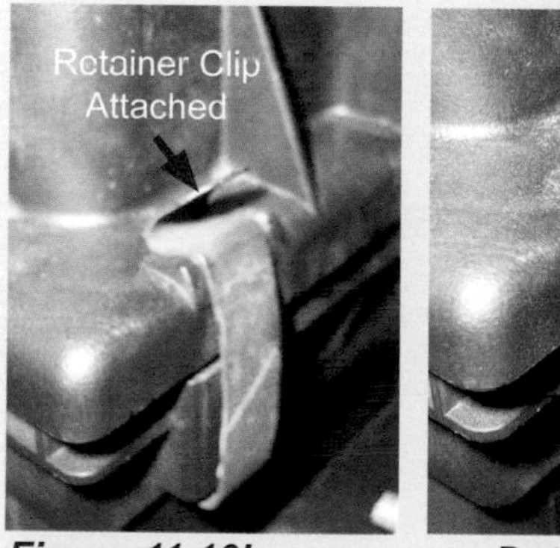

Figure 11.10b ***Detach Retainer Clips***

STEP 3	Remove the air filter housing cover and dirty air filter.

Figure 11.10c ***Remove Air Filter***

STEP 4	Use a vacuum to clean any dirt or debris from the air filter housing.
STEP 5	Install the new air filter and reassemble by reversing the procedure.

Figure 11.10 ***Changing an Air Filter***

Throttle Valve

The throttle valve, sometimes referred to as the butterfly valve, controls the airflow into the engine. The change in airflow increases or decreases engine power. More air and fuel equals more power. Less air and fuel equals less power.

Mechanical Throttle Controls. Some throttle valves are controlled by mechanical linkages, such as a cable that is connected to the accelerator pedal.

Electronic Throttle Controls. Many new vehicles use electronic throttle controls (ETC) to operate the throttle valve. This technology is often called drive-by-wire or throttle-by-wire. A sensor on the accelerator pedal sends information to the powertrain control module (PCM), which processes the request and sends the information to a motor on the throttle valve (***Figure 11.11***).

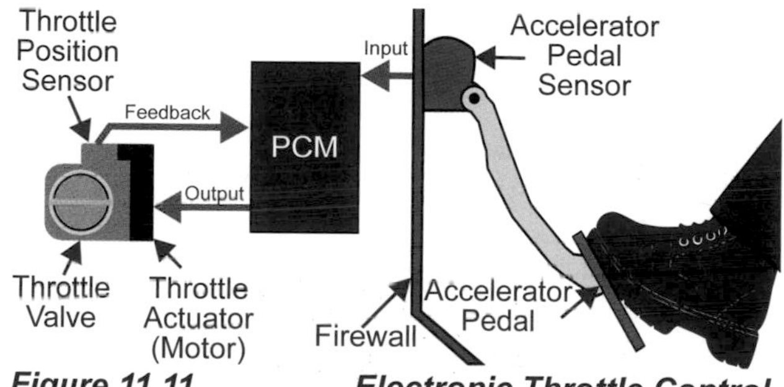

Figure 11.11 ***Electronic Throttle Control***

Powertrain Control Module

The powertrain control module (PCM) processes information from a variety of sensors to control the amount of fuel being injected, resulting in higher fuel economy and lower emissions.

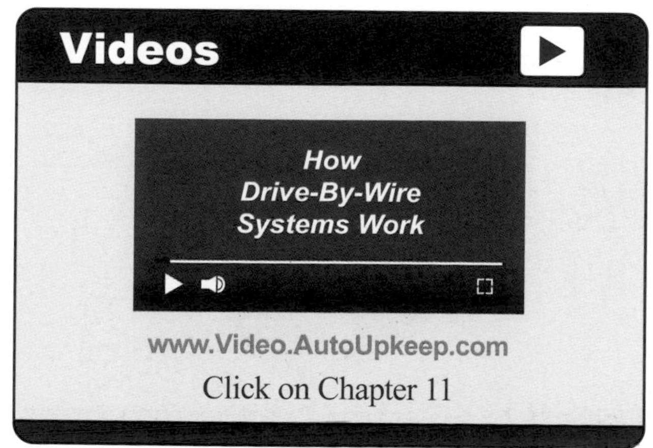

Sensors and Controls

Sensors and controls are used to measure the amount of air flowing into the engine, pressurize the fuel to the injectors, and maintain idle speed.

Manifold Absolute Pressure Sensor. Some engines use a manifold absolute pressure (MAP) sensor (***Figure 11.12***) to control fuel delivery. It converts engine vacuum/manifold pressure data to an electrical signal. The difference between the outside (atmospheric) pressure and the intake manifold pressure is defined as engine vacuum. That is why the term "absolute" is used in the name. It measures the absolute difference between atmospheric pressure and intake manifold pressure. This electrical signal tells the PCM how much of a load is on the engine, adjusting fuel delivery and timing as necessary. During acceleration (throttle open), engine vacuum is reduced - making it harder for fuel to enter the system, requiring a higher fuel pressure. During deceleration (throttle closes), engine vacuum is increased - making it easier for fuel to enter the system, requiring a lower fuel pressure.

Figure 11.12 Manifold Absolute Pressure Sensor
Courtesy of Spectra Premium, Inc. - www.spectrapremium.com

Mass Airflow Sensor. The mass airflow (MAF) sensor (***Figure 11.13***) is located in the cold air intake system. The MAF measures the volume (quantity) and mass (density) of air entering the engine. The MAF sends an electrical signal to the PCM to control fuel flow through the fuel injectors.

Figure 11.13 ***Mass Airflow Sensor***
Courtesy of Spectra Premium, Inc. - www.spectrapremium.com

Idle Speed Control. An idle air control (IAC) valve (***Figure 11.14***) or an idle speed control (ISC) motor is used to control idle speed. To maintain idle, it uses information from the PCM to adjust airflow past the throttle. Allowing more air to bypass the throttle increases idle speed. Allowing less air to bypass the throttle decreases idle speed. Vehicles with electronic throttle controls do this automatically using information from the PCM, as a result they don't need a separate speed control mechanism.

Figure 11.14 ***Idle Air Control Valve***
Photo: Bosch

Throttle Position Sensor. A throttle position sensor (***Figure 11.15***) is used to track the position of the throttle. It sends data to the PCM by monitoring how far the throttle is open or closed.

Figure 11.15 ***Throttle Position Sensor***
Photo: Bosch

Fuel Pressure Regulator. A fuel pressure regulator (***Figure 11.16***) is used to control the fuel system's pressure into the fuel injectors.

Figure 11.16 ***Fuel Pressure Regulator***
Photo: Bosch

Temperature Sensors. An engine coolant temperature (ECT) sensor monitors the temperature of the engine. An intake air temperature (IAT) sensor or a manifold air temperature (MAT) sensor measures the air temperature entering the engine. These sensors report data back to the PCM. This data is used to adjust the air-fuel mixture.

Technological Advancements

Automobiles are not very energy efficient. Losses occur in the engine, drivetrain, aerodynamics, rolling resistance, and braking. Technological advancements can increase efficiency and performance. This section focuses on:

- Gasoline Direct Injection
- Turbocharging
- Cylinder Deactivation

Gasoline Direct Injection (GDI)

Gasoline Direct Injection (GDI) is becoming the preferred fuel delivery method to maximize every drop of fuel. In a traditional engine, fuel and air mix together and then enter the combustion chamber through the intake valves. In a GDI engine, high-pressure fuel injectors deliver a fine mist of fuel directly into the combustion chamber (***Figure 11.17***). The fuel can enter the combustion chamber during the intake stroke (homogeneous charge) and/or during the compression stroke (stratified charge) depending on the engine load requirement. GDI engines burn leaner, have higher compression ratios, and increased power output. By eliminating wasted fuel on the intake manifold walls and by maximizing the energy of the fuel used in combustion, GDI engines decrease emissions (up to 15%) and increase fuel economy (up to 20%).

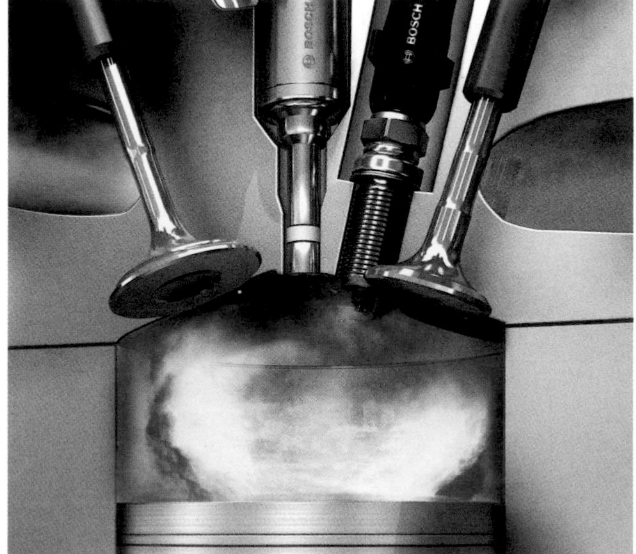

Figure 11.17 ***GDI Combustion Chamber***
Photo: Bosch

Turbocharging

A technology combination that is becoming popular in gasoline engines is GDI coupled with turbocharging. A turbocharger is a turbine and compressor (an air pump) attached to the exhaust system. The hot high velocity exhaust gases turn the turbine blades (***Figure 11.18***). The turbocharger's compressor uses this wasted energy of the exhaust system to pressurize the incoming air. When the air is forced and compressed into the combustion chamber, it provides more air for combustion. This process is called forced induction. When an engine does not have forced induction, it is called a naturally aspirated engine. With more air, more fuel can be used to provide a "boost" of power when needed. A smaller GDI turbo engine can replace a larger traditional engine without sacrificing performance.

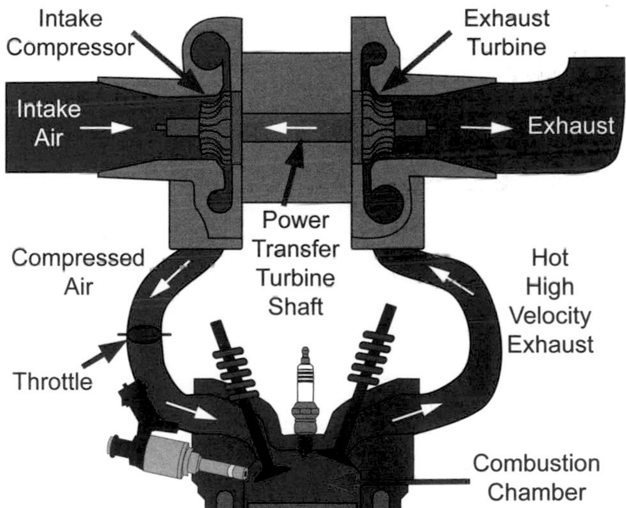

Figure 11.18 ***Turbocharger on GDI System***

Cylinder Deactivation

Cylinder deactivation (also known as displacement on demand, variable displacement, multiple displacement system, or active fuel management) uses engine control systems to shut off the air-fuel mixture to some of the engine's cylinders when they are not needed. For example, cruising at highway speeds takes less horsepower and torque than accelerating. When additional power is not needed, the intake and exhaust valves on half the engine's cylinders close. When the valves are closed, fuel is not being burned in those cylinders.

Petroleum Refining Process

Gasoline and diesel, like various other products (e.g., cosmetics, paints, nylon, and asphalt), come from crude oil (***Figure 11.19***). Crude oil is a nonrenewable energy resource. Crude oil goes through a series of processes before it is ready for your engine. This section focuses on:

- Separation
- Conversion
- Treatment
- Formulating or Blending

Separation

During the separation process (also called fractionation or distillation), crude oil is heated in a distillation column to separate various hydrocarbon compounds. Vapors rise in the distillation column. They are divided by their boiling points. These are called fractions.

Conversion

Next the fractions go through a conversion process. The hydrocarbon molecules are cracked, combined, or rearranged. Cracking is a process that changes the size and/or structure of the molecules. This conversion creates hydrocarbon streams, which are intermediate compounds.

Treatment

In the treatment stage, impurities and contaminants are removed from the streams.

Formulating or Blending

In the formulating or blending stage, different streams and additives can be combined to produce a finished product such as 87 octane gasoline for a particular fuel brand.

Gasoline Properties

Gasoline is a mixture of hydrocarbons (hydrogen and carbon) and is primarily used in internal combustion engines to propel most of today's automobiles. Gasoline engines are considered spark ignition engines. The fuel needs to be ignited to burn in the engine. This section focuses on:

- Octane
- Knocking
- Additives
- Oxygenates

Q & A ?

Octane and High Compression

Q: If the owner's manual says to use 91 octane fuel, can I use a lower octane fuel?

A: Some cars have high compression engines, requiring a mid-grade or premium fuel. The higher the octane number, the more the fuel resists "knocking" or "pinging" from premature ignition. Use the octane rating that the manufacturer suggests.

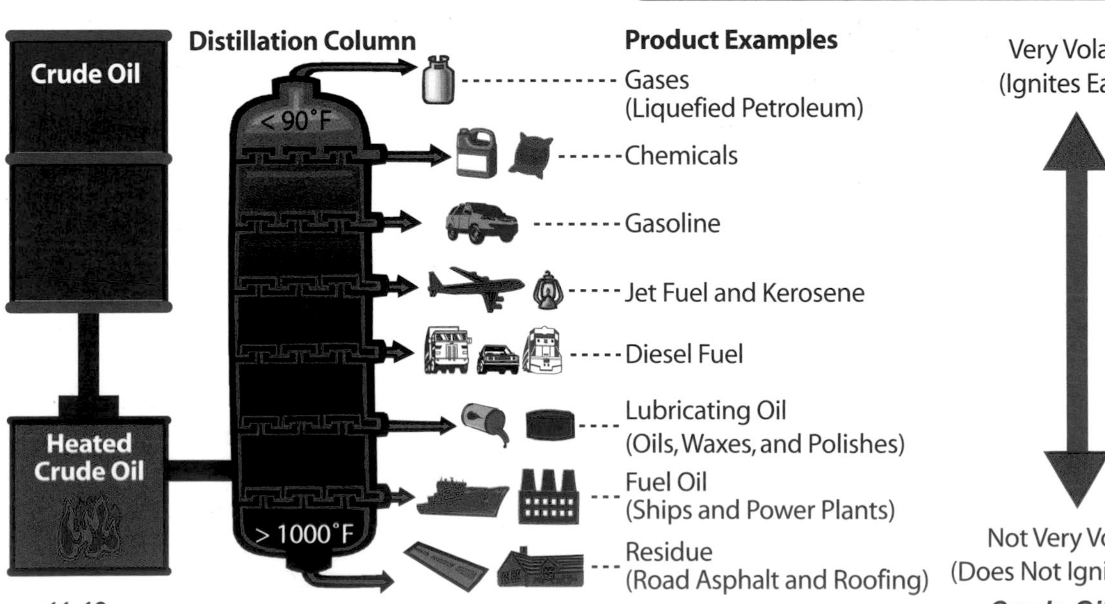

Figure 11.19 *Crude Oil Distillation*

Octane

Gas pumps are commonly labeled *regular*, *mid-grade*, or *premium*, which for the most part relates to the octane rating. Octane is defined as a resistance to detonate. The higher the octane number, the more the fuel resists detonation under pressure. The more the fuel resists detonation, the more complete the combustion is when the fuel ignites. Usually higher compression engines need higher octane fuels. Common octane numbers are regular 87, mid-grade (or plus) 89, and premium 93 (***Figure 11.20***). The octane requirement depends on the engine design, the altitude the vehicle is driven, and driving habits. Most automobiles require a minimum of 87 octane, but always check the owner's manual.

Figure 11.20 ***Common Octane Ratings***

Knocking

A knocking sound is created when fuel ignites prematurely. Anti-knock characteristics relate directly to octane ratings. The higher the octane rating the more the fuel resists knocking. It takes a higher temperature and more compression to ignite a fuel with a higher octane. Modern engines use knock sensors (KS), also known as detonation sensors, to identify when slight knocking begins to occur. When a sensor detects knocking (through engine vibrations), a signal is sent to the computer to retard the spark ignition timing until the knock is eliminated. This improves performance, reduces emissions, and avoids engine damage. Even though a knock isn't audible to the ear, it may be occurring.

Additives

Rust inhibitors are added to help metals resist rusting. Detergents are added to clean the fuel system. Different brands of fuel contain different additive packages.

Premier Additive Packages. High quality gasoline brands usually contain premier additive packages, including enhanced detergents. These detergents reduce deposits inside the engine, keeping the intake valves, combustion chamber, and fuel injectors clean.

Fuel System Cleaners. Running low quality gasoline can cause carbon deposits to form inside the fuel system. Some repair facilities offer fuel system cleaning services. You can also purchase aftermarket fuel system cleaners that you add to your gas tank to clean the fuel injectors and intake valves. These are designed to help restore engine performance.

Oxygenates

Oxygenates increase the octane rating in gasoline. Oxygenates include methyl tertiary butyl ether (MTBE), ethyl tertiary butyl ether (ETBE), tertiary amyl methyl ether (TAME), and ethanol. Gasoline burns cleaner when oxygenates are added, resulting in lower tailpipe emissions. Up until the late 1970s and early 1980s, tetraethyl lead was primarily used to increase octane levels. However, lead is toxic and shortened the life of catalytic converters by destroying the catalyst inside. After lead was phased out MTBE was primarily used, but it has also been banned in many places. MTBE has been found to contaminate drinking water from leaking gasoline storage tanks. Now ethanol use has significantly increased to replace MTBE. Ethanol is a grain alcohol, commonly made from corn or other starch-rich grains.

Gasohol. Gasoline commonly contains up to 10% ethanol (***Figure 11.21***). When gasoline and ethanol are mixed, it is called gasohol. Gasohol burns cleaner, emitting less air pollutants and greenhouse gases than 100% gasoline.

Figure 11.21 ***Ethanol Blended Fuel***

Diesel Properties

Diesel fuel is not only used in semi-tractors and heavy equipment, it is also used in many diesel cars and light trucks. Diesel fuel actually has more energy per volume than gasoline. This section focuses on:

- Cetane Number
- Diesel Grades
- Cloud Point
- CFPP
- Diesel Fuel Maintenance
- Ultra-Low Sulfur Diesel

Cetane Number

The cetane number relates to how well fuel ignites. This is different from gasoline octane ratings. The higher the octane number, the more the fuel resists detonation under pressure (***Figure 11.22***). Diesel fuels have a short time delay in the cylinder before igniting. As discussed in Chapter 1, diesel engines are compression ignition engines. Diesel is ignited by heat and pressure in the combustion chamber. When compared to lower cetane number fuels, diesel fuels with a higher cetane number have a shorter time delay from when the diesel is injected into the combustion chamber to the point when it ignites. Cetane numbers of 40 to 50 are the most common.

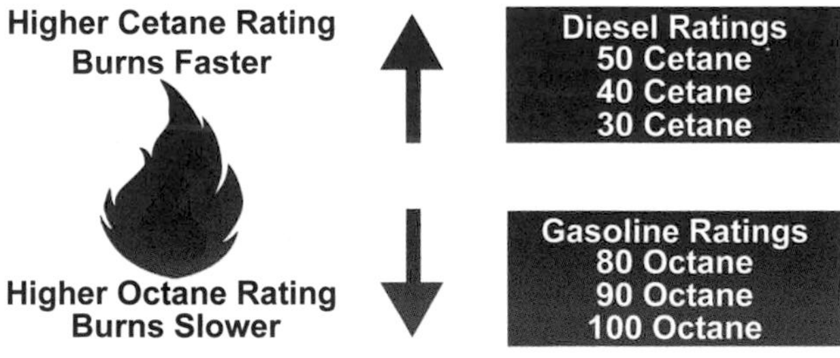

Figure 11.22 ***Octane vs. Cetane Comparison***

Diesel Grades

Two types of diesel fuels are used in cars and trucks: No. 1 and No. 2 (***Figure 11.23***). The American Society for Testing and Materials (ASTM) classifies these two grades. In the distillation process, No. 1 diesel fuel has a lower boiling point than No. 2 and thus vaporizes easier than No. 2. Therefore, No. 1 diesel fuel is commonly used when the outside ambient temperature is abnormally low. In cold climates many gas stations commonly provide No. 1 in the extreme winter, a mixture of No. 1 and No. 2 in the fall and spring, and No. 2 in the summer.

Figure 11.23 ***Diesel #2 Fuel Label***

Cloud Point

A natural substance found in diesel fuel is paraffin (wax). Paraffin can form wax crystals at cold temperatures. The temperature that this occurs is called the cloud point. The fuel will actually look cloudy once it has reached the cloud point. These wax crystals can clog a fuel filter.

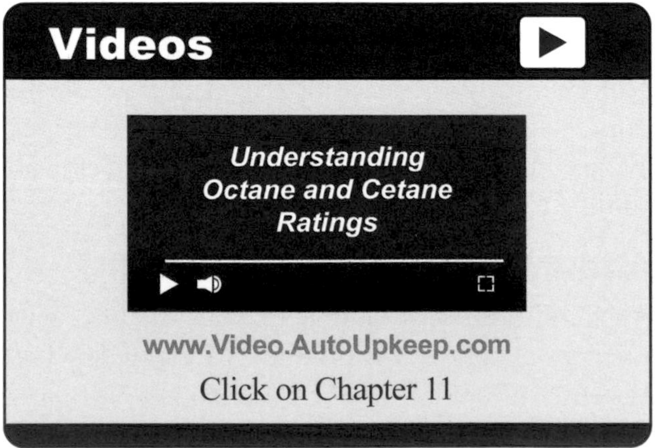

Cold Filter Plugging Point (CFPP)

The cold filter plugging point (CFPP) is the temperature that the fuel has reached where it will begin to clog the filter (***Figure 11.24***). When biodiesel is blended with conventional petroleum diesel above 5%, it will have a higher CFPP. Less than 5% blend has very little change on the CFPP.

Diesel Grade	Cold Filter Plugging Point
No. 1	-40 to -60 degrees F
No. 2	6 to 14 degrees F

Figure 11.24 *Cold Filter Plugging Point*

Anti-Gel Additives. No. 2 diesel fuel has a tendency to "gel" in cold climates. Anti-gel additives (***Figure 11.25***) lower the CFPP of the fuel. Wax dispersants are used to help prevent them from crystallizing (gelling).

Figure 11.25 *Anti-Gel Additives*

Diesel Fuel Maintenance

Removing water from diesel fuel is critical. Diesel fuel absorbs moisture from the air. It can hold some water in a solution, but at cooler temperatures it can hold less. The key is to keep the water in diesel within acceptable limits.

Saturation Point. When diesel fuel becomes saturated beyond its holding point, water settles in the tank. Water can also accumulate in storage tanks from condensation. Water in diesel fuel leads to rust and microbe (bacteria and fungi) problems, which can corrode parts and clog up filters. Water entering the engine can lead to fuel injection and engine problems.

Fuel Filters and Water Separators. Diesel vehicles have water separators (also called diesel fuel conditioning modules) and fuel filters. Water separators allow you to drain collected water. A warning light or message will inform you when you need to drain water from the system (***Figure 11.26***). Follow your owner's manual for service intervals.

Figure 11.26 *Water in Fuel Warning*

Ultra-Low Sulfur Diesel (ULSD)

Under Environmental Protection Agency (EPA) requirements, in 2006 there was a significant reduction of sulfur in diesel fuel. Burning sulfur contributes to air pollution. One of the greatest contributors to particulate matter (soot) emissions is the sulfur content in diesel. Ultra-low sulfur diesel (ULSD) contains a maximum of 15 parts-per-million (ppm) of sulfur, as compared to low sulfur diesel that allows up to 500 ppm of sulfur. Model year 2007 and later diesel engines require ULSD (***Figure 11.27***). These engines are designed with advanced emission systems to burn cleaner and pollute less. Fueling with higher sulfur diesel will damage a vehicle's more advanced catalysts and filters, voiding the engine warranty. ULSD is compatible with pre-2007 model vehicles. The disadvantage is that older diesel engines do not have the advanced emission systems to take full advantage of polluting less.

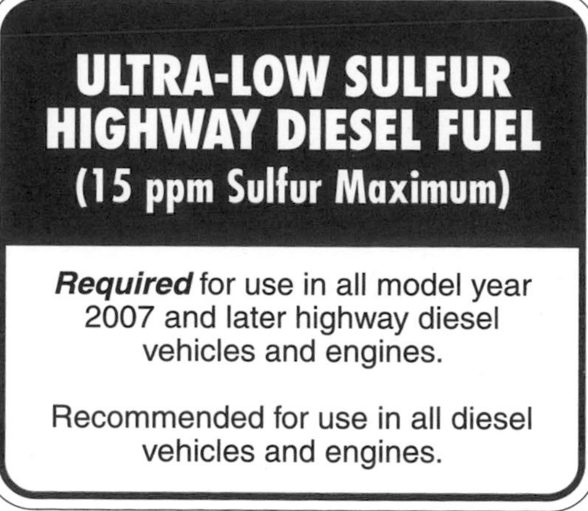

Figure 11.27 *ULSD Pump Sticker*

Refueling

Before refueling your automobile, check the owner's manual to be sure you put in the correct type and grade of fuel. Most automotive gasoline engines are designed to run on unleaded gasoline with an octane number of 87 or greater. Some high performance or high compression engines may require a higher octane fuel. The following is a general procedure to refilling a fuel tank (*Figure 11.28*).

Refueling	
STEP 1	As you arrive at the filling station, make sure you drive up to the fuel pump dispenser with the vehicle's fuel fill door lined up with the pump. ***Note: Commonly a directional triangle by the fuel gauge points to the fuel fill door side.***
STEP 2	Shut off the engine and engage the parking brake. ***Warning: Do not smoke.***
STEP 3	Open the fuel fill door. Some vehicles have a release button for the fuel fill door near the driver's seat.
STEP 4	Remove the fuel (gas) cap slowly. You may hear a hissing sound caused by the pressure in the tank equalizing with the outside pressure. Most fuel fill doors have a place to attach the fuel cap.

STEP 5	Read and follow the instructions on the fuel pump dispenser.
STEP 6	Do not overfill or "top off" the tank. Once the pump nozzle automatically shuts off, stop refueling. Fuel needs room to expand and overfilling can cause emission system problems in the vapor recovery system.
STEP 7	Before removing the gas pump nozzle, be sure all the fuel drips out of the nozzle's end. Spilled fuel contributes to air and ground pollution.
STEP 8	Hang up the nozzle on the pump.
STEP 9	Replace the fuel cap. Most manufacturers require the cap to be tightened until 1-3 clicks are heard. Check the owner's manual. If the cap is not tightened correctly, a malfunction indicator light (e.g., check fuel cap or check engine) may illuminate. Close the fuel fill door.

Figure 11.28 ***Refueling***

Fuel Prices

Fuel prices became a major concern in the 1970s, and have gained attention again as the price of crude oil fluctuates. Fuel prices (*Figure 11.29*) are influenced by taxes, marketing costs, distribution costs, geographical region, refinery productivity, supply, demand, crude oil prices, markup (i.e., profits), investor speculation of future prices, and world events. Every year more and more vehicles are put on the highways, increasing the demand for fuel. If the supply of fuel decreases and fuel demand increases, prices rise. If new oil reserves are found and technological advancements make vehicles more efficient, the supply may increase. This can cause the price to decrease.

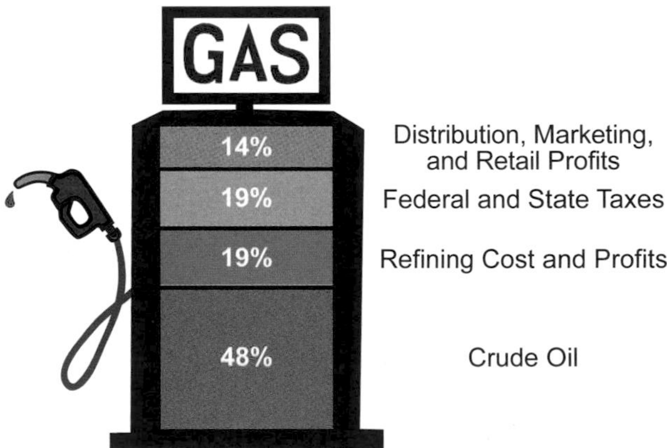

Figure 11.29 ***U.S. Gasoline Price Breakdown***

Q & A ?

Gasoline vs. Diesel Engine

Q: What are the main differences between diesel engines and gasoline engines?

A: Diesels (compression ignition engines) do not have spark plugs to ignite the fuel. Gasoline engines (spark ignition engines) usually produce higher horsepower, but diesels turn out more torque (crucial for pulling). Diesel engines are more fuel efficient and have a longer life, but tend to initially cost significantly more. Gasoline engines start better in extremely cold weather.

Fuel Saving Tips

There are many ways you can improve fuel economy (***Figure 11.30***) and reduce the amount of money you spend at the pump. For additional fuel saving tips go to www.fueleconomy.gov.

Improving Fuel Economy	
Checking Tire Pressure	Low tire pressure causes more frictional resistance, reducing fuel economy and increasing tire wear. Incorrect pressure can also increase the chance of a blowout.
Tuning-up the Engine	A properly tuned engine (replacing ignition components such as spark plugs) can improve your fuel mileage 4% on average.
Checking the Wheel Alignment	If the wheels are not contacting the road surface properly, fuel mileage will decrease due to increased friction.
Changing the Oil as Required	Clean engine oil has better cooling, cleaning, lubricating, and sealing properties, allowing an engine to run more efficiently. Use the recommended grade of oil for optimal efficiency.
Limiting A/C Usage	Running extra accessories puts more load on the engine, requiring more fuel. Use the air conditioner only when necessary.
Eliminating Brake Drag	If the brakes are dragging or rubbing, they cause more frictional resistance, reducing fuel economy. Avoid resting your foot on the brake pedal.
Avoiding Excessive Idling	Shut off your car if you plan to sit for an extended period of time. An engine idling for an hour can burn three gallons (11.36 L) of gasoline, creating unnecessary pollution. Vehicles with start-stop technology save fuel by shutting down at stops.
Combining Trips	Short trips increase engine wear and cause lower fuel economy because the engine does not reach an optimal operating temperature. Combining errands will also put fewer miles on your vehicle.
Moderating Speed	It is important to avoid abrupt acceleration and deceleration. "Stop and go" traffic reduces fuel economy. Using cruise control on the highway to keep your speed constant and putting the transmission in overdrive will increase fuel economy.
Checking the Cooling System	Running an engine too cool can lower fuel economy. The correct thermostat and maintenance will ensure proper operation.
Removing Weight and Accessories	Removing excess items will increase fuel economy. Every 100 lbs (45.36 kg) carried in your car decreases fuel economy by 1-2%. Also remove any accessories (e.g., ski racks) that decrease the aerodynamics of your vehicle.

Figure 11.30 ***Fuel Saving Tips***

Web Links

Energy Related Sites

U.S. Energy Information Administration
www.eia.gov

U.S. DOE - Fuel Economy Website
www.fueleconomy.gov

Summary

The purpose of the fuel system is to store, transfer, and then mix the fuel with air. Gasoline engines are spark ignition engines. Diesel engines are compression ignition engines. Various parts of the fuel system work together to supply clean fuel and air to the engine. Technological advancements like GDI and turbocharging are making it possible to build smaller engines that use less fuel and lower emissions, without compromising performance or torque. Fuel economy can also be increased through tune-ups, correct tire pressure, regular oil changes, and moderating your driving habits.

Activities

Fuel System

- Fuel System Part Identification Activity
- Fuel System Maintenance Activity
- Chapter 11 Study Questions

Activities and Study Questions can be completed in the *Auto Upkeep Workbook*.

Career Paths

Petroleum Engineer

Education: Bachelor's Degree in Engineering
Median Income: $129,990
Abilities: Strong science, math, analytical, and problem solving skills in technical areas.
Find your career at www.bls.gov/ooh.

Cooling System and Climate Control

Fuel for Thought

- What is the purpose of the cooling system?
- How does coolant circulate in an engine?
- How is heat transferred to the passenger compartment?

Introduction

Thousands of automobiles are stranded on the side of the road each year due to cooling system problems. Precautions can be taken to avoid this, including paying attention to the temperature gauge (***Figure 12.1***). Engine coolant carries away excess heat from the engine. Too much heat can destroy an engine, while an engine that is not at the proper operating temperature will run inefficiently. This chapter will identify and describe the importance of the cooling system, cooling system components, and passenger cabin climate control (also known as heating, ventilation and air conditioning or HVAC).

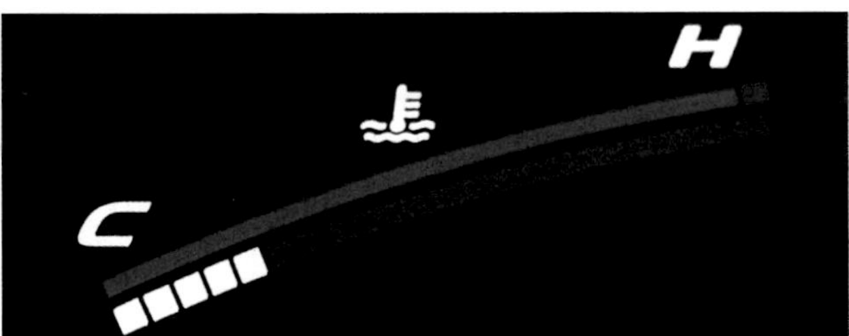

Figure 12.1 ***Temperature Gauge***

Videos

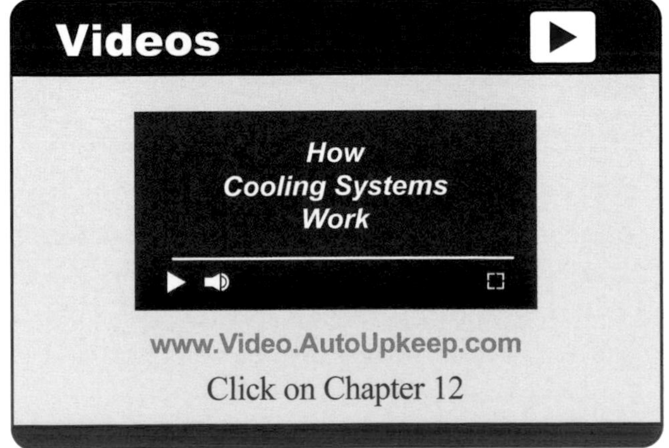

www.Video.AutoUpkeep.com

Click on Chapter 12

Objectives

Upon completion of this chapter and activities, you will be able to:

- Identify the purpose of the cooling system.
- Describe the cooling system's components.
- Define coolant properties.
- Explain how coolant flows in an engine.
- Describe how charge-air coolers work.
- Identify how active warm-up works.
- Test and service the cooling system.
- Change a passenger cabin air filter.

Tech Tip 

Coolant Temperature Light

The coolant temperature warning light comes on when your engine has reached a potentially damaging temperature. Do not ignore the warning.

Overheating an engine can warp and crack cylinder heads, overheat the engine oil, and cause excessive stress on engine components. If the temperature light stays on (or the gauge is in the HOT range), pull over to the side of the road and let the engine cool. Once the engine is completely cool, check the coolant level in the coolant recovery tank and the radiator.

Cooling System Purpose

The cooling system is designed to do four things:

- Reach Operating Temperature Quickly
- Maintain Operating Temperature
- Remove Excess Engine Heat
- Provide Passenger Comfort

Reach Operating Temperature Quickly

Fuel is wasted every second the engine runs below the most efficient operating temperature. The powertrain control module (PCM) communicates with the temperature sensor and regulates the other systems based on the coolant temperature. An engine running at the proper temperature will run cleaner (pollute less), smoother, and more efficient than an engine running too cool or too hot.

Maintain Operating Temperature

On today's computer controlled vehicles it is vital to maintain an efficient operating temperature. Too low of a temperature will cause the computer to run the vehicle with a rich air-fuel mixture. Excessively high temperatures can warp metal and crack gaskets, leading to major engine damage. Most vehicles run coolant at a temperature of around 195ºF (91ºC). Coolant temperature is controlled by a thermostat, which will be presented later in this chapter.

Remove Excess Engine Heat

Metal around the combustion chamber (where the fuel is ignited) can reach extremely high temperatures. Coolant circulates throughout the engine. To remove excess heat, coolant is transferred to the radiator where the movement of air dissipates the heat. A radiator fan is placed behind the radiator to draw air through the radiator fins.

Provide Passenger Comfort

Heat is transferred from engine coolant through the heater core to warm the passenger cabin.

Cooling System Components

This section focuses on:

- Radiator
- Radiator Cap
- Coolant Recovery Tank
- Thermostat
- Radiator Fan
- Coolant Temperature Sensor
- Radiator and Heater Hoses
- Clamps
- Water Pump
- Drive Belts
- Gaskets and Seals
- Heater Core

Radiator

The purpose of the radiator (***Figure 12.2***) is to remove heat from the coolant. When the temperature of the coolant reaches the opening rating of the thermostat, hot coolant enters the radiator by the upper radiator hose. The coolant runs down through various tubes. Air is drawn around the radiator tubes by a fan and by the motion of the vehicle. The flow of air cools the coolant in the radiator tubes so it can be returned to the engine.

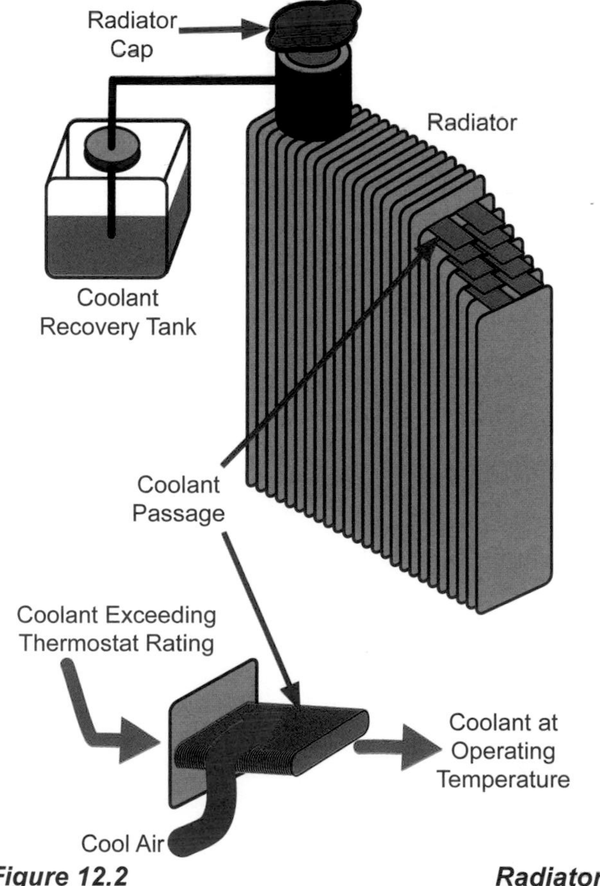

Figure 12.2 ***Radiator***

Radiator Cap

The radiator cap (***Figure 12.3***) is designed to maintain a constant pressure in the cooling system. The radiator cap allows expanding coolant to go to the coolant recovery tank. When the fluid has cooled, coolant is drawn back into the radiator through a vacuum valve in the cap. ***Note: Some vehicles do not have a radiator cap, only a cap on the coolant recovery tank.***

Figure 12.3 ***Radiator Cap***

Radiator Cap Pressure Rating. Most pressure caps are rated between 8 to 16 psi (55 to 110 kPa or 0.55 to 1.1 bar). Increasing pressure on the cooling system increases the boiling point of the coolant.

Overheating. Vehicles can overheat from climbing steep grades, idling for long periods of time, towing a trailer, or carrying heavy loads. Driving a vehicle with an overheated engine can cause serious damage and could even lead to a fire. If your vehicle is overheating first determine if there is steam or no steam coming from the engine compartment (***Figure 12.4***). Some vehicles will display a message in the driver information center. The message might say, "Engine Overheated Stop Engine" or "Engine Overheated Idle Engine".

Q & A

Radiator Hose Collapse

Q: Why would a radiator hose collapse?

A: The small vacuum valve in the radiator cap may not be working properly to maintain a constant pressure. As the antifreeze mixture begins to cool after engine shutdown, a vacuum is created. If the cap doesn't equalize this pressure, a radiator hose can collapse.

Warning: Never open the hood if steam is present, it can burn you. Never open a hot radiator cap, severe burns could result. Keep away from moving parts in the engine compartment.

Overheating - Engine Compartment Steam		
	YES - Steam	NO - Steam
STEP 1	Safely pull over. Turn on the hazard lights. Shut off the engine and get away from the vehicle.	Follow the manufacturer's instructions on whether to idle or shut off the engine. Turn off the air conditioning and accessories.
STEP 2	Continuing to drive the vehicle when it is overheated could cause a fire. Allow the engine to cool down completely.	Open the windows and turn on the heater to high. Running coolant through the heater core may help cool the engine down.
STEP 3	Only open the hood when no steam is present. Steam can cause severe burns.	If the engine continues to overheat, safely pull over. Turn on the hazard lights. Open the hood. Keep away from moving parts. If the vehicle has an electric fan, visually check or listen to see if it is running. If it isn't on, shut off the engine.
STEP 4	Once the engine has cooled completely, inspect the radiator hoses and radiator for leaks. Check the coolant level. Add the proper mixture if necessary. If leaks are found, call for roadside assistance.	
STEP 5	If there are no leaks and the coolant level has been corrected, restart the engine and monitor the temperature gauge. If it stays in the normal range you can resume driving.	
Note: Always follow your owner's manual.		

Figure 12.4 ***Steps for Engine Overheating***

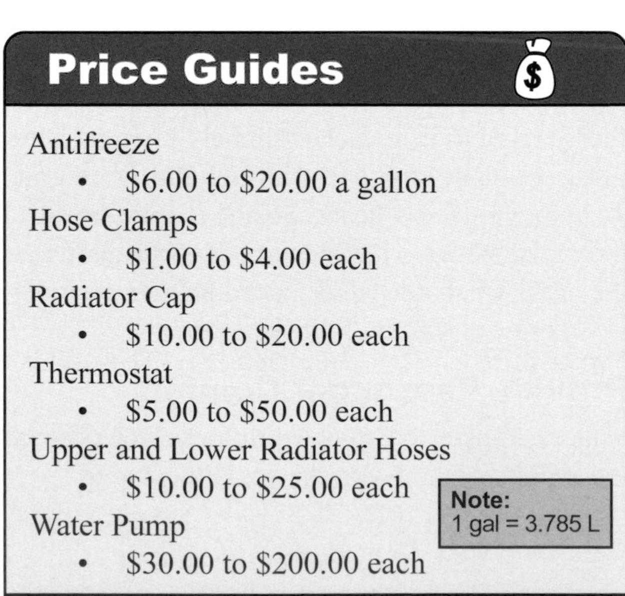

Price Guides

Antifreeze
- $6.00 to $20.00 a gallon

Hose Clamps
- $1.00 to $4.00 each

Radiator Cap
- $10.00 to $20.00 each

Thermostat
- $5.00 to $50.00 each

Upper and Lower Radiator Hoses
- $10.00 to $25.00 each

Water Pump
- $30.00 to $200.00 each

Note: 1 gal = 3.785 L

Coolant Recovery Tank

The coolant recovery tank (also called the expansion bottle, surge tank, reservoir, or reserve tank) (***Figure 12.5***) holds excess coolant during the cooling system operation. As pressure and heat build up, the coolant expands and is then transferred to the recovery tank. This prevents fluid being lost during cooling system operation, while keeping the maximum amount of coolant in the system at all times. A coolant recovery tank keeps outside air from being drawn into the engine block. Outside air may carry contaminants that can cause corrosion in the cooling system.

Figure 12.5 *Coolant Recovery Tank*

Thermostat

The thermostat is the brain of the cooling system. It senses the temperature of the coolant and allows fluid to exit from the engine to the radiator, controlling the temperature.

Conventional Thermostat. Conventional thermostats (***Figure 12.6***) are rated at a specified temperature – usually between 180-195ºF (82-91ºC). When an engine is cold, the thermostat is closed. Once the engine temperature reaches the thermostat rating, the thermostat opens.

Figure 12.6 *Conventional Thermostat*

Electrically Controlled Thermostat. Some vehicles use an electrically controlled thermostat (also called a map controlled thermostat). The powertrain control module (PCM) uses information to operate the thermostat according to different engine loads and temperature.

Radiator Fan

Radiator fans draw air through the radiator to cool the coolant. Fans are either mechanically or electrically driven.

Mechanical Fan. A mechanical fan is driven by a belt (***Figure 12.7***).

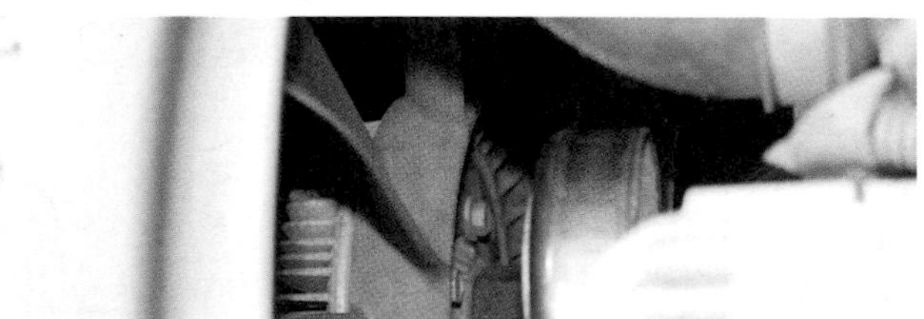

Figure 12.7 *Mechanical Radiator Fan*

Electrical Fan. An electrical fan is driven by an electric motor. Most newer vehicles use an electric fan (***Figure 12.8***) because it is more efficient and more suitable for front-wheel drive vehicles. ***Warning: Use caution when working near an electric fan. They can start without the engine running. Keep your fingers away from the fan area. If you need to work near an electric fan, disconnect your vehicle's negative battery cable.***

Figure 12.8 *Electric Radiator Fan*

Coolant Temperature Sensor

The engine coolant temperature (ECT) sensor (***Figure 12.9***) communicates with the powertrain control module (PCM). In the cooling system, the PCM uses this data to turn on or off the electric cooling fan. If your engine coolant is so low that it is not contacting the sensor, the gauge reading may not display that the engine is overheating. ***Note: Some older systems used a separate temperature sending unit (fan switch) to control the electric fan.***

Figure 12.9 *Coolant Temperature Sensor*
Photo: Bosch

Radiator and Heater Hoses

The upper and lower radiator hoses (***Figure 12.10***) connect the radiator to the engine. Cooled coolant is transferred from the radiator to the engine through the lower hose. Hot coolant is returned to the radiator by the upper hose. The upper hose connects to the water outlet that covers the thermostat. The lower hose connects to the water pump. ***Note: Some vehicles have a reverse-flow cooling system.*** Heater hoses are also used to transport heated coolant to the heater core that provides heat for the passenger cabin.

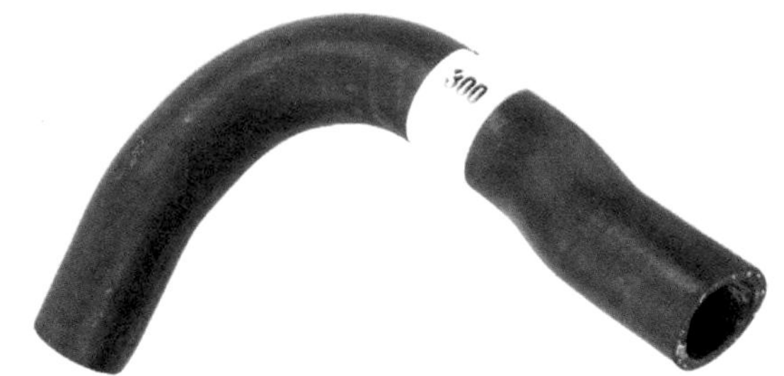

Figure 12.10 ***Radiator Hose***

Inspecting Hoses. Only inspect hoses when the engine is cold. First make sure the hose isn't kinked. A kinked hose reduces coolant flow. Next check the condition of the hoses. One cause of hose failure is called electrochemical degradation (ECD). ECD is caused by electrical reactions between engine metal and coolant. This electrical charge degrades the inside of the hose. Hoses can also become damaged from oil contamination, heat, abrasion (rubbing against something), and ozone. Look for swelling, rub marks, cracks, or excessively hard or soft hoses. In addition to the upper and lower radiator hose, also check the water pump bypass and heater hoses.

Servicing 

Radiator Hoses

- Inspect and change as recommended by the manufacturer

Clamps

A variety of clamps are used to attach radiator and heater hoses under the hood. Some clamps can be tightened with a screw. Tension band clamps use a tension band (***Figure 12.11***) and must be sized correctly to the hose. Use a pair of pliers to squeeze the clip ends together to remove a tension band clamp.

Figure 12.11 ***Tension Band Clamp***

Water Pump

The water pump (***Figure 12.12***), also called a coolant pump, is attached to the engine block. Its main purpose is to keep the coolant circulating. It draws cooled coolant in from the lower radiator hose and pushes it through the engine. An engine drive belt (V or serpentine), timing belt, electric motor, or gear rotates water pumps.

Figure 12.12 ***Water Pump***

Q & A 

Water Pump "Weep" Hole

Q: My car is dripping antifreeze around the water pump. What is the problem?

A: Water pumps have a built in "weep" hole. This hole is engineered in the water pump to signal the car owner when the internal seals have failed. When the water pump is leaking from this hole it is time for replacement.

Drive Belts

The crankshaft transfers the reciprocating (up and down or back and forth) motion of the pistons into a rotary (circular) motion that turns the crankshaft pulley with the drive belt. The drive belt then turns other pulleys (water pump, mechanical fan, power steering pump, alternator, and air conditioning compressor) (***Figure 12.13***). Worn or loose drive belts can cause slippage, leading to engine overheating.

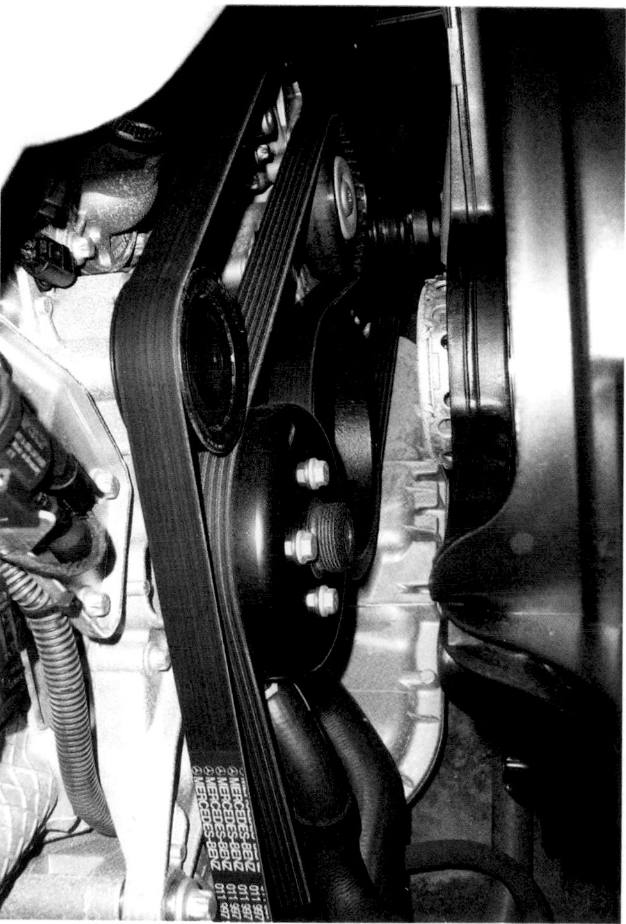

Figure 12.13 *Serpentine Drive Belt*

Gaskets and Seals

Gaskets and seals are placed in the joints of mated components. If any of the gaskets (***Figure 12.14***) or seals fail, fluid will leak. Some leaks can be fixed by retightening components, but most will need to be replaced.

Figure 12.14 *Thermostat Gasket*

Heater Core

The heater core (***Figure 12.15***) looks like a little radiator. It is normally mounted between the engine compartment and the passenger cabin on the firewall. Coolant from a warm engine flows through the heater core and radiates thermal heat energy. When you turn on the heater blower the heat is transferred into the passenger cabin of the vehicle through the heating/air conditioning ducts. If you notice a sweet odor in your car when you turn on your heat you may have a heater core leak. If it is leaking, it drips in the heater ducts and sometimes on the floor inside the car. When the blower is turned on, the odor circulates inside the passenger cabin. Check to see if your coolant level is low if you believe you have a leak.

Figure 12.15 *Heater Core*

Q & A ?

No Heat Inside Vehicle

Q: My car never seems to warm up inside. The heater blows plenty of air, but it is lukewarm at best. What do I need to do?

A: Check the temperature gauge to see if it is in the normal range. The thermostat controls the circulation of coolant in the engine. If the thermostat is stuck open, the coolant never gets a chance to warm up to the optimal temperature. Also, check to make sure your engine is not low on coolant. A clogged heater core or control valve can also restrict the circulation of coolant. Follow the manufacturer's recommendations for coolant flushes to avoid contaminants being built up in the coolant system. Another problem could be a malfunctioning HVAC blend door actuator that controls the flow of air.

Coolant Flow

The water pump forces coolant to flow throughout the engine (***Figure 12.16***). If the belt is slipping or not working properly the water pump will not circulate the coolant as needed and the engine will overheat. Coolant travels in passageways called water jackets (coolant voids) in the engine. Coolant, cooled from the car moving or from the radiator fan drawing in air across the radiator, flows from the radiator through the lower radiator hose, to the water pump, to the numerous water jackets in the engine, and then to the thermostat. If the coolant has reached operating temperature, the thermostat will open and allow the coolant to pass through the upper radiator hose back to the radiator to be cooled again. If the coolant has not reached operating temperature it will recirculate through the engine until it heats up to the thermostat's rating. Some coolant is also diverted from the engine through the heater core. Heat is transferred from the heater core to the passenger cabin when the inside heater blower is turned on.

Trouble Guide

Engine Overheating

- Coolant low
- Improper coolant mixture
- Clogged radiator fins
- Faulty thermostat (stuck closed)
- Restricted radiator hose
- Fan not working
- Faulty temperature sensor
- Faulty water pump
- Drive belt loose
- Faulty radiator cap

Engine Overcooling

- Faulty thermostat (stuck open)
- Faulty temperature sensor

Sweet Odor when Running Heat

- Heater core leak

Musty Odor when Running Air

- Dirty cabin air filter

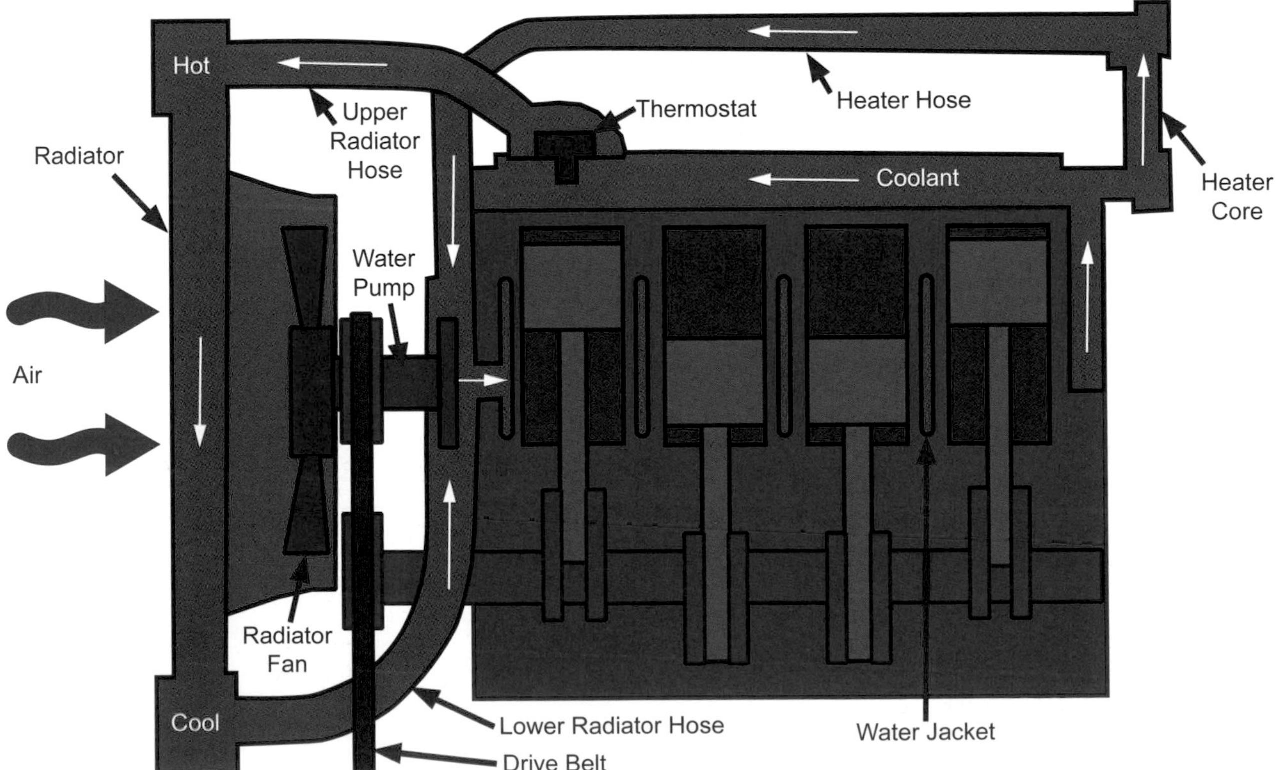

Figure 12.16 *Coolant Flow in an Inline 4 Engine*

Special Cooling Systems

Some vehicles have special cooling systems in addition to conventional engine cooling. This section focuses on:

- EV and HEV Cooling Systems
- Charge-Air Coolers
- Liquid Cooled AC Generators

EV and HEV Cooling Systems

As pointed out in Chapter 8, some electric vehicles (EVs) and hybrid electric vehicles (HEVs) use separate cooling systems for their high voltage batteries and power electronics (***Figure 12.17***). These additional cooling systems keep sensitive electronic components at acceptable temperatures.

Figure 12.17 Power Electronics Cooling System

Charge-Air Coolers

Charge-air coolers (intercoolers and aftercoolers) are air-to-air (***Figure 12.18***) or air-to-liquid heat exchangers. A supercharger or turbocharger compresses air for forced induction (discussed in Chapter 11). When air compresses, it heats up. A charge-air cooler reduces the air temperature before the air enters the engine. Cooler air is denser, allowing for more air and fuel to go into the combustion chamber which leads to more power.

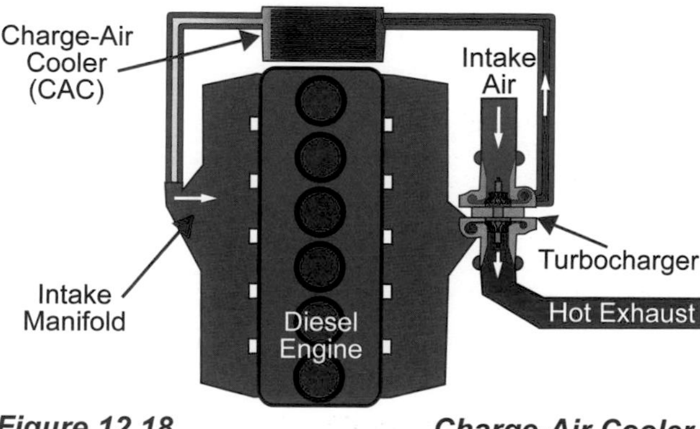

Figure 12.18 ***Charge-Air Cooler***

Liquid Cooled AC Generators

Some AC generators (also known as alternators) are liquid cooled (***Figure 12.19***). Liquid cooled alternators keep a more constant temperature and are less noisy than conventional air cooled alternators. Air cooling depends on engine speed, which can cause fluctuations in the alternator's temperature.

Figure 12.19 ***Liquid Cooled AC Generator***
Photo: Bosch

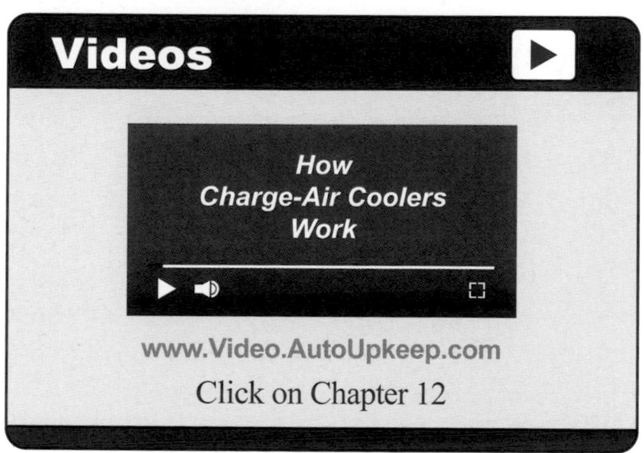

Videos
How Charge-Air Coolers Work
www.Video.AutoUpkeep.com
Click on Chapter 12

Coolant

Mainly two types of coolant are sold for automotive use: conventional antifreeze and extended life antifreeze (***Figure 12.20***). As presented in Chapter 8, antifreeze is manufactured in various colors and formulas (additive packages). ***Note: Always refer to the owner's manual to identify the correct antifreeze for a vehicle.*** Only use an antifreeze that is compatible with your engine. This section focuses on:

- Coolant Properties
- Coolant Mixing
- Coolant Testing and Service

Figure 12.20 ***Antifreeze***

Web Links

Antifreeze Related Sites

Peak Antifreeze
www.peakauto.com

Prestone Antifreeze
www.prestone.com

Zerex Antifreeze
www.valvoline.com

Tech Tip

Recycle Used Coolant

Used coolant is toxic and considered a hazardous waste. Take coolant to a service center that recycles it or wait until your community has a hazardous waste collection day. If you have to store coolant, do not leave it in open pans where pets or children can get into it.

Coolant Properties

Coolant is designed to prevent freezing and boiling, lubricate the water pump seal, and inhibit corrosion.

Prevent Freezing and Boiling. Pure water can be corrosive to engine components. Additionally, it freezes at 32°F (0°C) and boils at 212°F (100°C). If coolant freezes, it will expand, possibly bursting hoses and cracking engine components (radiator, heater core, or even the engine block). Also, the engine can run hotter than 212°F (100°C) and boiling causes problems. The solution to this is to use an antifreeze/water mixture.

Lubricates the Water Pump Seal. Coolant lubricates the water pump seal. As coolant ages it is contaminated with abrasive suspended solids, increasing wear on the water pump seal.

Inhibits Corrosion. Bare engine components are susceptible to corrosion. Coolant contains chemicals to minimize rust and corrosion from forming inside the engine.

Q & A

White Smoke

Q: I have white smoke coming from the tailpipe on my car, what could be wrong?

A: All cars, new ones included, may release a little white vapor when cold. Water vapor is a by-product from combustion. Water dripping from the tailpipe is also fairly common from condensation. If your car billows out white smoke after it is warm, you may have a problem. White smoke indicates that coolant is getting into the engine cylinders and burning with the air-fuel mixture. Another indication of burning coolant could be a low coolant level in the radiator or expansion bottle. A blown head gasket, cracked block, or cracked head can cause coolant to leak into the cylinders. To prevent severe engine damage, do not continue to drive your car. Have a technician look into the problem.

Coolant Mixing

In most climates a 50% antifreeze to 50% water mixture is recommended all year. This will give the coolant a freezing point of -34°F (-37°C) and a boiling point of about 226°F (108°C). When the cooling system is under pressure from the radiator cap, the boiling point raises to about 265°F (129°C) when the mixture is 50/50 (***Figure 12.21***). In a severely cold climate, 60% antifreeze to 40% water is necessary. ***Note: Use only distilled water when mixing.***

Antifreeze	Water	Freezing Point		Boiling Point with 15 lb. Radiator Cap	
		°F	(°C)	°F	(°C)
50%	50%	-34	(-37)	+265	(+129)
60%	40%	-62	(-52)	+269	(+132)
70%	30%	-84	(-64)	+276	(+136)

Figure 12.21 ***Freezing and Boiling Points***

Coolant Testing and Service

Coolant can be tested for strength and condition. The cooling system can also be tested for leaks using a pressure tester.

Testing Coolant Strength. A hydrometer tester measures specific gravity to determine coolant strength. Hydrometers have been found to be inaccurate when samples are taken at different coolant temperatures. In addition, they cannot be used with propylene glycol coolant. A more reliable tester is a refractometer (***Figure 12.22***), an optical device. It calculates freeze protection by measuring how light passes through the coolant sample. Refractometers are also temperature dependent unless they have an automatic temperature compensation feature.

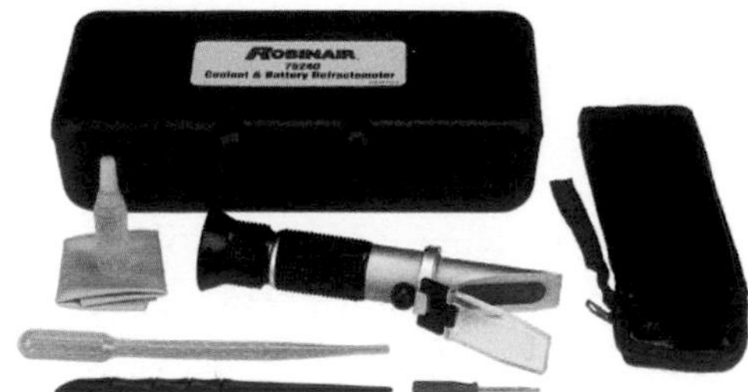

Figure 12.22 ***Refractometer***
Photo: Bosch Automotive Service Solutions, Inc.

Testing Coolant Condition. Test strips (***Figure 12.23***) can be used to test the coolant's pH. The pH scale, which goes from 0 (acidic) to 14 (alkaline) with 7 being neutral, measures how acidic or alkaline the coolant is. Be sure to read the instructions on the container to make sure the test strips are compatible with your coolant and to correctly interpret the sample. If coolant gets too acidic it becomes corrosive.

Figure 12.23 ***Coolant Test Strip***

Flushing the Cooling System. When the coolant's additives (e.g., corrosion inhibitors) are nearing depletion, it is time to drain, flush, and refill the cooling system. This can be done professionally with a flushing machine or at home with water. Dispose of coolant according to local laws and regulations.

Testing for Leaks. A special tool called a cooling system pressure tester can be used to find cooling system leaks.

Trouble Guide

Coolant Loss

- Crack in block or cylinder head
- Defective seal or gasket
- Engine overheating and boiling over
- Heater core leak
- Hole in hose or radiator
- Loose hose clamp
- Worn water pump

Servicing

Coolant (Antifreeze)

- Change conventional antifreeze every 2 years or 48,000 miles
- Change extended life antifreeze every 5 years or 150,000 miles
- Test once a year

Technological Advancements

Designing and implementing technologies to make the powertrain and heating, ventilation, and air conditioning (HVAC) system more efficient can be analyzed from a cost-value approach. Automotive manufacturers look at the cost to include a certain technology in relation to the value that it provides. In conventional gasoline or diesel powered vehicles, more efficiency leads to lower fuel consumption. If a conventional vehicle has start-stop technology, it may need auxiliary heating. In hybrid and electric vehicles, properly managing thermal energy reduces charging times, increases driving range, and increases passenger comfort. Other technological advances protect the engine from overheating. This section focuses on:

- Thermal Management
- Overheating Protection

Thermal Management

Advanced thermal management technologies are used to make engine and drivetrain components more efficient or to increase passenger comfort.

Active Grille Shutters. Active grille shutters (***Figure 12.24***) are used to improve aerodynamics and control airflow through the radiator. If the engine needs cooling, the grille shutters open and allow air to cool the radiator. If the engine is cool, they close. Grille shutters that are closed allow the engine to reach operating temperature quicker and also increase the aerodynamics of the vehicle, leading to better fuel economy.

Figure 12.24 ***Active Grille Shutters***
Courtesy of Ford Motor Company

Active Warm-Up. Especially important in cold climates, getting engine oil and transmission fluid to optimal temperatures enhances vehicle efficiency. An active warm-up device (***Figure 12.25***) is a heat exchanger. For example, some active devices use heat from the coolant and transfer it to the transmission fluid when needed. If the fluid gets too hot, it can also be put in a cooling mode. Other active devices are mounted in the exhaust system, using wasted heat from the exhaust to warm up fluids. One system, called exhaust gas heat recovery (EGHR), can be used to heat up powertrain fluids. It can also be used to heat up the heater core, warming the passenger cabin faster during cold temperatures.

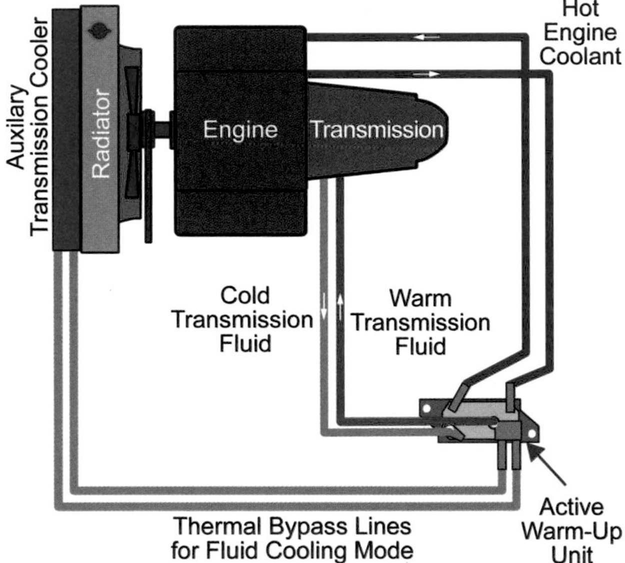

Figure 12.25 ***Active Warm-Up***

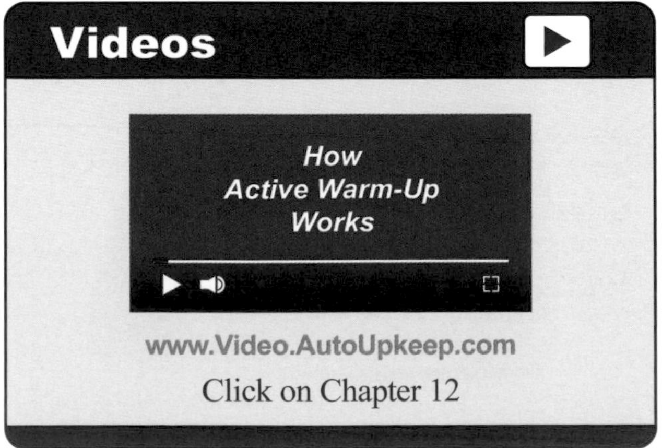

Supplemental Heaters/Heat Pumps. On electric vehicles (EVs), excess heat is not a major inefficiency as it is with internal combustion engines (ICEs). ICEs use wasted heat to warm the passenger cabin, but EVs need to use an electric heater or heat pump to warm the passenger cabin. Electric heaters use a resistive heating element to convert electricity to heat. Electric heaters can significantly reduce the driving range of an EV. A heat pump uses a refrigeration cycle to cool or heat the cabin, moving heat from one location to another.

Electric Water Pumps. Electric water pumps (***Figure 12.26***) can improve engine efficiency over conventional mechanical pumps. Electric pumps, run by electronic controls, only circulate coolant when needed. The mechanical counterpart water pump is running all the time, drawing away energy from the engine. Electric pumps can also continue to run after an engine is shut off, so hot coolant isn't trapped in the engine. ***Note: Electric and hybrid vehicles may have two or more electric water pumps.***

Figure 12.26 ***Electric Water Pump***
Courtesy of Gates Corporation - www.gates.com

Web Links 

Cooling System Related Sites

DANA Limited
www.dana.com

DENSO
www.denso.com

Gates Corporation
www.gates.com

MAHLE Group
www.mahle.com

Stant Corporation
www.stant.com

Overheating Protection

Overheating an engine can cause serious damage. One technology called fail-safe cooling allows you to drive the vehicle if it begins to overheat. It deactivates alternating cylinders in the engine and allows them to pump in air to cool them. If this mode is activated, you will have reduced power from the engine. This is designed to allow you to find a safe location to park your vehicle.

Cabin Air Filter

A cabin air filter (***Figure 12.27***) is used to clean the air coming into the HVAC system. This filter works similarly to a high efficiency filter in a home with a forced air furnace. It cleans the air in the HVAC system by removing pollen, dust, bacteria, and other contaminants. This cleaning increases the passenger cabin air quality. Without a filter or running the system with a dirty filter can cause the air quality inside the passenger cabin to be much worse than the outside air. If there is a reduction of air flow in the HVAC system, but the blower is working, the cabin air filter may be clogged. The filter is commonly located near the glove box or under the hood in the outside air intake for the HVAC system. Check the owner's manual for the location. See the Cabin Air Filter Activity in Chapter 12 of the workbook for cabin air filter change steps.

Figure 12.27 ***Cabin Air Filters***

Servicing 

Cabin Air Filter

- Change every 22,500 miles depending on the air quality and road conditions where the vehicle is driven

Air Conditioning

The air conditioning (A/C) system (***Figure 12.28***) removes heat and humidity from the air for passenger comfort. In hot weather it is dangerous to be in a vehicle without air conditioning, especially for children and pets. The following components work together to remove heat and dehumidify the air in an orifice tube A/C system:

- Refrigerant
- Accumulator
- Compressor
- Condenser
- Orifice Tube
- Evaporator

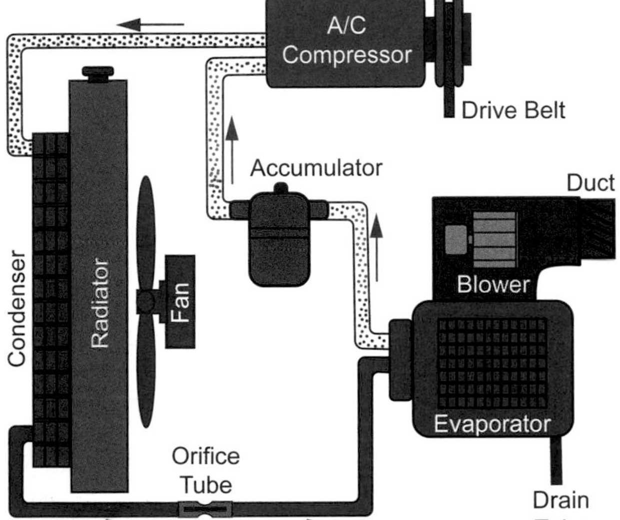

High Pressure Refrigerant Vapor
High Pressure Refrigerant Liquid
Low Pressure Refrigerant Vapor
Low Pressure Refrigerant Liquid

Figure 12.28 ***Orifice Tube A/C System***

Refrigerant

Refrigerant is in the A/C system to remove heat. During operation the refrigerant cycles through the system changing from a liquid to a vapor (absorbs heat) and then a vapor to a liquid (dissipates heat).

Recover and Recycle Refrigerant. You should not perform air conditioning work unless you have a special machine to recover and recycle the refrigerant and you have been trained and certified to perform this type of procedure. Service technicians are required by law to recover and recycle refrigerants in an effort to protect the environment.

Types of Refrigerant. Automotive refrigerants have changed over time. R-12 was used extensively in vehicles until the early 1990s. R-134a, a more environmentally friendly refrigerant, was phased in to replace R-12. R-134a is still an environmental concern when released into the atmosphere. New refrigerants, such as R-1234yf (***Figure 12.29***) and R-744 (CO_2), are being introduced to replace R-134a.

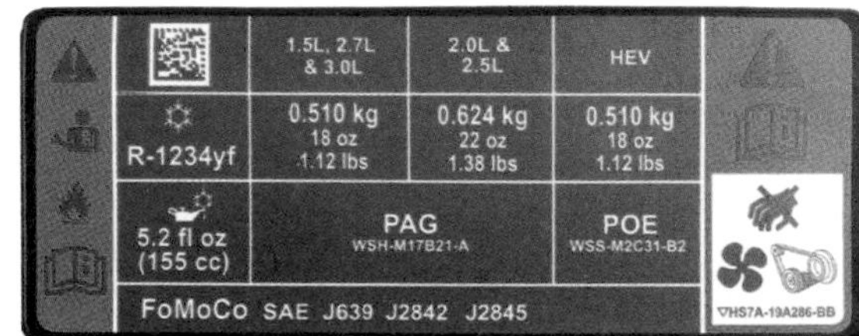

Figure 12.29 ***R-1234yf Refrigerant Label***

Accumulator

The A/C accumulator (***Figure 12.30***) cleans and stores refrigerant. It prevents refrigerant liquid from entering the A/C compressor. Some systems use a receiver-drier instead of an accumulator. They perform similar functions. However, an accumulator is installed on the low pressure side, while a receiver-drier is installed on the high pressure side.

Figure 12.30 ***Air Conditioning Accumulator***

Compressor

The A/C compressor (***Figure 12.31***) is commonly powered by a drive belt. An electromagnetic clutch is used to engage the pulley with the compressor shaft. If the clutch circuit senses low refrigerant or another problem, the clutch will not engage. The compressor pressurizes and recirculates refrigerant, which is sent to the condenser. A seized compressor may cause a turning belt to squeal. Since liquid cannot be compressed, only vapor enters the compressor.

Figure 12.31 **Air Conditioning Compressor**

Condenser

After the refrigerant in the evaporator absorbs heat from the air, the refrigerant is circulated by the compressor to the condenser to release that heat. The condenser, a heat exchanger, looks very similar to a radiator and is normally located in front of the radiator. If the air conditioner is not getting as cool as you think it should, make sure there is nothing in the condenser fins restricting air flow.

Orifice Tube

The orifice tube controls the refrigerant flow from the condenser to the evaporator. It changes the refrigerant from a high pressure liquid to a low pressure liquid. ***Note: Systems with a receiver-drier use an expansion valve instead of an orifice tube.***

Evaporator

The compressed refrigerant travels from the condenser to the evaporator, a heat exchanger, where heat is absorbed from the surrounding air. When you turn on the air conditioner blower this cooled air is transferred to the passenger cabin through the ducts. If the air recirculation switch is on, air will be pulled from inside the cabin making the system more efficient once the inside air is cool. Otherwise fresh air is pulled in from outside. A drain tube (***Figure 12.32***) allows condensation from humidity in the air to drain from the evaporator. The drain often leaves a water puddle on the ground that may look like a leak, especially if the A/C has been running on a humid day. If the drain becomes clogged it should be cleaned by probing it with a long dull object. If left clogged, the water can eventually work its way out onto the interior floorboards.

Figure 12.32 **Evaporator Drain Tube**

Summary

The cooling system is extremely important to the operation of the engine. The cooling system maintains efficient engine-operating temperature, removes excess heat, brings the engine up to operating temperature as quickly as possible, and provides warmth to the passenger cabin. Antifreeze prevents the coolant from freezing, increases the boiling temperature, lubricates components within the engine, and reduces the likelihood of corrosion. The heater core transfers heat from the engine to warm the passenger cabin. A cabin air filter cleans the air that blows through the cabin vent system. If your A/C doesn't work, take it to an ASE certified technician that has the proper equipment to find, repair, and recycle the refrigerant if necessary.

Activities

Cooling System and Climate Control

- Air Conditioning Activity
- Cabin Air Filter Activity
- Cooling System Activity
- Chapter 12 Study Questions

Activities and Study Questions can be completed in the *Auto Upkeep Workbook.*

Career Paths

Heating and A/C Technician

Education: Technical Training and ASE Cert.
Median Income: $45,110
Abilities: Understands system controls, testing equipment, and environmental regulations.
Find your career at www.bls.gov/ooh.

Ignition System

Chapter 13

Photo: Bosch

Fuel for Thought

- What is required for an engine to run?
- How have ignition system advancements reduced maintenance?
- What is an interference engine?

Introduction

The engine in a vehicle needs three things to run: air-fuel mixture, sufficient compression, and an ignition source (heat or spark). The air-fuel mixture is ignited by an electric spark in gas engines (***Figure 13.1***). Diesel engines use heat from compression to ignite the air-fuel mixture. This chapter focuses on gasoline engines. The ignition system on vehicles has changed over the years, but its purpose has been the same – to ignite the air-fuel mixture. The ignition system converts fuel's chemical energy into mechanical energy (wanted motion) and thermal energy (wasted heat). Ignition system advancements have been influenced by progressively stringent emission standards. This chapter gives you the knowledge to identify and perform basic maintenance procedures on a vehicle's ignition system.

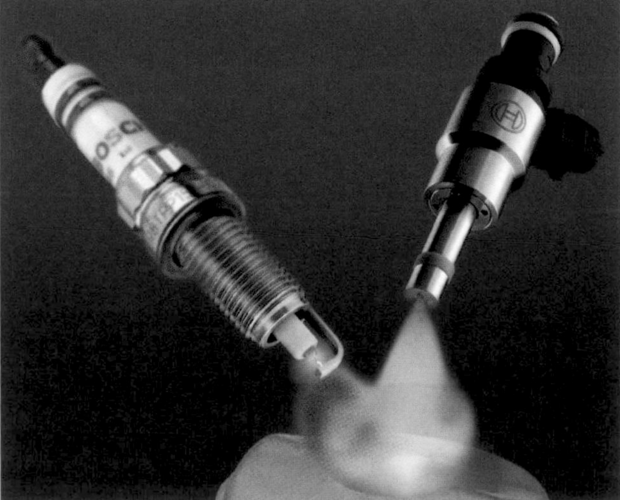

Figure 13.1 *Fuel Ignited by Spark Plug*
Photo: Bosch

Objectives

Upon completion of this chapter and activities, you will be able to:

- Define the purpose of the ignition system.
- Identify ignition system generations.
- Define and discuss the importance of the ignition system components while relating them to their respective generation.
- Differentiate between interference and non-interference engines.
- Test and perform basic service procedures on the ignition system.

Web Links

Ignition System Related Sites

ACDelco
www.acdelco.com

Autolite Spark Plugs
www.autolite.com

Bosch Auto Parts
www.boschautoparts.com

Champion Auto Parts
www.championautoparts.com

Denso Auto Parts
www.densoautoparts.com

MSD Performance
www.msdperformance.com

NGK Spark Plugs
www.ngksparkplugs.com

Standard Motor Products, Inc.
www.smpcorp.com

Ignition System Purpose

As mentioned earlier, an air-fuel mixture, sufficient compression, and an ignition source must all be present for an engine to run. The ignition system is designed to monitor and control the ignition to make the vehicle run smoothly. The purpose of the ignition system is to:

- Step Up Voltage
- Ignite the Air-Fuel Mixture

Step Up Voltage

One purpose of the ignition system is to step up low voltage supplied by the battery to a high voltage at the spark plug. High voltage is needed to ignite the air-fuel mixture in the combustion chamber. Some of the ignition system components carry low voltage (12-volts, the primary circuit) while others support high voltage (10,000 to 100,000 volts, the secondary circuit). High voltage is created with a coil, a step up transformer.

Ignite the Air-Fuel Mixture

Automotive engines are considered four-stroke engines (intake, compression, power, and exhaust). To get to the wanted power stroke (the stroke which gives the vehicle power to move), the engine must cycle through the other necessary strokes. Most automotive engines have four to eight pistons working together to provide the mechanical energy. Not only does the ignition system have to ignite the air-fuel mixture, it also needs to ignite it at the correct time.

Trouble Guide

Engine Misses

- Faulty spark plug wires
- Worn spark plugs
- Worn distributor cap or rotor
- Moisture on ignition components
- Loose or corroded electrical connection
- Poor ground
- Faulty knock or camshaft sensor

Ignition System Components

Changing technology has made major advancements in the ignition system. Over time some components were eliminated, others were added, while others stayed pretty much the same (***Figure 13.2***). The three ignition system generations that will be described later in this chapter are: Contact Point Ignition (CPI), Distributor Ignition (DI), and Electronic Ignition (EI). The following are common ignition system components:

- Battery
- Distributor Cap and Rotor
- Ignition Coil/ Coil Packs/Coil-On-Plug (COP)
- Spark Plug Wires
- Spark Plugs
- Ignition Module
- Powertrain Control Module (PCM)
- Crankshaft and Camshaft Sensors
- Knock Sensor
- Timing Belt, Chain, and Gears

Common Components	Ignition System Generation		
	CPI	DI	EI
Points/Condenser	YES	NO	NO
Distributor Cap/Rotor	YES	YES	NO
Spark Plug Wires	YES	YES	YES (NO on COP)
Ignition Coil	YES	YES	YES (Pack or COP)
Battery	YES	YES	YES
Spark Plugs	YES	YES	YES
Ignition Module	NO	YES	YES
Powertrain Control Module	NO	YES	YES
Crankshaft/Camshaft Sensors	NO	Some	YES
Knock Sensor	NO	Some	YES

Figure 13.2 ***Ignition System Components***

Battery

The battery, used in all three ignition generations, is a critical component in the electrical, starting, charging, and the ignition systems. Electrical energy must be present to ignite the air-fuel mixture. The problem is that a 12-volt DC battery does not have enough voltage to create the spark that is necessary in the combustion chamber, but it is the beginning point of power.

Distributor Cap and Rotor

The distributor cap and rotor (***Figure 13.3***), used on CPI and DI systems, distributes or sends high voltage to each spark plug. The rotor rotates inside the cap, connecting and sending high voltage to one terminal at a time.

Figure 13.3 ***Distributor Cap and Rotor***

Ignition Coil/Coil Packs/Coil-On-Plug

The ignition coil, used on all three generations, steps up low voltage to the high voltage needed to ignite the air-fuel mixture.

Ignition Coil. Some engines have only one coil (***Figure 13.4***), while others have a coil for each cylinder.

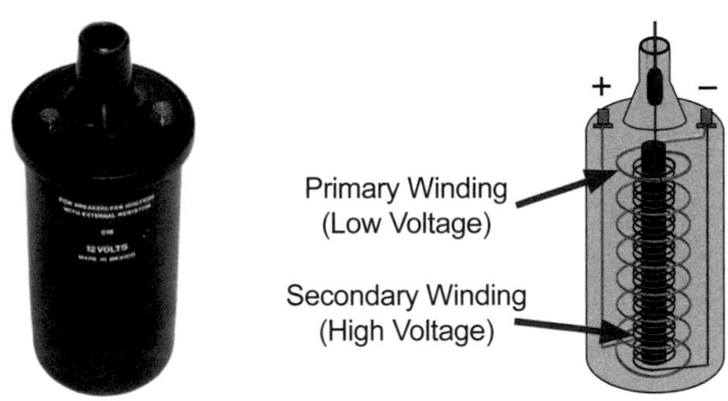

Figure 13.4 ***Ignition Coil***

Coil Packs. The EI generation has coil packs. These packs are a series of coils to induce voltage for each individual cylinder.

Coil-On-Plug (COP). Some EI systems use COP (***Figure 13.5***) technology. Spark plug wires are eliminated by using boots to connect the coils directly to the spark plugs. The COP ignition system is more reliable because high voltage plug wires often cause problems over time.

Figure 13.5 ***Ignition Coil-On-Plugs***

Spark Plug Wires

Spark plug wires (***Figure 13.6***) carrying high voltage electricity are used on all generations of ignition systems, except COP systems. On the CPI and DI systems, spark plug wires connect the distributor to the spark plugs at each cylinder. In the EI system, the spark plug wires connect the coil packs to the spark plugs.

Figure 13.6 ***Coil and Spark Plug Wires***

Tech Tip

Changing Spark Plug Wires

Changing spark plug wires is relatively easy. Engines have certain firing orders that cannot be mixed up. Remove and replace only one wire at a time, reusing the factory spark plug wire retainers. Follow the manufacturer's routing. Keep the wires away from the exhaust manifold and sharp metal edges. To inhibit corrosion, use dielectric grease in the boot end of each spark plug wire.

Servicing

Distributor Cap and Rotor

- Change every 25,000 to 50,000 miles

Spark Plugs

- On CPI systems, every 10,000 miles
- On DI systems, every 25,000 miles
- On EI systems, every 50,000 to 100,000 miles

Spark Plug Wires

- Change every 100,000 miles

Spark Plugs

The spark plug (***Figure 13.7***), used in all generations of ignition systems, completes the high voltage circuit. Spark plugs can be found at the end of spark plug wires or under coil packs on COP systems. Spark plugs are screwed into the engine head so their electrodes at the tip are exposed to the combustion chamber. Voltage at the spark plug needs to be great enough to arc across the gap between the electrodes. This spark is what ignites the air-fuel mixture. Most engines have one spark plug per cylinder, but some have two. The center electrode on a spark plug is commonly made of copper, platinum, or iridium.

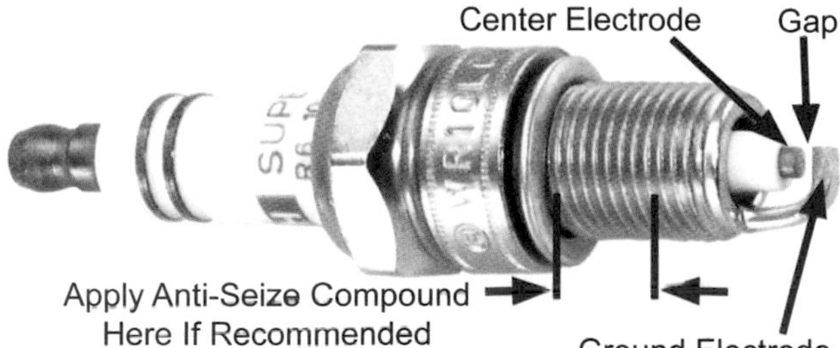

Figure 13.7 Spark Plug, Electrodes, and Gap

Gap. The gap between the center electrode and the ground electrode is usually between 0.020 to 0.080 of an inch (0.51 to 2.03 mm). Always check the service manual or the VECI sticker under the hood for the gap setting. See the Ignition System Activity in Chapter 13 of the workbook for spark plug installation steps.

Tech Tip 

Anti-Seize Compound

Some technicians use anti-seize compound on spark plug threads to prevent seizing that can result when different metals come in contact with one another, especially on vehicles with aluminum heads. Check vehicle and spark plug manufacturers' recommendations before applying. Using anti-seize compound can cause overtightening due to the increased thread lubrication. Some threads are engineered with corrosion protection, so applying anti-seize compound is not recommended.

Ignition Module

The ignition module (***Figure 13.8***), used on DI and EI systems, is basically a switch that turns the low voltage from the battery on and off to the ignition coil(s). It is a transistor that is timed and controlled by the PCM.

Figure 13.8 Ignition Module

Powertrain Control Module (PCM)

Advanced integration of the PCM is increasingly evident in the EI system. The PCM has taken over the vital role of precisely determining when the spark is needed to ignite the air-fuel mixture.

Input Data. Operating conditions are input by crankshaft, camshaft, throttle position, knock, and other sensors. Engine speed in revolutions per minute (RPM), throttle position, and coolant temperature are some of the data collected, compared, and used to determine the spark timing. The PCM monitors inputs from the sensors and makes adjustments as needed so the engine can operate efficiently. An ignition timing malfunction may be a sign of a loose, dirty, or worn sensor not sending the correct input information to the PCM.

Crankshaft and Camshaft Sensors

The crankshaft and camshaft sensors (***Figure 13.9***) are used on EI systems and some DI systems. They keep track of piston and valve positions in the engine to efficiently time the spark. The crankshaft position sensor relays information about the crankshaft position and engine speed. The camshaft position sensor signals which coil needs to fire and sequences fuel injection timing.

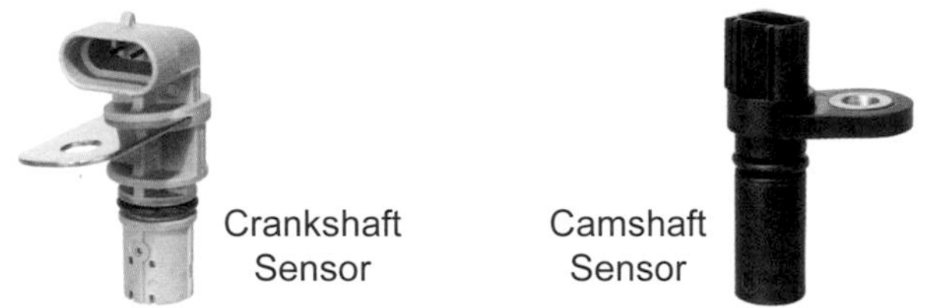

Figure 13.9 Crankshaft and Camshaft Sensors
Courtesy of Spectra Premium, Inc. - www.spectrapremium.com

Knock Sensor

A knock sensor (KS) (***Figure 13.10***) is used on all EI systems and some DI systems to detect uncontrolled detonation vibrations from spark timing that is too advanced. The PCM uses the KS signal to retard spark timing just enough for the knock vibrations to stop, allowing the timing to be as advanced as possible. See Chapter 11 for more on knocking.

Figure 13.10 Knock Sensor
Photo: Bosch

Apps
Ignition System Parts Lookup
www.AutoUpkeep.com/apps
Click on Chapter 13

Timing Belt, Chain, and Gears

Timing belts, chains, and gears (***Figure 13.11***) are used to keep the crankshaft and camshaft synchronized. This ensures the engine's exhaust and intake valves open at the correct time. The crankshaft, which is connected to the pistons, turns the camshaft. It takes two crankshaft rotations to turn the camshaft once.

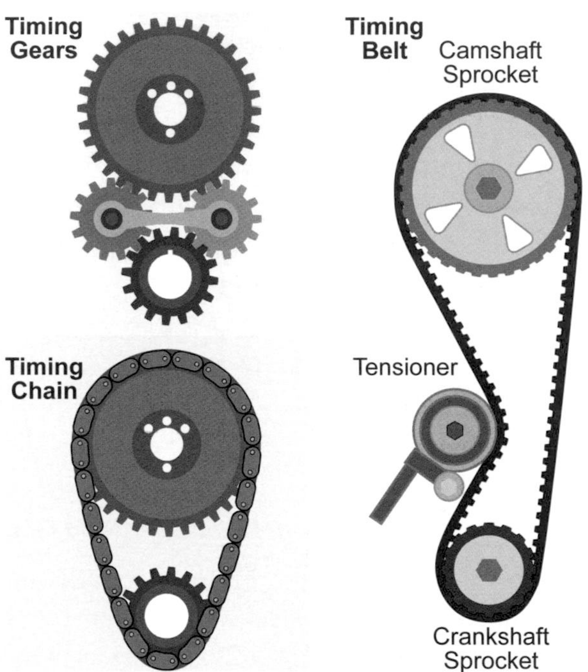

Figure 13.11 Timing Belt, Chain, and Gears

Timing Belt Replacement Intervals. Timing belts have replacement intervals, commonly between 60,000 to 105,000 miles or every 6 years. Your owner's manual may have two different interval schedules depending on how you use your vehicle: normal and a severe service interval (***Figure 13.12***). Always follow the manufacturer's service intervals.

Service	Typical Miles*	Vehicle Use
Normal	105,000 (169,000 km)	• City and Highway Driving • Typical Cargo Loads • Infrequent Towing • Mostly Flat Terrain
Severe	60,000 (97,000 km)	• Mostly City Driving • Heavy Cargo Loads • Frequent Towing • Mountainous or Hilly Terrain • Extreme Temperatures

*** Always refer to your owner's manual.**

Figure 13.12 Timing Belt Replacement Intervals

Interference Engines. Many engines are called interference engines (***Figure 13.13***). This means that the valves and pistons could come in contact with one another if the timing belt or chain breaks, skips, or is stripped out. The engine quits running and internal engine damage would result.

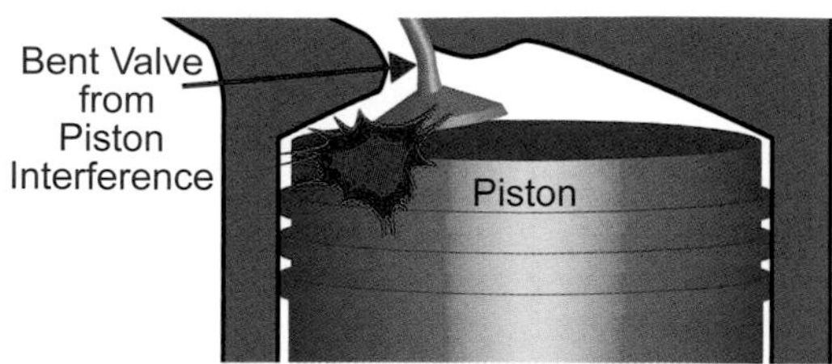

Figure 13.13 ***Interference Engine***

Non-Interference Engines. In non-interference engines (***Figure 13.14***), the valves cannot come in contact with the pistons if the timing chain or belt breaks, skips, or is stripped out. No internal damage results, but the engine will not run. This type of engine is also called a freewheeling engine.

Figure 13.14 ***Non-Interference Engine***

Causes of Timing Belt Failure. Extreme temperatures and adverse driving conditions, such as stop and go traffic, can impact timing belt life. Contamination from oil or other fluids can degrade the belt composition. Timing belts can also fail from worn tensioners and other components that are run off the belt. For example, on some vehicles the timing belt turns the water pump. If these components fail, the timing belt could fail.

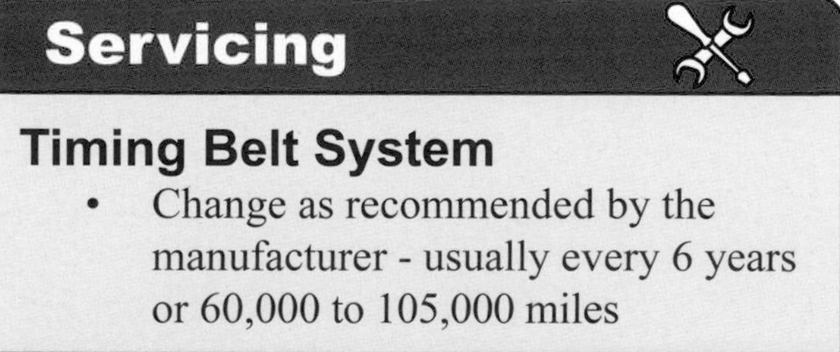

Servicing
Timing Belt System
• Change as recommended by the manufacturer - usually every 6 years or 60,000 to 105,000 miles

Servicing the Timing Belt System. It is usually recommended to replace the whole timing belt system (***Figure 13.15***) at the service interval. This includes the belt, idler, tensioner, and other components such as the water pump. These items wear too. If you put a new timing belt on with components that are near the end of their life, it may significantly reduce the life of the new timing belt.

Figure 13.15 ***Engine Timing Belt Component Kit***
Courtesy of Gates Corporation - www.gates.com

Ignition System Generations

Over the years automotive manufacturers have come a long way in making the "power" (ignition) stroke more reliable and efficient through advancements in technology. The purpose over time has been the same: to increase the voltage to induce a spark. It should be noted that the following dates of the ignition system generations are approximated. Depending on the automotive manufacturer, the implementation time of each ignition system generation may vary. The generations of the ignition system are commonly divided into the following eras:

- Contact Point Ignition (CPI) System
- Distributor Ignition (DI) System
- Electronic Ignition (EI) System

Contact Point Ignition (CPI) System

The CPI system (***Figure 13.16***) was common in vehicles from about 1920 to the mid 1970s. This system is considered a mechanical type ignition system because mechanical contact points in the distributor control the spark by opening and closing the primary circuit of the ignition coil. The condenser helps to suppress arcing between the points which can cause pitting and corrosion. Tune-ups during this age were frequent – sometimes every 5,000 to 10,000 miles (≈8,000 to 16,000 km).

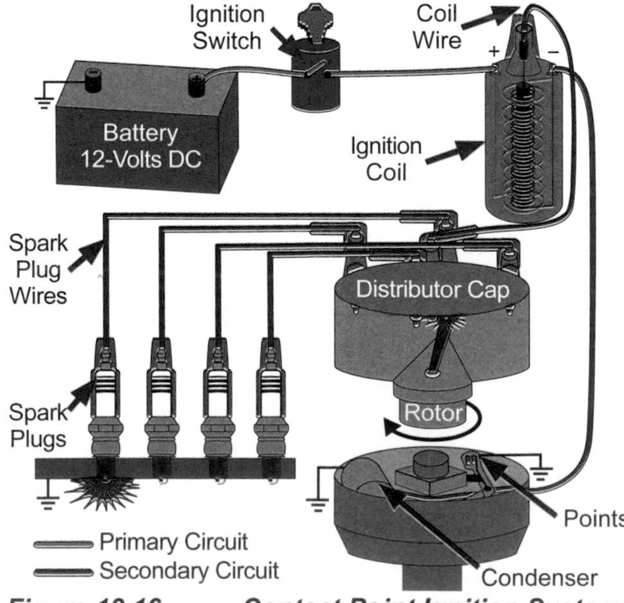

Figure 13.16 ***Contact Point Ignition System***

Distributor Ignition (DI) System

The DI system (***Figure 13.17***) was common in vehicles from about 1975 to the early 1990s. Tune-ups during this age were required about every 25,000 miles (≈40,000 km). The main advantage over the CPI system was the elimination of the contact points that physically rubbed on the distributor shaft. This elimination decreased the number of components that needed servicing. The DI system uses an ignition module to electronically control the spark.

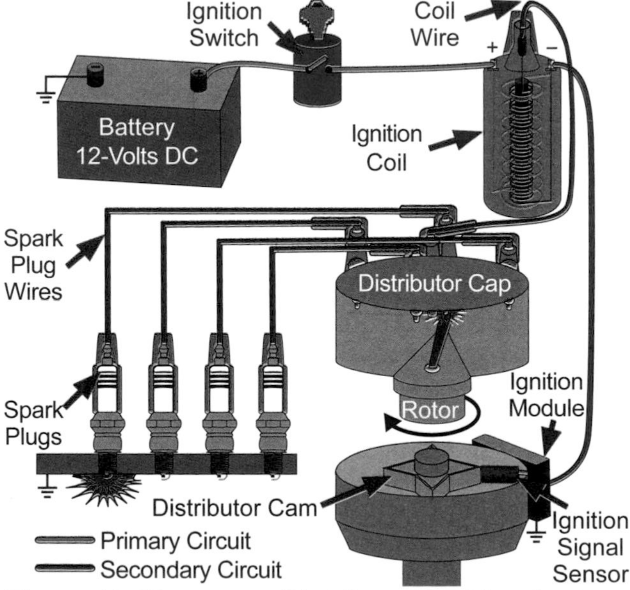

Figure 13.17 ***Distributor Ignition System***

Price Guides

Battery 12-volt DC
- $40.00 to $100.00

Coil Packs
- $100.00 to $200.00 per set

Distributor Cap and Rotor
- $15.00 to $30.00 per set

Ignition Coil
- $50.00 each

Ignition Module
- $40.00 to $200.00 each

Spark Plug Wire Set
- $20.00 to $80.00 per set

Spark Plugs
- $1.00 to $8.00 each

Electronic Ignition (EI) System

The EI system (also known as distributorless, direct, or computer-controlled coil ignition system) was actually introduced in the mid 1980s, but really became popular in the early 1990s. Tune-up intervals on EI systems vary, with some reaching or exceeding 100,000 miles (≈160,000 km). The advantages over the DI system are the elimination of a mechanical distributor, higher firing voltage, better timed spark, and a more efficient running engine. One example of an EI system is the coil-on-plug (COP) system (***Figure 13.18***). The COP unit, mounted directly on the spark plug, is controlled by the PCM. The PCM uses sensor input to precisely control the timing.

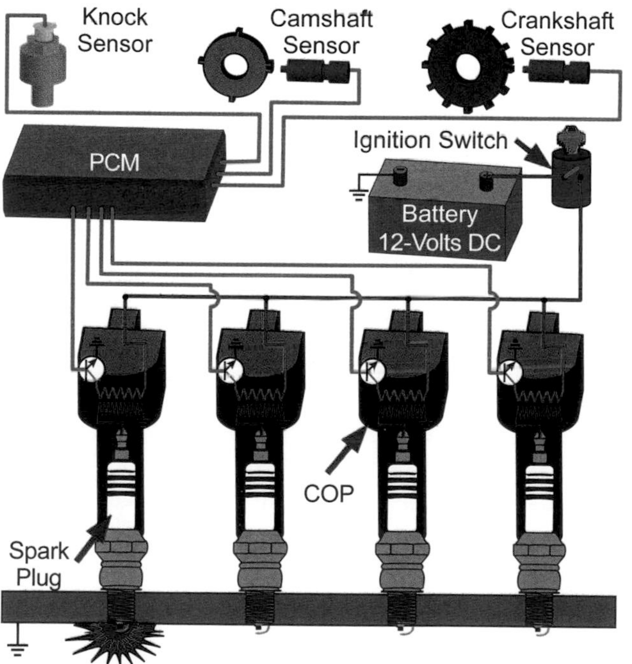

Figure 13.18 ***Coil-On-Plug EI System***

Trouble Guide

Engine Rotates, but No-Start

- Moisture on ignition components
- Worn or incorrectly gapped spark plugs
- Faulty ignition module or coil
- Cracked, burned, or corroded distributor cap or rotor
- Faulty crankshaft position sensor

Circuits Inside a Coil-On-Plug. The primary and secondary circuits are inside the coil-on-plug (***Figure 13.19***). Eliminating the distributor and coil/spark plug wires allows the COP system to operate very efficiently. The ignition module may also be integrated into the coil.

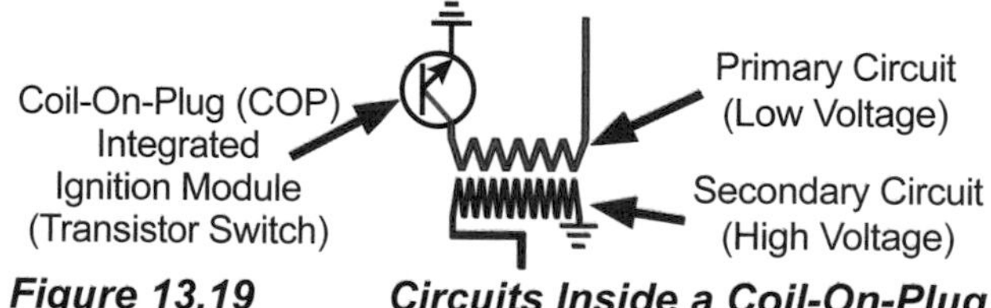

Figure 13.19 ***Circuits Inside a Coil-On-Plug***

Summary

The ignition system is designed to ignite the air-fuel mixture in the combustion chamber. Ignition systems have gone through three main generations: contact point, distributor, and electronic. The EI system allows cylinders to be controlled individually, providing reliability, lowering emissions, improving performance, and increasing fuel efficiency. Even though the ignition system may seem complex with sensors and control modules, there are things that the do-it-yourselfer can do to maintain and tune-up the engine to make it run smoothly.

Activities 

Ignition System

- Ignition System Activity
- Chapter 13 Study Questions

Activities and Study Questions can be completed in the *Auto Upkeep Workbook*.

Career Paths 

Engineering Technician

Education: Associate's Degree
Median Income: $61,130
Abilities: Problem solving, understands schematics, and use of electronic test equipment.
Find your career at **www.bls.gov/ooh**.

Suspension, Steering, and Tires

Fuel for Thought

- What are dependent and independent suspension systems?
- Why might the steering wheel of a vehicle pull to one side?
- What information is on a tire's sidewall?

Introduction

Most of the roads that we drive on are not perfectly smooth and straight. S-curves, potholes, speed bumps, construction zones, and weather conditions make it necessary for vehicles to have control mechanisms. A properly working suspension and steering system gives the operator and passengers of the vehicle a smooth and pleasant ride. Shocks, struts, springs, and tires all assist in controlling the automobile by keeping the tires in contact with the road. This chapter presents information about suspension, steering, and tires.

Objectives

Upon completion of this chapter and activities, you will be able to:

- Define the purpose and identify the functions of the suspension system.
- Define the purpose and identify the functions of the steering system.
- Inspect suspension and steering components.
- Discuss the importance of tires and explain their ratings.
- Describe different tread designs.
- Identify the non-repairable areas on a tire.
- Inspect and rotate tires.

Suspension System

The suspension system helps to control the up and down movement of the vehicle. During braking or going over bumps, the suspension system helps provide stability, safety, and control. This section focuses on:

- Dependent Suspension
- Independent Suspension

Dependent Suspension

A dependent suspension (***Figure 14.1***) is also known as a nonindependent, rigid, or solid axle system. This type of system is common on rear wheel drive vehicles, on the rear of some front wheel drive vehicles, and on the front of heavy trucks. When going over a bump with one wheel, the wheel on the other side also moves. One wheel's position is dependent on the other wheel.

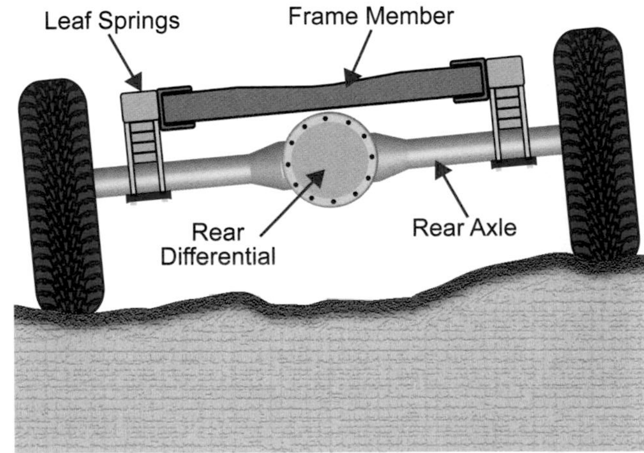

Figure 14.1 ***Dependent Suspension***

Independent Suspension

In an independent suspension (***Figure 14.2***), if one wheel hits a bump it moves independently from the other wheel. This type of system is widely used on passenger cars. It is also used on the front of light trucks and SUVs. Independent suspensions provide better ride and handling than dependent suspensions.

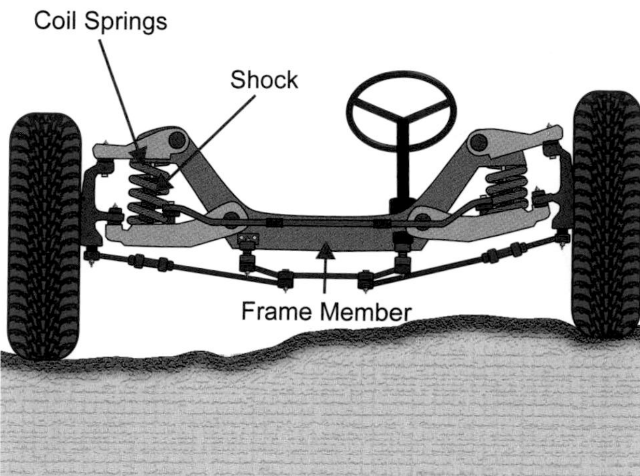

Figure 14.2 ***Independent Suspension***

Short-Long Arm. A short-long arm (SLA) system (***Figure 14.3***) is a type of independent suspension. This system is also called a double wishbone suspension. It gets its name from having two control arms of different lengths. The control arms use ball joints. Ball joints, which are connected to the steering knuckle, allow for turning and vertical movement.

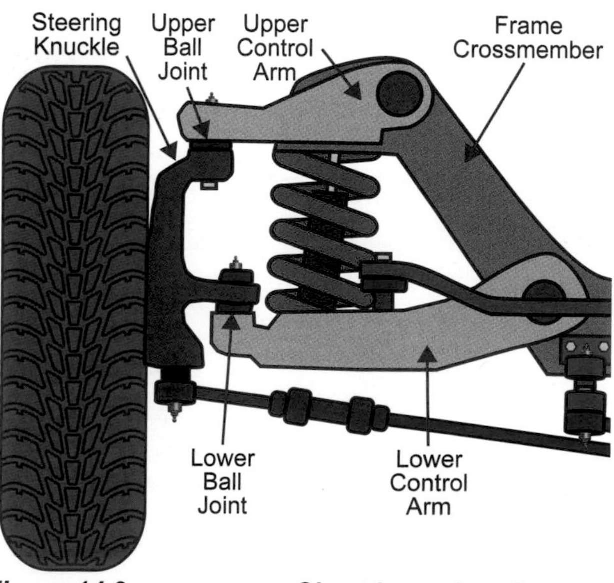

Figure 14.3 ***Short-Long Arm System***

MacPherson Strut. A MacPherson strut system (***Figure 14.4***) is a type of independent suspension. This system does not use an upper control arm or upper ball joint. Instead it uses a strut mount at the top. When this system is utilized on the front where turning is required, a bearing is incorporated into the strut mount. A MacPherson strut integrates the shock and coil spring together into one unit.

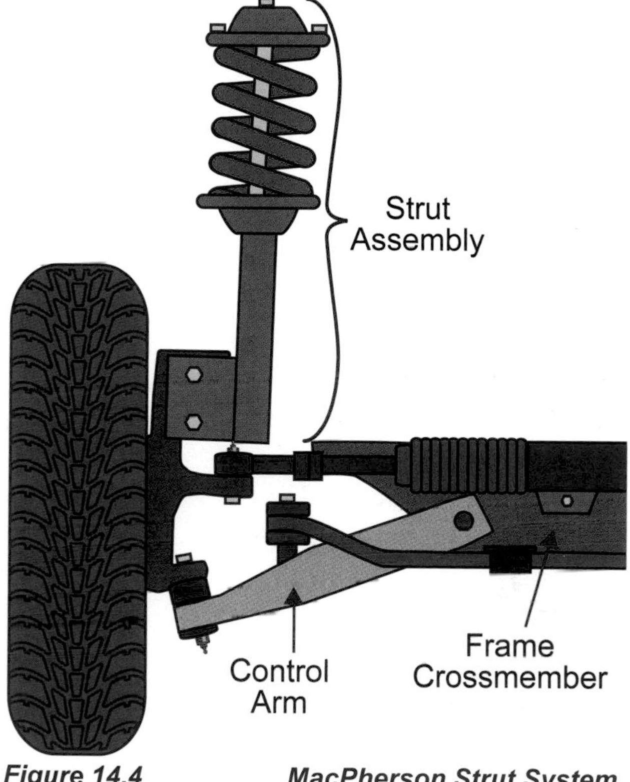

Figure 14.4 ***MacPherson Strut System***

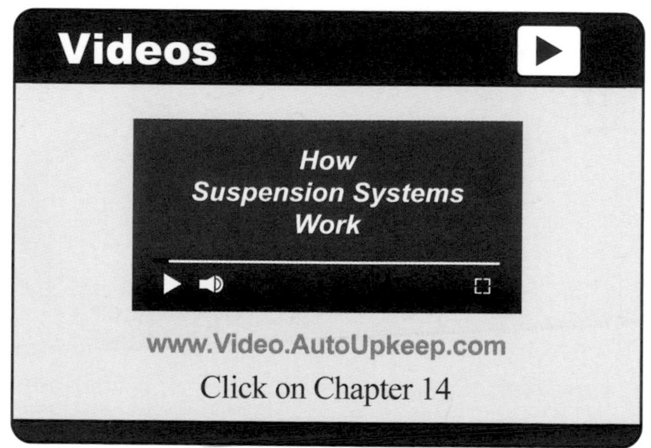

Suspension Components

The suspension components consist of many parts, all of which are attached to and become a part of the chassis. This section focuses on:

- Vehicle Design
- Axles
- Shock Absorbers
- Springs
- Struts
- Sway Bar
- Ball Joints

Vehicle Design

The vehicle must have a foundation to build upon.

Body-on-Frame. Some vehicles have a steel frame that runs the length of the vehicle (***Figure 14.5***). The body is then mounted onto the frame. This is a common design for trucks and full size SUVs.

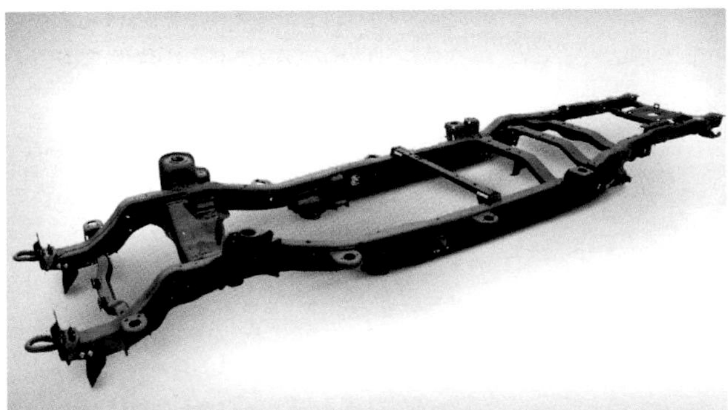

Figure 14.5 ***Frame***
Courtesy of Ford Motor Company

Unibody. Another design, called a unibody (***Figure 14.6***), combines the body and frame into one unit. This is a common design for passenger cars.

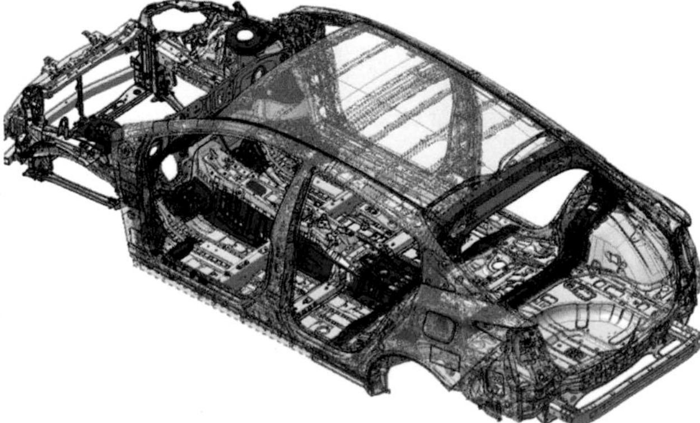

Figure 14.6 ***Unibody***
Photo: Toyota Motor Corporation

Axles

Axles work with suspension systems for a place to mount and hold tires in their proper orientation to the road. Shocks and springs also connect to axles to allow for up and down movement. Axles are classified as being either live or dead.

Live Axle. A live axle (***Figure 14.7***) is also part of the drivetrain system. It houses components that can transmit power to the wheels.

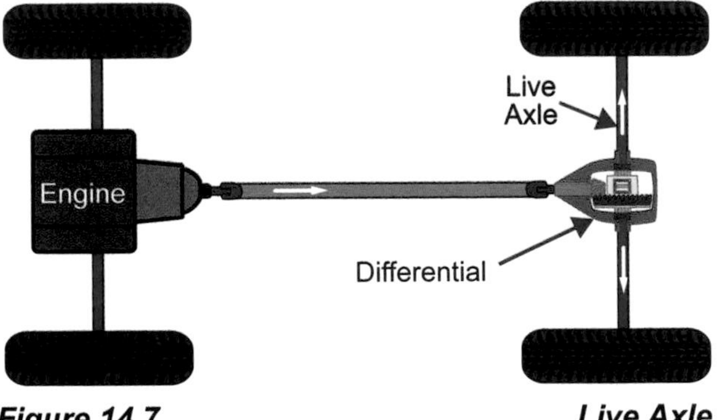

Figure 14.7 ***Live Axle***

Dead Axle. A dead axle (***Figure 14.8***) is not a part of the drivetrain system. It just holds the tires in position.

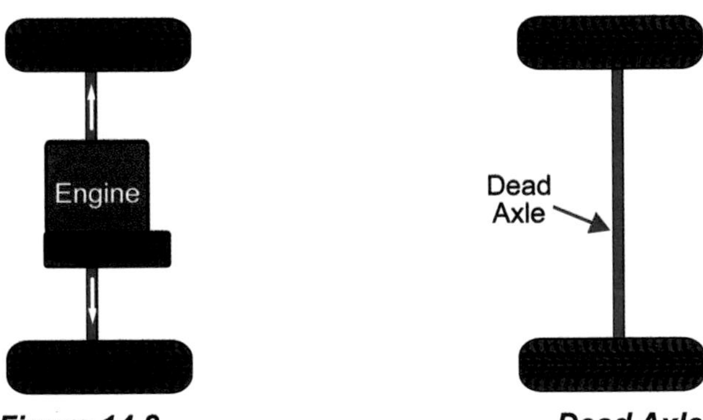

Figure 14.8 ***Dead Axle***

Price Guides

Coil Springs
- $175.00 a pair

Leaf Springs
- $300.00 a pair

Shocks
- $50.00-$100.00 a pair

Struts
- $150.00-$300.00 a pair

Shock Absorbers

A shock absorber (***Figure 14.9***), often referred to as a shock or damper, reduces (dampens) the number of oscillations (up and down movements) from uneven roads. Shocks keep the tires consistently and firmly in contact with the road when going over bumps. A good tire-to-road contact provides safe handling and braking. One end of the shock is connected to a stationary part on the frame or unibody, while the other is connected to a suspension component that moves.

Figure 14.9 ***Shock Absorber***

How Shocks Work. Shocks convert kinetic energy (energy of motion) to heat energy. Shocks have two chambers built inside them. When going over bumps, hydraulic fluid moves from one chamber to another through valves. These valves are small, putting a resistance on the fluid and slowing down the oscillations. Heat energy is created from the moving fluid (hydraulic friction). This heat is then dissipated from the fluid. Shocks continually go through resistance forces of compression and then extension (rebound).

Gas Charged. Gas charged shocks use a pressurized gas to help keep air bubbles or foam from forming. If foam forms inside the shock it will negatively impact performance.

Air Shocks. Air shocks are referred to as leveling or load-adjusted shocks. An air bladder on the shock is used to keep the vehicle level under heavy loads.

Magnetic Ride Systems. Magnetic ride systems (***Figure 14.10***) use motion sensors, special shocks, and a control module to modify the ride depending on the road surface. These shocks are filled with magneto-rheological (MR) fluid. This synthetic fluid contains suspended iron particles. Built into the shock is an electromagnetic coil. The fluid's viscosity can be changed by exposing the coil to an electric current, which creates a magnetic field. As the electric current is increased, the strength of the magnetic field increases which increases the viscosity (thickness) of the fluid. If the viscosity is higher, the fluid has an increased resistance to flow. The viscosity of the MR fluid impacts how fast or how slow it goes through the shocks internal passageways. The ability to change the current makes the MR fluid's viscosity variable, which makes the shocks extremely adaptable to road conditions. With computer controls, these adjustments can happen at 1000 times a second.

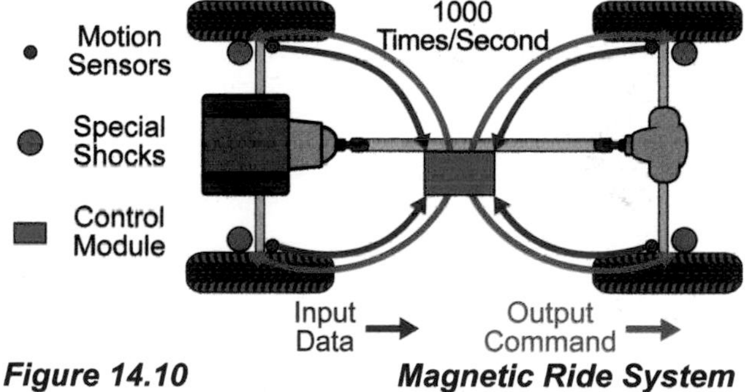

Figure 14.10 ***Magnetic Ride System***

Inspection. Excessive fluid leakage on a shock is a sign that it needs replacement. Also inspect the upper and lower mount bushings for wear.

Tech Tip

Bounce Test

To do a simple suspension test push down as hard as you can on one end of the vehicle and then let go. The vehicle should come to a rest after one cycle. If it cycles more than once, the shocks, struts, or springs could be worn out. This is a generic test and should be made in conjunction with a visual inspection.

Videos

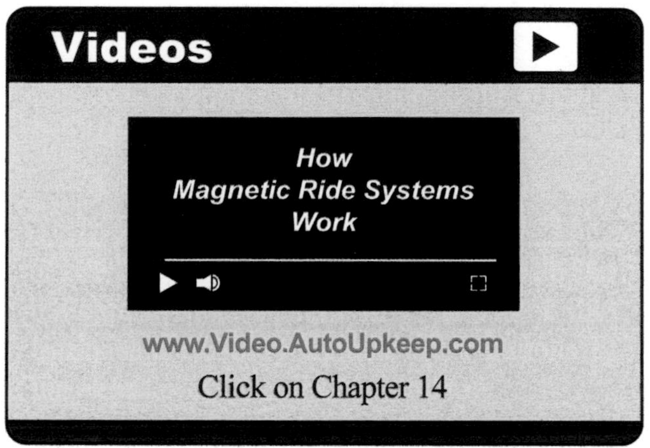

www.Video.AutoUpkeep.com

Click on Chapter 14

Springs

Springs support the weight of the vehicle while working in conjunction with shocks to absorb irregularities in the road surface. As the vehicle goes over bumps the springs are compressed (also called jounce) and then extended (also called rebound). Springs are designed as coil, semi-elliptical, air, and torsion bars.

Coil Springs. Coil springs (***Figure 14.11***) are common on the front and rear of vehicles.

Figure 14.11 *Coil Spring*

Leaf Springs. Semi-elliptical springs, usually called leaf springs (***Figure 14.12***), are common on the rear of trucks.

Figure 14.12 *Leaf Springs*

Air Springs. An air spring uses an air chamber to cushion the force. Vehicles with automatic leveling systems use compressed air springs.

Torsion Bar Springs. Torsion bar springs (***Figure 14.13***) are large rods of steel that twist, acting as a spring.

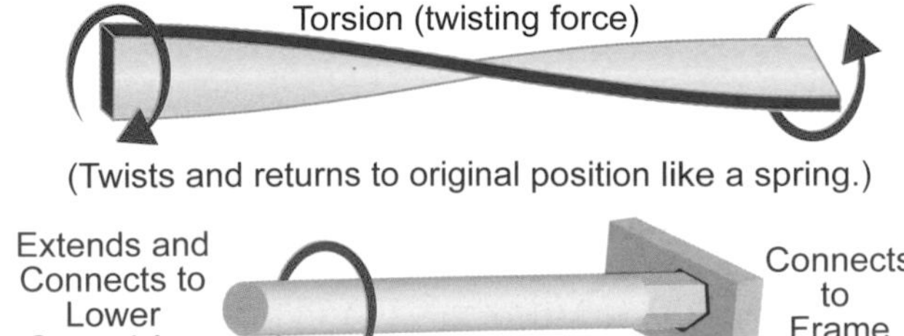

Figure 14.13 *Torsion Bar Spring*

Struts

Struts (***Figure 14.14***) are structural components that integrate the shock, spring, and upper control arm into one unit. They eliminate the need for individual shocks and springs on the front and/or rear of a vehicle, reducing the overall weight and space. Some vehicles have struts in the front and shocks and springs in the rear, while others have struts at each wheel.

Figure 14.14 *Strut*

Sway Bar

A sway (stabilizer) (***Figure 14.15***) bar adds stability and reduces body roll by connecting both lower control arms. It twists to transmit some movement from one side of the vehicle's suspension to the other.

Figure 14.15 *Sway Bar*
Photo: Toyota Motor Corporation

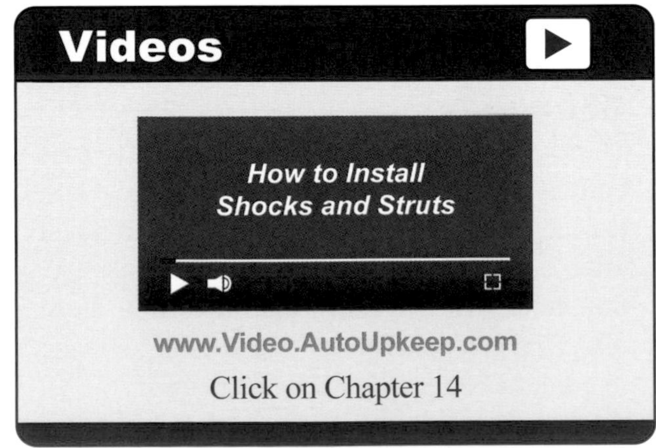

Videos
How to Install Shocks and Struts
www.Video.AutoUpkeep.com
Click on Chapter 14

Ball Joints

Ball joints (***Figure 14.16***) connect the control arms to the steering knuckle where turning and vertical movement is needed. They are designed to carry the weight of the vehicle. Ball joints are covered by a rubber boot, with many permanently sealed. Some ball joints may have a grease zerk to add grease. Check a vehicle's lube diagram for zerk locations.

Figure 14.16 ***Ball Joint***

Selecting the Correct Lubricating Grease. Some chassis components need grease, others may be permanently sealed. Grease is a lubricant that reduces friction and wear. Coating a component also protects it from rusting by preventing water infiltration. The National Lubricating Grease Institute (NLGI) certifies greases for different applications. Greases are graded for consistency and classified by performance criteria. Consistency grade numbers include 000, 00, 0, 1, 2, 3, 4, 5, and 6. The lower the number, the softer the grease. A common consistency grade for automotive maintenance is #2. The grease performance is classified using an American Society for Testing and Materials (ASTM) standard. You need to identify the grade consistency and the performance classification recommended in your owner's manual. Compare this to the NLGI certification label (***Figure 14.17***) on the grease tube (cartridge). Wheel bearing grease will start with the letter "G". Chassis grease starts with "L".

Figure 14.17 ***NLGI Certification Mark***

Grease Fittings. Grease fittings (***Figure 14.18***) are also called grease zerks or zerk fittings. Grease fittings have a spring-loaded one-way valve that allows grease to enter the component, but not come back out.

Figure 14.18 ***Grease Fittings (Zerks)***

Chassis Lubrication. A grease gun is used to lubricate chassis components that have grease fittings (***Figure 14.19***).

Greasing	
STEP 1	Use your owner's manual to select the proper grease.
STEP 2	Follow the grease gun manual to load the grease tube (cartridge) properly into the grease gun. Force a little grease out of the gun's nozzle to remove any possible dirt that is stuck in the tip. Wipe the nozzle clean with a shop rag.
STEP 3	Identify and locate the grease fittings. Look for points that pivot. Use a service manual if needed.
STEP 4	Clean the grease fittings with a shop rag, removing any dirt around the grease fittings.
STEP 5	Place the grease gun nozzle on the grease fitting. Just pump the grease gun enough until the rubber boot starts to swell. The boot should be firm when pressed with your finger. Do not overfill. Overfilling can cause the rubber to rupture on tight fitting boots. On components without tight fitting boots, grease may ooze out from the boot seal. This is normal.

STEP 6	Wipe off any excess grease that may have leaked out of the rubber boot. Excess grease can drop on the inside of the wheel, collect dirt, and throw the wheel off balance. If grease is coming out of the grease fitting, replace it and regrease.

Figure 14.19 ***Greasing***

Servicing

Lubricate Grease Fittings (Zerks)

- At every oil change

Steering System

The steering system controls the directional movements of the vehicle. The steering system, in conjunction with the suspension system, provides control and stability of the vehicle. The motion the operator makes at the steering wheel is transferred to the front wheels. This section focuses on:

- Parallelogram Steering
- Rack and Pinion Steering

Parallelogram Steering

A parallelogram system (***Figure 14.20***) is also called a pitman arm or recirculating ball system.

Rack and Pinion Steering

A rack and pinion system (***Figure 14.21***) commonly works in conjunction with struts to reduce space and weight.

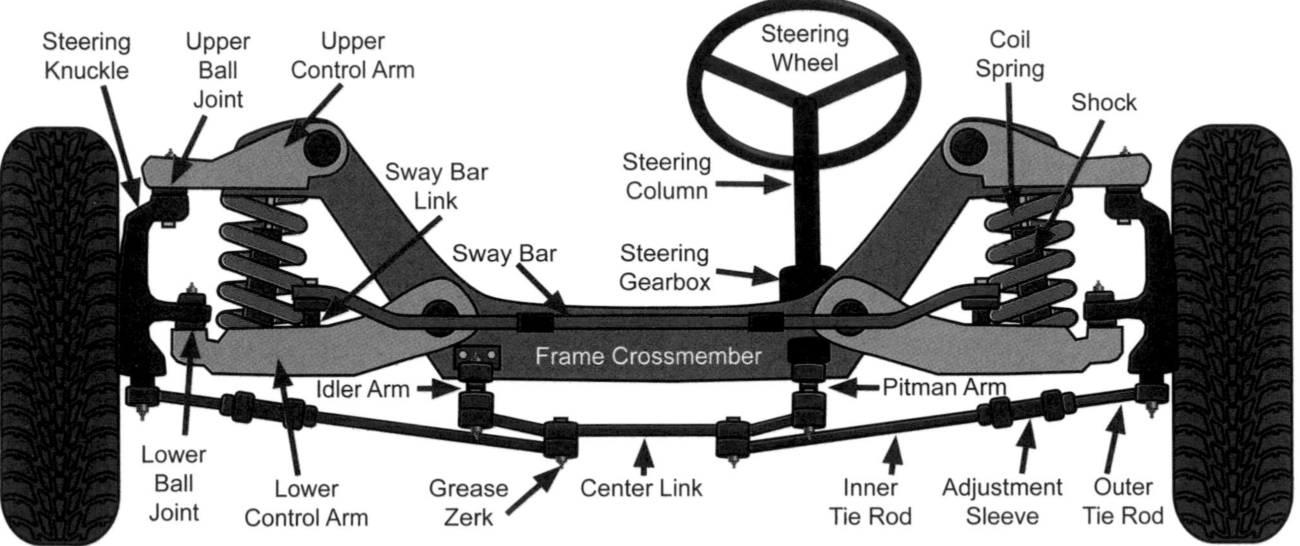

Figure 14.20 ***Parallelogram Steering Linkage with SLA Suspension Components***

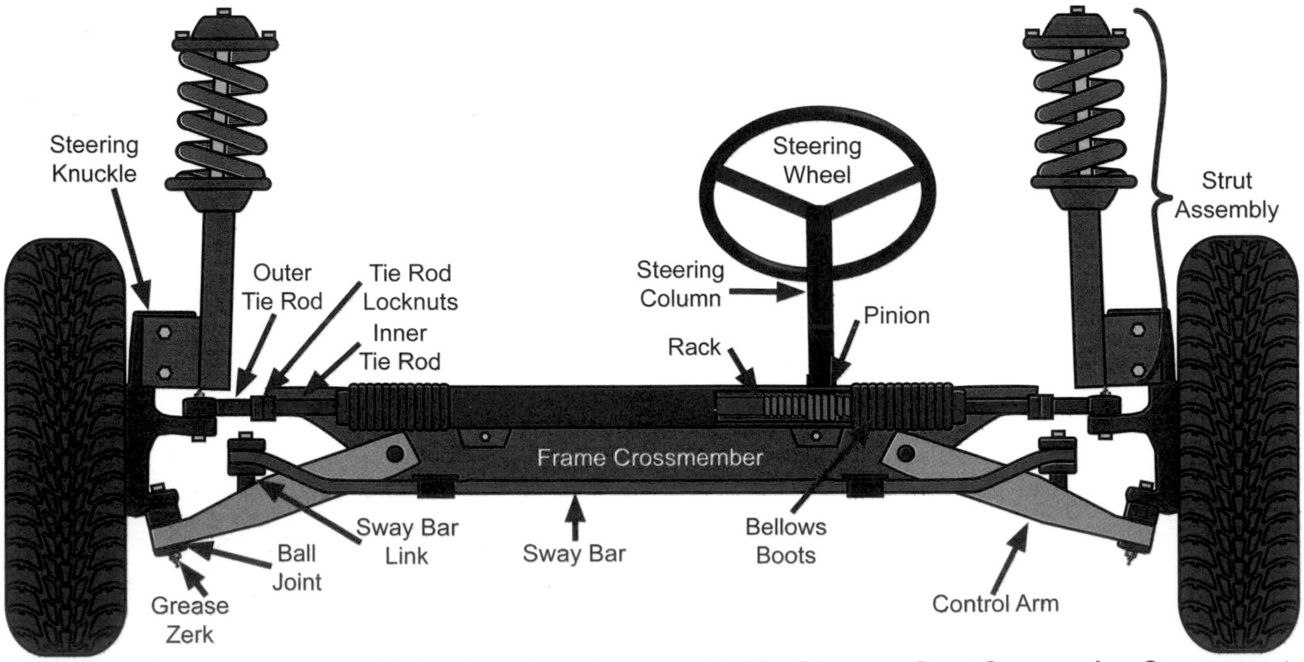

Figure 14.21 ***Rack and Pinion Steering Linkage with MacPherson Strut Suspension Components***

Steering Components

Some of the steering system components are connected to the frame of the vehicle while others need to move with the suspension. This section focuses on:

- Steering Wheel
- Steering Linkage
- Power Steering

Steering Wheel

The steering wheel allows the operator to control vehicle direction. Slight movements easily turn a 2,000+ lb (900+ kg) vehicle. Many vehicles have tilt and telescoping functions that aid in driver comfort. The steering wheel connects to the front wheels by steering linkage. ***Warning: Working on the steering wheel or column can be dangerous around airbags, so follow all manufacturer precautions.***

Steering Linkage

Steering linkage connects the steering shaft from the steering wheel to control the wheels.

Parallelogram Linkage. In a parallelogram linkage system, the steering wheel connects to the steering column. The steering column uses a shaft to connect to the steering gearbox. The pitman arm connects the steering gearbox to a center link. The center link is supported on the other side by an idler arm. Connected to the center link are inner and outer tie rods. An adjustment sleeve connects the two tie rods. This sleeve allows wheel toe (discussed later in this chapter) to be adjusted. The outer tie rod connects to the steering knuckle. This connection allows movements of the steering wheel to be transferred to the wheels.

Rack and Pinion Linkage. In a rack and pinion steering system, the steering wheel connects to the steering column. The steering column uses a shaft to connect to the pinion. The pinion meshes with the rack. The rack, a flat piece with teeth, is connected to the tie rods. The tie rods are adjustable, allowing for wheel toe to be changed. As the operator turns the steering wheel, the pinion turns, moving the rack to turn the vehicle.

Power Steering

Power steering reduces the amount of effort that a driver needs to exert when steering.

Hydraulic Power Steering. A power steering pump, which is commonly driven by a belt on the engine, provides fluid pressure to ease the force required by the operator to turn the steering wheel. It is necessary to periodically check the power steering pump reservoir fluid level. If there is a howling sound when turning the steering wheel the power steering fluid may be low.

Electric Power Steering (EPS). Some power steering systems are not mechanically belt driven. EPS (***Figure 14.22***) is becoming more popular. EPS systems allow the driver to have power steering even if the vehicle stalls or is shut down intentionally at stops. Using an EPS system increases fuel efficiency by 1-3% by reducing weight and mechanical losses. Being electrical, it also has built-in self diagnostic features.

Figure 14.22 Electric Power Steering System
Photo: Bosch

Trouble Guide

Hard Steering

- Low power steering fluid
- Loose belt

Howling Sound When Steering

- Low power steering fluid

Body Rolls Around Corners

- Defective shocks, struts, or springs
- Broken sway bar link or worn bushing

Squeaking Suspension

- Damaged or worn suspension bushings

Tires

Tires, part of the steering and suspension system, provide the connection to the road surface. They are designed to give passengers a comfortable ride and the needed traction (adhesive friction) to control the vehicle during acceleration, cornering, and braking. Tires are a critical component to driving safely. This section focuses on:

- Tire Sidewall
- Parts of a Tire
- Tire Sizes
- Tire Classification
- Tire Grading
- Tread Design
- Run Flat Tires
- Low Rolling Resistance Tires
- Light Truck Tire Load Range
- Spare Tire
- No Spare Tire

Tech Tip

Buying Tires

Always replace tires in pairs or complete sets. When pricing tires, include mounting, balancing, disposal, road hazard insurance (if desired), and tire valve stems or TPMS (Tire Pressure Monitoring System) service kits. Vehicles built after 2008 have tire pressure monitors that are part of the valve stem. Make sure your tires are registered so you will be notified of a safety recall. Tire sellers are required by Federal Law to complete registration for you or provide you with a tire registration form to mail yourself. ***Note: P-metric and Euro-metric tires with the same size (dimensions) may have different load ratings. Always make sure the tires you choose meet the load requirements of your vehicle.***

Tire Sidewall

A tire's sidewall (***Figure 14.23***) lists the size, ratings, and other information you may need when you buy new ones. Most cars will have passenger tires. Light trucks can come with either passenger or light truck type tires.

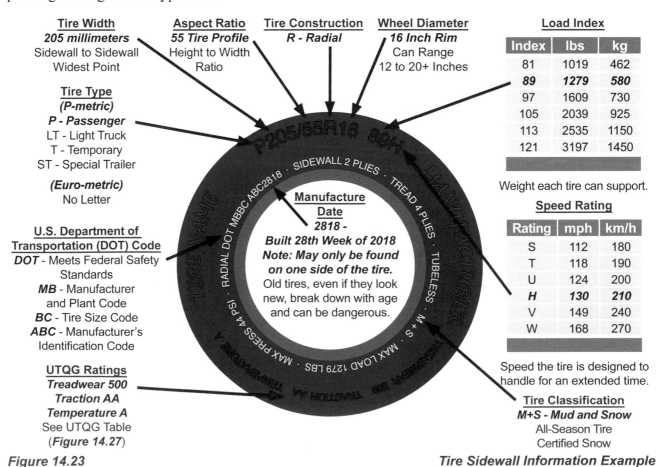

Tire Width
205 millimeters
Sidewall to Sidewall
Widest Point

Aspect Ratio
55 Tire Profile
Height to Width
Ratio

Tire Construction
R - Radial

Wheel Diameter
16 Inch Rim
Can Range
12 to 20+ Inches

Tire Type
(P-metric)
P - Passenger
LT - Light Truck
T - Temporary
ST - Special Trailer

(Euro-metric)
No Letter

U.S. Department of Transportation (DOT) Code
DOT - Meets Federal Safety Standards
MB - Manufacturer and Plant Code
BC - Tire Size Code
ABC - Manufacturer's Identification Code

UTQG Ratings
Treadwear 500
Traction AA
Temperature A
See UTQG Table
(***Figure 14.27***)

P205/55R16 89H
SIDEWALL 2 PLIES · TREAD 4 PLIES · TUBELESS · M+S · MAX LOAD 1279 LBS · MAX PRESS 44 PSI · RADIAL DOT MBBC ABC2818
TIRE NAME
MANUFACTURER
TREADWEAR 500 TRACTION AA TEMPERATURE A

Manufacture Date
2818 -
Built 28th Week of 2018
Note: May only be found on one side of the tire.
Old tires, even if they look new, break down with age and can be dangerous.

Load Index

Index	lbs	kg
81	1019	462
89	***1279***	***580***
97	1609	730
105	2039	925
113	2535	1150
121	3197	1450

Weight each tire can support.

Speed Rating

Rating	mph	km/h
S	112	180
T	118	190
U	124	200
H	***130***	***210***
V	149	240
W	168	270

Speed the tire is designed to handle for an extended time.

Tire Classification
M+S - Mud and Snow
All-Season Tire
Certified Snow

Figure 14.23 ***Tire Sidewall Information Example***

Parts of a Tire

The parts of a tire include the tread, grooves, sipes, shoulder, sidewall, bead, belts, and plies (*Figure 14.24*).

Tire Part Identification

Tread - The tread is the rubber that contacts the road.

Grooves - The grooves are designed to allow water to escape while driving on wet roads.

Sipes - Sipes (also called kerfs) are thin slits cut into the tread to provide additional traction.

Shoulder - The shoulder is the outer edge of the tread that connects to the sidewall.

Sidewall - The sidewall connects the shoulder to the bead. It is flexible to improve vehicle ride.

Bead - The bead is where the tire connects to the wheel.

Belts - The belts are the cords that run around the tire inside the tread section, giving the tread and tire strength.

Plies - A tire is made up of several layers of materials called plies. In a radial tire, the plies go from bead to bead at a 90 degree angle. The plies give the tire strength.

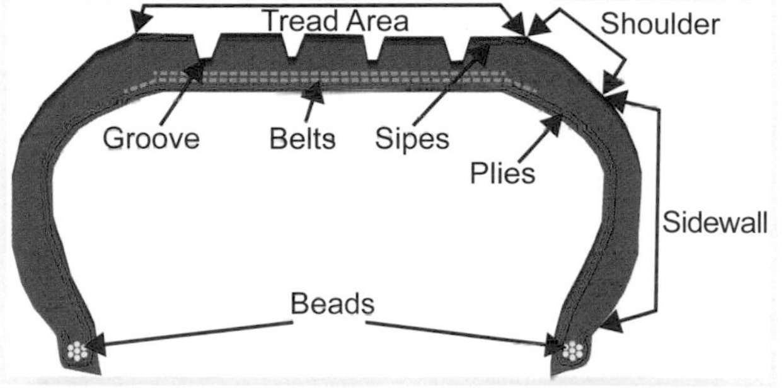

Figure 14.24 ***Parts of a Tire***

Tire Sizes

Tires come in a variety of sizes depending on vehicle size and weight. It is important to replace tires with the size recommended by the manufacturer. Having tires too big or too small will influence how a vehicle handles and may cause the speedometer to be inaccurate.

Tire Placard. The correct tire size is located on the tire placard (*Figure 14.25*) inside your driver's door or door jamb.

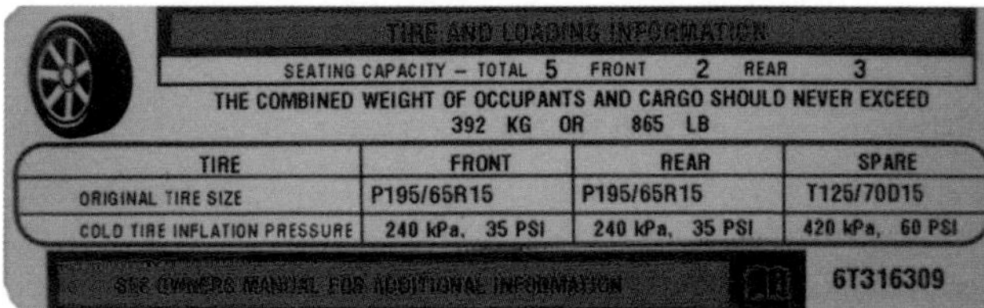

TIRE AND LOADING INFORMATION

SEATING CAPACITY – TOTAL 5 FRONT 2 REAR 3

THE COMBINED WEIGHT OF OCCUPANTS AND CARGO SHOULD NEVER EXCEED 392 KG OR 865 LB

TIRE	FRONT	REAR	SPARE
ORIGINAL TIRE SIZE	P195/65R15	P195/65R15	T125/70D15
COLD TIRE INFLATION PRESSURE	240 kPa, 35 PSI	240 kPa, 35 PSI	420 kPa, 60 PSI

SEE OWNERS MANUAL FOR ADDITIONAL INFORMATION 6T316309

Figure 14.25 ***Tire Placard***

Tire Classification

Tires are generally classified as all-season or snow tires. All-season tires will meet most consumer demands throughout the year. Snow tires have a more aggressive tread and are more flexible, giving them superior traction in the winter. An all-season radial may have a "M+S" (mud and snow) designation, but it is not a certified snow tire unless the tire's sidewall has a snowflake-on-a-mountain icon (*Figure 14.26*).

Figure 14.26 ***Certified Snow Tire Icon***

Tire Grading

All passenger (P) vehicle tires have UTQG (uniform tire quality grading) ratings established by the U.S. DOT to help consumers compare brands and types. The UTQG ratings are treadwear, traction, and temperature (*Figure 14.27*).

UTQG Ratings	BEST	↔	POOR
Treadwear - Tire's comparative tread life. A **500** tire should last five times as long as a **100** tire.	500+		100
Traction - Tire's comparative ability to grip a wet road. **AA** (superb), **A** (excellent), **B** (good), and **C** (poor).	AA	A B	C
Temperature - Tire's comparative ability to withstand heat. **A** resists the highest temperature.	A	B	C

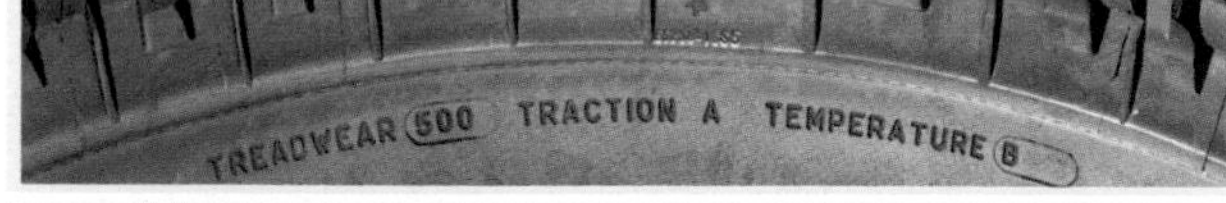

Figure 14.27 ***UTQG Ratings***

Tread Design

A tire's tread design is the arrangement of the independent tread blocks, grooves, and sipes on the tread.

Symmetrical Tire. On a symmetrical tire (***Figure 14.28***), the independent tread blocks and grooves have the same tread pattern across the whole tire. These are common on non-performance vehicles. Symmetrical tires can be rotated to any wheel position on the vehicle (as long as they are the same size), making them long lasting. They provide a quiet ride at a decent value.

Figure 14.28 *Symmetrical Tire*

Asymmetrical Tire. On an asymmetrical tire (***Figure 14.29***), the tread design changes from one side to the other. The outboard tread usually has larger blocks to help in cornering stability and traction on dry roads. The inside tread blocks are smaller, giving it good wet traction. Asymmetrical tires will be marked with an outside mark so the technician mounts it correctly. They can be rotated to any wheel position as long as they aren't also directional and as long as the outside tread stays out.

Figure 14.29 *Asymmetrical Tire*

Directional Tire. A directional tire (***Figure 14.30***), also called a unidirectional, is designed to roll in one direction. Directional tires have a "V" tread pattern that helps remove water faster to better resist hydroplaning. Hydroplaning occurs when the tire is lifted off the road by a thin film of water. During rotations they can be moved from front to back and vice versa as long as they are the same size. If you want to move them from side to side, they would need to be dismounted, flipped, and remounted on the wheel. The sidewall has a directional arrow on it.

Figure 14.30 *Directional Tire*

Asymmetrical and Directional. A tire that is both asymmetrical and directional (***Figure 14.31***) will have a dedicated inside and outside tread as well as being designed to roll in one direction. You could rotate them from front to back as long as they are the same size.

Figure 14.31 *Asymmetrical and Directional Tire*

Web Links
Tire Association Sites
Rethink Tires
www.rethinktires.ca
Tire and Rubber Association of Canada
www.rubberassociation.ca
Tire Industry Association (TIA)
www.tireindustry.org
U.S. Tire Manufacturers Association
www.ustires.org

Run Flat Tires

Some tires have the ability to maintain mobility when punctured. Three technologically advanced tires are self-sealing, self-supporting, and tire/wheel combination systems.

Self-Sealing Tire. A self-sealing tire (***Figure 14.32***) has a special lining inside that will permanently seal most small nail or screw punctures.

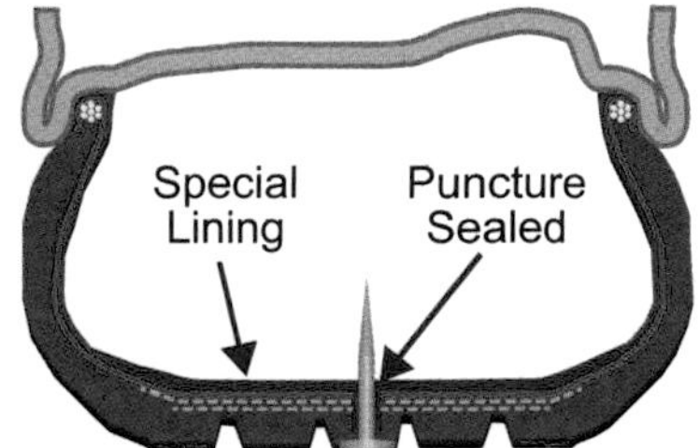

Figure 14.32 ***Self-Sealing Tire***

Self-Supporting Tire. A self-supporting tire (***Figure 14.33***) is designed with a stiff internal construction, generally carrying the weight of the vehicle for about 50 miles (80 km) even if the tire loses all air pressure.

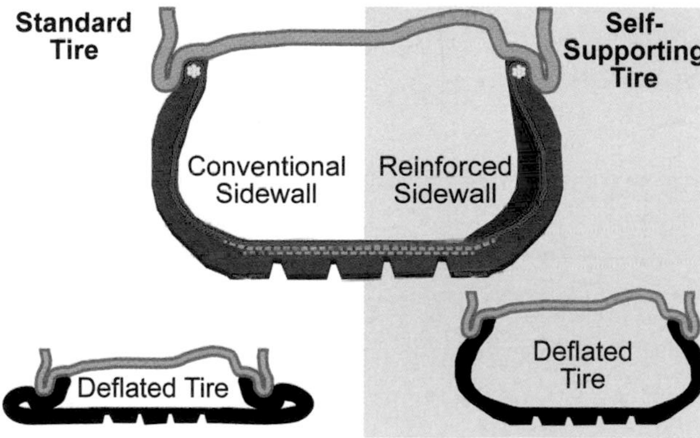

Figure 14.33 ***Self-Supporting Tire***

Tire/Wheel Combination System. A tire/wheel combination system (***Figure 14.34***) uses a special tire and wheel assembly that has a support ring to carry the weight of the vehicle if the tire loses air pressure. This assembly allows the vehicle to be driven about 125 miles (201 km) with no air pressure.

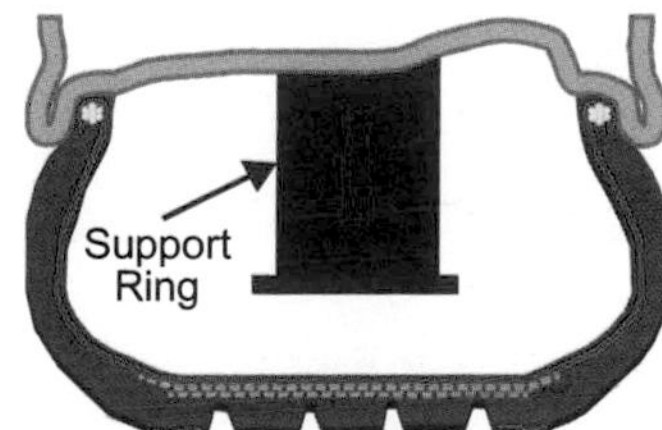

Figure 14.34 ***Tire/Wheel Combination System***

Low Rolling Resistance Tires

In an effort to meet Corporate Average Fuel Economy (CAFE) standards, automotive manufacturers commonly install low rolling resistance tires on new vehicles. It takes less energy to propel a vehicle with lower rolling resistance. Using low rolling resistance tires could save you 1.5% to 4.5% in fuel costs – depending on the vehicle. When purchasing replacement tires, you may want to consider low rolling resistance tires to optimize fuel economy.

Light Truck Tire Load Range

The load range, ply rating, and maximum inflation pressure determines the load that the tire can carry. Light truck tire sizes are often available in several load ranges (***Figure 14.35***). ***Note: The ply rating of a tire does not indicate the actual number of plies. It indicates the strength of the tire. Before load range letters were adopted in the tire industry, the ply rating was a way to compare two tires.***

Load Range	Ply Rating	Max PSI	Max kPa
B	4	35	241
C	6	50	345
D	8	65	448
E	10	80	552
F	12	95	655

Figure 14.35 ***Light Truck Tire Load Range***

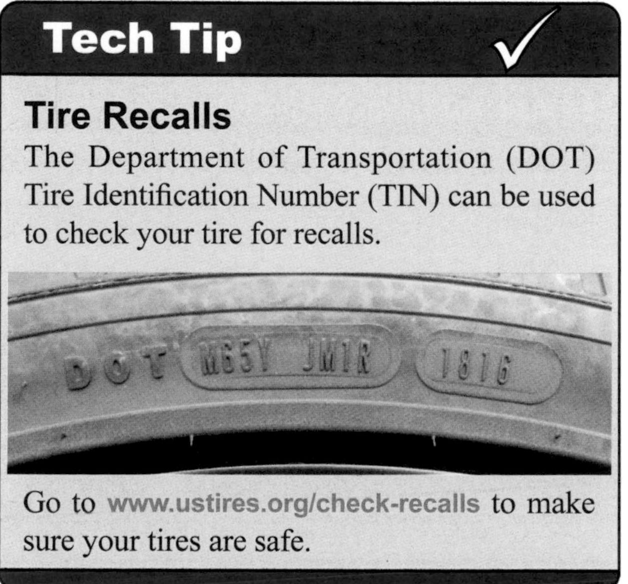

Tech Tip

Tire Recalls

The Department of Transportation (DOT) Tire Identification Number (TIN) can be used to check your tire for recalls.

Go to www.ustires.org/check-recalls to make sure your tires are safe.

Spare Tire

Spare tires come in three varieties: full size spare with matching wheel, full size spare with non-matching wheel, or a compact temporary spare. See Chapter 20 for Changing a Flat Tire steps.

Full Size Spare with Matching Wheel. A spare tire that is the exact same size with a wheel that matches the four on the vehicle is the most versatile, but also the most expensive. This type of spare should be included in a tire rotation pattern, increasing the overall useful life of all your tires.

Full Size Spare with Non-Matching Wheel. A spare tire may be the exact same size as the other tires on the vehicle, but mounted on a less expensive, usually steel, wheel (***Figure 14.36***).

Figure 14.36 *Full Size Spare*

Compact Temporary Spare. To save weight and space in the cargo area (trunk), most passenger cars come with a compact temporary spare – also called a "space-saver" or "donut" spare (***Figure 14.37***). These tires are for temporary emergency use only. Refer to the owner's manual and the spare tire sidewall for specific use. Most temporary spares are designed for very short distances that don't exceed 50 mph (80 km/h). ***Note: If you need to go past the tire's recommended distance, it is best to move the compact spare to a dead axle tire location. Different tire heights on a live axle may cause transaxle/differential damage.***

Figure 14.37 *Temporary Spare Tire*

No Spare Tire

Some cars no longer come equipped with a spare tire to save weight (increasing fuel economy), manufacturer cost, and cargo space. They may use run flat technology or come with an inflator kit (sealant) and mini air compressor (***Figure 14.38***). Free roadside assistance comes with most new vehicles for a specified amount of time.

Figure 14.38 *Inflator Kit and Air Compressor*

Trouble Guide

Vehicle Pulls to One Side

- Uneven tire pressure
- Defective tire
- Wheels out of alignment
- Brake caliper stuck

Tire Care and Maintenance

Inspecting your tires on a regular basis will help you identify their condition. Many things can cause abnormal tire wear: underinflation, overinflation, worn steering components, worn suspension components, tires out of balance, and tire misalignment. This section focuses on:

- Tire Wear Indicator Bars
- Wheel Alignment
- Tire Pressure
- Tire Repairs
- Age of Tire
- Tire Rotation
- Balancing

Tire Wear Indicator Bars

The design of tire tread, determines how well a tire will act on different road conditions, such as ice, water, mud, and snow. A tire with little tread is more likely to lose traction or hydroplane on wet roads. Tire wear indicator bars (***Figure 14.39***) run perpendicular to the tread providing a visual, tool free inspection of tread depth. Tread depth is measured in 32^{nds} of an inch or in millimeters. A tire is legally worn out when tread reaches 2/32^{nds} of an inch (1.6 mm), the same level as the indicator bars. Inspect your tires regularly to make sure they have plenty of tread.

Figure 14.39 ***Tire Wear Indicator Bars***

Wheel Alignment

Proper wheel alignment optimizes vehicle handling, maximizes fuel economy, and minimizes tire wear. If the wheels are properly aligned, the driver has to exert very little force to steer on straight, smooth roads. Wheel alignments should be performed when the vehicle pulls to the left or right, abnormal tire wear is noticed, new tires are installed, suspension or steering parts have been replaced, after an accident, hitting a curb, or going in the ditch. Terms used to describe how a tire aligns with the road are caster, camber, and toe.

Abnormal Tire Wear. Abnormal tire wear is effected by tire inflation, wheel balance, and wheel alignment (***Figure 14.40***).

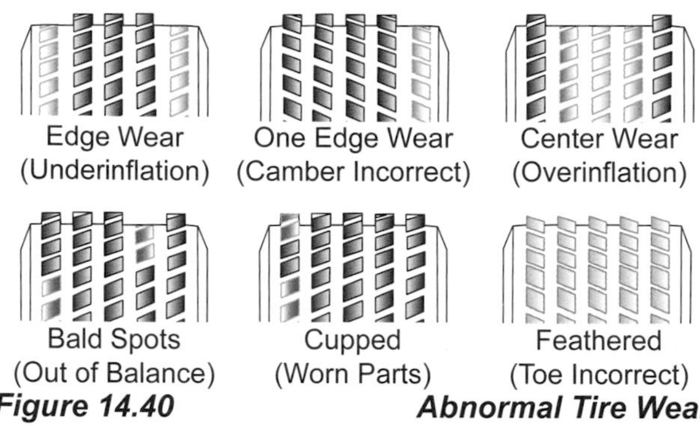

Figure 14.40 ***Abnormal Tire Wear***

Caster. Caster (***Figure 14.41***) is the steering axis angle - the forward or backward tilt from absolute vertical as viewed from the side of the vehicle. Forward tilt is negative caster while backward tilt is positive caster. Caster effects stability, control, and the steering wheel's ability to return to center.

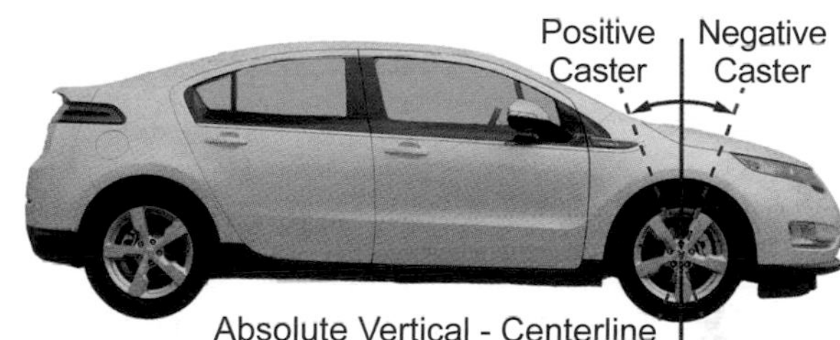

Figure 14.41 ***Caster as Viewed from the Side***

Camber. Camber (***Figure 14.42***) is the inward or outward tilt of the tire from absolute vertical when viewed from the vehicle's front. When the top of the tire leans outward, it has positive camber. When the top of the tire leans inward, it has negative camber.

Figure 14.42 ***Camber as Viewed from the Front***

Toe. When the front distance of a pair of tires is less than the back, it is defined as toe-in. When the front distance of a pair of tires is greater than the back, it is defined as toe-out (***Figure 14.43***).

Figure 14.43 ***Toe as Viewed from the Front***

Tire Pressure

Correct tire pressure is critical to tire wear and vehicle handling. A tire with low pressure dramatically increases the rolling resistance (which decreases fuel economy) and causes the tire to wear faster (due to excess heat). Tire pressure is based on tire type, vehicle weight, and ride performance desired. Tire pressure is measured with a tire pressure gauge in pounds per square inch (psi) or kilopascals (kPa).

Nitrogen. To help maintain optimal tire pressure, high purity nitrogen (over 93%) can be used instead of air (which is 78% nitrogen, 21% oxygen, and 1% water vapor and other gases). Nitrogen molecules are physically the largest in air, making them less permeable than standard air. Visit www.getnitrogen.org/why to learn more about using nitrogen in tires.

Tire Pressure Monitoring System (TPMS). A vehicle's TPMS is used to alert the driver if any tire is significantly low on pressure (***Figure 14.44***). Vehicles that have a gross vehicle weight ratio of less than 10,000 pounds (4,536 kg) and manufactured on or after September 1st, 2007 are required by the NHTSA to have a TPMS.

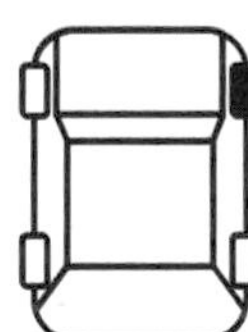

Figure 14.44 ***TPMS Indicators***

TPMS Sensor. A TPMS sensor (***Figure 14.45***) is commonly part of the tire valve stem. The battery, which is sealed into the sensor, usually lasts five to ten years.

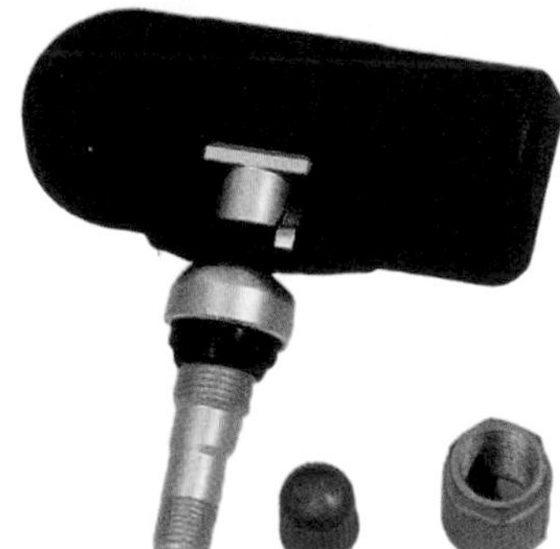

Figure 14.45 ***TPMS Sensor***

Tire Placard. The tire placard (***Figure 14.46***) identifies the recommended tire pressure. It should be on the driver's side door or jamb.

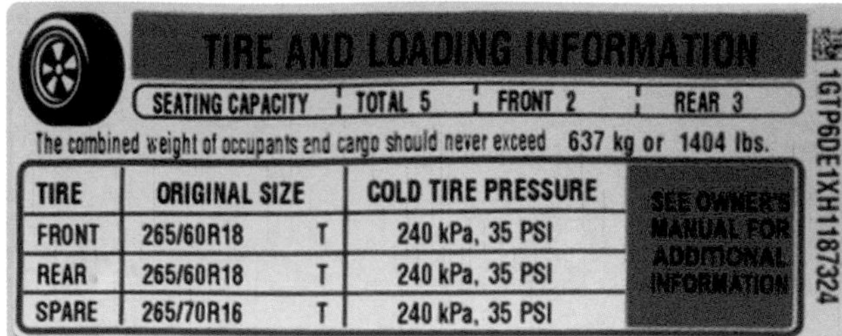

TIRE AND LOADING INFORMATION

SEATING CAPACITY | TOTAL 5 | FRONT 2 | REAR 3

The combined weight of occupants and cargo should never exceed 637 kg or 1404 lbs.

TIRE	ORIGINAL SIZE		COLD TIRE PRESSURE	SEE OWNER'S MANUAL FOR ADDITIONAL INFORMATION
FRONT	265/60R18	T	240 kPa, 35 PSI	
REAR	265/60R18	T	240 kPa, 35 PSI	
SPARE	265/70R16	T	240 kPa, 35 PSI	

1GTP6DE1XH1187324

Figure 14.46 ***Tire Placard***

Checking Tire Pressure. Use a quality air gauge to check the pressure in your tires, including the spare, at least once a month (***Figure 14.47***). Always check when tires are cold and before long trips.

Tire Pressure Check

STEP 1	Look in your driver's side door or other location as identified by the manufacturer for a tire placard that lists the correct pressure for each tire.
STEP 2	Check tire pressure when the tires are cold and you have access to an air compressor. Remove the valve stem cap.
STEP 3	Push the air gauge firmly onto the valve stem until you hear air rush into the gauge. Note the reading.

STEP 4	Add air if the reading is below the recommended pressure and repeat Step 3 and Step 4 as necessary. Do not overinflate.
STEP 5	If you added too much air, bleed some air from the tire. Many tire pressure gauges have a special tip for pressing in the valve to release air pressure. Repeat Step 3.
STEP 6	Once the tire is at the correct pressure, replace the valve stem cap and check the other tires.

Figure 14.47 ***Checking Tire Pressure***

Tire Repairs

The size and location of a tire puncture will determine if it can be repaired.

Repairable and Non-Repairable Area. Only small punctures in the tire tread area (***Figure 14.48***) can be repaired safely. The tire sidewall and shoulder experience too much stress from expansion and contraction as the tire rotates down the highway and therefore should not be repaired.

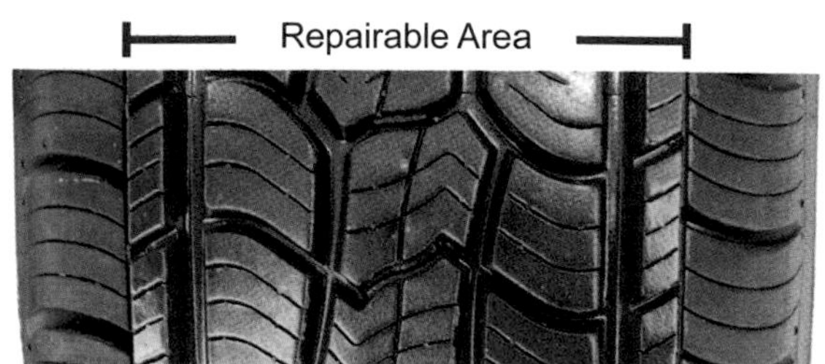

Figure 14.48 ***Repairable Area***

Patch/Plug Repair. A quality repair requires a patch/plug combination to seal and fill the hole (***Figure 14.49***). Service centers use speciality equipment to repair, change, and balance tires.

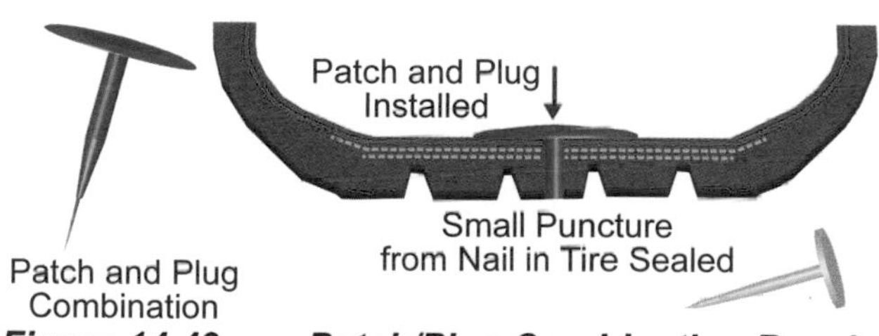

Figure 14.49 ***Patch/Plug Combination Repair***

Road Hazard/Repair Warranty. If you purchased a road hazard/repair warranty with your tires, your repair or tire replacement may be covered. Review your warranty booklet. After the free replacement period, tire warranties are prorated. This means that you would need to pay a percentage of the replacement depending on the remaining tread depth.

Age of a Tire

Tires are perishable items. This means that if you don't drive many miles each year, they could age out before wearing out. The rubber in a tire degrades over time. The tread of an old tire can dangerously separate from the rest of the tire. Some automotive manufacturers recommend replacing tires that are six years old, regardless of the tread left on them. The clock starts once the tire has been manufactured, not when it was installed on your vehicle. When you purchase new tires look at the manufacturer's date code (***Figure 14.50***). Be sure you are getting freshly made tires, not tires that have been sitting on the shelves for several years.

Figure 14.50 Tire Date Code - 51st Week of 2016

Price Guides

Radial Tires
- $40.00 to $250.00 each

Tire Repairs
- $10.00 to $30.00 (parts and labor)

Tire Rotation
- $20.00 to $40.00 (labor)

Tire Pressure Monitoring System Sensor
- $20.00 to $50.00 each (parts)

Tire Pressure Monitoring System Service Kit
- $5.00 to $10.00 each (parts)

Wheel Alignments
- $40.00 to $80.00 (labor)

Trouble Guide

Excessive Tire Wear

- Incorrect tire pressure
- Excessive speeds in turns
- Excessive braking
- Tires out of balance
- Suspension and steering components excessively worn
- Alignment incorrect

Vibration

- Out of balance tire
- Tire has broken belts

Tire Rotation

Moving tires from one location to another is called tire rotation. The front tires tend to wear faster than the back since they absorb turning forces, carry the engine weight, and support the added weight that shifts forward when braking. Rotating tires improves tire life by evening out tire wear. After rotating tires, check the tire pressure according to the tire placard on the vehicle.

Tire Rotation Pattern. Check the owner's manual for the rotation pattern (***Figure 14.51***).

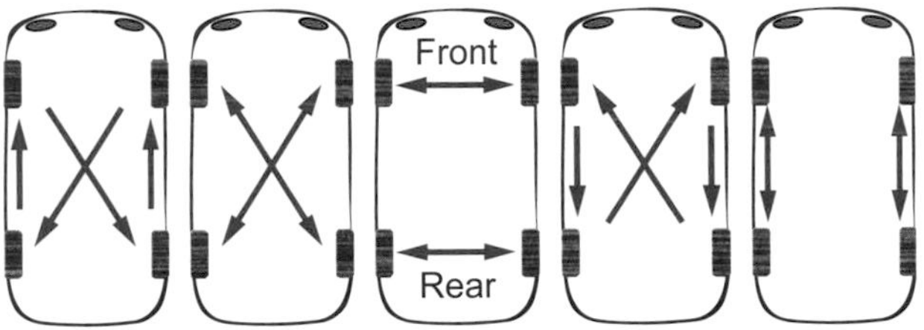

Figure 14.51 ***Example Tire Rotation Patterns***

Note: Some tires are directional, designed to roll in only one direction and should not be moved to the other side of the vehicle unless they are dismounted from the wheel, flipped, and remounted. An arrow on the sidewall indicates their forward rotation (Figure 14.52).

Figure 14.52 ***Directional Tire Arrow***

Lug Nut Design. A lug nut has a tapered end (***Figure 14.53***) that is faced toward the wheel.

Figure 14.53 ***Lug Nut Tapered End***

> **Servicing**
>
> **Tire Rotation**
> - Rotate every 7,500 miles

Lug Nut Torque Specification. Use a torque wrench (***Figure 14.54***) when retightening lug nuts. Torque refers to getting all of the lug nuts to the same tightness. Unevenly tightened lug nuts can cause rotor runout. Over-tightened lug nuts make it difficult to change the tire later, while under-tightened lug nuts may cause the wheel to come off. Find the correct torque specification in your owner's manual. Look under "Specifications", "Maintenance", "Wheels", or "Tire Rotation". ***Note: Always recheck lug nut torque within the first 100 miles after a tire rotation (or anytime the wheel has been removed and reinstalled).***

Figure 14.54 ***Torquing Lug Nuts***

Lug Nut Torque Patterns. It is important to torque the lug nuts in a star or crisscross pattern (***Figure 14.55***) with a torque wrench. See the Tire Inspection and Rotation Activity in Chapter 14 of the workbook for rotation steps.

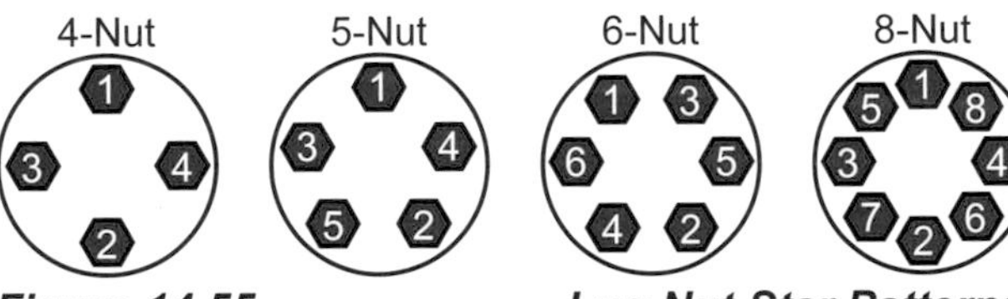

Figure 14.55 ***Lug Nut Star Patterns***

Wheel Lock (Antitheft) Lug Nuts. Vehicles with expensive custom wheels commonly have wheel lock (antitheft) lug nuts (***Figure 14.56***). A special key is used to remove and install the lug nut.

Figure 14.56 ***Wheel Lock Lug Nut and Key***

Resetting the TPMS. Some systems relearn the new tire location automatically, while others need you to use a compatible tool. Often called a TPMS reset, relearn, activation, or scan tool, it identifies the new location of the tire. Read your owner's manual to identify the TPMS relearn procedure for your vehicle.

Balancing

Once a tire is mounted on a wheel it needs to be balanced. This means the weight of the tire and wheel are evenly distributed. A tire and wheel that is out of balance may cause vibrations, increase tire wear, and shorten the life of suspension and steering components. A wheel balancer is used to identify where wheel weights (***Figure 14.57***) are installed on the wheel.

Figure 14.57 ***Wheel Weight***

Web Links

Tire Manufacturer Sites

BFGoodrich Tires
www.bfgoodrichtires.com

Bridgestone/Firestone Tires
www.firestonetire.com

Cooper Tires
www.us.coopertire.com

Dunlop Tires
www.dunloptires.com

Goodyear Tires
www.goodyear.com

Kelly Tires
www.kellytires.com

Michelin
www.michelinman.com

Pirelli Tires
www.pirelli.com

Toyo Tires
www.toyotires.com

Uniroyal Tires
www.uniroyaltires.com

Summary

The suspension system absorbs bumps in the road to give a smooth ride. The steering system allows the operator to control left and right motions of the vehicle. Tires can have symmetrical, asymmetrical, directional, or asymmetrical/directional tread designs. Tires provide the traction (adhesive friction) necessary for maneuvering. Knowing tire specifications can be beneficial when buying new tires. UTQG ratings make it easier for you to compare different tires. Abnormal tire wear patterns show possible problems with the vehicle. Suspension and steering components work in conjunction to provide a safe ride.

Activities

Suspension, Steering, and Tires

- Suspension and Steering Activity
- Tire Inspection and Rotation Activity
- Chapter 14 Study Questions

Activities and Study Questions can be completed in the *Auto Upkeep Workbook.*

Career Paths

Tire Manufacturing Engineer

Education: Bachelor's Degree
Median Income: $83,470
Abilities: Applies material science and technology to design, manufacture, and test tires.
Find your career at www.bls.gov/ooh.

Braking System

Fuel for Thought

- How are disc and drum brakes different?
- How do antilock brakes work?
- How do you know when brake pads need replacing?

Introduction

The braking system is designed to help the driver control the deceleration of the vehicle. While the suspension and steering systems control the ride and directional movements, the braking system is designed to slow or stop the vehicle. The braking system is crucial to the safe operation of the vehicle. This chapter identifies brake components and the principles of friction that assist in slowing a vehicle.

Web Links

Brake System Related Sites

ACDelco
www.acdelco.com

Bosch Auto Parts
www.boschautoparts.com

Brake Parts Inc.
www.brakepartsinc.com

EBC Brakes
www.ebcbrakes.com

Bendix Brakes
www.bendix-brakes.com

Meineke Car Care Centers, Inc.
www.meineke.com

Midas International Corporation
www.midas.com

Raybestos Brakes
www.raybestos.com

Wagner Brake Products
www.wagnerbrake.com

Objectives

Upon completion of this chapter and activities, you will be able to:

- Define the purpose and principles of the braking system.
- Identify the different types of brakes and their components.
- Identify brake fluid properties.
- Discuss the advantages of antilock brakes.
- Identify different types of advanced control and safety systems.
- Explain how the parking brake works.
- Safely perform basic inspections on the braking system.

Braking System Purpose

The braking system is designed to decrease the speed of a vehicle using kinetic (in motion) friction and keep it from rolling when stopped using static (at rest) friction. Friction is the force that resists motion between two touching objects (***Figure 15.1***). Friction between brake components slows or stops a vehicle by transferring the energy of motion (kinetic energy) to heat (thermal energy). This heat must be dissipated by the brake system into the air. Unlike the lubrication system, where minimizing friction is the goal, the braking system is designed to use friction for control.

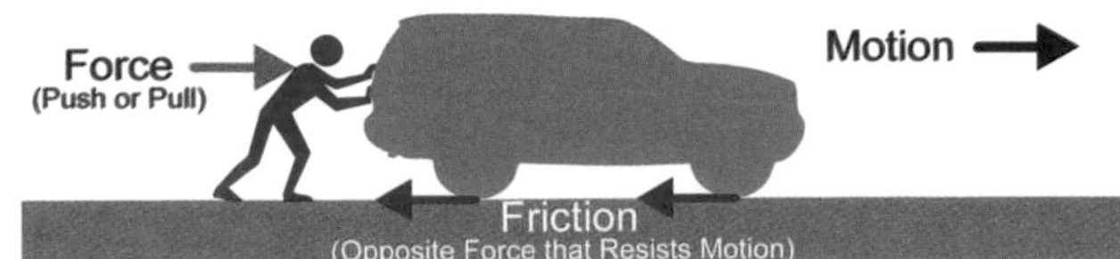

Figure 15.1 ***Friction***

Types of Brakes

Most vehicles use a hydraulic brake system. To become more fuel efficient, some vehicles use regenerative braking in addition to the hydraulic brake system. This section focuses on:

- Hydraulic Brakes
- Regenerative Braking

Hydraulic Brakes

Disc and drum are the two types of hydraulic brakes used on automobiles. Some vehicles have a combination of both types with disc brakes in the front and drum brakes in the rear. Other vehicles have disc brakes on all four wheels. When applying a force on the brake pedal, the system transfers pressure to the brake calipers (used in disc brakes) or wheel cylinders (used in drum brakes). This pressure is used to move the brake frictional materials to slow down the vehicle (***Figure 15.2***).

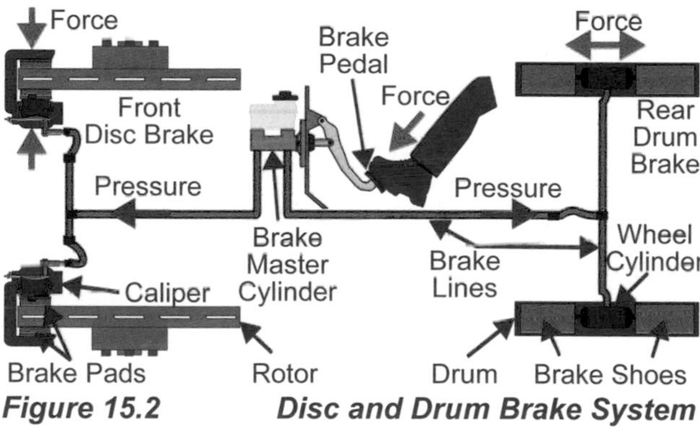

Figure 15.2 ***Disc and Drum Brake System***

Hydraulic Principles. The key principle in a hydraulic system is that fluid is not compressible (***Figure 15.3***). Pressure throughout the system is the same. Since air can be compressed, it will compromise the integrity of the system. Keeping air out of the system is extremely important. Technicians use a process called brake bleeding to remove any air that was introduced into the closed system during service or repair.

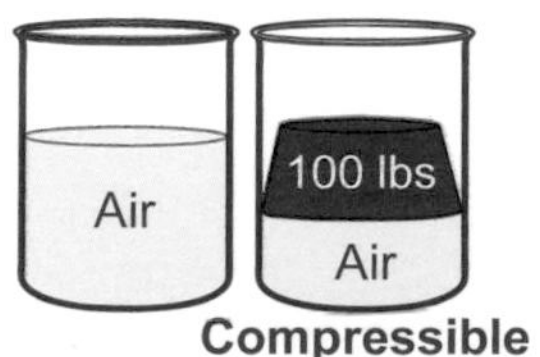

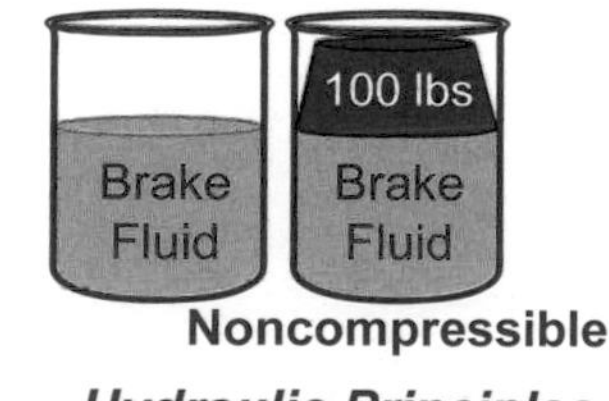

Figure 15.3 ***Hydraulic Principles***

Regenerative Braking

In addition to using a conventional hydraulic brake system, hybrid and electric vehicles use regenerative braking to capture kinetic energy that would otherwise be lost as heat from friction.

How Regenerative Braking Works. When applying the brakes in a hybrid or electric vehicle, the electric motor switches modes and becomes a generator (***Figure 15.4***). The kinetic energy of the wheels turns the motor/generator. The resistance that is created in the motor/generator from the electrical generation process, slows the vehicle. The regenerative and hydraulic brakes in these systems use computer controls with input from various sensors to work efficiently.

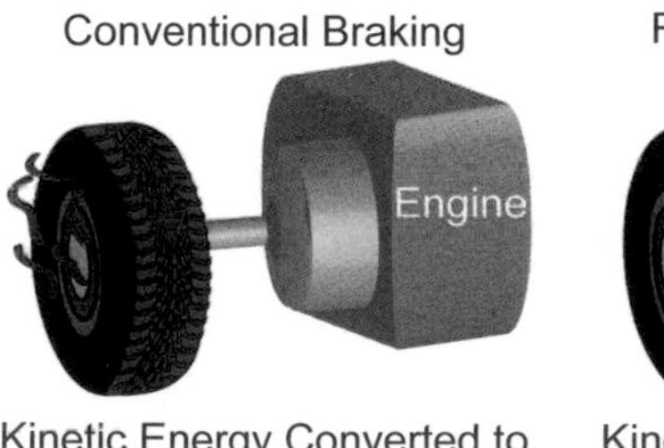

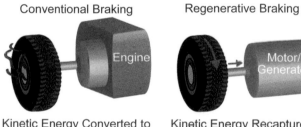

Figure 15.4 ***Regenerative Braking***

Benefits. By converting kinetic energy into electrical energy, a regenerative braking system increases the vehicle's electric range. In hybrid vehicles, the result is less fuel consumption. Regenerative braking also makes the frictional materials on the conventional brakes last longer. See Chapter 18 for more on regenerative braking.

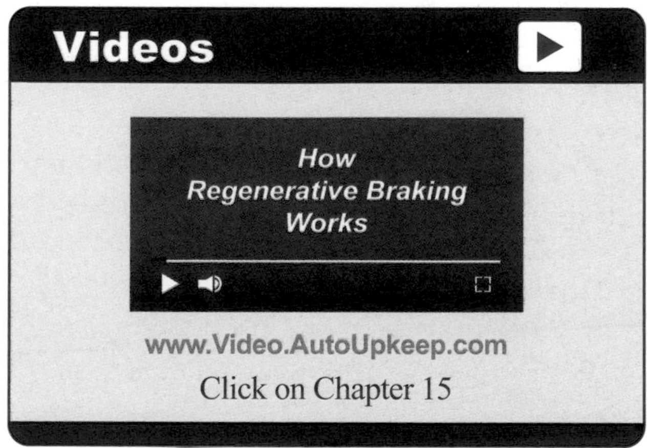

Brake Fluid

Hydraulic brakes depend on brake fluid. Brake fluid links braking system components through the brake lines. The fluid connects the master cylinder to the calipers (disc brakes) and to the wheel cylinders (drum brakes). This section focuses on:

- Types
- Checking
- Contaminates
- Service Intervals

Types

The most common brake fluid is DOT 3, but DOT 4, DOT 5, and DOT 5.1 are also available (***Figure 15.5***). Always refer to the owner's manual or brake master cylinder cap for the correct type of brake fluid. ***Warning: Use extreme caution when handling. Brake fluid is harmful to your eyes. Wear safety goggles and chemical resistant gloves. If brake fluid is spilled on a vehicle's finish, it will strip paint.***

Type	Minimum Dry Boiling Point	Minimum Wet Boiling Point*	Base
DOT 3	401°F (205°C)	284°F (140°C)	Glycol
DOT 4	446°F (230°C)	311°F (155°C)	Glycol
DOT 5	500°F (260°C)	356°F (180°C)	Silicone
DOT 5.1	500°F (260°C)	356°F (180°C)	Glycol

* @ 3.7% Water by Volume

Figure 15.5 Brake Fluid Type Specifications

Checking

Use the procedure listed in Chapter 8 to check and add brake fluid as necessary. A dash light may indicate when brake fluid is low (***Figure 15.6***).

Figure 15.6 Example Brake Fluid Low Indicators

Low Brake Fluid. Brake fluid may be low for two reasons. During normal brake wear, the brake fluid will be lower due to the frictional materials wearing. The pistons inside the calipers and wheel cylinders have to move further, so the fluid takes up the extra space. The other reason fluid would be low is if there was a leak. A leak in the system could cause your brakes to stop working.

Contaminates

Brake fluid must be clear of contaminates (***Figure 15.7***) to flow freely at high and low temperatures. Brake fluid fights corrosion, lubricates parts, and protects metal, plastic, and rubber components.

Brake Fluid System Contaminates	
Moisture	Brake fluid is designed to absorb and retain moisture to keep it from corrupting the brake system. Gradually, moisture absorbed by brake fluid will reduce the brake fluid's boiling point. To maintain the required temperature properties, only use brake fluid from a fresh sealed container and flush the system as recommended.
Dirt	To prevent dirt contamination, always clean the outside of the master cylinder reservoir before removing the cap and adding fluid.
Air	When brake components are replaced, air may get into the system. Air is compressible while brake fluid is not, making the brake pedal feel spongy and soft. Remove air by bleeding the system, pushing the air out of a "bleeder" at the caliper or wheel cylinder.

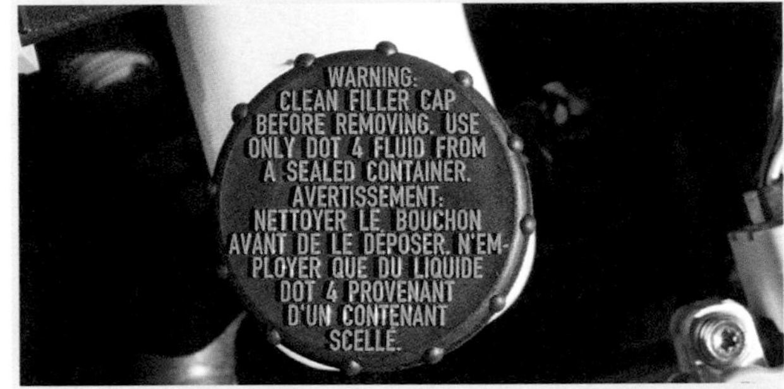

Figure 15.7 Brake Fluid System Contaminates

Service Intervals

Old brake fluid can cause brake components to deteriorate and create a hazardous driving condition. It is important to perform recommended brake fluid changes. Many manufacturers recommend changing the brake fluid every two to three years.

Servicing

Brake Fluid

- Change every 3 years, 45,000 miles, during brake service, or as recommended by the manufacturer

Braking System Components

Disc and drum brake systems both use a brake pedal, master cylinder, brake lines, and a frictional type material that slowly wears as the brakes are applied. ***Warning: Some brake frictional material contains asbestos. Wear an OSHA approved respirator when inspecting or replacing brake components at the wheels.*** The major difference between the disc and drum brake systems is the hardware at the wheels. This section focuses on:

- Brake Pedal
- Master Cylinder
- Brake Lines
- Disc Brakes
- Drum Brakes
- Wheel Speed Sensors

Brake Pedal

The force used on the brake pedal determines how much friction is created at the wheels. Force is defined as the pushing or pulling action of one object (driver's foot) upon another (brake pedal). The brake pedal is mechanically connected to a hydraulic unit called a master cylinder (***Figure 15.8***). Some brake pedals are height adjustable to aid in driver comfort.

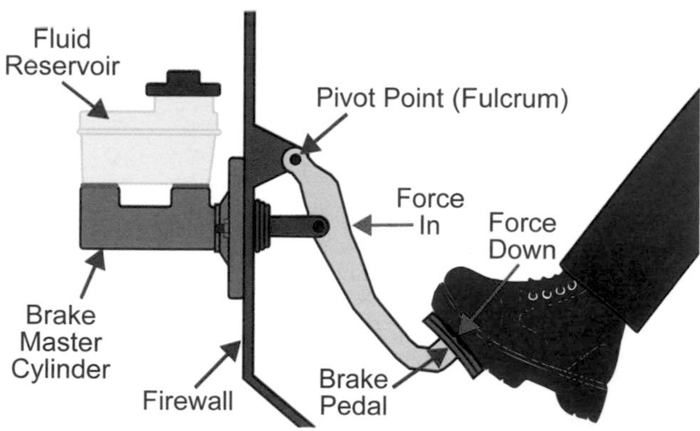

Figure 15.8 ***Brake Pedal Connection***

Trouble Guide

Pedal Travels to the Floor

- Low brake fluid
- Brake fluid leak
- Air in the brake system
- Incorrect drum brake shoe adjustment

Master Cylinder

The master cylinder (***Figure 15.9***) converts the mechanical force from the brake pedal to hydraulic pressure at the wheels. The master cylinder reservoir is where brake fluid is stored.

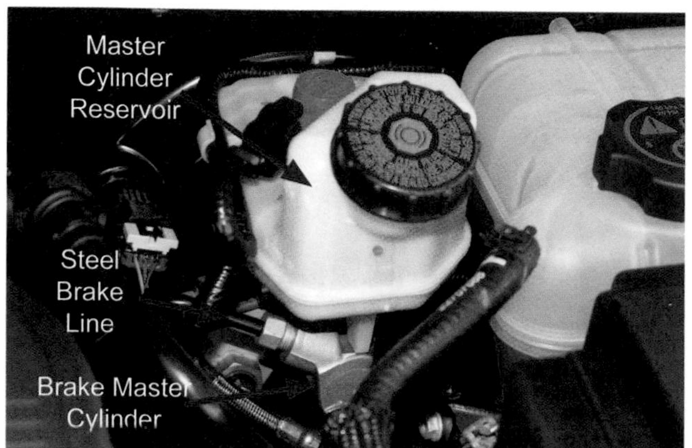

Figure 15.9 Brake Master Cylinder and Reservoir

Brake Lines

As force is exerted on the brake pedal, brake lines carry brake fluid under pressure from the master cylinder to each wheel. Once at the wheels, the fluid pressure is converted back to mechanical force in the caliper or wheel cylinder. This causes the brake pads or shoes to move against the rotating disc or drum at the wheels, creating friction to slow the wheel/tire unit. As long as the tires maintain friction (traction) with the road the vehicle will slow or stop.

Types. Steel brake lines and rubber hoses are used to transfer fluid to the wheels (***Figure 15.10***). Rubber hoses are used when a flexible connection is needed. For example, a rubber hose is used at each front wheel to allow the tires to turn.

Figure 15.10 ***Brake Lines***

Disc Brakes

The disc brake hardware at the wheel consists of a rotor, two brake pads, and a caliper (***Figure 15.11***).

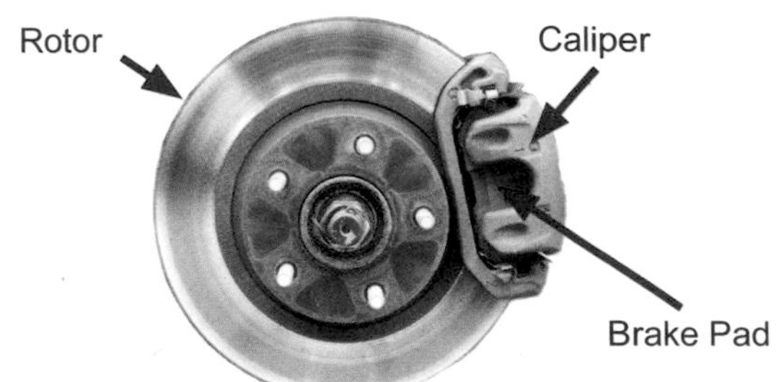

Figure 15.11 Brake Rotor, Pads, and Caliper

Rotor. The rotor, also called a disc, (***Figure 15.12***), connects to the wheel hub. Friction is produced when the brakes are applied. This friction creates a lot of heat, so rotors are often vented to help with cooling. When inspecting rotors check both sides for thickness, unevenness (disc thickness variation), cracks, and deep scoring. If a rotor measures thick enough, it may be possible to resurface it smooth. Replace or resurface rotors in pairs, so their thickness remains balanced and surface finish is consistent.

Figure 15.12 Brake Disc (Rotor)

Brake Pads. A set of brake pads (***Figure 15.13***) hug the rotor. As force is applied to the brake pedal, the brake pads hug the rotor tighter causing more friction.

Figure 15.13 Brake Pads

Servicing

Brake Pads and Shoes

- Inspect once a year
- Change when worn past specifications

Wear Indicators. Some brake pads are engineered with mechanical or electrical wear indicators as a replacement reminder. A mechanical indicator uses a thin metal strip against the rotor to produce a high pitched squeal once the pad wears down, without causing rotor damage. The electrical indicator uses an electrical contact in the pad. When the pad has worn to that electrical ground contact it completes a circuit and a dash indicator lamp (also called a MIL – malfunction indicator light) illuminates. If you don't replace worn brake pads you will soon hear a metal on metal grinding noise that will damage the rotors and create a braking hazard.

Caliper. The caliper, a type of hydraulic C-clamp with a piston, holds a brake pad on either side of the rotor (***Figure 15.14***). The caliper converts the fluid pressure in the brake lines to the mechanical motion of the pads against each side of the rotor.

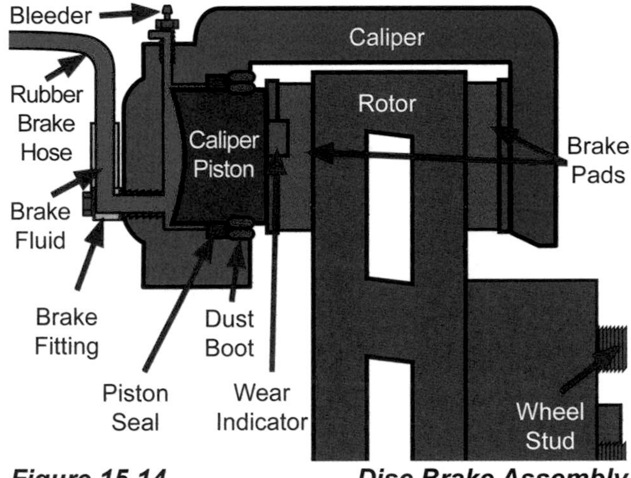

Figure 15.14 Disc Brake Assembly

Tech Tip

Brake Pedal Pulsation

If a pulsation is noticed when the brakes are applied, the rotors (discs) may have uneven wear. Disc thickness variation (DVT) is caused by rotor runout. Rotor runout can occur when lug nuts are unevenly torqued or if corrosion or dirt is between the rotor and the hub during installation. On drum brakes, the drum may be out-of-round.

Drum Brakes

The drum brake hardware at a wheel consists of a drum, two brake shoes, return springs, hold down springs, a wheel cylinder, and other miscellaneous hardware (***Figure 15.15***).

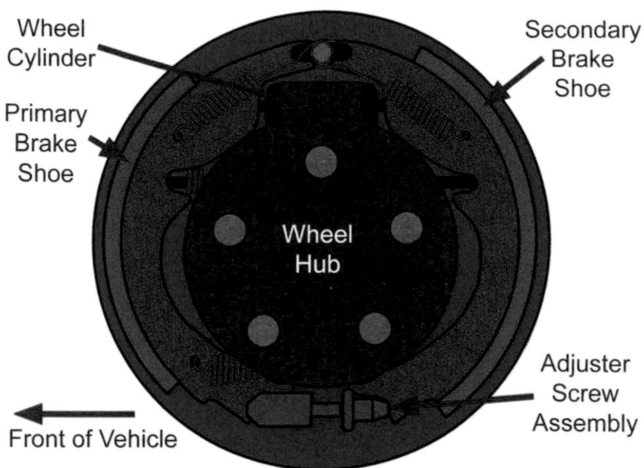

Figure 15.15 ***Drum Brake Assembly***

Brake Drum. The brake drum (***Figure 15.16***) connects to the wheel hub. If a newer vehicle has drum brakes, they are on the back wheels. Similar to rotors, it may be possible to resurface the drums if they are thick enough. The drums should be machined equally as a pair.

Figure 15.16 ***Brake Drum***

Trouble Guide

High Pitched Brake Squeal

- Disc brake pads worn out
- Hardened spots on pads or rotors
- Issues with shims, clips, or lubricant

Grinding Brakes

- Disc brake pads or shoes worn out

Pulsating Brakes

- Disc (rotor) thickness variation
- Excessive rotor runout
- Brake drum out-of-round

Brake Shoes. Inside the drum is a set of brake shoes (***Figure 15.17***). When force is applied to the brake pedal or the parking brake is engaged, the brake shoes are forced out against the brake drum creating friction to slow and stop the wheels.

Figure 15.17 ***Brake Shoes***

Wheel Cylinder. A wheel cylinder (***Figure 15.18***) converts the fluid pressure in the brake lines to the mechanical motion of the shoes against the drum.

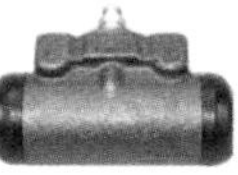

Figure 15.18 ***Wheel Cylinder***

Wheel Speed Sensors

Wheel speed sensors (***Figure 15.19***) monitor a toothed sensor ring (tone ring) to keep track of and compare the rotational speed of each wheel.

Figure 15.19 Wheel Speed Sensor and Tone Ring

Price Guides

Brake Fluid
- $4.00 to $12.00 a 12 oz. bottle

Brake Pads
- $30.00 to $75.00 a set (parts)

Brake Shoes
- $20.00 to $40.00 a set (parts)

Brake Rotor or Drum
- $50.00 to $100.00 each (parts)

Control and Safety Systems

The antilock brake system (ABS) was the first computerized system designed to help maintain tire traction, improving control and safety. The ABS uses sensors at each wheel (or in the differential) to monitor wheel speed, a hydraulic control unit (***Figure 15.20***) to regulate brake pressure, and a controller to command the system. Traction control and electronic stability control work from essentially the same ABS platform with added sensors. Many different types of safety and control devices are now available on vehicles. This section focuses on:

- Antilock Brake System (ABS)
- Traction Control System (TCS)
- Electronic Stability Control (ESC)
- Brake Assist System (BAS)
- Hill Start Assist (HSA)
- Autonomous Emergency Braking (AEB)
- Forward Collision Warning (FCW)
- Adaptive Cruise Control (ACC)
- Automatic Reverse Braking (ARB)

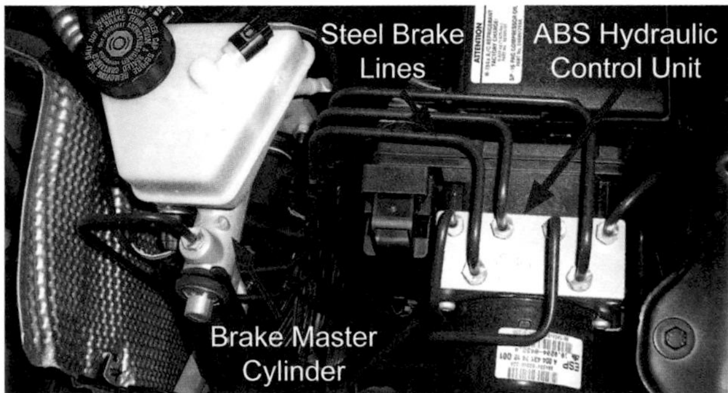

Figure 15.20 ***ABS Hydraulic Control Unit***

Antilock Brake System (ABS)

ABS minimizes wheel lockup (skidding) from too much force at the brake pedal. When a tire skids, braking distance increases and control of steering decreases. If a wheel speed sensor indicates that a wheel is about to lockup, the ABS hydraulic control unit releases pressure at that one wheel to help the tire maintain road traction. The rapid pressure adjustments of the ABS may make the brake pedal pulse. This is normal. Apply firm constant pressure and do not pump the brakes. ***Note: ABS does not always stop a vehicle faster, but it does help the operator maintain control.***

Traction Control System (TCS)

A traction control system (TCS) uses sensors to detect tire slippage during acceleration from a stop or when speeding up, the opposite of ABS (slipping during deceleration). A TCS adjusts the throttle input and applies braking force to slow a slipping wheel and help the tire regain traction with the road.

Electronic Stability Control (ESC)

Electronic stability control (ESC), required by the NHTSA for all 2012 and later vehicles, helps drivers maintain control during unstable situations such as attempting to avoid a crash or during unfavorable weather conditions. The ESC system uses information from sensors to improve the lateral stability in a vehicle by applying braking force at any wheel when instability is detected. This technology minimizes oversteer and understeer situations (***Figure 15.21***) which ultimately helps the vehicle stay on the intended course, lessening the chance of skidding and rollovers.

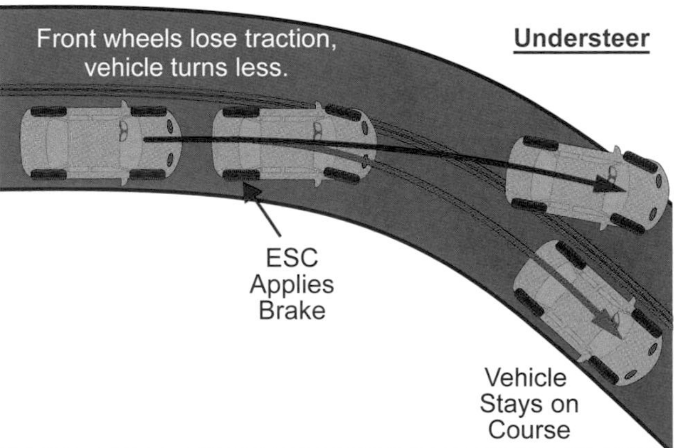

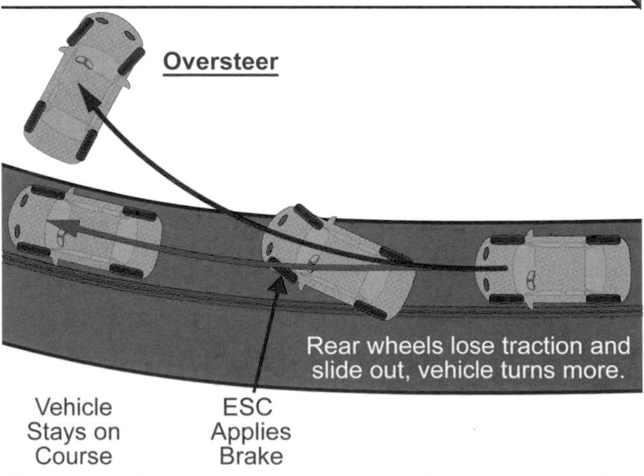

Figure 15.21 ***ESC Compensation***

Brake Assist System (BAS)

Many people do not push on the brake hard enough or fast enough during an emergency. The brake assist system (BAS) (***Figure 15.22***) is a safety control system that helps drivers stop in emergency braking situations. This system uses a control module to increase the brake pressure in the system when the driver is initiating an emergency stop. Sensors measures how fast and how hard the driver is pushing on the brake pedal to determine if it is indeed a panic stop. As the pressure increases, the ABS then activates to stop the vehicle safely and in a shorter distance.

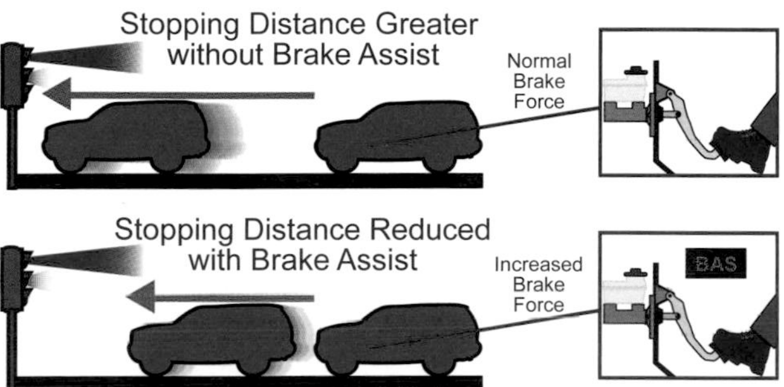

Figure 15.22 ***Brake Assist System***

Hill Start Assist (HSA)

Hill start assist (HSA) (***Figure 15.23***) helps drivers when they are stopped on a slope. When starting from a dead stop on a hill, a vehicle without HSA may roll forward or backward before the driver has a chance to accelerate. HSA uses sensors to detect when the vehicle is on a slope. It holds brake pressure during the transition time that it takes the driver to move his/her foot from the brake pedal to the accelerator pedal to prevent unwanted rolling. HSA will shut off after a preset time or when the driver presses the accelerator pedal.

Without HSA
Vehicle rolls backward until driver pushes the accelerator pedal.

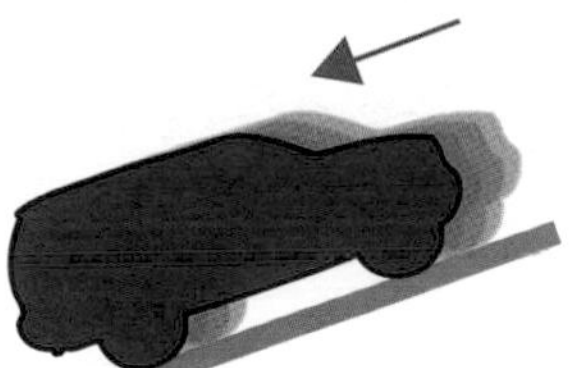

With HSA
Vehicle holds position until driver pushes the accelerator pedal.

Figure 15.23 ***Hill Start Assist***

Autonomous Emergency Braking (AEB)

Autonomous emergency braking (AEB) (***Figure 15.24***), also called automatic emergency braking, can stop a vehicle during a critical situation without the driver pushing the brake pedal. Radar, lidar (light detection and ranging), cameras, sensors, and other technologies are used to identify a possible collision. If a collision threat is identified, the system can act independently from the driver to avoid or lessen the impact by applying the brakes. Some AEB systems will also prepare the vehicle for impact. This technology is extremely effective at reducing and minimizing crash severity. Many auto manufacturers are putting AEB as standard equipment on vehicles.

Hazard Monitoring
Various sensors continuously monitor if the vehicle needs to slow down, calculating the closing distance (time-to-object).

AEB Independent Braking
As an emergency response, full braking pressure is automatically applied when a collision is imminent to avoid or lessen the impact.

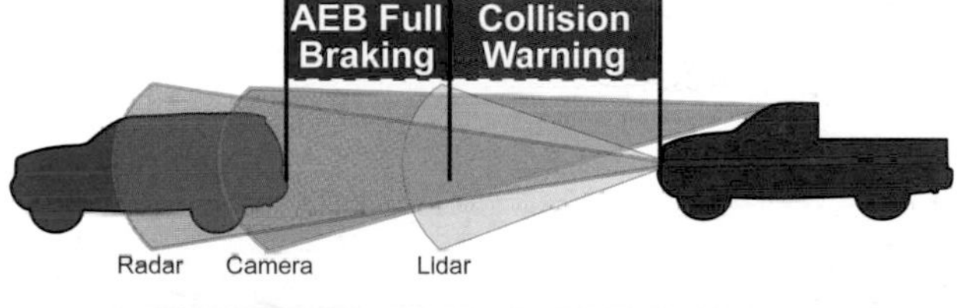

Figure 15.24 ***Autonomous Emergency Braking***

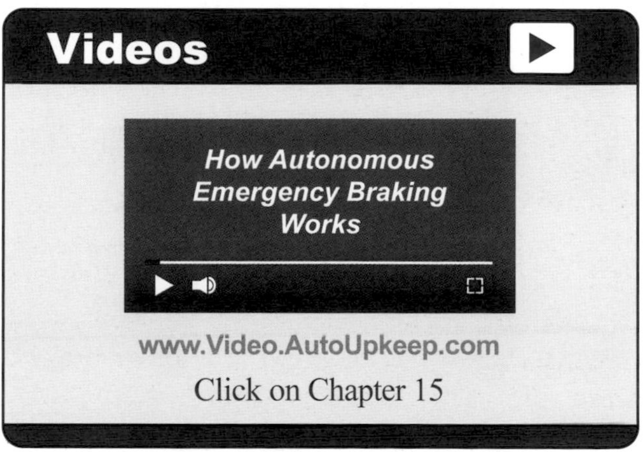

Driver must brake or steer quickly when alerted to avoid a collision.
Forward Collision Warning (FCW)

A forward collision warning (***Figure 15.25***), also known as forward collision alert, system uses similar technologies found in autonomous emergency braking systems to identify a potential collision. However, they are designed to alert the driver and not automatically and independently apply the brakes. When a collision is imminent, the system will use a visual display, audible alert, and/or seat vibration to notify the driver to apply the brakes.

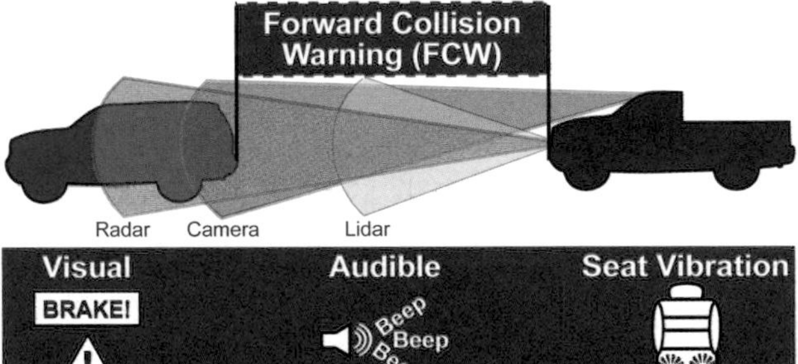

Figure 15.25 *Forward Collision Warning*

Adaptive Cruise Control (ACC)

An adaptive cruise control (ACC) system will automatically speed up or slow down based on driver initial settings when following another vehicle (***Figure 15.26***). This technology helps the driver maintain a safe following distance. Some systems even work in stop-and-go traffic, accelerating or braking when needed.

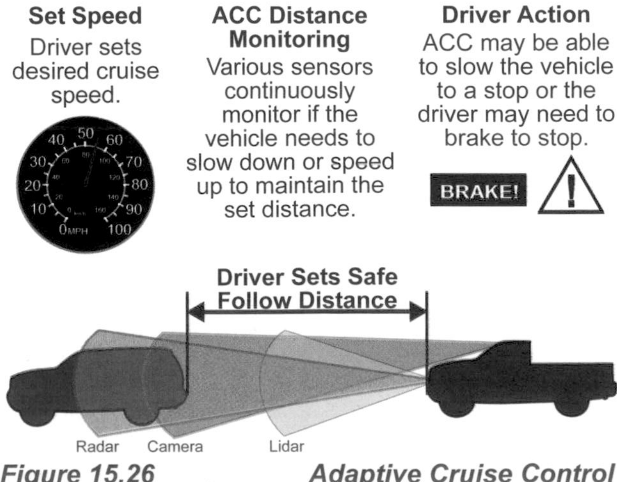

Set Speed
Driver sets desired cruise speed.
ACC Distance Monitoring
Various sensors continuously monitor if the vehicle needs to slow down or speed up to maintain the set distance.
Driver Action
ACC may be able to slow the vehicle to a stop or the driver may need to brake to stop.
BRAKE!
Driver Sets Safe Follow Distance
Radar
Camera
Lidar

Figure 15.26 *Adaptive Cruise Control*

Automatic Reverse Braking (ARB)

Rearview (backup) cameras (***Figure 15.27***), required on all vehicles made after May 2018, reduce the number of accidental backover accidents. Especially vulnerable are small children. Many blind spots exist behind a vehicle. A rearview camera can significantly increase the view for the driver while backing up. Using cameras and sensors, automatic reverse braking helps avoid collisions by automatically applying the brakes when an object is detected. ***Note: Not all vehicles with rearview cameras have automatic reverse braking. Read your owner's manual to find out if this technology is on your vehicle. Either way, be extremely cautious while backing up.***

Figure 15.27 *Rearview Camera*

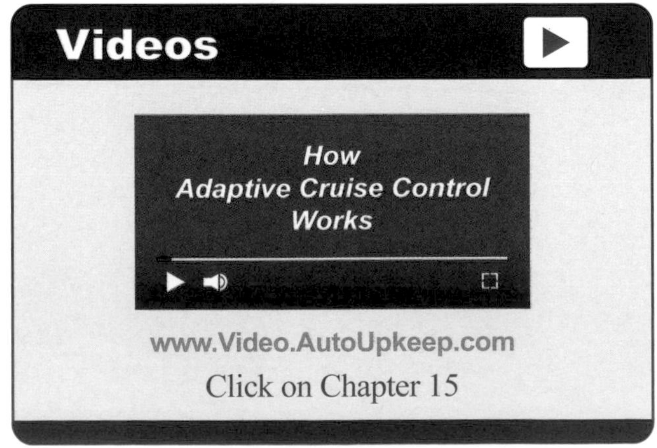

Click on Chapter 15

Parking Brakes

A parking brake engages shoes or pads at the rear wheels to keep the vehicle from moving when parked. However, instead of brake fluid as the connection, a mechanical cable or electric motor is used. This section focuses on:

- Mechanical Cable
- Electric Parking Brake (EPB)

Mechanical Cable

A hand lever (***Figure 15.28***) in the console or small pedal on the far left side of the driver's foot controls engages the cable. The cable allows the systems to work independently. To help keep the cable from corroding and seizing, use it whenever parking. If the brake lever or pedal moves more than normal, it may be an indication the cable or brakes are worn.

Figure 15.28 ***Hand Lever Parking Brake***

Electric Parking Brake (EPB)

An EPB uses an electric button located in the console (***Figure 15.29***) to signal a motor to pull the brake cable or directly engage advanced caliper motors when parking.

Figure 15.29 ***Electric Parking Brake Button***

Summary

Hydraulic brake systems use friction to slow and stop a vehicle. Regenerative braking captures kinetic energy to slow down a vehicle. Disc brakes use rotors, pads, and calipers. Drum brakes use drums, shoes, and wheel cylinders. Advanced technological systems such as antilock brakes, traction control, electronic stability control, brake assist, hill start assist, autonomous emergency braking, forward collision warning, adaptive cruise control, and automatic reverse braking have been installed on cars to maximize driver control and minimize accidents. The parking brake uses a mechanical linkage (cable) or motor instead of a fluid linkage (brake fluid).

Web Links

Safety Advocacy Sites

AAA Foundation for Traffic Safety
www.aaafoundation.org

Advocates for Highway and Auto Safety
www.saferoads.org

Insurance Institute for Highway Safety
www.iihs.org

KidsAndCars.org
www.kidsandcars.org

MyCarDoesWhat.org
www.mycardoeswhat.org

National Highway Traffic Safety Administration
www.nhtsa.gov

Activities

Braking System

- Braking Inspection Activity
- Chapter 15 Study Questions

Activities and Study Questions can be completed in the *Auto Upkeep Workbook*.

Career Paths

Brake Technician

Education: Technical Training or ASE Cert.
Median Income: $37,850
Abilities: Understands principles of electronics and hydraulics. Lathe operation experience.
Find your career at www.bls.gov/ooh.

Chapter 16: Drivetrain

Fuel for Thought

- What is the purpose of the drivetrain?
- How do transmissions work?
- What types of drivetrain configurations are available?

Introduction

The engine can provide all the power in the world, but if it isn't transferred to the wheels the vehicle will not move. Automobiles need to perform equally well under a variety of loads. The transfer of power needs to accommodate the conditions on the highway, the weight of the vehicle and its passengers, and the performance desired to accelerate. Today's automobile buyers can choose between rear-wheel, front-wheel, four-wheel, or all-wheel drivetrains. This chapter identifies the purpose of the drivetrain, drivetrain components, and types of drivetrains.

Objectives

Upon completion of this chapter and activities, you will be able to:

- Define the purpose of the drivetrain.
- Identify drivetrain components.
- Describe different drivetrain systems.
- Inspect drivetrain systems.

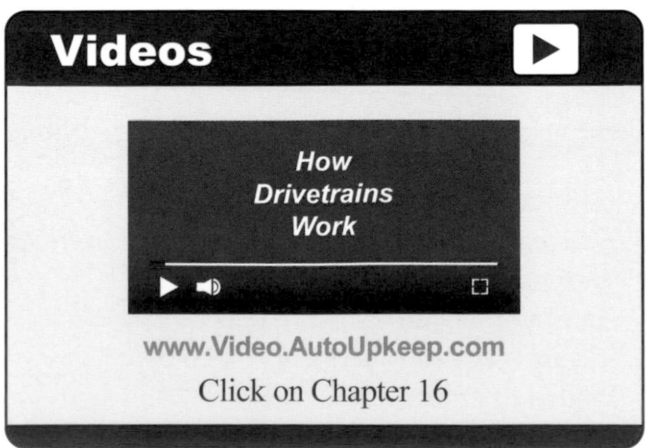

Purpose of the Drivetrain

The purpose of the drivetrain (***Figure 16.1***) is to transfer power from the engine to the wheels in order to propel the vehicle. This transfer needs to be done smoothly and efficiently. Without smooth transitions, the automobile would not be very comfortable or easy to drive. The drivetrain also helps to control the speed and power through gears.

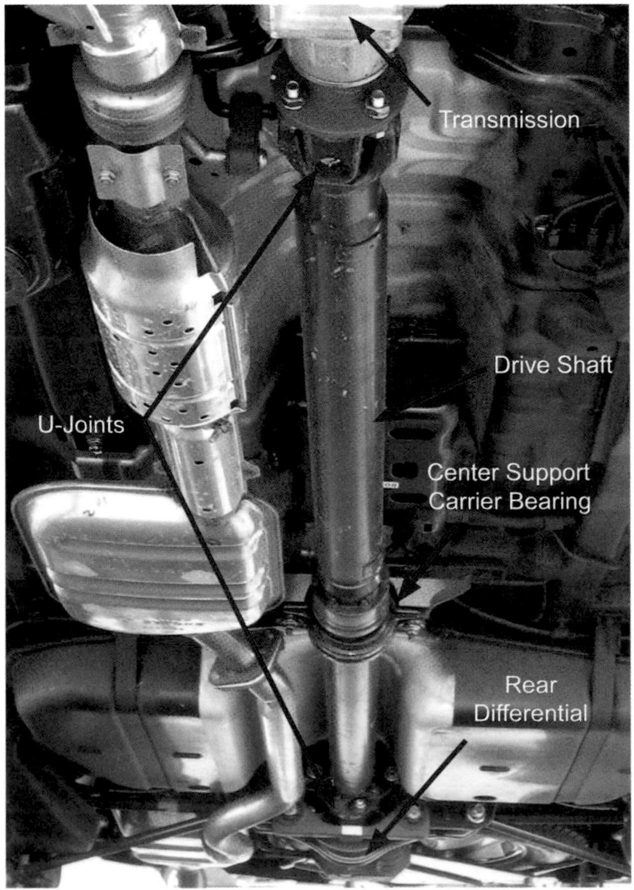

Figure 16.1 ***Drivetrain Components on a Rear-Wheel Drive Vehicle***

Gears

Gears are used in power transfer systems like transmissions and differentials. This section focuses on:

- Gear Sets
- Gear Ratio

Gear Sets

Gears, always engineered in sets, are used to change speed, torque, and direction of travel (***Figure 16.2***). Gears have teeth that prevent slippage. They have to correctly mesh, or lock together, to work properly.

Figure 16.2 ***Gear Set Example***

Gear Ratio

Gear ratio is a term used to describe the input (drive) gear speed relative to the output (driven) gear speed. The relative speed is dependent on the number of teeth on both gears (***Figure 16.3***).

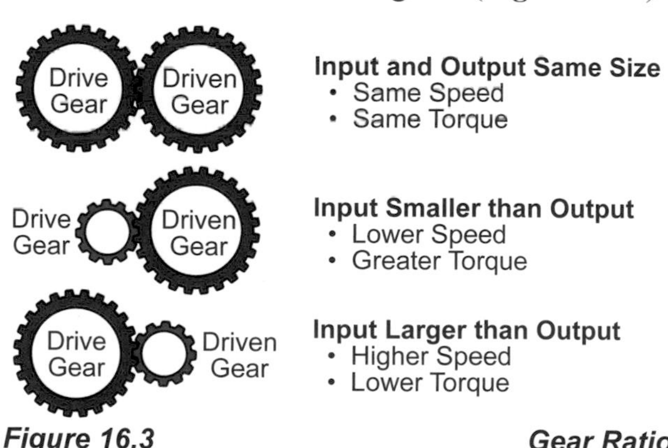

Figure 16.3 ***Gear Ratio***

Calculations

Determining Gear Ratios

Calculate a gear ratio by comparing the number of teeth on two gears (***Figure 16.2***).

$$\text{Gear Ratio} = \frac{\text{Driven Gear}}{\text{Drive Gear}} = \frac{\text{Output Gear}}{\text{Input Gear}} = \frac{24}{12} = 2$$

The gear ratio is 2:1. The drive gear rotates 2 times for every 1 time the driven gear rotates.

Engine Orientation

The way the engine mounts in the vehicle is called engine orientation, which impacts the types of drivetrain components used. This section focuses on:

- Longitudinal
- Transverse

Longitudinal

When an engine and its crankshaft are mounted parallel with the length of the vehicle, it is called a longitudinal engine (***Figure 16.4***). This type of engine placement is common on rear-wheel drive and four-wheel drive vehicles.

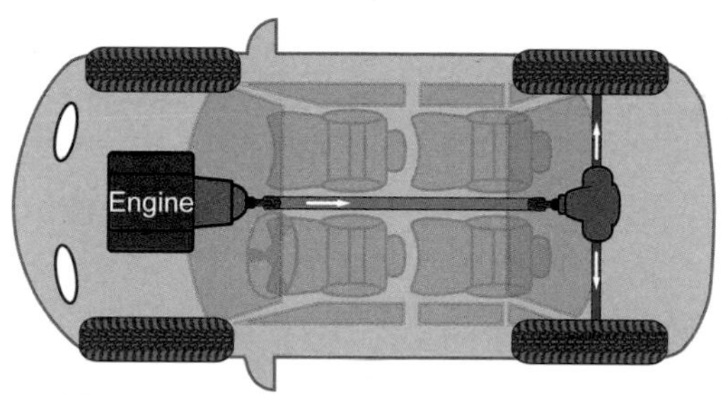

Figure 16.4 ***Longitudinal Engine***

Transverse

When an engine and its crankshaft are mounted perpendicular to the length of the vehicle, it is called a transverse engine (***Figure 16.5***). This type of engine placement is common on front-wheel drive vehicles.

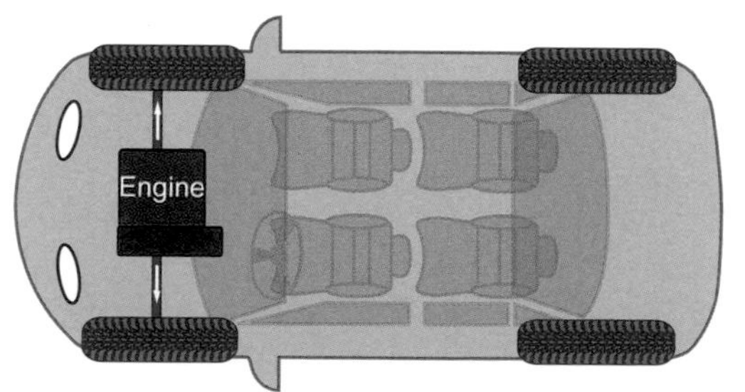

Figure 16.5 ***Transverse Engine***

Web Links

Drivetrain Related Sites

ETE Reman Transmissions
www.etereman.com

Spicer Drivetrain Products
www.spicerparts.com

Transmissions

A transmission can be manual, automatic, or continuously variable. Transmissions adjust the power to the wheels for different applications. Maintaining a steady speed requires less power than accelerating to that speed. This section focuses on:

- Manual Transmission
- Automatic Transmission
- Continuously Variable Transmission

Manual Transmission

In a manual transmission (***Figure 16.6***) the driver must use a clutch before shifting gears by hand with a gear stick shifter. The clutch is the connection between the transmission and engine.

Figure 16.6 ***Manual Transmission Cutaway***
Courtesy of Consulab - www.consulab.com

Clutch Parts. A manual transmission uses a clutch disc in conjunction with a pressure plate (***Figure 16.7***) to allow the operator to shift gears.

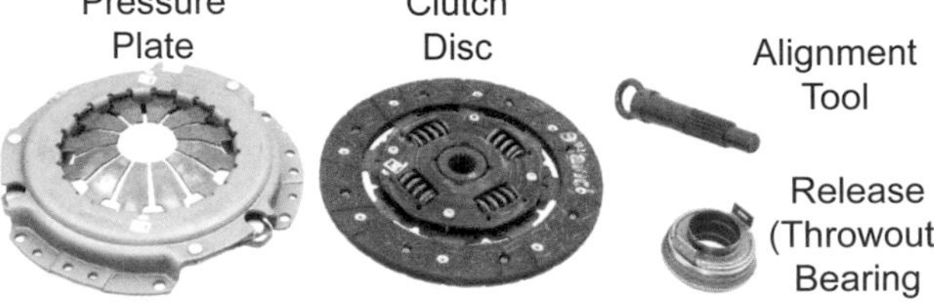

Figure 16.7 ***Clutch Components***

> **Trouble Guide**
>
> **Gears Difficult to Shift**
> - Worn clutch
> - Faulty clutch slave cylinder
> - Air in hydraulic clutch system
> - Worn blocking rings/synchronizers

Clutch Operation. When the clutch is engaged, the engine is driving the transmission (***Figure 16.8***). When the clutch is disengaged (when the clutch pedal is pushed down), the transmission is disconnected from the rotational motion of the engine's crankshaft. The pressure plate works with the clutch disc to aid in the engaging and disengaging process, allowing the operator to move the gear stick shifter and change from one gear to the next.

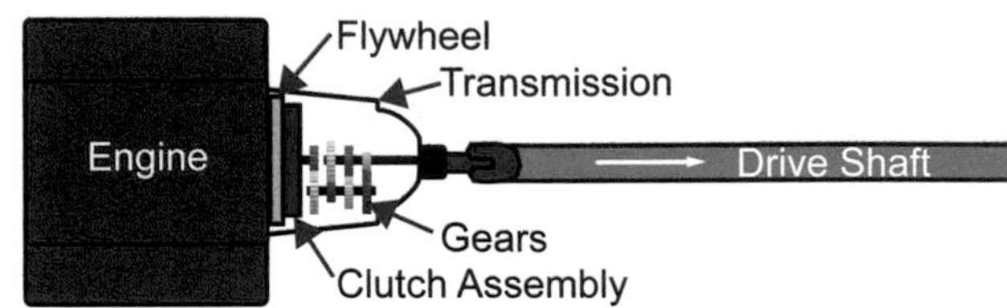

Figure 16.8 ***Clutch***

Shift Patterns. Manual transmissions commonly come in 4, 5, or 6 speeds (***Figure 16.9***).

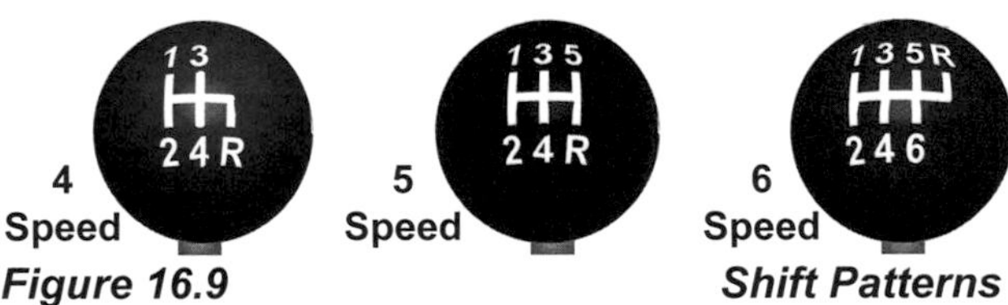

Figure 16.9 ***Shift Patterns***

Fluid Check. On most manual transmissions, a plug on the side of the transmission must be removed from under the vehicle to check the fluid. See Chapter 8 for more information on checking manual transmission fluid. Manual transmissions may take ATF, motor oil, synchromesh fluid, or heavyweight gear oil. Always read the owner's manual for fluid specifications.

> **Q & A**
>
> **Clutch Slipping**
>
> **Q:** My car struggles to speed up with my foot on the accelerator. When I downshift it doesn't help. There is also a burning smell.
>
> **A:** Your clutch and/or pressure plate may be worn out. When a clutch is slipping, you can get a burning smell and the car will not accelerate as designed.

Automatic Transmission

In an automatic transmission, the operator only has to select a forward or reverse gear to move the vehicle. Computer controlled electronic transmissions can calculate the most efficient time to shift. Automatic transmissions (***Figure 16.10***) commonly have 4, 6, 8, and even 10 speeds (forward gears).

Figure 16.10 Automatic Transmission Cutaway
Courtesy of Ford Motor Company

Fluid Coupling. Different than a manual transmission that uses friction from a clutch to connect the engine to the transmission, a torque converter uses fluid as the connection. To illustrate this concept, the inside of a torque converter operates like two fans facing one another. If one fan is plugged in, it acts like the driving force from the engine. The other fan that isn't plugged in will turn from the moving air (***Figure 16.11***).

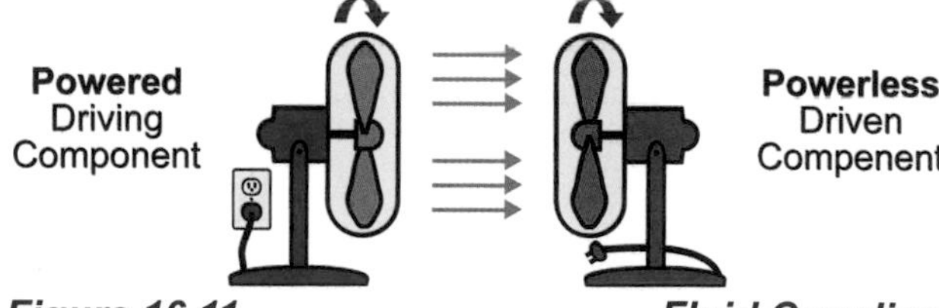

Figure 16.11 Fluid Coupling

Torque Converter. Instead of using air, the torque converter uses fluid (***Figure 16.12***). The input blade (driving component) is called an impeller. The output blade (driven component) is called a turbine. The impeller drives the turbine. The stator catches and redirects the fluid coming off the turbine back to the impeller. The impeller, turbine, and stator all have curved blades.

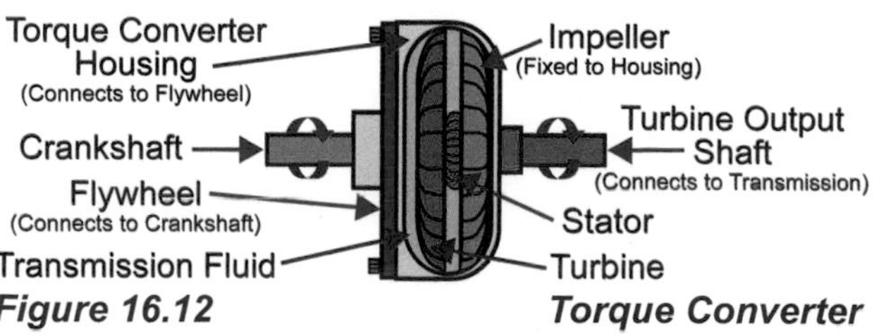

Figure 16.12 Torque Converter

Torque Converter Operational Stages. The torque converter operates in three stages: stall, acceleration, and coupling (***Figure 16.13***). A feature of a torque converter is that it can multiply torque.

Torque Converter Operational Stages	
Stall	Allows the vehicle to idle while still in gear (stopping at a stoplight). The impeller is turning, but the turbine is not.
Acceleration	Acts as a torque multiplier. The impeller is turning much faster than the turbine. The fluid coming off the turbine is caught by the stator and gets redirected back to the impeller.
Coupling (Lock-up)	The impeller and turbine lock together at cruising speed. This provides a direct connection from the engine's crankshaft to the transmission input shaft. This reduces heat and increases fuel efficiency.

Figure 16.13 Torque Converter Operation

Electronic Transmissions. Electronic transmissions still use the movement of fluid (hydraulics) inside the transmission, but the controls are operated by electronic devices. Using inputs from various sensors, a transmission control module controls the shifting (***Figure 16.14***). This improves shifting, performance, and fuel efficiency while reducing emissions.

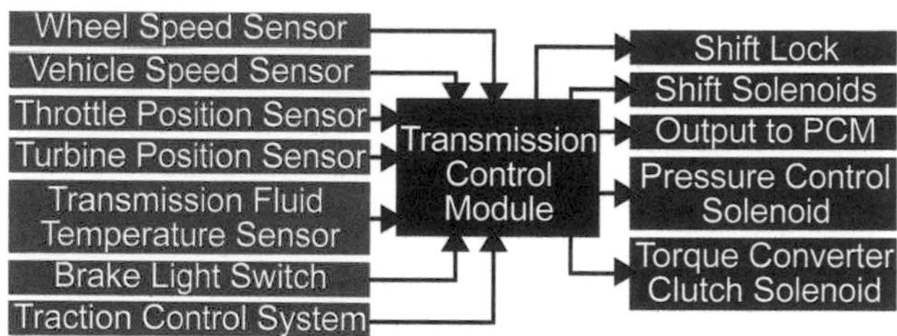

Figure 16.14 Transmission Control Module

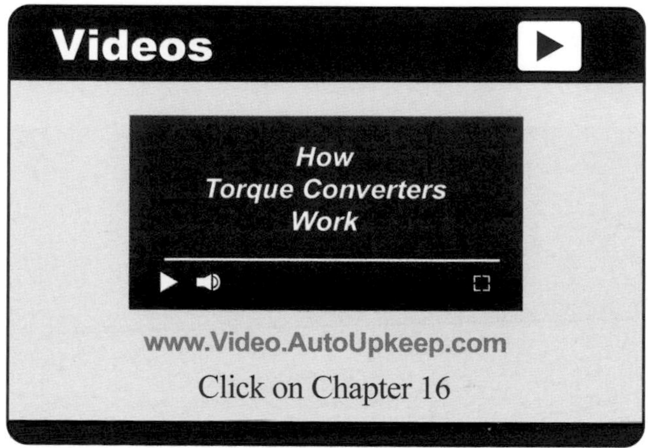

Transmission Coolers. Automatic transmissions generate a lot of heat. Excessive heat dramatically shortens the life of the transmission fluid. To remove excess heat, a transmission heat exchanger is used. This is also called a transmission oil cooler. The transmission fluid is directed to the radiator. The heat exchanger is built into the radiator. The transmission fluid and the coolant don't come in contact with one another, but heat is exchanged (***Figure 16.15***). In cold temperatures, the warm coolant helps the transmission fluid warm up to operating temperature. Some vehicles designed for towing or carrying heavy payloads often have an auxiliary cooler.

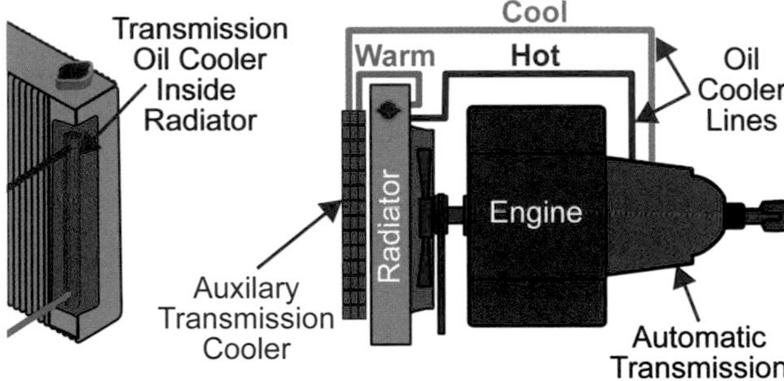

Figure 16.15 *Transmission Heat Exchanger*

Fluid Check. The fluid level on some automatic transmissions is checked with a dipstick under the hood (***Figure 16.16***), similar to an oil dipstick. See Chapter 8 for more information on checking automatic transmission fluid. New automatic transmission fluid is typically dyed a pinkish-red color to keep it from being confused with engine oil and to help find leaks. Always check the owner's manual for procedures and specifications. ***Note: To minimize the risk of internal damage from overfilling or adding the incorrect type of fluid, some automatic transmissions do not have a dipstick and must be checked with a special tool and/or procedure.***

Figure 16.16 *Automatic Transmission Dipstick*

Continuously Variable Transmission (CVT)

Instead of using gears, CVTs commonly use two variable speed cone-shaped pulleys in conjunction with a belt for an infinitely variable gear ratio (***Figure 16.17***).

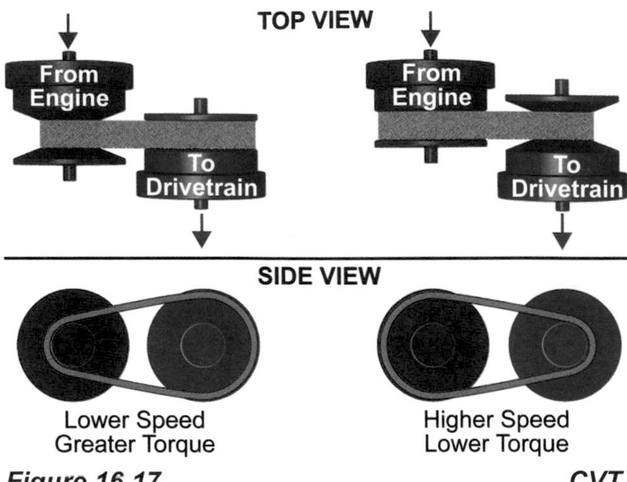

Figure 16.17 *CVT*

Benefits. CVTs have begun to appear on passenger cars as the advantages of their use have become more apparent (***Figure 16.18***).

Continuously Variable Transmission (CVT) Benefits Compared to an Automatic Transmission	
Smooth Ride	Acceleration and deceleration seamless. No gear shifting, hesitation, or jolt.
Improved Fuel Economy	Requires less fuel because engine runs consistently at levels of optimum power.
Increased Acceleration	Less power is lost because it is more efficient at adjusting energy required.
Reduced Emissions	Pollutes less by maintaining needed speed with minimal wasted RPMs.
Less Weight	Design is less complex with fewer parts.

Figure 16.18 *CVT Benefits*

Fluid Check. Since CVT fluid checking methods can vary, refer to your owner's manual for the proper procedure.

Transaxles

Commonly on front-wheel drive vehicles, the function of the transmission and differential is engineered into one component called a transaxle. By combining these functions into one unit, the transaxle can work more efficiently and be compact for transverse engine designs.

Transmission Fluid Servicing

Transmission fluid plays a vital role in cooling, cleaning, lubricating, and sealing transmission components. When servicing or adding fluid to a transmission, always check the owner's manual for recommendations. To maintain any transmission it is necessary to change the fluid as recommended. When inspecting fluid, excessive metal shavings are often a sign that the transmission needs further repairs.

Manual Transmissions. Manual transmissions require regular service intervals (***Figure 16.19***). They have a drain and fill plug, but no filter.

Manual Transmission Servicing	
STEP 1	Read a service manual specific to your vehicle on how to change the manual transmission fluid. Purchase the correct type and quantity of fluid. Wear appropriate personal protection equipment - safety glasses and disposable gloves.
STEP 2	Park on level ground. If you need to jack up the vehicle to gain access under it, jack up the front and back evenly. Use four jack stands to safely support the vehicle. The vehicle needs to be level in order to put the correct amount of new oil back into the transmission.
STEP 3	Find the fill plug and remove it with a wrench. Dip your finger in the fluid and put it on a clean paper towel. Next to your sample, put a clean drop of new fluid. This will allow you to visually compare the condition of the old fluid.
STEP 4	Place a drain pan under the drain plug. Remove the drain plug with a wrench. Allow the fluid to drain into the pan. Some drain and fill plugs have replaceable washers. If your transmission does, purchase the correct replacement washers.
STEP 5	Reinstall the drain plug with the new washer if applicable. Torque to the recommended specifications.
STEP 6	Refill the transmission with the manufacturer's recommended fluid. You may need to use a fluid transfer pump to perform this task. Once fluid comes out of the fill plug, the transmission is full.
STEP 7	Reinstall the fill plug with a new washer if applicable. Torque to the recommended specifications. Lower the vehicle.

Figure 16.19 Manual Transmission Servicing

Servicing

Transmission Fluid

- Change as recommended by the manufacturer

Automatic Transmissions. Automatic transmissions shift by themselves. They are more complex than manual transmissions. A filter is used to clean the fluid. Extracting all of the old fluid requires a special flushing machine (***Figure 16.20***). When having the transmission flushed ask for the pan to be cleaned and the filter removed and replaced. This will incur added cost, but will ensure a clean system. ***Note: Check your owner's manual to see if transmission flushing is recommended. Some manufacturers do not recommend using flushing additives and solvents, which may impact transmission durability.***

Figure 16.20 Transmission Fluid Exchanger
Photo: Bosch Automotive Service Solutions, Inc.

CVTs. Servicing CVTs can vary. Follow the procedures in a service manual specific to your vehicle. Be sure to use the recommended fluid.

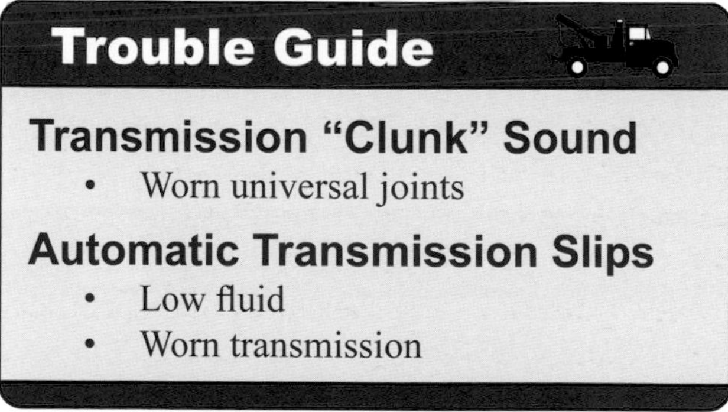

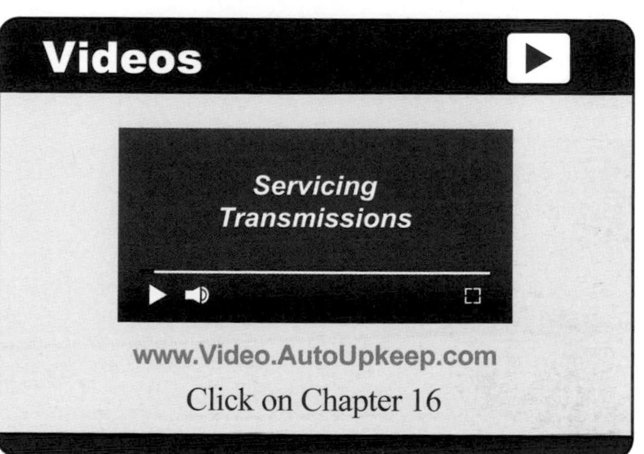

Driveline Components

Several components work together to transfer an engine's power smoothly and efficiently to a vehicle's wheels. This section focuses on:

- Drive Shafts
- Differential
- Transfer Case

Drive Shafts

Drive shafts are designed to transfer power from the transmission to the wheels.

Constant Velocity (CV) Axle Shafts. CV axle shafts are used on a variety of vehicles. On front-wheel drive vehicles a CV shaft (***Figure 16.21***) on each side connects the transaxle to each front wheel. Rubber boots protect the flexible CV shaft joint and hold grease for lubrication.

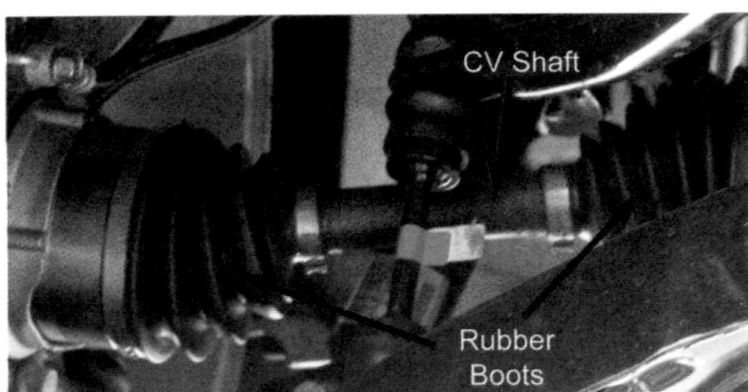

Figure 16.21 ***Constant Velocity Shaft***

Standard Drive Shaft. On rear-wheel drive vehicles, the standard drive shaft connects the transmission to the rear differential, which sends the power to the rear wheels through drive axles. Four-wheel and all-wheel drive vehicles usually have CV and standard drive shafts (***Figure 16.22***). Standard drive shafts are steel or aluminum tubes with welded ends.

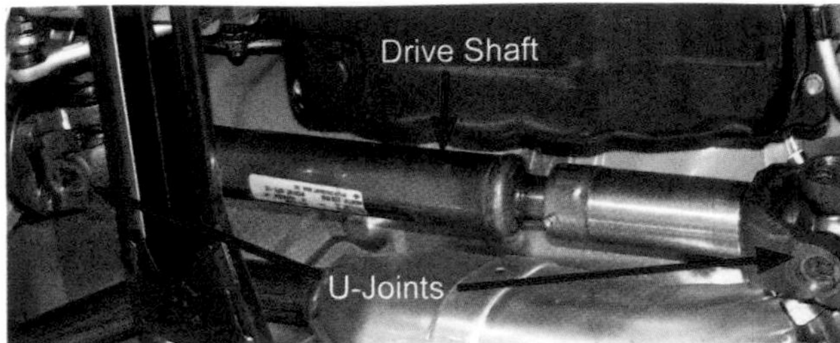

Figure 16.22 ***Standard Drive Shaft***

The standard drive shaft joints, called universal or U-joints (***Figure 16.23***), accept the moving chassis. U-joints can fail if they lose lubrication or eventually wear over time.

Figure 16.23 ***U-Joint***

Q & A

Clicking Noise

Q: What might cause a clicking noise when I turn sharply on my front-wheel drive car?

A: Worn CV joints can cause a clicking noise. The joints, covered by a boot at the end of the CV shaft, need to be flexible to allow for suspension movement and turning. If the boot gets torn, dirt and moisture may enter and the grease in the joint may come out. Foreign particles, with the absence of a sufficient quantity of grease, corrode and ruin the joint. Eventually if the joint is not replaced it will break and you will need to be towed.

Price Guides

Automatic Transmission Fluid (ATF)
- $2.00 to $5.00 a quart

Clutch and Pressure Plate
- $100.00 to $300.00 (parts)

CV Boot
- $15.00 to $45.00 each (parts)

CV Joint/Shaft
- $75.00 to $150.00 each (parts)

Manual Transmission Fluid/Differential Fluid
- $2.00 to $5.00 a quart

U-Joint
- $25.00 each (parts)

Note: 1 qt = 0.946 L

Differential

A differential (***Figure 16.24***) is a set of gears inside the axle housing that transfers the torque from the drive shaft to the wheels. The rear differential is located at the end of the drive shaft on a rear-wheel drive vehicle. Four-wheel drive vehicles have front and rear differentials. While turning, a vehicle's outer wheels rotate quicker than the inside wheels. The differential allows wheels to rotate at different speeds. If a vehicle didn't have a differential, drivetrain binding would occur.

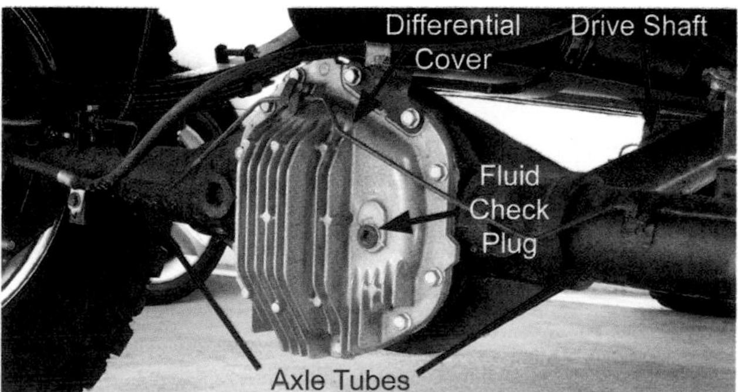

Figure 16.24 *Rear Differential*

Ring and Pinion. The gear sets used in differentials are ring and pinion gears (***Figure 16.25***).

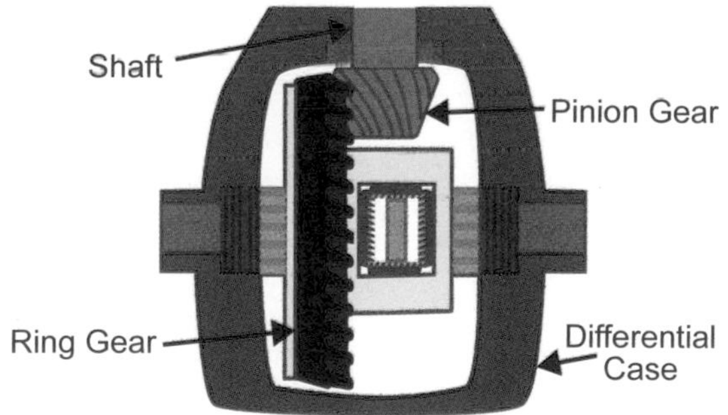

Figure 16.25 *Ring and Pinion*

Open Differential. In a standard (also called open) differential, one wheel can slip and rotate in low traction (***Figure 16.26***). This is especially disadvantageous on slippery road surfaces like ice. The wheel with traction will not turn.

Figure 16.26 *Open Differential*

Limited-Slip Differential. A limited-slip differential uses a mechanism (such as a clutch pack built into the differential) to apply torque to the wheel that isn't slipping, giving that tire traction.

Torque Vectoring Differential. A torque vectoring differential uses both mechanical and electronic devices to guide and influence the torque being sent to the wheels. These systems use a variety of sensors to input data needed to transfer torque to the proper wheel. Torque vectoring systems are especially useful while cornering, sending additional torque to the outside wheel while accelerating out of a curve (***Figure 16.27***).

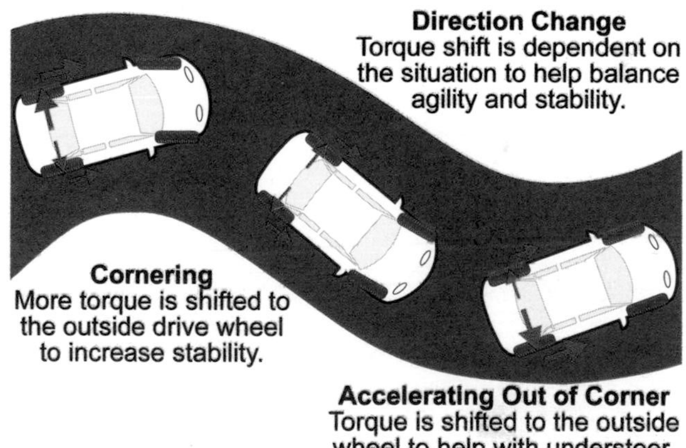

Figure 16.27 *Torque Vectoring*

Transfer Case

A transfer case allows power to be transmitted to a rear drive shaft and a front drive shaft. Two ranges are usually available - a high range for highway driving and a low range for off-road low speed conditions.

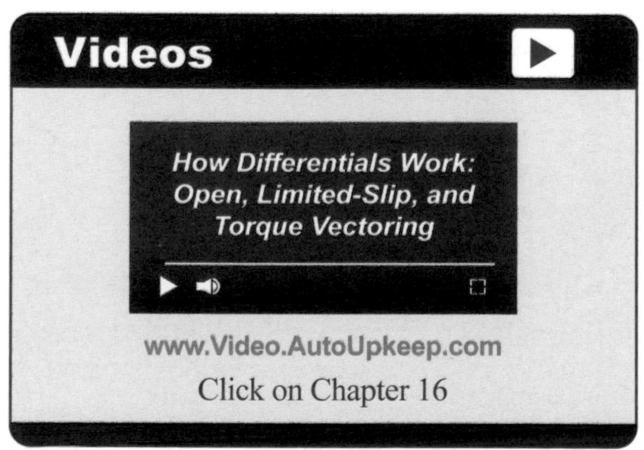

Drivetrain Systems

Drivetrain systems can be divided into the following categories:

- Rear-Wheel Drive
- Front-Wheel Drive
- Four-Wheel Drive
- All-Wheel Drive

Rear-Wheel Drive

On a rear-wheel drive (RWD) vehicle the power from the transmission is transferred through the drive shaft, through the differential, and then to the rear wheels (***Figure 16.28***). This was the standard on cars before the 1980s and still is the standard on most pickups.

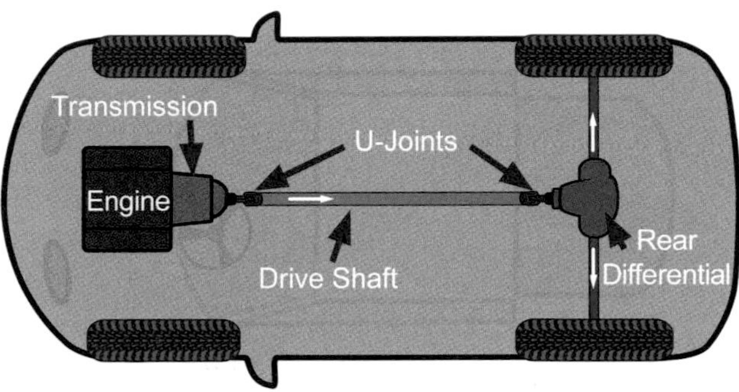

Figure 16.28 ***Rear-Wheel Drive***

Front-Wheel Drive

On a front-wheel drive (FWD) vehicle the power from the transaxle is transferred through the constant velocity shafts to the front wheels (***Figure 16.29***). This is the standard on most cars today. The weight of the engine on the front wheels gives front-wheel drive cars extremely good traction on diverse road conditions.

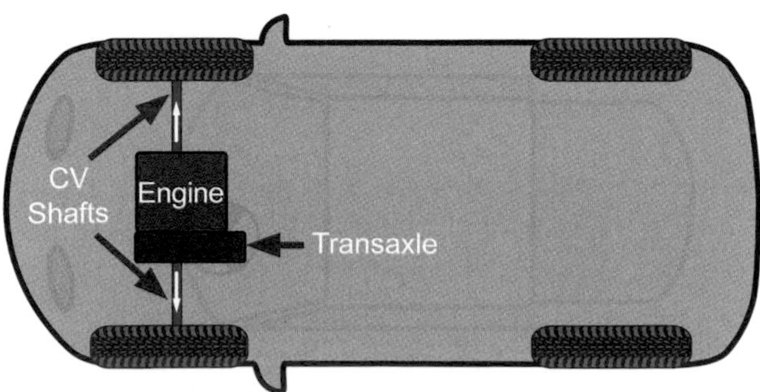

Figure 16.29 ***Front-Wheel Drive***

Four-Wheel Drive

On a four-wheel drive (4WD or 4x4) vehicle the power from the transmission is transferred to the rear and/or front wheels (***Figure 16.30***). On a four-wheel drive vehicle the operator has the choice of selecting either two-wheel drive or four-wheel drive. Many trucks have this option. Four-wheel drive vehicles have lower fuel economy than two-wheel drive vehicles. This is due to the addition of friction from the drivetrain turning more components. 4WD vehicles are designed for all-terrain use (on- or off-road).

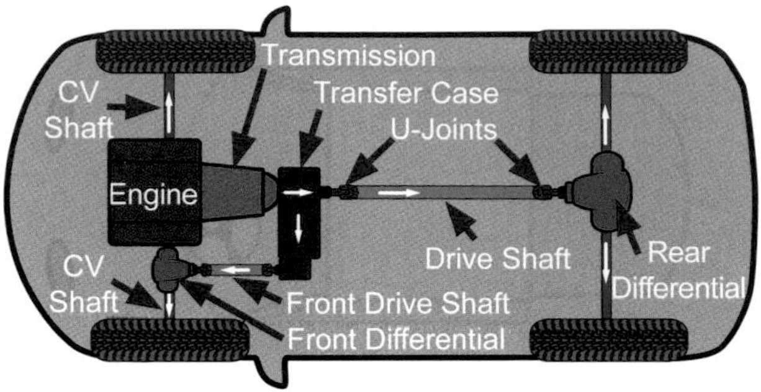

Figure 16.30 ***Four-Wheel Drive***

Torque Split Equally. When 4WD is selected, the transfer case splits the torque equally between the front and the rear axles - turning wheels at the same speed. This gives the vehicle superior traction on adverse on- or off-road conditions. ***Note: Once back on dry pavement, it is critical to put the vehicle back into 2WD or Auto/AWD to prevent drivetrain binding when turning.***

Range Selector. When off-roading, it may be beneficial to select a very low gear. Most 4WD vehicles will allow you to select from a high or low range. The range selector (***Figure 16.31***) will usually be labeled 2H or 2⬆ (2WD High Range), 4H or 4⬆ (4WD High Range), and 4L or 4⬇ (4WD Low Range). Low range will be slow, but will provide the gear reduction (higher torque) necessary to climb steep hills or when maximum power is necessary.

Figure 16.31 ***4WD Range Selector***

All-Wheel Drive

On an all-wheel drive (AWD) vehicle the power from the transmission is transferred to the front wheels and rear wheels. All-wheel drive systems are different from four-wheel drive systems. AWD vehicles are designed for all-weather use on roads.

Center Differential. Many AWD vehicles have a center differential. On some vehicles, the center differential, front differential, and transfer case may be built into one unit. This additional differential allows torque to be split at different amounts between the front and the back. For example, depending on the road conditions 40% of the torque may be sent to the front wheels and 60% to the back wheels. Some systems have driver controls, allowing the driver to select different modes (***Figure 16.32***). ***Note: The center differential allows you to drive on dry pavement without the drivetrain binding.***

Figure 16.32 Driver Controlled Center Differential

Intelligent AWD. Some AWD vehicles use advanced electronics to control the power transfer to the wheels. Speed sensors are mounted on each wheel to monitor wheel traction (***Figure 16.33***). These and other sensors send data to the powertrain control module. The benefit is when traction is lost at any one wheel, the power is automatically transferred to another. The result is superior traction and control.

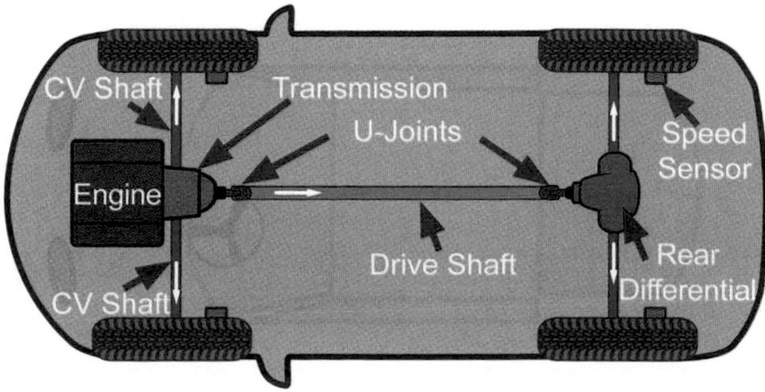

Figure 16.33 Symmetrical All-Wheel Drive

Types of Systems. There are different types of AWD systems. On-demand systems usually have power just to one axle until slippage occurs. Symmetrical systems send power to the front and rear at all times. Torque vectoring systems allow the system, through mechanical and electrical components, to vary the torque of each wheel. Unlike other AWD systems that rely on slippage to change the torque to the other wheel, a torque vectoring system is proactive (before a wheel slips). This can be done using a brake-based system or through a torque vectoring differential. Electric and hybrid electric vehicles use electric motors to apply on-demand AWD principles when needed.

Summary

Drivetrains transfer power from the engine to the wheels. Manual, automatic, and continuously variable transmissions are available. Gears, transmissions, drive shafts, and differentials are used to transmit the power. Vehicles can be front-, rear-, four-, or all-wheel drive. All-wheel drive vehicles have become popular because they have superior traction on diverse road conditions.

Activities

Drivetrain

- Drivetrain Activity
- Chapter 16 Study Questions

Activities and Study Questions can be completed in the *Auto Upkeep Workbook.*

Career Paths

Transmission Specialist

Education: Technical Training or ASE Cert.
Median Income: $37,850
Abilities: Computer knowledge, analytical skills, problem solving, and detail oriented.
Find your career at **www.bls.gov/ooh**.

Exhaust and Emission System

Fuel for Thought

- Why is it critical to move exhaust away from the passenger cabin?
- What is the function of the catalytic converter?
- Why is emission testing commonly required?

Introduction

Exhaust and emission systems on newer vehicles have become more complex than in the past. The emission system is used to monitor air-fuel ratios and has many benefits to the operator and the environment. For many years, automotive manufacturers were just concerned about getting the hot and toxic exhaust gases out to the side or rear of the vehicle. Today exhaust and emission systems are complex mechanisms that provide safety, efficiency, and concern for the environment. Periodically, exhaust and emission system components need replacing. This chapter focuses on identifying the components and purposes of the exhaust and emission system.

Objectives

Upon completion of this chapter and activities, you will be able to:

- Define the purpose of the exhaust and emission system.
- Identify and explain the components in an exhaust and emission system.
- Inspect exhaust and emission system components.

Exhaust and Emission Purpose

The exhaust and emission system is designed to deal with the inefficient by-products of the internal combustion process. The exhaust components dampen the sound of the engine (***Figure 17.1***). The emission components lower vehicle pollution categorized as tailpipe, crankcase, and evaporative emissions.

Web Links

Exhaust Sites

Bosch
www.boschautoparts.com

Dynomax Exhaust
www.dynomax.com

Gibson Performance Exhaust Systems
www.gibsonperformance.com

Hedman Performance Group
www.hedman.com

Nickson Industries (Exhaust Accessories)
www.nickson.com

Walker Exhaust Systems
www.walkerexhaust.com

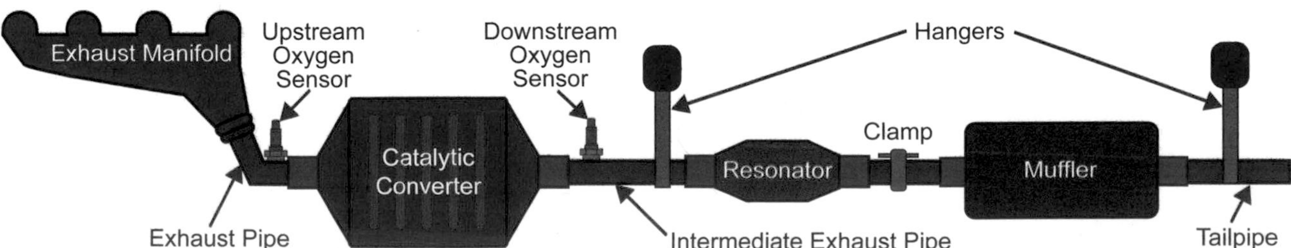

Figure 17.1 ***Exhaust System***

Exhaust Components

Exhaust system components presented are:

- Exhaust Manifolds
- Exhaust Pipes
- Muffler
- Resonator
- Exhaust Gaskets and Seals
- Hangers and Clamps

Exhaust Manifolds

An exhaust manifold connects directly to an engine's cylinder head. It harnesses the hot exhaust gases from combustion and guides them to the exhaust pipes. Inline engines have one exhaust manifold, while V configured engines have two (one for each bank of cylinders).

Standard Exhaust Manifolds. Standard exhaust manifolds are usually made out of cast iron. Each cylinder's exhaust collects together into one area relatively close to the cylinder head. An oxygen sensor may thread into the exhaust manifold to monitor oxygen levels in the exhaust gas. A shield may be used over the exhaust manifold to protect other components from the intense heat (***Figure 17.2***).

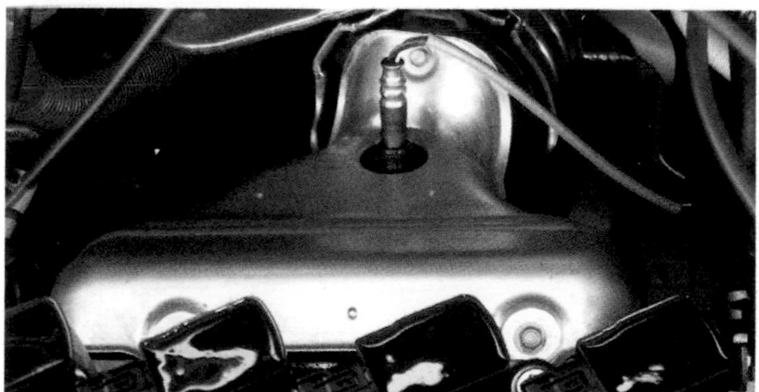

Figure 17.2 ***Exhaust Manifold with Heat Shield***

Price Guides 

Exhaust Clamps and Hangers
- $5.00 to $20.00 each (parts)

Exhaust Pipes
- $20.00 to $60.00 each (parts)

Muffler
- $25.00 to $100.00 each (parts)

Performance Headers. Headers (***Figure 17.3***) provide a more even and complete flow of exhaust out of the engine, equalizing exhaust backpressure and improving engine performance. Headers, designed from welded tubular steel, can be uncoated, painted, stainless steel, chrome, or ceramic-coated.

Figure 17.3 ***Exhaust Header***
Courtesy of Hedman Performance Group

Exhaust Pipes

Exhaust pipes are tubes of steel that connect components such as the exhaust manifold to the catalytic converter. The intermediate exhaust pipe connects the catalytic converter to the muffler. Another pipe, a tailpipe, expels the exhaust from the muffler.

Muffler

The muffler (***Figure 17.4***), usually oval or cylindrical in shape, is used to deaden the sound from the engine. It is basically a silencer to aid in the reduction of noise pollution and is located after the catalytic converter, but before the tailpipe.

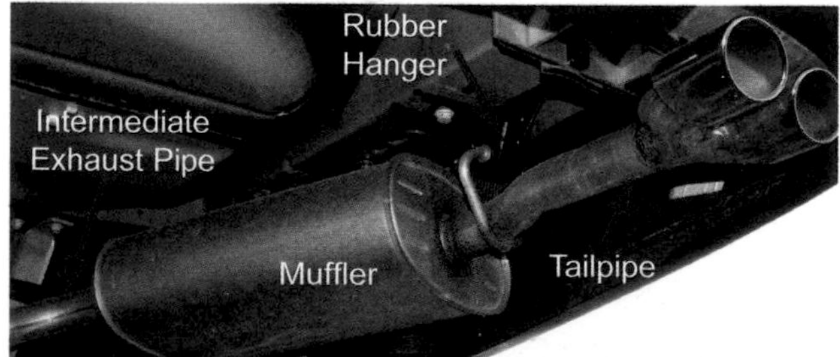

Figure 17.4 ***Muffler and Exhaust Pipes***

Trouble Guide

Excessively Loud Exhaust
- Hole in muffler or exhaust pipes
- Worn exhaust manifold gaskets
- Broken exhaust manifold bolts/studs

Resonator

Some vehicles have a second type of muffler called a resonator (***Figure 17.5***). A resonator helps absorb additional sound vibrations in critical areas of the exhaust system.

Figure 17.5 ***Resonator***

Exhaust Gaskets and Seals

A gasket or seal ring (also known as a donut) may be used where exhaust parts are joined to prevent exhaust leaks. If a gasket or seal is used between joining parts, always replace it with a new one when the joint is taken apart.

Q & A

Carbon Monoxide

Q: For no apparent reason I almost fell asleep driving. Does a car emit carbon monoxide as I drive it?

A: Yes, an exhaust leak could allow carbon monoxide (from incomplete combustion) to get in the vehicle. This odorless, colorless, deadly gas causes oxygen deprivation. Symptoms include headaches, shortness of breath, dizziness, fatigue, nausea, and confusion. Have the vehicle towed and then inspected by a qualified technician.

Hangers and Clamps

Exhaust clamps and hangers are used to connect and suspend the exhaust system components under the body of the vehicle.

Exhaust Hangers. As the engine runs, it vibrates. Exhaust hangers (***Figure 17.6***) have flexible rubber components to compensate for movement. If the exhaust system was connected solidly, stress cracks would develop.

Figure 17.6 ***Exhaust Hanger***

Exhaust Clamps. Exhaust clamps (***Figure 17.7***), usually a type of U-bolt, connect the exhaust pipes to the muffler and catalytic converter. On most new exhaust systems, welds instead of clamps are used.

Figure 17.7 ***Exhaust Clamp***

Servicing

Exhaust

- Inspect annually, replacing as needed

Tech Tip

Replacing Exhaust Components

Water, an exhaust by-product, tends to collect in and rust out the muffler. Most factory exhaust systems are welded assemblies from the catalytic to the tailpipe. It is relatively easy to replace everything from the catalytic back by bolting and hanging the parts in place, even if the muffler is the only worn out part. If you have a shop replace only the muffler, cutting and fabricating labor may cost as much as replacing the system as a unit.

Automotive Emissions

The by-products that are emitted from the automobile into the air around us are called automotive emissions. Vehicle emission control devices are used to reduce the level of emissions emitted by the automobile. This section focuses on:

- Types of Emissions
- Smog
- Federal Emission Standards
- California Emission Standards
- Smog Rating
- Standards and Classifications
- Vehicle Emission Control Information

Types of Emissions

Emissions are categorized as tailpipe, crankcase, and evaporative (***Figure 17.8***). During the combustion process, emissions are produced.

Types of Emissions	
HC	Hydrocarbons (HC), unburned or evaporated fuel, are toxic (cancer causing). When hydrocarbons combine with NO_X in the sun they contribute to ground-level ozone (a major part of smog).
NO_X	Various nitrogen oxides (collectively called NO_X) are formed from nitrogen and oxygen under high heat and pressure inside the combustion chamber. NO_X are the main component that cause smog and acid rain (NO_X and rainwater mixed).
CO	Carbon monoxide (CO), formed from incomplete combustion, is an odorless, colorless, deadly gas. It reduces the ability of blood to carry oxygen.
PM	Particulate matter (PM), also called particle pollution, includes fine particles, smoke, and soot commonly from burning diesel. Small microscopic particles are the most harmful. When breathed in, PM can get deep into your lungs and cause serious heath problems (heart disease, lung disease, decreased lung function, and other respiratory issues).
SO_2	Sulfur dioxide (SO_2) is created from burning fuels with sulfur, especially diesel. Sulfur dioxide impacts the respiratory system, which can make breathing difficult. Sulfur dioxide can lead to sulfur oxide (SO_x) formations, contributing to PM pollution.
CO_2	Carbon dioxide (CO_2) is not immediately harmful (the same gas exhaled when we breathe), but many scientists believe it is a greenhouse gas that contributes to climate change. Burning a gallon of gasoline produces about 19 pounds of CO_2. Burning a gallon of diesel produces about 22 pounds of CO_2.
H_2O	Water (H_2O) is produced during combustion.
O_2	The oxygen (O_2) content in the exhaust can be measured to diagnose the combustion process.

Figure 17.8 ***Types of Emissions***

Emissions Source. Automotive emissions come from the exhaust, engine crankcase (blow-by gases), and evaporative fuel vapors. Gasoline and diesel engines produce different levels of emissions (***Figure 17.9***).

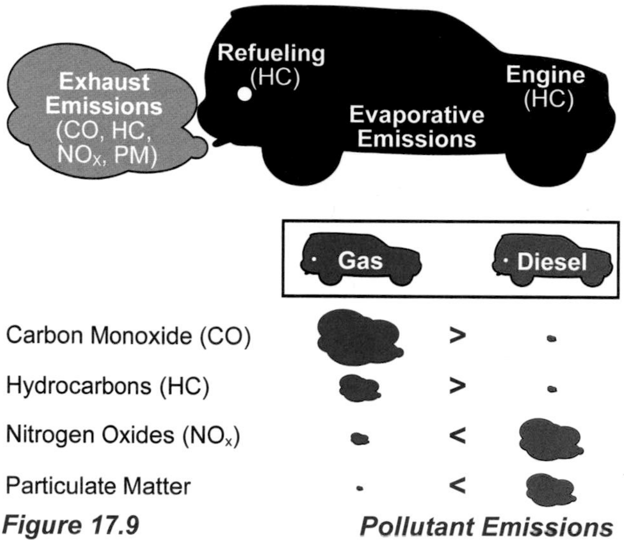

Figure 17.9 ***Pollutant Emissions***

Smog

Smog (***Figure 17.10***), also known as photochemical smog, is a lower atmosphere air pollution seen as a haze in the air. The word smog originally came from the two words **sm**oke and f**og**. Photochemical smog forms when HC and NO_X are exposed to sunlight. Smog can cause headaches, coughing, itching throat, burning eyes, and aggravate asthma. Some of the first smog conditions were recognized in Los Angeles, California in 1943.

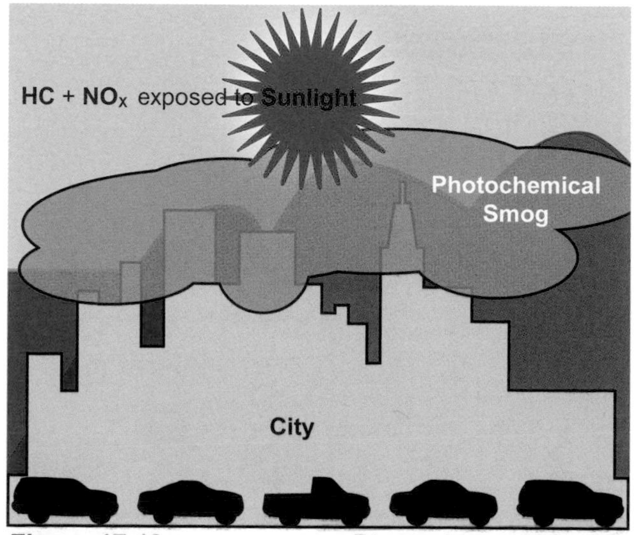

Figure 17.10 ***Photochemical Smog***

Federal Emission Standards

The first federal (USA) air pollution legislation, the Air Pollution Control Act of 1955, funded air pollution studies. The Clean Air Act of 1970 established requirements to control vehicle emissions. The Environmental Protection Agency (EPA), which was also created in 1970, continues to set standards for new vehicles. New standards are phased in over time. Advanced technologies make vehicles of today much cleaner than vehicles from 50 years ago.

California Emission Standards

In 1960, California established the Motor Vehicle Pollution Control Board. This entity was created to test and certify emission control devices for new cars sold in California. In 1967, then California Governor Ronald Reagan combined the Motor Vehicle Pollution Control Board and the Bureau of Air Sanitation into a new agency - California Air Resources Board (also known as CARB or ARB). One of the responsibilities of CARB is to establish vehicle emission standards. ***Note: In California non original/non conforming aftermarket parts that affect emissions must be CARB approved by an executive order.***

Smog Rating

All new vehicles are required to have a fuel economy and environmental label. On that label there is a smog rating (***Figure 17.11***). The range is from 1 (most polluting) to 10 (least polluting).

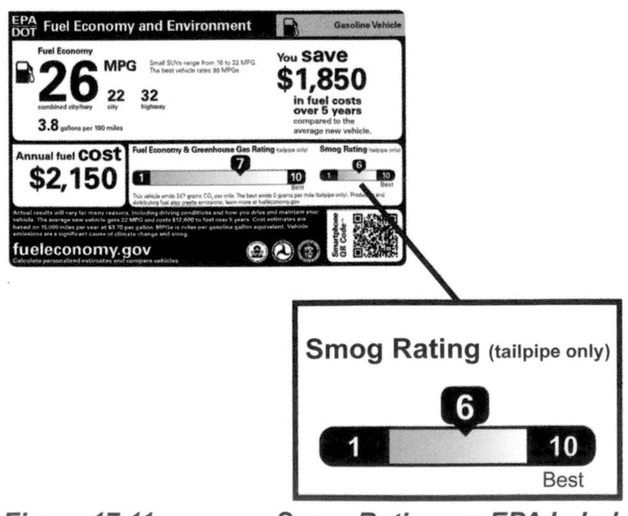

Figure 17.11 *Smog Rating on EPA Label*

Standards and Classifications

The Federal EPA and CARB both have ways to classify vehicles, identifying exhaust emission limits. The smog rating corresponds to the EPA and CARB standards.

EPA Tier 3. The Federal EPA groups emission standards under tiers and bins. Tier 3 is the current standard. The bin refers to non-methane organic gases + nitrogen oxides milligram limit per mile (or shortened to NMOG + NO_X mg/mi).

CARB. CARB's current standards are identified as Low Emission Vehicle III (LEV III). Unlike previous regulations, EPA's Tier 3 and CARB's LEV III standards have been harmonized so vehicles can be certified for all 50 states with one common set of standards (***Figure 17.12***). Some phase-in provisions exist in these latest requirements.

Emission Standards and Air Pollution Score For Passenger Cars, Light Duty Trucks, and Medium Duty Passenger Vehicles				
Smog Score	U.S. EPA Tier 3	CARB LEV III	NMOG + NOx (mg/mi)	CO (g/mi)
10	Bin 0	ZEV - Zero Emission Vehicle	0	0
9	Bin 20	PZEV - Partial Zero Emission Vehicle SULEV20 - Super Ultra Low Emission Vehicle Bin 20	20	1.0
8	Bin 30	SULEV30 - Super Ultra Low Emission Vehicle Bin 30	30	1.0
7	Bin 50	ULEV50 - Ultra Low Emission Vehicle Bin 50	50	1.7
	Bin 70	ULEV70 - Ultra Low Emission Vehicle Bin 70	70	
6	Bin 125	ULEV125 - Ultra Low Emission Vehicle Bin 125	125	2.1
5	Bin 160	LEV160 - Low Emission Vehicle Bin 160	160	4.2

Figure 17.12 *Emission Classifications*

Vehicle Emission Control Information

A vehicle emission control information (VECI) sticker is located under the vehicle's hood. A vehicle's emission classification is identified on the VECI sticker (***Figure 17.13***) based on the vehicle's model year (MY).

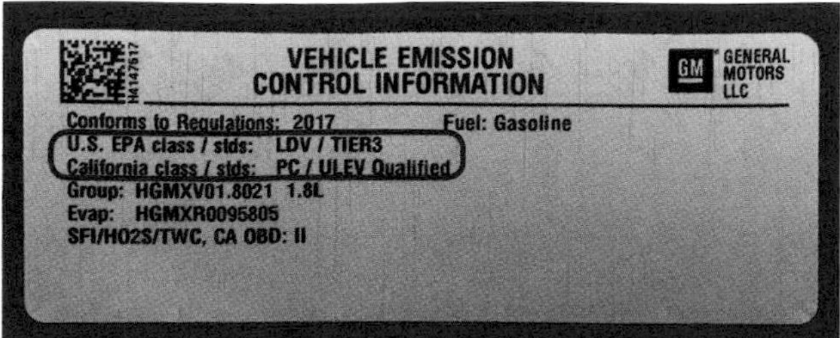

Figure 17.13 EPA and CARB Identified on VECI

Controlling Emissions

A properly running engine will emit fewer emissions than a poorly running engine. If combustion occurred completely and perfectly, only carbon dioxide (CO_2), nitrogen (N_2), water (H_2O), and heat would be emitted. But even a highly efficient finely tuned engine with the proper air-fuel ratio will produce some pollutants (***Figure 17.14***). The key is to minimize and control the undesirable emissions as much as possible. This section focuses on:

- Methods to Control Emissions
- Emissions Analyzers

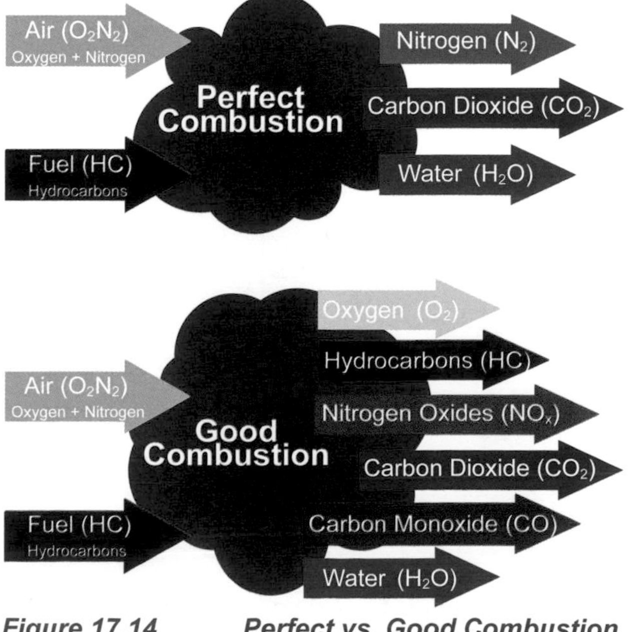

Figure 17.14 Perfect vs. Good Combustion

Methods to Control Emissions

Vehicle emissions can be minimized and controlled by having efficient engine designs, delivering the correct air-fuel mixture, and by treating the exhaust after combustion.

Emissions Analyzers

By identifying the gases coming out of the tailpipe, emission problems can be identified. Engine gas analyzers (***Figure 17.15***) are used to measure the level of the gases exiting the tailpipe. A five gas analyzer measures HC, NO_X, CO, O_2, and CO_2. HC, NO_X, and CO are regulated pollutants. O_2 and CO_2 are used to diagnose the system. HC and NO_X readings are given in parts-per-million. Whereas CO, O_2, and CO_2 are given as a percentage of the air. The levels give a technician an inside look at what is happening with the combustion process.

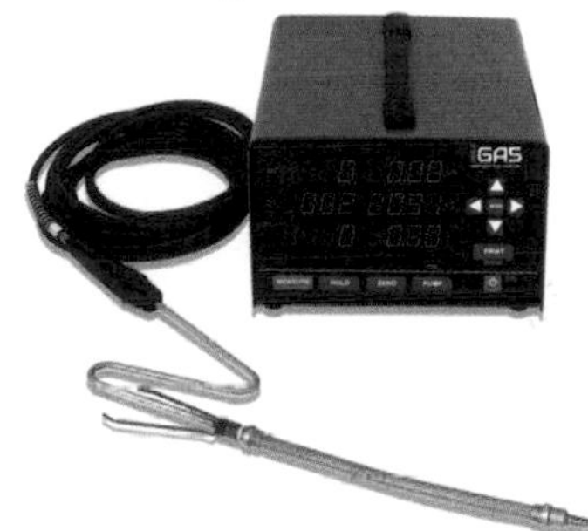

Figure 17.15 Five Gas Analyzer iGA5
Courtesy of Automotive Test Solutions, Inc. - www.automotivetestsolutions.com

Web Links

Emissions Related Sites

Automotive Electronics Services, Inc.
www.aeswave.com

Automotive Test Solutions, Inc.
www.automotivetestsolutions.com

California Air Resources Board
www.arb.ca.gov

Drive Clean
www.driveclean.ca.gov

Infrared Industries
www.infraredindustries.com

United States EPA
www.epa.gov

Emission Components

Vehicles produce a large amount of by-products harmful to our ecosystem. Emission system components reduce tailpipe, crankcase, and evaporative emissions (***Figure 17.16***). Emission system components presented are:

- Powertrain Control Module (PCM)
- Exhaust Gas Recirculation (EGR)
- Positive Crankcase Ventilation (PCV)
- EVAP/Charcoal Canister
- Catalytic Converter
- Oxygen Sensors

Price Guides

Catalytic Converter
- $100.00 to $1,000.00 each (parts)

EGR Valve
- $40.00 to $120.00 each (parts)

Oxygen Sensor
- $30.00 to $100.00 each (parts)

PCV Valve
- $5.00 to $25.00 each

Powertrain Control Module (PCM)

The use of a PCM (***Figure 17.17***) was originally spurred by the government requiring manufacturers to lower emissions and increase fuel economy. The PCM receives input from sensors and then provides accurate and immediate commands. If the catalytic converter or other emission component is not working properly or disconnected, the PCM will run the engine either too lean or too rich, increasing emissions and decreasing engine life.

Figure 17.17 ***Powertrain Control Module***

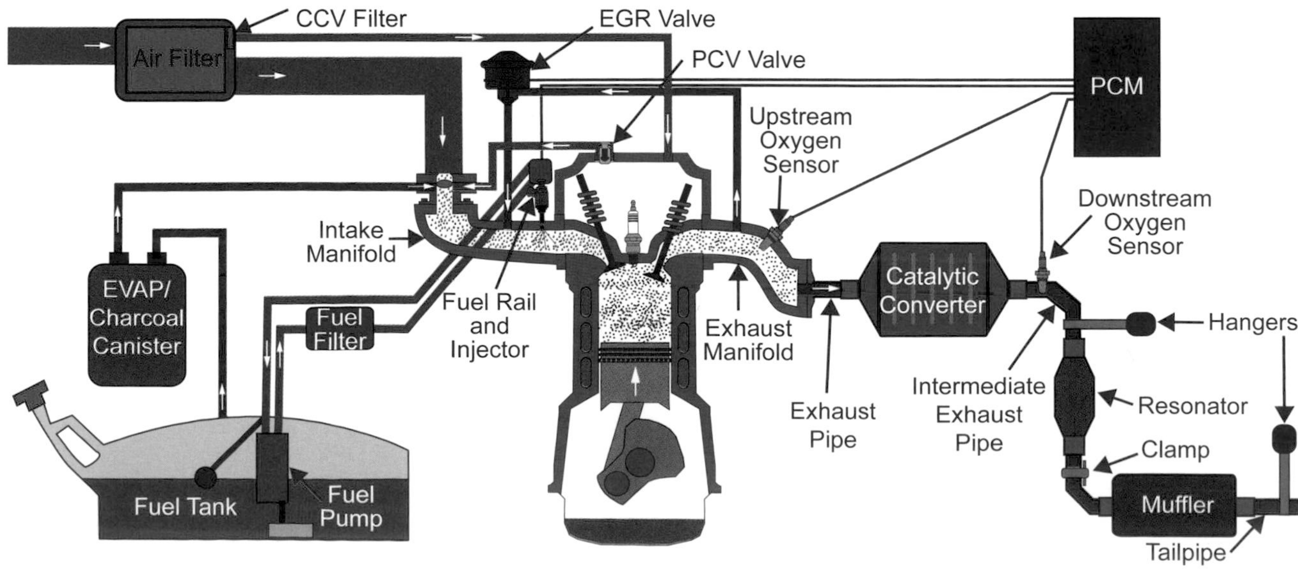

Figure 17.16 ***Exhaust and Emission System***

Exhaust Gas Recirculation (EGR)

Air that is drawn into the combustion chamber contains nitrogen (~78%), oxygen (~21%), and other gases (~1%). NO_X forms from high combustion chamber temperatures (above 2500°F or 1371°C) and pressure. The EGR valve, typically mounted on top of the engine (***Figure 17.18***), reduces NO_X (a tailpipe emission).

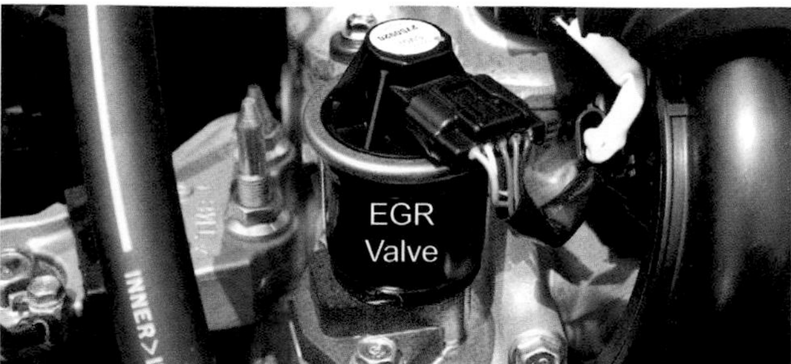

Figure 17.18 *EGR Valve*

How EGR Works. An EGR valve is generally closed when the engine is cold or when it is idling. When open, it reroutes a small amount (less than 10%) of inert (chemically inactive) exhaust gas to the intake manifold. This inert gas has a cooling effect on the air-fuel mixture's peak combustion temperature - reducing the formation of NO_X. The EGR valve on older systems is operated by a vacuum from the engine. Newer electronic EGR systems use the PCM with engine load and temperature input to adjust the EGR valve. An EGR valve stuck open can result in a rough idle or stalling. An EGR valve stuck closed may produce high NO_X and knocking.

EGR Cooler. Some vehicles use an EGR cooler (***Figure 17.19***) to reduce combustion chamber temperatures even further. An EGR cooler is an air-to-liquid heat exchanger.

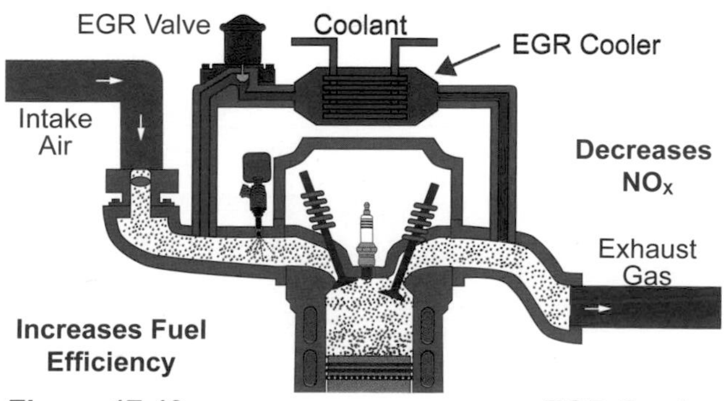

Figure 17.19 *EGR Cooler*

Positive Crankcase Ventilation (PCV)

During combustion, unwanted crankcase pressure is produced through blow-by. Blow-by is unburned fuel and water vapor that is forced past the piston rings and into the crankcase. To control crankcase emissions, a positive crankcase ventilation (PCV) system is used. A PCV valve (***Figure 17.20***) is commonly located in the valve cover. A hose connects the PCV valve to the intake manifold, redirecting unburned vapors from the crankcase back into the combustion chamber. These vapors mix with the air-fuel mixture and are burned. In addition to controlling emissions, reducing unburned fuel and water vapor in the crankcase provides other benefits. Water can turn oil into sludge, while unburned fuel can dilute oil. If not handled correctly, blow-by can cause corrosion and increase engine wear. To check the PCV valve, remove and shake it. A PCV valve that isn't plugged will rattle when shaken.

Figure 17.20 *PCV Valve*

EVAP/Charcoal Canister

An evaporative emissions (EVAP) control canister (***Figure 17.21***), also known as a charcoal or carbon canister, is used in the emission system to store hydrocarbons (e.g., fuel vapors from the fuel tank). When the engine is running the vapors are drawn into the intake air to be burned in the combustion chamber. On older vehicles it looks like a coffee can and is located under the hood. On newer vehicles it is located by the fuel tank.

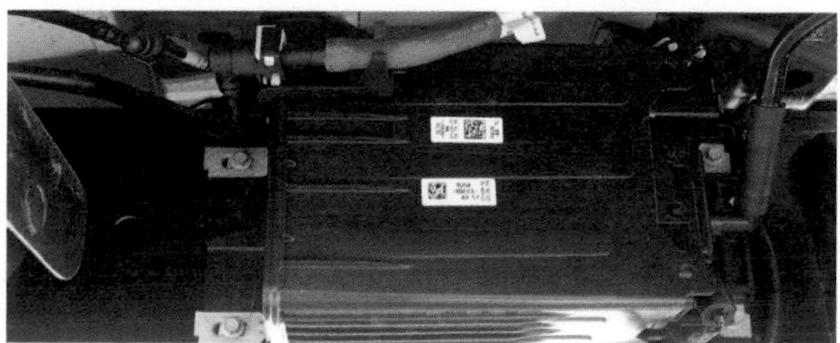

Figure 17.21 *EVAP Canister*

Catalytic Converter

The catalytic converter is located between the exhaust manifold(s) and muffler. It looks similar to a muffler and may have a heat shield.

Three-Way Converter (TWC). Most vehicles use a TWC (***Figure 17.22***). Oxygen sensors are required to regulate the air-fuel ratio close to stoichiometric (14.7 to 1) for it to efficiently reduce emissions.

Figure 17.22 *Three Way Catalytic Converter*

Catalyst. A TWC contains a catalyst. When very hot (over 500°F) it accelerates the chemical change of CO, HC, and NO_X into H_2O (water vapor), CO_2, and N_2 (***Figure 17.23***).

Figure 17.23 *Catalytic Converter*

Pre-Catalyst. Engines that burn ultra lean, like GDI engines, may also need a smaller pre-catalyst (warm-up converter). It is placed closer to the exhaust manifold, heating up to operating temperature faster, to better reduce NO_X.

Q & A

Catalytic Converter Clogged

Q: What causes a catalytic converter to fail?

A: Unburned fuel from a rich air-fuel mixture can overheat the converter and cause it to prematurely fail. Exhaust gases can be analyzed to see if the fuel mixture is correct. An overuse of some fuel additives can also shorten the converter's life. A loss of power, poor fuel economy, or engine/ignition misfire can be signs of a clogged converter..

Oxygen Sensors

Oxygen sensors (***Figure 17.24***), also known as O_2 or lambda sensors, are placed before, in, or after the catalytic converter. Some vehicles have four O_2 sensors. The O_2 sensor monitors the oxygen content in the vehicle's exhaust. It sends signals to the PCM to maintain a 14.7 to 1 (stoichiometric) air-fuel ratio. This ratio of air-fuel makes the engine run smooth, efficient, and in the end, pollute less.

Figure 17.24 *Oxygen Sensor*

Upstream O_2 Sensor. The O_2 sensor before the catalytic converter is called an upstream O_2 sensor. It monitors the combustion chamber efficiency.

Downstream O_2 Sensor. The O_2 sensor located in or after the catalytic converter is called a downstream O_2 sensor (***Figure 17.25***). It checks catalytic converter efficiency.

Figure 17.25 *Oxygen Sensors*

Servicing

Oxygen Sensors

- Change as recommended by the manufacturer

Trouble Guide

Engine Performance Issues

- Emission system malfunctioning

Diesel Emissions Technology

Diesel has more energy per gallon than any other type of fuel used in transportation. A diesel powered vehicle is about 30%+ more fuel efficient than a similar gasoline powered vehicle. This makes it an attractive engine design for vehicles. When compared to gasoline engines, diesel engines produce more NO_X and PM, but less HC and CO. Advanced technologies can make diesels pollute less. The diesel engine emission system works to reduce pollutants. This section focuses on:

- Diesel Emission Components
- Cleaner Diesel Fuel
- Advanced Engine Designs
- Aftertreatment Technologies

Diesel Emission Components

Because the level of each pollutant created by diesel engines varies greatly from gasoline engines, diesel emission systems are designed to work in unique ways. The components are different, although the end goal, minimizing pollution, is very much the same. New advances in technology are being developed, but not all diesel emission systems use the same technologies. Some aftertreatment components unique to diesel emission systems are the diesel particulate filter (DPF), the diesel oxidation catalyst (DOC), and the selective catalytic reduction (SCR) catalyst (***Figure 17.26***).

Cleaner Diesel Fuel

As you learned in Chapter 11, reducing the sulfur content in diesel made a significant difference in the amount of PM that a diesel engine emits. Ultra-low sulfur diesel contains only 15 parts-per-million (ppm) of sulfur, a 97% reduction from the previous standard of 500 ppm of sulfur (***Figure 17.27***). This reduction of sulfur led to more advanced engine designs and emission components.

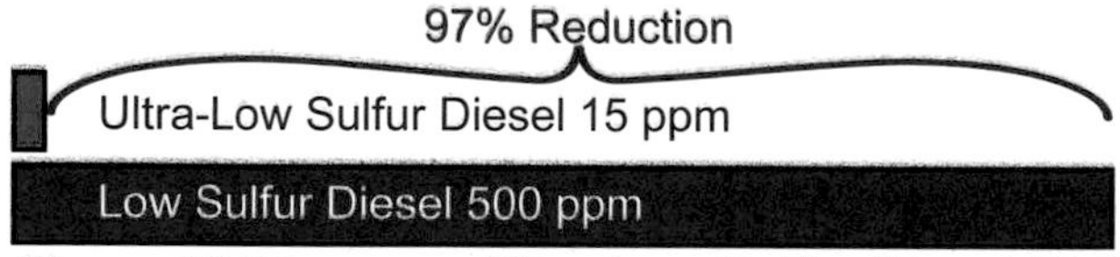

Figure 17.27 ***Ultra-Low Sulfur Diesel PPM***

Advanced Engine Designs

Advanced engine designs include such things as electronic controls, variable injection timing, turbocharging, common rail injection system, and reduced compression engines. Diesel engines are becoming more popular in passenger cars and light trucks. Some models (***Figure 17.28***) have a gasoline or diesel option.

Figure 17.28 ***Chevy Cruze***

Courtesy of Mayse Automotive Group - www.mayse.com

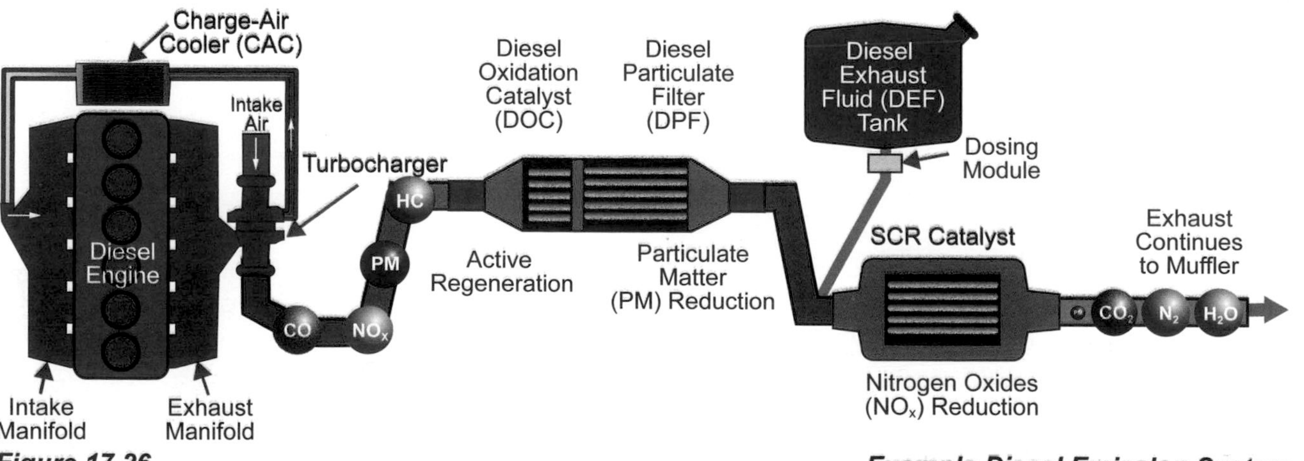

Figure 17.26 ***Example Diesel Emission System***

Aftertreatment Technologies

Engine aftertreatment technologies are used to reduce diesel emissions. Aftertreatment means that the pollution is treated after the combustion process, but before the exhaust exits the tailpipe. The following are example systems. Some automotive manufacturers use a combination of these technologies to meet emission standards.

Diesel Particulate Filters. A diesel particulate filter (DPF) (***Figure 17.29***) removes PM (soot) from the exhaust. These filters are automatically cleaned through passive and active regeneration. During passive regeneration, normal vehicle operating exhaust temperatures burn (oxidize) the soot. Active regeneration occurs when the computer controlled system has identified that the DPF is full of exhaust particles. During active regeneration, temperatures of the exhaust system are increased. This high heat eliminates the collected exhaust particles. Different vehicles use varying methods, so read your owner's manual to see how your DPF works.

Diesel Oxidation Catalyst. A diesel oxidation catalyst (DOC) is a catalytic converter for a diesel engine. By promoting oxidation, it reduces HC, CO, and the soluble organic fraction (SOF) of PM by converting them into CO_2 and water (H_2O).

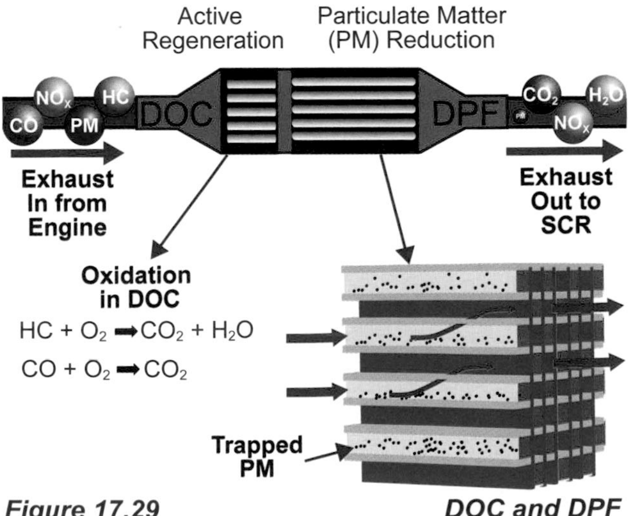

Figure 17.29 *DOC and DPF*

NO_X Storage Catalytic Converter. The NO_X storage catalytic converter temporarily stores the NO_X. When released, it converts NO_X to CO_2 and nitrogen (N_2).

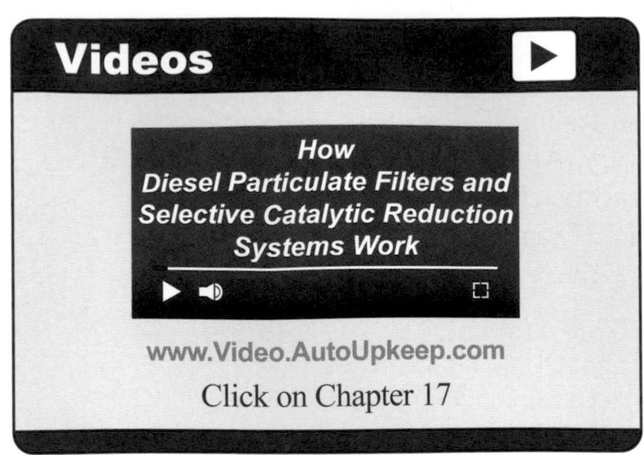

Selective Catalytic Reduction. Selective catalytic reduction (SCR) is used to reduce NO_X emissions. In a SCR system, diesel exhaust fluid (DEF) is injected in the exhaust system before the SCR catalyst. The DEF and the catalyst break NO_X down into nitrogen (N_2) and water (H_2O) (***Figure 17.30***).

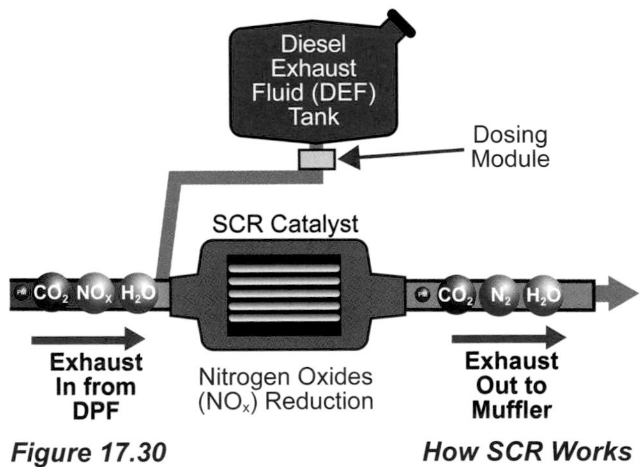

Figure 17.30 *How SCR Works*

Emission Testing

The National Ambient Air Quality Standards (NAAQS) are EPA outdoor air quality standards to protect human health. In areas not in compliance with NAAQS, vehicle Inspection and Maintenance (I/M) testing is mandatory to reduce HC, CO, and NO_X emissions. Vehicles that exceed set limits must be repaired (as a prerequisite to vehicle registration), retested, or retired. This section focuses on:

- I/M Testing
- I/M Test Preparation
- Emission Control System Warranty

I/M Testing

Each state has flexibility in designing their I/M, so testing requirements, standards, and methods vary. An enhanced I/M often includes a visual safety check in addition to tailpipe (***Figure 17.31***) and evaporative emission testing. Because of these standards, improvements in engine design, controls, and emission systems have reduced pollution from new vehicles by more than 95% compared to vehicles of the 1960s.

Figure 17.31 ***Emissions Testing***
Photo: Bosch

I/M Test Preparation

Before having your vehicle tested, plan to perform recommended preventative maintenance. If the on-board diagnostics (OBD) check engine light is on, the PCM detects an emission system component or engine issue and the vehicle is guaranteed not to pass testing. Never cut off emission components like the catalytic converter. It is illegal and will cause emission test failure. Vehicles are designed to run properly with emission components and will emit large amounts of pollution if any of these components are disconnected or removed.

Tech Tip

Help Passing an Emission Test

To better control pollution there may be a consumer assistance program to help qualified vehicle owners with emission related repairs. Financial assistance may also be offered for voluntarily retiring a vehicle if it does not pass emission testing and is not worth repairing. Check with your emission testing station to see if a program exists in your area.

Emission Control System Warranty

If a vehicle fails testing be sure to review the vehicle's emission control system warranty. Federal law requires the catalytic converter and PCM be covered for 8 years/80,000 miles (130,000 km) on 1995 and newer vehicles. Partial Zero Emission Vehicles (PZEV) carry a longer 15 years/150,000 mile emission control system warranty. To see a full list of emission-related components covered, read your warranty booklet.

Summary

As technology advances, the internal combustion engine will become more efficient and pollute less. Over time, exhaust system components have been added to lower noise, while emission system components have been added to convert harmful gases into more environmentally friendly by-products. I/M testing helps to keep vehicle emission levels regulated, minimizing pollution released into the environment. Consumers can reduce pollution by upgrading to a more efficient vehicle and by driving less.

Activities

Exhaust and Emission System

- Exhaust and Emission Activity
- Chapter 17 Study Questions

Activities and Study Questions can be completed in the *Auto Upkeep Workbook*.

Career Paths

Emissions Inspection Technician

Education: Technical Training or ASE Cert.
Median Income: $37,850
Abilities: Understands emission testing equipment and emission regulations.
Find your career at **www.bls.gov/ooh**.

Alternative Fuels and Designs

Chapter 18

Photo: Tesla

Fuel for Thought

- What is an alternative fueled vehicle?
- What is a renewable resource?
- What issues influence the usability of alternative fuels?

Introduction

Energy is used to propel vehicles. Energy cannot be created or destroyed, but it can be converted from one form to another. In a traditional internal combustion vehicle, gasoline or diesel is used as chemical energy in the combustion process. This chapter will identify the different types of energy sources used to propel alternative fueled vehicles. Examples include biodiesel, flex-fuel, natural gas, propane, bi-fuel, hybrid, electric, solar, and hydrogen fuel cell. Some alternative fuels are derived from petroleum (e.g., propane and natural gas), others are non-petroleum based using renewable energy. The most popular alternative designs are hybrid, electric (***Figure 18.1***), plug-in hybrid, and flex-fuel vehicles.

Figure 18.1 *Tesla Model 3*
Photo: Tesla

Objectives

Upon completion of this chapter and activities, you will be able to:

- Identify differences in automotive design, depending on the fuel source.
- Compare and contrast advantages and disadvantages between vehicle types.
- Compare petrobased and biobased fuels.
- Calculate the payback period on an alternative fueled vehicle.
- Predict the role of the automobile in 2050.

Tailpipe and Upstream Emissions

A Zero Emission Vehicle (ZEV) may not have emissions at the tailpipe, but the electrical generation may produce emissions. This really depends if the electrical power plant is run on coal (***Figure 18.2***), natural gas, nuclear, hydroelectric, biomass, geothermal, wind, solar, or some other source. These types of emissions are called upstream emissions. Conventionally fueled vehicles also have upstream emissions. Petroleum refining and distribution to gas stations are upstream emissions.

Figure 18.2 *Coal Power Plant*

Purpose of Alternatives

Automotive manufacturers are researching, developing, and mass-producing alternative vehicles to meet increasingly stringent EPA emission and fuel economy standards. This section focuses on:

- Gasoline Consumption
- Meeting Fuel Economy Standards
- Meeting Emission Standards

Gasoline Consumption

The U.S. consumes approximately 385,000,000 gallons of gasoline per day. To illustrate this, a semi tank trailer hauls about 9000 gallons (***Figure 18.3***). To refill gas stations in the U.S. each day, it takes about 42,800 trailer loads.

Figure 18.3 ***Semi Tank Trailer***

Meeting Fuel Economy Standards

With the goal of reducing energy consumption in the 1970s and beyond, the U.S. Congress enacted the Corporate Average Fuel Economy (CAFE) program. The CAFE program consists of two components: setting fuel economy standards for cars and light trucks (administered by the NHTSA) and calculating the average fuel economy for automotive manufacturers (the job of the EPA). If a manufacturer doesn't meet the current year standard, they have to pay a fine. Window sticker EPA fuel economy estimates and CAFE standards are different. The window sticker shows a tank-to-wheel or battery-to-wheel fuel economy, not taking into account the energy to produce and deliver a fuel. The CAFE fuel economy estimate is well-to-wheel, including an adjustment for alternatives that provides a higher miles per gallon of gasoline equivalent (MPGe).

Meeting Emission Standards

Over half of all air pollution in the U.S. originates from vehicles. In an effort to improve air quality, EPA emission standards require auto manufacturers to meet max allowable levels of tailpipe, crankcase, and evaporative emissions. See Chapter 17 for more information on emission standards.

Gasoline Gallon Equivalent

The energy content of fuels is rated in British Thermal Units (BTUs). One BTU equals the energy released by burning one wooden match. A gasoline gallon equivalent (GGE) is a measure used to compare the energy of an alternative fuel to gasoline (***Figure 18.4***). If the alternative fuel has less energy content, a vehicle would have to burn more of that fuel per mile.

Fuel	BTUs/Unit	GGE	Unit
Gasoline (Regular)	114,100	1.00	gallon
E85 (Ethanol)	81,800	1.39	gallon
E100 (Ethanol)	76,100	1.50	gallon
No. 2 Diesel	129,500	0.88	gallon
B20 (Biodiesel)	127,250	0.90	gallon
B100 (Biodiesel)	118,300	0.96	gallon
M100 (Methanol)	56,800	2.01	gallon
LPG (Propane)	84,300	1.35	gallon
CNG (Compressed Natural Gas)	900	126.67	cubic foot
Electricity	3,400	33.56	kilowatt hour
Hydrogen	51,500	2.198	pounds

Figure 18.4 ***Energy Content Comparison***

Calculations 

Gasoline Gallon Equivalent

Convert 10 gallons of gasoline to the equivalent gallons of E85 using the GGE factor.

	EXAMPLE	
Gallons of Gasoline		10 gallons
x GGE of E85 from table		x 1.39
= Equivalent E85 Gallons		**13.9 gallons**

This means that it takes 13.9 gallons of E85 to equal the energy content in 10 gallons of gasoline.

Biodiesel Vehicles

Biodiesel, an alternative to running 100% petroleum-based diesel (petrodiesel), is a renewable resource made from animal fats, vegetable oils, or recycled cooking grease through a refining process called transesterification. Straight vegetable oil (SVO) and waste vegetable oil (WVO) are not considered biodiesel until they have been transesterified. Soybean oil and WVO from restaurants are the most common sources of biodiesel in the United States. Biodiesel requires less energy to produce than ethanol, petrodiesel, or gasoline. Biodiesel can be burned at 100% or it can be blended with traditional petrodiesel. Biodiesel blends are given "B" designations. For example, B20 fuel is blended with 20% biodiesel/80% petrodiesel. Pure biodiesel (B100) is non-toxic and biodegradable. Using biodiesel is more environmentally friendly than petrodiesel, reducing pollution emissions and recycling carbon dioxide (***Figure 18.5***). It also has an increased lubricating ability, reducing friction in the engine.

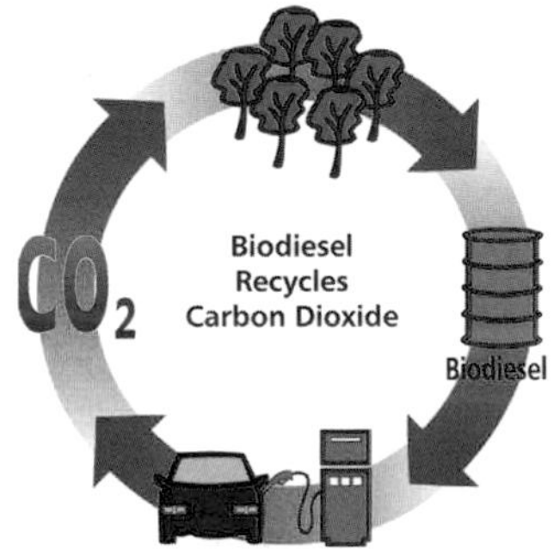

Figure 18.5 Biodiesel Recycles Carbon Dioxide
Source: U.S. Department of Energy EERE - www.eere.energy.gov

Tech Tip

Switching to Biodiesel

Biodiesel works as a cleaning solvent in a vehicle's fuel system. When switching from petrodiesel, biodiesel removes sludge and deposits. Residue cleaned out will end up in the fuel filter, which may result in a gradual loss of power when accelerating until the fuel filter is serviced or replaced.

Flex-fuel E85 Vehicles

E85 vehicles can burn a blended fuel that contains 85% ethanol and 15% gasoline (***Figure 18.6***). Ethanol is a grain alcohol made from renewable resources, commonly corn. Flex-fuel vehicle engines can be run on regular unleaded gasoline or any fuel that is blended with ethanol as long as the ethanol content does not exceed 85%. Millions of vehicles on the road today are flex-fuel compatible. Ethanol has less energy (BTUs) per volume than gasoline, resulting in lower fuel economy. E85 fuel contains about 81,800 BTUs per gallon (3.785 L), whereas gasoline has about 114,100 BTUs per gallon (3.785 L). Another disadvantage of using E85 is the limited number of refueling stations. Go to **www.afdc.energy.gov/locator/stations** to locate E85 refueling stations near you.

Figure 18.6 Ethanol E85 Logo
Courtesy of National Ethanol Vehicle Coalition

Q & A

E85 Compatible Vehicles

Q: How do I find out if my vehicle can run on ethanol?

A: All vehicles manufactured today and sold in the United States can burn at a minimum of 10% ethanol (E10). Many vehicles are also considered flex-fuel vehicles and can burn up to 85% ethanol (E85). Check the owner's manual or go to **www.fueleconomy.gov** to verify if your vehicle can burn E85.

Natural Gas Vehicles

Natural gas is regaining automakers' interest because it is abundant in North America, clean burning, and less expensive than gasoline. In 2017 there were over 150,000 natural gas vehicles (NGV) in use in the United States. Natural gas must be stored as either compressed natural gas (CNG) or liquefied natural gas (LNG) for use in vehicles. This section focuses on:

- CNG and LNG
- Fleets
- Conversion
- Refueling

CNG and LNG

Natural gas contains about 90% methane in pipeline form. Methane is the simplest hydrocarbon, making natural gas the cleanest fuel currently available for vehicles. CNG is compressed to around 3,600 psi (24,820 kPa) and stored in high pressure tanks (***Figure 18.7***). LNG is cooled to about -263°F (-164°C) in a process called liquefaction to condense it to a more pure liquid form. The liquid form is more dense, containing more energy than CNG, but is more complex to produce and transport.

Figure 18.7 ***Compressed Natural Gas Tank***
Courtesy of Ford Motor Company

Fleets

CNG and LNG have found their best fit so far in fleet vehicles, where it is easier to adapt to a reduced driving range and limited access to fast refilling stations. LNG is generally used in heavy-duty fleet vehicles like trains, transit buses, and semi-trucks. CNG is often found in fleet vehicles like cars, vans, trucks, and school buses. You can identify a CNG vehicle by its logo (***Figure 18.8***).

Figure 18.8 ***Compressed Natural Gas Logo***

Conversion

A gasoline engine has to be converted to run on CNG. Some automotive manufacturers offer a CNG prep package as an add-on option when ordering a vehicle (***Figure 18.9***). Then you work with a factory qualified vehicle modifier to have the CNG tank, fuel lines, and fuel injectors installed. The conversion cost is about $10,000. With near-zero emissions, CNG powered vehicles have extremely clean burning internal combustion engines.

Figure 18.9 ***Compressed Natural Gas Truck***
Courtesy of Ford Motor Company

Refueling

An extensive pipeline infrastructure already supplying homes for heating and cooking can be fitted with a compact CNG refilling station (***Figure 18.10***) that refills half a gallon per hour. A public access CNG refilling station must be used for a fast five minute refill. ***Note: Since CNG is in vapor and not liquid form, a gasoline gallon equivalent (GGE) is used to compare the energy of CNG to gasoline. It takes approximately 126.67 cubic feet or 5.7 pounds of CNG to equal the energy content of one gallon of gasoline.***

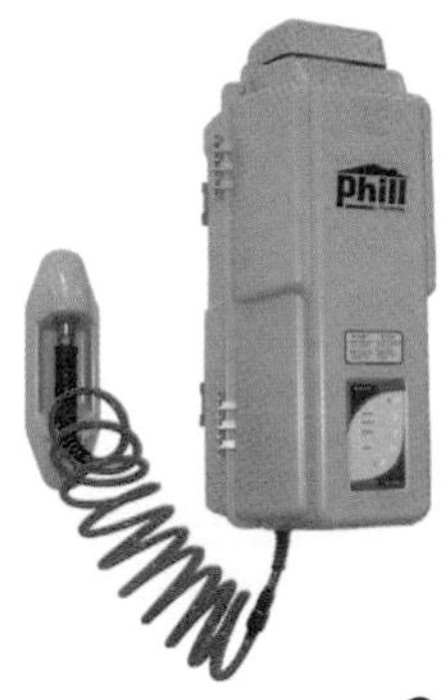

Figure 18.10 ***CNG Phill Station***
Courtesy of FuelMaker

Propane Vehicles

Propane, or liquefied petroleum gas (LPG), is also called autogas when used for vehicles. It is a by-product from two other energy processes: petroleum refining and natural gas processing. This section focuses on:

- Propane Use
- Fleets
- Clean Burning
- Refueling

Propane Use

Similar to natural gas, it is abundant in North America and is commonly used in homes in rural areas for heating, indoor cooking, and barbecues. Propane is colorless and odorless. An odorant is added as a leak detection safety measure. It is the most used alternative fuel, powering millions of vehicles worldwide.

Fleets

Many propane vehicles are used in fleets, converted from vehicles originally manufactured to run on gasoline (***Figure 18.11***).

Figure 18.11 ***Ford Fleet Vehicles***
Courtesy of Ford Motor Company

Calculations

Vehicle Cost Calculator

The U.S. Department of Energy provides an easy to use online Vehicle Cost Calculator at www.afdc.energy.gov/calc. The calculator tool compares the annual cost of ownership and emissions of any vehicle by make, model, and year. It includes most types of alternative vehicles.

Clean Burning

Propane is one of the simplest hydrocarbons (***Figure 18.12***), making it very clean burning. With minimal emissions, propane is also widely used in indoor commercial applications, such as forklifts. Propane vehicles have lower maintenance costs as compared to gasoline or diesel engines due to their clean burning engines. They emit less particulate matter (PM), nitrogen oxides (NO_X), carbon monoxide (CO), hydrocarbons (HC), and carbon dioxide (CO_2) as compared to a conventionally fueled engine.

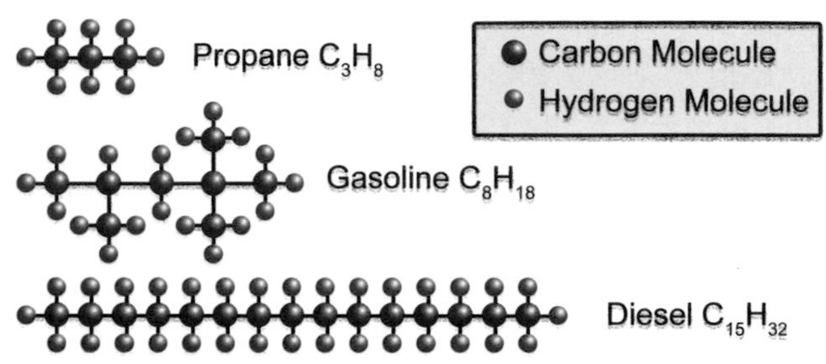

Figure 18.12 ***Hydrocarbon Comparison***

Refueling

One disadvantage is that propane contains less energy per volume than gasoline, so a vehicle's driving range is reduced unless additional storage capacity is added. Propane does not have an extensive pipeline delivery infrastructure like natural gas, but it is easily transported and stored under moderate pressure in tanks. Propane has more fueling stations (***Figure 18.13***) than any other alternative fuel, over 2500 in the U.S.

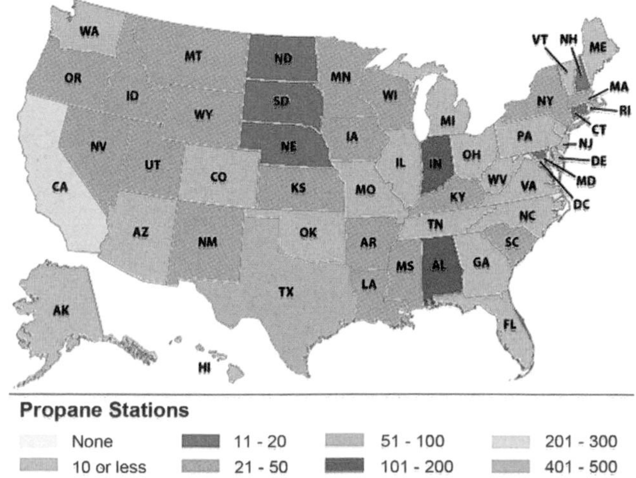

Figure 18.13 Propane Fueling Station Locations
Source: U.S. Department of Energy EERE - www.afdc.energy.gov

Bi-fuel Vehicles

Bi-fuel vehicles are different from flex-fuel vehicles. A bi-fuel vehicle has two separate fuel storage and delivery mechanisms. These are also called switchable systems, because you can switch from one type of fuel to another. The fuels are not mixed with one another, it only burns one type of fuel at a time. One type of fuel storage may be for gasoline or diesel while the other type may be for CNG or LPG. A vehicle that could run on gasoline and LPG would be considered a bi-fuel vehicle (***Figure 18.14***). Even though CNG and LPG are non-renewable, they are much cleaner burning than gasoline or diesel. Automotive manufacturers are producing bi-fuel (CNG and gasoline) vehicles to encourage the use of domestic supplied natural gas.

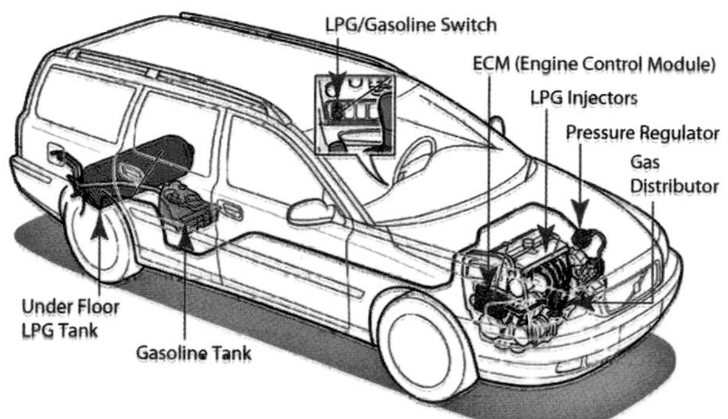

Figure 18.14 Propane/Gasoline Bi-fuel System
Source: U.S. Department of Energy EERE - www.afdc.energy.gov

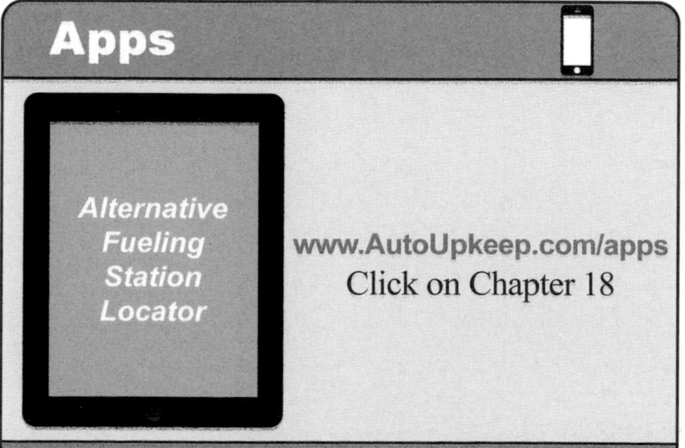

Mixed Fuel Vehicles

Mixed fuel, also referred to as dual fuel, vehicles are different from bi-fuel vehicles. In a mixed fuel vehicle, the engine runs on a combination of both fuels - a mixture of the two fuels. The fuel blend combusts together inside the engine. Some mixed fuel engines can run on the original fuel, the new alternative fuel, or a mixture of the two fuels. The powertrain control module (PCM) calculates how much of each fuel to use to optimize efficiency. This is called targeted blending. In a gasoline/natural gas mixed fuel vehicle, the PCM may use more natural gas during heavy load situations. In low load situations, it may use a blend that is more gasoline. The ability to shift the blend automatically to meet the demands of the engine load can increase the overall efficiency of the engine. The PCM may also blend the fuels depending on how much fuel is in each tank.

Web Links

Alternative Fuel Vehicles Sites

Autogas for America
www.autogasforamerica.org

CNG Now
www.cngnow.com

Energy and Environmental Research Center
www.undeerc.org

Growth Energy
www.drivingethanol.org

Methanol Institute
www.methanol.org

National Biodiesel Board
www.biodiesel.org

Natural Gas Vehicles for America
www.ngvamerica.org

Natural Resources Canada
www.nrcan.gc.ca

Propane Education and Research Council
www.propanecouncil.org

ROUSH CleanTech
www.roushcleantech.com

Hydrogen Powered Vehicles

Hydrogen was NASA's fuel choice for space shuttles. Vehicles can be powered by burning hydrogen in an internal combustion engine (ICE) or using it in a fuel cell. This section focuses on:

- Hydrogen
- Hydrogen Gas Production
- Hydrogen Internal Combustion Engine (H2ICE) Vehicles
- Fuel Cell Technology
- Fuel Cell Vehicles

Hydrogen

Hydrogen (H) is the simplest, lightest, and the most abundant element in the universe.

Atomic Number. Hydrogen has an atomic number of 1. The atomic number refers to the number of protons in the atom's nucleus (***Figure 18.15***).

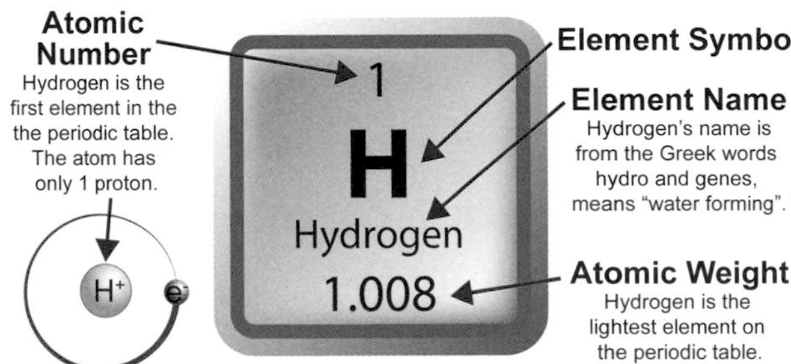

Figure 18.15 ***Hydrogen on Periodic Table***

Hydrogen Atom. Each hydrogen atom contains one negatively charged electron (e^-) and one positively charged hydrogen proton (H^+) (***Figure 18.16***).

Figure 18.16 ***Hydrogen Atom***

Hydrogen Gas. Hydrogen gas (H_2) is diatomic, meaning it contains two hydrogen atoms. The prefix "di" means two. It is a tasteless, odorless, and highly flammable gas. Hydrogen gas is also called molecular hydrogen. One hydrogen gas molecule (H_2) contains two hydrogen atoms. It is not found as a gas on Earth, it must be derived from other substances.

Molecular Formulas. A molecular formula is a way to identify how elements have combined. The formula uses the elemental symbol and a number, as a subscript, to identify the number of atoms of each element that are in the molecule. Hydrogen is always combined with other elements on Earth. For example, H_2O (hydrogen and oxygen) is water. It contains two hydrogen atoms and one oxygen atom. Hydrogen is also found in hydrocarbons. Octane used in gasoline has a molecular formula of C_8H_{18}, containing eight carbon atoms and eighteen hydrogen atoms.

Hydrogen Gas Production

Hydrogen gas is produced using steam reformation, gasification, and electrolysis.

Steam Reformation. The majority (about 95%) of hydrogen gas production is obtained from methane (CH_4) through a steam reformation process. Natural gas is mostly methane. It is where most of the methane comes from for hydrogen production. High temperature steam, in a device called a reformer, is used to separate the hydrogen from the carbon.

Gasification. Gasification uses organic materials like livestock wastes or agricultural crops to produce hydrogen gas. This process uses high heat to separate the hydrogen from the material.

Electrolysis. Electrolysis (***Figure 18.17***) is the process of running an electric current through water (H_2O) to separate the hydrogen from the oxygen.

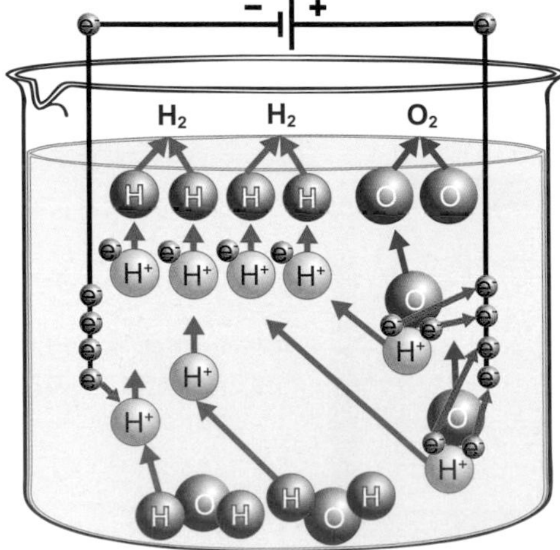

Figure 18.17 ***Electrolysis***

Hydrogen Internal Combustion Engine (H2ICE) Vehicles

Hydrogen can be burned in a modified internal combustion engine (ICE). Only a limited number of hydrogen ICE (H2ICE) vehicles have been built for research and development testing purposes. Automotive manufacturers are leaning towards fuel cell vehicles instead of H2ICE vehicles.

Fuel Cell Technology

A fuel cell, an electrochemical device, produces electricity by using a fuel and a chemical reaction. It does this without combustion by compounding hydrogen gas and oxygen. Fuel cells have three components: anode (where electrons are lost), electrolyte, and cathode (where electrons are gained). The electrolyte is a conducting substance that contains a catalyst. The catalyst causes the chemical reaction to occur. Fuel cells are classified by the electrolyte that they use.

Types of Fuel Cells. Various types of fuel cell membranes perform the function of extracting the electrons somewhat differently. However, the end result is the movement of electrons which is electricity. Currently several fuel cell types are under development for different applications from vehicles to power plants: proton exchange membrane (also known as polymer electrolyte membrane or PEM), direct methanol, alkaline, phosphoric acid, molten carbonate, solid oxide, and regenerative. PEM technology appears to be the most promising for automobiles.

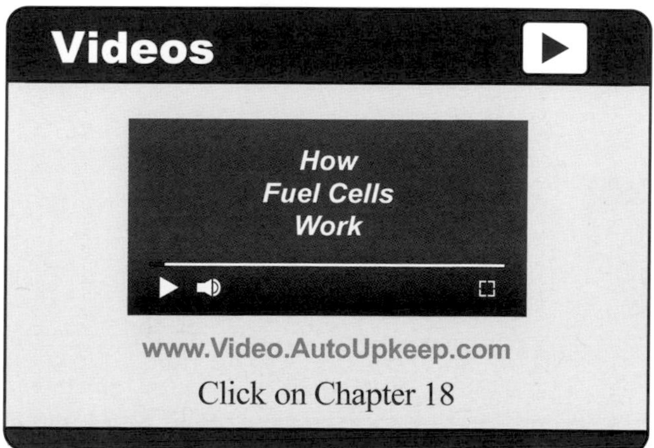

How a PEM Fuel Cell Works. A catalyst is used in a fuel cell to trigger a reaction that strips the electrons from hydrogen. After separation, the electrons are conducted on an anode (negative electrode). The electrons are attracted to the cathode (positive electrode), but they cannot flow through the proton exchange membrane (PEM) with the hydrogen ions (protons). The PEM only accepts protons. The electrons are routed through an external circuit, which includes an electric motor. Electricity is the flow of electrons, so the motor is powered as the electrons move toward the cathode (positive electrode). Upon returning to the fuel cell they reconnect with the hydrogen ions and join with oxygen to form water (H_2O) and heat (***Figure 18.18***). Water and heat are the only exhaust by-products of a fuel cell. Fuel cells are used in stacks to increase voltage.

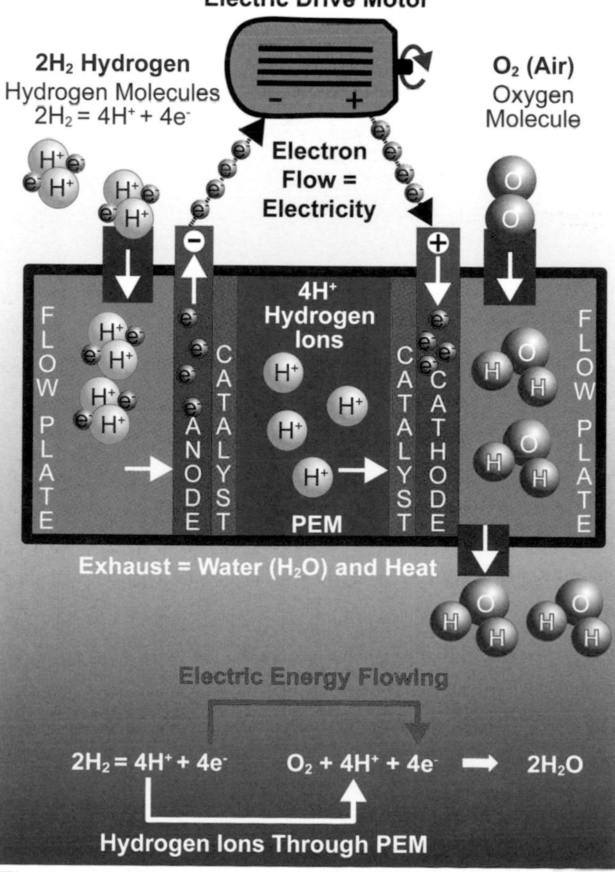

Figure 18.18 Hydrogen PEM Fuel Cell Operation

Fuel Cell Vehicles

A hydrogen fuel cell vehicle is an electric vehicle that gets its energy from hydrogen gas.

Production Vehicles. Fuel cell vehicles (***Figure 18.19***) are currently available to those that live or work near hydrogen fueling stations. To make fuel cell vehicles more appealing, manufacturers often include up to 3 years or $15,000 worth of fuel in the vehicle lease or purchase price. The key to expanding the number of fuel cell vehicles available is to increase the number of hydrogen fueling stations. Fuel cell vehicles have zero harmful tailpipe emissions and only take about 5 minutes to refuel.

2017 Fuel Cell Vehicles			
	Honda Clarity	Hyundai Tucson	Toyota Mirai
Available to Lease	Yes	Yes	Yes
Available to Purchase	No	No	Yes
Driving Range	366 miles	265 miles	312 miles
Combined MPGe	68 MPGe	50 MPGe	67 MPGe

Figure 18.19 ***2017 Fuel Cell Vehicles***

Major Components. A fuel cell vehicle has several components to make propulsion possible (***Figure 18.20***). A high pressure tank stores the hydrogen for the fuel cell. The fuel cell uses hydrogen gas and oxygen to produce electricity. Since a single fuel cell produces little voltage, multiple fuel cells are stacked together. The electricity is used to power the electric drive motor. A power control unit manages electrical flow.

Hydrogen Tank Safety. Hydrogen tanks need to withstand high pressure and accidental punctures. Automotive manufacturers are building carbon-fiber wrapped tanks. The tanks are placed strategically between the vehicle's frame. In an accident the vehicle is designed to absorb the forces of a crash to protect the tank. If a tank or line was punctured, the nature of hydrogen gas is that it disperses very quickly. Unlike gasoline which would pool under a vehicle if the tank was punctured, it only takes hydrogen gas about 30 seconds to escape out of a tank.

Hydrogen Fuel Cell Vehicle

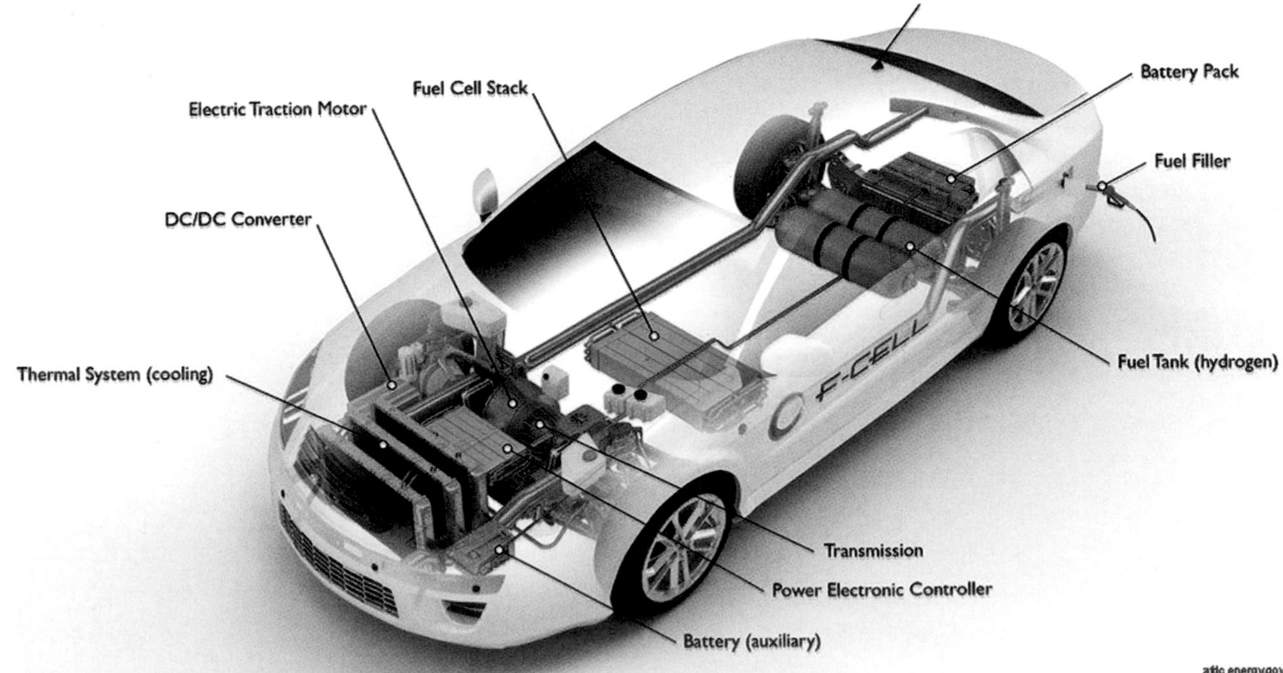

Figure 18.20 ***Hydrogen Fuel Cell Vehicle***
Source: U.S. Department of Energy - www.afdc.energy.gov

Hybrid and Electric Vehicles

Technological advances continue to improve the fuel efficiency of vehicles, but all new innovations are not created equal. With so many designs and combinations emerging, it can be a challenge to determine which technologies should be seriously considered when investing in a new vehicle. The internal combustion engine (ICE), especially in conventional vehicles, is inefficient, providing plenty room for improvement. Electric motor (EM) propulsion, even when pushing battery power to the limit, has limited nationwide recharging stations. By merging these systems in hybrid electric vehicles and optimizing the best of each, vehicles can better deliver the performance and range consumers expect. The table below summarizes some of the major advancements in conventional, hybrid, and electric vehicle technology (***Figure 18.21***) that allow vehicles to be cleaner (lower emissions) and more fuel efficient.

This section focuses on:

- Full Hybrid Electric Vehicles
- Plug-In Hybrid Electric Vehicles
- Mild Hybrid Electric Vehicles
- Hybrid Drivetrains
- Technological Advancements
- 100% Electric Vehicles
- Extended Range Electric Vehicles

Q & A ?

Quiet Vehicles

Q: How can a car be so quiet?

A: When there is no engine or when it is not running, there is very little noise. Drivers of hybrid and electric vehicles need to be more careful around pedestrians because it is not always easy to hear the car approaching.

Types of Vehicles						
	Conventional Vehicle	Mild/Belt-Alternator-Starter Hybrid	Full/Strong Hybrid Electric Vehicle	Plug-In Hybrid Electric Vehicle	100% Electric Vehicle	Extended Range Electric Vehicle
Propulsion Technology	ICE	ICE with Small EM	ICE with EM(s)	ICE with EM(s)	EM(s)	EM(s) with ICE Onboard Generator
Approximate Output of EM(s)	N/A	20 kW or Less	30 to 80 kW	30 to 80 kW	45 to 300 kW+	45 to 150 kW+
ICE Propels Vehicle	Yes	Yes	Yes	Yes	N/A	No
Sustained EM Only Mode	N/A	No	Yes	Yes	Yes	Yes
ICE and EM Can Connect Together to Propel Vehicle	N/A	Yes	Yes	Yes	N/A	No
ICE is an Onboard Generator Only	No	No	No	No	N/A	Yes
Start-Stop Technology	Some	Yes	Yes	Yes	N/A	N/A
Regenerative Braking	No	Yes	Yes	Yes	Yes	Yes
Plugs In	No	No	No	Yes	Yes	Yes
Fast Refuel	Yes	Yes	Yes	Yes	No	Yes
Example Vehicles	2017 Ford F-150	2017 Chevy Silverado with eAssist	2017 Toyota Prius	2017 Toyota Prius Prime	2017 Tesla Model S	2017 Chevrolet Volt

Figure 18.21 ***Conventional, Hybrid, and Electric Classifications***

Full Hybrid Electric Vehicles

A full hybrid electric vehicle (HEV) is any vehicle that has two or more distinct sources of power connected to the drivetrain (***Figure 18.22***). HEVs have been under development for a long time, with the first mass-produced Toyota Prius sold in 1997 in Japan. HEVs have increasingly gained attention in recent years. They are able to produce a higher than average range between fill-ups while reducing emissions. They also meet performance expectations of many drivers.

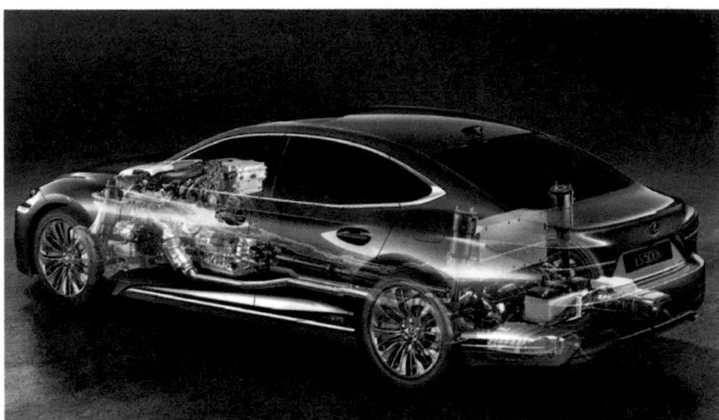

Figure 18.22 ***2018 Lexus LS 500h***
Photo: Toyota Motor Corporation

How Hybrids Work. Most HEVs have an internal combustion engine powered by fuel (commonly gasoline) and an electric motor powered by electricity from a high voltage battery pack. The engine and motor may provide power to the drivetrain individually or together (***Figure 18.23***). The battery pack is automatically recharged by surplus engine energy (from burning fuel in the ICE) and regenerative braking. Anytime the engine is running and full power is not needed surplus energy is available. Surplus energy can be sent through the generator directly to power the electric motor or stored in the high voltage battery pack.

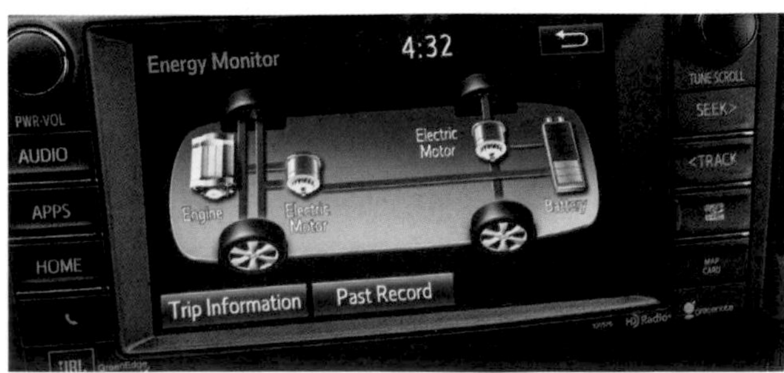

Figure 18.23 Hybrid Cruising Energy Distribution
Photo: Toyota Motor Corporation

Internal Combustion Engine. The engine is a hybrid's main power source, supplying power when driving conditions require more than the electric motor can provide efficiently. Gasoline is what provides the hybrid's energy, either directly from the ICE to the drivetrain or through surplus engine energy. The engine is sized for average power needs (not peak performance) and is engineered to run at a more constant and efficient speed than conventional vehicles. Start-stop technology shuts down the engine when not under a load, saving fuel. A conventional starter is not needed because the motor/generator is also used as the starter.

Electric Motor. The electric motor is a hybrid's alternative power source. The electric motor may be used independently during initial acceleration from a stop, traveling at low speeds, and stop and go traffic (city driving), when it is more efficient than the ICE. Power for the electric motor to propel the vehicle is provided by reusing otherwise wasted braking energy, surplus engine energy, and energy stored in the battery pack (***Figure 18.24***). The electric motor propels the vehicle when the ICE is least efficient and when additional or peak performance power is needed.

2017 Hybrids	Battery Type	Rating
Hyundai Sonata Hybrid	Lithium-ion polymer	270V
Toyota Prius	Lithium-Ion	207.2V

Figure 18.24 ***High Voltage Hybrid Vehicles***

Q & A ?

Hybrid Vehicle Upkeep

Q: What maintenance is required on a hybrid?

A: A hybrid needs maintenance similar to a conventional vehicle, like changing oil, replacing filters, adding fluids, 12V battery care, and rotating tires. Hybrid specific parts, such as the high voltage battery pack and electric motors, have been designed to last approximately 150,000 miles (≈240,000 km).

Plug-In Hybrid Electric Vehicles

HEVs and plug-in hybrid electric vehicles (PHEVs) both utilize an engine to eliminate range anxiety. Some people feel range anxiety when driving an all-electric vehicle that has a limited range. A hybrid's engine essentially allows for easy refueling and unlimited driving distances, just like a conventional vehicle.

Charge Port. A PHEV has the same components as a full HEV with the addition of an onboard DC charger. A charge port allows the user to recharge the high voltage battery pack by plugging into the electrical grid (***Figure 18.25***).

Figure 18.25 Prius Plug-In Hybrid Charge Port
Photo: Toyota Motor Corporation

Fuel Economy and Environment. The EPA's label identifies a PHEV's range and fuel economy when fueled by electricity or gasoline (***Figure 18.26***). The option of recharging the onboard high voltage battery pack by plugging in allows for longer distances in electric-only mode, reducing engine use. Whenever plugging into the grid for environmental benefits, the source of electricity should be considered. For example, electricity from a solar or wind power plant is cleaner than from a coal-fired power plant.

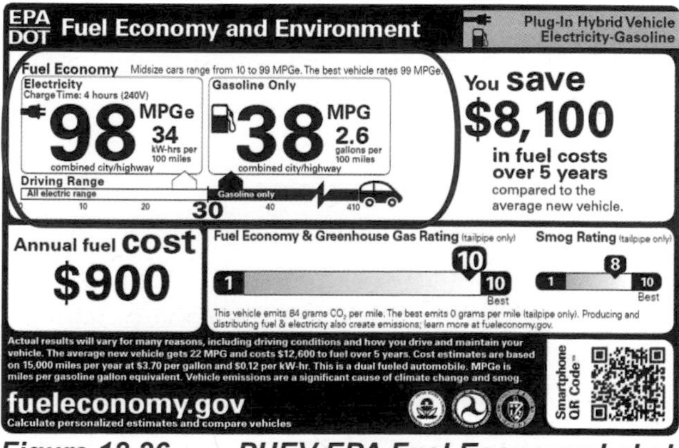

Figure 18.26 PHEV EPA Fuel Economy Label
Source: U.S. Department of Energy - www.fueleconomy.gov

Mild Hybrid Electric Vehicles

Mild hybrids with a small electric motor/generator (as compared to full hybrids) have the ability to crank over the engine, provide an on-demand acceleration power boost, and incorporate regenerative braking. The electric motor/generator is not sized to provide sustained electric-only mode, but by reducing peak demands on the engine it does allow the engine to be downsized (without losing performance). Mild hybrid vehicles also apply automatic start-stop technology.

Belt-Driven Electric Motor/Generator. In a belt-driven electric motor/generator system, the alternator and starter are combined into one unit. Also known as a belt-alternator-starter (BAS) system, the electric motor/generator connects to the engine via a serpentine belt and is mounted like a traditional alternator. GM calls their system eAssist (***Figure 18.27***).

Figure 18.27 eAssist

Crank-Driven Electric Motor/Generator. In a crank-driven electric motor/generator system, the unit is connected between the engine and transmission. Like the belt-driven system, the crank-driven electric motor/generator works with the engine to supply additional power when needed. Honda Motor Company calls their system Integrated Motor Assist (IMA) (***Figure 18.28***).

Figure 18.28 IMA on Honda Insight

Hybrid Drivetrains

As discussed in Chapter 16, a vehicle's drivetrain is designed to transfer power from the engine (or electric motor) to the wheels to move the vehicle. In a hybrid system, the drivetrain design determines how the electric motor and internal combustion engine (ICE) work together. Three systems are used: series, parallel, and series-parallel.

Series Drivetrain. In a series drivetrain, the vehicle's wheels are powered only by an electric motor/generator (MG). The ICE uses a generator to provide electrical power to the electric motor or recharge the batteries, but it isn't connected to the wheels (***Figure 18.29***). This is basically an electric vehicle with an onboard ICE powered generator.

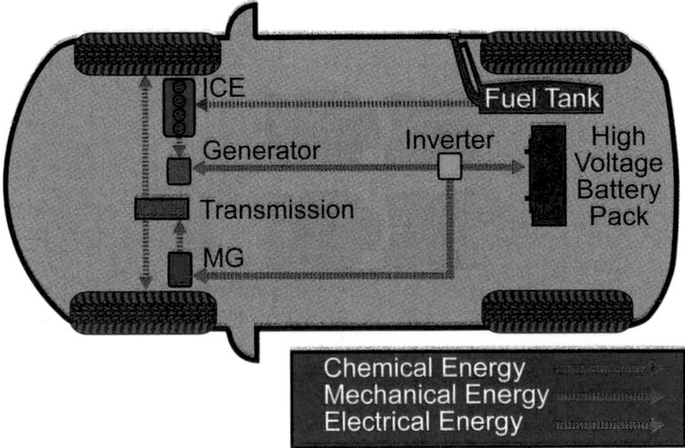

Figure 18.29 ***Series Drivetrain***

Parallel Drivetrain. In a parallel drivetrain (***Figure 18.30***), the vehicle's wheels are powered by the ICE and electric motor. Usually the electric motor/generator (MG) assists the ICE.

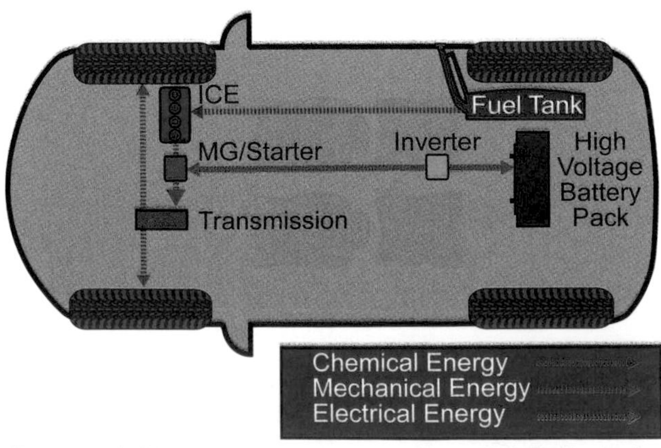

Figure 18.30 ***Parallel Drivetrain***

Series/Parallel Drivetrain. A series/parallel drivetrain allows the vehicle to operate like a series drivetrain or a parallel drivetrain (***Figure 18.31***). This drivetrain has two electric motors/generators (MG1 and MG2).

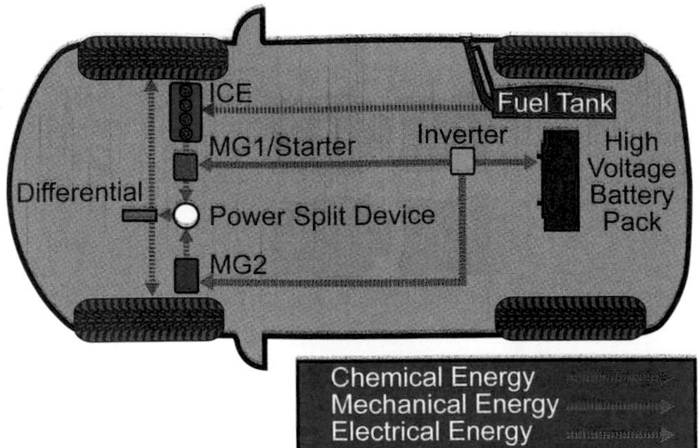

Figure 18.31 ***Series/Parallel Drivetrain***

A planetary gear set (***Figure 18.32***), also called a power split device, allows the electric motors (MG1 and MG2) and ICE to work independently or together. The ICE can drive the wheels mechanically (like a parallel drivetrain) or act like an onboard generator using electricity to drive the wheels (like a series drivetrain).

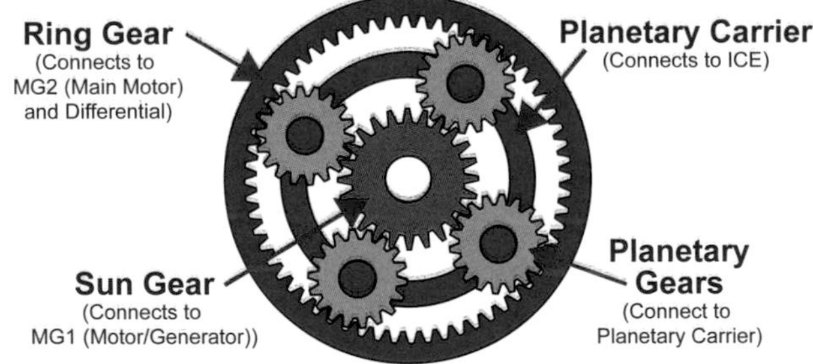

Figure 18.32 ***Planetary Gear Set***

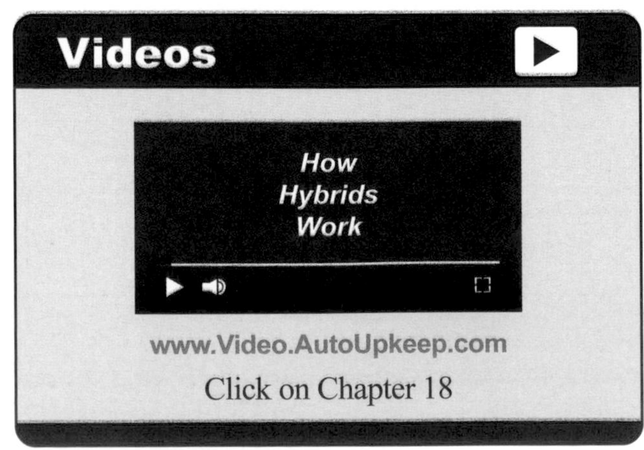

Videos
How
Hybrids
Work
www.Video.AutoUpkeep.com
Click on Chapter 18

Technological Advancements

With mass production, hybrid and electric vehicles have become more popular and affordable, especially as fuel costs and environmental concerns rise. Some common innovative technologies have made increased efficiency possible.

Start-Stop Technology. Start-stop technology, also known as an idle-stop system, automatically shuts down the engine at stops (when not under a load) and restarts upon acceleration. Reducing engine idle time saves up to 15% in fuel. A vehicle with the engine running, while sitting still, is the most inefficient way to burn fuel. Start-stop technology originated with hybrids, but is now also available on some conventional vehicles utilizing a specially adapted starter and programming. Start-stop technology is a very cost effective way to increase fuel economy and reduce emissions.

Regenerative Braking. Regenerative braking occurs when the electric motor acts as a generator to slow the vehicle and capture kinetic energy that would normally be lost as friction heat. This kinetic energy is converted to electrical energy to recharge the high voltage battery pack (***Figure 18.33***). Regenerative brakes do not replace conventional hydraulic brakes that are needed for more rapid stopping, but they do improve braking efficiency and reduce wear on conventional brake pads. To maximize regenerative braking, apply even pressure gradually when braking so the conventional brakes will not need to engage. Braking hard or braking and releasing repeatedly will not allow the system to work efficiently.

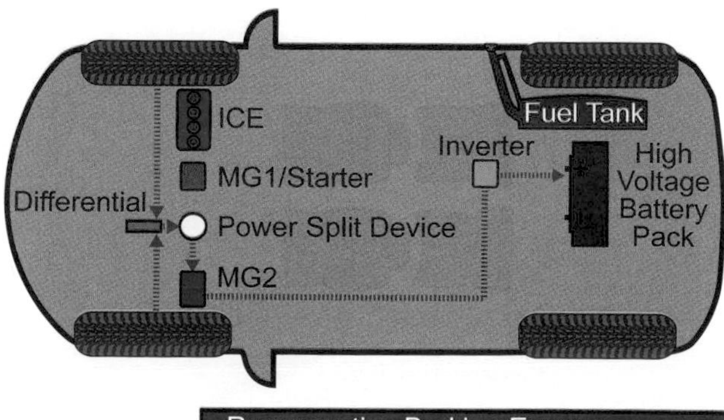

Figure 18.33 ***Regenerative Braking Energy***

High Voltage Battery Pack. Hybrid and electric vehicles have a standard 12V DC battery and a separate high voltage battery pack for storing energy. The battery pack is usually located where it is more protected against accidents (under the back seat, behind the back seat, in the trunk, or down the center console) (***Figure 18.34***).

Figure 18.34 ***Battery Location Label***

High voltage batteries, commonly nickel metal hydride (NiMH) or lithium-ion (Li-ion), can hold a great deal more energy than a standard lead acid battery. High voltage battery cables can be identified by their bright orange color. ***Warning: To avoid injury, shock, burn, or death the high voltage battery pack is equipped with a service disconnect*** (***Figure 18.35***).

Figure 18.35 ***High Voltage Service Disconnect***

Always follow manufacturer recommended precautions in the service manual and on warning labels (***Figure 18.36***) ***when servicing a hybrid or electric vehicle.***

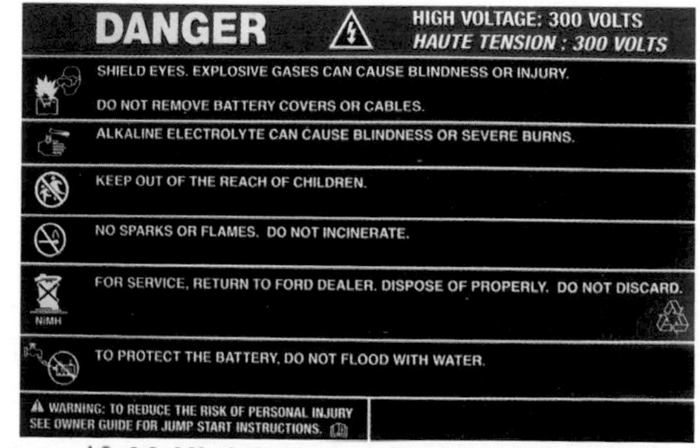

Figure 18.36 High Voltage Battery Warning Label

100% Electric Vehicles

Pure all-electric vehicles were actually extremely popular with city dwellers in the early 1900s until low cost, reliable internal combustion engines (ICEs) were developed. Electric vehicles (EVs) have gained attention once again. Most automakers have developed or are developing EVs as alternatives to ICE vehicles (***Figure 18.37***).

2017 EV Examples	EPA Estimated Range	Combined EPA Fuel Economy	Battery Rating
Hyundai Ioniq Electric	124 miles	136 MPGe	28 kWh
Chevrolet Bolt	238 miles	119 MPGe	60 kWh
Ford Focus Electric	115 miles	107 MPGe	33.5 kWh
Nissan Leaf	107 miles	112 MPGe	30 kWh
Mercedes-Benz B250e	87 miles	84 MPGe	28 kWh
Tesla Model S AWD - P100D	315 miles	98 MPGe	100 kWh

Figure 18.37 Electric Vehicle Specifications

Battery Technology. EVs have to be plugged in to recharge their high voltage/high capacity batteries. When driving, the chemical energy stored in batteries is converted to electricity to run electric motors that propel the vehicle. The release of mass-produced and practical EVs was dependent on high-capacity batteries. Lithium-ion batteries, used in current EVs, have a higher energy output and weigh less than older generation rechargeable batteries (e.g., nickel metal hydride). EV drivers may have range anxiety due to a limited nationwide fast recharging infrastructure. Time to recharge an EV's battery pack can vary from 15 minutes to 24 hours depending on the battery pack's state of charge, available charging voltage, the EV's onboard DC charger, and its battery capacity (***Figure 18.38***).

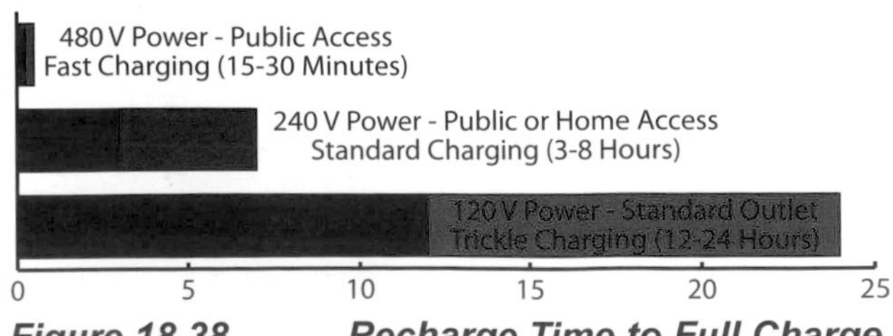

Figure 18.38 Recharge Time to Full Charge

Range. Range in an EV is greatly affected by driving style, cabin climate control, speed, cargo weight, and road topography. The dash on an EV may show estimated remaining drive range and the time to 100% charge based on a 120V, 240V, or 480V power source (***Figure 18.39***).

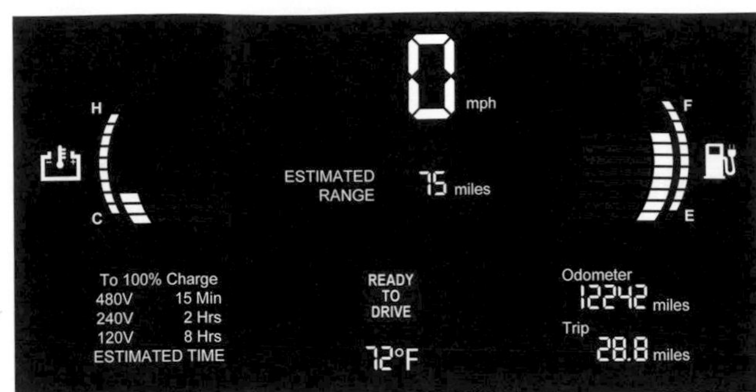

Figure 18.39 Electric Vehicle Dash Display

Electric Motor Drivetrain. In a common EV drivetrain, a large electric motor connects to constant velocity (CV) shafts that connect to the wheels. This is like a conventional vehicle, except the power source is the electric motor and not an ICE.

In-Wheel Electric Motor Drivetrain. An emerging electric drive configuration uses integrated in-wheel electric motors (***Figure 18.40***) that fit in the space behind the wheel. This direct drive system incorporates regenerative braking while eliminating the CV shafts and their drivetrain losses, making it even more efficient. Each wheel can work independently providing more control and performance than other drive systems.

Figure 18.40 Integrated In-Wheel Electric Motor
Image Courtesy of Protean Electric - www.proteanelectric.com

Advantages of the Electric Drivetrain. With a 100% EV you eliminate the need for refueling, there is no muffler to rust out, and you never need to perform a tune-up or oil change - just firmware updates. Electric motors provide a powerful, quiet, and smooth operation (***Figure 18.41***).

Figure 18.41 ***Tesla Electric Drivetrain***
Photo: Tesla

Sources of Electricity. Electric vehicles don't have tailpipe emissions, but the power plant providing the electricity may emit pollutants. The true well-to-wheel efficiency of electric vehicles really depends on where the source of energy originates. For example, if the source of electricity is mostly hydroelectric the vehicle is extremely efficient and environmentally friendly. However, if the majority of the electrical source is from a coal burning power plant, the environmental impact is greater. Each part of the United States has differing amounts of electricity sources. At www.afdc.energy.gov/calc a vehicle cost calculator determines where your electricity originates (***Figure 18.42***).

Electricity Sources - National Averages

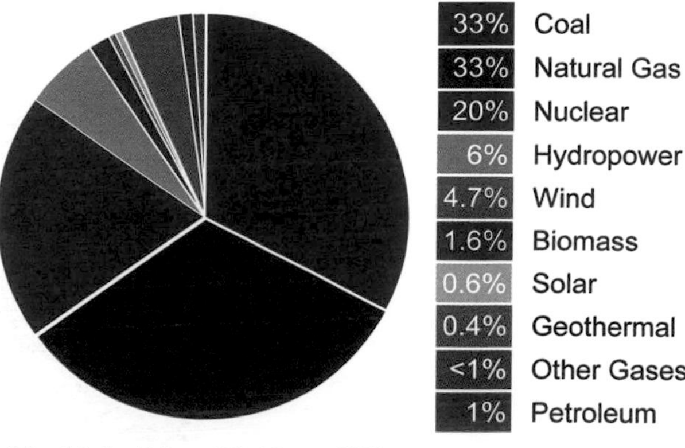

Figure 18.42 Electricity Sources - U.S. Averages
Source: U.S. Department of Energy EERE - www.afdc.energy.gov

Extended Range Electric Vehicles

Extended range electric vehicles (EREVs) are similar to plug-in hybrids except the internal combustion engine (ICE) is not designed to power the drivetrain directly. EREVs are designed to travel at all speeds in electric mode. Interest in EREVs is gradually increasing (***Figure 18.43***).

2017 EREVs	Electric Only Range	EPA Fuel Economy Electric	EPA Fuel Economy Gas	Li-ion Battery Rating
Chevy Volt	53 miles	106 MPGe	42 MPG	18.4 kWh
BMW i3 REx	97 miles	111 MPGe	35 MPG	33 kWh

Figure 18.43 ***EREV Specifications***

Chevrolet Volt. The Chevrolet Volt (***Figure 18.44***) allows for 53 miles of gas-free driving, after that the onboard 1.5 liter gasoline engine starts up to turn a generator to replenish the battery. This gives the Volt a 420 mile range.

Figure 18.44 ***Chevrolet Volt***
Courtesy of Mayse Automotive Group - www.mayse.com

BMW i3 REx. The BMW i3 REx has an electric only range of 97 miles. After that the onboard generator powered by a 0.65 liter two cylinder gasoline engine, located in the back, extends the range to 180 total miles (***Figure 18.45***).

Figure 18.45 ***BMW i3 REx***
Courtesy of BMW i

Solar Vehicles

Solar powered vehicles are basically all-electric vehicles that are powered by the sun's energy collected with hundreds of photovoltaic (solar) cells. The energy collected must be shared between running the electric motor and recharging the high voltage battery pack. Solar vehicles are currently impractical for common everyday use. Solar race challenges, such as the American Solar Challenge (***Figure 18.46***) and World Solar Challenge, are held to promote the fields of science and engineering and the development of renewable energy technologies.

Figure 18.46 ***Solar Vehicle***
Photo by Stefano Paltera/American Solar Challenge

Compressed Air Vehicles

Compressing air stores energy. Compressed air can be used in an engine to move the pistons, in contrast to an ICE that uses combustion. While a compressed air vehicle (***Figure 18.47***) may not have tailpipe emissions, upstream emissions are produced while refilling/compressing air. The vehicle's air tank may be refilled at home, at commercial refilling stations, or using an onboard compressor that runs on conventional fuel.

Figure 18.47 ***AIRPod***
Courtesy of Zero Pollution Motors on behalf of MDI - www.zeropollutionmotors.us

FlyDrive Vehicles

Are flying cars science fiction or reality? Some companies are working to make this a reality. To use this vehicle you would need a driver's license and a pilot's license. This section focuses on:

- Car/Gyroplane
- Car/Airplane

Car/Gyroplane

One company, PAL-V, began taking orders for a flying car in 2017 with expected deliveries in 2018 (***Figure 18.48***). The company indicates that the conversion from a driving mode to a flying mode or vice versa takes about 5 to 10 minutes.

Figure 18.48 ***PAL-V Liberty***
Courtesy of PAL-V - www.pal-v.com

Specifications. While in the air, the PAL-V Liberty is a gyroplane. A gyroplane is not the same as an airplane or a helicopter. Lift is generated by a wind-powered rotor. The engine drives the rear propeller to provide thrust (***Figure 18.49***). The force of the moving air spins the top rotor providing lift.

Specifications	Drive Mode	Fly Mode
Max Speed	100 mph	112 mph
Fuel Economy	31 mpg	6.9 gallons/hour
Engine Power	100 hp	200 hp
Maximum Range	817 miles	248 miles

Figure 18.49 ***PAL-V Specifications***

Car/Airplane

Other companies approach the FlyDrive experience differently. The prototype AeroMobil is a car and an airplane. Another company called Terrafugia is taking deposits on a vehicle called the Transition, with hopes to build an even more advanced vehicle called the TF-X.

Autonomous Vehicles

A vehicle that can drive without human input is autonomous (also know as self-driving, automated, or driverless vehicles). Many vehicles already have some level of autonomy such as autonomous braking, adaptive cruise, and park assist. Barriers exist to full autonomy. Regulatory agencies need to clarify laws and consumers will need to accept this technology. This section focuses on:

- Automation Levels
- How it Works
- Full Automation Vehicles

Automation Levels

Different levels of automation exist. The U.S. Department of Transportation adopted the SAE International definitions for its Federal Automated Vehicles Policy. These levels go from no automation to full automation (***Figure 18.50***). Levels 3 and above are identified as Highly Automated Vehicle (HAV) systems. Automotive manufacturers are expected to classify their systems accordingly.

Level	Defined
0 No Automation	The human driver does everything.
1 Driver Assistance	An automated system on the vehicle can sometimes assist the human driver to conduct some parts of the driving task.
2 Partial Automation	An automated system on the vehicle can actually conduct some parts of the driving task, while the human continues to monitor the driving environment and performs the rest of the driving task.
3 Conditional Automation	An automated system can both actually conduct some parts of the driving task and monitor the driving environment in some instances, but the human driver must be ready to take back control when the automated system requests.
4 High Automation	An automated system can conduct the driving task and monitor the driving environment, and the human need not take back control, but the automated system can operate only in certain environments and under certain conditions.
5 Full Automation	The automated system can perform all driving tasks, under all conditions that a human driver could perform them.

Figure 18.50 ***Automation Levels***
Source: NHTSA - www.nhtsa.gov

How it Works

By using cameras, radar, lidar (light detection and ranging), ultrasonic sensors, and a highly capable onboard computer, data is processed and hazards are identified more quickly than a human could sense them (***Figure 18.51***). It is projected that a car with full autonomy will be safer than with a human driver.

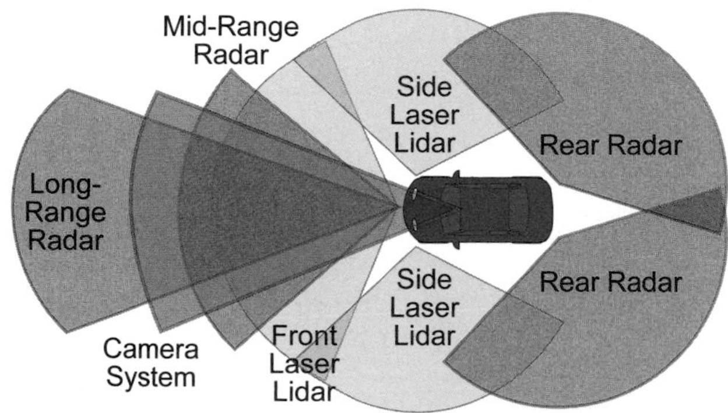

Figure 18.51 ***Autonomous Technologies***

Full Automation Vehicles

Since late 2016, all Tesla production vehicles have the necessary hardware to be fully self-driving. As new capabilities get fine tuned with real world data, Tesla rolls out features with over-the-air software updates.

Other Companies. Uber, Ford, GM, and others are also betting on autonomous vehicles. Ford is investing $1 billion (over 5 years) on an artificial intelligence company Argo AI. GM spent $1 billion on acquiring a company called Cruise Automation. Waymo is Google's (Alphabet's) self-driving division. Apple is also working on self-driving car technology.

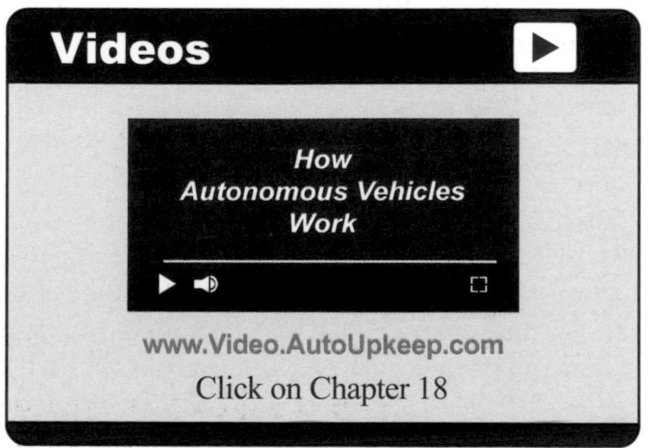

Technological Issues

With so many different energy sources and technologies, all of the advantages and disadvantages should be weighed. Factors are constantly changing as inventions and innovations occur. Ideally we are striving to use fuels and develop vehicles that are:

- Sustainable
- Renewable
- Practical
- Environmentally Friendly
- Affordable

Sustainable

The fuel source supply needs to meet the demand for it to be considered sustainable. Sustainable alternatives may include vehicles powered by solar, hydrogen, and electricity.

Renewable

Renewable energy resources are those that can be naturally replenished. Biodiesel (refined from animal fats and vegetable oil) and ethanol (made from corn) are renewable. Solar energy from the sun, electrical energy from wind and water, and hydrogen produced from the electrolysis of water are also renewable.

Practical

Being practical is where many of the alternatives have the most difficulty competing with gasoline and diesel. The infrastructure for supply is not readily available for many of the alternatives. The technology available for solar vehicles does not suitably meet our expectation of speed and range. Hydrogen fuel cell vehicles have a limited number of refueling stations.

Environmentally Friendly

Gasoline and diesel engines are major contributors to smog, acid rain, and greenhouse gases. Most alternative fuels and designs reduce harmful emissions, but do not eliminate them. An electric vehicle that gets its electricity from a coal-fired power plant isn't totally environmentally friendly. Upstream and tailpipe emissions need to be considered.

Affordable

The cost of a technology influences its development and popular acceptance. As the price of gasoline and diesel rise, more money is given to research alternatives. As the purchase price comes down on alternative vehicles, people are more willing to consider new technology.

Calculations

Fuel Economy Payback Period

If your reason for buying an alternative vehicle is to spend less at the gas pump, then you should determine the payback period. To illustrate let's compare vehicles with similar options, one is a conventional vehicle and the other is a hybrid.

Hybrid	60 MPG	$30,000 MSRP
Conventional	30 MPG	$24,000 MSRP
Difference	30 MPG	$6,000 MSRP

With gas at $3.60 a gallon, how many miles before the hybrid begins to save money?

EXAMPLES	Hybrid	Conventional
Gasoline Per Gallon	$3.60	$3.60
÷ Vehicle MPG	÷ 60	÷ 30
= Fuel Cost Per Mile	**= $0.06**	**= $0.12**

Fuel Cost Per Mile Difference	$0.12 - $0.06	**= $0.06**

	EXAMPLE
MSRP Difference	$6,000
÷ Fuel Cost Per Mile Difference	÷ $0.06
= Miles to Break Even	**= 100,000 Miles**

	EXAMPLE
Miles to Break Even	100,000 Miles
÷ Miles Driven per Year	÷ 15,000 Miles per Year
= Years to Break Even	**= 6.7 Years**

Considering only fuel costs, the break even point is 100,000 miles (≈160,000 km) or 6.7 years. If the price of gas increased the payback period would shorten. The payback period would also depend on actual fuel economy, purchase price, and upkeep.

Web Links

Alternative Vehicles Sites

AeroMobil
www.aeromobil.com

American Solar Challenge
www.americansolarchallenge.org

American Solar Energy Society
www.ases.org

California Air Resources Board
www.driveclean.ca.gov

California Energy Commission
www.energy.ca.gov

California Fuel Cell Partnership
www.cafcp.org

Center for Advanced Automotive Technology
www.autocaat.org

Fuel Cell and Hydrogen Energy Association
www.fchea.org

HybridCars.com
www.hybridcars.com

Motor Development International
www.mdi.lu

National Renewable Energy Laboratory
www.nrel.gov

National Fuel Cell Research Center
www.nfcrc.uci.edu

PAL-V
www.pal-v.com

Protean Electric
www.proteanelectric.com

Terrafugia
www.terrafugia.com

Tesla
www.tesla.com

The California Cars Initiative
www.calcars.org

U.S. DOE - Alternative Fuels Data Center
www.afdc.energy.gov

U.S. DOE - Fuel Economy Website
www.fueleconomy.gov

U.S. DOE - Efficiency and Renewable Energy
www.eere.energy.gov

Waymo
www.waymo.com

Zero Pollution Motors
www.zeropollutionmotors.us

Summary

The exponential growth of technology, crude oil prices, and consumer acceptance of new technology will drive the marketplace. From E85 to hybrids to 100% electric vehicles, changes are being made to make personal transportation more efficient and environmentally friendly. Continued technological advancements will help us work towards implementing better alternatives in the future.

Activities

Alternative Fuels and Designs

- Payback Period Activity
- Future Transportation Activity
- Chapter 18 Study Questions

Activities and Study Questions can be completed in the *Auto Upkeep Workbook*.

Career Paths

Mechanical Engineer

Education: Bachelor's Degree in Engineering
Median Income: $83,590
Abilities: Strong science, math, analytical, and problem solving skills in research and design.
Find your career at www.bls.gov/ooh.

AUTOMOTIVE ACCESSORIES

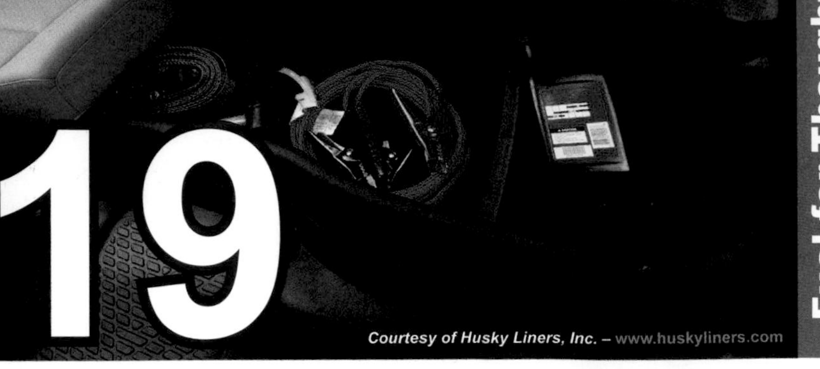

Courtesy of Husky Liners, Inc. – www.huskyliners.com

Fuel for Thought

- What types of accessories are available for your vehicle?
- How can accessories enhance the look of a vehicle?
- What accessories improve a vehicle's safety?

Introduction

Automotive accessories are an integral part of enhancing aesthetics, personalizing a vehicle, and often serve a practical purpose. They may also add comfort, convenience, protection, and safety. This chapter will identify some of the most common accessories and their functions.

Objectives

Upon completion of this chapter and activities, you will be able to:

- Identify automotive accessories.
- Explain different accessory functions.
- Estimate the cost of selected accessories for your vehicle.

Interior Accessories

Basic interior accessories include:

- Floor Liners
- Steering Wheel Covers
- Sun Shades
- Pet Travel
- Seat Covers
- Cargo Organizers
- Window Tint

Price Guides 

Floor Mats
- $20.00 to $80.00

Seat Covers
- $25.00 to $100.00

Window Tint
- $20.00 to $100.00 (parts)

Floor Liners

Floor mats and liners help protect a vehicle's carpet from dirt, mud, snow, salt, and other debris tracked in on feet. They can be easily removed and cleaned. If the floor mats begin to show wear, it is much less expensive to replace them than your vehicle's carpet. High quality floor liners (***Figure 19.1***) are molded to fit the contour of the floor and use floor mat retainers (especially on the driver's side), so they don't interfere with brake or gas pedal operation.

Figure 19.1 **Floor Liner**
Courtesy of WeatherTech – www.weathertech.com

Steering Wheel Covers

Steering wheel covers can be used for a custom look. A fabric cover may be used when a plastic or leather steering wheel is too hot in the summer sun or too cold in the winter. Make sure a cover fits snuggly and does not interfere with steering.

Sun Shades

Sun shades (***Figure 19.2***) are often used inside the windshield to block out the harmful ultraviolet rays that cause interiors to fade. They also reduce the inside temperature when a vehicle is parked in the sun. Mesh style shades can be used in the side windows to protect young children from the sun while driving.

Figure 19.2 ***Windshleld Sun Shade***
Courtesy of WeatherTech – www.weathertech.com

Pet Travel

Pet car seats, travel kennels, vehicle barriers, and seat belts (***Figure 19.3***) can all make transporting your pet safer. Keeping pets in a designated space minimizes distractions to the driver.

Figure 19.3 ***Pet Seat Belt***
Courtesy of HandicappedPets, Inc. – www.handicappedpets.com

Seat Covers

Seat covers protect the original seat fabric or provide a custom look inside the vehicle. Seat covers come in a rainbow of colors, designs, and material types. Specialty pet seat covers can also add safety and comfort for traveling pets.

Cargo Organizers

A wide variety of handy cargo organizers are on the market. Specialized net (***Figure 19.4***), truck cab, seat, console, clothing, and visor organizers help to keep items in place. Make sure you find one that fits properly and does not interfere with your ability to see and drive.

Figure 19.4 ***Trunk Net Organizer***

Window Tint

Window tint (***Figure 19.5***) is used to customize a vehicle, prevent interior fading, and keep you cooler in direct sun. Tint can be purchased in various shades. Dark tint makes it harder to see at night. Check your local laws to determine what shade and placement of tint is legal in your area. During installation do not trap any air, dust, lint, or other contaminants between the tint and the glass. Tinting requires patience, especially if your windows are curved. For quality results, consult a professional, research techniques, and follow directions.

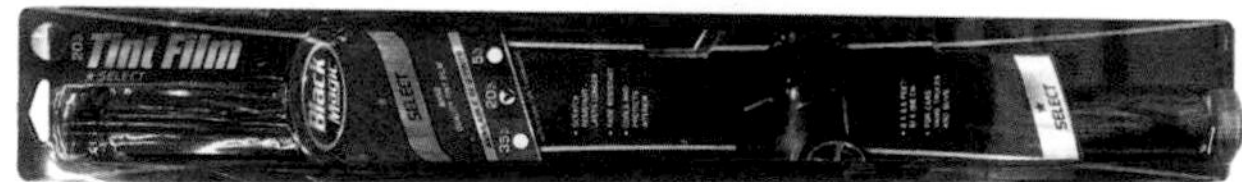

Figure 19.5 ***Window Tint***

Web Links

General Accessories Sites

Amazon.com
www.amazon.com

AutoAnything
www.autoanything.com

Gila Film Products (Window Tint)
www.gilafilms.com

Husky Liners (Floor Mats and Accessories)
www.huskyliners.com

WeatherTech
www.weathertech.com

Electronic Accessories

Basic electronic accessories include:

- AC/DC Converter
- Wi-Fi Hotspot
- Hands-Free Cell
- Audio Systems
- Entertainment Systems
- Navigation Systems
- OnStar
- Security and Alarms
- Remote Starters
- Camera Systems
- Keyless Entry
- Lights
- Engine Heaters
- Gauges
- Charging Docks

AC/DC Converter

If your vehicle did not come with a factory installed 120V AC accessory power outlet, you can use a plug-in power converter (***Figure 19.6***) to convert the 12V DC accessory plug to 120V AC power. This is an easy way to use a vehicle's power for laptops, cell phones, and other electronic devices. Make sure the converter's watt rating meets the power requirements of your electronic devices before plugging them in.

Wi-Fi Hotspot

Cellular technology continues to advance rapidly. In just the last few years it has become easier and less expensive to use the Internet while on the road. Because technology is advancing so fast you will need to research the current available options and consider the cost, ease of use, and signal strength to determine which option is best for you.

Built-in Wireless. Automotive manufacturers are increasingly offering new vehicles with Wi-Fi either standard or as an option. These built-in wireless systems provide some of the best signal strength and are easy to use. Most systems are offered with a free trial period and then require a subscription fee.

Other Wireless Options. There are several options for adding Wi-Fi if your vehicle does not already have it. These include using your smartphone as a hotspot, buying a portable hotspot (***Figure 19.7***), or installing a wireless automotive modem and router.

Figure 19.6 *AC/DC Power Converter*

Figure 19.7 *Wi-Fi Hotspot*

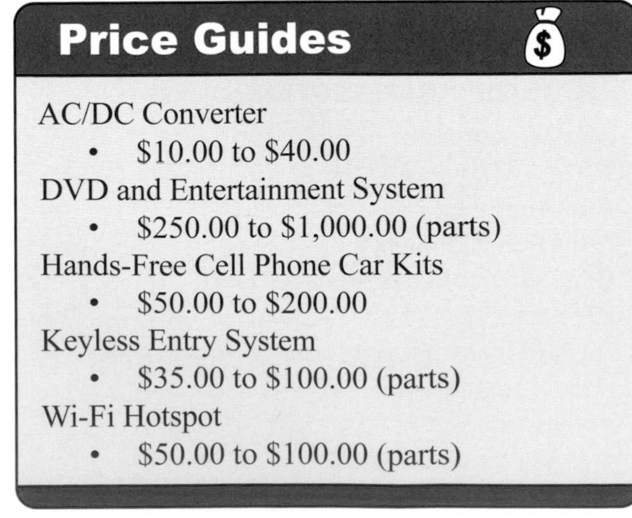

Price Guides

AC/DC Converter
- $10.00 to $40.00

DVD and Entertainment System
- $250.00 to $1,000.00 (parts)

Hands-Free Cell Phone Car Kits
- $50.00 to $200.00

Keyless Entry System
- $35.00 to $100.00 (parts)

Wi-Fi Hotspot
- $50.00 to $100.00 (parts)

Hands-Free Cell

Hands-free cell phone devices are safer to use than handheld cells, but both can be dangerous. A driver concentrating on a conversation is not as attentive to driving as someone that is not engaged in a conversation. Visit www.ghsa.org to learn about distracted driving (cell phone and texting) laws in your state. ***Note: Even if you are only a passenger, you still need to practice responsible vehicular use. Pay attention to your surroundings and the driver. Offer your assistance to the driver, especially if they are distracted by technology (cell phone, audio, navigation, etc.) to help keep everyone safer.***

Cell Phone Earpiece. Drivers often do not realize how much they rely on sound while behind the wheel. From sirens, to honking horns and screeching brakes, sound constantly helps you make driving decisions. Using just one earpiece (***Figure 19.8***) while driving still reduces your sensory input to outside noises, like an ambulance approaching. ***Note: In some states it is illegal to use a device in both ears while driving.***

Figure 19.8 *Cell Phone Earpiece*

Bluetooth. Bluetooth allows devices to communicate wirelessly with each other. With Bluetooth you can use your vehicle's speakers to hear a call for hands-free calling. Bluetooth can be added using a universal Bluetooth kit, connecting a vehicle specific adapter, or installing a stereo that has Bluetooth. Universal Bluetooth kits are inexpensive and compatible with any stereo that has an audio jack (AUX input).

Cell Phone Car Kits. Cell phone car kits may include wireless Bluetooth technology, a volume amplifying receiver, speakerphone, voice recognition, earpiece, automatic stereo mute, and a way to attach the device to the dash, visor, or headrest.

Audio Systems

Audio systems include basic AM/FM radios, HD radio (high definition digital), single CD players, multi-disk CD changers, MP3 players, WMA (Windows Media Audio), Apple CarPlay, Android Auto, and satellite radio (***Figure 19.9***). With Bluetooth connectivity you can also stream audio from another compatible device over your vehicle's speakers.

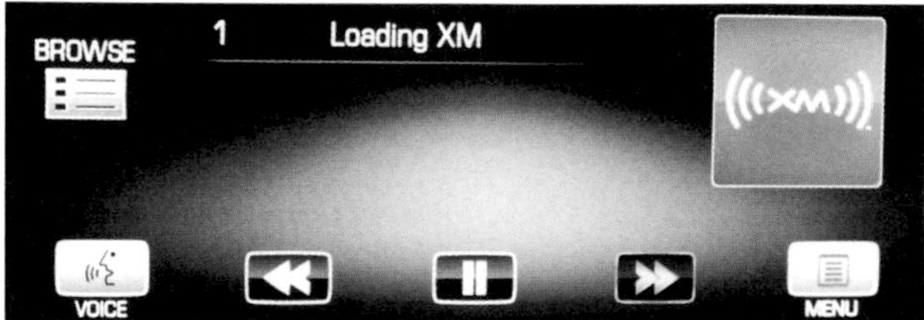

Figure 19.9 *Satellite Radio*

Speakers. Quality speakers can enhance the audio system in your automobile. Automotive speakers are generally grouped into two categories: component and multi-range speakers. Multi-range speakers have woofers and tweeters in one unit. Component speakers are single unit woofers or tweeters that are strategically mounted using a crossover unit for maximum clarity.

Entertainment Systems

DVD and entertainment gaming systems are available as portable units (***Figure 19.10***) or can be incorporated into a vehicle's passenger cabin. They are commonly located in a vehicle's ceiling or the back of headrests. A special input may be required to listen through your vehicle's audio system or you may be able to connect using Bluetooth.

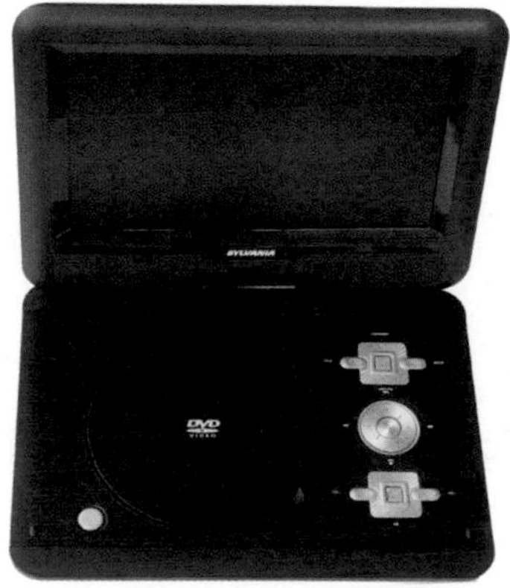

Figure 19.10 *Portable DVD Unit*

Navigation Systems

The Global Positioning System (GPS) is a navigational system comprised of 24 satellites orbiting the earth at about 7,000 miles per hour. The satellites continuously transmit radio signals that GPS receivers use to calculate a user's location. Three satellites are required to obtain latitude and longitude on Earth. This process is called trilateration. Four satellites are required to obtain latitude, longitude, and precise altitude. Standard GPS systems are accurate within 50 feet (about 15 meters). Advanced GPS systems that also use ground relay stations can improve accuracy by pinpointing the location within 3 to 10 feet (about 1 to 3 meters). Used with electronic maps, the receiver constantly sends signals to update a display (***Figure 19.11***) with upcoming roads, intersections, landmarks, airports, hospitals, and businesses.

Figure 19.11 ***GPS Display***
Courtesy of Ford Motor Company

Trouble Guide

GPS Inaccurate

- Update needed for outdated maps
- Satellites' signals interrupted
- Satellites' signals not available

Tech Tip

Navigate Safely

Do not input a new destination into a navigation system while driving. Some factory installed systems on new vehicles cannot be adjusted while the vehicle is moving.

OnStar

OnStar (***Figure 19.12***), installed as standard equipment since 2007 on General Motors vehicles sold in the United States and Canada, is a security and safety system. The three buttons allow for the driver to complete hands-free calling, talk to an OnStar advisor, or request emergency assistance. OnStar can also provide vehicle diagnostic information and maintenance intervals on some vehicles.

Figure 19.12 OnStar Security and Safety Buttons

Web Links

Electronic Accessories Sites

AutoMeter (Gauges)
www.autometer.com

Bosch Performance (Gauges)
www.boschperformance.com

Crutchfield (Audio)
www.crutchfield.com

Garmin International (GPS)
www.garmin.com

Gorilla Automotive Products (Security)
www.gorilla-auto.com

Hella (Lights)
www.hella.com

KC HiLiTES (Lights)
www.kchilites.com

LoJack Corporation (Security)
www.lojack.com

Magellan (GPS)
www.magellangps.com

ProHeat Products, Inc. (Engine Heaters)
www.proheatproducts.com

SiriusXM Satellite Radio (Audio)
www.siriusxm.com

Viper (Remote Starters)
www.viper.com

Webasto (Sunroofs and More)
www.webastosunroofs.com

Security and Alarms

As vehicle theft has increased, so has the technology to deter thieves. Alarms and security features can provide peace of mind. A wide range of alarm and security systems are available. The simplest of security devices can be used to lock your steering wheel. This visual deterrent may help a thief bypass your vehicle and pick an easier target. More sophisticated security systems disable the engine (***Figure 19.13***), track the vehicle, and notify the police.

Figure 19.13 ***Security System Window Decal***

Remote Starters

Remote starter systems can be accessed with a key fob, smartphone, or smartwatch app (***Figure 19.14***). They can start a vehicle on an extremely cold or hot day, defrosting a frozen windshield or cooling a hot passenger cabin from the comfort of your home or office. ***Warning: Carbon monoxide is poisonous, never start your vehicle and leave it running in a garage.***

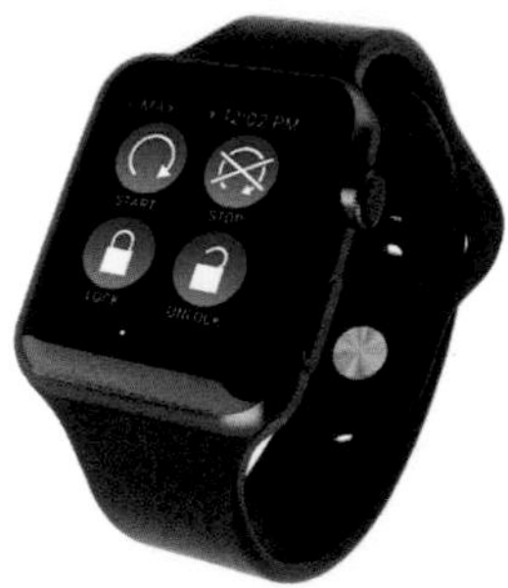

Figure 19.14 ***Remote Starter Apple Watch App***
Courtesy of Ford Motor Company

Tech Tip

Pollution from Remote Starters

Using a remote starter has a negative environmental impact because an idling engine increases air pollution. Many municipalities have anti-idling laws to reduce pollution.

Camera Systems

If your vehicle did not come with a backup camera system (***Figure 19.15***) you can add one. Wireless rearview cameras provide a much safer way to backup. There are many blind spots behind a vehicle that a camera can expose. Cameras can also provide monitoring when towing. On some systems the camera attaches quickly to your vehicle's back license plate holder and is wireless for ease of installation.

Figure 19.15 ***Rearview Camera System***
Courtesy of TadiBrothers - www.tadibrothers.com

Keyless Entry

Keyless entry systems, also known as remote entry systems, are popular on vehicles. Like any communication device, this system depends on a transmitter and a receiver. The receiver is mounted inside the vehicle and the transmitter is on the key, key fob (***Figure 19.16***), or smartphone app. To aid in security, keyless entry systems use a rolling code (also know as code-hopping) that can randomly generate millions of encrypted codes. The transmitter and receiver stay synchronized so they can communicate with one another.

Figure 19.16 ***Keyless Entry Transmitter***

Q & A

Keyless Entry Not Working

Q: What could be causing my keyless entry system not to work?

A: Periodically you will need to change the battery in the keyless remote. As the remote battery's life is near the end, it may work intermittently.

Lights

Fog, daytime running, and off-road lights can enhance driver visibility in a variety of conditions.

Fog Lights. Fog forms when water vapor condenses; it is basically a cloud that is near the ground. Fog makes visibility difficult. Fog lights are mounted low to the ground to get underneath the fog.

Daytime Running Lights. Many vehicles today come with automatic daytime running lights. Daytime running lights reduce multiple-vehicle daytime crashes.

Specialty Lights. Vehicles that are used for off-road purposes often use lights on a brush guard or specialized light bar to aid visibility (***Figure 19.17***). If you use specialty lights on the highway make sure they are aimed correctly so they don't blind oncoming traffic.

Figure 19.17 ***Off-Road Specialized Lights***
Photo: Toyota Motor Corporation

Price Guides

Engine Heater
- $30.00 to $60.00 (parts)

Fog Lights
- $40.00 to $150.00 (parts)

Navigation System
- $100.00 to $400.00

OnStar
- $200.00 (annual fee "Safe & Sound")

Remote Starter
- $40.00 to $100.00 (parts)

Security and Alarms
- $40.00 to $200.00 (parts)

Engine Heaters

Engine heaters are beneficial in cold climates, especially for diesel engines. In extremely cold temperatures, an engine may not start without one. Several types of engine heaters exist: dipstick, oil pan, hose heater, and block heater. All of them plug into 120V AC electrical outlets.

Oil Heaters. Dipstick heaters are electric dipsticks that warm engine oil. They should not be used on vehicles with plastic dipstick tubes. Magnetic oil pan heaters stick to steel oil pans, but not aluminum oil pans. Some oil pan heaters have a sticky pad that can be installed on all clean surfaces.

Coolant Heaters. A hose heater is installed in a radiator hose or heater hose, heating and circulating the coolant. A block heater (***Figure 19.18***) is installed into one of the engine's soft plugs (also known as freeze plugs). This type of heater consists of a heating element that heats the coolant. Block heaters are commonly installed in new cars as standard equipment in cold climates. Look under the hood or at the front of your vehicle for a 120V AC plug. Be sure to unplug the engine heater before driving away.

Figure 19.18 ***Engine Block Heater***

Tech Tip

Engine Heater and Emissions

Warm engine coolant conducts heat to other components. In addition to enhancing the ability to start an engine, engine heaters also reduce tailpipe emissions. A cold engine releases more pollution than a warm one.

Gauges

A vehicle may come with a variety of gauges already mounted as part of the instrument cluster. Aftermarket gauges (***Figure 19.19***) can also be added. Tachometer, oil pressure, water temperature, voltmeter, and ammeter gauges are the most popular types that are added to vehicles.

Figure 19.19 ***Gauges***
Photo: Bosch Automotive Service Solutions, Inc.

Charging Dock

A 240V AC home charging dock (***Figure 19.20***) is an accessory for an electric vehicle (EV). Most EVs include a standard 120V AC charging cable, but charging time is much less using a 240V AC charger. It takes about 12 to 24 hours to recharge a depleted battery from a standard 120V AC outlet. The same charge using a 240V AC system takes only 3 to 8 hours.

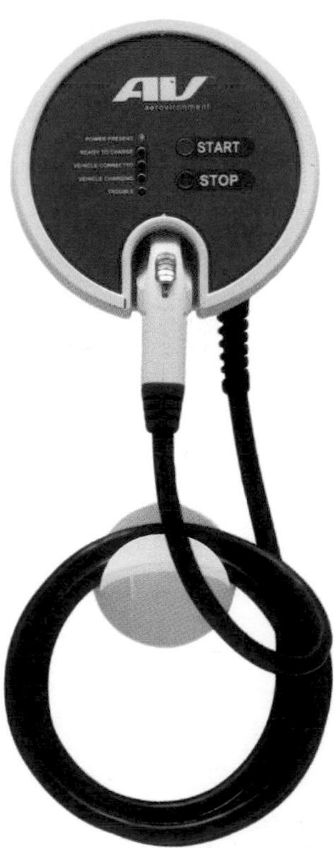

Figure 19.20 ***AeroVironment EVSE-RS 240 Volt Home Charging Dock***

Exterior Accessories

Basic exterior accessories include:

- Hood Protectors
- Running Boards and Nerf Bars
- Brush Guards/ Push Bars
- Truck Bed Accessories
- Car Covers
- Splash Guards and Mud Flaps
- Wind Deflectors
- Spoilers
- Undercoating and Rustproofing
- Wheel Customizing
- Wheel Lock Lug Nuts
- Grille Inserts
- Vehicle Graphics

Hood Protectors

A hood protector (also known as a bug shield) (***Figure 19.21***) can be installed to protect the hood of the vehicle, provide a cleaner windshield during bug season, or for aesthetics. Bug shields come in a variety of colors, clear, or tinted (smoked gray). Most bug shields are made from rugged acrylic.

Figure 19.21 ***Hood Protector***
Courtesy of WeatherTech – www.weathertech.com

Price Guides 

Bug Deflector
- $45.00 to $100.00 (parts)

Car Cover
- $50.00 to $250.00

Mud Flaps
- $10.00 to $40.00 (set of 2)

Running Boards
- $50.00 to $350.00 (parts)

Sunroof Deflector
- $35.00 to $100.00 (parts)

Running Boards and Nerf Bars

Running boards, nerf bars (***Figure 19.22***), and steps are commonly added to trucks and SUVs to give the driver and passengers an added step in entering a high-sitting vehicle. They also provide a custom look often desired by car enthusiasts. They are made from stainless steel, aluminum, fiberglass, and ABS plastic. Some vehicles even have automatically extending running boards that retract in when the door is closed.

Figure 19.22 ***Nerf Bar***
Courtesy of Dee Zee, Inc. - www.deezee.com

Brush Guards/Push Bars

A brush guard is a push bar (***Figure 19.23***) with mounted headlight protectors. Some brush guards (also called grille guards) are one piece units. These chrome or colored bars are usually added for aesthetics or to mount additional driving lights. Brush guards often give trucks and SUVs a more rugged off-road look.

Figure 19.23 ***Brush Guard***
Courtesy of Dee Zee, Inc. - www.deezee.com

Truck Bed Accessories

A wide range of truck bed accessories are available. Tonneau covers, tie down systems, tool storage devices, bed liners, cargo mats, bed rails, and truck bed caps are just some of the widely popular bed accessories.

Custom Cargo Liners and Truck Bedliners. Liners are made to custom fit trunk, cargo areas, and truck beds (***Figure 19.24***). They help protect factory carpet and finishes from spills and wear.

Figure 19.24 ***Custom Truck Bedliner***
Courtesy of Dee Zee, Inc. - www.deezee.com

Web Links

Exterior Accessories Sites

AZTrucks, Inc. (Truck Accessories)
www.aztrucks.com

Century Fiberglass, Inc. (Bed Covers)
www.centurycaps.com

Covercraft (Car Covers and More)
www.covercraft.com

Coverking (Custom Covers)
www.coverking.com

Dee Zee, Inc. (Truck Accessories)
www.deezee.com

JC Whitney
www.jcwhitney.com

Leer (Bed Covers)
www.leer.com

Lund International (Shields and More)
www.lundinternational.com

WeatherTech (Automotive Accessories)
www.weathertech.com

Westin (Truck Accessories)
www.westinautomotive.com

Ziebart International (Rustproofing and More)
www.ziebart.com

Spray-on Liners. A spray-on (***Figure 19.25***) liner helps to create a seamless protective coating that can often resist corrosion and chemical damage. It creates an easy to clean surface that can withstand rugged use.

Figure 19.25 ***Spray-on Liner***

Tie Down Systems. Most trucks come with tie downs, but you can add more to work with your specific cargo (***Figure 19.26***).

Figure 19.26 ***Truck Bed Tie Down***
Courtesy of Dee Zee, Inc. - www.deezee.com

Tonneau Covers. A tonneau cover (***Figure 19.27***) helps protect the truck bed and anything carried in it. It also reduces aerodynamic drag, increasing fuel economy.

Figure 19.27 ***Tonneau Cover***
Courtesy of WeatherTech – www.weathertech.com

Car Covers

Car covers are most frequently used when people are storing classic or collector vehicles (***Figure 19.28***). High quality fitted car covers can help protect a vehicle's exterior finish from rain, snow, dust, sunlight, and airborne pollution. To properly install a car cover make sure the vehicle's finish is clean, dry, and not hot. Never drag the cover across the finish, unfold it from the roof center down. Dirt under the cover can scratch the finish if the cover moves. Don't leave a cover on when it is windy. If the cover becomes wet, take it off to dry to avoid marking the finish.

Figure 19.28 ***Custom Car Cover***
Courtesy of Coverking - www.coverking.com

Splash Guards and Mud Flaps

Mud flaps (***Figure 19.29***) help protect a vehicle's finish from rocks and other debris that are thrown up from the tires. They are made from plastic, rubber, or metal. Once only common on large trucks, they are now specially molded to fit all types of cars and luxury vehicles.

Figure 19.29 ***Mud Flaps***
Courtesy of Husky Liners, Inc. – www.huskyliners.com

Wind Deflectors

Sunroof and side window wind deflectors (***Figure 19.30***) made out of acrylic plastic, are not just for looks. When going down the highway with the sunroof or window open they reduce dust, turbulence noise, and wind by redirecting the flow of air. Fresh air can come in and noise is minimized. Deflectors also provide some shade and rain protection.

Figure 19.30 ***Wind Deflectors***
Courtesy of WeatherTech – www.weathertech.com

Spoilers

Rear spoilers (***Figure 19.31***) are added to give a custom look to vehicles. In the past they were common on sports cars, but are gaining attention on a variety of two door coupes and four door sedans.

Figure 19.31 ***Spoiler***
Courtesy of Ford Motor Company

Tech Tip 

Custom Spoilers

If you are planning on installing a spoiler keep in mind that it may drastically limit your view from your rearview mirror. Also if the spoiler was not designed for your vehicle it may increase drag, lowering fuel economy.

Undercoating and Rustproofing

Automotive manufacturers go to great lengths to rustproof vehicles during manufacturing. Rust (iron oxide) is formed when oxygen and water come in contact with iron. Since iron is used to make steel, rust can form on unprotected steel. To rustproof a vehicle more thoroughly, rust-inhibitors can also be sprayed inside body panels.

Corrosion Perforation. Most vehicles have corrosion perforation warranties for a designated period of time. Since perforation means hole formation, before the warranty applies, the steel would have to completely rust through (***Figure 19.32***).

Figure 19.32 ***Corrosion Perforation***

Undercoating. Undercoating (***Figure 19.33***) can be added to the underside of the vehicle to deaden road noise and lessen the chance of rust forming.

Figure 19.33 ***Undercoating***

Tech Tip 

Undercoating a New Vehicle

Many new vehicles come from the manufacturer with a good rustproof coating, making it unnecessary to pay for this additional dealer applied option.

Wheel Customizing

Adding custom wheels is one way to personalize a vehicle. In the past, most vehicles came with standard steel wheels covered by hubcaps. Common sizes were 13″, 14″, 15″, and 16″. Today, the most common custom wheels are painted, chrome (***Figure 19.34***), and polished aluminum. Custom wheel sizes come in a variety of sizes: 17″, 18″, 19″, 20″, 22″, 24″, 26″, and 28″. Costs for a set of custom wheels range from a couple hundred to several thousand dollars.

Figure 19.34 ***Custom Chrome Wheel***

Wheel Lock Lug Nuts

Wheel lock lug nuts are commonly put on vehicles with expensive alloy wheels. Lock lug nuts come in packs of four, one for each wheel. A special coded key tool (***Figure 19.35***) is used to remove the lug nuts. It is a good idea to keep this tool locked in the glove box or center console.

Figure 19.35 ***Locking Lug Nut Key Tool***

Tech Tip

Locking Lug Nut Key Tool

If you take your vehicle to a repair facility to have the tires rotated or serviced make sure the technician returns the lug nut key after the service is performed. Sometimes when technicians get busy they forget about returning the key. Also, if a technician uses an impact wrench on your lug nut key it may become damaged. You will need this key to install the spare if you have a flat.

Grille Inserts

A grille insert can be installed on some vehicles to warm up the engine quicker in cold climates. Most styles snap easily into the grille. Be sure to remove the air restricting grille inserts when the outside temperature warms up. You can also change to a mesh insert in the summer to prevent bugs from clogging up the radiator fins.

Vehicle Graphics

Vehicle stripes (***Figure 19.36***) and wraps are the ultimate custom expression for your ride, ranging from mild to extremely wild. Businesses increasingly use wraps for brand awareness marketing. The graphics are commonly made from vinyl film and stick with adhesive pressure activation. They last around 5-7 years with various factors affecting performance: surface preparation, installation, sun exposure, environmental conditions, and maintenance. They are removable with heat and/or chemicals from most surfaces.

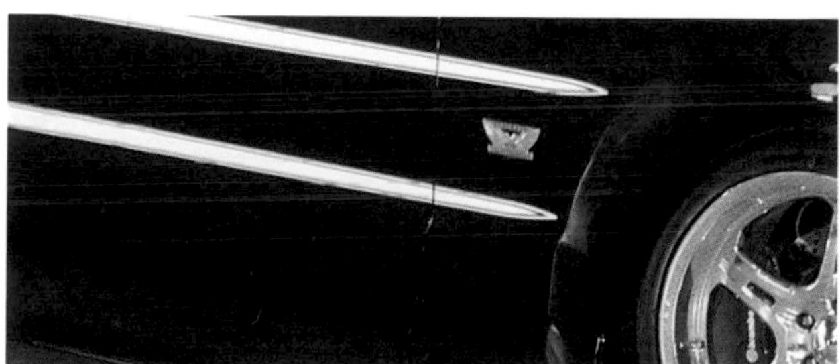

Figure 19.36 ***Vehicle Graphic Stripes***

Web Links

Performance Accessories Sites

American Eagle Wheel Corporation
www.americaneaglewheel.com

American Racing Custom Wheels
www.americanracing.com

Center Line Forged Wheels
www.centerlinewheels.com

JEG's High Performance
www.jegs.com

Summit Racing Equipment
www.summitracing.com

Weld Wheel Industries
www.weldwheels.com

Hauling and Towing Accessories

Basic hauling and towing accessories include:

- Cargo Carriers
- Ratchet Straps
- Trailer Brake Controllers
- Trailer Brake Wiring and Plugs
- Trailer Hitches
- Towing Mirrors
- Tow Straps
- Winches

Cargo Carriers

If you are an outdoor enthusiast or just need extra cargo space, you may want to add a cargo rack to your vehicle. Racks can be mounted on the roof, trunk, trailer hitch (***Figure 19.37***), or in the bed of a pickup. They allow you to safely and easily transport items that may be too large for inside or would take up needed passenger room. Outside vehicle mounting systems reduce fuel economy, but may be the best option for some cargo. ***Note: Before mounting any rack, you need to make sure the carrier and cargo will not exceed the vehicle's weight rating.***

Figure 19.37 **Cargo Hitch Rack**

Roof Rack. Roof racks (***Figure 19.38***) transport items (e.g., luggage, coolers, kayaks, skis, and surfboards) on top of a vehicle. A roof rack may provide the most stable and versatile location for some items, but it does not provide protection from the wind, weather, and the road.

Figure 19.38 **Roof Rack**

Rooftop Cargo Box. Rooftop cargo boxes (***Figure 19.39***) transport items in a protected shell. They are commonly made to be weathertight and aerodynamic for reduced drag and noise.

Figure 19.39 **Roof Carrier**

Hitch Rack. If your vehicle has a trailer hitch, adding a hitch rack (***Figure 19.40***) may be the easiest way to augment cargo space. Racks located behind the vehicle are more aerodynamic, creating less wind resistance, when compared to a roof rack. Some hitch racks are specially designed to transport a wheelchair or mobility scooter.

Figure 19.40 **Equipment Hitch Rack**
Photo: Tesla

Trunk Rack. Trunk racks fit most cars with the advantage of no overhead lifting.

Price Guides

Bike Rack
- $30.00 to $200.00

Ratchet Tie Downs
- $10.00 to $40.00

Rustproofing
- $200.00 to $400.00

Towing Mirrors - Extension Style
- $20.00 to $50.00 (pair)

Wheel Lock Lug Nuts
- $15.00 to $50.00

Ladder Rack. Ladder racks may be your best option for accommodating larger items like ladders, kayaks, and canoes (***Figure 19.41***).

Figure 19.41 ***Ladder Rack***
Courtesy of Dee Zee, Inc. - www.deezee.com

Ratchet Straps

Ratchet tie down straps (***Figure 19.42***) are used to securely hold cargo in place. They come in different sizes, lengths, ratings, and styles.

Figure 19.42 ***Ratchet Tie Down Straps***

Web Links

Hauling and Towing Accessory Sites

Draw-Tite Hitches
www.draw-tite.com

Hopkins Mfg. Corp. (Towing and More)
www.hopkinsmfg.com

Ramsey Industries
www.ramsey.com

Reese Hitches
www.reeseprod.com

Tekonsha Brake Controllers
www.tekonsha.com

Warn Industries, Inc. (Winches and More)
www.warn.com

Yakima Products (Roof Racks)
www.yakima.com

Trailer Brake Controllers

When towing a trailer with independent brakes, a brake controller is necessary. The brake controller adjusts the power to the electrically operated trailer brakes during deceleration. Some trucks have brake controllers as standard equipment (***Figure 19.43***).

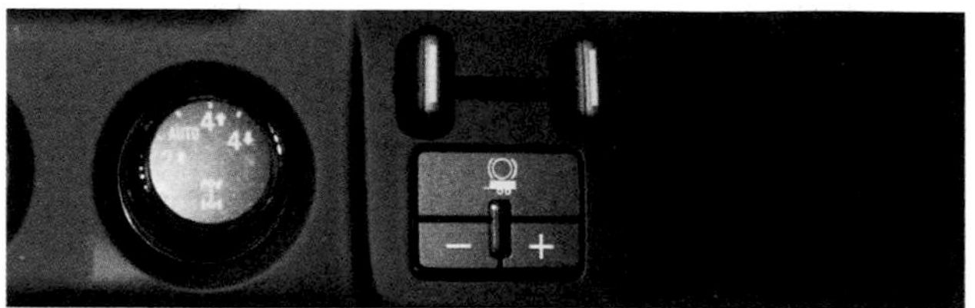

Figure 19.43 ***Trailer Brake Controller***

Trailer Brake Wiring and Plugs

Electricity is necessary to power the running and brake lights on a trailer. Several types of trailer wiring plugs are available: 4, 5, 6, or 7 pole (***Figure 19.44***). On vehicles that tow lightweight trailers, a four pole flat plug is the most common. On vehicles that tow larger heavyweight trailers, a seven pole round plug is commonly used.

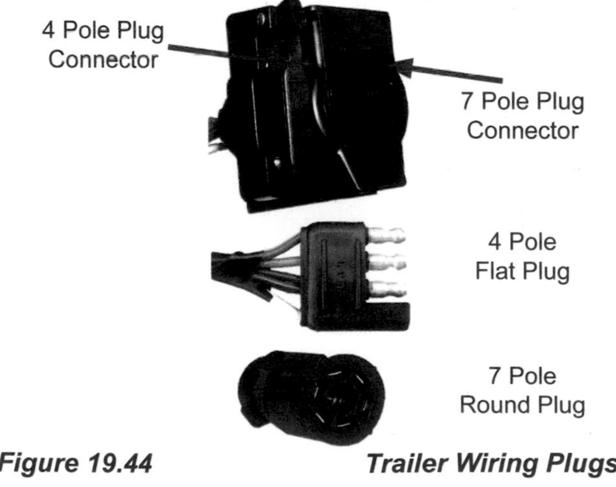

Figure 19.44 ***Trailer Wiring Plugs***

Tech Tip

Trailer Light Check

Trailer wiring can easily become corroded or damaged. To be on the safe side, the brake lights and turn signals should be visually inspected every time before you tow.

Trailer Hitches

Trailer hitches (***Figure 19.45***) are used to pull boat, snowmobile, motorcycle, utility, and recreational trailers.

Figure 19.45 ***Class V Hitch***

Hitch Classes. Trailer hitches are commonly classified into five classes (***Figure 19.46***). The style that you install depends on the vehicle.

Class	Receiver	Tongue Weight* (TW)	Gross Trailer Weight* (GTW)	Vehicle Type
I	1¼"	200 lbs (91 kg)	2000 lbs (907 kg)	Mid-sized Cars, Compact Trucks
II	1¼"	300 lbs (136 kg)	3500 lbs (1588 kg)	Mid-sized Cars, Compact Trucks
III	2"	600 lbs (272 kg)	6000 lbs (2722 kg)	Full-sized Cars, Mid-sized Trucks, Mid-sized SUVs
IV	2"	1000 lbs (454 kg)	10000 lbs (4536 kg)	Full-sized Trucks, Full-sized SUVs
V	2"	1200 lbs (544 kg)	12000 lbs (5443 kg)	Full-sized Trucks, Full-sized SUVs
	2½"	1800 lbs (817 kg)	18000 lbs (8165 kg)	Full-sized Trucks
	3"	2100 lbs (953 kg)	21000 lbs (9525 kg)	Full-sized Trucks

*May vary depending on hitch manufacturer.

Figure 19.46 ***Trailer Hitch Classifications***

Bed Mount Hitches. Specialty bed mount hitches are used on heavy-duty trucks to pull fifth wheel and gooseneck trailers. Refer to the owner's manual to identify the maximum towing capacity and the correct trailer hitch.

Ball Mount Receivers. Some hitches have ball mount receivers (***Figure 19.47***). Receivers come in 1¼", 2", 2½", and 3".

Figure 19.47 ***Ball Mount Receiver***

Trailer Hitch Balls. Trailer hitch balls (***Figure 19.48***) come in three basic sizes: $1\frac{7}{8}$″, 2″, and $2\frac{5}{16}$″. These sizes relate to the ball diameter. The trailer tongue size determines the ball size needed.

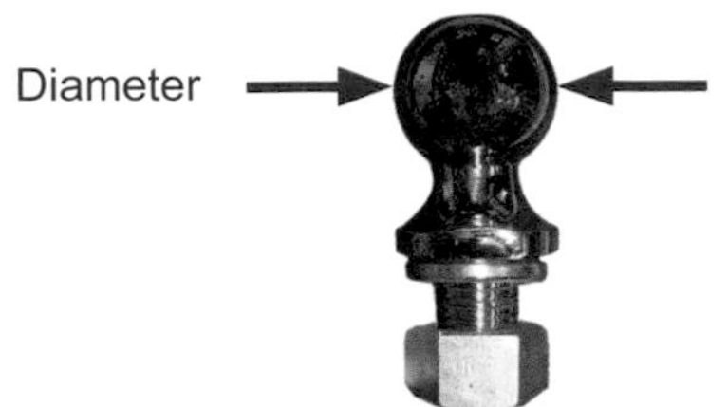

Figure 19.48 ***Trailer Hitch Ball***

Trailer Safety Chains. Safety chains (***Figure 19.49***) attach to a trailer tongue to prevent runaway trailers. Safety chains hook onto the vehicle's hitch or frame to keep the trailer connected to the vehicle if the trailer tongue slips off or breaks away from the trailer ball. A runaway trailer could cause serious injury and damage. Safety chains need to be attached loose enough so they do not bind when turning, but tight enough so they do not drag on the road. ***Warning: Never tow anything without properly attaching approved safety chains.***

Figure 19.49 ***Trailer Tongue with Safety Chains***

Towing Mirrors

Towing mirrors can completely replace the original equipment manufacturer's (OEM) style mirrors or can be installed as extensions on the existing mirrors (***Figure 19.50***). Both styles help the driver see around large trailers. They often extend out from the doors much farther than standard mirrors.

Figure 19.50 ***Towing Mirrors - Extension Style***

Tow Straps

Tow ropes or straps (***Figure 19.51***) can be used for emergency towing and moving vehicles short distances at a slow speed. Tow bars or dollies should be used for any long distance towing. ***Warning: Never use an ordinary rope to tow a vehicle.***

Figure 19.51 ***Tow Strap***

Tech Tip

Tow Rope/Strap Rating

Never use just anything to tow a vehicle. Tow ropes and straps are rated for a reason. Never stand where a tow rope can snap back at you. Use the tow rope to get the vehicle to the side of the road. Call a tow truck for transporting the vehicle to an automotive repair shop.

Winches

A winch (***Figure 19.52***) can be added to a vehicle that is used for off-road conditions. The size of winch (pulling power and line strength) depends on the vehicle's weight and what it intends to pull. Add-on winch systems are electrically or hydraulically driven.

Figure 19.52 ***Winch***

Summary

Vehicle accessories can be for function and/or aesthetics. Be sure the accessories you add are designed specifically for your vehicle. Remove accessories when not being used. Adding unnecessary weight and drag impacts fuel economy.

Activities

Automotive Accessories

- Automotive Accessories Activity
- Chapter 19 Study Questions

Activities and Study Questions can be completed in the *Auto Upkeep Workbook.*

Career Paths

Electronics Installer

Education: Technical Training
Median Income: $55,160
Abilities: Mechanical, electrical, and programing aptitude. Fast learner and detail oriented.
Find your career at www.bls.gov/ooh.

Common Problems and Roadside Emergencies

Chapter 20

Fuel for Thought

- What are common automotive problems?
- What should you do during a roadside emergency?
- What can be done to avoid an accident?

Introduction

This chapter will cover some of the most common problems that automobile owners encounter. It will also cover what to do during roadside emergencies. You can often see, hear, smell, or feel a problem arising before it leaves you stranded on the side of the road (***Figure 20.1***). Sometimes the solution is so simple it is often overlooked. Being familiar with the various systems that keep a vehicle operating properly will better prepare you to diagnose problems. Use your senses and pay attention to your vehicle. Most importantly, your safety and the safety of your passengers should always be the top priority.

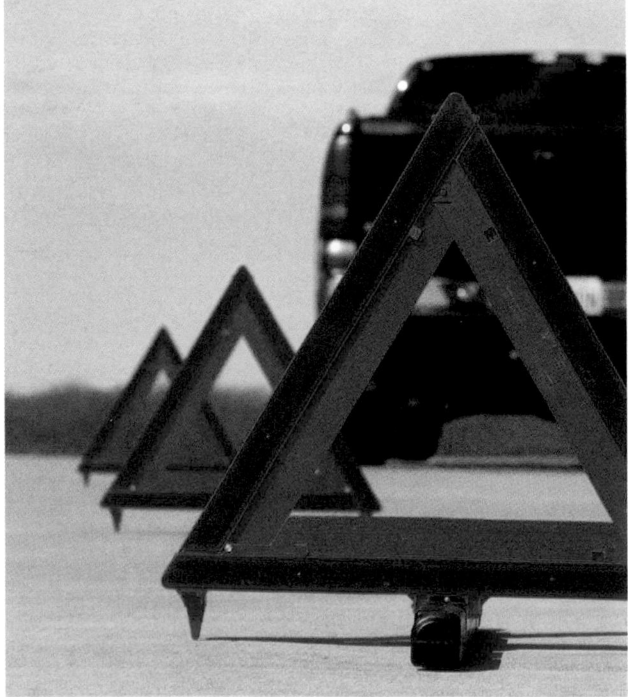

Figure 20.1 *Roadside Emergency*

Objectives

Upon completion of this chapter and activities, you will be able to:

- Identify common automotive problems.
- Explain how OBD systems are used.
- Use an OBD II scan tool.
- Replace a headlight.
- Clean a battery.
- Inspect and replace wiper blades.
- Prepare for a road trip.
- Prepare for roadside emergencies.
- Jump-start a vehicle safely.
- Change a flat tire.

Q & A

Technical Service Bulletins

Q: What is a technical service bulletin?

A: A technical service bulletin (TSB) is a written advisory statement by a vehicle manufacturer to assist dealerships in diagnosing reoccurring problems. TSBs can save you time diagnosing problems. They are separate from safety or emissions recall notices and can address anything from suspension vibrations to engine misfires. To search for TSBs and recalls visit the National Highway Traffic Safety Administration website at www.safercar.gov.

Diagnosing Problems

At times it may be difficult to get a problem to duplicate for a technician. Keeping a record of possible symptoms and any maintenance performed will help. This section focuses on:

- On-Board Diagnostics
- Malfunction Indicator Lights
- Fluid Leaks
- Tailpipe Smoke
- Unusual Smells
- Unusual Sounds

On-Board Diagnostics

On-board diagnostics (OBD) have been in many vehicles since the 1980s. In 1996 a new OBD II system was mandated standardizing some aspects. An OBD II compliant 16 pin data link connector (DLC) (***Figure 20.2***) is accessible from the driver's seat. It is usually under the dash near the steering column or a sticker is placed in that area to direct you to the DLC location.

Figure 20.2 ***Data Link Connector for OBD II***

OBD II Scan Tool. A scan tool (***Figure 20.3***) plugs into the DLC and retrieves any diagnostic codes that have been stored in the powertrain control module (PCM). Some scan tools (also called code readers) are very basic, retrieving only the diagnostic trouble code (DTC). They can cost less than $20. Other scan tools are highly sophisticated, providing DTC information along with advanced diagnostics such as built in features to view live data streams. These tools help technicians diagnose the root cause of the problem. Technicians can even create vehicle system reports for their customers. These scan tools can cost more than $5,000. Between the low end and high end models are a vast number of choices.

Figure 20.3 ***OBD II Scan Tool***
Photo: Bosch Automotive Service Solutions, Inc.

OBD II App. Another way to access your OBD II system is by using a smartphone or tablet app. You need to purchase a wireless adapter (also called an OBD II dongle) (***Figure 20.4***) that will communicate with the app. After you plug the wireless adapter into the vehicle's DLC, it uses a Wi-Fi or Bluetooth signal to connect to your smartphone or tablet. Be sure the devices are compatible with one another.

Figure 20.4 ***OBD II Wireless Adapter***

PCM Communication. The powertrain control module (PCM) communicates problems to the driver through malfunction indicator lights (MILs). MILs vary how they illuminate to help identify the urgency of a problem (***Figure 20.5***).

Malfunction Indicator Light Signals	
Quick Single Flash	Driver action not required. May indicate a temporary glitch in the system. No problem actually present.
Steady Illumination	Driver attention required. If MIL stays on, there is a problem. The vehicle should be scanned as soon as possible to determine the cause. Repair the vehicle as needed.
Rapid Flashing	Driver should immediately take action. Vehicle load and speed need to be decreased. If MIL does not quickly go back to steady illumination with reduced demand, pull off the road, shut the engine down, and have the vehicle towed for repair. ***Note: A condition is occurring that may damage the catalytic converter.***

Figure 20.5 ***Malfunction Indicator Light Signals***

Malfunction Indicator Lights

MILs and gauges act as problem or potential problem indicators. They communicate important information to you from your vehicle's computer system and should never be ignored. This section reviews some common warning and informational indicator lights that may illuminate on your vehicle's dashboard (***Figure 20.6***). ***Note: If there was a glitch in the system and the problem detected is no longer occurring, it may be possible for the OBD II system to turn the malfunction indicator off automatically.***

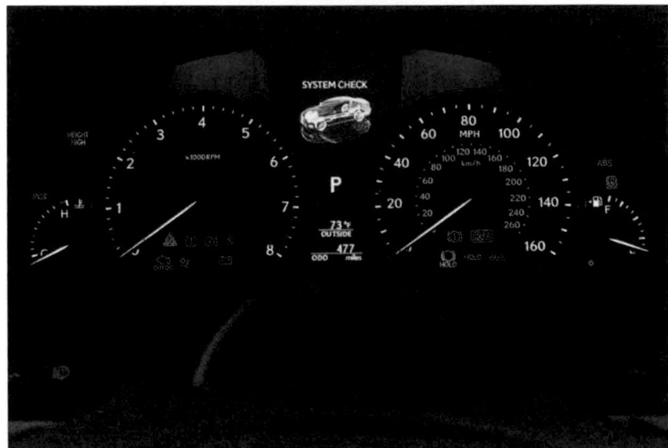

Figure 20.6 **Dashboard Indicator Lights**
Photo: Toyota Motor Corporation

Review Your Owner's Manual. Learn what the MILs on your specific vehicle mean by reviewing your owner's manual (***Figure 20.7***). If you know why a light comes on it will help you understand what you need to do about it. The light may indicate a potential safety problem or could mean you should pull over and shut the engine off before serious damage occurs.

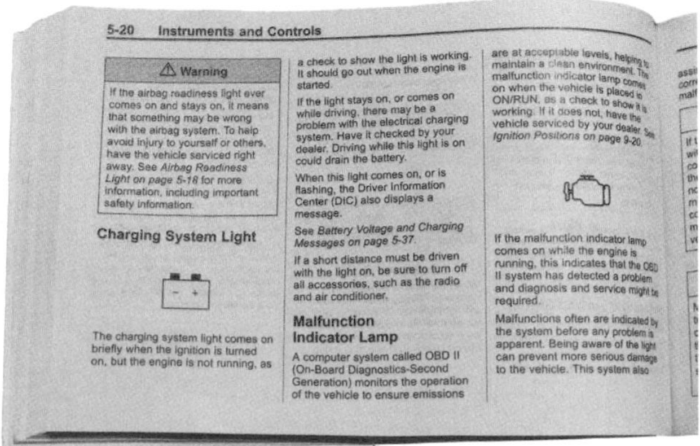

5-20 Instruments and Controls

⚠ Warning

If the airbag readiness light ever comes on and stays on, it means that something may be wrong with the airbag system. To help avoid injury to yourself or others, have the vehicle serviced right away. See *Airbag Readiness Light on page 5-18* for more information, including important safety information.

Charging System Light

The charging system light comes on briefly when the ignition is turned on, but the engine is not running, as a check to show the light is working. It should go out when the engine is started.

If the light stays on, or comes on while driving, there may be a problem with the electrical charging system. Have it checked by your dealer. Driving while this light is on could drain the battery.

When this light comes on, or is flashing, the Driver Information Center (DIC) also displays a message.

See *Battery Voltage and Charging Messages on page 5-37*.

If a short distance must be driven with the light on, be sure to turn off all accessories, such as the radio and air conditioner.

Malfunction Indicator Lamp

A computer system called OBD II (On-Board Diagnostics-Second Generation) monitors the operation of the vehicle to ensure emissions are at acceptable levels, helping to maintain a clean environment. The malfunction indicator lamp comes on when the vehicle is placed in ON/RUN, as a check to show it is working. If it does not, have the vehicle serviced by your dealer. See *Ignition Positions on page 9-20*.

If the malfunction indicator lamp comes on while the engine is running, this indicates that the OBD II system has detected a problem and diagnosis and service might be required.

Malfunctions often are indicated by the system before any problem is apparent. Being aware of the light can prevent more serious damage to the vehicle. This system also

Figure 20.7 **Owner's Manual**

Check Engine Indicator. The check engine light, service engine soon light, or icon resembling an engine (***Figure 20.8***) illuminates if the PCM detects an emission system or engine performance problem, triggered by sensors. It could be anything from a loose gas cap to a failing catalytic converter to an engine misfire. Check the gas cap first. Some vehicles even have a special check fuel cap light. A check engine light that stays on steady is a sign that a technician's service is needed soon. Under most conditions you can still drive the vehicle. However, the longer you drive it the more damage you could cause, along with emitting additional pollution. A blinking light is a sign of a serious problem, so check the owner's manual. The manufacturer may suggest having the vehicle towed in for repair. In the future, new OBD systems may transmit a signal to a highway monitor to enforce emissions compliance.

Figure 20.8 **Check Engine Light**

Coolant Temperature Indicator. If the coolant temperature exceeds the normal operating range, a warning light (***Figure 20.9***) should come on or the indicator on a gauge should move to the red area. Serious engine damage could result from driving an overheated engine. ***Note: If your engine coolant is so low that it is not contacting the engine coolant temperature sensor, a warning may not display even though your engine is overheating.*** See Chapter 12 for what to do when an engine is overheating.

Figure 20.9 **Coolant Temperature Light**

Tech Tip ✓

Check Engine Light

If a check engine light is on, some automotive parts stores and repair facilities will hook up a scan tool to retrieve DTCs for free.

Low Fuel Indicator. When the low fuel light (***Figure 20.10***) turns on a vehicle may have only a gallon of fuel left, but it depends on the vehicle. It is best to refuel before this light comes on.

Figure 20.10 *Low Fuel Light*

Oil Pressure Indicator. Do not drive your vehicle if the oil pressure light (***Figure 20.11***) is illuminated. Low oil pressure can cause immediate engine damage. Check your oil level and add if low. If the light still does not go off, have the vehicle towed to a service facility.

Figure 20.11 *Oil Pressure Light*

Electric Power Steering (EPS) Indicator. If the fault light for the electric power steering illuminates (***Figure 20.12***), there is a problem within the system. You will still be able to steer the vehicle, but it may take an increased effort to turn the steering wheel. Have a technician inspect the system.

Figure 20.12 *Electric Power Steering Light*

Low Tire Pressure. A tire pressure monitoring system (TPMS) light comes on when a tire is significantly low on pressure (***Figure 20.13***). Check the pressure in all the tires with a tire pressure gauge. Figure out why the tire is low, add air, or get the tire repaired.

Figure 20.13 *TPMS Indicators*

Powertrain Fault Indicator. The wrench is generally a powertrain related light (***Figure 20.14***) indicating that there is a fault in the powertrain (engine, transmission, or drivetrain).

Figure 20.14 *Powertrain Fault Light*

Charging System Indicator. The charging system light (***Figure 20.15***) indicates that the battery is not being recharged. This does not necessarily mean that the battery is malfunctioning. The problem may be another part of the charging system, such as the AC generator (alternator).

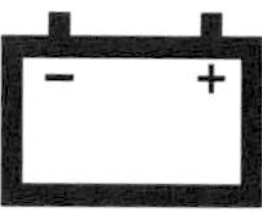

Figure 20.15 *Charging System Light*

Brake Warning Indicator. If the brake light (***Figure 20.16***) is on and the parking brake is not engaged, check the brake fluid level. If the fluid level is fine, have a technician inspect the system.

Figure 20.16 *Brake Warning Light*

Antilock Brake System Indicator. If the ABS light (***Figure 20.17***) comes on, have a technician check for DTCs and inspect the brake system. The conventional part of the brake system will still be operational.

Figure 20.17 *Antilock Brake System Light*

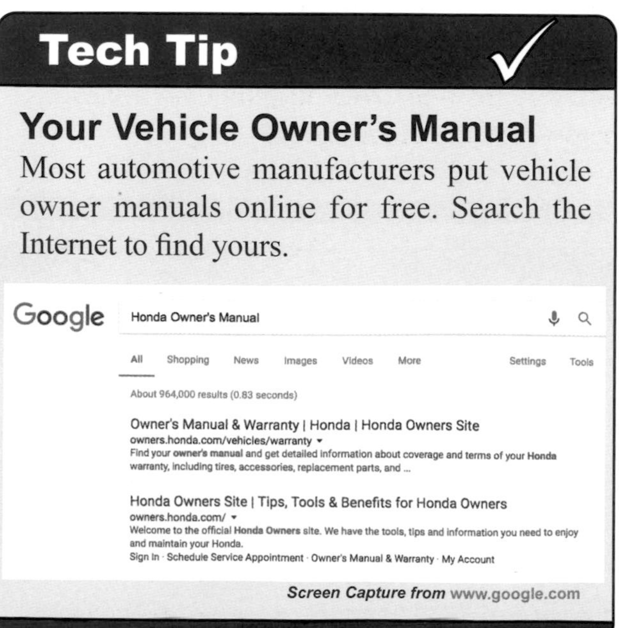

Tech Tip

Your Vehicle Owner's Manual

Most automotive manufacturers put vehicle owner manuals online for free. Search the Internet to find yours.

Screen Capture from www.google.com

Fluid Leaks

A spot on the driveway (***Figure 20.18***) can give you insight into an occurring problem. Don't ignore a leak just because it starts out small.

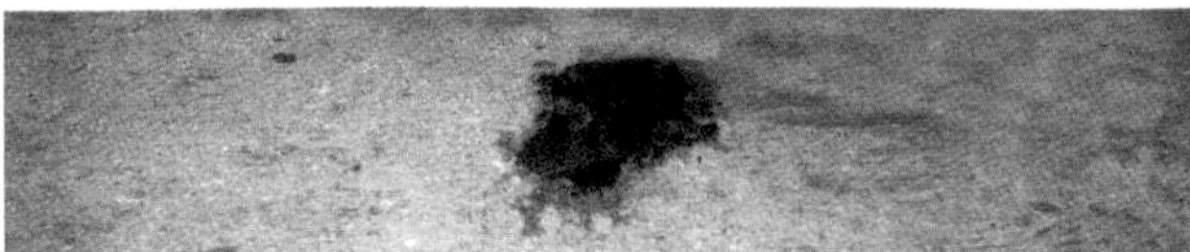

Figure 20.18 ***Spotting a Leak***

Fluid Color. Note the fluid's color (***Figure 20.19***), approximate amount, location, and texture to help determine if a component is failing, needs to be retightened, or serviced.

Fluid Leak	Black	Golden Brown	Red	Orange	Green
Oil	●	●			
Automatic Transmission			●		
Manual Transmission	●	●	●		
Differential	●	●			
Power Steering		●	●		
Coolant			●	●	●

Figure 20.19 ***Fluid Leak Color Indicators***

Tech Tip

Clear Fluid Drip

If you see clear fluid dripping from your car after you have run the air conditioner, don't worry. This is just water condensation.

Q & A

Oil Dripping After Oil Change

Q: I had my oil changed. It looks like my drain plug is leaking oil. Why?

A: Some oil plugs have a rubber O-ring or gasket (washer). Over time this gasket can become cracked. If the plug is tight, this gasket may need to be replaced.

Tailpipe Smoke

Tailpipe smoke (***Figure 20.20***) can be an indicator of faulty components or engine problems.

Smoke	Problem
Black	Black smoke is usually an indication of the engine getting too much fuel (running rich). Excess fuel may be entering the combustion chamber. A faulty fuel injector, fuel pressure regulator, PCV valve, clogged catalytic converter, vacuum leak, overdue tune-up, or various engine control sensors could cause the engine to run rich.
Blue	Blue smoke indicates oil burning. This usually signifies that the piston rings or valve guide seals may be worn. When the piston rings or valve guide seals are worn, oil can enter the combustion chamber. The oil is then burned with the air-fuel mixture. The engine may need rebuilding.
	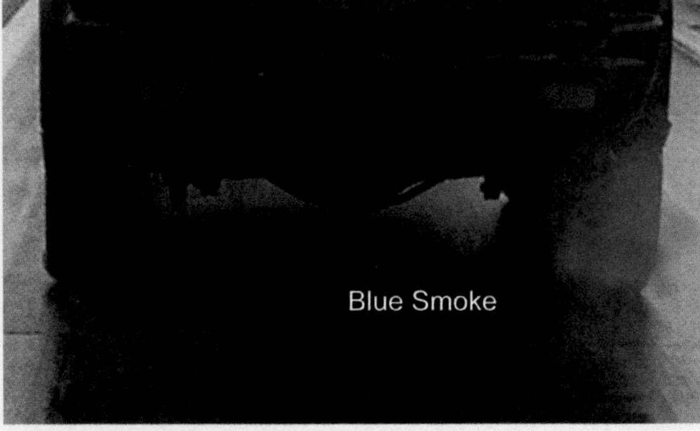
White	White smoke indicates that coolant is getting into the combustion chamber and burning with the air-fuel mixture.

Figure 20.20 ***Tailpipe Smoke Color Indicators***

Tech Tip

Check Vehicle Warranty

If you are having trouble with your vehicle, check the warranty. You may have complete bumper-to-bumper coverage. If so, take it back to the dealer and let them address the issue. Emission related warranties are often longer than powertrain and bumper-to-bumper warranties. Read the warranty that covers your vehicle. Commonly it is divided into the following categories: bumper-to-bumper, emissions, powertrain, corrosion-perforation, and roadside assistance.

Unusual Smells

If you smell (***Figure 20.21***) something abnormal, check it out.

Smell	Problem
Rich Fuel	A rich fuel smell when attempting to start is a sign of a flooded engine. If you continue to crank over the engine, more fuel will be sprayed into the cylinders fouling out the spark plugs and contaminating the oil. Let the vehicle sit for a period of time so the gasoline can evaporate off the spark plugs.
Rotten Egg	A rotten egg/sulfur smell is usually linked to a faulty catalytic converter or other component in the emission system.
Sweet	Smells that have a sweet odor to them may indicate a coolant leak. Take the vehicle to a service center to have the cooling system pressure tested.
Burning	A burning smell can signify an electrical problem. Your vehicle could have an electrical short or a failing electrical component.

Figure 20.21 ***Unusual Smell Indicators***

Web Links

Automotive Parts Sites

AC Delco Replacement Parts
www.acdelco.com

Advance Auto Parts
www.advanceautoparts.com

Aftermarket Auto Parts Alliance
www.alliance1.com

Auto Parts Warehouse
www.autopartswarehouse.com

AutoZone, Inc.
www.autozone.com

CARQUEST Auto Parts
www.carquest.com

JC Whitney
www.jcwhitney.com

National Automotive Parts Association (NAPA)
www.napaonline.com

O'Reilly Auto Parts
www.oreillyauto.com

Pep Boys
www.pepboys.com

RockAuto, LLC
www.rockauto.com

Unusual Sounds

Do not ignore sounds (***Figure 20.22***) coming from your vehicle. If you heed a warning sound you may be able to avoid your vehicle leaving you stranded or needing expensive repairs.

Sound	Problem
Squeal From Engine When Accelerating	A squeal from the engine when accelerating generally indicates a loose or glazed belt. When accelerating the belt is forced to rotate faster and may be slipping. Inspect and replace serpentine belts, stretch belts, or V-belts as required.
Howl	A howl that is coming from a wheel and increases with acceleration, may be a worn wheel bearing.
Knocking	Internal engine problems may have occurred. Take the vehicle to a qualified technician for diagnosis.
Pinging While Accelerating	A pinging sound while accelerating is a sign of low octane rating in the fuel. At the next fill up, put in a mid-grade or premium fuel to see if the pinging sound goes away.
Rattling	Loose or worn belt or belt tensioner may cause a rattle. Replace components as necessary.
Screech From Wheel Area	If you hear a screech from the wheel area, the brake pads may be worn. Take the vehicle to a service center as soon as possible when brake problems occur.
Loud or Rumbling Muffler	A rumbling sound coming from underneath the car could indicate a hole in the exhaust system. Inspect and replace components as necessary because a hole in the exhaust can pose a carbon monoxide hazard. Inside most mufflers are baffles to help reduce noise. You may not see any visible holes as a muffler rusts from the inside out, but it can become increasingly louder.
Engine Clicking	Clicking valvetrain noise is caused by low oil pressure or too thick of oil viscosity in cold temperatures. Check oil level and pressure. Use a lower viscosity oil in cold temperatures as recommended by the manufacturer.
Clicking When Turning	A clicking sound when turning (moving vehicle) on a front-wheel, four-wheel, or all-wheel drive, signifies worn constant velocity (CV) joints. A clicking sound when turning (stationary vehicle) may point to a worn strut mount or steering linkage part.
Clunk In Trunk	The annoying clunk noise coming from the trunk area during rapid braking may be as simple as a loose spare tire or jack rolling around as the vehicle changes speeds.

Figure 20.22 ***Unusual Sound Indicators***

Common Problems

Common automotive problems can range from your car not starting to the wipers not cleaning the windshield. It is important to know when it is safe to drive your vehicle and when you should have it towed to a repair facility. This section focuses on:

- Engine Overheating with Steam
- Shaking
- Steering
- Automotive Lights
- Wipers
- Windshield Chip
- Leaking Tire
- No-Start Conditions
- Battery Cables and Terminals

Engine Overheating with Steam

An engine overheating with steam may be caused by a burst radiator hose, a faulty water pump, blown head gasket, or a leaky radiator. If the engine begins to steam you should pull over safely and shut it down. Severe overheating can lead to more costly repairs. ***Warning: Never open the hood when steam is present, it can burn you. Never open a hot radiator cap.*** Once the engine is cool, check the radiator and heater hoses (***Figure 20.23***). A leaking hose is an easy fix. If the radiator is leaking through the radiator fins, you will probably need a new radiator. One of the more complex scenarios is an internal engine leak. If the engine is leaking coolant internally the probable cause is a blown head gasket or cracked cylinder head.

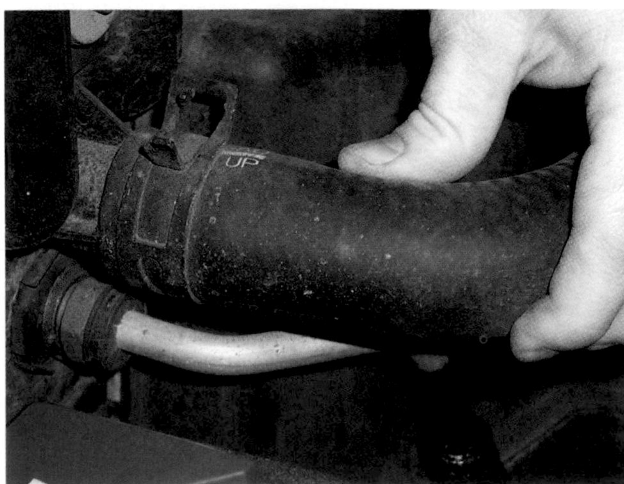

Figure 20.23 ***Check Radiator Hose***

Shaking

A shaking or vibrating automobile can cause a potentially dangerous driving situation. Tires out of balance, belts broken in tires, worn suspension and steering components, transmission problems, worn CV joints or U-joints, broken motor or transmission mounts, and engine misfires can cause shaking and vibrations while driving. Try to determine if it is engine, drivetrain, brake, or suspension components that are the culprit.

Steering

If your vehicle is pulling in one direction, you may have a steering system or tire problem. A simple thing to check is the tire pressure. Look at the tire placard to find the correct tire pressure. See Tire Pressure Check steps in Chapter 14. If the tire pressure was the culprit, you need to determine why that tire lost pressure. You may have a nail puncture or faulty valve stem that is leaking air. If the vehicle still pulls after you have inflated the tires properly, you may have a defective tire, worn steering component, or incorrect wheel alignment.

Price Guides 

Auto Club Membership (Roadside Assistance)
- $50.00 to $150.00 (annually)

Change Flat Tire
- $25.00 to $50.00 (labor)

Jump-Start
- $25.00 to $50.00 (labor)

Roadside Emergency Kit
- $40.00 to $80.00

Snow Traction Cables or Chains
- $25.00 to $75.00 pair

Tow
- $50.00 to $100.00 (local tow)

Unlock
- $25.00 to $50.00 (labor)

Wiper Blades
- $10.00 to $25.00 each

Automotive Lights

Vehicles have several lights that will burn out over time. The most common ones that cause inconvenience and a safety hazard when burned out are headlights, turn signal lights, and brake lights (***Figure 20.24***).

Figure 20.24 ***Taillight Unit***

Light Bulbs. Light bulbs (***Figure 20.25***) are generally not too expensive and take only a few or no tools to replace. Most involve disconnecting a bulb's socket and electrical connector, removing the burned out bulb, and replacing it with the new bulb. A service manual will describe the specific procedure for your vehicle. See Chapter 9 for more information on lights.

Miniature Bulbs

Push-in

Bayonet

Figure 20.25 ***Types of Light Bulbs***

> **Trouble Guide**
>
> **Light Not Working**
> - Blown fuse
> - Burned out bulb
> - Loose wire
> - Corroded socket or connector

Headlight Bulb Replacement Steps. The following is a general procedure for replacing a headlight bulb (***Figure 20.26***).

Headlight Bulb Replacement

STEP 1	Open the hood and look behind the headlight assembly. You should only have to turn the bulb socket or a retainer clip that holds the bulb in place a quarter turn.

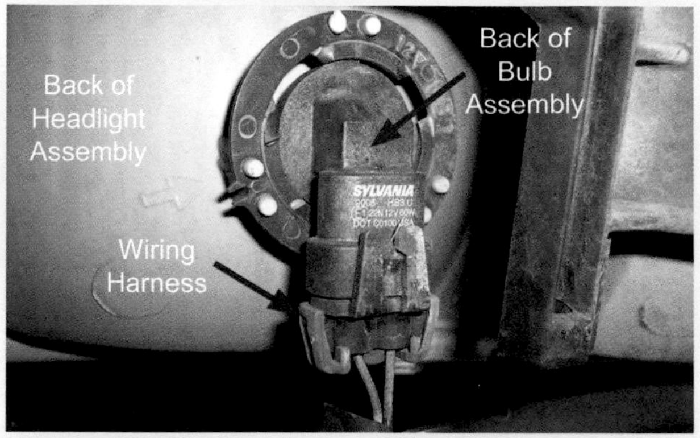

Figure 20.26a ***Back of Headlight Assembly***

STEP 2	After the retainer clip is removed or bulb assembly is turned, carefully pull on the bulb. It may seem a little snug. It has a rubber O-ring gasket that keeps it tight.

Figure 20.26b ***Remove the Bulb***

STEP 3	Once the bulb is removed, lift up on the clips that hold the electrical wiring harness to release the bulb.

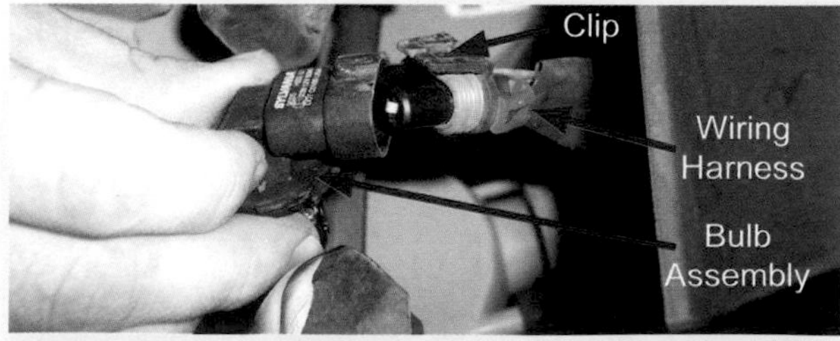

Figure 20.26c ***Release Bulb from Harness Clip***

STEP 4	Remove and replace the bulb. Do not touch the glass part of the new bulb. It will shorten the life.
STEP 5	Reverse the procedure to install the new bulb and reconnect the wiring harness assembly.
STEP 6	Once the new bulb is installed be sure to test the headlights.

Figure 20.26 ***Replacing a Headlight Bulb***

Wipers

Old, worn, damaged, or dirty wipers can cause a dangerous driving condition. If you don't check your windshield wipers, you may not know they should be cleaned or replaced until you need them (***Figure 20.27***).

Figure 20.27 Windshield Wipers on a Rainy Day

Worn or Damaged Wiper Blades. Over time the rubber on wipers dries out, making them stiff. Without being flexible, the wipers have a tendency to skip, streak, split, or squeak across the windshield (***Figure 20.28***). Wipers are relatively inexpensive and usually simple to replace.

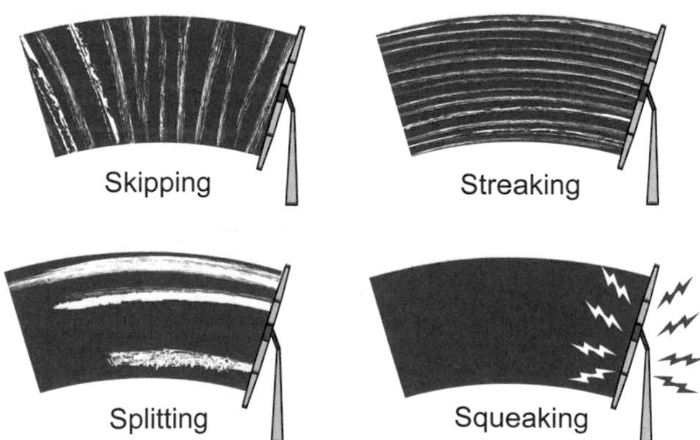

Figure 20.28 Worn or Damaged Wiper Blades

Servicing

Windshield Wipers

- Check at oil change intervals
- Change once a year or as needed

Inspecting Wiper Blades. Inspect wiper blades for damage by running your finger down the edge of the blade. Look for cracks, tears, or missing pieces. Exposure to environmental factors found in the desert (extreme dry heat, dust, and sand) and cold climates (freezing temperatures, ice, snow, and road salt) can dramatically increase wiper deterioration. A good wiper should clean the window thoroughly (***Figure 20.29***) and greatly improve visibility. While driving you make split second decisions based on what you see, so a clear view is important.

Figure 20.29 Improve Visibility
Picture: Bosch

Buying Wiper Blades. It is best to replace wipers in pairs and the whole blade, not just the rubber "refill" component. If the metal pivoting points have worn out, the blade will apply uneven pressure across the windshield. To identify the size of wiper blades, measure the length in inches or millimeters (***Figure 20.30***). Wipers may come with several adapters to fit multiple automotive models. Many vehicles have back window wipers that also need replacement.

Figure 20.30 Wiper Size Visible on Package

Frozen Wipers. Anytime it is snowing or below freezing make sure the wipers are not frozen down before turning them on. Lift them up carefully so you don't rip the rubber blade or bend the wiper arm. Turning the wipers on before clearing snow (***Figure 20.31***) or ice could burn out the wiper motor, strip the wiper arms, or blow the wiper fuse. If the wiper is really frozen down hard and you are unable to break it free, turn on the windshield defrost to melt the ice first. It is also a good practice to always allow the wipers to go to the "park position" before shutting off the ignition.

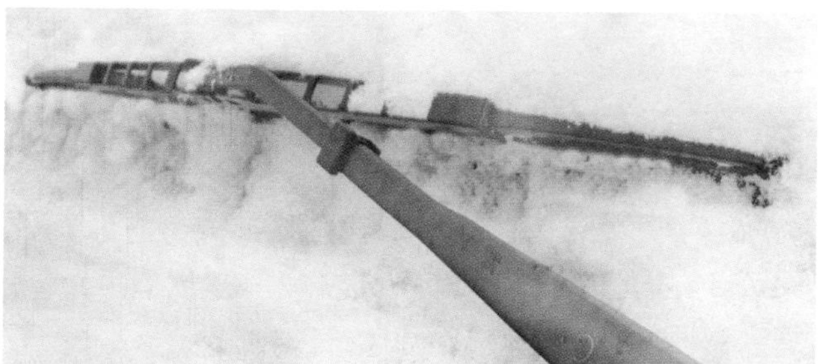

Figure 20.31 ***Frozen Wipers***

Types of Wiper Arms. Several different wiper arm designs are used to connect to the wiper blade (***Figure 20.32***).

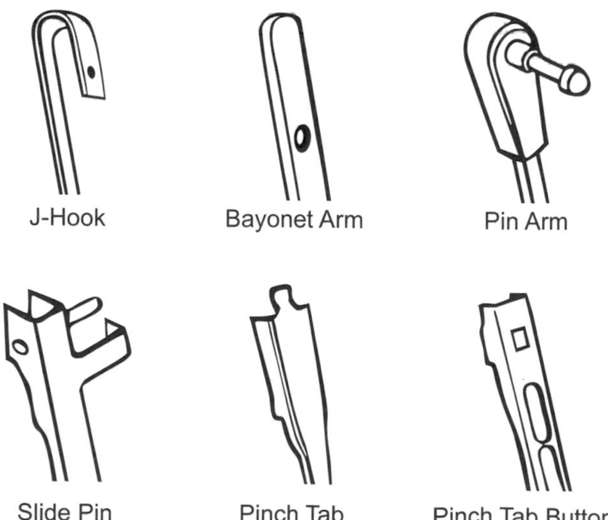

Figure 20.32 ***Types of Wiper Arms***

Wiper Blade Replacement. To determine the proper method of installation refer to the owner's manual or the example that matches your wipers on the new wiper instruction sheet. The following is a general procedure for replacing wiper blades on a hook style wiper arm (***Figure 20.33***).

Wiper Blade Replacement

STEP 1	Raise the wiper blade assembly up from the windshield and locate the lock assembly.

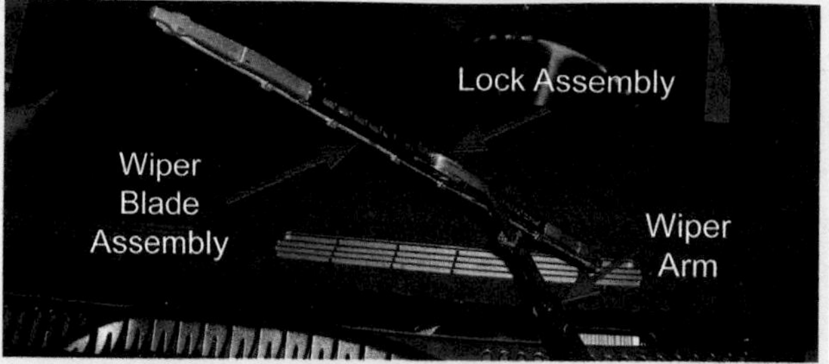

Figure 20.33a ***Wiper Blade Assembly Raised***

STEP 2	A wiper blade may have a little cover over the blade lock assembly. If yours has a cover, push the cover tabs to release the cover.
STEP 3	The hook style blade assembly has a lock tab that needs to be pressed and held down.

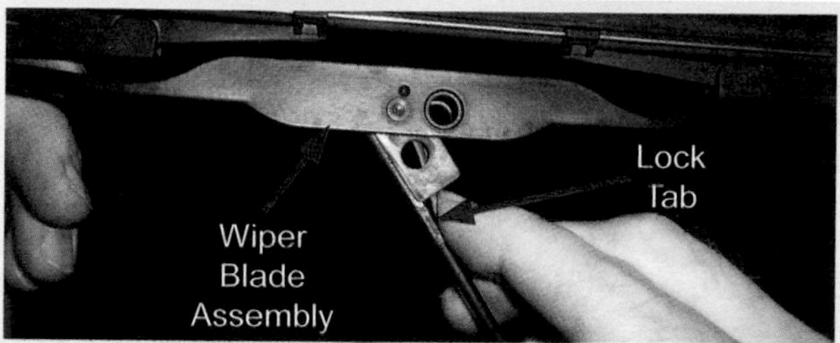

Figure 20.33b ***Press Lock Tab Down***

STEP 4	Move the blade assembly toward the wiper arm to release the wiper arm hook.

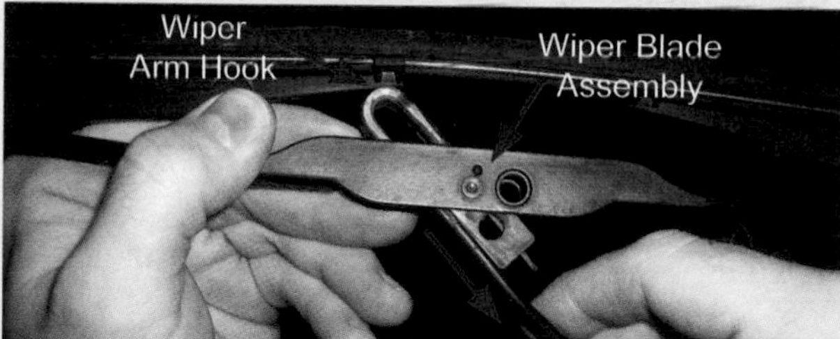

Figure 20.33c ***Move Blade Assembly***

STEP 5	Remove the old blade assembly once it is free from the wiper arm hook.

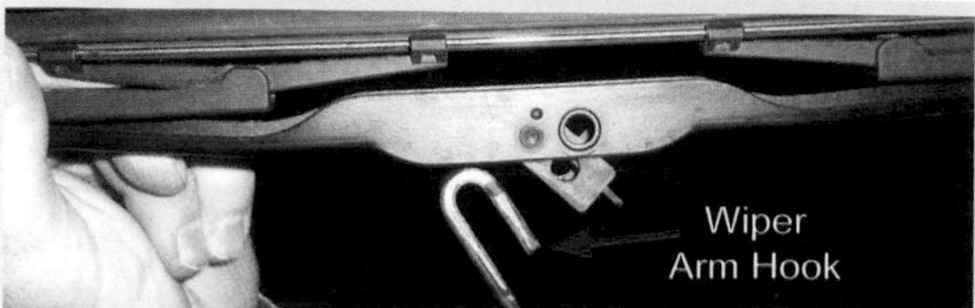

Figure 20.33d ***Release Blade Assembly***

STEP 6	Reverse the procedure to install the new wiper blade assembly and repeat the above steps for other wipers on the vehicle.
STEP 7	Check the windshield washer fluid reservoir, add fluid as needed, and test the wipers.

Figure 20.33 ***Replacing Wiper Blades***

Windshield Chip

At some point you will be driving down the road and hear a large whack from a flying rock or other debris hitting your vehicle's windshield. Then you will notice the chip. It may start out small and seem insignificant, but it is important to repair it as soon as you can. A small chip can quickly turn into a large crack (***Figure 20.34***), which requires a costly windshield replacement, instead of a $10 do-it-yourself (DIY) repair.

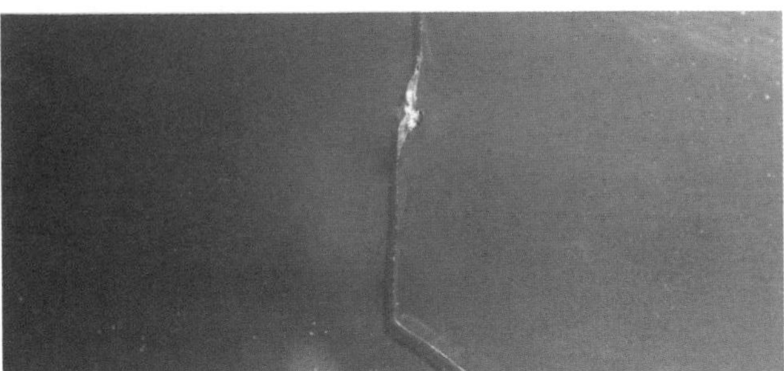

Figure 20.34 ***Small Chip Turned into Crack***

Temporary Fix. If you can't get the repair done right away, put a piece of clear packing tape over the chip on the outside. This will help to keep the chip from expanding and keep dirt and grime out, so a quality repair can be completed. When a repair is done, if any dirt or water is trapped in the chip it will cause the area to be cloudy. Changes in temperature can cause the chip to crack farther so time is of the essence.

Chip Repair. If a chip is small enough, there are inexpensive DIY chip repair kits (***Figure 20.35***) available. The key is to keep the chip clean and keep any air from being trapped as you fill the void. If the chip is in your sight line, then it may be best to have a professional repair done.

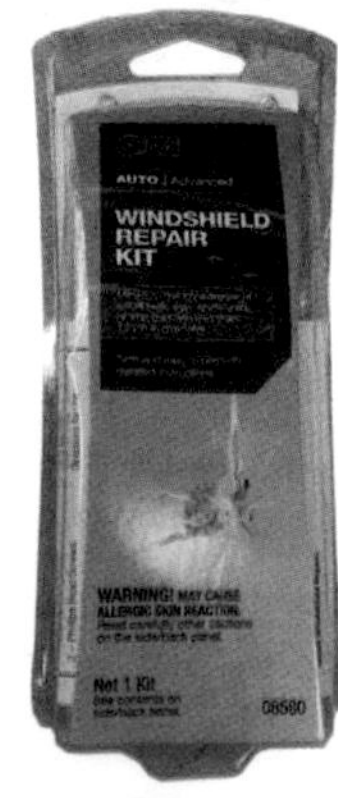

Figure 20.35 ***Windshield Repair Kits***

Leaking Tire

If a tire is low you should locate the leak. Look for any obvious sidewall, tread, or wheel damage. Make sure there are no foreign objects embedded in the tread. If you can't see the leak source, the following easy steps may help (***Figure 20.36***).

Finding a Tire Leak

STEP 1	Put about a teaspoon of dish detergent in a spray bottle with water. Slowly squirt the tire, working all the way around the tire tread.

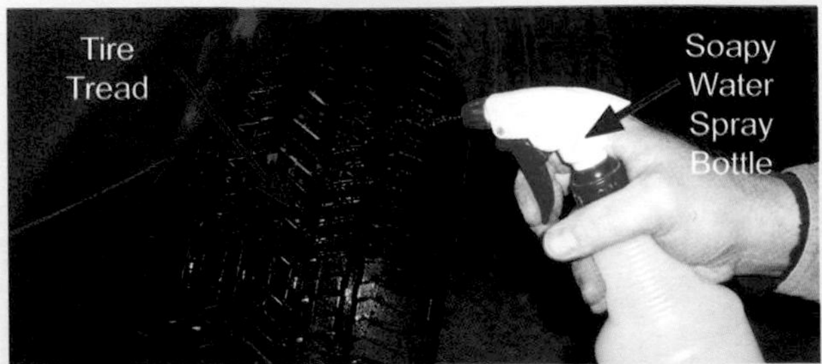

Figure 20.36a ***Spray Tire with Soapy Water***

STEP 2	Don't forget to spray the valve stem and bead (the connection between the rubber tire and the rim) which are common culprits for slow leaks.

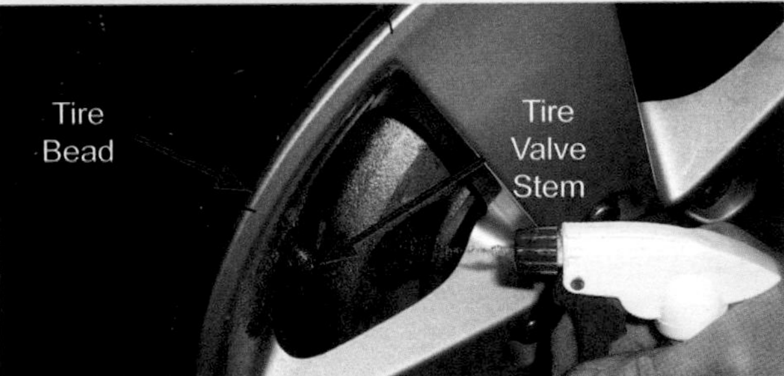

Figure 20.36b ***Spray Tire Valve Stem and Bead***

STEP 3	As you spray the tire you will see many bubbles from the soap, but look carefully. Eventually the leak will start to blow a pile of bubbles.

Figure 20.36c ***Air Leak Pile of Bubbles***

STEP 4	Note the location of the leak in reference to the wheel and distance from the valve stem. Check if you bought a road hazard warranty. Take the tire to a service facility for replacement or repair. See Chapter 14 Tire Repairs to determine if the leak is in a repairable area of the tire.

Figure 20.36 ***Finding a Tire Leak***

No-Start Conditions

One thing you may encounter is a no-start situation (***Figure 20.37***). During one type of no-start situation the engine will not crank. In the other, the engine will crank but will not start.

No-Start Conditions	
Will Not Crank (Dead Battery)	If the engine will not crank over, you may have a dead battery. Turn on the headlights to see if you have electrical power. If you don't have any electricity, the headlights or interior light may have been left on and drained the battery over time. See the Battery Activity in Chapter 9 of the workbook to learn how to test the battery. If the battery is dead, recharge the battery with a battery charger or jump-start the car and drive it for 15 to 20 minutes to recharge the battery.
Will Not Crank (Battery has Charge)	Check the battery cables to make sure they are tight. If you have battery power but the vehicle will still not start you may need to replace the starter.
Cranks, But No Start	If your engine cranks over but will not start, then the engine may not be getting fuel or spark. This type of situation usually warrants a call to a repair shop.
Key Will Not Turn	The key will not turn in the ignition if there is pressure on the steering wheel, the steering wheel is locked, the gear shifter is not in park, or you are not applying the brake.

Figure 20.37 ***Vehicle No-Start Conditions***

Q & A ?

AC Generator or Battery

Q: My car will not start. When I turn the key there is a clicking sound. With a jump-start it starts right up. After jump-starting, I ran it for 20 minutes and then shut it off. When I tried to start it again, it just clicked. I jump-started it again, but let the cables stay attached for 10 minutes. Now the car starts several times with no problem. What is happening here?

A: Sounds like an AC generator (alternator) problem. When you left the cables on for 10 minutes the other car's charging system may have recharged your battery. See the Charging Activity in Chapter 9 of the workbook to learn how to test your alternator.

Battery Cables and Terminals

One of the most common problems in vehicles over three years old is battery failure. Battery failure is often caused by poor connections, corrosion, improper maintenance, and age. Although many batteries are considered maintenance-free, you still need to keep the battery terminals and cables free of corrosion. Always make sure the clamps and battery mounts are securely connected. The following is a general procedure for cleaning a battery (***Figure 20.38***). See the Battery Activity in Chapter 9 of the workbook for more detailed information.

Battery Cleaning	
STEP 1	Apply the parking brake. Remove key from the ignition. Visually inspect the battery for loose battery cables, corroded terminals, deposits on connections, cracks or leaks in the case, and frayed or broken cables. Remove your rings and watch. ***Warning: Battery electrolyte irritates skin and will eat through clothing. Always wear gloves, a respirator, and safety goggles.***
STEP 2	Prepare a baking soda solution. Mix about one tablespoon of baking soda per pint (≈0.5 L) of water.
STEP 3	If you need to remove the cables to get at all of the corrosion, remove the negative cable first and then the positive.
STEP 4	On top post batteries, use a battery post cleaner tool to remove corrosion from the posts after the cables have been removed.

STEP 5	Scrub the cables, terminals, and surface of the battery with the baking soda solution and a parts brush.
STEP 6	Rinse away all of the baking soda solution with clean water and dry the battery and cables.
STEP 7	If you have removed the cables, reattach them by installing the positive cable first and then the negative cable.
STEP 8	Use an anti-corrosive spray over the cable ends to minimize corrosion coming back.

Figure 20.38 ***Cleaning a Battery***

Roadside Emergencies

Even with a well maintained vehicle, you can still end up stranded on the side of a road unpredictably. It is important to prepare your vehicle and learn how to keep you and your passengers safe in an emergency. This section focuses on:

- Trip Checklist
- Safety Kits
- Vehicle Fire
- Accidents
- Animal Collision
- Broken Belt
- Dead Battery
- Jump-Starting
- Lockout
- Burst Radiator Hose
- Running on Empty
- Flat Tire
- Traction in Snow

Trip Checklist

Before you leave in your vehicle on a trip, prepare by going through a road trip checklist (***Figure 20.39***). Do this early to allow time for needed vehicle repairs. Let someone know your travel route and when you are expected to arrive.

Road Trip Checklist	
☐	Check all fluids for the proper level.
☐	Inspect the hoses for leaks.
☐	Inspect the belts for tearing, glazing, cracking, or incorrect adjustment.
☐	Inspect the battery terminals for corrosion.
☐	Check the tire pressure, tread depth, and condition (including the spare tire).
☐	Inspect the wiper blades.
☐	Assemble an emergency kit (**See next section**).
☐	Listen and look for exhaust leaks.
☐	Inspect the brake pads.
☐	Check all lights, including flashing hazard lights.
☐	Test the A/C system for proper operation.
☐	Inspect the air filter.
☐	Test coolant for freeze and boilover protection.
☐	Check maintenance records. Perform preventative maintenance (e.g., oil change) as required.
☐	Make sure current registration and insurance information is in the vehicle.
☐	Hide a spare key on the vehicle using a magnetic key holder or make sure your keyless entry app is updated.
☐	Place a cell phone car charger in the vehicle.
☐	Update GPS or print a map for your route.

Figure 20.39 ***Road Trip Checklist***

Safety Kits

Prepare your vehicle for emergencies and winter weather. You may find yourself stranded late at night in a parking lot, alongside a desolate road, or in a ditch. Leave your vehicle only as a last resort. If you cannot call for help with a cell phone and someone offers assistance, ask them to contact the police or a tow company for you. ***Warning: Never get into a stranger's vehicle.***

Emergency Kit. An emergency roadside kit should be in every vehicle (***Figure 20.40***).

Figure 20.40 ***Emergency Kit***

Emergency Kit Checklist. Carry an emergency kit in your vehicle at all times. Certain essential items can help you get through an unexpected situation (***Figure 20.41***).

Emergency Kit Checklist	
☐	Cell Phone, Charge Cord, and Contact Numbers
☐	Protein/Energy Bars and Bottled Water
☐	Heavy Duty Jumper Cables
☐	Road Flares, Reflective Triangles
☐	Fluorescent Distress Flag and Sign
☐	Disposable Gloves and Work Gloves
☐	Fire Extinguisher
☐	Safety Vest
☐	First Aid Kit
☐	Flashlight with Spare Batteries
☐	Hand Wipes and Shop Towels
☐	Basic Tool Kit (Tire Pressure Gauge, Pliers, Screwdrivers, and an Adjustable Wrench)
☐	Jack, Chocks, and Lug Wrench
☐	Emergency Whistle
☐	Electrical Tape and Duct Tape

Figure 20.41 ***Emergency Kit Checklist***

Winter Safety Kit. Winter driving can be especially hazardous. Before it gets cold outside and the snow is blowing, put a winter safety kit (***Figure 20.42***) in your vehicle. This should be in addition to your emergency kit. Even if you call for help, it may take time for help to arrive, especially in severe weather conditions.

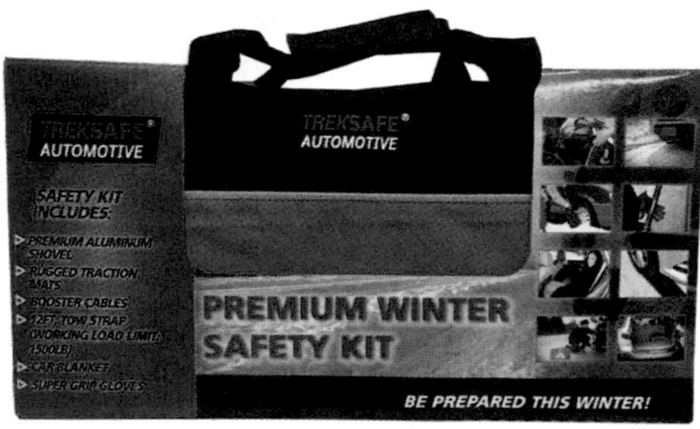

Figure 20.42 ***Winter Safety Kit***

Winter Safety Kit Checklist. Winter specific items can be helpful for cold weather survival and safety (***Figure 20.43***).

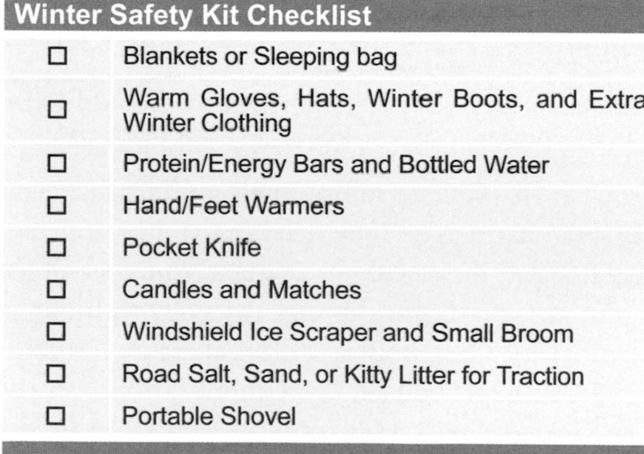

Winter Safety Kit Checklist	
☐	Blankets or Sleeping bag
☐	Warm Gloves, Hats, Winter Boots, and Extra Winter Clothing
☐	Protein/Energy Bars and Bottled Water
☐	Hand/Feet Warmers
☐	Pocket Knife
☐	Candles and Matches
☐	Windshield Ice Scraper and Small Broom
☐	Road Salt, Sand, or Kitty Litter for Traction
☐	Portable Shovel

Figure 20.43 ***Winter Safety Kit Checklist***

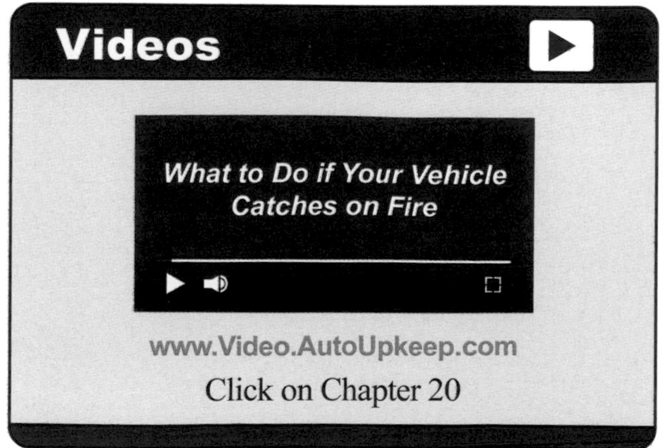

Videos
What to Do if Your Vehicle Catches on Fire
www.Video.AutoUpkeep.com
Click on Chapter 20

Vehicle Fire

Vehicle fires (***Figure 20.44***) are often caused by mechanical or electrical malfunctions. They occur more frequently than most people realize. When driving down the road if you suspect your vehicle is on fire, smell something burning, see smoke, or see flames in or around your vehicle act quickly. Try to stay calm and not panic. Safely pull off to the side of the road, turn off the engine, and exit the vehicle immediately. Do not waste time thinking about how to save your vehicle. Get out as fast as you can and get far away from the fire. Call 911 for help. ***Warning: Never open the hood. Air rushing in can make the fire much worse. Do not attempt to put out the fire. It's not worth the risk.***

Figure 20.44 ***Vehicle Fire***

Emergency Exit Tool. It is possible that the electrical system may not function to unlock doors or roll down the windows. You may have to unlock a door manually or break a window. An emergency exit tool (***Figure 20.45***) has a steel hammer head designed to break side window glass. On the other end of the tool is a razor sharp blade to cut through seat belts if needed. Keep the tool where you can reach it easily, but away from small children. Another option in an emergency is to pull out a headrest and use the metal rods as a tool to break a window.

Figure 20.45 ***Emergency Exit Tool***

Accidents

If you are in an accident, try to remain calm. Do not leave the accident. Check for injuries.

Safety. Turn on your hazard lights to warn other drivers. Use a cell phone to call 911 or other assistance. If no one is hurt and the accident was minor, move the cars (if possible) to the side of the road out of traffic. If you have safety cones, reflective triangles, or flares in an emergency kit, set them out to warn oncoming traffic.

Gather Information. After safety considerations have been taken, wait for police to arrive. Take pictures of vehicles, the scene (***Figure 20.46***), and any contributing factors to the accident. Record audio/video or write down what you remember. Get witness contact information. Ask for the name and badge number of the responding officers and the police report number.

Figure 20.46 *Accident*

Exchange Information. Exchange information with the other party (***Figure 20.47***). ***Note: Discuss the specifics of the accident only with the police. Be polite. Do not accept blame or accuse the other party.***

Accident Information Exchange Checklist	
☐	Full Name (Include Names of Passengers)
☐	Address, Email, and Phone Number
☐	Insurance Company, Policy Number, Agent Name, and Phone Number
☐	Driver's License Number
☐	Vehicle's Make, Model, Year, Color, and VIN
☐	License Plate Number

Figure 20.47 *Information Exchange Checklist*

After the Accident. Call your insurance company. If you believe you may have been injured, visit a doctor and contact a lawyer for advice. Additionally, re-read your insurance policy.

Animal Collision

Vehicle collisions with large animals like deer can cause significant damage and personal injury. Hundreds of thousands of accidents happen each year involving animals.

Active Times. October through December are very active months for car-deer collisions due to the deer rutting (mating) season. Drivers need to be particularly attentive during the evening hours and around sunrise. If you see one deer on the side of the road or running, be cautious. Deer commonly run in groups.

Driving Tips. Follow all posted speed limits, use high beams when possible, always wear your seat belt, and be especially cautious in designated animal crossing areas (***Figure 20.48***). Do not swerve into oncoming traffic or off the road to miss a deer or animal. Brake firmly and honk your horn.

Figure 20.48 *Deer Crossing Sign*

Collision. If you do collide with an animal, don't touch it. It may be injured and could cause you personal harm. You may need to call law enforcement. After the accident, contact your insurance agent to see if the damage to your vehicle is covered by your policy. Comprehensive policies cover damage caused by vehicle-animal collisions. Also check your policy deductible to see if it makes sense to have the insurance company pay for the damage.

Videos
What to Do After an Automobile Accident
www.Video.AutoUpkeep.com
Click on Chapter 20

Broken Belt

On many vehicles today, only one main belt (called a serpentine belt) runs most or all of the engine's vital systems and accessories. The serpentine belt often turns the water pump, air conditioning compressor, and AC generator (alternator). On vehicles with hydraulic power steering, it will also turn a power steering pump. If this belt breaks, you should not drive the vehicle. You will need a tow to a local repair facility or you will need to replace the belt on the side of the road. If you drive the vehicle, you risk overheating the engine and draining the battery. If the vehicle has hydraulic power steering, the vehicle will require more effort to turn. The following is a general procedure for replacing a belt (***Figure 20.49***).

Web Links

Transportation Safety Sites

Advocates for Highway and Auto Safety
www.saferoads.org

Bureau of Transportation Statistics
www.bts.gov

Insurance Information Institute
www.iii.org

Insurance Institute for Highway Safety
www.iihs.org

National Highway Traffic Safety Administration
www.nhtsa.gov

U.S. Department of Transportation
www.transportation.gov

Belt Replacement

STEP 1	Apply the parking brake. Remove the key from the ignition. Disconnect the negative battery cable.
STEP 2	Review the belt routing diagram which is commonly on an engine compartment label.

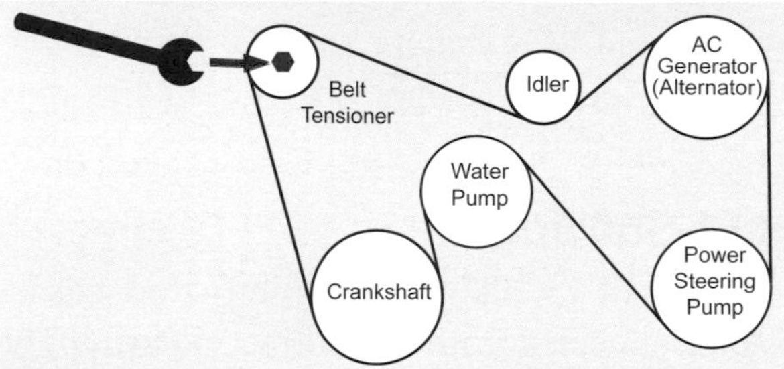

Figure 20.49a ***Belt Routing Diagram***

STEP 3	Find the belt tensioner. Be careful when using a wrench or ratchet to release the tensioner, it uses a spring mechanism to keep the belt tight.
STEP 4	Once tension is released, slip the belt off. Check the tensioner bearing and spring for wear. Make sure all of the accessory pulleys rotate freely.

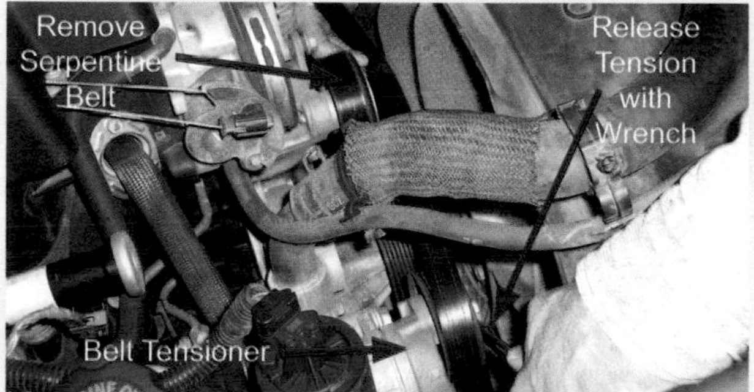

Figure 20.49b ***Relieving Tension***

STEP 5	Route the new belt, lining up the ribs in the grooves, use a wrench to relieve tension, position belt, and then carefully release the belt tensioner.

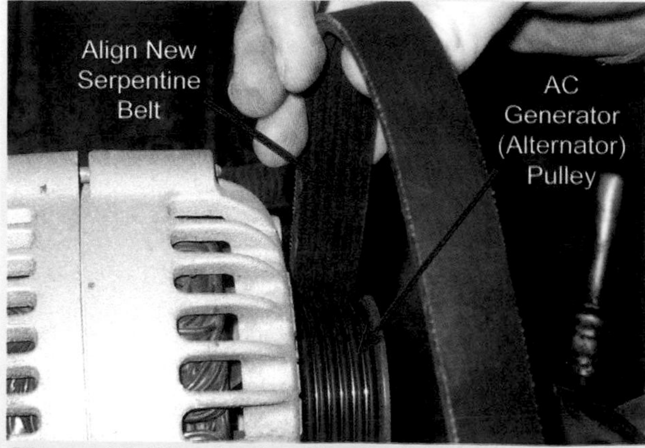

Figure 20.49c Lining Up the Ribs and Grooves

STEP 6	Double check to make sure the belt is positioned correctly. Reconnect the negative battery cable.

Figure 20.49 ***Replacing a Belt***

Dead Battery

A dead battery is usually caused when the driver forgets to turn off the headlights or interior cabin light. It can also be caused by leaving a door ajar or if there is something draining the battery. If you have a dead battery and you know it was caused by leaving a light on, you should only need a jump-start.

Jump-Starting

Vehicles can be damaged if jump-start cables are not connected with the correct polarity. The red jumper cable clamps should always go to the positive battery terminals (+) and the black jumper cable clamps should always go to the negative battery terminal (–) and bare metal (ground). ***Warning: Jump-starting can cause serious injury and damage. If you are unsure about how to do it, call for roadside assistance.***

Remote Jumper Block. If the battery is not easily accessible, there may be a designated remote jumper block terminal for the positive jumper cable connection (***Figure 20.50***).

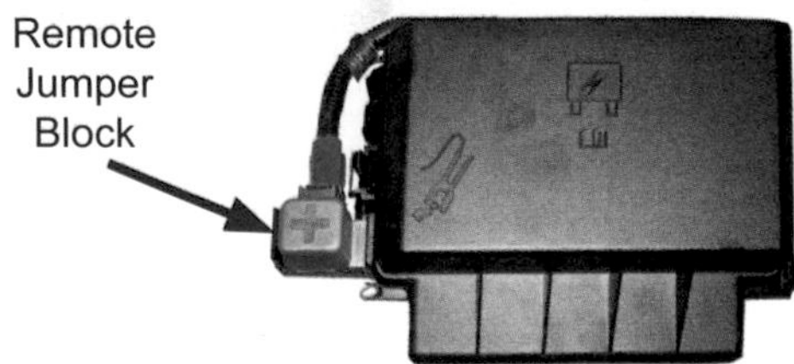

Figure 20.50 ***Remote Jumper Block***

Negative Jump-Start Attachment. A vehicle may also have a designated negative jump-start attachment for the ground (***Figure 20.51***).

Figure 20.51 ***Negative Jump-Start Attachment***

Jump-Starting Steps. The following are steps for connecting jumper cables (***Figure 20.52***). Check the owner's manual first for any specific recommendations and then complete each step of the jump-start procedure carefully. ***Warning: Never try to jump-start a battery that is low on electrolyte or that is frozen.***

Jump-Start Pre-Inspection and Setup

- Put on eye protection and inspect the discharged/weak battery for damage, cracks, loose connections, or bad cables. Correct any problems.
- Make sure the batteries are the same voltage.
- Maneuver the vehicle with the good battery so the jumper cables reach both batteries. The vehicles should not be touching.
- Turn off the ignition switch, lights, and accessories on both vehicles, place them in park or neutral, and engage the parking brakes.

Steps for Connecting the Cables

STEP 1	Connect one positive jumper cable (red) to the positive terminal (+) on the discharged/weak battery.
STEP 2	Connect the other positive jumper cable (red) to the positive terminal (+) of the booster/good battery.
STEP 3	Connect the negative jumper cable (black) to the negative terminal (–) of the booster/good battery.
STEP 4	Connect the other negative jumper cable (black) to a clean/bare metal part of the discharged/weak vehicle's engine block or frame for a good ground connection.

BE SURE VEHICLES DO NOT TOUCH

STEP 1
STEP 2
Weak Battery
Good Battery
Positive Jumper Cable Ends (Red)
Negative Jumper Cable Ends (Black)
STEP 3
Bare Metal
STEP 4

Always make the connection to bare metal or the engine block last. Be at least 18 inches away from battery. Once the vehicle has started disconnect this clamp first.

Starting

- Start the engine of the booster vehicle and rev it slightly. Let it charge for a few minutes.
- Start the engine of the vehicle with the discharged battery. Do not crank the engine for more than 20 seconds at a time. Starter damage could result.

Steps for Disconnecting the Cables

- Carefully disconnect the jumper cables in reverse step order (4-3-2-1). Hold the clamps away from the vehicles' parts and other cable clamps.

Finishing Up

- Let the engine of the discharged/weak vehicle run.
- Put away the jumper cables.
- Determine why the battery failed.

Figure 20.52 ***Jump-Starting Procedure***

Lockout

Locking keys inside a vehicle is common on older vehicles with a traditional key. Use a magnetic key-holder to store a spare someplace on the vehicle body or frame. If you don't have an extra set, many towing companies have tools to unlock your door without damaging the window or paint. Some locksmiths also specialize in this service. If you have a service like OnStar, you can call the toll free number and a representative will send a cellular signal to your vehicle's computer module to unlock the doors. Your vehicle may have an app that allows you to unlock it (***Figure 20.53***). If your vehicle's battery is dead and the keys are locked inside, the car doors will not unlock with the remote signal or app. Do not break a window to get inside the vehicle. Commonly it only takes minutes for an experienced tow driver or locksmith to enter a vehicle.

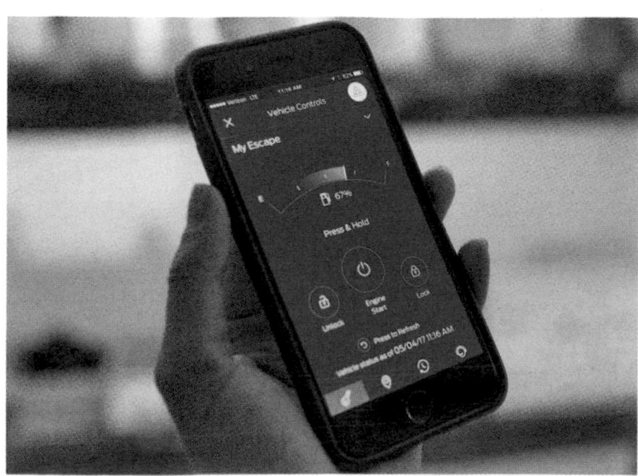

Figure 20.53 *Smartphone App*
Courtesy of Ford Motor Company

Burst Radiator Hose

Cooling system failure is a common cause of roadside emergencies. If a hose bursts, pull off to the side of the road. Shut off the engine so you don't risk overheating it. See Chapter 12 for more information about engine overheating. Coolant can be extremely hot (***Figure 20.54***). ***Warning: Never open the hood if steam is present. Never open a hot radiator cap. Severe burns could result. Keep away from moving parts in the engine compartment.*** You will need to call a tow truck or get the replacement part and fix it on the side of the road. If you do replace the hose, complete the repair when the engine is cool. Also, refill the radiator and coolant recovery tank with the proper coolant mixture (usually 50% water to 50% antifreeze).

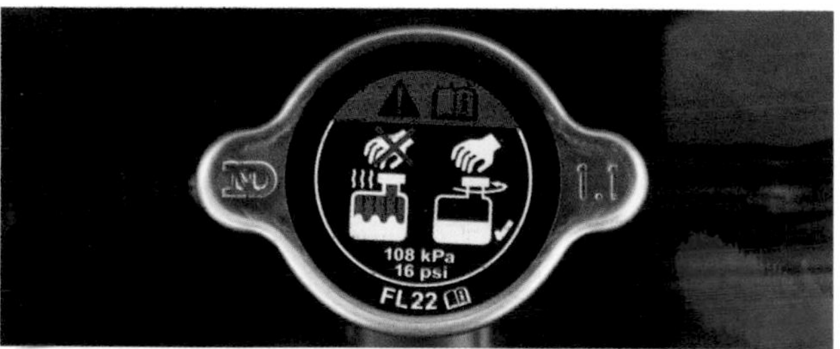

Figure 20.54 *Radiator Cap Warning*

Running on Empty

Most drivers run out of fuel at least once in their driving career, not knowing just how far they can go when the fuel gauge drops to "E". Keep in mind that running a tank low repeatedly can accelerate electric in-tank fuel pump wear. Fuel acts as a cooling system for the fuel pump and when the fuel is low the pump does not cool as effectively. If you do run out, never put gas in an unapproved container. Some gas stations will loan an approved gas can (***Figure 20.55***) if you leave a deposit.

Figure 20.55 *Approved Container*

Flat Tire

Encountering a flat tire is a common roadside emergency. If you anticipate that a tire is going flat, firmly grasp the steering wheel and pull onto the road's shoulder or as far off the road as possible. If there is a nearby driveway or side street, turn to get to the least traveled road. Be prepared by checking your vehicle's spare tire pressure and condition periodically. Depending on the location, whether you are on a busy freeway or desolate rural road, may impact your decision to use a liquid spray, change the tire, or call a tow truck. ***Warning: Changing a driver's side tire on a busy highway is dangerous.***

Changing a Tire Steps. If your vehicle is in a safe spot, use the following general procedure (***Figure 20.56***) along with the specific procedure in the owner's manual to change the tire. If you do not feel comfortable or safe, call a tow truck for assistance.

Changing a Flat Tire

STEP 1	Park where the ground is flat, solid, and level. Set the parking brake and turn on the hazard lights.
STEP 2	Review the owner's manual tire change steps. Get out your spare tire, jack, and lug wrench.

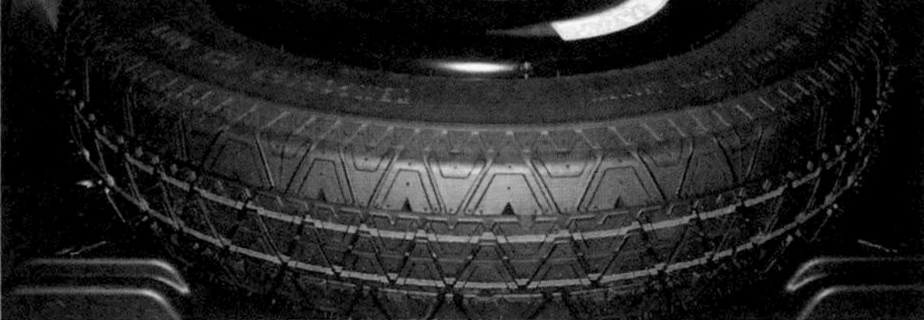

Figure 20.56a ***Spare Tire in Trunk***

STEP 3	If your wheel has a wheel cover, read the owner's manual if you cannot determine how it comes off.
STEP 4	Break the lug nuts loose about a 1/2 turn each counterclockwise. A 4-way lug wrench makes it easier if they are tight.

Figure 20.56b ***4-Way Breaking Lug Nuts Free***

STEP 5	Align the notch in the top of the jack with the designated jacking location. Turn the handle to lift the vehicle until the flat tire is off the ground.

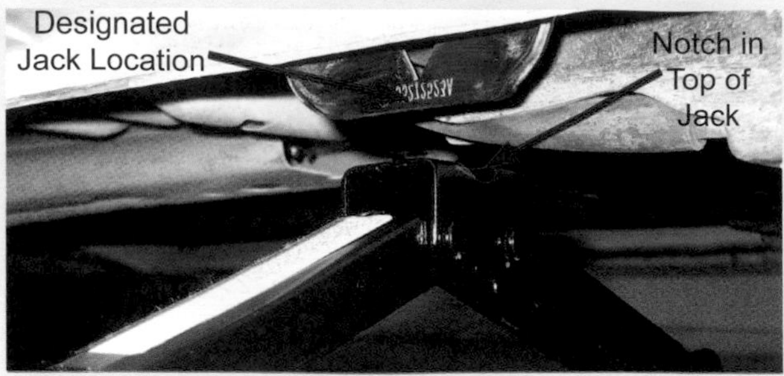

Figure 20.56c ***Align Jack with Jacking Point***

STEP 6	Remove lug nuts and keep them in a safe location. Put on gloves.
STEP 7	Lift off the flat tire and lay it on the ground under the vehicle. If the jack failed, it could help to keep the vehicle from crushing you.

Figure 20.56d ***Flat Tire Used for Added Safety***

STEP 8	Carefully lift the spare tire onto the wheel studs and thread the lug nuts (tapered end towards wheel) on clockwise with your fingers until tight. Move the flat tire out from under the vehicle.
STEP 9	Slowly lower the vehicle just until the spare tire touches the ground. With the lug wrench, securely tighten the lug nuts using a star pattern.
STEP 10	Lower the vehicle completely and remove the jack. Double check to make sure you tightened all the lug nuts. Put away the jack, tools, and flat tire.
STEP 11	Remember to have the lug nuts torqued once you reach a service facility.

Figure 20.56 ***Changing a Flat Tire***

Tech Tip

Driving on a Flat Tire

Driving on a flat tire can ruin the tire and wheel. It is much less expensive to fix a flat or replace a tire than to also replace the wheel.

Q & A ?

Temporary Spare Tire Speed

Q: How fast can you drive on a spare tire?

A: Most temporary spare tires are designed for a maximum speed of 50 mph (80 km/h). Only use it to reach a facility that can repair or replace your original tire. Before putting your spare away, check the air pressure. It is common that the air pressure in a temporary spare is higher than in regular tires. Always read the tire placard for the specific pressure.

Liquid Tire Spray. Liquid sprays (***Figure 20.57***) that are inserted into the tire valve are only recommended for temporary emergency fixes. The liquid can corrode the inside of the wheel and throw the tire off balance. After use, the tire should be taken off the wheel so the inside can be dried, patched, and rebalanced. Prior to service, inform the tire technician if you used a liquid tire spray. Special precautions need to be taken to avoid injury. ***Note: Do not use liquid tire sprays on vehicles with tire pressure monitoring systems (TPMS), unless it says "TPMS Safe".***

Figure 20.57 *Liquid Tire Spray*

Traction in Snow

When driving in cold climates it is best to be prepared for unexpected snowy weather conditions. Tire traction devices can keep you on the road when you would otherwise not be able to get traction. Before buying tire traction devices for your tires, check the owner's manual for the recommended style. There are different classes of traction devices and they must be sized to your vehicle's tires. Some are made with cables and others with metal chains. One company, AutoSock®, developed a textile tire cover.

Installation. Install snow traction devices (***Figure 20.58***) according to their instructions. Make sure they are tight. If they loosen up while going down the road they can be a hazard and damage your vehicle.

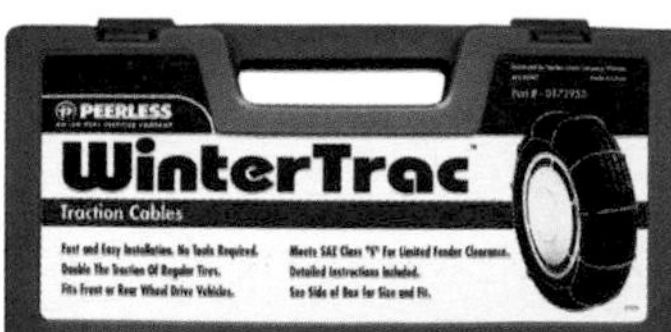

Figure 20.58 *Tire Traction Cables*

Summary

Common problems and roadside emergencies can range from minor mechanical issues to serious accidents. The key to getting through these often difficult and stressful situations is to be prepared and stay calm. Analyze the situation and find an appropriate solution. Keep in mind that vehicles can be replaced. Human safety needs to always be the number one priority.

Activities

Common Problems and Roadside Emergencies

- Changing a Flat Tire Activity
- Jump-Starting Activity
- Lighting Activity
- Replacing Wipers Activity
- On-Board Diagnostics Activity
- Chapter 20 Study Questions

Activities and Study Questions can be completed in the *Auto Upkeep Workbook.*

Career Paths

Tow Truck Driver

Education: Technical Training

Median Income: $38,000

Abilities: Excellent driver, customer service skills, safety conscious, and ingenuity.

Find your career at www.bls.gov/ooh.

Workbook Activities

Chapter 1
Car Identification Activity
Identify an automobile by make, model, year, and type.

Owner's Manual Activity
Locate and use an online owner's manual.

Chapter 2
Buying a New Automobile Activity
Differentiate between MSRP, dealer invoice, and dealer cost.

Buying a Used Automobile Activity
Research prices, reliability ratings, and safety ratings on used automobiles.

Chapter 3
Automotive Expenses Activity
Calculate automotive expenses.

Chapter 4
Repair Facilities Activity
Choose a quality repair facility. Interpret a repair invoice.

Chapter 5
Automotive Safety Activity
Identify the location of emergency and safety equipment.

Safety Data Sheet Activity
Locate and interpret a safety data sheet.

Personal Protection Equipment (PPE) and Fire Safety Activity
Identify the importance of using PPE.

Chapter 6
Tools and Equipment Activity
Identify basic tools that are used in automotive shops.

Service Manual Activity
Navigate an online service manual.

Chapter 7
Interior Cleaning Activity
Clean the inside of a vehicle.

Exterior Cleaning Activity
Clean the outside of a vehicle.

Waxing Activity
Wax the finish on a vehicle.

Chapter 8
Fluid Level Check Activity
Safely check the fluid level in various vehicle components.

Chapter 9
Ohm's Law Activity
Use ohm's law to calculate volts, amps, or ohms.

Wiring Diagram Activity
Locate and interpret a wiring diagram.

Battery Activity
Safely clean and test the battery.

Charging Activity
Safely test the alternator and replace the belt.

Starting Activity
Safely test the starter.

Chapter 10
Oil and Filter Change Activity
Safely change the oil and filter on a vehicle.

Chapter 11
Fuel System Part Identification Activity
Use an online auto parts catalog to identify fuel system parts.

Fuel System Maintenance Activity
Identify the components of the fuel system. Change the air filter, PCV valve, and fuel filter.

Chapter 12
Air Conditioning Activity
Inspect and identify the components within the air conditioning system.

Cabin Air Filter Activity
Replace the cabin air filter on a vehicle.

Cooling System Activity
Safely test, inspect, and service the cooling system. Observe thermostat operation.

Chapter 13
Ignition System Activity
Install spark plugs. Inspect, test, and install spark plug wires. Inspect and install distributor cap and rotor on a distributor system.

Chapter 14
Suspension and Steering Activity
Safely inspect and perform basic service procedures on suspension and steering components.

Tire Inspection and Rotation Activity
Safely inspect tires for wear. Rotate tires.

Chapter 15
Brake Inspection Activity
Safely inspect disc brakes.

Chapter 16
Drivetrain Activity
Safely inspect drivetrain components.

Chapter 17
Exhaust and Emissions Activity
Safely inspect exhaust and emission components.

Chapter 18
Payback Period Activity
Calculate payback period.

Future Vehicle Activity
Predict the role of the automobile in 2050.

Chapter 19
Auto Accessories Activity
Estimate the cost of accessories for a vehicle.

Chapter 20
Changing a Flat Tire Activity
Safely change a flat tire.

Jump-Starting Activity
Safely jump-start a vehicle.

Lighting Activity
Replace various lights on a vehicle.

Replacing Wipers Activity
Replace wipers on a vehicle.

On-Board Diagnostics Activity
Safely retrieve diagnostic trouble codes (DTCs) from an OBD II system using a basic scan tool.

Acronyms/Abbreviations

′ Foot
″ Inch
4WD Four-Wheel Drive
A/C Air Conditioning
AAA American Automobile Association
ABS Antilock Braking System
AC Alternating Current
ACC Adaptive Cruise Control
ACEA European Automobile Manufacturer's Association
AEB Autonomous Emergency Braking
AGM Absorbed Glass Mat
ANSI American National Standards Institute
API American Petroleum Institute
ARB Air Resources Board
ARB Automatic Reverse Braking
ASE Automotive Service Excellence
ASTM American Society for Testing and Materials
ATF Automatic Transmission Fluid
AWD All-Wheel Drive
B Biodiesel
BAS Belt-Alternator-Starter
BAS Brake Assist System
BBB Better Business Bureau
BCI Battery Council International
BTS Bureau of Transportation Statistics
BTU British Thermal Unit
C Celsius
CA Cranking Amps
CAA Clean Air Act
CAFE Corporate Average Fuel Economy
CARB California Air Resources Board
CCA Cold Cranking Amps
CCV Crankcase Ventilation
CFPP Cold Filter Plugging Point
CI Compression Ignition
CPI Contact Point Ignition
CNG Compressed Natural Gas
CO Carbon Monoxide
CO_2 Carbon Dioxide
COP Coil-On-Plug
CV Constant Velocity
CVT Continuously Variable Transmission
dB Decibels
DC Direct Current
DEF Diesel Exhaust Fluid
DI Distributor Ignition
DLC Data Link Connector
DMM Digital Multimeter
DOC Diesel Oxidation Catalyst
DOHC Dual Overhead Cam
DOT Department of Transportation
DPF Diesel Particulate Filter
DRL Daytime Running Lights
DTV Disc Thickness Variation
E Ethanol
e.g. For example
ECU Engine Control Unit
EEC Electronic Engine Control
ECM Electronic Control Module
ECT Engine Coolant Temperature
EGHR Exhaust Gas Heat Recovery
EGR Exhaust Gas Recirculation
EI Electronic Ignition
EM Electric Motor
EPA Environmental Protection Agency
EPS Electric Power Steering
EREV Extended Range Electric Vehicle
ESC Electronic Stability Control
ETBE Ethyl Tertiary Butyl Ether
EV Electric Vehicle
EVAP Evaporative Emissions
F Fahrenheit
FCW Forward Collision Warning
ft Foot
FWD Front-Wheel Drive
GDI Gasoline Direct Injection
GGE Gasoline Gallon Equivalent
GPS Global Positioning Systems
H Hydrogen
H2ICE Hydrogen Internal Combustion Engine
H_2O Water
HC Hydrocarbons
HEV Hybrid Electric Vehicle
HID High-Intensity Discharge
HOAT Hybrid Organic Acid Technology
HVAC Heating, Ventilation, and Air Conditioning
i.e. That is
IAC Idle Air Control
IAT Inorganic Acid Technology
IBS Intelligent Battery Sensor
ICE Internal Combustion Engine
IIHS Insurance Institute for Highway Safety
I/M Inspection and Maintenance
IMA Integrated Motor Assist
ILSAC International Lubricant Standardization and Approval Committee
ISG Integrated Starter/Generator
KBB Kelley Blue Book
kg Kilogram
km Kilometer
km/h Kilometers Per Hour
kPA Kilopascal
KS Knock Sensor
lb Pound
LED Light-Emitting Diode
Lidar Light Detection and Ranging
Li-ion Lithium-Ion
Li-poly Lithium-Ion Polymer
LNG Liquefied Natural Gas
LPG Liquefied Petroleum Gas
LT Light Truck
m Meter
M+S Mud and Snow
MAF Mass Airflow
MAP Manifold Absolute Pressure
MIL Malfunction Indicator Light
mm Millimeter
MPG Miles Per Gallon
MPGe Miles Per Gallon Equivalent
MSDS Material Safety Data Sheet
MSRP Manufacturer's Suggested Retail Price
MTBE Methyl Tertiary Butyl Ether
MY Model Year
N Nitrogen
NADA National Automotive Dealers Association
NATEF National Automotive Technicians Education Foundation
NHTSA National Highway Traffic Safety Administration
NIHL Noise-Induced Hearing Loss
NiMH Nickel Metal Hydride
No. Number
NO_x Nitrogen Oxides
NSC National Safety Council
O_2 Oxygen
OAT Organic Acid Technology
OBD On-Board Diagnostics
OEM Original Equipment Manufacturer
OSHA Occupational Safety and Health Administration
P Passenger
PCM Powertrain Control Module
PCV Positive Crankcase Ventilation
PDR Paintless Dent Repair
PEM Proton Exchange Membrane
PFI Port Fuel Injection
PHEV Plug-in Hybrid Electric Vehicle
PM Particulate Matter
PPE Personal Protection Equipment
R Radial
R Resistance
RPM Revolutions Per Minute
RWD Rear-Wheel Drive
SAE Society of Automotive Engineers
SCR Selective Catalytic Reduction
SDS Safety Data Sheet
SI International System of Units
SI Spark Ignition
SLA Short-Long Arm
SRS Supplemental Restraint System
ST Special Trailer
SUT Sport Utility Truck
SUV Sport Utility Vehicle
SVO Straight Vegetable Oil
T Temporary
TAME Tertiary Amyl Methyl Ether
TBI Throttle Body Injection
TCS Traction Control System
TPMS Tire Pressure Monitoring System
TSB Technical Service Bulletin
TWC Three-Way Converter
U-Joint Universal Joint
ULSD Ultra-Low Sulfur Diesel
UTQG Uniform Tire Quality Grading
USB Universal Serial Bus
V Volt
VECI Vehicle Emission Control Information
VIN Vehicle Identification Number
WMA Windows Media Audio
WVO Waste Vegetable Oil

Text Features

Q & As

Career Paths

Web Links

Procedures

Trouble Guides

Calculations

Tech Tips

Servicing

Glossary

A

ABS – Antilock Braking System, a system used to minimize wheel lockup when braking to maximize driver control.

AC – Alternating Current, a type of electrical current where electron (electricity) flow changes direction (alternates) back and forth.

Aftermarket part – a term used to identify a replacement part made by a company that did not originally make the part for the vehicle when the vehicle was assembled.

Alternator – a device, also called an AC generator, that converts mechanical energy to electrical energy to recharge the battery.

Amperage – measured in amperes (or amps), is the strength (quantity of electrons) in the electrical circuit.

Antifreeze – also called coolant, is a substance with its main ingredient glycol, which has a high boiling point and a low freezing point when mixed with water.

API – American Petroleum Institute, a trade organization that represents oil and natural gas stakeholders that, among other things, develops consensus standards within the oil and gas industry (e.g., engine oil service ratings).

Asymmetrical – one side is different than the other.

Automatic transmission – a transmission that shifts automatically from one gear ratio to another without the assistance of the driver.

Autonomous vehicles – vehicles that can drive without human input.

B

Battery – a device that stores chemical energy.

Blow-by – combustion gases that leak past the piston rings and into the crankcase.

Brake fluid – a hydraulic fluid used in automotive brake systems that withstands high temperatures and freezing.

BTU – British Thermal Unit, a measurement of the amount of energy released burning one wooden match.

C

Camber – a term used during wheel alignments to identify the tilt of the top of a wheel/tire assembly.

Carnauba – a wax, commonly found in automotive waxes, made from the carnauba wax palm (Copernicia prunifera) plant.

Caster – a term used during wheel alignments to identify the forward or backward tilt from absolute vertical as viewed from the side of the vehicle.

Catalytic converter – a device used to convert carbon monoxide, hydrocarbons, and nitrogen oxides into water vapor, carbon dioxide, and nitrogen.

Chamois – a leather towel, commonly made from sheepskin, used to dry a vehicle after washing.

Circuit – a path for electricity to flow that includes a power source, a conductor, and a load.

Conductor – a material that easily allows electron movement (electricity) from one point to another.

Contaminates – something that is impure.

Corrosivity – ability to corrode or dissolve.

Crude oil – a fossil fuel that is also known as petroleum, a substance mainly containing carbon and hydrogen (hydrocarbons) found naturally in the earth that is used to make gasoline, diesel, kerosene, and a wide range of products.

Current – the quantity of electrons moving through a conductor measured in amps.

CV shaft – Constant Velocity shaft, a drive shaft commonly used on front-wheel and all-wheel drive vehicles that allows for power transfer to the wheels while also allowing for suspension movement and turning.

CVT – Continuously Variable Transmission, a type of automatic transmission commonly utilizing a chain or belt system that does not have a limited number of gear ratios like traditional automatic transmissions.

D

dB – decibel, a measurement of the loudness of sound.

DC – Direct Current, a type of electrical current where electrons (electricity) flow in one direction.

Deductible – the amount you must pay when you make an insurance claim.

Depreciation – a term used to describe how an asset has its value reduced over time.

Diesel – a fuel (chemical energy) made from crude oil that has an energy content of approximately 129,500 BTUs per gallon.

Diesel, Rudolf – invented the diesel engine that eliminated a spark plug by instead using high compression to ignite the fuel.

Diodes – an electronic device that allows electricity to flow in only one direction.

Directional – one direction.

Disc thickness variation – subtle variation in thickness of the disc (rotor).

Distillation – the process of using heat to refine crude oil to make a variety of products.

E

Electricity – the movement of electrons through a conductor.

Electrolysis – process of running an electric current through water to separate the hydrogen from the oxygen.

Electrolyte – a water and sulfuric acid solution in an automotive lead acid battery.

Energy – the fuel stored or used to perform work.

Engine configuration – the design of the engine block, most commonly inline or V shaped.

Engine (internal combustion) – a machine where fuel (chemical energy) is burned inside a combustion chamber within the engine to produce motion (mechanical energy).

Engine (motor) oil – a substance, made from crude oil and/or synthetic compounds, that lubricates, cools, cleans, and seals moving parts inside an engine.

Engine size – the size of the engine calculated from the combined volume of all the cylinders.

F

Firewall – the divider, commonly made of steel with insulating material, between the engine compartment and the passenger cabin.

Force – a push or pull, the interaction between objects.

Forced induction – the process of forcing and compressing air into the combustion chamber.

Ford, Henry – entrepreneur and founder of Ford Motor Company that successfully mass-produced cars on a moving assembly line in the early 1900s.

Fuse – an overcurrent protection device that safeguards electrical components.

G

Gasoline – a fuel (chemical energy) made from crude oil that has an energy content of approximately 114,100 BTUs per gallon.

GDI – Gasoline Direct Injection, a type of fuel injection where high-pressure fuel injectors deliver a fine mist of fuel directly into the combustion chamber.

Gear – engineered in sets, have teeth that mesh with one another to change speed, torque, and direction of travel.

GGE – Gasoline Gallon Equivalent, a measure used to compare the energy of an alternative fuel to gasoline.

H

Heater core – a small heat exchanger that provides heat from engine coolant to the passenger cabin.

Horsepower – the work needed to lift 550 pounds a distance of 1 foot in 1 second.

Hybrid – a vehicle that uses more than one method for propulsion or power.

Hydroplane – when a thin film of water causes the tire tread to lose traction with the road.

I

Ignitability – easily combustible.

Ignition coil – a step up transformer used to convert a low voltage of the battery into a high voltage at the spark plugs to ignite the air-fuel mixture.

Independent suspension – a type of suspension that allows the wheel/tire assembly to move up and down without relying on movements from another wheel/tire assembly.

Insulator – a material that resists the flow of electrons (electricity).

Insurance – a policy that provides protection against financial loss when accidents occur.

Interference engine – an engine where the valves and pistons could come in contact with one another if the timing belt or chain breaks, skips, or is stripped out.

K

Key fob – commonly a decorative or useful item kept with keys that may contain a transmitter for use in keyless entry and/or push button keyless ignition systems.

Kinetic energy – energy of motion.

L

Load – in electricity, the resistance in a circuit.

Longitudinal engine – an engine that is mounted parallel with the length of the vehicle.

M

MacPherson – a type of strut that integrates the shock and coil spring together into one unit.

Manual transmission – a transmission that requires the driver to manually shift gear ratios with a gear stick shifter and a clutch.

Master cylinder – a component in the braking system that converts movement from the brake pedal to hydraulic pressure.

MIL – an acronym for Malfunction Indicator Light, illuminates when a problem or potential problem exists within one of the vehicle's systems.

MPGe – Miles Per Gallon of gasoline equivalent, a measure used to compare energy usage in advanced technology vehicles to the MPG rating in conventional vehicles.

MY – Model Year, the year of a vehicle's pollution standards conformance, found on the VECI sticker under the hood.

O

Octane rating – a number visible on a gasoline pump, the higher the number the more the fuel resists igniting (an antiknock quality that resists premature combustion).

OEM part – Original Equipment Manufacturer, used to identify a replacement part that is made by the same company as the original part when the vehicle was assembled.

Oil – see engine oil.

Open – in electricity, a break in the circuit.

OSHA – an acronym for the Occupational Safety and Health Administration, a governmental organization that was created to help prevent work related deaths, illnesses, and injuries.

Otto cycle – named after Nikolaus Otto, the most common internal combustion engine design for automobiles which consists of four piston strokes (intake, compression, power, and exhaust).

P

Parallel – an electrical circuit with two or more paths.

PCM – Powertrain Control Module, the main computer on an automobile that processes data from sensors and sends commands to engine and transmission controls.

Photovoltaic cells – solar arrays that convert sunlight directly to electrical energy.

Polish – a product used to remove minor scratches and oxidation on painted surfaces.

Potential energy – stored energy, energy of position.

Power – the rate at which work is done.

R

Reactivity – unstable under normal conditions.

Rebuilt part – a replacement part that has been fixed by removing and replacing the defective component(s), but has not necessarily been completely reworked.

Recall – a notice informing the owner that a service needs to be completed to remedy a defective or unsafe component or design.

Refrigerant – a compound used in the A/C system of an automobile that changes from a liquid to a gas, absorbing heat when evaporated and dissipates heat during condensation.

Regenerative braking – a type of braking where a generator is used to recapture energy that would be normally lost when the driver is attempting to slow down the vehicle.

Remanufactured part – a replacement part that has been completely disassembled, inspected, and wearable parts replaced.

Resistance – usually measured in ohms (Ω), a measure used to identify the degree of an opposing electron flow (electricity).

Runout – the slight up and down or side to side movement in error when a part rotates.

S

SAE – Society of Automotive Engineers, a professional organization that establishes standards (e.g., engine oil classifications).

Saturation – beyond it holding point.

Series – an electrical circuit with a single path.

Serpentine belt – the most common type of drive belt (flat belt with grooves on one side and smooth on the other) used on today's automobiles to turn the alternator, power steering, A/C compressor, and other components.

Short – in electricity, a shorter less resistant, unintended and unwanted path.

Starter – a device that converts electrical energy to mechanical energy to turn over (crank) an engine.

Stoichiometric mixture – the mass ratio of 14.7 parts of air to 1 part of fuel, the ideal mixture for combustion.

Symmetrical – same on both sides.

System – parts that work together to perform a specific task.

Synthetic oil – oil made from chemically derived base stock (molecular engineered) with additives that create an oil with exceptional lubricating abilities.

T

Technical service bulletin – also called a TSB, a written advisory statement by a vehicle manufacturer to assist dealerships in diagnosing reoccurring problems.

Toe – a term used during wheel alignments to identify the outward (toe out) or inward (toe in) position of the front edge of a wheel/tire assembly.

Torque – a rotational force used to turn an object around an axis, fulcrum, or pivot point.

Transverse engine – an engine that is mounted perpendicular to the length of the vehicle.

U

Unibody – a design that combines the body and frame into one unit.

UTQG – Uniform Tire Quality Grading ratings, used to compare treadwear, traction, and temperature capabilities between different tires.

V

Viscosity – the measure of resistance of a fluid to flow (e.g., low viscosity oils flow easier than high viscosity oils).

Voltage – the electrical potential measured in volts.

W

Wax – a product used to protect an automobile's exterior finish.

Wheel chock – a device used to block a wheel to help keep a vehicle from rolling.

Windshield washer fluid – specially formulated fluid which resists freezing that is added to the windshield washer reservoir, assisting in cleaning the windshield.

Work – the transfer of energy from one object to another.

Z

Zerk fitting – a fitting that can be greased using a grease gun commonly found on a steering or drivetrain component.

Index

C

D

E

J

K

L

Auto Upkeep

Maintenance, Light Repair, Auto Ownership, and How Cars Work

Edition
4th

Michael E. Gray
and
Linda E. Gray

Order Info

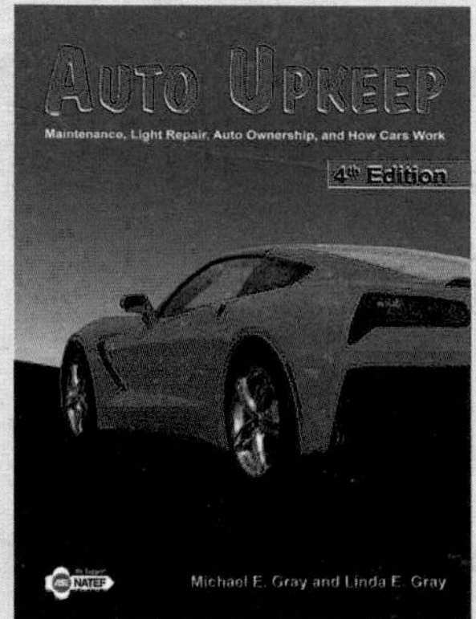

Textbook

ISBN: 978-1-62702-011-4
Paperback, 288 Pages

ISBN: 978-1-62702-016-9
Hardcover, 288 Pages

Paperback Set

ISBN: 978-1-62702-014-5
Includes:
- 1 - Paperback Textbook
- 1 - Paperback Workbook

Hardcover Set

ISBN: 978-1-62702-017-6
Includes:
- 1 - Hardcover Textbook
- 1 - Paperback Workbook

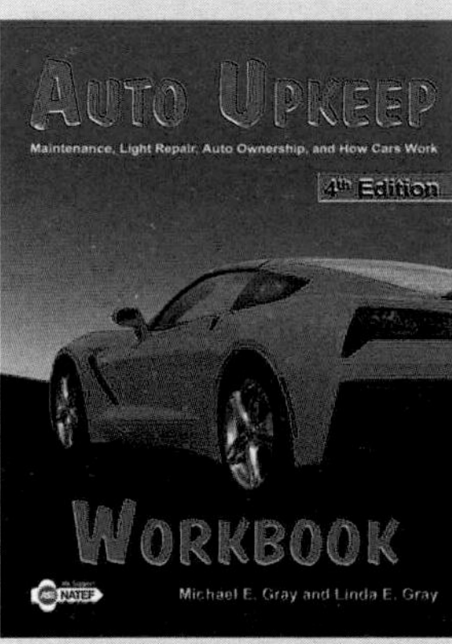

Workbook

ISBN: 978-1-62702-012-1
Paperback, 176 Pages

Instructor USB

ISBN: 978-1-62702-013-8
Includes:
- Course Syllabus Outline
- Competency Profile
- NATEF Correlation Matrix
- PowerPoint Slides
- Lab Activities
- Study Questions
- Chapter Tests
- Exams and Final
- Answer Keys

Auto Upkeep is Excellent For:

- Introductory Automotive Programs and Classes
- Homeschool Students
- New Drivers
- Boy Scouts - Automotive Maintenance Merit Badge
- Girl Scouts - Car Care Badge
- 4-H Automotive Programs
- Car Care Clinics and Seminars
- Automotive Workshops
- Adult and Consumer Education Classes
- Driver Education Classes
- Afterschool Programs

Discount pricing and order information available at:

www.AutoUpkeep.com **(800) 918-READ**